In March 2023, Silicon Valley Bank collapsed as central banks struggled to control inflation by increasing interest rates and selling bonds, leaving commercial banks with unexpectedly significant losses. The global financial system is under severe strain, and another banking crisis has become more likely. Have we learned the accounting lessons from previous crises? All the banks that collapsed in the 2008/2009 financial crisis had clean audit reports. Surely, contemporary, globally regulated accounting has improved, and now directs attention towards financially stressed institutions? Sadly, it does not.

Rob Bryer's new book, *Accounting for Crises*, explains why by providing a compelling, historically rigorous case that, by allowing overstating reported profits and understating their risk, accounting theory facilitated and aggravated both the 1929 and 2008 financial crises. More concerning, Bryer carefully explains that accounting practice in 2023, in spite of new regulations, would serve exactly the same function today. Current "fair value" rules, for example, allowed SVB to avoid reporting losses on its financial assets.

As with Bryer's previous books, policy makers, academics, historians and anyone who want to understand how accounting functions in society should read *Accounting for Crises*.

Christine Cooper
Professor of Accounting, University of Edinburgh Business School, Edinburgh, United Kingdom

A tour de force: Engaging seriously with Marx's actual crisis theory — rather than potted versions — and marshalling the author's deep knowledge of accounting and its history, *Accounting for Crises*, explain why the United States was the epicentre of both the Great Depression and the Great Recession. The interplay of the tendential fall in the rate of profit, "moral hazard" and "swindling" is central to Rob Bryer's explanation, as is the role of accounting theory. The first three factors were stressed also by Marx; the last is Bryer's original contribution.

Andrew Kliman
Emeritus Professor of Economics, Pace University, New York, USA

Rob Bryer presents an insightful narrative that offers a captivating new perspective on the economic history of the United States. He demonstrates that major financial crises can be traced back to the shortcomings of accounting methods. By setting out rigorously argued linkages between accounting theory and its economic consequences, Bryer challenges conventional thinking and highlights the ongoing significance of Marx in comprehending the history and present-day problems of capitalism. *Accounting for Crises* deserves a wide audience.

Steven Toms
Professor of Accounting, Accounting and Finance Division,
Leeds Business School, The University of Leeds,
Maurice Keyworth Building, Leeds,
United Kingdom

ACCOUNTING FOR CRISES

A Marxist History of American Accounting Theory, c.1929-2007

Frontiers of Accounting and Financial History

Print ISSN: 2737-5706
Online ISSN: 2737-5714

Accounting and financial history underlies the history of all organisations, civilisations, politics, institutions and societies. Its ambit is, therefore, very wide in scope and chronology. However, the study of accounting and financial history is mainly centred within the realm of social science faculties in universities where the institutional norm is for researchers, including accounting and financial historians, to produce journal articles for specialists in the same field. Many serious scholars see this journal fetishism as a limitation, and there is an appetite for producing more substantial works that enable the accounting and financial historian to engage with their subject matter in greater depth. Furthermore, while the subject's remit is very wide, a relatively small and specialised audience reads most of what accounting and financial historians produce in journals. This series, therefore, a) gives scholars the opportunity to explore their subject matter in greater depth; and b) reach a wider audience, given the fundamental nature of the subject. The focus will, therefore, be on single-authored works rather than edited volumes, and the subject matter will be eclectic in its composition. Proposals are encouraged from accounting and financial historians and all those interested in exploring the frontiers of this broad, changing and exciting subject.

Published

Vol. 2 *Accounting for Crises: A Marxist History of American Accounting Theory, c.1929 to 2007*
by Robert Arthur Bryer

Vol. 1 *Creating the "Big Mess": A Marxist History of American Accounting Theory, c.1900–1929*
by Rob Bryer

Frontiers of Accounting and Financial History – Vol. 2

ACCOUNTING FOR CRISES

A Marxist History of American Accounting Theory, c.1929-2007

Rob Bryer
Warwick Business School, UK

World Scientific

EW JERSEY • LONDON • SINGAPORE • BEIJING • SHANGHAI • HONG KONG • TAIPEI • CHENNAI • TOKYO

Published by

World Scientific Publishing Co. Pte. Ltd.
5 Toh Tuck Link, Singapore 596224
USA office: 27 Warren Street, Suite 401-402, Hackensack, NJ 07601
UK office: 57 Shelton Street, Covent Garden, London WC2H 9HE

Library of Congress Cataloging-in-Publication Data
Names: Bryer, Robert, author.
Title: Accounting for crises : a marxist history of American accounting theory, c.1929 to 2007 / Rob Bryer, Warwick Business School, UK.
Description: New Jersey : World Scientific, 2023. | Series: Frontiers of accounting and financial history, 2737-5706 ; Vol. 2 | Includes bibliographical references and index.
Identifiers: LCCN 2022048813 | ISBN 9789811267062 (hardcover) | ISBN 9789811267079 (ebook) | ISBN 9789811267086 (ebook other)
Subjects: LCSH: Saving and investment--United States--History. | Speculation--United States--History. | Financial crises--United States--History. | Accounting--United States--History. | Fisher, Irving, 1867–1947. | Marxian economics--United States--History.
Classification: LCC HC110.S3 B794 2023 | DDC 339.4/30973--dc23/eng/20221228
LC record available at https://lccn.loc.gov/2022048813

British Library Cataloguing-in-Publication Data
A catalogue record for this book is available from the British Library.

Cover photograph: A Great Depression soup line.

For any available supplementary material, please visit
https://www.worldscientific.com/worldscibooks/10.1142/13163#t=suppl

Desk Editors: Jayanthi Muthuswamy/Thaheera Althaf

Typeset by Stallion Press
Email: enquiries@stallionpress.com

Preface

Historians have not convincingly explained modern capitalism's two major economic crises, the Great Depression of the 1930s and the Global Financial Crisis (GFC) of 2008–2009. *Accounting for Crises* offers a new explanation, why both began and were more severe in the USA ("America"), based on an accounting interpretation of Marx's theory of crises. It explains their origins in capitalists' control of accumulation, which reveals important overlooked roles for Irving Fisher's accounting theory, which by allowing discretion in accounts, in the context of falling rates of profit, encouraged "swindling", overstating reported profits and understating their risk, which facilitated and aggravated both crises. Framed by Fisher's theory, during the 1920s American accounting theorists justified management's discretion, which *Creating the "Big Mess"* (the companion volume) concluded it used to conservatively smooth earnings. Fisher's theory, *Accounting for Crises* shows, also underlay the popular new theory of investment that justified valuing shares using reported earnings, which encouraged their manipulation and legitimised "speculation". This, it argues, underlay America's exceptional late-1920s stock market boom, 1929 Great Crash, and the depth and length of its Great Depression. Prominently associated with the boom, Fisher became unpopular after the crash, his name disappearing from public debate. Nevertheless, the book concludes, his theory hindered economic recovery, weakened 1930s reforms, undermined accounting regulation from the late-1930s, and following his rehabilitation from the late-1950s, it underlies the Financial Accounting Standards Board's conceptual framework, which by allowing off-balance-sheet accounting for securitization-SPEs, fostered the 2007 "credit crunch" that triggered the 2008–2009 GFC.

About the Author

Rob Bryer is Emeritus Professor of Accounting at Warwick Business School, Warwick University, in the UK. He has a BA in Business with a major in Accountancy, and holds a PhD in Operational Research from Warwick University. He has researched and taught accounting for over 40 years. His research interests are accounting theory and accounting history, on which he has published 27 refereed journal articles, 6 books and 4 invited book chapters. He is an Editorial Board Member of *Accounting History*, *Accounting History Review* and *Critical Perspectives on Accounting*.

Acknowledgements

My thanks to Professor David McCullom-Oldroyd (Newcastle University, UK) for inviting me to explore the history of American accounting theory, for his encouragement, helpful comments, and editorial guidance. Many thanks also to Professor Stephen A. Zeff (Rice University, USA) for his helpful comments on the preliminary draft. Special thanks to Vin Bryer, my intellectual partner *sine qua non*.

I thank the following organisations for permission to quote from their published works.

The American Accounting Association for permission to quote from "A Tentative Statement of Accounting Principles Affecting Corporate Reports", *The Accounting Review*, 1936, 11(2), 187–191; Paton, W.A. and A.C. Littleton (1940). *An Introduction to Corporate Accounting Standards*. Columbus, Ohio; and Perry, R.E. (1993), Accounting for securitizations, *Accounting Horizons*, 7(3), 71–82; The American Institute of Certified Public Accountants for permission to quote from Myers, J.H., (1962). Reporting of leases in financial statements, Accounting Research Study No. 4, Carey, J.L. (1969). *The Rise of the Accounting Profession: To Responsibility and Authority, 1937–1969*, and Stewart, J.E. and B.S. Neuhausen (1986). Financial instruments and transactions: The CPA's newest challenge, *The Journal of Accountancy*, 162(2), 101–111; material from the FASB Special Report, The Framework of Financial Accounting Concepts and Standards, copyrighted by the Financial Accounting Foundation, 401 Merritt 7, PO Box 5116, Norwalk, CT 06856-5116, and material from Financial Accounting Standards Board (1978), *Objectives of Financial Reporting by Business Enterprises*. Statement of Financial

Accounting Concepts No. 1. Stamford, Conn., copyrighted by the Financial Accounting Foundation, 401 Merritt 7, PO Box 5116, Norwalk, CT 06856-5116, are used with permission; New Left Review for permission to quote from Marx, Karl, 1978. Capital: A Critique of Political Economy, Vol. 2, Harmondsworth: Penguin Books; Ohio State University Press for permission to quote from Previts, G.J. and B.D. Merino (1998). *A History of Accountancy in the United States: The Cultural Significance of Accounting*; Penguin Random House for permission to quote from Galbraith, J.K. (1961). *The Great Crash 1929*. Harmondsworth: Penguin Books, copyright © John Kenneth Galbraith, 1955. Reprinted by permission of Penguin Books Limited, and HarperCollins Publishers; The Taylor and Francis Group LLC (Books) US for permission to quote from Berle, A.A. and G.C. Means (1932). *The Modern Corporation and Private Property*. New York: Macmillan, and Bevis, H.W. (1965). *Corporate Financial Reporting in a Competitive Economy*. London: Collier-Macmillan; Taylor and Francis Group for permission to quote from Cerbioni, F., M. Fabrizi and A. Parbonetti. (2015). Securitizations and the financial crisis: Is accounting the missing link? *Accounting Forum*, 39(3), 155–175, copyright © 2014 University of South Australia, reprinted by permission of Taylor & Francis Ltd., http://www.tandfonline.com on behalf of University of South Australia.

Contents

Preface		vii
About the Author		ix
Acknowledgements		xi
List of Figures		xv
List of Tables		xvii
List of Abbreviations		xix
Chapter 1	Accounting Theory and Crises	1
Chapter 2	Marx's Theory of Crises	21
Chapter 3	The Great Collapse 1929–1933	69
Chapter 4	Accounting for the 1929 Stock Market Crash	87
Chapter 5	Accounting Theory and Reform in the Great Depression	125
Chapter 6	"People's Capitalism" and the Rise and Fall of GAAP	185
Chapter 7	The Profitability Crisis and the FASB's Conceptual Framework	261
Chapter 8	Accounting for the Global Financial Crisis	333

Conclusions 403

Bibliography 405

Index 433

List of Figures

Figure 2.1:	Marx's Theory of Crises	59
Figure 3.1:	Standard and Poor's Index of Common Stocks 1920–1934	70
Figure 3.2:	NYSE Securities Issued 1920–1930	80
Figure 3.3:	Corporate, Individual and Non-Corporate Debt Divided By GNP (Current Prices)	81
Figure 3.4:	Corporate, Individual and Non-Corporate Debt and GNP (Current Prices)	81
Figure 3.5:	Brokers' Loans and Consumer Debt 1919–1930	82
Figure 4.1:	"Earnings" and "Dow Theory" in Barron's Weekly, 1921–1942	102
Figure 4.2:	S&P 500 Weekly Index, October 1928–October 1934	114
Figure 7.1:	US Inflation 1940–1995	266
Figure 7.2:	UK Historical and Current Cost Profits 1968–1977	271
Figure 8.1:	The Securitisation Process	363
Figure 8.2:	Total and Subprime Home Mortgage Originations and Securitisations	394
Figure 8.3:	Relative Subprime Securitisation Rates	395

List of Tables

Table 2.1: Accumulation and Wages: Constant OCC and S/V 31

Table 2.2: Accumulation and Employment: Rising OCC and S/V 33

Table 2.3: Marx's Schemas — First Example 39

Table 2.4: Marx's Initial Schema 42

Table 2.5: Marx's Unbalanced Initial Schema for Expanded Reproduction 42

Table 2.6: Capitalist Accumulation: Year 1 43

Table 2.7: Capitalist Accumulation: Year 2 45

Table 2.8: Indefinite Growth 48

Table 5.1: Profits and Dividends 1929–1938 176

Table 7.1: Value to the Owner Rules 273

Table 8.1: Financial and Operating Policies 343

Table 8.2: Myers' In-Substance Purchase and Right of Use Asset 355

Table 8.3: Myers' Extreme Lease Examples 357

Table 8.4: Common Features of SPEs 364

List of Abbreviations

AAA	American Accounting Association
AAUIA	American Association of University Instructors in Accounting
AFL	American Federation of Labour
AIA	American Institute of Accountants
AICPA	American Institute of Certified Public Accountants
APB	Accounting Principles Board
ARB	Accounting Research Bulletin
ARS	Accounting Research Study
ASC	Accounting Standards Committee
ASR	Accounting Series Release
BIS	Bank for International Settlements
CAP	Committee on Accounting Procedure
CCA	Current Cost Accounting
CMA	Capital Maintenance Adjustment
CPA	Certified Public Accountant
CPP	Current Purchasing Power
DM	Discussion Memorandum
ED	Exposure Draft
FAS	Financial Accounting Standard
FASB	Financial Accounting Standards Board

FEI	Financial Executives Institute
FIN	Financial Accounting Interpretation
FTC	Federal Trade Commission
GAAP	Generally Accepted Accounting Principles
GFC	Global Financial Crisis
GPLA	General Price-Level Accounting
HC	Historical Cost
HCA	Historical Cost Accounting
IASB	International Accounting Standards Board
IFRS	International Financial Reporting Standards
L-C-M	Lower of Cost or Market
LIFO	Last-In-First-Out
LTFRP	Law of the Tendential Falling Rate of Profit
NRV	Net Realisable Value
NYSE	New York Stock Exchange
NYSSCPA	New York State Society of Certified Public Accountants
OCC	Organic Composition of Capital
PV	Present Value
QSPE	Qualifying Special Purpose Entity
RC	Replacement Cost
RCA	Replacement Cost Accounting
ROI	Return on Investment
ROU	Right of Use
SEC	Securities and Exchange Commission
SFAC	Statement of Financial Accounting Concepts
SFAS	Statement of Financial Accounting Standard
SPE	Special Purpose Entity
SSAP	Statement of Standard Accounting Practice
TSSI	Temporal Single-System Interpretation
VIE	Variable Interest Entities
VIU	Value-In-Use

Chapter 1

Accounting Theory and Crises

Since capitalism's development into its modern form of stock markets and large management-controlled companies — from the 1880s in Britain, and 1920s in the USA ("America") — there have been two major depressions, severe economic crises, the Great Depression of 1929–1932 following the 1929 stock market crash, and the 2008–2009 Global Financial Crisis (GFC) following the 2007 "credit-crunch".[1] Historians have not explained them convincingly. *Accounting for Crises* offers a new explanation, why both began and were more severe in America, based on an accounting interpretation of Karl Marx's theory of crises, which explains accounting's roles in creating their preconditions, in facilitating and aggravating them, and in promoting economic recovery. Market economies, according to mainstream economists, should have no crises, which if they occur have monetary or financial causes that reforms could prevent, but they see no directly causal roles for accounting that, most agree, simply provides investors with potentially useful information for valuing financial securities.[2] Marx by contrast, who studied political economy to understand capitalism's crises, argued that reforms could not prevent them because their underlying cause was capital "accumulation", capitalism's dedication to economic growth.[3] Accounting plays a key role in Marx's

[1]Economists generally distinguish "depressions" from less severe "recessions" (Roberts 2016, p. 1).

[2]Unless otherwise specified, in what follows "accounting" means financial accounting (or "reporting").

[3]Marx distinguished "crises" ("depressions") from short-term "business cycles" ("recessions") (Kliman 2017, p. 227).

theory of capitalism — how it controls the production of surplus value by holding management accountable to the stock market for the rate of profit (Bryer 2017, 2021a) — and in his theory of crises, which the book argues explains them as the consequences of capitalist control. Marx's theories of capitalism and crises are controversial, but the criticisms are misplaced, the accounting interpretations suggest, and using them to study the history of financial reporting reveals its significance and the lessons. Based on Ladislaus Bortkiewicz's (1906/7) claim that Marx's value-price transformation is "inconsistent", many scholars have rejected his theory of value. The basis of Marx's theory of crises is his "law of the tendential falling rate of profit" (LTFRP) (Kliman 2012, 2015, 2017), but many accept that Nobuo Okishio (1961) "disproved" it. The book, however, builds on demonstrations by Temporal Single-System Interpretation's (TSSI) supporters that Marx's transformation is consistent, and Okishio did not disprove the LTFRP (Kliman 2007; Bryer 2017), to give an accounting interpretation of his theory of crises. It uses this interpretation to explain American accounting theory's roles in facilitating and aggravating the Great Crash and Depression, and the "credit-crunch" and GFC. Explaining capitalism's inevitable crises to workers, Marx argued, would convince them to replace it with socialism.

Accounting in different forms also plays an important role in Marx's theory of history, an evolutionary theory of "modes of production". Each mode of production has different "social relations of production", slavery, feudalism and capitalism, which meant different ways of extracting surplus labour, as production, rent, or profit, appropriate to different levels of the "forces of production", and appropriate "superstructures", legal and ideological systems of control, including appropriate accounts (Bryer 2019, Chapter 2). Throughout history different forms of accounts have played important roles in controlling the social relations of production (Bryer 2019), but in capitalism, which extracts surplus value from free wageworkers, accounting is central, and during the late-19th century British capitalism, Marx's model, built an appropriate superstructure of accounting control (Bryer 2017; 2021a, Chapter 2). By holding management accountable to what Marx called "total social capital", the capital market, for the rate of profit, accountants' return on investment (ROI), according to Marx's theory of capitalism the late-19th century British system of accounting regulation was functional for capitalists. This, however, does not mean capitalism functioned smoothly. Capitalism inevitably had crises, severe disruptions to the accumulation of capital because according to Marx's theory of crises, Chapter 2 argues, the accounting superstructure controls individual capitals to strive relentlessly for the maximum rate of profit, the maximum rate of capital accumulation. Capitalist accumulation produces tendencies to "underconsumption", "overproduction" and "disproportionality", Marx argued, which made capitalism fragile and precarious for workers, which made crises possible. They are inevitable because capital accumulation also produces a tendency for the rate of profit to fall, which he argued indirectly causes a financial crisis that triggers an economic crisis because capitalists and managers resist it by making risky investments, increasing debt, speculation, and "swindling", unethical behaviour, including manipulating accounts. According to the accounting interpretation of Marx's theory of capitalism shareholders collectively control individual capitals using published accounts (Bryer 2017, pp. 37–40), which management has incentives to manipulate, whereas to control the circulation of capital it requires objective rate of profit accounts. According to the accounting interpretation of Marx's theory of crises, accounting control promotes capital-intensive investments to increase labour productivity that produces a tendency for the rate of profit to fall. Management resists falling rates of profit because it is accountable for target-rates based on earlier higher rates, which encourages risk-taking and, if possible, "swindling" published accounts, overstating profit and understating risk to inflate share prices, encouraging speculation. Historians can therefore test Marx's theory of crises by investigating whether objective rate of profit accounts generated their possibility, and manipulated published accounts facilitated and made them worse, the focus here.

To explain the roles of accounting in the Great Crash and Depression and the credit-crunch and GFC, *Accounting for Crises* builds on *Creating the "Big Mess"* (Bryer 2021b), which argued that accounting theory underlay American management's late-1920s manipulations of published accounts. Marx used his theory of value to explain core features of late-19th century British accounting, which gave him an accounting theory of capitalist control (Bryer 2017), which *Creating the "Big Mess"* used as the benchmark to judge American accounting theory. Because accounting is a key element of capitalism's superstructure it hypothesised that accounting theory, by undermining management's accountability, would have negative economic consequences (Bryer 2021a, p. 5). *Accounting for Crises* supports that hypothesis by showing Irving Fisher's accounting theory legitimised speculation, and theorists facilitated "swindling" by giving management discretion, which produced crises, but reforming accounting to prevent them, it concludes, is not possible. *Creating the "Big Mess"* argued that Marxian accounting would eliminate discretion, but it would be ideologically unacceptable and would not abolish crises, but in Marx's theory it increases their possibility, and would not prevent speculation or other forms of swindling. Marxian accounting would have shortened the Great Depression and produced a "second", but shorter, "Great Depression" in the early-1980s "profitability crisis", and avoided the GFC, *Accounting for Crises* argues, but increased their severity, which also makes it unacceptable because the Great Depression showed that a severe depression, as it nonetheless was, radicalises workers, threatening unwelcome political consequences.

Capitalists and their agents see only capitalism's "phenomenal forms", of "capital", "profit", "cost", etc., Marx argued, "inverted" appearances of an invisible underlying "essence", the historically-determined calculative mentality and social relations of production (Bryer 2017, 2019). Based on British evidence, he concluded, according to the accounting interpretation, that although their categories were ideological, from the mid-19th century capitalists developed coherent, generally accepted accounting principles, which were inchoate and not comprehensive, but were functional. Late-19th century British accounts held management accountable for ROI, which limited its scope for risk-taking, speculation and swindling. This helps to explain why although Britain had "a long series of financial crises … [in] 1825, 1836-7, 1847, 1857, and 1866", it had lesser "episodes" in 1873, 1878, 1891, 1907, 1914, and 1931, why "from 1866 onwards there were essentially a hundred years of financial stability without any [major] financial crises" (Capie 2014, p. 11). British financial crises became milder because joint stock banks and the Bank of England learned to manage the system, but also because governments implemented a statutory framework (Capie 2014), including for financial reporting. Consistent with Marx's theory that crises would be short because destroying and devaluing capital would promote recovery, from the mid-19th century Britain developed and enforced "conservative" accounting for stewardship (Bryer 2021a, Chapter 2), not for "speculators" (Maltby 2000). During the 19th century, America by contrast had frequent financial crises and was the centre of the Great Depression and GFC, and there *Creating the "Big Mess"* argued, during the 1920s, framed by Fisher's accounting theory, theorists made British principles incoherent, which produced a "big mess". Fisher's theory responded to the ideological problem facing late-19th and early-20th century America created by the growth of "big business", provoking widespread social unrest, political protest and resistance, with an accounting critique of Marx's theory of capitalism (Bryer 2013b; 2021a, Chapter 3). This provided a neo-classical economics alternative that theorists used to justify a wide variety of methods which management used to manipulate profits (Bryer 2021a, Chapter 9). In the context of a falling rate of profit this "big mess", *Accounting for Crises* argues, facilitated the late-1920s stock market boom and 1929 crash, and aggravated the 1930s depression.

Prominently associated with the 1920s stock market boom, Fisher became unpopular after the 1929 crash, his name disappearing from public and scholarly debate. Nevertheless, his theory survived the Great Crash and Depression, Chapters 4 and 5 argue, which limited accounting reform in the 1933 and 1934 Securities Acts passed in response to the collapse in investors' confidence in reported earnings, which underlay the 1929 crash. Strongly criticised after the crash, facing calls for "uniformity" and government control, the accounting profession survived as a private-sector activity in the Securities Acts, which required independent auditors, thanks to the intervention of George Oliver May, for many years the senior Price Waterhouse partner in America, who became its "philosopher" and self-appointed leader. May successfully defended the profession using an interpretation of Fisher's theory derived from John B. Canning (1929) by arguing investors had not understood accounting's "limitations" — that balance sheets did not report economic value, and accounting's role in share valuation was limited to the income statement. Management selects methods, May argued, which independent accountants certify are consistent with "accepted accounting principles", to reflect "earning capacity", an estimate of "steady-state" dividends, which investors can use for share valuation. During the 1930s, Fisher's theory saved the profession from government control, but by limiting accounting reform restricted capital devaluation and the recovery, and from the late-1930s constrained professional regulation, steering it away from British principles based on the "cost theory of value" and stewardship, towards economic valuation and, ultimately, "decision-usefulness".

Following the 1929 crash, from the late-1930s with Securities and Exchange Commission (SEC) encouragement, accountants shifted towards historical cost accounting (HCA) and "stewardship", and introduced regulatory guidance. However, Fisher's theory had infiltrated the Securities Acts, and Chapters 6 argues it infiltrated the profession's Committee on Accounting Procedure (CAP) from the late-1930s to the late-1950s, thanks to William A. Paton's influence, allowing continued management discretion, bringing the CAP's downfall in 1959 and its replacement by the Accounting Principle Board (APB), which suffered the same fate. When the APB failed to control management discretion, in crisis the profession created the Financial Accounting Standards Board (FASB) in 1973, and following Fisher's intellectual rehabilitation in the late-1950s, and accounting theory's revival in the 1960s, Chapter 7 argues, his theory framed its conceptual framework, which abolished "stewardship", replacing it with "decision usefulness" to assert investors' supremacy. This victory, however, was Pyrrhic. Management retains discretion, a taken-for-granted "fact" whose ideological origins are invisible to regulators, observers and scholars (cf. Cardao-Pito and Ferreira 2018, p. 172). An important consequence, the final chapter argues, was that, facing low profit rates, from the early-1980s banks used the FASB's framework to design "sophisticated" financial instruments, particularly "special purpose entities" (SPEs) to "securitize" mortgages, which they could account for "off-balance sheet" and report "gains". The FASB endorsed this accounting in 1996, and the "money machine" it created facilitated the "swindling" that led to the credit-crunch that triggered the GFC.

The first lesson from the books' Marxist history is for capitalists. Socially rational accounting is impossible in modern capitalism because the only ideologically acceptable accounting theory is pathological. Pathology is the study of disease, which in Marxian accounting means not holding management accountable for the rate of profit, which allows swindling, which facilitates and aggravates crises. Fisher's theory undermines accountability because it is an ideologically-distorted managerial representation of capitalism, *Creating the "Big Mess"* argued, designed to reconcile America's simple commodity producers and semi-capitalist manufacturers to late-19th century big business and money capitalism, and undermine support for socialism. Its price, *Accounting for Crises* concludes, is an accounting theory that sanctifies managerialist ideology as unalterable reality, which means financial accounting has no coherent generally accepted comprehensive theory (Jones 2015), and never will.

The second lesson from history is for workers. Accounting history supports Marx's aim in developing the LTFRP, which for him was "the most important law of political economy" because explaining to workers how it underlay capitalism's "bitter contradictions, crises, [and] spasms" would create the necessary "mental conditions" for socialism (1973, pp. 748–749). Understanding the role of accounting theory in facilitating crises should convince them that a society in which rational accounting is impossible has outlived its usefulness. Marx's LTFRP is potentially politically significant because, if true, capitalism's ability to deliver economic progress is inherently limited, but one reason for worker indifference is that Marxists often claim it is false. TSSI proponents refute this claim by, in effect, showing its basis is incorrect accounting, but this is not widely understood (Kliman 2007; Bryer 2017, Chapter 4). Some Marxists seek to demonstrate the LTFRP empirically and use it to explain crises (e.g., Kliman 2012; Roberts 2016; Carchedi and Roberts 2018), but these studies generate controversies and to deal with them also requires understanding Marxian accounting. Fisher's theory facilitates crises, *Accounting for Crises* concludes, but cloaks their reality, represents them as "financial", preventable by reforms, misleading workers, generations of reformers, radicals and even many Marxists, rather than inevitable crises that society can eliminate only by replacing capitalism.

Explaining the Great Crash and Depression

The late-1920s stock market boom and 1929 crash was the "greatest cycle of speculative boom and collapse in modern times" (Galbraith 1961, p. 9). Historians offer "numerous explanations" for the stock market boom, "probably too many", there is "little consensus" (White 1990b, p. 143; Hughes and Cain 1998, p. 440), but most agree with John Kenneth Galbraith who blames it on "irrational" speculation: "illusion replaced reality and people got rimmed" (1961, p. 9). The Great Depression was the deepest and most protracted economic, political and social crisis of the 20th century, creating "disturbances so severe as to call into question the further development of the capitalist system itself" (Foley 1986, p. 142). To contemporaries and historians, 1930s American capitalism was a "system gone haywire" (Dawley 1991, p. 4). Many have studied the causes (e.g., Galbraith 1961; Schlesinger 1957; McElvaine 1984; Bernstein 1987; Dawley 1991), and there are many explanations, including Marxist.

Galbraith's *The Great Crash 1929* remains the classic history of the boom and crash, and his view that "We do not know why a great speculative orgy occurred in 1928 and 1929" (1961, p. 187) is widely accepted. Economic historians agree, "even such a primary question as what caused the 1929 crash cannot be answered with confidence" (Hughes and Cain 1998, p. 440), and probably never will. The 1929 crash, some like Galbraith argue, caused the Great Depression. Some blame failures in monetary policy, and some weakness in banking. Most emphasise sharply increasing inequality in income and wealth causing under-consumption, a slump in demand when the bubble burst, undermining wealthy and middle class investors' confidence and willingness to consume and invest; over-investment in production capacity causing sectoral and global imbalances; poor economic policies and political leadership; and history. However, "there is no consensus" (McElvaine 1984, p. 26). It remains "The puzzle of the 1930s" (Bernstein 1987, p. 1), "precisely why the Great Depression lasted almost an entire generation" (Lichtenstein *et al.* 2000, p. 368). To explain the "irrationality" of the stock market boom and solve the 1930s "puzzle", important ingredients missing from current explanations Chapters 3–5 argue are Marx's theory of crises and Fisher's accounting theory. As its influence spread during the 1920s, Fisher's theory encouraged over-investment, speculation and swindling, but it survived to stave off the threat of "socialism" implicit in the demand for government control of accounting following the crash, and hinder economic adjustment during the 1930s.

The Great Depression began in America, historians agree, was uniquely intense and prolonged there (Bernstein 1987, p. 2), which we must understand as the product of its political, economic and social history, the "tumultuous" years from the late-19th century. From the Gilded Age to the Roaring Twenties big business corporations transformed a society of independent farmers and small manufacturers into "corporate capitalism" (Dawley 1991, pp. 1–2), giant corporations employing large fixed capitals, financed by Wall Street, employing wageworkers, many immigrants from southern and eastern Europe. America's transition to capitalism provoked resistance and demands for change, stimulated economic, racial and ethnic tensions and many "struggles for justice" (Dawley 1991) under the banners of populism, progressivism and socialism, but all foundered on the continuing, dogmatic, widespread commitment to *laissez-faire*, to free markets, small government and individualism. Social historians sympathetic to Marx's historical materialism (Dawley 1991, fn. 9, p. 432), stress the importance of American ideology, of Americanism, particularly its ruling elite's, middle classes', and many workers' devotion to *laissez-faire*. Accounting historians use America's commitment to *laissez-faire* to explain the failure to provide a British-type legal framework to regulate accounting during the 1920s. Social historians use *laissez-faire* to explain the failure of politicians to respond quickly or effectively to popular demands for reform, why the ruling elite ruthlessly repressed those who opposed them, and its slow and limited response to the 1930s crisis (Dawley 1991; Lichtenstein *et al.* 2000; McElvaine 2009). "In every case, reform struggles ran up against one aspect or another of the liberal state" (Dawley 1991, p. 2). *Laissez-faire* explains why only the "necessity of circumstance" of the 1930s drove "the United States from the individual toward the social, from personal liberty towards social security, from less government toward more government", why "Americans were dragged kicking and screaming toward social responsibility" (Dawley 1991, p. 5), including, we will see, in accounting.

Capitalism had "gone haywire". Its devotion to free market economics, to *laissez-faire*, to "100 percent Americanism" had failed to deliver the promised ever-growing prosperity, yet historians show it hindered even Franklin D. Roosevelt, even during the Second New Deal from 1934 when he is widely credited with saving capitalism from communism or fascism. In the face of popular revolt, Roosevelt started a "fledgling welfare state and imposed new regulations on industrial relations", intervened in the economy, fostered unions' growth and increased the regulation of business, the stock exchange and accounting. From the 1930s, America had "liberalism with a social face" (Dawley 1991, p. 4), had avoided "socialism", that is, government regulation of business. Rather than social "liberty" or "equality", the "watchword" guiding reform was "*security*", which produced a form of "social liberalism" (Dawley 1991, pp. 4–5). In the face of evidence contradicting *laissez-faire*, many Americans stuck blindly to it, historians have repeatedly shown, and even radical reformers accepted its limits, but questions remain. Why did "most Americans … shun … social responsibility", "tolerate vast inequalities in wealth in the name of individual opportunity", have an "inveterate attachment to personal liberty", believe "That government is best which governs least" (Dawley 1991, p. 5)? *Laissez-faire* during the early-1930s eventually provoked worker militancy, unions and social and political unrest, but why was the "evolution of New Deal liberalism" enough to "stave off some kind of breakdown of the system" (Dawley 1991, p. 9)? To answer these questions, Alan Dawley accepts, there "is no doubt that deep mental structures and long-term processes deserve attention", that historians must engage in "historical materialism", but doubts "Whether these methodologies can encompass the actual historical process" (Dawley 1991, p. 8).

They can, the book argues, because according to the accounting interpretation of Marx's theory of history the "deep mental structures" historians must study are underlying calculative mentalities, which are signatured by the ways the owners of the means of production calculated surpluses (Bryer 2000, pp. 137–143; 2012, pp. 513–514; 2019, Chapter 2). Historians can observe the phenomenal forms produced by the social relations of production and the superstructure of control, particularly accounting. America's social relations and accounts changed in long-term processes of class conflict as it made the transition from simple commodity production to advanced capitalism (Bryer 2012, 2013a, 2013b), a historical process that Fisher's accounting theory, constructed as a critique of Marx to undermine American socialism, distorted to provide an appealing alternative concept of capitalism (Bryer 2012, 2013a, 2013b). Historians can therefore seek to integrate "deep mental structures" in "the actual historical process" through a Marxist history of Fisher's accounting theory. This answers the challenge of the well-known contemporary journalist, Walter Lippmann (1914, p. 313), who in his youth flirted with socialism, that "even if Karl Marx captured the secret of social evolution (which is doubtful) … the necessity still remains of showing concretely how the key unlocks the American difficulty". Understood as a key to unlocking the link between accounting and social reality, the success of Fisher's theory as a criticism of Marx would explain why many Americans found it difficult to recognise social reality. From this perspective, Chapter 5 argues, Roosevelt did not "save" American capitalism, that this accolade should go to Fisher's accounting theory.

The "fact that there was something rotten in the state of American capitalism" in the 1930s was not just "utterly incomprehensible to neoclassical economists" (Dawley 1991, p. 335). Through a large expansion in university education in accounting and economics during the first three decades of the 20th century, at varying levels of consciousness, Fisher's neoclassical vision of capitalism gripped its ruling elite, politicians, intellectuals and middle classes (Bryer 2013b; 2021a, Chapters 3 and 4). Influential and popular during the 1920s, America's most famous economist, closely associated with the stock market boom and engaged in benefiting from it, Fisher's "reputation crashed" following the 1929 crash (Tobin 2005, p. 25). Economists, business leaders and bankers "still esteemed Fisher" (Allen 1993, p. 258), but until the late-1950s his name "was without honour in his own university" (Tobin 2005, p. 25). In the 1940s, references to him "vanished from macroeconomics" (Dimand and Geanakoplos 2005, p. 10). Although rarely cited, his theory remained influential, and in the 1930s, interpreted and promulgated by G.O. May, saved American capitalism, blunted demands for radical change, for government control of big business and the capital market, the key to which was controlling accounting.

Complaints about accounting became vociferous after the 1929 crash, but the SEC, established in 1934, began to clean up the "mess" only from the late-1930s. Historians have not considered the impact of accounting theory in blunting and shaping reform. Some highlight the SEC's creation as an important New Deal reform, but focus on its regulation of stock exchange practices, but most ignore it, and economists discount its importance. Galbraith (1961, p. 9) noted, "Congress passed some tolerably astringent legislation, including the Securities Exchange Act of 1934", but thought, "It was not, at the time, especially necessary". Capital markets researchers and agency theorists agree (Bryer 2021a, pp. 381–388). Contrary to the contemporary popular view, they argue, "There is no substantial evidence to support the contention that accounting was culpable in the stock market crash of 1929" (Dillon 1984, p. 6), or the Great Depression. History, however, shows accounting was culpable in two ways. First, *Creating the "Big Mess"* argued, management used accounting theory to justify profit smoothing. Second, the consequence, *Accounting for Crises* argues, was fooling wealthy and middle-class shareholders who used Fisher's "new-era theory" of security valuation to value shares using earnings, which encouraged speculation and management "swindling", representing companies as safer and more profitable than they were. Management's unaccountability allowed overinvestment in the 1920s and after the crash weakened investors' confidence, which prevented new investment, but allowed overcapacity throughout the 1930s.

Crises would be temporary, Marx argued, because facing an unacceptably low rate of profit capitalists would cut back production, capacity and costs, would "devalue capital" to restore the rate of profit, which would regenerate investment and growth. Capitalists would reallocate capital from markets and technologies producing losses or low profitability to new markets and technologies offering higher returns and the process of expansion would begin again. Crises, Marx predicted, would become more serious as capitalism developed and became more extensive and integrated. However, he did not predict capitalism's catastrophic economic collapse, its cataclysmic end, because his study of British capitalism revealed that capitalists used functional, socially objective accounts of "cost price" and "profit" to hold management and workers accountable for required ROI (Bryer 2006, 2017), which Chapter 2 argues meant they would be self-correcting. In

America, by contrast, reacting to a falling general rate of profit, and historically low corporate profit rates, Chapters 3–5 argue, pathological accounts sent its economy "haywire". Vulgar economics' infiltration of accounts would have surprised Marx, who saw the possibility of accounting swindling, observing it in British railway accounts, but assumed capitalists would quickly learn to prevent it. Capitalists failed to learn in America because to defeat the threat of socialism they accepted Fisher's accounting theory, which distorted capitalist reality, depicting it as simple commodity production and money capitalism (Bryer 2013b).

After the 1929 crash, criticisms of accounts and accountants discredited the economic valuation, balance sheet approach that Fisher's theory had spawned during the 1920s. G.O. May nevertheless, Chapter 5 argues, drew on Fisher's theory, switching the focus from balance sheets to "earning capacity", to the profit and loss account ("income statement"). May used a simplification of Canning's (1929) concept of accounting income to define the "nature" of accounting, to limit criticism of practice, to prevent government control of accounts and auditing. Accounting's role in share valuation, May argued, was providing investors a measure of "earning capacity" under current conditions based on "conventions" or "generally accepted principles" that management choose to give an "indication" of future earnings. Intelligent shareholders could improve on these steady-state forecasts to value a corporation's shares, but because this was accounting's objective, not producing the factual statement of position and progress that many assumed, May defended practitioners by stressing its inherent "limitations" for investors, as theorists had (Bryer 2021a). Because accounts reflected a process of independent judgement based on expert knowledge and experience, management must take responsibility for selecting the appropriate methods and independent accountants must give their opinion whether they were consistent with "generally accepted principles". During the 1930s, May's interpretation stemmed the criticism and undermined critical, potentially radical analyses of the problem of controlling big business, particularly Adolf A. Berle and Gardiner C. Means', *The Modern Corporation and Private Property* (1932), because it denied them an operational theory of social control. For the same reason, Fisher's theory defeated the radical demand of resurgent unions in the 1940s led by the United Auto Workers to "open the books" (Bryer 2016).

From the Golden Age to the Global Financial Crisis

World War II pulled America out of depression. The late-1940s to the early-1970s was a Golden Age of high rates of profit and economic growth. It ended, Marxists argue, with a "profitability crisis", a sharply falling rate of profit from the late-1960s that hit a historical low in the early-1980s, and high levels of inflation, producing recessions in the mid-1970s and early-1980s, ended by government interventions to boost the rate of profit and prevent a second Great Depression (Kliman 2012; Roberts 2016). Government intervention, however, Andrew Kliman (2012) argues, prevented sufficient destruction and devaluation of capital to restore the rate of profit to allow historical growth rates to continue. Instead, from the 1970s there was low economic growth and frequent debt-fuelled financial crises resolved by government-sponsored debt expansions, leading to the 2008–2009 GFC. Chapters 7 and 8 support Kliman's explanations of the "profitability crisis" and GFC, but add roles for accounting theory.

To restore investors' "confidence", badly undermined by the 1929 crash, the accounting profession came under pressure from 1937 from the SEC, academics and financial press, to clear up accounting's "mess". In 1939, it reformed the CAP to seek to reign in management's discretion, on which May, Paton and A.C. Littleton justified "stewardship", "cost" and "conservatism", and outlawed egregious abuses. After World War II, the New York Stock Exchange (NYSE) promoted "people's capitalism", to propagandise widespread share ownership and entice back still wary investors. However, Fisher's continuing influence, Chapter 6 argues, meant the CAP's many "Accounting Research Bulletins" (ARBs), failed to curb management's discretion, which it increasingly used as the rate of profit fell from the mid-1950s. Accounting methods proliferated as the CAP dealt with issues on a case-by-case basis (Storey and Storey 1998, p. 31). Disagreements flared over deferred taxation, historical cost (HC) versus current value, general price-level adjustments and unusual items (Zeff 1999, p. 92), which undermined investors' confidence and the profession's credibility, which led to the CAP's replacement in 1959 by the APB. However, as the rate of profit fell sharply in the 1960s, management's insistence on discretion provoked conflicts over leases, pooling-of-interests, inflation accounting, and many other issues, which threatened the profession's "economic success story" as "people's capitalism" became a reality (Carey 1969b, p. 58), leading to the APB's replacement in 1973 by the FASB. In crisis, after an intensive academic campaign, to limit management's discretion, the profession in effect accepted required embracing Fisher's theory.

University of Chicago economists rehabilitated Fisher's reputation from the late-1950s, and his theory of capital and income underlies the dominance of "financial economics" in mainstream financial reporting theory today. A new generation of accounting scholars, dubbed the "normative apriorists", a school that peaked in the 1960s and early-1970s (Mouck 1995, p. 55), came forward do battle with management discretion, proposing fundamental change. Drawing on Fisher, Paton and Canning, financial accounting's objective, they argued in various ways, should be what the FASB called "decision-usefulness", operationalised leading authorities argued by "current value accounting" in various forms (e.g., Edwards and Bell 1961; Staubus 1961, Mattessich 1964; Chambers 1966; Sterling 1970). This school gave birth to the "information perspective" in the late-1960s that integrated accounting as "information" into Fisher's theory of financial markets as markets for equalising preferences for borrowing and lending (Mouck 1995, p. 65). This "new" perspective drew on Paton's (1922) and Canning's (1929) interpretation of Fisher's theory as a branch of statistics, that accounting should have "predicting ability", which it reformulated as "decision-usefulness", which the FASB used to write its conceptual framework in the late-1970s and early-1980s. The FASB's framework was a Pyrrhic victory, however, Chapter 7 shows, because despite the best endeavours of the best minds, its key concepts covertly give management discretion. The framework, it argues, allowed management to avoid devaluing capital by ditching "current cost accounting" (CCA) during the "profitability crisis" of the 1970s and early-1980s, and Chapter 8 that it allowed banks to account for "securitization" SPEs off-balance sheet which facilitated the credit-crunch and GFC.

The FASB wrote its framework in the context of the "profitability crisis" and high inflation. Management demanded some form of "inflation accounting" to reduce reported profits in the face of wage demands, Chapter 7 argues, and make the case for tax cuts, which prompted an "inflation accounting debate" (Tweedie and Whittington 1984). Capitalists should measure the rate of profit using replacement cost accounting (RCA), according to Marxian accounting, and late-19th century British principles, and some 20th century accounting scholars, inchoately agreed (Bryer 2021b, pp. 49–57). US accounting theorists argued for accounts adjusted for "specific prices", usually RCs, or "general price-level accounting" (GPLA), also known as "current purchasing power accounting" (CPP), or prominently (Paton 1922; Sweeney 1936) for both. When the UK Accounting Standards Steering Committee (1973) and the FASB (1974) proposed CPP/GPLA accounting, favoured by some large companies, the British government established a Committee of Enquiry into whether RCA was preferable, and the SEC in 1974 required key RCA disclosures. In 1975 the UK's "Sandilands Committee" recommended RCA, which it called "current cost accounting", but took its justification from the economic theory of valuation popularised by Professor James Bonbright of Columbia University in *The Valuation of Property* (1937), his analysis of "value to the owner", influenced by Fisher's theory. This introduced management discretion into measuring replacement cost (RC) and allowed lower values using net realisable value (NRV) and PV. When CCA's RCA element revealed sharply lower profits and dividends paid from capital, its origins in economic theory allowed management to agitate for "monetary adjustments" to counteract and camouflage these effects, which the UK's Accounting Standards Board (ASC) accepted in Statement of Standard Accounting Practice (SSAP) 16 *Current Cost Accounting* (1980). The FASB followed the UK's lead in withdrawing its 1974 GPLA proposals, producing Financial Accounting Standard (FAS) 33 *Financial Reporting and Changing Prices* (FASB 1979) requiring CCA and GPLA. CCA motivated UK plant-closures in the mid-1970s and early-1980s (Bryer and Brignall 1986), and initially US analysts used it (Berliner 1983; Norby 1983). However, as the inflation rate fell following neoliberalism's ascendance in the US and UK, and economic policies prevented another Great Depression, management used theorists' criticisms of RC to agitate for abolishing CCA, which the SEC, FASB and ASC accepted in the mid-1980s. The rate of profit's failure to recover to pre-1970s levels shows insufficient devaluation of capital, Marxists argue, which history supports because theory allowed management to resist implementing RCA and ditch it.

Accounting theory also contributed to the GFC, the final chapter argues, by helping US banks find new ways to resist low rates of profit from the 1980s. Influenced by John H. Myers' (1959, 1962) contributions to revenue recognition and lease accounting, based on Paton's (1922) and Canning's (1929) "asset" definitions, banks used the FASB's asset definition, which allows both Paton's and Canning's, to create new financial instruments. An important innovation was "securitization" of banks' mortgages, transferring them to a "special purpose entity" (SPE) that sold the cash flow rights to outside investors. The SPE used the proceeds to pay the bank that accounted for the transfer as a "sale" usually booking a "gain". The banks built on FAS 76 *Extinguishment of Debt* on "in-substance defeasance" and FAS 77 *Reporting by Transferors for Transfers of Receivables with Recourse*, issued in 1983, based respectively on Paton's definition of an asset as the control of use-values with PV, and Canning's definition as legal or equitable control of access to future cash flows. FAS 125 *Accounting for Transfers and Servicing of Financial Assets and Extinguishments of Liabilities* (FASB 1996) approved off-balance sheet accounting for "qualifying special purpose entities" (QSPEs), drawing on Paton's definition to argue that banks did not control SPEs, and Canning's to justify treating transferring cash flow rights as a "sale". By justifying off-balance sheet accounting, the chapter concludes, accounting theory justified extensive "swindling", which facilitated the credit-crunch and GFC.

Overview

Chapter 2 gives an accounting interpretation of Marx's theory of crises, which explains the presentation of his theory of capitalism in the three Volumes of *Capital*, and his conclusion that the underlying cause of crises is accumulation, and contrasts it with leading critical interpretations. The chapter explains Marx's "general law of capitalist accumulation" presented in Volume 1 as workers' first accounting lesson in crises: wages and unemployment are the "dependent" variables; capital accumulation is the "independent" variable. It explains his controversial "schemas" of expanded reproduction in Volume 2, as interlinked departmental profit and loss accounts that reveal a major source of workers' precariousness in capitalism is the absence of a central controller. It explains Marx's value-price transformation in Volume 3 as his theory of accounting results control by total social capital, and gives an accounting explanation of his theory of crises based on the consequences of a falling rate of profit leading to an inevitable financial and economic crisis.

Chapter 3 applies Marx's theory of crises to the Great Collapse in America, 1929–1932. It outlines the historical context of the 1920s boom, 1929 crash and 1930s depression, and uses the accounting interpretation to evaluate historians' and orthodox Marxists' explanations. The evidence, it concludes, supports Marx's theory, which explains the origin of the crisis in reactions to the falling general rate of profit from the mid-1920s and historically low corporate profit rates, increased concentration and centralisation, an increased rate of exploitation, increased borrowing, and exceptional "speculation" and "swindling".

Chapter 4 analyses the impact of accounting theory on the 1920s stock market boom and 1929 crash. Fisher's theory influenced practice during the "lawless decade", *Creating the "Big Mess"* argued, that Henry Rand Hatfield's, Paton's and others' proliferated accounting options gave "explanatory justifications for accepted procedure" (Previts 1980, p. 110), theoretical excuses that management and accountants used to justify "conservative" accounting and profit-smoothing. This accounting and Fisher's "new-era theory" of security analysis, the chapter argues, explains shareholders' "speculative" behaviour. Accounting practice contributed to the boom by suppressing risk, undermining management's accountability for capital, allowing the overinvestment, underconsumption and sectoral imbalances that underlay the depression. Accounting theory contributed to the "speculative" bubble by legitimating valuing shares using reported earnings, and loss of confidence in their integrity explains the 1929 crash.

Chapter 5 analyses the role of Fisher's theory in saving capitalism from "socialism" through the limits it imposed on reform during the Great Depression, particularly the 1933 and 1934 Securities Acts' reform of accounting, which was heavily criticised after the crash. During the 1932 election, Roosevelt promised accounting reform as an integral part of capital market regulation. Berle and Means' influential *The Modern Corporation and Private Property*, published in 1932 argued that the owners of large corporations did not "control" them, and was critical of accounting. One of Roosevelt's "brains trust" advisers, Berle had radical aims, but Fisher's theory prevented him from formulating radical proposals. G.O. May, the chapter argues, persuasively interpreted Fisher's theory to defend the profession, and May tutored Berle on accounts, which by denying him an operational definition of "control", undermined his and others' criticisms of accounts and their radical aims, which saved the profession from government control and business from "socialism". The price during the 1930s was the profession's rejection of demands for "uniformity", allowing continued management discretion, manipulating accounts to overstate the rate of profit. To restore investor confidence and counter union-militancy, in 1937 an exasperated SEC demanded "conservatism" and that the profession produce "generally accepted accounting principles" (GAAP).

Chapter 6 examines the SEC's, the profession's and academics' search for GAAP from the late-1930s. To assert management's accountability they promoted a version of British conservatism — HC, realisation and matching — and May, Paton and Littleton, and others, emphasised accounting's "stewardship" function. The high point was Paton and Littleton's *Introduction to Corporate Accounting Standards* (1940), an influential attempt to articulate accounting principles without an explicit theory of value. This and similar attempts at formulating a theory of "stewardship", "historical cost", "revenue" and "expense", ruled American accounting increasingly badly for the next 30 years. This was because accountants, academics and the SEC interpreted "stewardship" using May's interpretation to mean accounting's primary objective was valuation using the income statement, that "earning capacity" measured management's "accomplishment", and concluded accounting did not have or need a theory of balance sheet valuation. Accepting Fisher's economic entity concept, according to May's and Paton and Littleton's interpretation, management select accounting policies to reflect its estimate of "earning capacity", requiring only their disclosure and consistent application. In the Golden Age with high rates of profit and economic growth the CAP cleared up the mess from the 1920s, but as the rate of profit fell from the mid-1950s and inflation increased another mess began to appear, which given management's ideological hegemony and intransigent control of accounting, "generally accepted accounting principles" were unable to prevent. The Security Acts' objective of "disclosure" for "fair" pricing left accounting open to recapture by Fisher's theory, which began following a resurgence in neoclassical accounting theory from the late-1950s. By the early-1960s, to curb management's discretion, which threatened "people's capitalism", a new generation of academics built on Hatfield, Paton, and Canning who, with Fisher increasingly in the foreground, provided the intellectual basis of the FASB's framework (Whittington 1977; Zeff *et al.* 1979; Mills 1994). By the late-1960s, facing a legitimacy crisis, the profession accepted theorists' call, in effect, to seek intellectual hegemony by embracing Fisher's theory. In 1971, the AICPA appointed a "blue ribbon" committee of leading accountants and academics, the "Trueblood Committee", to determine financial reporting's objective, which concluded it should be "decision-usefulness".

Chapter 7 examines the FASB's framework that implemented the Trueblood recommendations in the context of the 1970s and 1980s profitability crisis. It outlines the Marxist measurement debate, whether to calculate the rate of profit using HCAs or CCAs, and highlights the apparent contradiction between Marx arguing that capitalists should use RCA and the fact that management and investors continued to use HCA. It explains accounting theory's influence on management's domination of the 1970s and 1980s inflation accounting debate, how it used theory to water-down and camouflage the effects of the RCA elements of CCA, and to ditch it in the mid-1980s. The chapter explains the FASB's abolition of "stewardship" and its replacement with "decision-usefulness", and reinstatement of Fisher's theory of balance sheet valuation, replacing HC, "revenue-expense" accounting, with "asset-liability" accounting. The FASB's framework took overt control of accounting choice from management, but resorting to Fisher's theory, the chapter concludes, meant the profession's victory was Pyrrhic because within it management covertly retains discretion.

Chapter 8 examines the influence of the FASB's framework on accounting for securitization SPEs that it argues facilitated the "swindling" from the 1990s that underlay the 2007 credit-crunch, triggering the 2008–2009 GFC. It applies Marxian consolidated accounting to securitization SPEs, which it uses to judge US GAAP, which allowed off-balance sheet accounting and fair value "gains" on retained interests, concluding that banks should have consolidated their SPEs, and should not have reported "gains". It explains the origins of the FASB's standards for SPE accounting in Paton's and Canning's "asset" definitions, and shows how bankers used the discretion they allowed to justify swindling by overstating profits and understating capital, violating the realisation principle, basing management-bonuses on discretionary "gains", ignoring credit-standards, and failing to conduct due-diligence. The FASB's framework, insiders recognised, had created a "machine" for generating "gains" and keeping assets and liabilities off-balance sheet, which bankers exploited for personal gain. This experience shows, the book concludes, that socially rational accounting is impossible within modern capitalism, whereas a coherent, generally accepted and comprehensive set of Marxian accounting standards for Day 1 of socialism remains a possibility if critical accountants take Marx's theories of history and capitalism seriously.

Chapter 2

Marx's Theory of Crises

By holding management accountable for ROI late-19th century British accounting was functional for capitalists collectively, according to Marx's theory of capitalism (Bryer 2021a, Chapter 2), but this does not mean British capitalism functioned smoothly. Marx argued against the political economists that capitalism's normal functioning, its dedication to capital accumulation, to economic growth, inevitably produced crises, Marxists agree, but they disagree about what he meant, and many argue his theory of crises, if he had one, is confused, inconsistent, or at best under-developed. By contrast, building on accounting interpretations of Marx's theories of value and history (Bryer 2017, 2019), the chapter argues he proposed a coherent accounting theory of crises open to empirical testing. Individual capitals use accounts to control their "valorisation processes" of producing and realising profit, Marx understood from Frederick Engels, and argued that as capitalism developed individual capitals became elements of "total social capital", today's capital market, accountable for the rate of profit, accountants' ROI (Bryer 2017, Chapter 3). Accounting is a key element of capitalism's superstructure (Bryer 2019, Figure 2.1, p. 35), which drives capitalists and their agents to seek the maximum rate of profit, which promotes continuous increases in the forces of production, particularly technology, but produces inevitable crises, disruptions to accumulation. This chapter gives an accounting interpretation of Marx's theory of crises, explains accounting's roles in producing, exacerbating and ending them. The following three chapters use it to explain accounting's roles in facilitating the boom during the Roaring Twenties, triggering the Great Crash, and deepening and extending the Great Depression; the final three chapters use it to explain accounting regulation from the late-1930s, and accounting's roles in facilitating the credit-crunch and GFC.

Like the classical political economists, mainstream economists today have no theory of crises because they assume economies naturally seek "equilibrium" and crises are the consequence of interference or external events. There are many non-mainstream theories, including Marx's (Cobb 2015), but "there is no generally agreed Marxist theory of crisis" (Clarke 2012, p. 90). Marx's writings on crises have long been controversial (Fine 1975, p. 55; Cullenberg 1994, pp. viii, 1; Clarke 1994, pp. 4–10, 14–72; 2012, p. 90; Kliman 2017, p. 225). He uniquely argued, all agree, that crises were inherent and inevitable consequences of capitalism's functioning, its relentless accumulation of capital, which defined its limits and pointed to the necessity of socialism. Prominent Marxists, however, argue he had no coherent theory, and failed to explain how crises were inevitable, nowhere "present[s] a systematic and thoroughly worked-out exposition of a theory of crisis" (Clarke 1994, p. 5). "It is generally assumed", as Simon Clarke (1994, p. 9) says, "Marx never developed a systematic theory of crisis, an assumption that has left his successors free to construct their various interpretations of Marx's crisis theory from scattered, and not entirely consistent, fragments". According to Clarke and others, "Marx's writings on crisis are indeed fragmentary and confused", his discussions "certainly do not provide a consistent and rigorous theory of crisis", that "there is no doubt that Marx's theorising is undeveloped, and that his discussion is often inconsistent and confused" (Clarke 1994, pp. 10, 138; Fine 1975, p. 55; Harvey 2006, p. 179). The dominant orthodox Marxist interpretation is "underconsumptionist" (Kliman 2012, pp. 12, 151), but Marxists often see Marx "associating" crises with a falling rate of profit, "overproduction", "underconsumption" and "disproportionality", "without ever clearly championing one or the other theory" (Clarke 1994, p. 5), yet conclude he predicted capitalism's inevitable collapse.

Critics of Marx's theory of crises also criticise his theory of value for being metaphysical, claim that his value-price transformation is inconsistent and his LTFRP is false. TSSI-supporters rebut these criticisms (Kliman 2007). The accounting interpretation supports their rebuttals (Bryer 2017, Chapters 4 and 5), and the chapter supports their interpretation of Marx's crises theory, particularly Kliman's (2007, 2012, 2015, 2017; see also Kliman *et al.* 2013). TSSI-supporters reject the underconsumptionist interpretation (e.g., Kliman 2012), see a coherent production-based theory of inevitable crises (e.g., Kliman 2015), which the accounting interpretation articulates as Marx's explanation of the consequences of capitalist control of society's valorisation process, which national income accounts (e.g., Kliman 2012, 2015; Roberts 2016; Carchedi and Roberts 2018) and other accounting evidence, later chapters argue, supports. A key element of capitalism's superstructure in Marx's theory, critics overlook, is accounting, management accounting focused on controlling the production of surplus value, and financial accounting focused on reporting results to shareholders, Marx's "functioning capitalists" (Bryer 2017, 2019), which explains why, we will see, he did not argue that crises were logically or theoretically inevitable. Crises were historically inevitable given capitalism's pursuit of ROI. This produced its contradictory tendencies, to expand production limitlessly, but constrain it within the limits of profitability, and its tendencies towards a falling rate of profit, speculation and "swindling", including manipulating accounts, produced inevitable financial crises that triggered economic crises. Capitalism was vulnerable to crises because accumulation produced "disproportionality", unbalanced development, created tendencies to "overproduction" and "underconsumption", its "dynamics" in seeking maximum ROI. There were external causes (famine, disease, war, etc.), but crises arose indirectly, Marx argued, because capitalism's pursuit of surplus value by increasing labour productivity created a tendency for the rate of profit to fall, and capitalists' reactions inevitably produced a financial crisis triggering an economic crisis. A falling rate of profit means falling accumulation (productive investment), lower economic growth (incomes), which capitalists respond to by reducing interest rates, increasing debt, making riskier investments, speculation and swindling, which create a financial crisis, which triggers an economic crisis and the destruction of capital, paving the way to recovery.

In his mature works (from *Grundrisse*), Marx did not predict a catastrophic crisis, that the rate of profit would fall so low that capitalism could not continue, causing a socialist revolution. The LTFRP's significance for Marx lay in the consequences of the reactions it provoked in capitalists and their agents, those producing crises, and those that overcame them. The LTFRP, he concluded, was "the most important law of political economy" because showing that it underlay capitalism's "bitter contradictions, crises, spasms" would create the necessary "mental conditions" for socialism (Marx 1973, pp. 748–749; 1981, p. 319; 1991, p. 104). To explain crises to workers, the chapter argues, Marx in effect explained them as the consequence of capitalist accounting control, which confronted capitalists and their agents with the "phenomenal forms" produced by its social relations of production. Crises were self-correcting, Marx argued, by destroying and devaluing capital, but would be educational for workers who come to understand and abolish them by abolishing capitalism because the "irrationality of … [the] system becomes most evident at times of crisis" (Harvey 2006, p. 203). As Marx put it, "The violent destruction of capital not by relations external to it, but rather as a condition of its self-preservation, is the most striking form in which advice is given to be gone and [make way] for a higher state of social production" (1973, pp. 749–750), and a higher state of accounting control (Bryer 2019, Chapter 8).

The chapter first outlines the accounting interpretation of Marx's theory of capitalist control, which it argues explains the progression of his presentation through the volumes of *Capital* and his conclusion that the underlying cause of crises is capitalist accumulation. Second, it explains Marx's "general law of capitalist accumulation" presented towards the end of Volume 1 as the workers' first accounting lesson in crises, which was that wages and unemployment are the "dependent" variables, and capital accumulation is the "independent" variable. The third section explains his controversial "schemas" of expanded reproduction presented at the end of Volume 2, as interlinked "departmental" profit or loss accounts that reveal major sources of workers' precariousness in capitalism are "unbalanced growth", "production for the sake of production" (Kliman 2011), for increased surplus value, not workers' consumption, and the absence of a central controller. Orthodox Marxists interpret Marx's schema as a blueprint for socialist planning (Harvey 2013, pp. 376–378), but according to the accounting interpretation Marx did not advocate central planning (Bryer 2019, pp. 281–283). Its necessary absence in capitalism corrects the common view that Marx intended his schemas to explain crises by the improbability of "balanced growth". The fourth section interprets his value-price transformation in Volume 3 as a theory of results control by total social capital, the accounting basis of the LTFRP, which adds technical, labour-saving change to production-for-the-sake-of-production. Finally, the chapter explains Marx's theory of crises in Volume 3 as the consequences of a falling rate of profit. Following chapters use the accounting interpretation to explain the 1929 crash and Great Depression, and the 2007 credit-crunch and GFC.

An Accounting Interpretation

Marx and Engels began their economic studies in the 1840s to explain capitalist crises, and this was Marx's aim when he began *Grundrisse* in 1857. When he worked out his theory of surplus value he immediately used it to articulate a theory of history as evolving "modes of production", the combination of the forces and social relations of production controlled by a "superstructure" of law, including accounting, and ideology (Bryer 2017, 2019). He then elaborated and "proved" his theory of value by using it to explain the capitalist "economic categories" or "phenomenal forms" he found in political economy, but critically in capitalists' accounts, how capitalists used them to control the valorisation process (Bryer 2017), and used this, what follows argues, to explain crises, which were the consequence of its functioning. Marx's analyses of accounting for value revealed the possibility of the LTFRP as the consequence of the tendency to increase the rate of profit by increasing labour productivity using machinery, etc., increasing the proportion of constant capital, and that the indirect consequences of the accounting control-induced reactions to it inevitably caused crises.

Marx's Theory of Accounting Control

Marxists debate why Marx in December 1862 decided to change the title of his *Critique of Political Economy* to *Capital* and the logic of its presentation. According to the accounting interpretation, changing to *Capital* reflected his discovery from studying double-entry bookkeeping (DEB) and capitalist accounts in the early-1860s that he could understand, correct and transcend Quesnay's *Economic Tableau* by constructing and explaining society's and individual capital's accounts with his theory of value (Bryer 2017, pp. 64–71). Being confident he could explain real capitalist's accounts using his theory of value was important for presenting his argument. Knowing it would explain the economic categories in actual accounts meant he could simplify the presentation. He could first explain surplus value and capital accumulation assuming prices equalled values, leaving to last explaining why individual capitals earned the general rate of profit in reality where prices did not necessarily equal values (Bryer 2017, pp. 71–75).

According to David Harvey (2006, p. 156) Marx provided "three major 'models' of the dynamics of accumulation set out in *Capital*", each offering "a particular 'window' or vantage point from which to view an extraordinarily complex process". Volume 1's model focuses on the production of surplus value, emphasises social and technical change and class conflict, but takes realisation for granted; Volume 2's model focuses on circulation and expanded reproduction, but ignores class conflict; in Volume 3 "the intent ... is to ... build a model that integrates production-distribution relationship with production-realization requirements" (Harvey 2006, pp. 156–157). Seeing Marx as an economic "model" builder, Harvey is critical of his "restrictive assumptions", and failure to integrate them theoretically. According to the accounting interpretation, however, Marx gives three perspectives on capitalist accounting that complement and reinforce each other, three different views of the same thing, integrated aspects of capitalist accounting control, not different "models" requiring theoretical integration. Marx started by explaining the accounts of what in *Grundrisse* he called "capital-in-general" and in *Capital* Volumes 1, 2 and early-parts of 3, "aggregate social capital" or the "collective capitalist", of which the individual commodity or capital is a representative part. For most of Volume 3, by contrast, Marx explained the accounts of "many capitals" forming a "total social capital", of capitalism as a living whole, as the aggregate capital in motion. The accounting logic of *Capital*, in short, is that workers first learn how capitalists-in-general's accounts control the production and circulation of commodities and, second, how total social capital controls competing individual capitals by holding them accountable for the rate of profit (Bryer 2017, Chapter 3).

This accounting logic explains Marx's presentation in *Capital*, starting from an abstract analysis of the commodity in Volume 1 as an element of "aggregate social capital" and ending with a real-world analysis of "many capitals" in Volume 3. Marx's argument, as Mattick says, has a "complex structure" because it is "a critique of political economy", a demonstration that it "represents an inversion of the true state of affairs", its claim that capitalism is merely a "market economy", and an explanation of the differences between appearances and underlying reality (2008, p. 214). According to political economists, capitalists made profits from the market, but Marx argued this was impossible, that it must originate in production (Mattick 2008, p. 214). The "challenge" was to provide "an analysis of the functioning of the social system ... [that did] justice at once to the individual character of capitalist entities — the absence of any overall planning mechanism — and to the fact that they are constrained in their operations by their relation to the rest of the system" (Mattick 2008, p. 215). Marx met the challenge "by the power of abstraction", "begins by representing the system as made up of 'aliquot parts', as a way of examining the features shared by all capitalist firms" that "abstracts from all the features that, in reality, differentiate firms" (Mattick 2008, p. 215). This abstraction gave Marx the foundation of a general system of accounting.

In Volume 1, he explained how an individual capitalist as a representative of all capitalists combined, "capital-in-general", produces and accounts for surplus value, assumed to be equal to profit, and in Volume 2 how individually and collectively through "departments" capitalists account for its circulation and realisation. In Volume 3, by contrast, he explained how with the development of the joint stock company and "total social capital", the aggregate capitalist as a living individual, the capital market, the capitalist's generally accepted accounting calculations mean that competition between individual capitals distributes surplus value to give them all the general rate of profit (Bryer 2017, pp. 78–92). Marx's accounting solution to the "transformation problem", the transformation of values into prices of production, is his theory of capitalist accounting control by total social capital that holds individual capitals accountable for the general rate of profit or required ROI (Bryer 2017, Chapter 5). Neglected by Marxists, Marx conceptualised total social capital using what Piaget (1971) called the method of "operational structuralism", a structured totality formed by the functioning of its parts according to laws that explained the totality in motion (Bryer 2017, pp. 80–81). Understanding Marx's theory "dialectically" rather than as only a question of abstract logic (Kennedy 2001), that is, stuck at the level of capital-in-general, as a historical theory of social control, through markets, but also capitalist accounting, shows that his theory of crises is neither inconsistent nor confused.

Marx's Accounting Theory of Crises

Driving the dynamics of capitalist accumulation, according to the accounting interpretation, is accountability for the rate of profit, because underlying it Marx's analyses revealed were three interrelated accounting ratios (Foley 1986, p. 92):

$$\frac{s}{C}=\left[\frac{s}{v}\right]\left[\frac{v}{v+c}\right]\left[\frac{v+c}{C}\right].$$

Marx decomposed the rate of profit (s/C) into the product of the rate of surplus value (s/v), the division of value added ($v + s$); the organic composition of capital ($v/[v + c]$), the proportion of variable to total capital; and the rate of turnover of capital ($[v + c]/C$), how many times the capitalist sold and recovered the capital each year; where s = surplus value, C = total capital employed, v = variable capital (production wages), c = constant capital (non-labour cost of production, materials, fixed asset depreciation, etc). Capitalists do not see the value form of these variables, but have their own version of Marx's formula in prices, without the organic composition of capital (OCC), usually called the "DuPont formula" after Donaldson Brown, DuPont corporation's chief accountant, who developed it in 1912, that ROI = $p/S \times S/C$, where p = profit and S = sales (Bryer 2013b, p. 310).[1]

A weakness of empirical studies that decompose rate of profit movements into changes in s/v, $v/[v + c]$ and $[v + v]/C$ is that "since these variables themselves have multiple potential causes, this does not provide a satisfactory *causal* explanation of movements in the rate of profit" (Kliman 2017, p. 231). The decomposition does, however, provide a satisfactory basis for explaining accountability to capitalists for results, who leave it to management to seek to understand and control the causal relationships. Similarly, what follows argues, Marx's decomposition provides a satisfactory general framework for explaining crises as the indirect consequences of a falling rate of profit without requiring multi-causal explanations of each variable, which are necessary for specific cases (e.g., Kliman 2012, pp. 133–138). In short, Marx's variables do "explain" the rate of profit because they are its components, but they do not explain themselves. Using them, Marx's analyses of individual capitals as competing elements of capital-in-general, accountable to total social capital for required ROI revealed, we will see, that capitalism had tendencies to "disproportionality", unbalanced growth, "underconsumption", insufficient demand, and "overproduction", excessive commodities, which made it vulnerable to any interruption to accumulation, from accidents, wars, etc., but critically, from inevitable financial crises. A falling rate of profit

[1] For capital-in-general, we can straightforwardly measure Marx's value categories in prices. Profit does not necessarily equal surplus value for individual capitals, but we can observe socially necessary labour time in capitalist calculations of cost-prices and profits (Bryer 2017, pp. 148–168).

would lead to "overproduction of capital", producing more surplus value than capitalists can profitably reinvest (Marx 1981, p. 360), indirectly generating a financial crisis, triggering an economic crisis revealing the underlying fragility. Driving these tendencies, Marx argued, was the aim of unlimited accumulation: the general rate of profit, required ROI, is the minimum.

To maximise ROI individual capitals in effect seek to increase profit, Marx argued, by increasing the "rate of surplus value", or "rate of exploitation" expressed in prices, seeking "absolute surplus value" from cutting wages and extending working time, but particularly by producing "relative surplus value", cutting costs by increasing labour productivity by employing additional constant capital, particularly fixed capital, increasing profit margin, and by increasing the turnover of capital through expanding output and sales. Reducing workers' proportion of the value created ($v + s$) increases the need for capitalists to employ a growing surplus value by additional productive investment, what Marx called the tendency to "underconsumption", which created the "possibility" of crises (Kliman 2012, p. 166). Increasing the rate of turnover by expanding production increases competition and the difficulty of realising surplus value on the market, which Marx called the tendency to "overproduction". Lack of a central controller allows "disproportionality" between "departments" of the economy producing means of production and means of subsistence. However, it was the persistent tendency to increase labour productivity by increasing the OCC, which, although it generated counter-tendencies would, Marx argued, produce periods with a falling rate of profit leading to inevitable financial and economic crises.

The General Law of Capitalist Accumulation

From 1857–1858 in *Grundrisse*, through the *Economic Manuscripts* of 1861–1865, and eventually in the three volumes of *Capital*, Marx worked out his theory of crises. By 1867, he had an acceptable draft of Volume 1. However, he and Engels knew much work remained to finish Volume 2 and prepare it and Volume 3, where he dealt with crises, for publication. Wanting to make an immediate political impact in Volume 1 could explain why at the last minute Marx added a closing chapter, "The General Law of Capitalist Accumulation", where he "situates the principal significance of industrial crises" (Clarke 1994, p. 244).

There Marx explains the functioning of the "capitalist system" from the workers' perspective, assuming inevitable crises, how it ensures in the process of accumulation "The production of surplus-value, or the making of profits, is the absolute law of this mode of production" (1976, p. 769). This system, Marx argued, controlled workers' wages in relation to profits by producing a "relative surplus population or reserve army" of increasingly insecure and impoverished workers.

In Chapter 25 of Volume 1, having explained that the purpose of capitalist production is endless "accumulation", investment of surplus value to increase the production of more surplus value, which here equals profit, Marx turned to "consider the influence of the growth of capital on the fate of the working class" (1976, p. 762). He started by defining the "composition of capital", the "most important factor ... and the changes it undergoes in the course of capitalist accumulation" (Marx 1976, p. 762), which plays a major role in the LTFRP of Volume 3. If the OCC is constant, accumulation means adding more variable capital, that is, more workers, "multiplication of the proletariat", and rapid accumulation can therefore mean rising wages (Marx 1976, p. 764). However, this will always be checked, Marx argued, because the "absolute law" of "the making of profits" meant, "labour-power can be sold only to the extent that it preserves and maintains the means of production as capital" (1976, p. 769). Marx (1976, fn. 7, p. 769) agreed with the contemporary historian John Wade that "If the rate of wages is such as to reduce the master's gains below the average profit of capital, he will cease to employ them, or ... only [with] a reduction in wages". Thus, Marx explained, workers should understand, contrary to political economists' view that high wages caused accumulation to slow down or stop, "To put it mathematically: the rate of accumulation is the independent, not the dependent variable; the rate of wages is the dependent, not the independent variable" (1976, p. 770), movements Marx knew capitalists observed in their accounts and reacted to:

> If the quantity of unpaid labour supplied by the working class and accumulated by the capitalist class increases so rapidly that its transformation into capital requires an extraordinary addition of paid labour, then wages rise and, all other circumstances remaining equal, the unpaid labour diminishes in proportion. But as soon as this diminution touches the point at which the surplus labour that nourishes capital is no longer supplied in normal quantity, a reaction sets in: a smaller part of revenue is capitalized, accumulation slows down, and the rising movement of

wages comes up against an obstacle. The rise of wages is therefore confined within limits that not only leave intact the foundations of the capitalist system, but also secure its reproduction on an increasing scale". (Marx 1976, p. 771)

From studying *Capital* Volume 1 workers would understand the accumulation story told by capitalist society's accounts, for example, starting from the example Marx constructed to transcend Quesnay's Economic *Tableau* (Bryer 2017, Table 3.3, p. 67), the data for year 1 shown in Table 2.1.[2] In subsequent years assume capitalists reinvest all profit, that

Table 2.1: Accumulation and Wages: Constant OCC and S/V

	Year 1 £bn	**Year 2 £bn**	**Year 3 £bn**	**Year 4 £bn**	**Year 5 £bn**
Variable capital (wages)[1]	233.33	326.66	457.33	640.26	1,254.91
Constant capital (materials, etc.)[2]	933.33	1,306.67	1,829.33	2,561.06	3,585.47
Surplus value (profit)[3]	466.67	653.33	914.66	1,280.52	250.98
Production	1,633.33	2,286.66	3,201.32	4,481.84	5,091.37
Means of subsistence	233.33	326.66	457.33	640.26	1,254.91
Means of production	933.33	1,306.67	1,829.33	2,561.06	3,585.47
Capital investment	466.67	653.33	914.66	1,280.52	250.98
Sales	1,633.33	2,286.66	3,201.32	4,481.84	5,091.37
Number of workers (millions)[4]	100	140	196	275	385
Rate of profit	0.4	0.4	0.4	0.4	0.1
s/v	2.0	2.0	2.0	2.0	0.2
OCC	4.0	4.0	4.0	4.0	2.9

Notes:
[1]Starting from year 1 data, wages in year t = wages in year $t - 1 + [0.2 \times$ surplus value in $t - 1]$.
[2]Starting from year 1 data, constant capital in year t = constant capital in year $t - 1 + [0.8 \times$ surplus value in $t - 1]$.
[3]Surplus value in t = wages in $t \times 2$.
[4]Starting from year 1 data, in years 2–4, with wages constant the number of workers in t = variable capital in t/£2,333 per worker. In year 5, wages increase by 40% from £2,333 to £3,260 per worker.
Source: Created by the author based on Marx and Engels (1985, pp. 485–487, 490–491).

[2]The £ billions for values/prices and millions for workers are illustrative. Marx worked his example in "millions" for values (Bryer 2017, p. 68).

the OCC, rate of surplus value and wages are constant until year 5 when a shrinking "reserve army" secures a (40 percent) wage increase reducing the rate of profit below the general rate of 40 percent, requiring wages to fall back for accumulation to continue (see Tables 2.1 and 2.2). This is what Marx called "overproduction", producing more capital than capitalists can employ at the required rate of profit. From the capitalists' viewpoint, the wage increase in year 5 made the increase in variable and constant capital from year 4–5 of £1,639bn (see Table 2.1) "overproduction" because capitalists did not earn their required rate of profit.

Individual capitals see wage increases breach the "limit" in their accounts, Marx knew, observing the fall in the rate of profit from 40 percent to 10 percent, and they react. Wage rises caused by rapid accumulation, Marx warned workers, would always be temporary, only a loosening of the "golden chain", at best a reduction in "the amount of unpaid labour the worker has to supply" (1976, p. 769), which capitalists resist with all means, particularly increasing the OCC reducing demand for workers and wages. Workers should expect the OCC to increase, successive increases in productivity by applying science, concentrating and centralising capital facilitated by the credit system, and the cheapening of commodities, but also the creation of an growing "reserve army" of workers who, unless organised, would become increasingly impoverished as capitalists became wealthier (Marx 1976, pp. 773–781). Workers could understand this accumulation story by extending society's accounts (see Table 2.2). Assume wages fall back in year 6 to restore the rate of profit; that labour productivity and rate of surplus value doubles every year, and the OCC increases, so that by year 10 employment falls back to year 1 levels, replenishing the reserve army, while capital accumulation continues (see Table 2.2).[3]

Marx did not discuss the LTRP in Volume 1, noting only that a rising OCC made overproduction more likely, but pointed out that with expanded accumulation prices fell, which was an integral part of its operation. He explained in Chapter 14 in Part 4 of Volume 1 on "Relative Surplus Value", that capitalism fostered "over-production", commodities capitalists cannot turn into capital, on which they cannot earn the required rate of profit, a condition exacerbated by the factory system. Workers knew its "tremendous capacity for expanding with sudden immense leaps, and its

[3]Labour productivity is the proportion of the total value produced in a year advanced as variable capital, which falls from 0.143 [£946.56/£6,625.95] in year 6 to 0.07143 [£662.59/£9,276.33] in year 7 and halves every year thereafter (see Table 2.2).

Table 2.2: Accumulation and Employment: Rising OCC and S/V

	Year 6 £bn	**Year 7 £bn**	**Year 8 £bn**	**Year 9 £bn**	**Year 10 £bn**
Variable capital (wages)	946.56	662.59	463.82	324.67	227.27
Constant capital (materials, etc)	3,786.26	5,963.35	8,812.51	12,662.19	17,954.33
Surplus value (profit)	1,893.13	2,650.38	3,710.53	5,194.74	7,272.64
Production	6,625.95	9,276.33	12,986.86	18,181.60	25,454.24
Means of subsistence	946.56	662.59	463.82	324.67	227.27
Means of production	3,786.26	5,963.35	8,812.51	12,662.19	17,954.33
Capital investment	1,893.13	2,650.38	3,710.53	5,194.74	7,272.64
Sales	6,625.95	9,276.33	12,986.86	18,181.60	25,454.24
Number of workers (millions)	406	284	199	139	98
Rate of profit	0.4	0.4	0.4	0.4	0.4
s/v	2.0	4.0	8.0	16.0	32.0
OCC	4.0	9.0	19.0	39.0	79.0

Source: Created by the author.

dependence on the world market, necessarily give rise to the following cycle: feverish production, a consequent glut on the market, then a contraction of the market, which causes production to be crippled" (Marx 1976, p. 580). They knew the "uncertainty and instability to which machinery subjects the employment, and consequently the living conditions, of the workers becomes a normal state of affairs, owing to these periodic turns of the industrial cycle" (Marx 1976, pp. 580, 582). Workers should understand that capitalists remorselessly compete for market share, which "is directly proportional to the cheapness of the product", which meant "the use of improved machinery for replacing labour-power, and the introduction of new methods of production" (Marx 1976, p. 582). He warned, as the reserve army grew "there also comes a time in every industrial cycle when a forcible reduction of wages beneath the value of labour-power is attempted so as to cheapen commodities" (Marx 1976, pp. 580, 582). He wanted "workers [to] learn the secret of why it happens that the more they work, the more alien wealth they produce, and … the more the productivity of their labour increases, the more does their very function as a means for the valorization of capital become precarious" (Marx 1976, p. 793). They should "discover that the degree of intensity of the competition amongst themselves depends wholly on the pressure of the relative surplus population" (Marx 1976, p. 793). He urged unions to "organize co-operation between the employed and the unemployed in order to obviate or to weaken the ruinous effects of this natural law of capitalist production on their class" (Marx 1976, p. 793).

According to Harvey (2006, pp. 161–166), Marx's general law of capitalist accumulation "rests upon certain strong and quite restrictive assumptions", particularly that workers' real standard of living does not increase, and population grows with accumulation, and therefore he ignores the "sociological, demographic and geographical aspects of labour supply". According to Harvey (2006, pp. 164–165), "Marx seems to be trapped in the same general swamp of ignorance with respect to the process of reproduction of labour power as were his contemporaries", overlooking that Marx was analysing the accounting system from the capitalists' perspective in which workers appeared as a cost to be minimised. Harvey (2006, p. 166) admits, in effect, that his criticisms are beside the point "considering Marx's main purpose in building this first model of accumulation", which he does not see was to analyse capitalists' accounting control. He agrees, "What Marx demonstrates, convincingly, rigorously and brilliantly, is that if misery, poverty and unemployment are found under capitalism, then they have to be interpreted as the product of this mode of production and not attributed to 'nature'" (Harvey 2006, p. 166), but does not attribute this to its control superstructure. Likewise, Volume 2, according to Harvey, we will see, "is argued imaginatively and tentatively rather than rigorously", makes "restrictive assumptions", and he follows the dominant view that Volume 3's crises theory was merely "a preliminary sketch", which is "plagued by … ambiguities" (2006, pp. 157, 170, 177, 179). However, to understand the tendencies for an increasing OCC and overproduction, workers would have to study Volumes 2 and 3 of *Capital* where Marx progressively elaborated his explanation of the capitalist accounting system, and then turned to its consequences for crises.

Expanded Reproduction

Towards the end of Volume 2, having articulated the major categories of circulating and fixed capital, in Chapters 20 and 21 Marx drew on capitalist accounting to construct his "reproduction schemas" to show that accumulation, "expanded reproduction", by interdependent "departments", made capitalism even more precarious for workers. In Volume 3, he built on this to argue that competition, the LTFRP, and accounting control by individual capitals and total social capital, means capitalism has inevitable crises. Seeing the capitalist mode of production as an accounting control system that drives and curtails accumulation to maximise ROI, explains Marx's controversial conclusion in Volume 3 that "The *real barrier* of capitalist production is *capital itself*" (1998, p. 245). In capitalists' accounts, "capital and its self-expansion appear as the starting and the closing point, the motive and the purpose of production; that production is only production for *capital* and not *vice versa*, the means of production are not mere means for a constant expansion of the living process of the *society* of producers" (Marx 1998, p. 245). Capitalist control therefore meant, "The means — unconditional development of the productive forces of society — comes continually into conflict with the limited purpose, the self expansion of the existing capital" (Marx 1998, p. 245). The capitalist mode of production is "a historical means of developing the material forces of production and creating an appropriate world-market and is, at the same time, a continual conflict between this its historical task and its own corresponding relations of social production" (Marx 1998, p. 245) controlled by the objective of producing the maximum rate of profit.

In Part 3 of *Capital* Volume 2, "The Reproduction and Circulation of the Total Social Capital", Marx outlined "The Object of the Inquiry" (1978, pp. 425–427), to progress beyond "an individual capital" (1978, p. 429). This was necessary because, "the circuits of individual capitals are interlinked, they presuppose one another and condition one another, and it is precisely by being interlinked in this way that they constitute the movement of the total social capital. … What we now have to consider is the circulation process of the individual capitals as components of the total social capital, i.e., the circulation process of this total social capital. Taken in its entirety, this circulation process is a form of the reproduction process" (Marx 1978, pp. 429–430). Referring back to Volume 1, Chapter 24 where he argued competition compelled individual capitals to expand production, particularly by increasing constant capital to produce relative surplus value, Marx turned to show that "what occurs in the case of an individual capital must occur in the overall annual reproduction" (1978, p. 565).

Reproduction Schemes

In Volume 2, Part 3, Marx turned to aggregating individual capitals performing different economic functions, taking a step nearer to reality. He worked out a "schematic presentation of accumulation", constructed consistent "reproduction schemas", the "tableau" of an economy with two "departments", Department 1 producing means of production, and Department 2 means of subsistence (Marx 1978, pp. 568, 581), creating what many economists see as an innovative approach to "macroeconomic modelling" (Harvey 2013, pp. 372–373). In his "reproduction schemas" in Chapter 21, "Accumulation and Reproduction on an Expanded Scale", according to most economists Marx analysed the necessary conditions for uninterrupted accumulation, "what proportions of social capital must be allocated to different functions to sustain smooth reproduction" (Foley 1986, p. 77). His answer, they conclude, was "an appropriate division … between the production of means of subsistence and the production of further means of production", which depends on the OCCs, rates of surplus value, proportions of profit reinvested, and time lags (Foley 1986, pp. 85–86). To economists his schemas "represent … the first ever model of balanced economic growth", which leaves the "problem … that [they] … are contained in notes … [that] were far from being finished, comprising disparate tables and models, with no summary available from Marx of the purpose … [which] left … scholars to make their own interpretations" (Trigg 2014, p. 215). As Kliman says, seeing the "reproduction schemes as balanced-growth models is widely, almost universally, accepted nowadays" (2011, p. 35). Some think Marx "intended to depict capitalism as a system in 'perpetual balanced growth'", but many argue he wanted "to highlight how implausible it is, how difficult it would be to achieve it in reality", but either way, "recent interpreters almost invariably agree that the reproduction schemes themselves depict a process of balanced growth" (Kliman 2011, p. 35).

The accounting interpretation supports Kliman's contrary view that "the schemes … can plausibly be understood as an unbalanced-growth model" (2011, p. 35), that is, for accumulation, initially Department 1 must grow faster than Department 2, "production for the sake of production", as we will see. This is important because, "If the unbalanced-growth interpretation is plausible, it puts to rest the allegation that Marx's discussion of reproduction and the remainder of Capital are necessarily internally inconsistent", shows that "Marx can be regarded as a consistent non-equilibrium theorist" (Kliman 2011, pp. 35–36). It is possible "Marx depicted balanced growth only in order to highlight its implausibility", but "no textual support for this interpretation seems to exist" (Kliman 2011, p. 36). Marx's schemas, we will see, "depict a continual balance between supplies and demands", and "he does at times refer to the difficulties involved in achieving such a balance (see, e.g., Marx 1981, pp. 571, 593, 596). In contrast, he seems never to comment on obstacles to balanced growth" (Kliman 2011, p. 36). However, this may be because, like supply and demand imbalances, this was obvious. What follows supports Kliman's (2011, p. 46) conclusion that Marx's aim was to explain to workers why capitalist accumulation did not mean increased consumption, to critique Adam Smith's "trickle down" economics, but Marx, it adds, also intended to show that with no central controller capitalists solved their accounting control problem by acting collectively.

Capitalist accumulation, Marx's schemes showed, meant "production for the sake of production", that in pursuing surplus value production of means of production took precedence over means of subsistence. As Kliman (2011, p. 52) says, "when understood as a model of unbalanced growth, the reproduction schemes complement Marx's (197[6], p. 742) vision, articulated in Capital, Vol. 1, of the capitalist system as a system of production for the sake of production: 'Accumulate, accumulate! That is Moses and the prophets! … Accumulation for the sake of accumulation, production for the sake of production: this was the formula in which classical economics expressed the historical mission of the bourgeoisie in the period of its domination'". Explaining this did not give Marx his theory of crises, which he based on technical labour-saving changes. However, it posed the capitalists' collective accounting control problem, and explaining how they solved it in reality, with many competing capitals in the context of total social capital, provided the basis for the LTFRP, and with no central controller, his schemas also showed that "balanced" growth in capitalism would be an "accident".

Marx's two "departments" are not industries, sectors or firms, nor specific use-values, which can often function as means of subsistence or means of production, for example, capitalists can use corn to produce food or for seed, and use steel in building factories or houses (Foley 1986, p. 77). For accumulation to occur, Marx assumed money and the appropriate use-values exist at the end of one period for use in the next, that there must have "already been reproduction on an expanded scale" (1978, p. 566). The realisation of surplus value means one set of capitalists has stocks of money and another has stocks of commodities of equal value, which they use to increase the constant and variable capital advanced to each department in the appropriate proportions. At any time, "One section … is transforming its potential money capital, which has grown to an appropriate size, into productive capital, i.e., using the money it has hoarded up by the realization of surplus-value to buy means of production, additional elements of constant capital; while another section is still occupied with hoarding up its potential money capital" (Marx 1978, p. 568). Capitalists with money or commodities are "buyers and sellers respectively, and each of the two in this exclusive role" (Marx 1978, p. 568). Hoarding money could restrict buying, but Marx assumed sales and purchases "balance" (1978, pp. 568, 570).

In simple reproduction, department 1 capitalists sell means of production in return for means of consumption. "Say however that A (department I) converts his surplus product into money by selling it to a B belonging to department II. This can only happen if A(I), after he has sold means of production to B(II), does not go on to buy means of consumption; i.e., only by a unilateral sale on his part", which seen as simple reproduction meant "under-consumption from department II's viewpoint", "relative over-production in department II" (Marx 1978, pp. 577–578). However, this was not how capitalists' saw it. As Marx explained, "it was presupposed in our presentation of simple reproduction that the entire surplus-value in departments I and II was spent as revenue", but now "one portion of surplus-value is spent as revenue, and another portion transformed into capital. Only with this precondition does real accumulation take place" (1978, p. 579). However, as we will see, "the idea that accumulation is achieved at the expense of consumption … is an illusion that contradicts the essence of capitalist production, in as much as it assumes that the purpose and driving motive of this is consumption, and not the grabbing of surplus-value and its capitalization, i.e., accumulation" (Marx 1978, p. 579). Clearly, "The capitalist cannot spend the value of his surplus product on means of consumption, and at the same time himself productively consume the surplus product, i.e., incorporate it into his productive capital" (Marx 1978, p. 579). Showing how productive consumption allowed the "grabbing of surplus-value and its capitalization", which potentially increased capitalists' consumption, was the key question, and to answer it Marx turned, in effect, to capitalist accounts to construct "systematic schema".

Table 2.3 presents Marx's "First Example". He assumed department 1 invests 50 percent of its surplus value (profit) into additional capital every year, whereas at the beginning of the first year department 2 invests 20 percent of its starting profit of £750, and 30 percent thereafter. The departments have different compositions of capital (c/v) (£4,000/£1,000 = 4 for department 1, and £1,500/£750 = 2 for department 2), different rates of profit ($s/[c + v]$), £1,000/[£4,000 + £1,000]) = 20 percent in department 1, and £750/[£1,500 £750] = 33.33 percent in department 2, and the same rate of exploitation ($s/v = 1$). Marx assumed no technological change, so these accounting ratios are constant. Marx worked out his solution

Table 2.3: Marx's Schemas — First Example

			c	Δc	v	Δv	s	u	**Total**
1st year	Beginning	I	4,000		1,000		1,000		6,000
		II	1,500		750		750		3,000
	End	I	4,000	400	1,000	100		500	6,000
		II	1,500	100	750	50		600	3,000
2nd year	Beginning	I	4,400		1,100		1,100		6,600
		II	1,600		800		800		3,200
	End	I	4,400	440	1,100	110		550	6,600
		II	1,600	160	800	80		560	3,200
3rd year	Beginning	I	4,840		1,210		1,210		7,260
		II	1,760		880		880		3,520
	End	I	4,840	484	1,210	121		605	7,260
		II	1,760	176	880	88		616	3,520
4th year	Beginning	I	5,324		1,331		1,331		7,986
		II	1,936		968		968		3,872
	End	I	5,324	532	1,331	133		666	7,986
		II	1,936	194	968	97		677	3,872
5th year	Beginning	I	5,856		1464		1,464		8,784
		II	2,129		1,065		1,065		4,259
	End	I	5,856	586	1,464	146		732	8,784
		II	2,129	213	1,065	107		745	4,259

Note: c = constant capital; v = variable capital; s = surplus value; u = capitalists' consumption.
Source: Created by the author from Harvey (2013, p. 367) and Marx (1978, pp. 586–589).

through successive "schemas", in effect working through the departments' accounts, calculating the implications of accumulation for both for five years (Table 2.3).

In simple reproduction, department 1 supplied department 2 with constant capital in exchange for means of subsistence to allow department 1 to advance variable capital and for its capitalists' consumption: "$I(v + s) = \mathrm{IIc}$" (Marx 1978, p. 478), the variable capital and surplus value of department 1 must equal the constant capital of department 2. Starting from the initial schema, in year 1 department 1 exchanges 1,500 constant capital for 1,500 means of subsistence, which is simple reproduction. For accumulation, $c_2 + \Delta c_2 = v_1 + \Delta v_1 + [1 - (p_1 s_1)]$, where c_2 is department 2's constant capital, v_1 is department 1's variable capital, p_1 is the proportion of profit (s_1) it reinvests (Harvey 2013, p. 367). "If we assume that … half the surplus-value in department I is accumulated, i.e., 500, then we get in the first place (1,000v + 500s)I or 1,500I(v + s) to be replaced by 1,500IIc; there then remains in department I, 4,000c + 500s, the latter having to be accumulated. The replacement of (1,000v + 500s)I by 1,500IIc is a process of simple reproduction and has already been examined in connection with the latter" (Marx 1978, p. 586). To make the transition from simple reproduction, department 1 retains 500s, which means in year 2 it advances 400 for additional constant capital and 100 for additional variable capital. In year 2, therefore, department 2 must buy an additional 100 of constant capital from department 1, which requires it to advance an additional 50 for variable capital, leaving its capitalists with 600 for consumption at the end of year 1 (Marx 1978, p. 586). In year 1, therefore, with accumulation the exchange, $c_2 + \Delta c_2 = v_1 + \Delta v_1 + [1 - (p_1 s_1)]$, is 1,500 + 100 = 1,000 + 100 + 500. In year 2, department 1's variable capital and surplus value increase to 1,100, increasing department 1 capitalists' consumption by 50 to 550, requiring department 2 to buy an additional 50 of constant capital, which requires it to advance an additional 25 for variable capital. To cover the increase in department 1's variable capital of 110, department 2 must also buy an additional 110 constant capital from department 1 requiring it to invest another 55 in variable capital, leaving its capitalists 560 for consumption from their surplus value of 800 (Marx 1978, pp. 587–588). In short, 800 – 50 – 25 – 110 – 55 = 560 is left for consumption by department 2 capitalists, which increases its retention rate from 20 percent to 30 percent of surplus value ([800 – 560]/800). In year 2, therefore, the exchange is 1,600 + 160 = 1,100 + 110 + 550. In year 3, department 1's accumulation requires department 2's capitalists to retain 264 and consume 616 from the surplus value of 880 (880 – 55 – 27.5 – 121 – 60.5 = 616) (Marx 1978, p. 588), so the exchange is 1,760 + 176 = 1,210 + 121 + 605. Marx worked all five years using this procedure, starting from department 1's accumulation and tracing through the necessary consequences for department 2, calculating "all the actual and potential transfers" (1978, p. 588).

Marx's focus in Volume 2, Marxists often argue, was working out a series of "balanced" exchanges, based on his notes that were "unfinished" but, according to the accounting interpretation, only in the sense that he gave little attention to their presentation, his "schemas" largely appearing as continuous text. Critics often seek to "improve" Marx's presentation using mathematics, re-presenting his schemas as mathematical models, and they dispute his aim, what he intended to contribute to his theory of crises. However, they fail to recognise that Marx's schemas are, in effect, a series of interlinked departmental profit and loss accounts, based on DEB. Representing Marx's schemas as capitalists' accounts, what follows argues, reveals his aims, what he thought he had established. These were, first, that capitalist accumulation was "unbalanced", "production for the sake of production" in pursuit of increased surplus value. Second, capitalism did not have a central accounting controller, which would be necessary for "balanced" accumulation, and therefore to explain how it functioned in reality required seeing accounting control not as supervision, but results control by total social capital.

Unbalanced Growth

Marx said his aim was to show what "occurs in the case of an individual must also occur in the overall annual reproduction" (1978, p. 565), that his theory of value would explain how it occurs. In an individual capital's accounts the production of value, cost of production and profit mark-up, conventionally appear on the left, as uses of capital, as "debits", and the sources, sales, on the right, as "credits". Presenting Marx's schema as accounts shows, first, his "initial schema for reproduction on an expanded scale" is unbalanced. Second, to make the transition from simple to expanded reproduction requires "unbalanced" growth, faster growth in department 1, and extending them beyond the transition demonstrates the aim was increased surplus value.

Marx (1978, p. 586) began with a "schema of simple reproduction", which he amended by reducing department 2's OCC from 4 to 2,

Table 2.4: Marx's Initial Schema

(A) Schema of simple reproduction:								
I.	4,000*c*	+	1,000*v*	+	1,000*s*	=	6,000
II.	2,000*c*	+	500*v*	+	500*s*	=	3,000
Total							9,000
(B) Initial schema for reproduction on an expanded scale:							
I.	4,000*c*	+	1,000*v*	+	1,000*s*	=	6,000
II.	1,500*c*	+	750*v*	+	750*s*	=	3,000
Total							9,000

Source: Marx (1978, p. 586).

Table 2.5: Marx's Unbalanced Initial Schema for Expanded Reproduction

Dr	**Accounting ratios**	**£bn**	**Cr**	**£bn**
Department 1				
Wages		1,000	Department 1	4,000
Means of production		4,000	Department 2	1,500
Profit		1,000		
Production		6,000	Sales	5,500
Rate of profit	0.2			
s/v	1.0			
OCC	4.0			
Department 2				
Wages		750	Department 1 workers' consumption	1,000
Means of production		1,500	Department 2 workers' consumption	750
Profit		750	Department 1 capitalists' consumption	1,000
			Department 2 capitalists' consumption	750
Production		3,000	Sales	3,500
Rate of profit	0.3333			
s/v	1.0			
OCC	2.0			

Source: Created by the author from Marx (1978, p. 586).

increasing its surplus value to create the "Initial schema for reproduction on an expanded scale" (see Table 2.4).

Marx's initial schema is "unbalanced" because, as the accounts in Table 2.5 show, unlike the simple reproduction schema, neither department's accounts balance. In simple reproduction, department 1 capitalists exchange 2,000*c* for 1,000*v* for workers and 1,000*s* of capitalists' means of consumption. In Marx's initial schema for expanded reproduction, department 1's capitalists exchange only 1,500*c*. To change from simple reproduction to accumulation, demand (sales) for department 2's means of subsistence must fall by £500, whereas demand (sales) for department 1's means of production must increase by £500. For accumulation, production of means of production must expand compared to simple reproduction, and production of means of subsistence must contract.

To make the transition from simple reproduction to accumulation Marx assumed department 1 retains £500, 50 percent of its starting profit of £1,000, in stocks (inventories) of means of production, and department 2 retains £150, 20 percent of its starting profit of £750, as stocks of means of subsistence (see Table 2.6).

Table 2.6: Capitalist Accumulation: Year 1

Dr	Accounting ratios	£bn	Cr	£bn
Department 1				
Wages		1,000	Department 1	4,000
Means of production		4,000	Department 2	1,500
Profit		1,000	Stocks – Department 1[1]	400
			Stocks – Department 2[2]	100
Production		6,000	Sales	6,000
Rate of profit[3]	0.2			
s/v[4]	1.0			
OCC[5]	4.0			
Retention rate[6]	0.5			
Department 2				
Wages		750	Department 1 workers' consumption	1,000
Means of production		1,500	Department 2 workers' consumption	750
Profit		750	Department 1 capitalists' consumption[7]	500
			Department 2 capitalists' consumption[8]	600
			Stocks – Department 1[9]	100
			Stocks – Department 2[10]	50
Production		3,000	Sales	3,000
Rate of profit[11]	0.3333			

(*Continued*)

Table 2.6: (*Continued*)

	Accounting ratios
s/v[12]	1.0
OCC[13]	2.0
Retention rate[14]	0.2
C_1/C_2[15]	2.22222

Notes:
[1]Stocks – Department 1 = 0.5 × £1,000 × 0.8 = £400.
[2]Stocks – Department 2 = 0.2 × £750 × 0.67 = £100.
[3]Rate of profit = £1,000/[£1,000 = £4,000] = 0.2.
[4]s/v = £1,000/£1,000 = 1.
[5]OCC = £4,000/£1,000 = 4.
[6]Retention rate = £500/£1,000 = 0.5.
[7]Department 1 capitalists' consumption = 0.5 × £1,000 = £500.
[8]Department 2 capitalists' consumption = (1 – 0.2) × £750 = £600.
[9]Stocks – Department 1 = 0.5 × £1,000 × 0.2 = £100.
[10]Stocks – Department 2 = 0.2 × £750 × 0.334 = £50.
[11]Rate of profit = £750/[£750 + £1,500] = 0.3333.
[12]s/v = £750/£750 = 1.
[13]OCC = £1,500/£750 = 2.
[14]Retention rate = £150/£750 = 0.2.
[15]Proportionality ratio = department 1 capital (C_1)/department 2 capital (C_2) = [£1,000 + £4,000]/[£750 + £1,500] = 2.2222.
Source: Created by the author from Marx (1978, pp. 586–589).

The production and sales accounts show that Marx's schemas balance within and across departments. According to Harvey, "The necessary balances are defined by a 'beginning and end-of-year' accounting procedure which ignores everything that goes on in between. The accounting also presumes that all capital exists in the form of commodities that are totally used up during the production period — no capital exists as money, as inventories or as fixed capital carried over from one period to the next" (2006, p. 170). However, department 1's balance sheet would show its capitalists starting year 1 with £6,000 in money capital and ending it with the £5,400 in money and £600 in commodity stocks or money, and department 2's capitalists starting with £3,000 money capital and ending with £2,850 in money and £150 in commodity stocks or money. Adding fixed capital would not change the principles. During year 1, department 1's capitalists exchange £1,500 of constant capital in return for £1,500 of means of consumption, i.e., $c_2 = v_1 + [(1 - p_1)s_1] = £1{,}000 + £500$. The accounts show "the constant formation of commodity stocks is indispensable, in the hands of their respective producers themselves, in order to keep the machinery of reproduction going" (Marx 1978, p. 580). At the end of year 1, one set of capitalists hold stocks of money and others hold stocks of use-values. Those with money advance it in each department to hire more workers and buy additional commodities from the other set, in appropriate proportions of constant and variable capital that allow both departments' capital to grow in balance. Capitalists with money buy additional constant capital from department 1's stock of £500, £400 by department 1 and £100 by department 2, and buy additional means of subsistence from department 2's stock of £150, £100 by department 1, and £50 by department 2, to grow their capitals to the end of year 2 (see Table 2.7).

Table 2.7: Capitalist Accumulation: Year 2

Dr	**Accounting ratios**	**£bn**	**Cr**	**£bn**
Department 1				
Wages[1]		1,100	Department 1	4,400
Means of production[2]		4,400	Department 2	1,600
Profit[3]		1,100	Stocks – Department 1[4]	440
			Stocks – Department 2[5]	160
Production		6,600	Sales	6,600
Rate of profit[6]	0.2			
s/v[7]	1.0			
OCC[8]	4.0			
Retention rate[9]	0.5			
Department 2				
Wages[10]		800	Department 1 workers' consumption	1,100
Means of production[11]		1,600	Department 2 workers' consumption	800
Profit[12]		800	Department 1 capitalists' consumption[13]	550
			Department 2 capitalists' consumption[14]	560
			Stocks – Department 1[15]	110
			Stocks – Department 2[16]	80
Production		3,200	Sales	3,200

(*Continued*)

Table 2.7: (*Continued*)

	Accounting ratios
Rate of profit[17]	0.3333
s/v[18]	1.0
OCC[19]	2.0
Retention rate[20]	0.3
C_1/C_2[21]	2.29167

Notes:
[1]Department 1 wages = £1,000 + [0.5 × £1,000 × 0.2] = £1,100.
[2]Department 1 means of production = £4,000 + [0.5 × £1,000 × 0.8] = £4,400.
[3]Department 1 profit = £1,100 × 1 = £1,100.
[4]Stocks – Department 1 = 0.5 × £1,100 × 0.8 = £440.
[5]Stocks – Department 2 = 0.3 × £800 × 0.6667 = £160.
[6]Rate of profit = £1,100/[£1,100 = £4,400] = 0.2.
[7]s/v = £1,100/£1,100 = 1.
[8]OCC = £4,400/£1,100 = 4.
[9]Retention rate = £600/£1,100.
[10]Department 2 wages = £750 + [0.2 × £750 × 0.3333] = £800.
[11]Department 2 means of production = £1,500 + [0.2 × £750 × 0.6667] = £1,600.
[12]Department 2 profit = £800 × 1 = £800.
[13]Department 1 capitalists' consumption = 0.5 × £1,100 = £550.
[14]Department 2 capitalists' consumption = (1 – 0.3) × £800 = £560.
[15]Stocks – Department 1 = 0.5 × £1,100 × 0.2 = £100.
[16]Stocks – Department 2 = 0.3 × £800 × 0.3333 = £80.
[17]Rate of profit = £800/[£800 + £1,600] = 0.3333.
[18]*s/v* = £8000/£800 = 1.
[19]OCC = £1,600/£800 = 2.
[20]Retention rate = £240/£800 = 0.3.
[21]Proportionality ratio = department 1 capital (C_1)/department 2 capital (C_2) = [£1,100 + £4,400]/[£800 + £1,600] = 2.29172.
Source: Created by the author from Marx (1978, pp. 586–589).

Accumulation initially required unbalanced growth, the accounts show, production-for-the-sake-of-production. To accumulate, department 1 must grow faster than department 2: "the transition from simple to expanded reproduction requires production of means of production to grow faster than production of consumer goods" (Kliman 2011, p. 33). In Marx's example, department 1 grows by 10 percent during the transition from period 1 to 2 [6,600/6,000], whereas department 2 grows by 6.7 percent [3,200/3,000]. Department 1's higher growth is small and brief, the transition occurs in one-year, because Marx does not include fixed capital (Kliman 2011, p. 40). However, as Kliman shows, "If … a relatively large share of capital were fixed, a larger increase in the relative size of department I would be needed in order to sustain a much smaller growth rate, and the transition from simple to expanded reproduction would be of considerably longer duration", which describes capitalism's growth history (2011, p. 40; 2012, pp. 174–175).

After the transition, both departments grow by 10 percent every year. For balanced growth, year 2's accounts show department 2 capitalists must retain 30 percent of profits in commodities and money at the end of year 2, to allow both departments to increase constant and variable capital the following year, whilst also maintaining their accounting ratios (Table 2.7). Harvey says, "Something odd happens to this reinvestment function…. In order to keep the system in balance, capitalists in department 2 have to raise their rate of reinvestment in the second year and every year thereafter from 20 to 30 percent" (2006, p. 169). This adjustment is not "odd", but results from Marx's method of accounting for the capital flows, given his assumptions and the law of value, rather than beginning with a mathematical abstraction. Marx recognised department 2's accumulation rate imposed a limit to growth, so he increased it from 0.0666 [0.2 × 0.333] in year 1 to 0.1 [0.3 × 0.333], to keep up with department 1 [0.5 × 0.2 = 0.1] (see Tables 2.6 and 2.7). Having calculated year 2's necessary exchanges, Marx noted, "If things are to proceed normally, accumulation in department II must take place quicker than in department I, since the part of I($v + s$) that has to be exchanged for commodities IIc would otherwise grow more quickly than IIc, which is all that it can be exchanged for" (1978, p. 588). To prevent this imbalance between demand and supply, from year 1 to year 2 he has department 2's stocks grow by 26.7 percent [£190/150], whereas department 1's grow by 20 percent [£600/£500] (Tables 2.6 and 2.7).

Repeating the process, Marx showed, "growth can occur indefinitely, despite a relative decline in consumption demand by means of an increase in the demand for machines to produce new machines, and a relative expansion of machine production", which contradicts the underconsumptionist theory that capitalist economic growth "*must* eventually be held back by limited consumption demand" (Kliman 2012, pp. 162, 164). Marx's accounts demonstrate "there exists a final part of output, means of production that will be used to produce additional means of production, which themselves produce even more means of production, and so on", and that an increased rate of growth "generally requires an expansion of this final part of output in relation to the total" (Kliman 2012, pp. 162–163). Table 2.8 shows department 1 grows by 46 percent over the 5-year period, whereas department 2 grows by 42 percent, and that department 2's stocks grow faster than department 1's, which comes at the expense of slower growth in department 2's capitalists' consumption.

Table 2.8: Indefinite Growth

	Year 1	**Year 2**	**Year 3**	**Year 4**	**Year 5**	**Growth (Year 5/Year 1)**
Department 1						
Dr	£bn	£bn	£bn	£bn	£bn	
Constant	4,000	4,400	4,840	5,324	5,856	1.46
Variable	1,000	1,100	1,210	1,331	1,464	1.46
Surplus value	1,000	1,100	1,210	1,331	1,464	1.46
Production	6,000	6,600	7,260	7,986	8,784	1.46
Cr						
Sales: Department 1	4,000	4,400	4,840	5,234	5,856	1.46
Sales: Department 2	1,500	1,600	1,760	1,936	2,129	1.42
Stocks: Department 1	400	440	484	533	586	1.46
Stocks: Department 2	100	160	176	193	213	2.13
Sales	6,000	6,600	7,260	7,896	8,784	1.46
Department 2						
Dr						
Constant	1,500	1,600	1,760	1,936	2,129	1.42
Variable	750	800	880	968	1,065	1.42
Surplus value	750	800	880	968	1,065	1.42
Production	3,000	3,200	3,520	3,872	4,259	1.42
Cr						
Department 1 workers	1,000	1,100	1,210	1,331	1,464	1.46
Department 2 workers	750	800	880	968	1,065	1.42
Department 1 capitalists	500	550	605	665	732	1.46
Department 2 capitalists	600	560	616	678	745	1.24
Stocks: Department 1	100	110	121	133	146	1.46
Stocks: Department 2	50	80	88	97	107	2.12
Sales	3,000	3,200	3,520	3,872	4,259	1.42

Source: Created by the author from Marx (1978, pp. 586–589).

Marx aimed to show capitalism could grow smoothly, some argue, just like Keynesian economists who debate whether with appropriate policies and technologies it could (Harvey 2013, pp. 371–375). Marxists often argue, as Duncan Foley (1986, p. 84) puts it, that a "general proportionality condition for expanded reproduction ... is the foundation for Marx's results in *Capital*". Mathematically, the "general proportionality condition" is that $C_1/C_2 = (1 - k_2)(1 + p_1q_1)/[(1 + q_1) - (1 - k_1)(1 + p_1q_1)]$, where C_1 and C_2 are the capital invested in departments 1 and 2, k_1 and k_2 are the compositions of their capitals, p_1 is the proportion of profit reinvested in department 1, and q_1 is its profit mark-up (Foley 1986, pp. 81–84). In Marx's initial schema for expanded reproduction C_1/C_2 = [£1,000 + £4,000]/[£750 + £1,500] = 2.2222 (Table 2.5), whereas for balanced accumulation after the transition Marx, in effect, worked out from his accounts that it must be $2.2917 = (1 - 0.3334)(1 + \{0.5 \times 0.2\})/[(1 + 0.2) - (1 - 0.2)(1 + \{0.5 \times 0.2\})]$. Marx, however, did not claim he had demonstrated a "general proportionality condition" for "balanced growth". As Kliman (2011, p. 47) says, "the textual evidence suggests that Marx did not intend to develop a balanced-growth model", but it seems unlikely "he evinced no interest in, and probably failed to notice, the fact that his examples eventually settled into a state of balanced growth". He extended the example beyond the transition, the accounts suggests, because to demonstrate the aim was increased surplus value and potential capitalists' consumption required a period of balanced growth. Over the 5 years, Marx concluded by pointing out, total surplus value increased from 1,750 to 2,782, and "The surplus-value consumed was originally 500 for department I and 600 for department II, a total of 1,100; in the final year it is 732 for department I and 745 for department II, altogether 1,477. It has thus grown in the ratio of 100:134" (1978, p. 589). Marx arguably extended the example, therefore, because whereas in simple reproduction capitalists consumed 1,500 a year (Table 2.4), expanded reproduction approached this (1,477) only by year 5. Without the prospect of increased profits and consumption, why would capitalists accumulate? To explain expanded reproduction capitalists must act collectively, as total social capital, Marx implied, share the initial falls in consumption and the future increases, which he turned to in Volume 3.

Rather than a balanced-growth model, most Marxists conclude, Marx meant to show its improbability, "depicted balanced growth only in order to highlight its implausibility" (Kliman 2011, p. 36). There is no textual support for this, but there is that he demonstrated the need to explain how capitalists act collectively despite the absence of a central controller. Economics-inspired critics like Harvey (2013, p. 368) overlook this when they emphasise "the schemas are totally unrealistic", that Marx evidently "cooked the figures to fit his case". Harvey complains, "By modelling accumulation in highly simplified stock terms", while it gives "analytical tractability" means ignoring "the circulation of variable capital and surplus value", and the exclusive focus on "value exchanges" means ignoring money exchange values and use-values, particularly the need for "viable technology", technical change that does not disrupt the balance (2006, p. 170). He complains of "other restrictive assumptions built into Marx's model", and the failure to use "modern mathematical techniques" to enable their relaxation, of the many "issues that Marx raises but does not resolve" (Harvey 2006, p. 170). Like other critics, as Mattick (2008, p. 213) says, "lurking in the background is a comparison of Marx's argument to the modes of analysis of modern mathematicised economics, and in fact … academic economics has importantly shaped Harvey's thinking", not capitalist accounting. Marx's accounts deal with capital flows because in capital-in-general money exchange values equal value exchanges, and while Marx assumes no technical change, adding extra "realism" or employing mathematics would not change the unbalanced transition and control problem they reveal. Rather than mathematics, Marx used capitalist accounts to find the general proportionality condition that would allow "balanced" accumulation, but to demonstrate capitalists' collective aim of increased surplus value, not because he expected capitalism to grow smoothly. Because, in reality, money and money capital introduced many "possibilities of crisis … on the basis of the spontaneous pattern of this production, this balance is itself an accident" (Marx 1978, pp. 570–571).

Because capitalism is "spontaneous", has no central controller to impose all the necessary conditions, supervise every individual capital to maintain all the necessary ratios, Marx's accounts showed that in reality capitalism was prone to imbalances of supply and demand as competing individual capitals, accountable to total social capital only for ROI, strove for the maximum. Despite his criticisms, Harvey (2006, pp. 171, 174) concludes, "Marx was most certainly not trying to build a framework to model the actualities of the capitalist growth process". Nobody could disagree that Marx designed the schemas "to yield us *theoretical* insights", but according to Harvey, these are that "Capital circulates, as it were, through the body of the labourer as variable capital and thereby turns the labourer into a mere appendage of the circulation of capital itself. The capitalist is likewise imprisoned within the rules of the circulation of capital, because it is only through the observance of these rules that reproduction and expansion of constant capital and the production of further surplus value is ensured. We are, in short looking at the rules that govern the reproduction of capital" (Harvey 2006, p. 175). In Marx's schemas workers are mere appendages, and represented as such, as costs, in capitalist accounts, and they reveal the "rules that govern reproduction", the necessary accounting values and ratios. However, these are rules that individual capitals could not follow to balance supply and demand, by simply observing the "rules of the circulation of capital", the accounting principles based on the law of value. These rules imprison workers and capitalists, but they do not ensure balanced accumulation. Working within capital-in-general Marx knew his "technical analysis" had shown only the "possibilities of disruptions and dislocations" (Harvey 2013, pp. 366, 373). He constructed the accounts of "total social capital" in Chapters 20 and 21 of Volume 2, but knew this was only the formal result of assuming the opening data and relationships and working through the departmental accounts to the aggregate social capital. Showing expanded reproduction was possible did not explain how capitalism functioned in reality, where "social reason asserts itself only *post festum* … [and] great disturbances may and must constantly occur" because there is no "need of society to calculate beforehand" (Marx 1997, p. 314). Marx, in short, accepted that because capitalism had no central controller, was not simply capital-in-general, his accounting had not explained how it functioned in reality with competition between many capitals, according to operational laws. Marx knew capitalists transcended hoarding through the "credit system", money capital, and used it to pursue accumulation through relative surplus value, which meant a tendency for falling rather than the constant rates of profit he assumed in Volumes 1 and 2, and roles for money capital in producing inevitable crises.

To explain capitalist reality, in *Capital* Volume 3 Marx built on his accounting for capital-in-general in Volumes 1 and 2 a theory of accounting control of "many capitals" by "total social capital", the totality in motion as a living individual (Bryer 2017, Chapters 5–7), and the inevitable crises a falling rate of profit produced. Knowing that analysing accumulation within capital-in-general would lead to only the possibility of crisis, Marx dropped the assumptions of no technical change and constant, different departmental rates of profit, and turned to the LTFRP because "Here … we once again stand on firm ground" (1991, p. 104). The LTFRP was "firm ground" because it connected value theory to the real world of many capitals in competition. In this world, dominated by total social capital and results control for maximum ROI through expanded reproduction, but now for relative surplus value through continuous investment in labour-saving technology increasing the OCC, Marx's value theory explained why the rate of profit tended to fall, which inevitably produced crises. Adam Smith, David Ricardo and other classical political economists accepted the rate of profit tended to fall as capitalism developed, and Marx agreed, but claimed his LTFRP was the first explanation. The LTFRP is "extremely controversial", particularly Marx's rate of profit definition, and the nature of his "law" (Kliman 2017, pp. 225, 229–231), disagreements that stem from not recognising his theory of capitalism's accounting control superstructure.

The Law of the Tendency for a Falling Rate of Profit

Marxists often interpret Marx's "law" to mean the rate of profit must inevitably fall. However, as Kliman *et al.* say, "the law is not a *prediction* of what must inevitably happen, but an *explanation* of what does happen; it explains why the rate of profit does tend to fall in the long run" (2013, p. 3). This is why Marx does not "claim … to have proved that the rate of profit *must* fall in the long run", in all circumstances, but was "the first to … successfully *explain why* the rate of profit tends to fall in the long run" (Kliman *et al.* 2013, p. 5). Marx was the first to get the accounting right, show that "if and when it does exhibit a long term decline the capitalist mode of development of the forces of production is the dominant cause of that decline" (Kliman *et al.* 2013, p. 5). For Marx, the rate of profit falls "only under particular circumstances", a rising OCC and constant s/v, that outweigh "counteracting tendencies", but "it can fall for other reasons, such as rising wage rates" (Kliman *et al.* 2013, p. 5). Marx does not claim its logical inevitability and, therefore, "the fact that the laws of mathematics and logic do not rule out cases in which the rate of profit rises does not invalidate the LTFRP, because this law doesn't assert that the rate of profit must fall, come what may. It explains why it does fall, when this happens" (Kliman *et al.* 2013, p. 6), as the result of capitalist accounting control, we will see, which also explains the consequences, his theory of inevitable crises.

The Law Itself

In *Capital* Volume 3, Part 3, Marx explained his "law" that "The progressive tendency for the rate of profit to fall is … simply *the expression, peculiar to the capitalist mode of production*, of the progressive development of the social productivity of labour" (1981, p. 319). To cut costs capitalists increase labour productivity by investing in machines, etc., which increases the "technical composition of capital", which tends to rise over time, along with the "value composition", the ratio of constant to variable capital, whereas the amount of new value added by labour falls as commodities contain less labour and more means of production. For the economy as a whole value equals price and profit equals surplus value, so as Kliman (2017, pp. 226) puts it, Marx's "basic idea" was that "when productivity increases less labor is needed to produce a product, so it can be produced more cheaply. As a result prices tend to fall. And when prices tend to fall, so do profits and the rate of profit". Marx expressed the LTFRP as the relationship between the rate of profit, the rate of exploitation, and the organic composition of capital. If the total capital turned over in a year = $c + v$, the rate of profit = $(s/v)/(c/v + 1)$, where c/v is the OCC. The rate of profit therefore varies directly with the rate of exploitation, and inversely with the OCC. To understand how the LTFRP works we must understand Marx's accounting, particularly his RCA, which supports the TSSI's refutation of the "Okishio theorem" (Bryer 2017, Chapter 4). Marx (1991, pp. 266–274) appears to have worked out his LTFRP from a critique of Sir George Ramsay's claim that increased labour productivity would cause the rate of profit to rise. Refuting it, Marx discovered, required a detailed accounting analysis of the effect of changes in the prices of constant capital on the rate of profit, which required what accountants today call "capital maintenance adjustments" (CMAs) (Bryer 2017, pp. 126–138).

Marx's accounting demonstrates the possibility of a falling rate of profit from increasing relative surplus value by investing in constant capital to increase labour productivity (Bryer 2017, pp. 142–146). Generalising increases in productivity through increasing the OCC that compete away relative surplus value restores the rate of profit, but if the rate of exploitation falls back to historical norms, the changed OCC means the rate of profit falls (Bryer 2017, Table 4.19, p. 145). This accounting answers the "standard criticisms" that there is no reason to expect the OCC to rise faster than the rate of exploitation, capitalists would not invest in profit-reducing investments, or revert to older methods, and generalising productivity gains through competition could not reduce the rate of profit, which many regard as "proved formally by Okishio" (Clarke 1994, pp. 68–69). Individual capitalists have no choice about striving to increase the rate of profit by increasing relative surplus value, Marx agreed, and have no choice but to compete. In the *Economic Manuscripts* he noted, "no capitalist voluntarily employs a new mode of production, even though it may be much more productive, and however high the ratio in which it increases the rate of surplus value, if it reduces the rate of profit" (Marx 1991, p. 147). The innovator makes an extra profit from lower costs of production and selling at or below the commodity's value because "his mode of production stands above the socially average level. Competition generalises this and subjects it to the general law. Then the fall in the rate of profit takes place, a law which is therefore completely independent of the will of the capitalist" (Marx 1991, pp. 147–148), which Engels incorporated as a "supplementary remark" in *Capital* Volume 3 (1981, p. 259). Okishio argued this was impossible, but Kliman (2007) refutes Okishio's claim (1961) by showing his "simultaneous" accounting is incorrect, does not measure Marx's rate of profit. As Kliman (2017, pp. 229–230) says, Okishio "failed to prove that 'the' rate of profit cannot fall for the reasons Marx claimed, [because] the rate of profit that cannot fall is conceptually different from the rate to which his law refers". Using RCA for Marx's example the rate of profit falls following a rise in labour productivity when competition generalises it, and then reverts to the original rate and "annuls" the decrease, but only if the rate of exploitation does not revert to historical norms (Bryer 2017, Table 4.19, p. 145). Competing away relative surplus value restores the rate of profit, but increasing OCC, and "Then", as Marx said, through competition and class struggle pushing the rate of exploitation back to historical norms, the rate of profit falls, which is how capitalists and critics see it, as driven by wage increases, forgetting the earlier increase in the OCC. Capitalists would not seek to avoid the fall by reverting to lower labour productivity methods because this would reduce wages and profits (Bryer 2017, Table 4.19, p. 145).

Having explained why increasing the OCC with a constant or more slowly increasing rate of exploitation reduced the rate of profit, the difficulty was, as Marx repeatedly emphasised, "to explain why this fall is not greater and more rapid. There must be some counteracting influences at work, which cross and annul the effect of the general law, and which give it merely the characteristic of a tendency" (1978, p. 227; 1971, p. 365; 1981, p. 339; 1991, p. 111).

Counteracting Influences

Counteracting tendencies arise because "capitalists try, by all the means at their disposal, to find ways of sustaining their profitability" (Clarke 1994, p. 214). As Marx put it, "the same influences which produce a tendency in the general rate of profit to fall, also call forth counter effects, which hamper, retard and partly paralyse this fall. The latter do not do away with the law, but impair its effect" (1998, p. 237). Without counter-tendencies, "it would not be the fall of the general rate of profit, but rather its relative slowness, that would be incomprehensible. Thus, the law acts only as a tendency. And it is only under certain circumstances and only after long periods that its effects become strikingly pronounced" (Marx 1998, p. 237). One counter-tendency was that rising labour productivity tends also to cheapen the means of production and workers' consumption goods, which tended to increase profitability. The rate of exploitation may rise, but increasing surplus value from this was limited by the length of the working day, Marx pointed out, and the total would fall if the number of workers fell below a certain point even if they "live on air" (1991, p. 356). If 100 workers, for example, work 4 hours surplus labour a day the total surplus value they produce is 400 hours, whereas if increased labour productivity reduces the workers employed to 50, they can produce 400 surplus hours only if they work 8 hours a day for nothing, and any fewer than 50 workers produces less (Kliman 2017, p. 226).

The tendency for the rate of profit to fall, Marx argued, prevails "under certain conditions and only after long periods" over the counteracting factors (Clarke 1994, p. 213). Marx "assumed increasing composition of capital would outweigh any influence of an increasing rate of exploitation, and so took it for granted that the secular tendency was for the rate of profit to fall", because he accepted political economists' view that it had fallen (Clarke 1994, p. 214). The counteracting influences "could always" cause the rate of profit to rise, critics argue, so Marx was wrong to "privilege" the "law" over the counteracting influences, but the criticism is a "strawman" because "his law has an explanatory function; it does not assert that the fall in the rate of profit is inevitable" (Kliman 2017, p. 228; 2015, p. 244). Believing that it does, "Unfortunately", according to Harvey, Volume 3's "model makes very little reference to the findings of the second volume, and therefore lacks firm grounding", and "has to be treated … as a preliminary and quite incomplete stab at understanding a difficult and complex problem" (2006, p. 157). Not seeing the accounting foundation for Volume 3's "model" in Volumes 1 and 2, or the LTFRP and the counteracting tendencies as consequences of capitalism's system of accounting control, Harvey sees "a good deal of confusion as to the exact epistemological status of the law" (2006, p. 180). Kliman (2017, p. 225), by contrast, concludes that Marx's "law" is an "explanatory principle", which is consistent with the accounting interpretation in which the epistemological status of the LTFRP is that it explains the observable consequences of a system of accountability for the rate of profit.

Consequences

The falling rate of profit, classical political economists predicted, would eventually lead to stagnation whereas Marx argued it would produce crises (Kliman 2017, pp. 226–227). Marx's theory "is unique in that it suggests that economic crises are inevitable under capitalism because they are not caused by 'relations external to it', that is, by factors than can be eliminated while keeping the system intact. To do away with crises, a different socio-economic system is needed" (Kliman 2017, p. 227), new social relations and superstructure of control. The capitalist superstructure controls the social relations, which develops the forces of production, which makes crises inevitable. When a falling rate of profit occurs, Marx argued, it was because the development of the forces of production had changed the OCC, and the control system that produced it meant crises were inevitable. Marx worked out his explanation of capitalist accounting in 1862–1863 (Bryer 2017). He did not need a distinct theory of crises, he discovered, but had a theory of capitalism as a contradictory and unstable mechanism of social control that in its evolution inevitably produced crises as an emergent property. Predictably, it was in *Grundrisse*, written in 1857–1858, when he first became interested in accounts, that he began the process of abstractly specifying the necessary links between the fundamental contradictions of capitalism, between production of use-values and valorisation, the forces and social relations of production, and crises, to discover their "inner necessity", where he first worked out his LTFRP. "Marx immediately links … [the] fall in the rate of profit to the eruption of crises, without giving any indication of precisely how the fall in the rate of profit might precipitate a crisis" (Clarke 1994) because it took him until 1865 to fully work out.

Marxists have often concluded, "Nevertheless Marx presents an apocalyptic vision of the fate of capitalism as the result of the fall in the rate of profit. At this point the system of wage labour becomes a fetter on the development of social wealth, and is cast off, as the result of the development of the contradictions of the capitalist form of production itself" (Clarke 1994, pp. 148, 164). However, as Kliman says, "There seems to be no textual evidence that supports the legend that he claimed that this tendency would cause capitalism to collapse in an automatic or quasi-automatic manner" (2015, p. 244). Harvey (2006, p. 191) suggests, "at certain points Marx seems to indicate that capitalism indeed faces such a fate (*Grundrisse*, p. 750)", "the ultimate catastrophe". However, Marx actually says, "these regularly recurring catastrophes lead to their repetition on a higher scale and ultimately to its violent overthrow" (1973, p. 750). In light of his view that the LTFRP was the most important "law" because using it to explain crises to workers would lead to socialism, he meant the "repetition" of "catastrophes", that is, crises, would educate workers to overthrow capitalism "violently", but not necessarily physically.

Consistent with the hypothesis that his encounter with capitalist accounting in the late-1850s gave him the basis of his theory of crises, "While Marx had been attentive to every hint of a crisis in the 1850s, in the 1860s he paid much less attention to everyday economic developments, and regarded the onset of crisis much more prosaically" (Clarke 1994, p. 248). According to Clarke (1994, p. 248), this was because of changing political interests: "From this point on Marx's political activity and revolutionary hopes were focused not on the expectation of a catastrophic revolutionary crisis, but on the slow development and progressive politicisation of an organised movement of the working class". However, only from the late-1850s had Marx worked out that the revolutionary task was to explain crises. Marx's reappraisal is consistent with him theorising capitalism as a mode of production, as a system of social control, how capitalists control the valorisation process and exploit workers by purchasing their labour power, extract surplus value in production and realise it on the market, maximising ROI by seeking relative surplus value. This drives its historical tendencies, which are the constant expansion and revolutionising of production by new technologies to increase labour productivity, disproportionality, underconsumption, overproduction, the LTFRP and its counteracting influences, particularly constant pressure to increase the rate of exploitation, the production of surplus population, and the centralisation and concentration of capital. In addition to increasing relative surplus value, which automatically increased the rate of exploitation, "The most important counteracting tendencies which Marx considers are those mobilised by the capitalist in the desperate attempt to stave off a fall in the rate of profit" (Clarke 1994, pp. 216–217). He stressed the lengthening of the working day, the employment of women and children, and the intensification and exploitation of labour to increase the production of surplus value, not by increasing the productivity of labour, but by reducing the paid portion of the working day. None of this, however, as his critics emphasise, and Marx knew, explained the inevitability of crises.

Explaining Crises

There was no inevitability to underconsumption, overproduction, disproportionality or a falling rate of profit. What were inevitable, according to Marx, were the capitalists' pursuit of maximum ROI, and the consequences of their responses to a falling rate of profit. Clarke (1994) and others recognise that capitalists resist the fall, but conflating capital-in-general with total social capital, rejecting value theory and the LTFRP, fail to see how a fall in the rate of profit causes financial and economic crises. Clarke (2012, p. 94) agrees with Anwar Shaikh's (1978) complaint of a 1970s debate that "none of the contending theorists provided any explanation of why a fall in the rate of profit should provoke a crisis", as he and others conclude Marx had not. For Marx a falling rate of profit "is not the cause of the crisis", as Clarke (1994, pp. 225–226) says, not the direct cause, which he is right, we will see, according to Marx, in part "arise from speculation provoked by the concentration of capital", but concludes this only "makes such crises more likely". Kliman (2007, 2012, 2015, 2017), by contrast, argues that in Marx's theory a falling rate of profit indirectly but inevitably causes crises. The accounting interpretation supports Kliman, adding that what make crises inevitable in the face of a falling rate of profit are the accountability consequences, those that result from accountability, and from its absence.

Indirect Causation

Given tendencies to disproportionality, underconsumption and overproduction, "The lynchpins of Marx's theory of capitalist economic crisis",

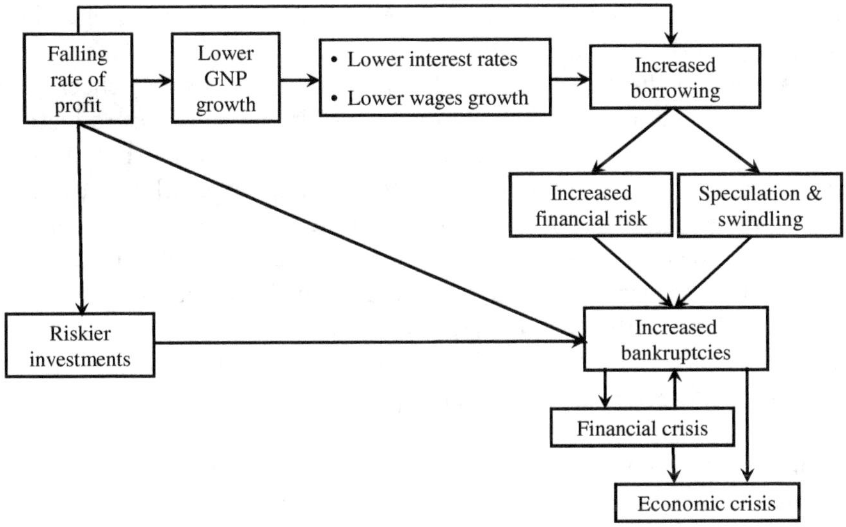

Figure 2.1: Marx's Theory of Crises

Source: Created by the author.

Kliman argues, are the "LTFRP …, the operation of the credits markets and the destruction of capital" (2012, p. 13). A falling rate of profit reduces "capitalists' willingness to invest in production (Marx 1991, p. 349), but his crisis theory is not one in which a fall in the rate of profit causes a fall in the rate of accumulation, which then causes an economic crisis, in a mechanical fashion" (Kliman 2015, p. 244). Marx's theory "regards a fall in the rate of profit as an *indirect* cause of crises, it leads to crises only in conjunction with financial market instability and instability caused by low (as distinct from falling) profitability" (Kliman 2012, p. 13; 2017, p. 227), does not require that profit rates are currently falling, but are historically low. Following Kliman (2012, pp. 13–27; 2015; 2017), Figure 2.1 summarises Marx's theory.

Financial Crises

A falling rate of profit indirectly causes crises through capitalists' and their agents' reactions. It means lower growth in incomes (GNP), leading to lower interest rates, which encourage increased borrowing by capitalists and managers, which increases financial risk and encourages speculation and "swindling", and lower wage growth encourages borrowing by workers. When the rate of profit falls capitalists invest less because "being the goad of capitalist production … its fall checks the formation of new independent capitals", and it "breeds overproduction, speculation, crises, and surplus capital alongside surplus population" (Marx 1998, p. 240). Capitalists "want to maintain [at least] their existing rate of profit" (Kliman 2015, p. 244), so if the rate falls, accountable for a target ROI based on earlier higher rates, they resist. They "may need to maintain it in order to be able to repay their debts" (Kliman 2015, p. 244) because a low profit rate reduces the financial margin of safety for unforeseen losses, which directly increases bankruptcy risk. Low profit rates also indirectly increase bankruptcy risk by encouraging riskier investments promising higher rates, "new capital investments and new adventures, to secure some kind of extra profit" (Marx 1991, p. 367), and increased competition to maximise production to lower costs and increase market power, borrowing to leverage profits, and speculation (Kliman 2012, pp. 14–20). A falling or historically low profit rate, in short, "leads indirectly to crisis by encouraging speculation and overproduction", which eventually leads "to a … financial crisis … in which a substantial volume of debt cannot be repaid … [which] is … the immediate cause of the economic downturn" (Kliman 2012, p. 20; 2015, p. 244).

Financial and economic crises are the consequences of capitalism's functioning, the results of "the process of capital's movement considered as a whole" (Marx 1981, p. 117), according to the accounting interpretation of competing individual capitals under accounting control, its functioning as "total social capital". Financial accounting developed alongside the "credit system", particularly stock markets and the separation of ownership from control (Bryer 2021a, pp. 21–34), which Marx argued amplified the tendencies to centralisation and overproduction, and promoted "gambling" and "swindling" that caused crises, in which we will see accounting played important roles. In *Capital* Volume 1 he noted, "with capitalist production an altogether new force comes into play — the credit system, which … soon becomes a new and terrible weapon in the battle of competition and is finally transformed into an enormous social mechanism for the centralisation of capitals" (Marx 1996, p. 621), which he analysed in Volume 3. Along with the credit system came the concentration and centralisation of capital, and with this the separation of ownership from control, which gave further impetus to overproduction by employing managers who are less risk averse. The credit system was "the principal lever of overproduction and excessive speculation ... because a great part of the social capital is applied by those who are not its owners, and who therefore proceed quite unlike owners who, when they function themselves, anxiously weigh the limits of their private capital" (Marx 1981, p. 572). The credit system promotes "excessive speculation", bubbles that exaggerate booms and slumps because separating ownership and control introduced "what is now called *moral hazard* — that is, failure to 'anxiously weigh' whether your investment behaviour is too risky" (Kliman 2012, p. 19), because managers are not personally liable for failure.

Separating ownership from control meant for Marx, as Kliman emphasises, "that moral hazard is *the* problem that makes the credit system 'the principal lever of overproduction and excessive speculation'" (2012, p. 20). A falling rate of profit increased moral hazard. It fostered increased concentration of capital since "a large capital with a lower rate of profit accumulates more quickly than a small capital with a higher rate of profit" (Marx 1981, p. 359). Concentration caused the rate to fall further, which pushed smaller capitalists into speculation, and generated "a so-called plethora of capital" — "an expression used only with reference to the interest-bearing capital, i.e., money capital" (Marx 1981, pp. 349, 607). Additional money capital came "essentially" from small capitals, "capital for which the fall in the rate of profit is not outweighed by its mass", for "newly developing offshoots of capital", or "a plethora which places capitals incapable of action on their own at the disposal of the managers of large enterprises in the form of credit" (1998, pp. 249–250). New "offshoots" offer higher rates of profit, but are riskier, and increasing large enterprises' debt increases their financial risk. Money capital also accumulated as the rate of profit fell because "capital ... released by a fall in the price of the elements of production, raw materials, etc. If the industrial capitalist cannot expand his reproduction process immediately, a portion of his money capital is expelled from the circuit as superfluous and is transformed into loanable money capital" (Marx 1998, p. 504; see Bryer 2017, Chapter 4). According to the LTFRP, prices and the rate of profit fall together. As profit is "converted into money capital only when it is not immediately able to find a place for investment in the expansion of business", for example, due to "lack of spheres for investment" (Marx 1998, pp. 504–505), a falling rate created money capital. As these were "circumstances, which are independent of actual accumulation but nevertheless accompany it", Marx concluded, "there must be a continuous plethora of money capital in definite phases of the cycle and this plethora must develop with the development of credit", further expanded by the banks (1998, p. 505) during the speculative boom.

Driven by a falling rate of profit, crises were therefore inevitable, there "must develop overtrade, overproduction, and excessive credit … in forms that call forth a reaction" (Marx 1998, p. 505). The credit system breaks the barrier to production of individual ownership, creates the world market and extends capitalist relations around the globe. The crises it generated demonstrated the need for socialism, for "the new form of production", by which according to the accounting interpretation Marx meant new social relations of production and system of accounting control (Bryer 2019, Chapter 8). The credit system "accelerates the material development of the productive forces and the creation of the world market, which it is the historical task of the capitalist mode of production to bring to a certain level of development, as material foundations for the new form of production" (Marx 1981, p. 572). Its development into a "colossal system of gambling and swindling" showed the need for change, but the credit system nevertheless provided the basis for the new mode of production:

> … credit accelerates the violent outbreaks of this contradiction, crises, and with these the elements of dissolution of the old mode of production. The credit system … on the one hand … develops the motive of capitalist production, enrichment by the exploitation of others' labour, into the purest and most colossal system of gambling and swindling, and restricts ever more the already small number of the exploiters of social wealth; on the other hand however it constitutes the form of transition towards a new mode of production. (Marx 1981, pp. 572–573)

Joint stock companies were for Marx a key element of the credit system and, converted into worker cooperatives, of socialism (Bryer 2019, pp. 308–313, 330–333). To expose their "dual" or "ambiguous nature" (Marx 1998, p. 439) it was necessary to explain their role in facilitating crises. First, the moral hazard from "swindling" created by separating ownership from control, and second, the opportunities for speculation opened by "fictitious" capital.

By "swindle" or "swindling" Marx meant fraud and "something like 'finagling' or 'deceptive business practices', not necessarily fraudulent" (Kliman 2012, fn. 9, p. 209; 2017, p. 227), that is, deceptive, unethical, unscrupulous or unprincipled practices. Management of joint stock companies, Marx observed in *Capital* Volume 3, could for example "swindle" itself increased wages. "On the basis of capitalist production, a new swindle with the wages of management develops in connection with joint-stock companies, in that, over and above the actual managing director, a number of governing and supervisory boards arise, for which management and supervision are in fact a mere pretext for the robbery of shareholders and their own enrichment" (Marx 1981, p. 514). With the concentration and centralisation of capital came the separation of ownership and control, the development of financial accounting, and for Marx "swindling" included manipulating accounts. In *Capital* Volume 3, he saw the 1845–1846 British railway "mania" as a "great railway swindle" (Marx 1981, p. 538), having in Volume 2 criticised railway companies' depreciation accounting, vitally important for calculating railway companies' rate of profit. Marx observed, "The transfer of repair costs to the capital account instead of the current account is a well-known device through which railway directors artificially rack up their dividends", but "experience", he concluded, provided the solution (1978, p. 257). Citing 1850s and 1860s authorities, the answer was to debit construction costs to capital, and depreciation and repairs to revenue, and expenditures for completing a line, Marx agreed, were not "expenses due to wear and tear", but "should be debited to capital" (1978, pp. 257–258; see Bryer 2017, Chapter 6). He gave "some evidence of the broad limits within which clever directors can manipulate the concepts of repairs and replacement in the interest of their dividends" (Marx 1978, p. 259). To prevent manipulations, railway companies, Marx (1978, p. 258) agreed with the authorities, should "charge each year's revenue with the depreciation", which they did not during and after the "mania" (McCartney and Arnold 2003), which supports the interpretation that by "great railway swindle" in Volume 3 he meant unscrupulously not accounting for depreciation (Bryer 1991, 2022b).

"Swindling" and "gambling" (speculation) were for Marx symptoms of an impending crisis, the boom's collapse, which causes a financial crisis. "It is only when debts finally cannot be repaid that a crisis erupts" (Kliman 2012, p. 21), when as Marx put it, "The chain of payment obligations at specific dates is broken in a hundred places, and this is still further intensified by an accompanying breakdown of the credit system, which had developed alongside capital. All this therefore leads to violent and acute crises, sudden forcible devaluations, an actual stagnation and disruption in the reproduction process, and hence to an actual decline in reproduction" (1981, p. 363). Crises occur when speculative investments collapse, which makes it appear that their origins lay in the credit markets, whereas for Marx they lay in production (Clarke 1994, pp. 169–170). Stock market speculation and gambling by lesser capitalists centralised capital: "credit lends ... the ... appropriation of social property by a few ... more and more the aspect of pure adventurers. Since property here exists in the form of stock, its movement and transfer become purely a result of gambling on the stock exchange, where the little fish are swallowed by the sharks and the lambs by the stock-exchange wolves" (1998, p. 437). Smaller capitals speculated when faced with a falling rate of profit, Marx argued, because the concentration of capital meant their rate of profit was already lower than the general rate (Clarke 1994, p. 231). In *Theories of Surplus Value*, "Once it has reached a certain level, this rising concentration in turn brings about a new fall in the rate of profit. The mass of the lesser, fragmented capitals are therefore ready to take risks. *Hinc* crisis" (Marx 1991, p. 112). In *Capital* Volume 3, "At a certain high point this increasing concentration in its turn causes a new fall in the rate of profit. The mass of small dispersed capitals is thereby driven along the adventurous road of speculation, credit frauds, stock swindles, and crises" (Marx 1998, p. 249). The big losers were smaller capitalists and workers, whereas larger capitalists survived and would, Marx argued, take advantage of falling prices, which would end the crisis and restart the accumulation process.

Self-Correcting Crises

For Marx, "Crises were the superficial and transient expression of the most fundamental contradiction of the capitalist mode of production" (Clarke 1994, p. 280), so "When Adam Smith explains the fall in the rate of profit from an over-abundance of capital, an accumulation of capital, he is speaking of a *permanent* effect and this is wrong. ... Permanent crises do not exist" (Marx 1969, p. 497). From the early 1860s, he came to see crises as regular events, albeit growing in scale and ferocity as capitalism expanded, which implies individual capitals produce and publish objective accounts (Bryer 2017, Chapters 4–5; 2021a, Chapter 2) that, with competition, ensured the rate of profit ruled. Capitalists and accountants agreed, "The rate of profit is the motive power of capitalist production. Things are produced only so long as they can be produced with a profit" (Marx 1998, p. 258). For Marx, therefore "crisis … is not a pathological phenomenon appearing on the surface of capitalist society, but the normal and regular means by which prices and production are adjusted in order to make possible the renewed reproduction of capital" (Clarke 1994, p. 196). As Clarke says of *Capital*, etc., crises stem from "the contradiction between the tendency to develop the forces of production without limit, and the subordination of production to the valorisation of capital, while the effect of the crisis is always to restore the rate of profit through the devaluation of capital and the destruction of productive capacity" (1994, p. 234). Both are accounting processes. Capitalism, as Marx put it *Grundrisse*, is "a contradiction-in-process" (Clarke 1994, p. 234), but according to the accounting interpretation, a contradiction embedded in its social relations and superstructure, in its system of accounting control.

Crises would be self-correcting, Marx argued in *Theories of Surplus Value*, because the "depreciation of *values*" imposed losses on individual capitals from lower selling prices, and "real destruction", the non-use or physical destruction of assets, losses he knew should appear in accounts. First, physical destruction: "In so far as the reproduction process is checked and the labour-process is restricted or in some instances is completely stopped, *real* capital is destroyed. Machinery which is not used is not capital. Labour which is not exploited is equivalent to lost production. Raw material which lies unused is no capital. Buildings (also newly built machinery) which are either unused or remain unfinished, commodities which rot in warehouses — all this is destruction of capital. … Thus their use-value and their exchange value go to the devil" (Marx 1969, p. 495). Second, if the "reproduction process is checked" so that use-values and exchange values "go to the devil", capitalist enterprises cease being "going concerns" so accountants value their assets at typically lower selling prices (Bryer 2021, Chapter 2), as Marx did, which was what he meant by "destruction" from the "depreciation of values" (1969, pp. 495–496). For Marx, the "devaluation of capital … [is] achieved through deflation of commodity prices, bankruptcies, and corporate consolidations" (Mattick 2008, p. 221; Kliman 2017, p. 227). Importantly, Marx argued, as Harvey puts it, "in conditions of crisis the use value of fixed capital can often be acquired for almost nothing, which means that the exchange value that capitalists have to advance to acquire fixed constant capital from their fallen competitors falls dramatically" (2006, p. 201), to "distress" or "fire sale" prices. In short, in a crisis commodity selling prices fall below cost of production, capitalists become bankrupt, cannot repay their debts, which forces them to sell productive capital below RC, which produces a "devaluation in the capital they represent" (Marx 1981, pp. 362–363). Devaluation requires accounts that hold management accountable for losses, which produces an appropriate destruction of value, for example, writing down finished commodities and fixed assets for sale to lower of cost or market (L-C-M). Fictitious capital values, the market prices of shares and debt, also fall in a crisis as the prospects for profits decrease, and the likelihood of bankruptcies increases. For going concerns, low bond and share prices present the moneyed interest with opportunities, which "enriches itself at the cost of industrial interest", that simply "transfer[s] … wealth from one hand to another", which also requires accounts, but changing the owners "acts favourably upon reproduction" because the "parvenus" are "mostly more enterprising" (Marx 1969, p. 496).

Concluding Comments

The still dominant view is that Marx's theory of crises is fragmentary, at best unfinished, just the "first cut" (Harvey 2006, cf. Mattick 2008), which he gave up as hopeless by the publication of *Capital* Volume 1 (Clarke 1994). By contrast, according to Kliman (2012), Marx's theory is coherent and testable, according to the accounting interpretation as a theory of capitalists' accounting control of the production and distribution of surplus value. By explaining capitalist's accounts in Volumes 1 and 2, using them to explain the general law of capitalist accumulation and expanded-reproduction, and in Volume 3 the value-price transformation by individual capitals' accountability for ROI to total social capital, and the LTFRP, he connected his theory of value with the real world of competing capitals. The precarity generated by capitalist control, coupled with the accountability consequences of a falling rate of profit and responses to it, the chapter argued, was Marx's theory of inevitable financial and economic crises. The remainder of the book uses it to explain the Great Collapse in America, 1929–1933, and the 2008–2009 GFC.

In Britain after the "great railway swindle" principled and increasingly regulated accounts (Bryer 2021a, 2022b) limited "swindling" and speculation, according to the accounting interpretation, so its crises were relatively infrequent and transient. In America, by contrast, while sophisticated management accounting systems pursued relative surplus value, during the 1920s (Bryer 2013a), financial accounting failed to hold management accountable for ROI, allowed widespread "swindling", which Chapter 3 outlines, and Chapters 4 and 5 argue in detail, stimulated unprecedented "speculation", financial crisis, and a long depression. Chapter 3 examines the historical context and alternative explanations of the stock market boom, the Great Crash and Depression, the Great Collapse. The evidence, it argues, supports the accounting interpretation, which explains the crisis by capitalists' reactions to the falling general rate of profit from 1924 and historically low corporate rates: increased concentration and centralisation, increased rate of exploitation and borrowing, and exceptional "speculation" and "swindling".

Marx saw the potential of vulgar political economy for distorting fixed capital accounting when he criticised Smith's distinction between fixed and circulating capital (Bryer 2013b, pp. 576–579). However, he did not anticipate it infiltrating accounting practice, allowing management to engage in "swindling" on a vast scale, and grip not just small capitalists, but the middle classes and wealthy, the "moneyed interest" and the "industrial interest", which would see their capitals dramatically devalued in the 1929 crash and depression. Marx did not imagine that not just bankers, traders and smaller capitalists, as in Britain from the 1820s to the 1860s, but many wealthy and well-to-do stock market investors, America's total social capital, would "gamble" on the indefinite accumulation of capital and lose. To explain the stock market boom's exceptional breadth and height, and the depression's depth and length, historians must allow for the amplifying effects of Fisher's accounting theory, Chapters 4 and 5 argue, the historically specific American ingredient that allowed and encouraged "swindling" by manipulating accounts on a vast scale, in producing and exacerbating the crisis. We can observe this process, Chapters 6–8 argue, repeated in the history of the 2007 credit-crunch and 2008–2009 GFC.

Chapter 3

The Great Collapse 1929–1933

The stock market collapse began in October 1929, triggering a financial crisis that pushed the American economy sharply into recession, followed by "restrictive fiscal and monetary policy ... and protectionism [that] interacted to break the unstable prosperity and accelerate the downward movement" (Devine 1990, p. 166). Government, business and pundits claimed it would be short, but by Autumn 1930 unemployment was over 15 percent, farm prices plunged bringing closures, bankruptcies, and evictions; large companies laid off thousands of workers at a time, and breadlines appeared in the cities. Demands for help swamped relief agencies, and hundreds of thousands of destitute Americans took "to the roads" (Zieger 1994, p. 11). By 1933, national income and manufacturing output in America had fallen by half, farm prices by 40 percent, exports by a third in value, and unemployment had risen from two million in 1930 to 15 million, a quarter of the workforce (Renshaw 1991, p. 6). It was "the greatest economic collapse in the history of the industrial world" (McElvaine 2009, pp. 26–27). When the NYSE reached the bottom in July 1932, it had fallen 82 percent from the high in September 1929 (Figure 3.1), from a total value of $90 billion to $16 billion (Seligman 1982, p. 1), a loss it did not recover until the mid-1950s.

Historians have advanced numerous explanations of the late-1920s share price boom but it "remains, as the conventional wisdom always maintained, the great peculiarity" (Hughes and Cain 1998, p. 448), an unexplained mystery. The most popular explanations of the Great Depression are various forms of underconsumptionist theory (Duménil *et al.* 1987, p. 18; McElvaine 2009, p. 28). There are Marxist (e.g., Baran

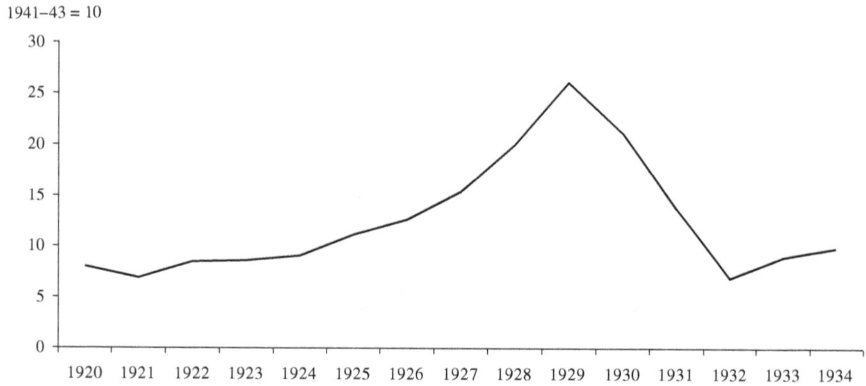

Figure 3.1: Standard and Poor's Index of Common Stocks 1920–1934
Source: Historical Statistics of the United States, Series X, pp. 492–498.

and Sweezy 1968; Devine 1983, 1994) and non-Marxist, Keynesian versions (e.g., Galbraith 1961; McElvaine 2009). Increasing income inequality, underconsumptionists argue, meant increasing dependence on luxury spending and investment, so when the stock market unexpectedly collapsed in 1929, consumption fell as investors lost confidence (McElvaine 2009, pp. 48–49). However, this does not explain why they did, and why the economic collapse was sudden and recovery slow. According to the accounting interpretation, the stock market collapsed in October 1929 because investors lost confidence in continued "earnings" growth, and in the integrity of accounting, and the economy collapsed because confidence had encouraged the build up of unsustainable debts, and its loss caused a large debt-deflation.

The chapter first outlines the historical context of the Great Collapse, the "New-Era" and its contradictions, particularly those created by its development into the "common stock era", using the accounting interpretation to criticise the most popular explanations. It then examines the evidence of a falling rate of profit, increasing financial risk and speculation during the 1920s, and evaluates the alternative Marxist explanations. The evidence, it concludes, is consistent with the accounting interpretation, which Chapter 4 supports with an accounting history of the boom and 1929 crash.

Historical Context

From the 1870s, a persistent increase in America's OCC correlates with a falling rate of profit (Roberts 2016, Figure 2.3, p. 43), which fell steeply in the 1880s (Duménil and Lévy 1994, Figure 20, p. 21), producing countervailing tendencies — the appearance of "big business", increased concentration, attacks on labour, capital-intensive investment and cost management. Nevertheless, by 1914 the rate of profit had fallen back to the 1880s lows. World War I and the Roaring Twenties pushed it back to the highs of the 1890s, peaking around 1924, but the rate of profit then trended down, this time leading to a severe financial and economic crisis. Did the 1930s crisis mean there was a long "delay" in the operation of Marx's "law" (Devine 1994)?

Large-scale crises were inevitable, Marx argued, in advanced capitalism with a developed credit system, a stock market, separating ownership from control, capital concentration and centralisation, the formation of a total social capital, which emerged in America during the 1920s (Bryer 2021a, pp. 138–151). America had many financial and economic crises from the 1880s to the 1920s (Roberts 2016). Before ownership and control separated, when capitalists took their own risks and insisted on "conservative" accounting, crises were relatively restricted and brief, but when management took the risks, and thanks to accounting theory became increasingly unaccountable, in a few years America had produced a system-threatening crisis. What was different in the "New-Era", what follows argues, was the influx of middle class and wealthy investors into the stock market coinciding with a falling general rate of profit and historically low corporate profit rates from the mid-1920s, which investors and managers resisted by increased debt and exceptional "speculation", driven by exceptional "swindling" of accounts.

The New-Era and its Contradictions

To many, the notion of a New-Era had a factual foundation in economic fundamentals, which appeared as a "decade of apparently limitless economic advance" (Hughes and Cain 1998, p. 440), the Roaring Twenties. GNP growth averaged 6 percent a year in real terms from 1921 to 1929, from trough to peak, and unemployment was low, averaging around 4 percent excluding the recession years of 1921 and 1924 (Hughes and Cain 1998, p. 444). Real GNP growth averaged 4.7 percent and unemployment averaged 3.7 percent from 1922 to 1929 (White 1990a, p. 69; Hughes and Cain 1998, Table 23.2, p. 444). Driving growth were large-scale commercial and industrial corporations employing new process technologies that appeared and dominated most sectors, which turned to the capital markets, making large bond and stock issues, rapidly dominating the equities market (Chandler 1977; White 1990a, p. 69; 1990b, p. 146; Michie 2006, pp. 176–177). In 1929, GNP growth peaked at 6.8 percent and unemployment had dropped to 3.2 percent (White 1990b, p. 146). During the 1920s middle and upper-class consumers purchased many consumer durables, as did workers, often on credit, which increased 8.3 percent annually from 1922 to 1929 (Hughes and Cain 1998, p. 441). Automobile production, like most other consumer goods, "increased dramatically in the 1920s" (Hughes and Cain 1998, p. 443). Leftover capacity from the war, a boom in investment, and the real-subsumption of labour, significantly increased manufacturing output growth, with only a small interruption in 1924, and a levelling from 1926 to 1927, and prices were relatively stable (Hughes and Cain 1998, Table 23.1, p. 443). Real weekly earnings of industrial workers grew by around 15 percent from 1922 to 1929 (Brody 1980, p. 62), whereas between 1923 and 1929 "corporate profits soared upward of 62 percent and dividends rose by 65 percent" (McElvaine 1984, p. 39). During the 1920s, labour productivity increased faster than wages (Brody 1980, p. 62), particularly in manufacturing, so profits increased: "These profits sustained the spending of the well-to-do, and they also nourished at least some of the expectations behind the stock market boom. Most of all they encouraged a very high level of capital investment" (Galbraith 1961, p. 192).

However, this picture was flattering. Agricultural output increased only slowly, prices fell, and agricultural incomes fell throughout the 1920s; house prices and building fell from 1927; the coal industry was shrinking in output and employment; the growth in demand for automobiles slackened from around 1925; textile production fell (Allen 1993, p. 180). The mechanisation of the 1920s "reduced demand sharply for non skilled and even skilled labor. The idea of 'technological unemployment' appeared first in the later 1920s" (Hughes and Cain 1998, p. 445). The markets for consumer durables and housing became "saturated" from around 1928, and fewer profitable investment opportunities in plant and machinery appeared. As the rate of profit fell from 1924 the rate of growth in real GNP significantly slowed, falling from 8.9 percent a year from 1921 to 1925 to 3.2 percent from 1925 to 1929 (Hughes and Cain 1998, Table 23.2, p. 444). As incomes became more unequal, growth increasingly depended on capital investment and luxury spending, not mass consumption, because as Galbraith put it, "The rich cannot buy great quantities of bread. If they are to dispose of what they receive it must be on luxuries or by way of investment in new plants and new projects" (1961, p. 195).

However, "Since the upper income strata received the lion's share of the income during the 1920s, there was a large stock of saving in search of a return" (Hughes and Cain 1998, p. 449), which became an increasing problem. In 1922, the top 1 percent of income recipients took 12 percent of all personal incomes and provided 49 percent of all savings, but by 1929, they took 13.7 percent of all income and provided 80 percent of all savings (Hughes and Cain 1998, p. 441).

For underconsumptionists like Galbraith, "It follows that anything that interrupted the investment outlays — anything, indeed, which kept them from showing the necessary rate of increase — could cause trouble" (1961, p. 193). Through the second half of the 1920s, most of the large increases in dividends went to the 1 percent richest, which combined with large tax handouts, "increase[d] their disposable income nine times faster than that of the population as a whole" (Dawley 1991, p. 338). In 1929, "income from capital (essentially dividends and capital gains) was the primary source for the top 1 percent of the income hierarchy" (Piketty 2014, p. 301). Some observers then thought, and many historians agree, this fuelled an engine of speculation and crisis that in combination with the limits imposed by *laissez-faire* on boosting mass consumption, produced and then deepened the recession. According to Dawley, "The result of all these elements combined — overproduction, maldistribution, speculation, inadequate welfare — was a crisis waiting to happen. The crux of the problem was that the laboring masses had too little income to purchase the fruits of their rising productivity, while the corporate rich had too much capital to invest profitably" (1991, p. 341). Galbraith blamed the "blow … struck by the stock market crash" for the depression because "This high-bracket spending and investment was especially susceptible, one may assume, to the crushing news from the stock market in October 1929" (1961, pp. 195, 203). Given the "weaknesses of the economy", Galbraith concluded, the stock market played a critical "role … in the great tragedy of the thirties" because its "collapse … affected in the first instance the wealthy and well-to-do … a vital group. … Anything that struck at the spending or investment by this group would of necessity have broad effects on expenditure and income in the economy at large" (1961, p. 203). The wealthy were critical to the boom, and their losses during the crash were portentous for the economy, and for themselves, but why they, the well-to-do and the middle classes engaged in "speculation" remains a mystery.

According to Galbraith, "Far more important than the rate of interest or the supply of credit is the mood. Speculation on a large scale requires a pervasive sense of confidence and optimism and conviction that ordinary people were meant to be rich. People must also have faith in the good intentions and even in the benevolence of others" (1961, p. 187). Finding no substantive basis for confidence or faith, the speculation he concludes was an irrational mania, and the crash an irrational panic that inflicted a damaging blow on an "exceedingly fragile" economy (Galbraith 1961, p. 204). However, the "mood" that underlay the "speculative" boom, Chapter 4 argues, came from Fisher's new-era theory of investment that focused "investors" on "earnings" growth. Similarly, the cause of the crash, and the blow it struck to the reproductive process, in addition to its economic impacts, was loss of "faith" in continued earnings growth, and critically, in accounting's integrity and the institutional structure it purported to support. Loss of faith in accounting, Chapter 4 argues, extended the crash by drying up needed investment funds for new industries to rebalance the economy.

Galbraith's explanation of *The Great Crash 1929* (1961) remains widely accepted (e.g., White 1990a, 1990b). An "irrational", self-induced and self-deluding "euphoria", "hysteria", "luminous insanity", or "mania", Galbraith argued, appeared during the rapid economic growth and stable prices of the 1920s, which induced the public to invest in common stocks, who became convinced that stock prices would increase, and changed their behaviour, from buy-and-hold to "speculation". The boom became self-reinforcing because, Galbraith argued, it created "the vested interest in euphoria [that] leads men and women, individuals and institutions to believe that all will be better, that they are meant to be richer and to dismiss as intellectually deficient what is in conflict with that conviction" (1961, pp. xii–xiii). The bubble burst in October 1929 when sellers outweighed buyers and prices inevitably fell, which caused an equally irrational panic. However, as White (1990a, p. 68; 1990b, p. 145) says, "While Galbraith's book makes for compelling reading, there remain many unanswered questions. There is little discussion about how much fundamentals contributed to the bull market and what might have triggered the speculative mania", particularly earnings and dividends. The key question is "whether fundamentals or a bubble drove the bull market", but because the answer requires explaining investor behaviour, "An econometric resolution of this question is unlikely", so we must use "qualitative evidence" that, White concludes, "favors the view that a bubble was present in the 1929 market" (1990a, p. 67). As he says, "all descriptions are vague about when the speculative boom began and what might have triggered the change in investor behaviour" (White 1990b, p. 144), but his work is no exception. His approach is to show that "Most of the factors cited by [other] historians played trivial or insignificant roles" (White 1990a, p. 67), which leaves a speculative boom. White (1990a, 1990b) overlooks the accounting evidence, which we will see supports his, Galbraith's, and others' conclusion (e.g., Fisher 1930; Kindleberger 1978) that the boom from c.1927 to 1929 was a "speculative" bubble detached from "fundamentals", particularly realistic earnings expectations, but not that it was an "insane", "irrational", self-delusion, or simply an "enthusiasm" (Michie 2006, p. 177). The boom became detached from the reality of a falling rate of profit by an accounting illusion created by Fisher's theory. One of those with a "vested interest in euphoria", in creating the "conviction that God intended the American middle class to be rich" (Galbraith 1961, p. 35) was, we will see, Fisher himself.

In the "conventional view", which Fisher supported, "the economy was basically sound but that excessive speculation by the public at large brought old-time American capitalism to grief" (Hughes and Cain 1998, p. 447). Some historians see the 1929 crash "as a cause of the [economic] Collapse", as "an exogenous shock" (Devine 1994, p. 121). Speculation, in this view, was excessive in relation to deteriorating fundamentals and recognising this reality delivered a blow to the economy that pushed it into depression. Marx would agree, as Galbraith argued, that the crash revealed the economic fragility of the Roaring Twenties, that "the economy was fundamentally unsound" (1961, p. 104), but for Marx because the rate of profit was falling, and he would therefore agree that the blow struck by the stock market crash was endogenous. The same factor that caused the boom ("irrationality" according to Galbraith), the falling rate of profit in Marx's theory, eventually produced a financial crisis, and then exacerbated the recession. Marx would also have agreed with Galbraith, there is "an essential unity in economic phenomena; no Chinese wall separates the fiduciary from the real" (1961, p. 26), separates the stock market from production. The accounting evidence, we will see, supports Galbraith's view that the boom was not simply "froth" beneath which "more serious forces were at work … shaping things up for a serious depression"; rather, "the crash and speculation that made it inevitable had an important effect on the … malperformance of the economy in the ensuing months and years" (1961, p. 26). Marx's theory, however, requires historians to go beyond Galbraith's and others' list of increasing income inequality, an unstable corporate structure, weak banks, international financial problems and economically-illiterate politicians (1961, pp. 186–202), to include the consequences of a falling rate of profit, including "swindling" by means of distorted accounts. Galbraith argues, "No one was responsible" for the boom and the bust, that they were "the product of the free choice and decisions of thousands of individuals", that "the latter were not led to the slaughter" (1961, p. 28). However, an insufficiently emphasised feature of the crash was the extent to which *all* "Investors suffered monumental losses" (Dillon 1984, p. 1), the middle classes, the well-to-do, and particularly the wealthy; that it was not lambs led to slaughter, but lions. As Galbraith (1961, pp. 163, 135) said, the crash "blighted the fortunes of many hundreds of thousands of Americans", particularly the "well-to-do and wealthy who were being subject to a levelling process comparable in magnitude and suddenness to that presided over a decade before by Lenin". It was, as Fisher said, "*A Rich Man's and Poor Man's* [sic] *Panic*" (1930b, p. 8).

Important economic consequences, Galbraith recognised, flowed from the involvement of the upper reaches of American society in the boom and bust — it did not involve workers except in its consequences. However, he did not consider, and nor has anyone else, whether a falling rate of profit and their shared experiences and ideology could explain the origin of the "speculative mania", the crash, and its impact on the depression. The entanglement of the wealthiest and therefore the best educated in the stock market supports the hypothesis they were not gullible because they were ignorant, that what made them gullible was their exceptional, ideologically loaded higher education in business, economics and accounting (Bryer 2013b, 2021a). An overlooked link between the "fiduciary" and "real", between the boom, bust, depression and people's choices, is Fisher's accounting theory, which Chapter 4 argues was not only exploited by the "many Wall Streeters who helped to foster this insanity" (Galbraith 1961, p. 28), but by corporate management, politicians, the press, and academics, including Fisher.

The Common Stock Era

From 1900 to 1930, giant corporations listed on the NYSE run by professional managers and owned by dispersed shareholders came to dominate the financial system (Bryer 2021a, Chapter 4). The change occurred through two equity-financed merger waves, the first around 1900, and the second in the 1920s, and by expansion, which produced a massive concentration and centralisation of capital. Because banking regulations prevented banks from making large long-term loans to only a few large corporations, or taking equity stakes, or trading in equities, corporations turned to retained earnings, to bonds, and particularly to issuing common stocks, and the commercial banks took to investment banking, "became more like agents, simply issuing and distributing companies' securities" (Rappoport and White 1993, p. 551).

From 1925 to 1929, the NYSE was flooded with common stock issues from large corporations "to finance new plant and equipment" (White 1990a, p. 69). The rapid growth in equity financing during the later 1920s reduced corporate demand even for working capital loans from banks. In response, the large banks began to provide an increased array of financial services, including securities trading, avoiding legal restrictions on equity trading by forming wholly-owned "affiliates" that "allowed them to freely enter all aspects of investment banking and the brokerage business" (White 1990b, p. 146), many acting, in effect, as cheap brokers for the middle classes. Banks sold bonds to the investing public and lent "extensively to those holding securities, whether financial intermediaries, like brokers or individual investors", loans using securities as collateral rising "strongly" in the 1920s (Michie 2006, p. 177). To attract middle-class investors, commercial banks organised an increasing number of "investment trusts", supposedly to offer them the decreased risk of a diversified portfolio, but in practice they changed from "fixed" to "managed" trusts that actively speculated (White 1990b, p. 147). From around 1926, many "investors" moved away from the traditional focus on investing in bonds and preference shares and a buy-and-hold approach to few selected equities of stable and well-established companies, and began to "speculate" in common stocks.

The middle classes' participation, White argues meant, "many of the new investors they served lacked experience in buying stock and monitoring firms, thus creating a favorable condition for a bubble" (1990a, p. 70). This, however, does not explain the participation of the wealthy that if they lacked experience had access to those who did not. Adding to investors' problems, some argue, "fundamentals — usually measured as expected future dividends – became difficult to assess" (Rappoport and White 1993, p. 551; White 1990a; 1990b). One feature of the boom was the importance of firms using new production technologies, such as General Motors, RCA Corporation, and the utilities, that promised higher earning and dividends, which White argues, "made fundamentals more difficult to evaluate, thus setting the stage for a bubble" (1990a, p. 81). RCA Corporation "had never paid a dividend", whereas "stocks of railroad companies, which embodied a well-known technology and produced steady dividends, showed little sign of a bubble" (Rappoport and White 1993, p. 551). However, we could as justifiably argue that uncertainty should have prevented a bubble because assuming uncertainty caused it begs the question of how investors came to believe they could nevertheless value shares using reported earnings growth. According to White and others, a boom based on fundamentals turned into a bubble detached from them because inexperienced stockholders in an uncertain world irrationally believed they could forecast future dividends! By contrast, Chapter 4 argues, many believed they could value shares using earnings because Fisher's "new-era theory" of security valuation, which became dominant from around 1925, redefined "speculation" to mean "investment". Fisher's theory took away the notion of gambling associated with shares to mean "security-investment", gave it an aura of "security" by linking share values to earnings. From 1925 to 1929, Fisher endlessly argued that past and expected earnings justified the rise in stock prices, and continued to argue after the crash, "the market went up principally because of sound, justified expectations of earnings, and only partly because of unreasoning and unintelligent mania for buying" (1930b, p. 53).

The Falling Rate of Profit

The most important factor underlying the stock market boom, Fisher was right, was the growing earnings reported by large corporations, the leading sectors of the American economy. Sectors whose profit shares were increasing, were manufacturing, mining, electric light, power and gas, construction, transport, communication, trade, finance, services, and miscellaneous sectors (Devine 1994, p. 141; fn. 53, p. 186). Employers with government support launched an offensive against labour from 1920 (Bryer 2013b; Devine 1994, pp. 134, 143–149), seeking to reverse the decline in the rate of profit that had occurred by 1919. Backed by deflationary policies and *laissez-faire*, with a plentiful supply of labour the big corporations attacked unions and political militancy, boosted labour productivity through large investments in fixed capital and new technologies, and imposed tighter management control, curbing the growth in real wages. This strategy succeeded in increasing manufacturing's share of profit in value during the 1920s (Devine 1994, p. 148). Large leading corporations had high rates of profit during the First World War when they invested in expansion and labour saving technologies, and continued investing throughout the 1920s. Cheap and docile labour and the rising prosperity of the middle and upper classes meant the "industrial and corporate" sectors had relatively "high and rising profit shares and rates" in the later-1920s, but their profit rates fell in 1926, and remained below historical highs (Devine 1994, p. 149, Diagram 3-B, p. 151, Diagram 3-C, p. 152, Diagram 3-D, pp. 153, 156). The general rate of profit peaked in 1924, from when it fell, significantly from 1926 to 1928, and sharply in 1930 and 1931 as the depression took hold, and was negatively associated with the OCC (Roberts 2016, Figure 3.1, p. 53; Appendix 1, pp. 273–274).

The OCC rose during the 1920s because "a process of overinvestment relative to consumption occurred, in which accumulation surged forward despite stagnant real wages and slowing consumer demand" (Devine 1994, p. 120). During the early stages of the depression, contemplating "the fact that industries, at present, are, many of them, overequipped", Rex Tugwell, an economist and member of Roosevelt's "brains trust", mused, "Somehow they have been able to get hold of enough investment funds to build more plants and install more machinery than they ever use" (1933, p. 203). Evidence of falling capacity utilisation is consistent with overinvestment, particularly in manufacturing (Devine 1994, p. 157). During the 1920s, while overall capacity utilisation returned to pre-war levels, capacity levels in manufacturing did not (Devine 1994, p. 154). One reason was that "in the last years of the decade, the ratio of manufacturing investment in plant and equipment rose relative to manufacturing production. Interestingly, the ratio of manufacturing investment to industrial production surged in the last quarter of 1929. Investment was overshooting (as production fell) and would soon be cut back dramatically" (Devine 1994, p. 160). During the 1920s, William Trufant Foster noted, "Far from being profligate, the nation wasted its substance in riotous saving" (McElvaine 2009, p. 40). Dividends increased, but reinvestment of profits increased more, became "the principal use to which excess profits were put in the twenties" (McElvaine 2009, p. 40). Investment ran at "a high level throughout the years 1925–1929, dipping below 15 percent of GNP only in 1928 … [which] helped keep the economy in temporary balance during the boom years" (McElvaine 2009, p. 40), but capacity utilisation fell from 91 percent in 1925 to 83 percent in 1929 (Baran and Sweezy 1968, Table 11, p. 232).

Increasing Financial Risk

As the rate of profit fell from 1924, so did interest rates: "from the early twenties to the end of 1927 interest rates declined, even though corporations, real estate owners, and state and local governments were large net borrowers" (Federal Reserve Bank of St Louis 1965, p. 5). Increased borrowing by corporations coincided with the falling rate of profit, particularly in 1926–1927 (see Figure 3.2).

Corporate borrowing fell when interest rates rose as the boom took off and the authorities sought to restrain it: "During the economic boom lasting from the fall of 1927 to the fall of 1929, interest rates again moved higher. Yields on four- to six-month commercial paper rose from 4.00 percent to 6.25 percent, and interest rates on highest grade corporate bonds increased from 4.50 percent to 4.80 percent" (Federal Reserve Bank of St Louis 1965, p. 5). The excess of bond and note issues over equity issues, having fluctuated around $1,700 million from 1921 to 1925, increased to $2,144 million in 1926 and $3,031 million in 1927, increasing gearing ratios and financial risk. Historians agree, "Part of the instability of capitalism in the late-1920s was due to … excessive leverage" (Devine 1994, p. 121; for example, Galbraith 1961, pp. 195–196; Sobel 1968, p. 89). Bond and note issues fell in 1928 and 1929 as corporations took advantage of the boom to issue large amounts of common stock, but over the whole economy debt continued to rise as a proportion of GNP (see Figure 3.3).

Prices and nominal GNP rapidly increased in 1920, which pushed the debt ratio down, whereas the recession of 1921–1922 pushed it back up.

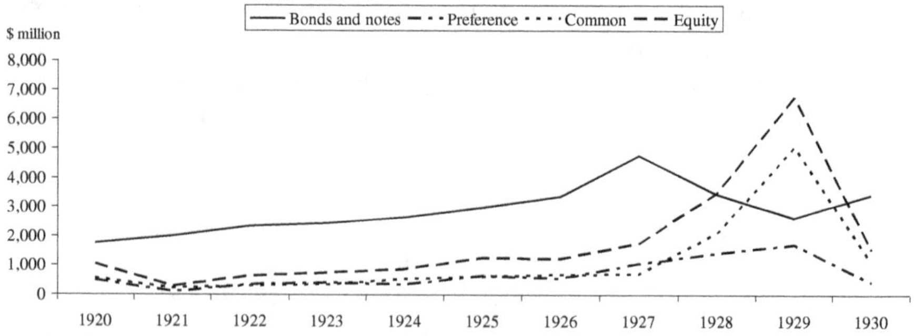

Figure 3.2: NYSE Securities Issued 1920–1930

Source: Historical Statistics of the United States, Series X, pp. 510–515.

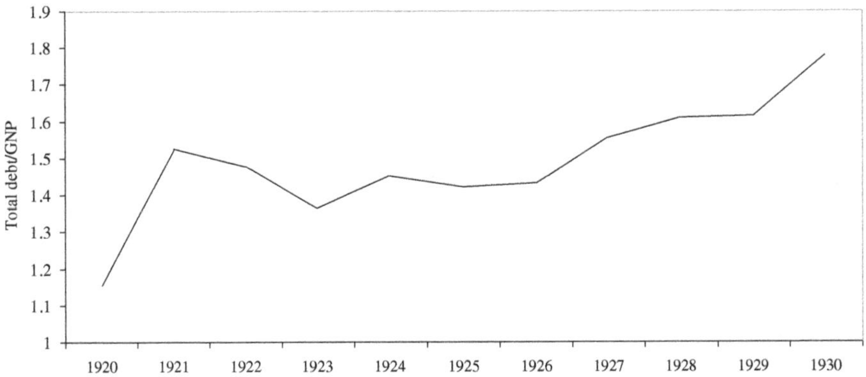

Figure 3.3: Corporate, Individual and Non-Corporate Debt Divided By GNP (Current Prices)

Source: *Historical Statistics of the United States*, Series F 1–5, X, pp. 393–409; author's calculations.

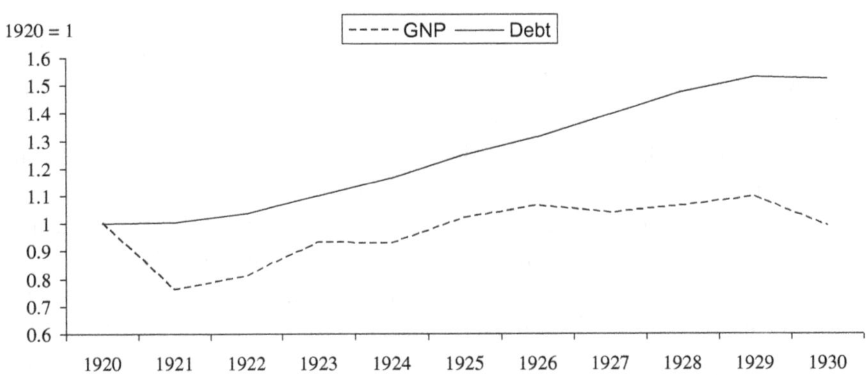

Figure 3.4: Corporate, Individual and Non-Corporate Debt and GNP (Current Prices)

Source: *Historical Statistics of the United States*, Series F 1–5, X, pp. 393–409; author's calculations.

Real growth resumed from 1922, which stabilised the ratio until 1926, from when as real growth slowed total debt increased to 1930, and the gap between their growth rates widened (Figure 3.4). Alongside increasing debt the business failure rate, which had fallen to 93 per 1,000 firms in 1923, trended upwards to reach 122 failures per 1,000 in 1929 (Hughes and Cain 1998, Table 23.6, p. 449). Consumer debt increased throughout the 1920s, and brokers' loans significantly increased in 1925 and 1926, but rapidly increased as the stock market boom took off in 1927, which many leading historians "believe … helped to create the bubble" (White

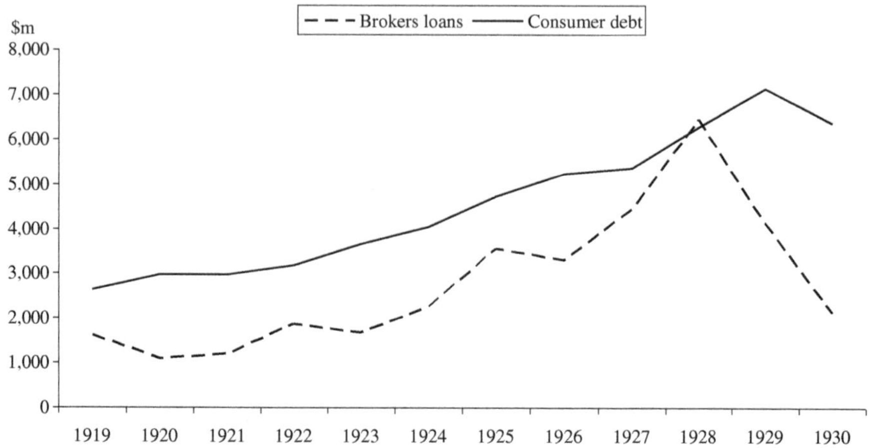

Figure 3.5: Brokers' Loans and Consumer Debt 1919–1930

Source: *Historical Statistics of the United States*, Series X 547–50, pp. 551–560.

1990a, pp. 74–75; Figure 3.5). Historians see increasing consumer debt as evidence of underconsumption, and brokers' loans as evidence of speculation, but the question is what was driving them.

Rather than debt-availability, the underlying causes of debt-expansion and speculation according to Marx's theory were the falling rate of profit from 1924 and the disjuncture between investors' expectation of continuously growing earnings and the reality. During the later-1920s large listed corporations' profit rate was rising, but remained below historical highs, encouraging managers to increase leverage, make risky investments, and engage in "swindling", earnings management, facilitated by theorists (Bryer 2021a), and Fisher's new-era theory gripped middle class and wealthy investors, encouraging risky leveraged-speculation, borrowing to buy shares. However, as Michie says, while "Inevitably, lending on this scale to support the purchase of securities fostered a speculative boom", the constant ratio of loans to the market values of securities from 1926 to 1929 shows it was "speculative enthusiasm ... that lay behind the boom, rather than profligate credit from brokers" (2006, p. 177). Brokers' loans increased in step with the NYSE index (White 1990a, Figure 4, p. 76).

Alternative Marxian Explanations

The difficulty facing orthodox Marxian underconsumptionist explanations of the crisis by "overinvestment" is the long gap between cause and effect.

Devine argues, "a long-term fall in the economy-wide profit rate (up to the end of the 1910s) encouraged an intense effort to boost profit rates, which was largely successful in the leading sectors (manufacturing, the corporate sector) until 1929" (1994, p. 143). By 1929, the latent problems of growing income inequality and slow growth of mass consumption, according to this view, "came to the surface, causing the collapse. This theory follows the classic falling-profit-rate-and-then-underconsumption sequence …, but there is a long delay associated with the 'then'" (Devine 1994, p. 128). To explain the Great Collapse by underconsumption, as Devine says, "The lag is crucial to the story, since the accumulated fixed capital, luxury goods, and consumer debt that allowed this long delay (roughly a decade) also meant the deepening of imbalances that helped make the U.S. Collapse so Great" (1994, pp. 143, 121).

Why was there a long "delay", of arguably 20 years, from c.1910 to 1929? One delay was World War I when profit rates dramatically increased and another, to everyone's surprise, was the economic boom of the 1920s. Certainly, "the Big Bull market itself could be explained partly by … increasing income inequality … by giving income to those most able and apt to speculate; at the same time, rising corporate profit rates inspired the price of equities to rise" (Devine 1994, p. 164), but this ignores the effects of historically low corporate profit rates and the falling general rate. According to orthodox Marxism, as Devine says, "Such bubbles (and their popping) are not mysterious but are a normal outcome of unfettered stock-market behavior, while the stock market itself is a commonplace accouterment of capitalism" (1994, p. 121), but this means the timing is unexplained. Devine argues, "the speculative dynamic of the stock market, as studies of the 1929 … crash … [show] cannot be simply explained by economic information about 'fundamentals' (such as the dynamics of the profit rate)" (1994, p. 122), because "Speculation (normal to capitalism) and a laissez-faire system of finance (more specific to this era) also encouraged this boom" (1994, p. 164). He therefore avoids the question: "when the real economy itself resembles a bubble, the question of whether or not price-equity [sic] ratios were justified by 'fundamentals' is not very important to the tale" (Devine 1994, p. 164). However, rather than take America's "era-specific", "*laissez-faire* system of finance" for granted, and assume "speculation" was "normal", according to the accounting interpretation historians can explain them and their roles in producing the economic collapse.

First, the evidence supports Marx's theory that the falling rate of profit leads to falling interest rates, falling wages, increasing debt and speculation. The collapse produced debt defaults, price deflation and economic crisis. Marx would have agreed with Fisher, the "Leading economist of the Depression era … [who] argued that the predominant factor leading to the Great Depression was over indebtedness and deflation" (Roberts 2016, p. 48). Second, ignored by Fisher and Marxists, during the later-1920s for the first time in history valuing common stocks using "earnings" became widely accepted and, Chapter 4 argues, stimulated "speculation". Why investors came to believe they could value shares using earnings, why the meaning of "investment" changed to encompass and justify mass "speculation", is important because this belief coupled with extensive profit smoothing extended the bubble and delayed the crisis thereby increasing its severity, whereas Devine (1994) provides no satisfactory explanation for the "delay". His explanation, that it was "the accumulated fixed capital, luxury goods, and consumer debt that allowed this long delay (roughly a decade)" (Devine 1943, p. 143) is circular: we cannot explain the "delay" by these accumulations, but must explain them by the "delay". Innocent of the risks, consumers borrowed, luxuries accumulated, and investors financed more investment than they would have, Chapter 4 argues, if management had not manipulated reported earnings, tilting the trend upwards.

Concluding Comments

The economic evidence is consistent with Marx's theory. The accounting evidence, the following two chapters argue, shows it was more than high rates of profit following the post-war recession encouraging overinvestment (Devine 1994, p. 160), that management's unaccountability amplified the 1920s boom and 1929 crash, and extended the 1930s depression. Fisher's accounting theory, which underlay his new-era investment theory, led investors to "speculate", and helped by accounting theorists encouraged management to manipulate accounts, to engage in "swindling", which ended in a collapse in confidence in the integrity of reported earnings that began in October 1929 and continued to the end of the 1930s. Fisher's theory and accounting practice allowed overinvestment, fuelled "speculation", a stock market boom boosting middle class consumption and encouraging the accumulation of debt, which ended in financial and economic collapse when the "earnings" driven bubble burst.

The rate of profit began falling and indebtedness increased from around 1924. As the general rate fell, and corporate profit rates remained historically low, Chapter 4 argues, bankers, corporations, politicians and academics, including Fisher, exploited his accounting theory to encourage middle class, well-to-do and wealthy investors to "speculate" in common stocks. Evidence of accounting practice is consistent with widespread "swindling" by earnings manipulation from the mid-1920s to take advantage of the flexibility theorists allowed (Bryer 2021a, Chapter 9). This amplified the boom, and when investors discovered it, seriously undermined their "confidence", which prolonged the depression. The crash "drastically devalued" the wealthy and middle classes' capital and depressed their incomes, "and, by virtue of high unemployment and rapid deflation it generated, so biased the already unequal distribution of purchasing power as to virtually eliminate consumer and investor confidence" (Bernstein 1987, pp. 30–31). It was not only loss of economic "confidence", that "Idle plant and unemployed workers dampened entrepreneurial spirits and depressed the rate of net investment", and consumption, but also that "capital markets, because of massive bank failures and *public suspicion*, were in no position to float large equity issues and loans" (Bernstein 1987, pp. 30–31, emphasis added). The Great Crash revealed the economy's fragility, which immediately collapsed, and the importance of confidence in accounting, which also collapsed, which Chapter 5 argues helps explain why the economy did not rapidly recover as Marx's theory predicts.

After the crash, many agreed the 1920s had demonstrated management's, the stock market's and accountants' inability to work in investors' interests without state regulation. American stockholders found to their cost there is a world of difference between an efficient capital market and efficient companies producing the maximum return on capital (Bush 2005, p. 14), between the appearance of safe and ever-more valuable shares in large corporations with continuously growing earnings, and the reality. Investors' outrage after the crash and criticisms of practices during the 1920s made accounting reform politically *necessary*, not just *expedient* as some scholars suggest (Dillon 1984; Watts and Zimmerman 1979). Outrage against accountants, Chapter 5 argues, came from an inchoate realisation, particularly by wealthy investors, that the profession had failed to hold management accountable, but Fisher's theory rendered the reforms ineffective, which saved capitalism but prolonged the depression.

Chapter 4

Accounting for the 1929 Stock Market Crash

During the 1920s increasing numbers became "preoccupied with the single-minded pursuit of riches", came to believe that "'God intended the American middle class to be rich' … 'without work'" (McElvaine 2009, p. 42). From around 2 million in 1920, stockholders increased to around 5–6 million in 1927, and 9–11 million by 1930 (Twentieth Century Fund 1935, Table 7, p. 50; Hawkins 1963, p. 145). Share ownership was unequally distributed, like wealth in general: "the 500,000 to 600,000 dividend receivers, and presumably about the same number of stockholders, with net incomes over $5,000 received in the years 1925–1929 between 75 and 85 percent of the total dividends going to individuals" (Twentieth Century Fund 1935, p. 55). The "100,000 persons whose net incomes were above $25,000 per year, or about 1 percent of the estimated total number of stockholders, owned … half of the total stocks in the hands of individuals, the remaining millions of stock holders owning the other half" (Twentieth Century Fund 1935, p. 55). Investors with incomes above $5,000, the wealthy and "moderately well-to-do", who owned "no less than three-quarters" of all stocks, must have speculated because the "great bulk of stocks is in the hands of the wealthy and well-to-do", whereas "the bulk of the 'stockholders' owned only a few shares" (Twentieth Century Fund 1935, pp. 55, 60; McElvaine 2009, pp. 43–44). Around 1.5 million stockholders had a broker's account, mostly in New York, of which probably less than 1 million were active speculators (Galbraith 1961, p. 102). Enticing the wealthy, the moderately well-to-do and middle classes into the market was a "new-era theory" of security analysis promoted by Irving Fisher, which emphasised the role of earnings in share valuation, and the earnings growth reported from 1925 to 1929. Widespread profit smoothing justified by leading theorists' critique of British principles, framed by Fisher's theory of accounting, supported this trend (Bryer 2021a, Chapter 9).

The chapter first explains the "new-era theory", the central role of earnings, its popularity and Fisher's role in promoting it. The chapter then examines and rejects the alternative view that investors ignored earnings and relied on share price trends, and explores the accounting origins of the bubble, the role of reported earnings in explaining investor behaviour. Investors' confidence in earning growth underlay the "speculation" and boom, it concludes, and loss of faith in the integrity of reported earnings caused the crash in October 1929 and the fall in share prices to 1932. Chapter 5 examines the consequences for the profession, its near demise as a private-sector activity, and the role of Fisher's theory in saving it. Remaining chapters examine the consequences of Fisher's continuing influence.

New-Era Theory

Twenty-two months after the stock market reached the bottom in July 1932, Benjamin Graham and David L. Dodd published their classic work on *Security Analysis*, in which they "set forth the difficulties inherent in efforts to apply the analytical technique to speculative situations", to common stocks (1934, p. 299). The crash, they argued, showed "security analysis" was "a somewhat questionable aid to speculative judgement, or a highly illusory method of aiming at values which defy calculation" (Graham and Dodd 1934, p. 300). They gave readers a history lesson in which the "traditional approach" to investment, based on the "security" of property and dividends, gave way to "an entirely different concept of common-stock selection, the so-called 'new-era theory', which beneath its superficial plausibility will hold possibilities of untold mischief in store" (Graham and Dodd 1934, p. 300). The theory's redefinition of investment created mischief because it "abolished the fundamental distinctions between investment and speculation" (Graham and Dodd 1934, p. 309). In the new definition, words meant their opposite: "Speculation … meant looking forward; investment was allied to 'vested interests', — to property rights and values taking root in the *past*" (Graham and Dodd 1934, p. 306).

Before the First World War, according to Graham and Dodd, the basis of common stock investment was "factual". It was confined to stocks that "(1) … showed a satisfactory record of continued dividends; (2) the earnings were reasonably stable and averaged substantially in excess of the dividends paid; and (3) each dollar of stock was backed by a dollar or more of actual investment in the business" (Graham and Dodd 1934, p. 302). Having scrutinised the stock for "elements of weakness" including in management, the "emphasis would be … upon the … the average earnings in relation to price, and the stability and trend of the earnings" (Graham and Dodd 1934, pp. 303–304). Like the bondholder, the common stock investor, also wanted "a stable business, and one showing an adequate margin over dividend requirements", but had an ownership interest, for which accounting "asset values" were essential (Graham and Dodd 1934, pp. 304, 306). Anyone "considering purchasing a partnership or shares in a private undertaking will always start with the value of that interest as shown 'on the books', i.e., the balance sheet, and will then consider whether or not the record and prospects are good enough to make such a commitment attractive" (Graham and Dodd 1934, p. 306). The same accounting approach, Graham and Dodd argued, "was formerly taken in ... [making] an investment … [in] common stock … [when] investors asked themselves: 'Is this … a desirable purchase at the premium above book value, or the discount below book value, represented by the market price?'" (1934, p. 306). Therefore, for example, one of the "protective functions of security analysis was to discover whether … the value of the fixed assets … on the balance sheet … fairly represented the actual cost or reasonable worth" (Graham and Dodd 1934, p. 306), in effect, to verify their capital values for which the business was accountable to its owners. However, between 1927 and 1929 "the basis of valuation employed by the stock-buying public departed more and more from the factual approach and technique of security analysis and concerned itself increasingly with the elements of potentiality and prophecy" (Graham and Dodd 1934, p. 300). This "new theory" spread during the late-1920s to become the dominant approach:

> "During … the latter stage of the bull market culminating in 1929, the public acquired a completely different attitude towards the investment merits of common stocks … and … the earnings record … took on an entirely novel complexion. The new theory or principle may be summed up …: 'The value of a common stock depends entirely upon what it will

> earn in the future'. … That past earnings were significant only to the extent that they indicated what changes in the earnings were likely to take place in the future". (Graham and Dodd 1934, p. 307)

The "corollaries" were that "the dividend rate should have slight bearing upon the value", and "since no relationship apparently existed between assets and earning power, the asset value was entirely devoid of importance" (Graham and Dodd 1934, p. 307). Consistent with acceptance of the new theory, for the first time "many … prominent companies traded on the exchanges that did not pay dividends and caught the public's attention", particularly utility companies (White 1990b, pp. 148–149). Moreover, it gave many corporations, particularly in new and expanding industries, an incentive to manipulate profits to show a trend increase. Graham and Dodd observed, "A new conception was given central importance — that of *trend of earnings*", so the "past was important only in so far as it showed the direction in which the future could be expected to move" (1934, p. 309). Companies wanted to report a "continuous increase in profits" because to believers it proved "the company was on the upgrade and promised still better results in the future than had been accomplished to date. Conversely, if the earnings had declined or even remained stationary during a prosperous period, the future must be thought unpromising, and the issue was certainly to be avoided" (Graham and Dodd 1934, p. 309). New-era theory had thereby turned "speculation" into "investment": "'new-era investment', … was almost identical with speculation as popularly defined in preboom days" (Graham and Dodd 1934, p. 309). It meant buying common stocks rather than bonds, "emphasizing enhancement of principal instead of income, and stressing the … future instead of … the established past" (Graham and Dodd 1934, pp. 309–310). Because new-era investment was "simply old-style speculation confined to common stocks with a satisfactory trend of earnings", Graham and Dodd witheringly concluded, the "impressive new concept underlying the greatest stock-market boom in history appears to be no more than a thinly disguised version of the old cynical epigram: 'Investment is successful speculation'" (1934, pp. 309–310).

New-era theory, Graham and Dodd (1934, p. 312) suggested, originated from data "in the small and rather sketchy volume", *Common Stocks as Long-Term Investments*, by Edgar Lawrence Smith, which was published in 1924. Common stocks tended to increase in value, Smith argued, because "they earned more than they paid out in dividends, and thus the reinvested earnings added to their net worth … *compounded*" (Graham and Dodd 1934, p. 312). Fisher (1925, p. v), however, noted in the preface to Kenneth S. Van Strum's, *Investing in Purchasing Power*, that Smith built on views "some of us expressed … in 1912 in a book entitled 'How to Invest When Prices are Rising'". To Van Strum (1925, p. 244), who added to Smith's evidence, Fisher was the "Most prominent among early exponents of the doctrine … that in a large majority of cases stocks proved to be better investments than bonds". Fisher had argued in several publications "during periods of rising commodity prices, the debtor gains and the creditor loses — equities in property increasing and equities in dollars decreasing in value, when measured from the viewpoint of purchasing power", which meant "stocks increase and bonds decrease in real value during such periods" (Van Strum 1925, p. 244).

Fisher latched onto Smith and Van Strum's findings. He claimed, "It was only as the public came to realize, largely through the writings of Edgar Lawrence Smith, that stocks were to be preferred to bonds during a period of dollar depreciation, that the bull market began in good earnest to cause a proper valuation of common shares" (Fisher 1930b, p. 99). "These various publications, especially Smith's and Van Strum's", Fisher claimed, "are rightly having a profound influence on the investing world" (1925, p. v), that Smith's book was "excellent" because it had "thrown a bombshell into the investing world" (Fisher 1930b, pp. 200, 202–203). Its foundation was his accounting theory. Framed by it, Paton (1922) emphasised the "statistical" role of earnings as a forecast of future earnings, which as Canning (1929) concluded, implied earnings had "predicting value", which opened a business opportunity for Fisher selling his theory of investment, and his, Smith and Van Strum's new-era theory, which influential politicians, business leaders and other academics accepted and promoted.[1] Fisher's entity theory taught that corporations did not have "income". Rather, they produced "incomes" for their stakeholders, a rate of interest on a "capital value" for investors, based on forecast "realized earnings", the source of stockholders' "income", and the value of their "capital", its market price, was the PV of expected dividends (Bryer 2013b). Fisher's theory promulgated the money capitalist's mentality, the circuit of money capital M-M′, justifying "speculation" by valuing shares

[1]Canning began his PhD in 1920, submitted in 1928, and published it as *Economics of Accountancy* (1929); Fisher was Canning's "mentor" (Zeff 2000a, p. 25).

using earnings, which provided that "indispensable element of substance" necessary for the creation of the "classic speculative bubble" (Galbraith 1961, p. 32).

In 1925, Fisher "began his campaign to let the world know that common stocks were fully as safe as gilt-edged bonds and a better investment. His optimism about the economy showed in his argument that common stock recorded the inevitable progress of the economy and would yield greater profits than bonds" (Allen 1993, p. 185). To strengthen the case, "In the *Magazine of Wall Street* … [Fisher] recast Smith's calculations in a form to give, in terms of purchasing power, the 'rate of return realized' on the bonds and common stocks studied by him" (Fisher 1925, p. v). Fisher was part, Frederick Drew Bond noted in *Stock Movements and Speculation*, first published in 1928, of "a publicity campaign" (1930, p. 186). Bond observed, "at first disconnected and discontinuous, [it] arose with the purpose of convincing prospective buyers of common stocks that such shares were as secure or nearly as secure as bonds, and that a diversified collection of such common stock was certain to appreciate in value in the future. Verbally, the appeal was to investors; actually it was to the type of buyer who wants both 'a good buy and a sure thing'" ([1928] 1930, p. 186), in traditional vocabulary, a "speculator". Bond, a traditionalist investor, we will see, judged Smith's work "hardly statistically conclusive", and noted "An attempt to supply this deficiency was made in a more elaborate work, *Investing in Purchasing Power* by Kenneth S. Van Strum, with a foreword by Professor Irving Fisher" (1930, pp. 186–187). Fisher also backed up the campaign from 1925 with his widely publicised theory of business cycles, which was, essentially, that they were a monetary phenomenon governments could avoid by controlling the money supply and, if they did, expansion of production could continue indefinitely (Allen 1993, pp. 181–184, 207, 209).

Given Fisher's stature as "one of the leading economists and statistical analysts in the world", and "as a monetary economist … second to none", courted by Washington (Allen 1993, p. 185), his efforts had a significant impact. As Graham and Dodd (1934, p. 313) put it, the new-era theory "exploited … [Smith's] finding", which "plausibly explained the growth of common stock values as arising from the building up of asset values through the reinvestment of surplus earnings". "Paradoxically", like Fisher, it "refused to accord the slightest importance to the asset values behind the stocks it favored", and like Fisher "threw out of account … earnings … except in so far as they were regarded as pointing to a *trend* for the future" (Graham and Dodd 1934, p. 313). Graham and Dodd had no doubt that during 1927–1929 the new-era theory gripped the public, observing "that since the trend-of-earnings theory was at bottom only a pretext to excuse rank speculation under the guise of 'investment', the profit-mad public was quite willing to accept the flimsiest evidence of the existence of a favorable trend. Rising earnings for a period of five, or four, or even three years only, were regarded as an assurance of uninterrupted future growth and a warrant for projecting the curve of profits indefinitely upward" (Graham and Dodd 1934, p. 315). Consistent with a "swindling" reaction to the falling rate of profit, Graham and Dodd concluded, "The craze for a showing of rising profits resulted in the promotion of many industrial enterprises that had been favored by temporary good fortune" (1934, p. 315). Similarly, established companies had an incentive to manage earnings, and it was largely through published accounts, we will see, that "the gospel of common stocks as safe and satisfactory investments was preached to and avidly accepted by the American public" (Graham and Dodd 1934, p. 316).

Exploiting the "common stock era", from 1925 Fisher changed from "a university professor to business publicist and financial tycoon, from small businessman to a board member of important corporations, and stock market prophet" (Allen 1993, p. 179). He became a "millionaire", worth more than $10 million on paper before the crash, spending his time on commerce, industry, the stock market and boardrooms, writing about "money, making money, and financial markets" (Allen 1993, pp. 179–180). Fisher made "several years' study of the stock market" before publishing "in the newspapers ... weekly and daily index numbers of stock prices, sales and values" (1930b, p. vii). He founded the "Index Number Institute" that sold share indexes and a chart of prices and sales weekly, and included a signed article by Fisher on current economic subjects, so "By 1929 several million newspaper readers had that economic information available to them" (Allen 1993, p. 210). Fisher, for example, published weekly price index numbers for share prices and the "purchasing power of money" in *Barron's* from 1921 to 1928, which also published books and articles in his praise (e.g., Van Strum 1925, 1926). "To all who would listen, Irving Fisher praised investment in the stock market in common stocks as safe and sound, profitable to the individual as well as helpful to America. In some of his writings for the Index Number Institute he suggested investment trusts", for whose popularity in America, "Fisher can claim some credit" (Allen 1993, p. 207). In 1925, he noted, "Several

Investment Trusts have already sprung up" as one of "various plans for offsetting, so far as possible, the evils of instability", claiming, "In steadiness of real income, or purchasing power, a list of diversified common stocks surpasses bonds" (Fisher 1925, pp. vi–vii).

Invented in England and Scotland in the 1880s, investment trusts were "the most notable piece of speculative architecture of the late twenties, and one by which, more than any other device, the public demand for common stocks was satisfied" (Galbraith 1961, pp. 72–73). In the early-1920s, "trusts were trusts — the investor bought an interest in a specified assortment of securities which were then deposited with a trust company. ... But as the twenties wore along, such niceties disappeared. The investment trust became an investment corporation" (Galbraith 1961, p. 74) that raised equity, borrowed and speculated. He advocated a diversified portfolio, but Fisher's theory helped engineer this change, and he led by example. From 1925 "Fisher had played the ... fashionable common-stock game of the day, borrowing on margin with only 10 percent down and buying more stock" (Allen 1993, p. 180). He made his views widely known. For example, in December 1928 the *New York Herald Tribune Magazine* published an article by Fisher, which the national press broadcast, in which his answer to the question, "'Will Stocks Stay Up in 1929?' ... was yes" (Allen 1993, p. 206). Fisher wrote articles defending his views. For example, on 20 March 1929, in the *New York Times*, he criticised Sir George Paish's prediction of a financial crash and recession in America (Allen 1993, p. 210).

When the stock market began to falter from September 1929, Fisher spent much of his time reassuring the public that the economy was sound and stocks were not overpriced (Allen 1993, pp. 210–213). On the 15 October 1929, "Professor Irving Fisher of Yale made his immortal estimate: 'Stock prices have reached what looks like a permanently high plateau'", and added, "I expect to see the stock market a good deal higher than it is today within a few months" (Galbraith 1961, pp. 95, 116). On the 21 October 1929, "now ... recognized as [one of] Wall Street's official prophets", in New York "Professor Fisher said that the decline had represented only a 'shaking out of the lunatic fringe'. He went on to explain why he felt that the prices of stocks during the boom had not caught up with their real value" (Galbraith 1961, p. 119). In December 1929, Fisher gave a speech to the New Haven Chamber of Commerce in which he repeated his claim: "The market is now far below the intrinsic worth of stocks, and will doubtless rise towards the higher plateau of 1929 as a new set of buyers becomes convinced of this fact" (Allen 1993, p. 212). He repeated it in a rushed-out book, his limited apology and vigorous self-defence, *The Stock Market Crash And After* (Fisher 1930b, p. vii), where he argued the crash "was just a technical correction: he attributed the panic almost exclusively to margin accounts and saw no reason to be pessimistic" (Previts and Merino 1998, fn. 86, p. 455). Fisher began his defence by playing what he believed was his strongest card, restating the implications of his accounting theory for share valuation:

> To begin at the beginning: Since every stock price represents a discounted value of the future dividends and earnings of that stock, there are four reasons that may justify a rise in the price level of stocks:
>
> (1) Because the earnings are continually plowed-back into the business instead of being declared as dividends, this plowing-back resulting in an accumulation at compound interest, so to speak;
> (2) Because the expected earnings will increase on account of technical progress within the industry;
> (3) Because less risk is believed to attach to those earnings than formerly;
> (4) Because the 'basis' by which discounting is made has been lowered. (Fisher 1930b, xxii)[2]

On this foundation, Fisher based his case: "all four of these causes were at work, tending to raise the prices on the stock market during the years preceding the panic of 1929", which meant, "what was once speculation or mere gambling in common stocks has changed towards safer investment. The intrinsic value of stocks, present and future, has increased" (1930b, pp. xxii, 208). Whereas traditional investment required a price-earnings ratio of around 10, for Fisher "for the new type of rapidly expanding corporation the price-earnings ratio might be anywhere up to 100 to one, or literally to infinity in the initial stages of investment when earnings are not being realized" (1930b, p. 88). He asserted, "the price-earnings ratio should reflect not only current earnings, but expected earnings. That is why the price earnings ratio should not be fixed to any standard, but wholly with reference to expected earnings of different

---

[2]That is, holding a diversified portfolio (Fisher 1930b, pp. 98, 203–207).

stocks" (Fisher 1930b, p. 91). The annual growth in earnings from 1922 to 1927 of 9 percent, the growth of dividends of 6.8 percent, and their prospects in 1929 when earnings increased by 20 percent, he argued, justified from two-thirds to three-quarters of the 1929 stock market peak, and predicted earnings would continue growing (Fisher 1930b, p. 259; Allen 1993, p. 214). Science, invention, scientific management, cooperative labour and a stable price level all underlay earnings growth by lowering unit costs, and there was the justifiable expectation it would continue. All this, he argued, in effect, justified the "speculation" that broke out in 1928 and 1929, the abandonment of interest in "all aspects of property ownership … except the prospect for an early rise in price. Income from property, or enjoyment of its use, or even its long-run worth … [became] academic" (Galbraith 1961, p. 46).

Evidence "investors" adopted the money capitalist mentality, fixated on the circuit M-M′, was that "People were swarming to buy stocks on the margin — in other words, to have the increase in price without the cost of ownership" (Galbraith 1961, p. 49), were "speculating". Fisher was one of them. From 1925 to 1929 "he engaged in a large number of stock transactions, both buying and selling" (Allen 1993, p. 207). Fisher proved wrong in his predictions and his personal speculations: "Cruel facts made Fisher look foolish and gullible" (Allen 1993, p. 181). The stock market plunged shortly after Fisher's book came out in February 1930, and by early 1931 he was probably bankrupt, in part because the Internal Revenue Service pursued him for tax on his impressive-looking past speculative "gains" (Allen 1993, pp. 207, 237). However, his new-era theory's influence over the wealthy and the well-to-do during the 1920s helps explain why "investors became concerned with accounting reports of earnings and dividends payments in addition to reports of assets owned" (Dillon 1984, p. 118), why they used earnings to value shares and "speculate". Investors' fixation with earnings became clear around 1927, when "most emphasis was placed on the earnings statement", probably because, as Dillon suggested, of "the new emphasis on earnings in determining security prices" (1984, pp. 118, 188). During the pre-SEC era, Ely and Waymire found, "investors value sample firms primarily based on earnings" (1999, p. 41), but according to Merino and Neimark (1982, fn. 21, p. 41), and others, "average investors" were "indifferent" to earnings and relied on "market trends". The evidence, however, suggests investors turned briefly to "trend charts" only after the crash when they lost faith in the integrity of reported earnings.

Earnings Trends or Trend Charts?

When the "trusts" came under popular attack big business began making voluntary accounting disclosures, and "began to encourage widespread stock ownership and to promote the concept that the stockholder was indeed the owner of the corporation" (Merino and Neimark 1982, pp. 36–38). However, the problem and "A major deterrent to widespread stock ownership was the widely held belief that the average investor was unable to understand corporate financial data and, thus, to invest intelligently" (Merino and Neimark 1982, p. 38). The solution, some argued, was the "average investor" accepting share prices established by an "elite" who they could trust because of "self-imposed 'moral regulation'" (Merino and Neimark 1982, pp. 38–39). Most corporations voluntarily disclosed some earnings data and a simplified balance sheet, which was sufficient, their supporters argued, as "a mechanism by which a responsible fiduciary group (bankers or the government) could keep the 'unscrupulous' few under control" (Van Antwerp 1913, 650ff). There was "skepticism of most progressive reformers toward the utility of financial disclosure to investors", but in this vision, "a knowledgeable few" disciplined businesses to protect the many (Merino and Neimark 1982, p. 39).

"Acceptance of a two-tiered market structure", Merino and Neimark argue, "contributed to what became by the 1920s the widespread advocacy of trading rules based on trends in prices and trading volumes rather than on 'intrinsic' analysis" (1982, p. 41). However, while true for investment trust followers, it was not true generally. Investment trusts were increasingly important, particularly for the modest investor, but were only part of the market. There were around 40 in 1921, and 750 by 1929 (White 1990a, p. 69) when they marketed around $3 billion, around third of all new capital issues that year (Galbraith 1961, p. 75). Belief in a two-tiered market, "respect for financial genius", was the foundation of the investment trusts, who as the 1920s wore on, "more and more speculators saw as centers of intelligence — or at least inside information" (Galbraith 1961, p. 79; McElvaine 2009, p. 45). "The conviction that the market had become the personal instrument of mysterious but omnipotent men was never stronger", particularly during summer 1929 when many pool and syndicate operations manipulated the market (Galbraith 1961, p. 103). Investment banks, commercial banks, brokerage firms, securities dealers "were busy giving birth to new trusts", and "aware of their reputation for omniscience, as well as its importance" in maintaining the trust's shares at a premium, "they lost no opportunity to enlarge it", particularly by recruiting professors of "financial genius" (Galbraith 1961, pp. 76, 79–80). One had three professors, including Irving Fisher, but he was not alone: it was "a golden age for professors" (Galbraith 1961, p. 80; Bond 1930, p. 183). Finding many willing and worthy academics to recruit, "Confidence in the investment judgement of the managers of the trusts was very high", and necessarily because trusts sold non-voting stock or assigned rights to management-controlled voting trusts (Galbraith 1961, pp. 74–75). The managed trusts were secretive, most traded "on the curb" or on other markets, requiring even less disclosure than NYSE. They would not reveal the stocks they selected in case this "set off a dangerous boom in the securities they promoted" (Galbraith 1961, p. 75). They had, as Bond put it, "mostly the character of speculative pools operating under the form of a corporation" (1930, p. 189), usually a commercial bank's subsidiary. Like the legendary company that offered stock during the South Sea Bubble "For an Undertaking which shall in due time be revealed", which "is said to have sold exceedingly well", the managed investment trusts were "undertakings the nature of which was never to be revealed, and their stock also sold exceedingly well" (Galbraith 1961, p. 75).

The popularity of investment trusts reflected belief in a "two-tier" market, but the advice often given to the "independent speculator", Merino and Neimark argue, was also to "trail the trend in the stock market and liquidate when the group in control liquidates", and not engage in "financial statement analysis" (1982, fn. 21, p. 41), not use accounting data. They cite Bond (1928, 1930) who they say, "provides an excellent example of the investment advice offered to market participants in the 1920s" (Merino and Neimark 1982, fn. 21, p. 41). Bond, they argue, "advised against financial statement analysis as a basis for trading decisions, believing that, at best such analysis could only indicate sources for further inquiries that most investors were unable to conduct" (Merino and Neimark 1982, fn. 21, p. 41). However, Bond recommended trailing the market precisely because "investors" were, in his view, foolishly speculating, using what Merino and Neimark call "financial statement analysis", but they called "investigation". First published in 1928, Bond's book, *Stock Movements and Speculation*, explained stock market prices, market movements and trends, and offered tips on speculation. Bond's concern, in effect, was that independent speculators were "new-era" analysts, took a naïve interest in reported earnings. This was new-era theory's advice, not to engage in traditional "security analysis", but focus on earnings trends. Writing during the 1928 boom, Bond sought to persuade independent speculators *not* to engage in "investigation", recognising that the "number of speculators among the public who like to confirm a belief in a stock's desirability by an 'investigation' has plainly increased" (Bond 1930, p. 142). Bond pointed out, "The public has been urged to become familiar with the balance sheet and earnings statement of a company", but "Often the business investigation of a company is simply impossible to conduct to a satisfactory end without authority from the courts to inspect the books. Yet, the average outside speculator imagines, by reading a so-called 'analysis' printed in a big and expensive volume, that he is making an 'investigation'" (1930, p. 143). The fallacy, Bond argued, was "reasoning as an investor while acting as a speculator" (1930, p. 146), which, consistent with popular acceptance of new-era theory, was a popular confusion. Bond noted, "A curious psychological point was that the members of these masses, differing from the oldtime speculators had, nearly all of them, the singular notion that they were 'investors', and that their purchases of stock for the rise were 'investments'" (1930, pp. 182–183). Bond observed, "In fact, these words, before the end of the boom, almost supplanted the word 'speculator' and its derivatives, to the amusement of the great bankers who brooded over the scene" (1930, pp. 182–183).

Bond urged a "market trend trading rule", but this does not mean he thought investors were "indifferent to financial disclosure" (Merino and Neimark 1982, fn. 21, p. 41), and nor did leading observers. Merino and Neimark argue, "A great deal of testimony supporting the widespread use of ... trading rules is available in the US Senate Committee on Banking and Currency hearings" (1982, fn. 21, p. 41). They cite, "For example, see the testimony by Charles Wright a NYSE specialist (US Congress, Senate 1934, 389ff), and from the later 1955 hearings, the testimony by Ronald E Kaehler president of the San Francisco Exchange, regarding his experience as a floor trader from 1927 to 1930 (US Congress, Senate, 1955, 237ff)" (Merino and Neimark 1982, fn. 21, p. 41). Pool operators' aim Wright admitted was to increase prices by "creating a market", to induce speculators and investors to buy, but although he followed the market, he did not argue investors did, and he generally considered accounting data:

> The Chairman. In any of these stock transactions, Mr. Wright, did you trouble to look after the operations of the company issuing the stock, whether it was a successful enterprise or not, what capital they had, what assets, what liabilities?
>
> Mr. Wright. As a general rule, we did, Senator.

In 1955, Kaehler recalled that as a trader from 1927 to 1930 he followed the "trend of the market". However, he distinguished floor traders from other investors and speculators:

> The Chairman. If that was your approach to it, why do you think everybody else looked at the income and the dividends before they bought stock?
>
> Mr. Kaehler. I think there is a distinction between trading on the floor of the exchange and investing either for yield or for appreciation. (US Congress, Senate 1955, pp. 237–238)

Some academics, such as Fisher, devised and used "charts" to predict share prices. In 1925, Fisher began collecting daily and weekly stock prices and other measures, and wrote "a draft of 'A Formulary for Anticipating Short-time Changes in Market Action'. He and others used it to predict what would happen in the market" (Allen 1993, p. 188), but he mainly advocated earnings trends. The use of trading rules by some academics, specialists, and floor traders does not mean the investing or speculating public used them, or, if they did, that they used only such rules. Merino and Neimark noted writers, including John Maynard Keynes (1936) and Galbraith (1961), who "have suggested that trades, investment advisers, and pool and syndicate managers behaved as if the average investor followed a 'market-trend' trading rule and was indifferent to financial disclosure" (1982, fn. 21, p. 41). Behaving "as if" the average investor followed a market-trend rule, however, says nothing about the investors' actual attitudes. As evidence for this, Merino and Neimark (1982, p. 42) cite the Twentieth Century Fund (1935, pp. 645–646): "It is just this tendency on the part of the public to base its security operations more and more upon what is actually going on in the market that enables pool managers and other manipulators to entice their naive victims to the slaughterhouse". Merino and Neimark conclude, "Given the quality of the financial information that was being reported at the time, investors were not necessarily behaving irrationally in dismissing financial reports as a source of investment information" (1982, p. 42). However, the Twentieth Century Fund was discussing "Chart Reading", the fact that "there has grown up in recent years a technique known vaguely as 'chart reading'" (1935, p. 643), that support for "technical study" appeared only after the crash of 1929, during the depression's early years.

"Chart reading", or "technical analysis", goes back at least to around 1900: "The precursor of all technical principles was the Dow Theory, which evolved as a result of the work of Charles H. Dow, editor of the *Wall Street Journal* from 1889 to 1902, and his followers" (Levy 1966, p. 83). Books by William P. Hamilton (1922) and Robert Rhea (1932) sought to popularise the basic concepts. From 1902 to 1929, Hamilton wrote editorials in *The Wall Street Journal* and *Barron's*, "discussing and forecasting major trends in the U.S. stock market. Hamilton cited his predecessor Charles Dow's theory of stock market movements as the explicit basis for market predictions. In his 1922 book, *The Stock Market Barometer*, Hamilton further explains the basic outlines of the theory" (Brown *et al.* 1998, pp. 1312–1313), but these efforts had little impact. The most notable literary event in the history of technical analysis was the publication of Rhea's *Dow Theory*, by *Barron's* in 1932, which articulated and refined Dow's theories. While the "basic outlines of the Dow Theory may be gleaned from Hamilton's book and editorials, Robert Rhea's reduction of the Dow Theory as 'theorems' is a useful guide" (Brown *et al.* 1998, p. 1313). In 1934, Graham and Dodd surmised, "the vogue of … 'technical study' has increased immensely during the past ten years", from "about 1927", when traditional "security analysis suffered a distinct and continuous loss of prestige", but added, "chart reading apparently increased the number of its followers *even during the long depression*" (1934, p. 608, emphasis added). In 1935, the Twentieth Century Fund associated the popularity of "chart reading" with the depression — "the chartist has come into his own *in the last few years*" (1935, p. 644, emphasis added) — and with loss of faith in the "usual economic and statistical data", which we will see was true of published accounts following the crash:

> … there has grown up *in recent years* a technique known vaguely as 'chart reading', which because of its widespread and growing usage in brokerage circles deserves some explanation. … It has gained a

> relatively large following and has undergone more or less continuous refinement of technique in recent years. *This growth appears to have been, in part at least, the result of the bewilderment of most market prognosticators the face of the developments of the depression period.* In these years, most precedents upon which the average Wall Street observer relied were broken. Current interpretations of the usual economic and statistical data failed to prove a useful guide. (Twentieth Century Fund 1935, p. 643, emphases added)

Interest in "chart reading" increased after the crash, after the public's "bewilderment", loss of faith in reported earnings' integrity. The proportion of total records published by *Barron's (Weekly)* between 1921 and 1942 using "Dow Theory" was low before the publication of Rhea's book in 1932, whereas the proportion containing the word "earnings" was high (more than 30 percent) from 1923 to 1929 (Figure 4.1).[3] However, whereas the relative frequency of "Dow Theory" increased, the frequency of "earnings" decreased from 1930, consistent with interest in "earnings" being high until the 1929 crash and then decreasing to 1935. The relative decline

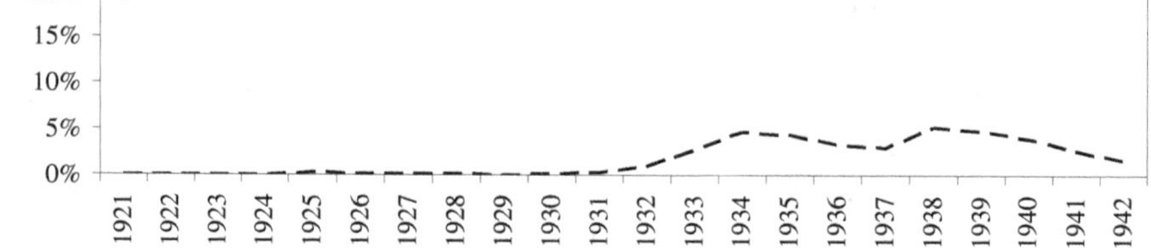

Figure 4.1: "Earnings" and "Dow Theory" in Barron's Weekly, 1921–1942

Source: Author's calculations from ABI-Inform Global.

[3] *Barron's* "carries a few articles whose subjects are of wide and general interest …, but much the larger … space is devoted to the sort of company analysis and comment that is to be found in the *Wall Street Journal* and on the Dow-Jones news ticker" (Twentieth Century Fund 1935, p. 620). I estimate the total annual records in *Barron's* containing words by searching for records containing "the", the commonest English word.

in investors' interest in "earnings" halted around the Securities Acts of 1933 and 1934, consistent with their passage halting falling confidence in accounting, and interest in earnings began reviving, but declined again from 1938, consistent with accountants and managers resisting its implementation, then increased following the SEC's intervention forcing professional regulation of accounting standards from 1940, as we will see in Chapters 5 and 6. There were also increases in the frequency of records including "chart" from 1930, "Trend Line" from 1932, and increased use of "Technical Analysis" from 1933 (ABI-Inform Global).[4] Technical analysis had "Many sceptics", including Graham and Dodd, who were "inclined to dismiss the whole procedure as akin to astrology or necromancy", but discussed it because when they were writing "the sheer weight of its importance in Wall Street requires that its pretensions be examined" (1934, p. 608).

"Dow Theory", "charts", "trend lines" and "technical analysis" were increasingly popular after the 1929 crash, but before it the new-era theory's focus on "earnings" was overwhelmingly more popular, if only because it was supported by a large stream of accounting data, particularly "earnings" and "analysis". It is true, "only a small proportion of the millions of security holders have the time, the patience and the technical training to enable them to analyse corporate statements and make intelligent decisions on the basis thereof" (Twentieth Century Fund 1935, p. 61). Only a relatively small proportion of investors and speculators could afford to subscribe to the "financial manuals" (Twentieth Century Fund 1935, p. 612).[5] However, there were only relatively few well-to-do and wealthy investors who owned around 80 percent of all stocks and could afford the best advice money could buy. For the vast majority, "most corporations in which the public holds substantial interests regularly publish balance sheets and operating statements", who distributed them direct to stockholders, and filed them with the NYSE (Twentieth Century Fund 1935, pp. 564, 576, 579). The financial press deluged investors, speculators and the public, with accounting information. Twentieth Century Fund found, "It is very largely through

[4] "Trend line" appeared in 1930 and 101 times up to 1942; "technical analysis" four times from 1921 to 1931, but 16 times from 1932 to 1942; "chart reading" first appeared in 1930 and nine times to 1939 (ABI-Inform Global).

[5] The main publishers were Fitch Publishing Company, Moody's Investors Service, Poor's Publishing Company, the Standard Statistics Company, and William B. Dana Company (Twentieth Century Fund 1935, pp. 610–611).

the financial press in all its various aspects that the mass of data having a direct bearing upon investment and speculative policies reaches the public" (1935, p. 615).

The "financial press" included the *Wall Street Journal* and its and others' "news ticker services". In addition to "write-ups", the "point of view" these services promoted, a valued "feature of the ticker services", was "the forecasts of earnings of individual companies ... ordinarily published shortly before the earnings statements of the corporations in question are due to appear" (Twentieth Century Fund 1935, pp. 618–619). The "public" valued them because "The closeness with which it is possible for these specialists to tell the public some weeks in advance approximately what the earnings of a number of corporations will be for a given period, leaves little doubt that they are in close touch with the management of the enterprise in question. It is thus not often that the report of the quarterly earnings catches the general market greatly by surprise. This work is to be regarded as a real service to the investment and speculative market" (Twentieth Century Fund 1935, pp. 618–619). In addition to many statistics, financial magazines, particularly the *Commercial & Financial Chronicle* published, "relatively complete corporation reports" (Twentieth Century Fund 1935, pp. 619–620). During the 1920s, the daily press gave greatly increased coverage to "financial developments", and "Financial Services" blossomed. Twentieth Century Fund had no doubt that the "American public is bombarded with advice about securities" (1935, pp. 615–616, 619–620, 622, 630). Many financial services publishers provided, as one of them put it, "detailed analysis and forecast of sales, price, profit margin and earnings trend, with similar condensed analysis of the leading corporations, ... with suggestions for purchase, holding or sale" (Twentieth Century Fund 1935, p. 630). This plethora of "earnings" information during the 1920s, which could feed the new-era theory, makes it questionable whether during the 1920s the wealthy, well-to-do or middle-class were "dismissing financial reports as a source of investment information" (Merino and Neimark 1982, p. 42). Market-trading rules made speculators vulnerable to market-rigging (Merino and Neimark 1982, p. 45), but focusing on earnings made them vulnerable to accounting manipulation.

Earnings and the Boom

G.O. May had no doubt "An outstanding characteristic ... [of] the enormous volume and extravagantly high prices which characterized the dealings in corporate stocks in the period running up to 1929 … was the new emphasis laid on earning capacity as the measure of value of such securities" (1932, p. 337). In his view, "we have seen during periods of inflation and deflation this truth applied in a most reckless and ill-advised manner, not only by investors, but by many who have undertaken to advise others" (May 1932, p. 337). May admitted, "Such people were no doubt right when they argued that earning capacity was usually the main criterion on value. They may have been right … that the fair value of securities of a given type was a multiple — ten, fifteen, or twenty — of the earning capacity attached to the security" (May 1932, p. 337). However, they were "hopelessly wrong" when they assumed the "earnings capacity was fairly measured by the past or prospective earnings for a comparatively short period, without any adequate knowledge of the way in which the figures of earnings employed in their calculations were derived" (May 1932, p. 337). As May pointed out, "The combination of the concept of income as including capital gains and that of capital value as a multiple of income-producing capacity obviously may and, indeed, did in the financial boom of 1928 and 1929 produce fantastic results" (1943, p. 29). In another lecture in 1932, May complained, "in recent years there has, to my mind, grown up a tendency to attach an altogether too much importance to the earnings reported annually by corporations as an index of future earning capacity and, consequently, of the value of the business. This tendency has, I think, incidentally had the effect of magnifying the swings in the market price of stocks" (1936, p. 8).

The "fantastic results" and "swings" of 1928 and 1929, May argued, were the products of accounting methods and widespread ignorance: "Nothing has astonished me more in conversations with men fairly well versed in financial matters than their failure to appreciate the importance of methods of accounting in relation to corporate earnings and to capital values predicated on earnings" (1932, p. 337). They failed to understand, May lectured, that at best "the value of the income account depends on its being a fair indication of the earning capacity of the business under the conditions existing during the year to which it relates" (1932, p. 345), that earnings were at best a steady-state forecast (see Chapter 5). May's comments are consistent with popular acceptance of new-era theory. Believing it made even "fairly well versed" wealthy and well-to-do investors and their agents' expectations vulnerable to manipulation. It allowed management and influential outsiders and insiders to manage expectations, which could explain why dividends began to disconnect from share prices from around 1927 (Rappoport and White 1993, p. 552). Share prices sharply increased, but dividends did not, which White concluded, "seems to imply that managers did not share the public's enthusiasm", but few warned of unrealistic expectations (White 1990b, pp. 154, 158).

The consensus among econometricians during the 1980s was that stock prices "move closely enough with their fundamentals, measured by dividends, to support the efficient market hypothesis", that there was no evidence of "persistent bubbles" (Rappoport and White 1993, p. 549). Against this, Rappoport and White (1993) see "unusually high" rates charged for brokers' loans as evidence of a bubble. During the boom, many bought stocks on credit. Investors took "margin loans" from brokers who obtained "brokers' loans" to finance it — both "call" and "time" loans from banks and the stock exchange floor. Rappoport and White argued there were "unusually high premia over other money market rates during the course of the 1928 to 1929 stock market boom" which meant, "lenders required larger premia because they thought that stock prices might collapse during the term of a loan and jeopardize the collateral" (1993, p. 550). In their view, "These results imply that even if investors in the stock market believed it to be driven by fundamentals, lenders were apprehensive and attached significant risk to a large stock market decline" (Rappoport and White 1993, p. 550). However, their results could also imply that lenders increased interest rates on call loans to take a share of large capital gains, as high interest rates would not insure lenders against a crash, as the failure of many of the banks who provided the loans (Michie 2006, pp. 183–185) demonstrated after the crash. Shares provide "collateral" for a loan only if they maintain their market value to meet any "margin requirement" less than 100 percent. Margin requirements did increase from "perhaps 25 to 40 or 50 percent" at the boom's height, which shows scepticism but not disbelief in stock prices, whose volatility increased only after the crash (Rappoport and White 1993, pp. 557–558). Therefore, it does not necessarily follow that "there was a sharp divergence in opinion between lenders and investors", or that "some managers ... shared the lenders' skepticism" (Rappoport and White 1993, p. 550) and predicted the crash.

Many contemporaries and historians blamed the speculation on "easy credit", including Fisher (1930b, p. 218), who borrowed heavily (Allen 1993, p. 214). Galbraith and others argued that fuelling the public's eagerness to buy stocks was a large expansion of credit in the form of margin loans and brokers' loans (time and increasingly call loans) encouraging investors to take on dangerous levels of debt (1961, pp. 46–50). Credit in general was tight. Nevertheless many lenders, including investment trusts and corporations, funnelled large amounts of credit to the stock market via brokers' loans, and the rates they charged increased sharply during the later stages of the boom, "suggesting that it was the rising tide of speculation that attracted funds, not any independent credit creation" (White 1990b, p. 162). Galbraith also accepted "it takes more to start a speculation than a general ability to borrow money" (1961, p. 55). Rejecting easy credit, to explain the dramatic rise in share prices, the "surviving candidate is that a bubble appeared" (White 1990b, p. 167). However, by identifying the bubble by the high call rates Rappoport and White admit, "Our findings are not … immune from … criticism that movements in stock prices can be produced by dynamics of fundamentals seen by agents, but not by econometricians" (1993, p. 550). They defend their interpretation because "neither contemporary observers nor current researchers have been able to identify a dramatic economic or policy event that could have altered fundamentals sufficiently to explain the extraordinary movement in stock prices", and date the bubble from March 1928, the standard historical view (Rappoport and White 1993, pp. 550, 553). For example, according to Seligman, "It was only during the final year of the Coolidge administration that the market began to exhibit its manic quality" (1982, p. 2).

However, "skepticism" about the existence of a "bubble", Rappoport and White are right, "might be supported by evidence from contemporary academic observers, including Charles Dice and Irving Fisher, who saw new advances in technology and managerial and industrial organization driving the boom" (1993, p. 550), particularly evidence of Fisher's influence. Judging by the success of his new-era theory the "speculation" began around 1927. We can observe the change in "fundamentals as seen by agents" that produced the "bubble" as the change in their shared belief in current and future earnings as the basis of economic value, which made them vulnerable to earnings management. If earnings "indicate" future earnings and dividends, believers could differ about the realistic multiple, and some judged "superior", political, business, financial and academic leaders, particularly influential insiders, the "big men who put stocks up and put them down", who "became more and more omnipotent in the popular or at least in the speculative view" (Galbraith 1961, p. 41). Mass retailing of shares began in 1925. From 1927, the influx of middle class investors began, the wealthy reinvested their dividends, and "speculation" took hold. The Twentieth Century Fund produced a "price index, earnings index, and price-earnings rates", for 25 common stocks, 1925–1932 (1935, Chart 4, p. 172) that show the separation of market prices from reported earnings around mid-1927.

During the 1920s, accountants "were becoming aware … that investors … were using accounting statements" to value shares, that "Using the income statement to evaluate the investment value of common stocks was perhaps the most important use made during the 1920s", and management responded, "attempts were being made" to make accounts "more useful" (Dillon 1984, pp. 108, 120). In 1928, Paton applauded the "improvements [that] were made in the 1920s" (Dillon 1984, p. 107), noting "accountants on all sides laying great stress on the arrangement of items in statements and reports" (Paton 1928, p. 252). There was, he thought, a "general recognition of the need for discarding archaic arrangements and for developing elasticity of reports, with a view to the use of the most effective setup from the standpoint of the particular audience for which a report is intended" (Paton 1928, p. 252). Corporations were "experimenting with such comparative statements, graphs and charts" (Paton 1928, p. 252). Paton had no doubt what the focus should be: "there is one ratio, or group of ratios, involving both balance sheet and income statement data, which seem to me to rank far and above any and all other percentages in general significance. That is the return … realized by the enterprise to the capital investment", of which the most popular was the "rate of common stock earnings to common stock equity" (Paton 1928, p. 254). Dominating them all, "This is the outstanding fact, *earning power*" (Paton 1928, p. 254), and common stock earnings was the foundation, as Graham and Dodd observed, "on which the entire edifice of value has come to be built" (1934, p. 352).

Consistent with new-era theory, "The investment value of a corporation's stock was frequently expressed in the 1920s … in terms of the ratio between the market price of the stock and the corporation's earnings per share" (Dillon 1984, p. 121). As Dillon (1984, p. 121) says, "Canning's remarks", that "ultimate statistical effects … must result from the succession of periodic measures" (1929, p. 93), "are representative of the [1920s] opinion that accounting reports should provide insights into future expectations as well as historical facts". As Canning put it, "All measures of income for periods less than … the duration of the enterprise are approximate indexes only. These indexes are good or bad to the degree that they enable or fail to enable a future income to be anticipated reliably rather than the degree to which they approximate the measure that will be, or may ultimately be determined to have been, the real gross income for the period reported on" (1929, p. 213). Canning observed "the very great variety of forms and statistical arrangements of income statements [which] must be bewildering to all except those who have made a professional study of accounts" (1929, p. 136). Even if they had, many would have been none-the-wiser. Observers pointed out how easy it was to manipulate earnings (Hatfield 1927, pp. 245–246; Graham and Dodd 1934, p. 354). Looking back over a 40-year career, Main judged "Good accounting, during these decades, has been conservative; substantial reserves have been created; and businessmen have prided themselves on presenting balance sheets which are understatements of the fixed assets. … Accounting, during many of these decades was secretive, and the accounting secrets were carefully guarded" (1944, p. 390). Not privy to them and convinced earnings trends were dividend forecasts, many "speculated".

Consistent with investors fixated on earnings trends, observers thought it was possible to influence share prices by manipulating earnings. Berle and Means (1932, p. 183) highlighted a prominent example: "Litigation is now pending in connection with the Gillett Safety Razor Co., occasioned in part by the fact that this company transferred inventory to subsidiaries at a price yielding a paper profit, and reported such profits as 'earnings'. The subsidiary of course ultimately showed a loss. The parent company's shares, however, had a brilliant stock market career for a time on the strength of the apparent earnings". Overall, until the mid-1920s share prices reflected a relatively constant multiple (price-earnings ratio). However, from 1927, when large numbers of middle-class investors appeared, the multiple increased significantly, particularly for utilities. Utility companies dominated the second merger wave of 1919–1928 during which 1,200 mergers gave control of 6,000 independent companies (McElvaine 2009, pp. 37–38). Utilities were central to the boom, and took the early brunt of the collapse (White 1990a, Figure 2, p. 71), and were assiduous account manipulators (Bryer 2021a, p. 364). The first merger wave around 1900 created big industrial corporations to reap economies of scale, but the second "brought together … firms doing the same thing in different communities. Local electric, gas, water, bus, and milk companies were united in great regional or national systems", as were food stores, variety stores, department stores and motion picture companies, using the holding company to centralise management and control (Galbraith 1961, p. 70). Fisher acclaimed "The Age of Mergers" from 1922 to 1927, which "for economical reasons ... have had much to do with the increase in the stock price level during the long Bull market" (1930b, p. 101), but their consolidated accounts were often manipulated (Bryer 2021a, pp. 370–373). Fisher observed, "public utilities ... mergers are responsible for the increase of stock prices to something like 26 times earnings up to the market crash in October ... as against only 13½ to 1 for the average of the whole market during the first nine months of 1929" (1930b, pp. 101–102), consistent with exceptional manipulation of utilities' expected earnings growth and risk.

After the crash, despite the "superior economies of mergers, and the consequent increase in the price level of their securities", Fisher recognised, big businesses were not popular, were "still on trial before the bar of public opinion" (1930b, p. 113), and belatedly argued, "Publicity is the sovereign remedy against merger evils today" (1930b, p. 114). Only after the crash did he call for "publicity of corporate accounts" (Fisher 1930a, p. 115). Fisher opined, "The value of fuller corporate publicity has in a measure been shown in the recent stock market by the greater stability of railroad than other listed issues. American railroads must report earnings frequently under standard methods of bookkeeping prescribed by the Interstate Commerce Commission. The investor knows with a railroad security just about what he is buying" (1930b, p. 114). He complained, rightly, "This is by no means the case with industrial securities, and the investor is forced to speculate on the accuracy of published industrial corporations" (1930b, p. 114), but for the wrong reason, and was wrong that railroad and, by inference, utility holding company accounts, were superior. As the Twentieth Century Fund pointed out, "Public utilities ... have no uniform standards for making reports, as the different states vary in their requirements" (1935, p. 579), and railroad accounts were rarely audited independently. "It is the opinion of some able students of the subject, moreover, that the annual reports of the railroad companies to their stockholders, although they contain more detail ..., are rather less informative than the more carefully prepared annual reports of industrial corporations" (Twentieth Century Fund 1935, p. 580). Problems with consolidated accounts meant all sectors were bad, but utilities were particularly bad: "The information contained in such reports is often so meagre as to be almost useless to the stockholder. In numerous instances, indeed, instead of disclosing, the report succeeds in concealing the real conditions" (Twentieth Century Fund 1935, p. 580).

In 1926, William Z. Ripley, professor of political economy at Harvard University, criticised poor disclosure, receiving wide publicity for his advice to investors to "Stop, Look, Listen!", but was an almost lone voice. Oblivious to such advice, from the mid-1920s, "investors were shifting their money from productive capital to what Hoover, then secretary of commerce, aptly damned as 'an orgy of speculation'", warning of "the growing tide of speculation" even in 1925 (Seligman 1982, p. 4; Dawley 1991, pp. 338–339), mainly confined to the wealthy. Efforts to encourage the middle classes to take part began "by the middle of the decade … [when] securities salesmen were telling potential customers that buying stock on margin was no different than paying for a radio on time" (Sobel 1968, p. 46). However, the real speculation began when the wealthy began investing dividends back into the stock market, "especially after 1927 … [when] the stock exchanges were flooded with individuals who had no previous experience in buying and selling securities. By then the dream of great wealth and of a limitless bull market seemed more real than fanciful" (Sobel 1968, p. 47). To realise this dream, thinking of themselves as money capitalists, borrowing at a low rate and investing in an asset with a higher rate of return, to many seemed obvious (McElvaine 2009, p. 44).

To maintain earnings growth, many large corporations and investment trusts did likewise, dramatically increased their debt levels, so that "by the late twenties, several large companies found themselves in a pleasant spiral: the more they borrowed, the higher their earnings; the higher their earnings, the more they could borrow. This fact was not lost on most corporate treasurers" (Sobel 1968, p. 89). Reported secured debt of American corporations increased from $67 billion in 1925 to almost $77 billion in 1929 (Sobel 1968, p. 89). *Barron's* published an essay submitted to its competition for the best essay on "Investing for the businessman", which while not the winner it found "so interesting" it purchased it for publication (9 January 1928, p. 5). The author, Robert G. Wiese (1928, p. 5), had an MA in Economics from Yale, and like Fisher argued that equities would earn higher returns than bonds because "Common stocks profit by issuing bonds". This, combined with Fisher's other factors, "diversification" that "eliminates the risk", the "compound interest effect in the value of common stocks due to the reinvesting into the business of undistributed earnings" and "corporations grow in size and earning power", Wiese (1928, p. 5) concluded, meant all was well in the new-era.

He reassured readers, “While it is true that the stock market is at a relatively high level and that in the past we have seen the valleys follow the peaks, yet we must remember two things. First, equities in America’s leading corporations never before have been so valuable as now. Second, that the public is being educated to using common stocks as an investment medium; consequently they are selling on a much different basis than they have in the past, and they will continue to do so” (Wiese 1928, p. 5). During the first three-quarters of 1929, this was how it looked. “Profits were high and the size of the firms indicated a certain stability”, and there was “every reason to hope for still greater profits, and to believe that new industries would grow rapidly. And these beliefs were quickly transformed into higher prices” (Sobel 1968, p. 38), shortly followed by the crash.

Explaining the Crash

By early 1929, Galbraith argued, it was evident to “men of wisdom” that “a roaring boom was in progress in the stock market”, and because “like all booms it had to end”, that they should do something to end it (1961, p. 51). A crash was inevitable because “When prices stopped rising — when the supply of people who were buying for an increase was exhausted — then ownership on margin would become meaningless and everyone would want to sell. The market wouldn’t level out; it would fall precipitately” (Galbraith 1961, p. 51). However, Galbraith’s explanation assumes prices were artificially high because demand was artificially high, without asking whether this was because expectations of future earnings were artificially high.

Some in authority, Galbraith argued, “wanted the boom to continue. They were making money” and probably “had an intimation of the personal disaster that awaited them when the boom came to an end”, but some “saw, however dimly, that a wild speculation was in progress and that something should be done” (1961, pp. 51–52). He criticised President Coolidge, who “neither knew nor cared what was going on. A few days before leaving office in 1929, Coolidge cheerily observed that things were ‘fundamentally sound’ and that ‘stocks were cheap at current prices’” (Galbraith 1961, p. 53). Galbraith (1961, pp. 53–54) criticised Andrew W. Mellon, Secretary of the Treasury from March 9, 1921 to February 12, 1932, “a passionate advocate of inaction”, and the Federal Reserve Board as a “body of startling incompetence”. The Fed twice cautioned banks against borrowing money to lend for speculation, which Hoover, now president-elect, supported (Seligman 1982, p. 4). However, it did not press the point, and its warnings had little effect. Galbraith criticised Charles E. Mitchell, head of the National City Bank, one of the two largest commercial banks, with a reputation as "an aggressive and highly successful investment banker", director of the New York Federal Reserve Bank, who unabashedly "was for the boom" (Galbraith 1961, p. 63). In March 1929, Mitchell defied the Fed by announcing his bank would borrow from it to support margin loans (Seligman 1982, p. 4). His and Coolidge's interventions implied the earnings multiple should be even higher. Share prices increased during the summer by around 25 percent, "the market sailed off into the wild blue yonder" (Galbraith 1961, p. 68). Coolidge's cheery remarks, "had helped to undermine the boards' tentative efforts at 'moral suasion'" (Seligman 1982, p. 4). Moreover, Coolidge, Mellon, Mitchell and others were self-interested, but Galbraith makes no allowance for the fact that, as Fisher and others repeatedly pointed out, as far as everyone knew the "fundamentals", particularly earnings growth, was "sound". Galbraith was right that if the Fed had "been determined to do something, it could for example have asked Congress for authority to halt trading on margin" (1961, p. 58), but neither the Fed nor anyone else had reason to act.

The S&P 500 index peaked on 2 September 1929 at 31.83 and did not hit the bottom of 4.41 until 9 July 1932 (Figure 4.2).[6] The "bubble" began to deflate suddenly, largely unexpectedly, and inexplicably to scholars, from 7 October, and particularly on 24 October 1929 ("Black Thursday") when investors panicked because the ticker ran late in heavy trading (White 1990b). Prices recovered briefly for a few days, but significantly worsened on the 28th and particularly 29th of October ("Black Tuesday"), from when they began their descent to the bottom (Galbraith 1961, pp. 121, 133; White 1990a, p. 68). The crisis intensified as corporations and investment banks, which had provided over half the margin loans, recalled them (Bond 1930, pp. 194, 196; Galbraith 1961, pp. 135–134; Merino and Neimark 1982, p. 45). Why did the "bubble" burst, and why was it that "The singular feature of the great crash of 1929 was that the worst continued to worsen" (Galbraith 1961, p. 130)? Why did bankers fail to prevent it? Having tried and failed to support the market, "Few men

[6] *The New York Times* Industrial Index used by Galbraith also peaked on 2 September 1929 at 452, and hit the bottom of 58 on 8 July 1932 (1954, p. 161).

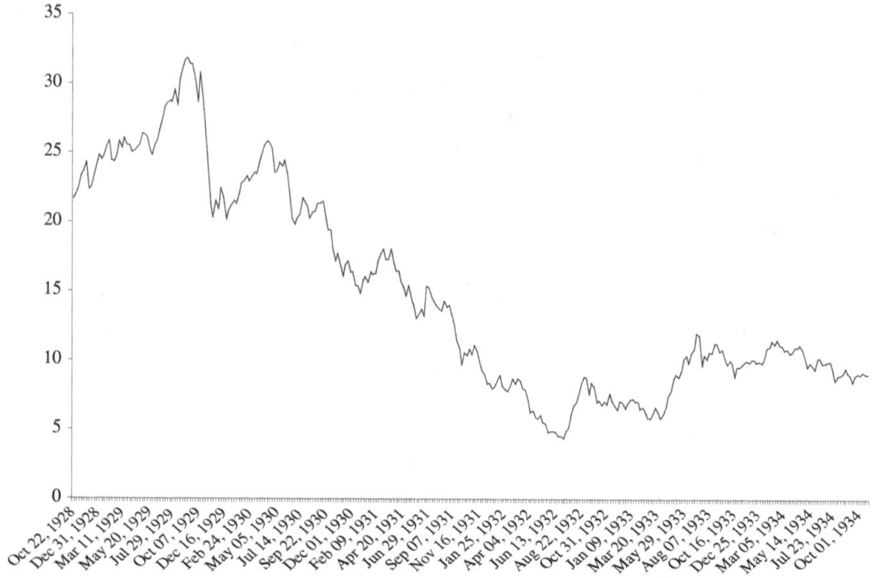

Figure 4.2: S&P 500 Weekly Index, October 1928–October 1934

Source: https://finance.yahoo.com.

have ever lost position so rapidly as did the New York bankers in the five days from 24 October to 29 October" (Galbraith 1961, p. 135). The "bubble" burst and swept bankers aside because investors and speculators stopped believing in earnings growth and in reported earnings' integrity, and revising these beliefs produced a continuing decline in stock prices. Investors and speculators were flying blind, with a disbelief in "fundamentals".

Galbraith and others see the crash as an endogenous collapse of expectations, that "the stock market was inherently unstable and anything could have shattered the public's confidence" (White 1990a, p. 78). However, as White says, "Yet something did convince investors that their expectations of future price increases were no longer justified. Contemporary pundits offered many explanations, including the excessive issues of new stock, decisions by government regulators, the Smoot–Hawley tariff, foreign stock markets, and declining brokers' loans", but they are "minor or irrelevant factors in the crash" (1990a, p. 78). Instead, White concludes, evidence of a downturn in the business cycle prompted a revision in expectations. Galbraith criticised the "accepted view of events" that "by the autumn of 1929 the economy was well into a depression" and, "Finally, down came the stock market", which is "but a mirror which, perhaps belatedly, provides an image of the underlying or *fundamental* economic situation" (1961, p. 111). The fall in economic activity was minor, Galbraith suggests, and became the "accepted view" only because it supported Wall Street's desire to avoid any responsibility for the depression (1961, pp. 111–112). He therefore concluded, "any satisfactory explanation of the events of the autumn of 1929 and thereafter must accord a dignified role to the speculative boom and ensuing collapse. Until September or October of 1929, the decline in economic activity was very modest", and "A depression, serious or otherwise, could not be foreseen when the market fell" (Galbraith 1961, pp. 112–113). It was a "spontaneous decision to get out", possibly, Galbraith suggests, prompted by advertisements in the New York papers on the 22 September 1929 on the perils of "OVERSTAYING A BULL MARKET", but "What first stirred these doubts we do not know, but neither is it very important that we know" (1961, pp. 114–115).

Galbraith's conclusions are questionable. First, stockholders did not have to foresee a depression to lose faith in current prices, but come to believe that the earnings growth expectations on which share prices depended had been undermined. The market eventually reacted to "fundamentals" not because stockholders could foresee the future, but because they stopped believing in the past. Second, as White (1990a, p. 80) says, the "inadequacy" of Galbraith's explanation "leads back to the question whether any abrupt change in dividends or earnings might have set off the crash". When the rate of profit fell from 1924 (Roberts 2016, Figure 3.1, p. 53), management's manipulations delayed revision in earnings expectations, which extended the boom. Management created "hidden reserves" and used them to report earnings growth, particularly in 1928 and 1929 (Bryer 2021, Chapter 9). It was not until the third quarter of 1929, therefore, after evidence that production and earnings growth were slowing that share prices began to fall, and with loss of faith in the integrity of reported earnings, keep falling. Evidence consistent with an exceptional delay in America is that the stock price indexes for London, Paris and Berlin began falling around the beginning of 1929 (Fisher 1930b, Chart 5, p. 33; White 1990a, Figure 6, p. 80). During 1929, in America "The quarterly dividends of the Dow-Jones industrials show healthy increases in late-1929, rising 12.8 percent in the third quarter and

11.6 percent in the fourth. The first drop of 6.3 percent appears only in the initial quarter of 1930" (White 1990a, pp. 80–81), but current dividends were not of primary concern to Fisher and his new-era theory followers. More important was earnings, and here there was cause for concern, although not necessarily because, as White (1990a, p. 80) suggests, with other information it signalled an "oncoming recession", but because it undermined growth expectations. White argues, "there was evidence of an oncoming recession. In the absence of any quarterly earnings, the Federal Reserve's index of industrial production may be used as a proxy. This first dropped in July 1929. In August and September, some of the Federal Reserve's other indices began to fall" (1990, pp. 80–81). He concludes, "This mixed news and rising real interest rates, at home and abroad, spelled an incipient recession; and it was all that was necessary to cause stockholders to revise their expectations" (White 1990a, pp. 80–81). With hindsight, "The peak of the business cycle has been dated from August 1929. The decline in all the Federal Reserve's indices came only when the October figures were published after the crash" (White 1990a, fn. 15, p. 80).

Quarterly earnings reports were available for 25–50 percent of the corporations listed on the NYSE, the Twentieth Century Fund (1935, pp. 590–591) estimated, and for others they would have been available to insiders. Twentieth Century Fund analysed a sample of 25 common stocks of large corporations for which quarterly accounting data were available. This shows a slackening of earnings growth from around mid-1929, but share prices continued rising to early September, followed by sharply falling earnings from the end of 1929 (1935, Chart 4, pp. 172, 176). "Publication of quarterly statements is usually made within about five weeks after the close of the quarterly period" (Twentieth Century Fund 1935, p. 591), so second quarter earnings would begin appearing around the first week in September. Coincidentally, "On 3 September, by common consent, the great bull market of the nineteen twenties came to an end"; "never again did the market manifest its old confidence" (Galbraith 1961, p. 108). Adding fear to uncertainty, in early-October 1929 the realisation dawned on sophisticated investors that the falling earnings figures could themselves not be trusted. Following two highly publicised events, one in the US and one in Britain, that to knowledgeable investors indicated widespread manipulation of accounts, by the end of October, as third-quarter results began to appear confirming the slackening second-quarter earnings, confidence evaporated, and in early-1930 investors panicked. In short, the evidence suggests these two factors — slowing reported earnings growth, and loss of faith in their integrity — caused the timing of the crash, just as their opposite had caused the boom.

Timing the Crash

The S&P 500 index fell from 30.76 on 7 October 1929 to 20.3 on 11 November 1929 (Figure 4.2). In the context of growing criticism of accounting during the later-1920s, particularly Ripley's (1927) attacks, but also others' (Bryer 2021a, pp. 177–179, 347–375), evidence that undermined earnings' integrity could explain the popular "lore", as Galbraith (1961, p. 114) put it, highlighting two events which individually or together triggered the October crash. One was the "unprecedented … refusal on 11 October of the Massachusetts Department of Public Utilities to allow Boston Edison to split its stocks four to one" (Galbraith 1961, p. 114). Corporations with high share values often saw stock splits as "desirable, since they increased the marketability of the stock" and "often accompanied by dividend increases and favorable publicity … the price of the new shares is usually somewhat higher than the equivalent old shares" (Sobel 1968, p. 100). For Boston Edison, however, the Department refused, arguing, "the present value of the stock, 'due to the action of speculators', had reached a level where 'no one, in our judgement … on the basis of its earnings, would find it advantageous to buy it'" (Galbraith 1961, p. 114). Galbraith accepted these "uncouth words" "could have been important", but concluded, "it could also be that the inherently unstable equilibrium was shattered simply by a spontaneous decision to get out" (1961, p. 114). Alternatively, they may have provided evidence undermining knowledgeable investors' faith in the integrity of reported earnings more widely.

Galbraith overlooked the Department's criticism that "the company has been paying out practically all its earnings in dividends, without adequate reserves to depreciation and surplus" (*Barron's Weekly*, 21 October 1929, p. 23). This may have struck a chord because Ripley had prominently criticised earnings management, including by utilities, by varying "depreciation to smooth out the curve of net earnings" (1927, pp. 179–181, 184–245, 321). The Department's decision "jolted the investing public by the terms of its unanimous denial of the application", the "warning to the public that Edison stock, and, by implication, similar public utility stocks, were overpriced" (*Barron's Weekly*, 21 October 1929, p. 23). The company "pointed out that, far from setting inadequate depreciation reserves, it had actually been establishing reserves 50 percent greater than those suggested by the Department of Public Utilities" (*Barron's Weekly*, 21 October 1929, p. 23), which accepted "those suggested" were inadequate, and did not answer the criticisms that its depreciation charges and other "reserves" were inadequate. Despite Boston Edison's "impressive answer" its shares fell "from a high of 375½ the day before the announcement to a low of 290 on Wednesday [16th October], and its influence was reflected in liquidation of various public utility securities in Wall Street during the week" (*Barron's Weekly*, 21 October 1929, 23). After the crash, the NYSE informally "urged" companies to "desist from the practice of constantly revising depreciation charges in relation to earnings" (Parrish 1970, p. 41). Boston Edison's policy, however, continued. In 1933, *Barron's* noted it "has no established rule or rate for determining the amounts to be credited to depreciation reserves, but at the end of each fiscal year transfers to the credit of this account what ever amount is authorized by the executive committee" (27 February 1933, p. 15). For 1932, as the Department said was typical, this made earnings after depreciation equal to dividends: "With the $2,400,000 appropriated for depreciation reserve deducted from 1932 income the balance was equal to $12.40 a share. Dividends paid aggregated $12.40 a share" (*Barron's Weekly*, 27 February 1933, p. 15).

Shaking faith in accounting's integrity could also explain the other equal-ranking "lore", the importance attributed to the collapse of the British enterprises of Clarence Hatry and his arrest on 20 September 1929 for securities fraud (Galbraith 1961, p. 114). This, as *Barron's* put it, "started a wave of pessimism in London and of British liquidation both there and here" (9 December 1929, p. 10). Hatry and his associates issued forged securities to obtain loans to avert a financial crisis (Walker 1977, pp. 80–81), which received much publicity. Galbraith accepted, "conceivably" the Hatry affair could have helped cause the sharp fall in share prices from the end of September 1929, but like Boston Edison, he thought a "spontaneous" decision upsetting the "inherently unstable equilibrium" was as likely (1961, pp. 113–114). Galbraith overlooked that the Hatry scandal questioned the reliability of British financial reporting, which was widely seen as superior to the American system, which therefore could have undermined American financial reporting's credibility. The *Accountant's* reviewer of "Ripley's attack on American reporting practices" was "happy to believe that were a British investor given the utmost facility he would be unable to frame an indictment against British big business even fractionally as serious as the charges which Professor Ripley levels at American corporations" (Walker 1977, p. 80). Fisher (1930b, pp. 31, 229–230) thought, "the failure of the issuing house of Hatry in London ... was the signal for a recession on the London Stock Exchange", caused by a "gigantic forgery of stock certificates", which helped produce panic in America. More likely, in America, as in Britain, as Robert G. Walker said, "the Hatry failure was of special significance, for it shocked the British securities markets and focused public attention on the adequacy of regulatory mechanisms. And it seems that the Hatry failure paved the way for stock exchange involvement in the regulation of corporate financial reporting" (Walker 1977, p. 80).

Given its impact, as Walker (1977, p. 81) says, "Ironically the Hatry affair did not itself provide hard evidence of the deficiencies in financial reporting though it did underline the absence of any mechanism for policing reporting practices". However, the problem it revealed was "the key company in the Hatry group had delayed publication of its annual report before the collapse, and hence the group's grave financial position had been concealed from the investing public .... Disclosure of the fact highlighted the ineffectiveness of the administrative processes adopted by the Registrar of Companies to follow up overdue financial statements ... and the lack of any stock exchange rules setting deadlines for publication of reports to shareholders" (Walker 1977, p. 81). Delaying publication of accounts was a bigger problem in America. Twentieth Century Fund found for NYSE listed companies "there has been considerable improvement in the frequency of published reports", but only somewhere between the quarter that published quarterly reports in 1923, and the half that did so by 1933 (1935, pp. 590–591). For the others who published only annual reports, "Promptness has been lacking, ... which appear at periods ranging between one and six months after the end of the fiscal year, sometimes even longer" (1935, pp. 591–592). More portentous for America, however, the Hatry affair roused "misgivings about the hazards of investing in subsidiaries" (Walker 1978, p. 80).

In January 1930, the London Stock Exchange appointed a Special Sub-committee to investigate the affair that highlighted problems with "groups": "The Stock Exchange initially responded to the Hatry affair by being cautious about listing the stocks of firms which were part of 'groups'" (Walker 1977, p. 81). It "indicated" it would "henceforth 'be disinclined' to grant permission to deal in the shares of a subsidiary company until after the publication of the first annual report of the parent company" (Walker 1977, pp. 81–82; 1978, pp. 80–81). Hatry had floated a subsidiary and delayed publishing the parent's accounts — consolidated accounts were not required — which meant the parent could easily manipulate the subsidiary's accounts. Holding companies were uncommon in Britain, but widespread in America, so possible manipulation of British accounts using "groups", an American problem, critics had highlighted, could have undermined British investors' confidence in American consolidated accounts, who liquidated their investments in New York, raising the question, "Did Britons Foresee the Recent Crash?" (*Barron's Weekly*, 9 December 1929, p. 10). *Barron's* concluded, "The date of Hatry's arrest was a matter of luck — bad for Hatry, perhaps, but fine for British speculators in 'Yanks'" (9 December 1929, p. 10), but did not explain why problems with a British company should cause British speculators to liquidate in New York, and why American speculators followed them.

American shareholders apparently lost interest in earnings from around the end of October 1929, Fisher observed, noting US Steel's record reported earnings for the third quarter "made no impression", "The market had no ear for such news" (1930b, pp. 9–10). For Fisher this meant, "the panic [of the 24th October] was 'technical' in its character and highly artificial. This may be understood from the fact that industrial shares had achieved their highest earnings of their history" (1930b, p. 15). Fisher (1930b, pp. 68–69) noted Hoover's Committee on Recent Economic Changes had found the average increase in earnings of 600 corporations for the third quarter of 1929 was 14 percent greater than the same quarter in 1928. For all of 1929, Fisher claimed, "*Profits Rise Faster Than Stocks*" (1930b, p. 69). The market ignored this "good news" because, in his view, it was "deafened by the stentorian voices of banks calling up brokers and individuals to repay their loans" (Fisher 1930b, p. 10), but there are better grounds for concluding American investors simply stopped believing in reported earnings, and simultaneously stopped believing in Fisher.

After Fisher's *The Stock Market Crash and After* came out in February 1930 "the stock market … resumed its downward plunge not to recover for years" (see Figure 4.2) "taking Fisher with it" (Allen 1993, pp. 214–215). Galbraith (1961, p. 95) ridiculed Fisher's "immortal estimate: 'Stock prices have reached what looks like a permanently high plateau'. Irving Fisher was the most original of American economists.

Happily there are better things — his contribution to index numbers, technical economic theory, and monetary theory — for which he is remembered". By May 1930, Fisher was in deep financial difficulties because of the rapidly shrinking value of his stock speculations and his high borrowings. His personal bubble had burst. The powerful shunned him, the knowledgeable criticised him, and the public laughed at him. He now received no replies from Hoover to his letters (of May and July 1930), whereas they had previously corresponded (Allen 1993, p. 220). In his book and elsewhere Fisher "tried hard to explain why he had been wrong. Early in November 1929 he suggested that the whole thing had been irrational and hence beyond his prediction" (Galbraith 1961, p. 165). On the 9 November 1929 the editor of *The Commercial and Financial Chronicle* "observed with succinct brutality: 'The learned professor is wrong as he usually is when he talks about the stock market'" (Galbraith 1961, p. 165). His book "attracted little attention" (Galbraith 1961, p. 165). Fisher corresponded with Hoover in 1931 about his ideas for ending the depression, and even visited him (Allen 1993, p. 237), but Hoover did not listen. Fisher had supported Hoover's election partly because of his support of prohibition, but also because "Hoover lined up with big business, with which Fisher also identified as his wealth grew and his involvement with the stock market and corporate America developed" (Allen 1993, pp. 205–206). In spite of his impeccable intellectual and ideological credentials, however, as his son's biography observed, "his suggestions for remedying the defects of our creaking economy were given a cold reception" (Fisher 1956, p. ix). To the public, revelations about Fisher's speculations in "several younger enterprises ... make him appear rather gullible" (Fisher 1956, p. 263), particularly in a legal case that indicted a promoter for misrepresentation. When Fisher appeared to give testimony, which "was filling the front pages of the New York papers", his son "overheard two strangers discussing the lurid details at the table next to mine in a restaurant. One of them summed it all up thus: 'Gosh, he's supposed to know all the answers, and look how he got burned'" (Fisher 1956, p. 268).

Evidence directly linking a loss of faith in the integrity of accounting with plunging share prices is that "Within ten weeks of the October stock market crash, six members of Congress introduced bills to regulate corporate financial statements, margin loans, or short sales of securities" (Seligman 1982, p. 5). Moreover, whereas the NYSE had "peremptorily rejected" May's offer in 1926 to cooperate in accounting reform, in spring 1930 it approached the American Institute of Accountants (AIA) (Grady 1962, pp. 58–59). "Times had changed. The stock market had suffered a massive decline in the previous October", after which "Some had cited inferior accounting and reporting practices as a cause" (Zeff 1972, pp. 120–121). Over the coming months many more claimed, "Loose accounting practices had contributed to the debacle", that "*Laissez-faire* had prevailed in broad areas of accounting practice as in the rest of the economy" (Carey 1969a, p. 182). Following the crash, seeking to restore confidence, "The Exchange had accelerated its drive to improve financial disclosures of listed companies and since December 1929, had been trying to persuade one of its largest listed companies, Allied Chemical and Dye Corporation, to eliminate several deficiencies" (Zeff 1972, p. 121). In May 1930, the Exchange made clear it had "become concerned about the variety of accounting methods that were employed by different corporations to reflect similar transactions" (Zeff 1972, p. 121). In a speech to the National Association of Securities Commissioners on 20 May 1930, J.M.B. Hoxsey from the NYSE illustrated the problem by pointing to the "eight different methods known to us for accounting for the issuance of periodic stock dividends" (Zeff 1972, p. 121), which all knew was the tip of an iceberg.

Also consistent with investors' loss of faith in accounting is that after the crash the profession, through G.O. May, the following chapter shows, sought to deflect criticism by "educating" investors in the "limitations" of accounting, whereas NYSE leaders had resisted this during the later-1920s (Merino and Neimark 1982, fn. 33, p. 47). Hoxsey wrote to "May (February 3, 1928) … [such education] would erode confidence in annual reports, tearing away the moorings on which people have built their faith" (Merino and Neimark 1982, fn. 33, p. 47). Roosevelt promised during his 1932 election campaign to replace "lax state corporation laws" (Seligman 1982, p. 42), "to require … true earnings, true liabilities and true assets of the corporation itself" (Merino and Neimark 1982, fn. 30, p. 46). His government passed the Securities Acts of 1933 and 1934 that introduced a regulatory regime, putting financial accounting under potential government control. The SEC lost patience with the profession's refusal to accept "responsibility" in 1937. It eventually forced accountants to help restore investor confidence through setting and enforcing "generally accepted principles of accounting" (GAAP), but the Securities Acts and their accounting principles were limited, the following and subsequent chapters argue, by their framing within Fisher's theory of accounting, which left management in control.

Concluding Comments

Accepting Fisher's new-era theory made investors vulnerable, not only, like Fisher, to expectations management, in his case self-induced, but to accounting manipulations because theorists framed by his theory had provided management with justifications (Bryer 2021a, Chapter 9). Fisher even found room in defending his "plateau" vision for some ill-informed criticism of accounting. He was right, the investor in industrial securities "is largely forced to speculate on the accuracy of published industrial corporation statements", but his claim that "Our best companies particularly have often understated their earnings by charging excessive depreciation, and so on" (1930b, pp. 114–115), revealed his limited understanding. Fisher did not understand that many companies had conservatively smoothed their earnings reports, many to produce an upward trend.

Fisher illustrated the flexibility of his "conservatism" when in April 1931 he "had his accountant draw up a balance sheet … which showed that he had a net worth of $1.25 million. The asset side, however, showed their value at the acquisition costs of the asset, not their current value, which was in fact much lower than their costs. Still, he told Margie [his wife] with typical Fisher optimism that he believed they were conservative figures" (Allen 1993, p. 237). If Fisher had used a "reasonable current value for the assets", that is, L-C-M, "his net worth would have been close to zero, or possibly even negative" (Allen 1993, p. 237). However, as the manager of his household, Fisher in effect chose to waive L-C-M in reporting to his wife, which was an option in American accounting, justified by theorists framed by his theory of accounting (Bryer 2021a)!

Chapter 5

Accounting Theory and Reform in the Great Depression

The Great Depression provoked "sneers of cynicism" (Galambos and Pratt 1988, p. 100) and "turbulent" protests in which communists, socialists and other "anticapitalist" radicals "often provided leadership" (Zieger 1994, p. 19). Demonstrations, anti-eviction actions, relief riots and street marches did not turn into a political movement, but "made it abundantly clear" to political leaders and capitalists "that working people would fight", and if leaders did nothing "could turn to corps of energetic, articulate radicals for support" (Zieger 1994, p. 19). In 1930, workers punished Republicans at the polls, and in 1932 punished Hoover, electing Democrats and Franklin D. Roosevelt as president. From 1933, a resurgence of organised labour, militancy and political activism, was deflected from "socialism" only around 1950, holding the line at "managerial rights" (Zieger 1994, pp. 15, 20, 108). Nobody — politicians, intellectuals, union leaders or workers — could overturn management's rights (Bryer 2016), including over accounts.

The depression's causes, depth and length puzzle historians. They agree, "to find the most telling causes of the Depression, we must look within the borders of the United States" (McElvaine 2009, p. 35), where industrial production fell much more than in Sweden, France and Britain, and its unemployment rate was higher than all industrialised nations (Bernstein 1987, fn. 3, p. 3). Within America, we find management's distinctive lack of accountability to stockholders and workers' tight accountability, inequality, overinvestment and underconsumption, which produced conditions for the depression and, the chapter argues, continued lack of management accountability prolonged it. America's unequal income distribution meant it was "heavily dependent upon confidence and the spending and investment of the well-to-do", which the crash "most effectively undercut" (McElvaine 2009, pp. 48–49), as did criticisms of management, the stock exchange and accounting. The influence of Fisher's theory on policymakers compounded the problems by limiting efforts to intervene in the crisis, imposing limits to reform by thwarting government control of accounting. Fisher's theory helped create the crisis and prolong it, but in G.O. May's hands, it saved capitalism, the managerial capitalism that emerged during the 1920s, leaving management's power virtually untouched.

The chapter first explains how Fisher's theory undermined government's responses to the depression, particularly any idea of controlling big business through accounting. Second, it examines Fisher's influence on accounting and auditing reform in the Securities Acts 1933 and 1934, which legitimated management's discretion and prevented government control of auditing. Third, it examines accountants' reluctant implementation of the Acts, leading an exasperated SEC in 1937 to demand they produce and enforce GAAP, shift towards British principles. From the late-1930s, however, following chapters show Fisher's theory undermined the development of GAAP, and after World War II, management's discretion threatened "people's capitalism" and the profession, which led to the FASB's conceptual framework that limited management's overt discretion, but gave it back covertly through "asset-liability" accounting.

Managing the Great Depression

To business leaders, neoclassical economists and politicians the 1920s boom was "ultimate proof of the political *economy* of Adam Smith" (McElvaine 2009, p. 29), so the Great Crash and Depression left them, and almost everyone else, dumbfounded. To Keynesians and most Marxists it was an underconsumption crisis caused by widening inequality in income and wealth. They agreed "there was a dangerous imbalance between the increasingly socialized forms of mass production/mass reproduction and the still private forms of ownership and control" (Dawley 1991, p. 342), requiring vigorous government action. It was clear to some then and historians since, that "Too much of the value of what was being produced (and, hence, of effective demand) was going into too few pockets" (McElvaine 2009, p. 31). Most business leaders, politicians and intellectuals, however, clung to *laissez-faire*, continued to worship "the god of the marketplace", which is why, although the "do-nothing approach came to be totally discredited", which "severely undermined [neo]classical economics" (McElvaine 2009, p. 30), this did not undermine its framing of accounting.

Managerial Liberalism

New-Era politicians "handed leadership over to the great corporations" because from the Revolution "liberty and property had been linked as nowhere else" (Dawley 1991, p. 342), which did not change. As the 1930s progressed the spectacle of "*rentiers* clipping dividend coupons and the unemployed rummaging through garbage cans" eventually forced a "reckoning with liberty", "pierced the armor of New Era boosterism, punctured America's self-image as the land of equal opportunity", but it is doubtful whether this "punched holes in the theory of *laissez-faire*" (Dawley 1991, p. 342). Very few called, like Theodore Dreiser in *Tragic America*, for "a fundamental change in our government", and he made clear, "Not [to] Communism or Socialism, necessarily, but something similar and suited to the American temperament and certainly not with the money lords directly or indirectly reaping the profits" (1932, pp. 182, 193). Most business leaders and politicians, including "increasing numbers of the elite", eventually realised, "if they were to preserve their power … the liberal state would have to be modified" (Dawley 1991, p. 342), but it was not abandoned. Roosevelt's expansion of the federal bureaucracy by increasing economic and business regulation, beginning a welfare state, recognising labour as a "great estate", certainly "amounted to a significant restructuring of the liberal state" (Dawley 1991, p. 343). Historians also credit Hoover with "saving capitalism by changing the liberal state" (Dawley 1991, p. 343), but what follows argues this accolade should go to May's interpretation of Fisher's theory. With it framing dispassionate thinkers, and even leading radicals, the liberal state flexibly withstood the blows and undermined the resurgence of "socialism", helped Roosevelt to save capitalism, but the price was ineffective public policy and institutionalising the ideological corruption of accounting.

Historians see Hoover as the "prime architect" of "managerial liberalism", "the idea of state assistance to capitalist planning", but also struggling to "preserve the spirit of independence", sticking to the "dogma of individual self-reliance", which limited his attempts to help farmers and ruled out direct relief to the poor (Dawley 1991, pp. 344–349). In responding to the depression his "biggest mistake was to place his main hope in corporate self-management", in "corporate paternalism", to "maintain the sound American tradition" (Dawley 1991, p. 349). His promise of "welfare capitalism" proved empty "as companies jettisoned their meagre unemployment pay, pensions, and health benefits" and cut pay despite promising Hoover they would not (Dawley 1991, pp. 349–350). The destitute grew, the unemployment lines lengthened, but initially there was protest, not revolt. Unions had not recovered from the "devastating defeats in 1919–1922", so workers "remained for a long time in the supine position" (Dawley 1991, p. 352). The American Federation of Labor's (AFL) membership fell from nearly 5 million in 1919 to under 3 million in 1933, leaving "radical unionists … [to keep] up a drumbeat of demands on the government to come to the aid of the jobless and destitute" (Zieger 1994, p. 23). AFL leaders began to break from "voluntarism" in 1931, George Barry of the Printing Pressmen declaring, "our capitalistic system requires radical reorganization", calling for unemployment compensation (Zieger 1994, p. 24). Farmers protested after prices plummeted in 1931, organised "farm strikes", and in 1932 the Farmers Union called for a debt repayments moratorium and an alliance with unions because "both were 'exploited by the capitalistic owners of the means of production and distribution'" (Dawley 1991, p. 353).

Hoover became unpopular for giving money to banks and food to pigs, but neither to the people. Many blamed him, the financial markets and big business for the depression (McElvaine 2009, p. 121). Roosevelt won the 1932 presidential election by a landslide, but like Hoover "ran as a fiscal conservative", and "If he had any philosophy, it was close to the managerialism of the New Era, but without the boosterism" (Dawley 1991, pp. 357–358). After the 1932 election the AFL's president, William Green, told a Congress committee that if it did nothing for working people the labour movement would call a "universal strike", and when challenged that this "threatened class war", Green admitted, "yes, … it would be that …. That is the only language that a lot of employers ever understand is the language of force" (Zieger 1994, p. 24). There was a "red scare" in the winter of 1932–1933, but still "no revolution on the horizon" (Dawley 1991, pp. 354–355). In January 1933, strikes broke out in key Detroit automobile plants, responding to wage cuts. Ruthless corporations, helpful public authorities, and an "antilabor press" eventually defeated the strikers, but their action left activists with a "sense of their own power" (Zieger 1994, pp. 24, 25). Experts had pronounced it dead and buried, but from such beginnings, the labour movement sprang into life. With grudging but critical help from Roosevelt, union membership soared from 1932, now embracing not just craft workers but hundreds of thousands of workers in mass-production industries, organised by the new and more radical Congress of Industrial Organizations (Zieger 1994, p. 26). To many the possibility of socialism or fascism seemed real. Throughout the 1930s unionists, journalists, government officials and academics, "puzzled over the mood of the working people. ... Would the broken promises of the golden twenties cause embittered workers to abandon the American system" (Zieger 1994, p. 27) and choose socialism, something politicians, businesses and America's best brains dedicated themselves to preventing.

The Brains Trust

In March 1932, Roosevelt created a "brains trust" to guide policy headed by Raymond Moley, professor of political economy at Columbia University, some favouring increased government-regulation of big business. Moley came from a populist-progressive background, was a William Jennings Bryan supporter, was against "the Interests" and "Wall Street", had read and reread Henry George's *Poverty and Progress*, did his PhD with historian Charles Beard, and had "flirted with socialism" (McElvaine 2009, p. 124). Moley wrote Roosevelt's "Forgotten Man" radio speech in April 1932 that "placed Roosevelt clearly among those who saw lack of demand — underconsumption — as the key, and some form of redistribution of income as the solution", which "struck some as radical talk" (McElvaine 2009, p. 125). Moley accepted large corporations as inevitable and was against "trust-busting", but for federal "controls to stimulate and stabilize economic activity" (Seligman 1982, p. 40). He advised Roosevelt there was "no room in this country for two reactionary parties", that the Democratic Party should align itself with the middle and lower classes, proposed Roosevelt's "New Deal", and had him promise "to protect the welfare of the people against selfish greed" (McElvaine 2009, pp. 127, 130, 133).

Economist Rexford Tugwell, a Roosevelt brains-truster also from Columbia, agreed with Moley, "we are a long way down the road to a system of monopolies", but argued, "we should allow it to evolve and should manage it publicly rather than go back to a state where no social management existed" (Seligman 1982, p. 40). Tugwell, "the most radical of Roosevelt's academic advisers", "a maverick" who in 1927 "had seen the future" in Russia (McElvaine 2009, p. 126), argued, in effect, the popular Marxist view that "the depression had been caused, in part, by the misallocation of capital. Overexpansion of plant facilities had raised prices, but there was no corresponding increase in consumer purchasing power", and "the need for a 'system of planning' [w]as all but self-evident" (Seligman 1982, pp. 40–41). Tugwell agreed with J.A. Hobson, influenced by Marx, who argued, "underconsumption is a basic flaw of capitalism" (McElvaine 2009, p. 126). Tugwell called for a system that "allocated to specific industries capital sufficient to produce an amount of goods which would be taken by consumers at the price possible with capacity production", so "the surplus capital could then be assigned to other industries" (1933, p. 204), and proposed an "Economic Council" to provide "integrated industrial planning" (Seligman 1982, p. 41). The alternative to *laissez-faire*, Tugwell took-for-granted, was government supervision of capital, which "might be done through the Federal incorporation of businesses" (1933, p. 206). Having organised an industry into an "association", Tugwell's "controlling body ... would have powers of investigation and review of association policies", and "would need to require common accounting systems", by which he meant "Expansion and contraction, price policies, standards of wages, and working conditions would be worked out ... in budgetary fashion quarterly" (Tugwell 1933, pp. 212, 215). Tugwell's state, as Lenin had argued (Bryer 2021c), would control big business using budgets. Influenced by Tugwell, under political pressure in the nomination race, Roosevelt made a "move to the left", called for a "more equitable distribution of the national wealth" (McElvaine 2009, p. 127).

Adolf Berle, Columbia University Law School professor "and the brains truster with the greatest technical familiarity with corporate finance, urged Roosevelt in May 1932 to establish a federal board that would 'exact full information about securities sold'" (Seligman 1982, p. 41). He argued for a federal incorporation act "for the purpose of regulating corporations through a Federal Trade Commission with sharpened teeth" (McElvaine 2009, pp. 127–128). Although the "most moderate", Berle was committed to the "Social Gospel" of Matthew 6:10: "Thy will be done on earth as it is in heaven". However, although his analysis was radical, his proposals were not because, through May, Fisher's theory blunted them. "Roosevelt disagreed" with Berle and Tugwell's planning approach because he had "the instincts of a progressive politician", but consistent with May and Berle in practice, saw the problem as Louis Brandeis had as one of "publicity" (Seligman 1982, p. 41). He made clear in a speech in 1932, "I plead not for class control, but for a true concert of interests" (McElvaine 2009, p. 125). Roosevelt called for "common participation ... planned on the basis of a shared common life", and only "committed himself to the long-held populist and progressive goal of superseding lax state corporation laws with more stringent federal standards" (McElvaine 2009, p. 125; Seligman 1982, p. 42), but Fisher's theory blunted even this moderate aim.

Roosevelt's New Deal

Roosevelt's victory, the biggest since Lincoln's in 1864, was not an overt shift to the left: communists and socialists polled no more votes than Eugene Debs did in 1912 although the electorate was much bigger, but Roosevelt's radicalism provided an alternative, which many socialists, etc., voted for (McElvaine 2009, p. 133). Many, including some Wall Street conservatives, hailed the "Roosevelt revolution" as the "answer to proletarian revolution" (Dawley 1991, p. 359), a threat business, union and farmers' leaders, politicians and intellectuals had feared or predicted since the end of 1931 as protests and violence escalated through 1932 (McElvaine 2009, pp. 90–94, 135). In his first 100 days, Roosevelt's administration "gave the banking system the kiss of life, put industry on the road to recovery, doled out jobs and relief, stabilized agriculture, and, most important, restored confidence in government" (Dawley 1991, p. 359). The 1933 National Industrial Recovery Act, Section 7(a), "declared that workers had the right to bargain collectively with their employers through representatives of their own choosing" that activists quickly used to form unions under the slogan "The President wants you to join a union" (Zieger 1994, p. 29). Adopting New-Era managerialist ideas, Roosevelt promoted "state-assisted capitalist planning", not the radicals' planned economy, "limited state regulation in the tradition of progressivism", aimed at "fair competition" (Dawley 1991, pp. 361–364).

Roosevelt accepted Louis Brandeis' view in *Other Peoples' Money* that "the moral delicts of the bankers would be curbed when fully exposed to public scrutiny", that "Sunlight is ... the best of disinfectants" (Seligman 1982, pp. 41–42). However, this meant *laissez-faire* was not completely "a thing of the past", that there was no "transforming

[of] national political sentiment from a *laissez-faire* ideology … to a regulatory-reform ideology" (cf. Dawley 1991, p. 368; Seligman 1982, p. 2). Opposition to the New Deal "was the touchstone around which extreme *laissez-faire* liberalism transformed itself into modern ultraconservatism", but even radicals did not want socialised ownership and control, but "planning for the masses rather than planning for the capitalists", and even leading liberal academics like John Dewey pushed only "mild socialist ideas" (Dawley 1991, p. 369). "Some businessmen called the President 'a traitor to his class', and his 'New Deal' was attacked as socialism" (Carey 1969a, pp. 181–182), but New Dealers were unified around the "mission to save liberal capitalism" and never contemplated equalising wealth (Dawley 1991, p. 370). Unsurprisingly, as their policies had little impact, "labor peace ended with a bang in 1934. From one end of the country to another, industrial workers recovered a long-lost militancy", clocking-up 1,800 work stoppages involving 1.5 million strikers, some generating "a lethal bitterness rarely matched in American history" (Dawley 1991, p. 372; Zieger 1994, p. 33). Working class activists discovered the AFL provided "only dilatory and unresponsive leadership", and the National Recovery Administration (NRA) did not protect their right to collective bargaining, was anti-union, and could do nothing to prevent employers who "waged no-holds-barred warfare against the new locals, firing activists, imposing company-controlled organizations, and refusing to bargain" (Zieger 1994, pp. 34–35, 38). Senator Robert Wagner, seeing strong unions as a way of increasing wages to help recovery, introduced a Bill in 1935 to strengthen Section 7(a) by creating an independent agency with enforcement powers. When the Supreme Court declared the NRA unconstitutional, because the "events of 1934 had clearly revealed that the potential for labor unrest and even for violent confrontation lay close to the surface", as part of his "Second New Deal" from 1935, Roosevelt passed the Labor Relations Act (Zieger 1994, p. 39). Employers continued to fight unions, but deaths and serious injuries decreased from 1937 (Zieger 1994, p. 40).

Roosevelt also passed the Social Security Act providing limited government assistance to the poor and needy, but "Most businessmen … attacked public welfare as if it flew the red flag of socialism", and continued to extol individual "thrift" (Dawley 1991, p. 379). Even mild social reforms "looked like 'creeping socialism'", which shows "they still saw the world in terms of nineteenth century liberalism" (Dawley 1991, p. 380). The New Deal responded to "popular demands for social justice", but "was careful not to infringe too much upon the privileges of wealth" (Dawley 1991, p. 385), and the key question is why, when it achieved little, this worldview also restrained radical intellectuals and worker activists. Was it the inevitable outcome of the "balance of forces" — lack of a civil service, suspicion of big government, *laissez-faire* bias in the courts, antistatism in big business (Dawley 1991, pp. 385–386) — or were these "forces" themselves the consequence of individualism and *laissez-faire*? Why was it that "Not all the checks on the New Deal came from its enemies. Among the most important came from within" (Dawley 1991, p. 394)? An important reason, what follows argues, was framing by Fisher's theory, embedded in the business world and accounting practice, in the universities, and even radical and informed opinion, beyond the reach of worker activists, which meant the means of controlling big business capitalism eluded reformers, so that "public ownership" and "control" became a *non-sequitur*. Because they could see no way short of popular enlightenment or totalitarianism, they "barely trenched upon the dominance of corporate capital" (Dawley 1991, p. 408). Acceptance of May's view that accounts were a matter of "opinion", and Paton's that control meant "the power to direct" so only the state, or effective popular demand with judicial backing, could "control" corporations, following sections argue, explain the limited reform proposed by Berle and Means (1932) and achieved by the 1933 and 1934 Securities Acts.

Controlling Big Business

By 1900, references to separating ownership and control "were the common currency of European economists and businessmen" (Hannah 2007, p. 422). In America, however, debate began with Ripley's *Stop, Look, Listen!* in 1926, and intensified only after Berle and Means' *The Modern Corporation and Private Property* appeared in 1932, which starkly concluded, big businesses' owners typically did not "control" them, that "security holders and in particular the stockholders, performs the function of risk-takers" (1932, pp. 300–301), not controllers. Accounting theorists had discussed the separation of ownership from control (Bryer 2021a), and this limited Berle and Means' thinking, who never saw stockholders as a collective, Marx's total social capital. They saw a world of individuals or groups of shareholders and never considered whether shareholders are passive as individuals, but active collectively, the living "thing" that uses accounts to control management and workers. Nor crucially, therefore, did they conceive of replacing the capital market with society, replacing capitalist control with democratic social control of big business, even though this, we will see, was Berle's goal.

Berle and Means' book was the first systematic study of the "divorce of ownership from control" in America, that is, from Marx's perspective, of America's transition to advanced capitalism, to widely dispersed ownership, professional managers and free wageworkers, during the 1920s. When May put down his administrative duties at Price Waterhouse in 1926 to deal with the threat posed by the accounting issues raised by Ripley, he joined the Social Science Research Council of America, suggested they form a Committee on Corporate Relations, and this funded Berle's research that began in 1927 (Grady 1962, pp. 47–48). May chaired this committee and "helped to define the objectives of the research designed to assess the implications for America of the increased public ownership of investment securities" (Miranti 1990, p. 140). Although, as Miranti pointed out, "the committee's membership originally included many who favored a more active role for government in regulating the financial markets", such as Ripley, initially a member, "Those who seemed not to favor broadening government's role became a majority by 1928" (1990, p. 141). Miranti noted, "All were friends or professional associates of Chairman May. They were united … in the belief that private institutions were appropriate for solving society's most serious problems" (1990, p. 141), but Berle was not necessarily one of them — May (1943, p. 71) later described Berle as "neither an accountant nor a rugged individualist". According to Carey (1979, p. 30), "Among Mr. May's acquaintances was the brilliant young Columbia University law professor, A.A. Berle" who, we will see, did not propose government regulation of the financial markets, business or accounting, because May convinced him of the "limitations" of accounting. Carey surmised, "Somehow Mr. May must have learned that the book was being written, and found opportunity to talk with Berle before it was published" (1979, p. 30), which framed his thinking. Carey observed, "While Berle was highly critical of current accounting practices, the criticism was somewhat tempered by … modifications of an otherwise devastating indictment [that] were clear evidence of George O. May's diplomatic influence" (Carey 1979, pp. 30–31), colouring Berle's understanding of accounting's "limitations". Berle thanked May for his "wide experience" and "shrewd comments" (Berle and Means 1932, pp. li, liv). Therefore, while Berle "stressed the need for more objective information", and proposed "requiring large public companies to file audited financial statements and for mandating some accounting principles", we will see, he did not advocate government control, but adopted May's "vision of market governance" through "increased regulatory powers for the NYSE" (Miranti 1990, pp. 141–142). May's influence was important because Berle later rightly claimed his and Mean's "book, describing property in the stock markets, became the foundation for the Federal legislation begun in 1933" (Berle and Means 1968, p. 252), even though he was dissatisfied with the outcome. Carey called it "almost a blueprint for the Securities Acts" (1979, p. 31). Berle was dissatisfied because although his analysis was radical, implicitly "socialist", May's "shrewd comments", the profession's view that "uniform" accounting was impossible, blunted his proposals for controlling big business, prevented him formulating a convincing programme for government or social control.

Berle, a lawyer, and Means, an economist, readily adopted Fisher's entity concept and thought of "control" as action control over the corporation's use-values (including labour), control over its administration, production and distribution. Theorists like Paton (1922) had defined "control" as the "power to direct", and so did Berle and Means. Berle (1926, p. 257) accepted Ripley's view that "control of great corporations was rapidly passing from the hands of the stockholders into the hands of small groups". By "control" Berle meant, "a corporation so far as control is concerned retains some features of an overgrown partnership; and it has been considered that every participant in the enterprise was entitled to his share in the management" (1926, p. 259), in supervision. Hence, as he saw it, America faced the dilemma "of securing … the benefits of continuous, compact, and able direction, and of avoiding … the hazard of unchecked power" (Berle 1926, p. 260). Berle and Means emphasised the "fundamental shift" was the change of "physical control", "Physical control over the instruments of production has been surrendered in ever growing degree to centralised groups who manage property in bulk, supposedly, but by no means necessarily, for the benefit of the security holders. Power over industrial property has been cut off from the beneficial ownership of this property" (Berle and Means 1932, p. 8). "Control" meant "actual control", legal and effective action control. They deduced, "Five major types can be distinguished, though no sharp dividing line separates type from type. These include (1) control through almost complete ownership, (2) majority control, (3) control through a legal device without majority ownership, (4) minority control, and (5) management control" (Berle and

Means 1932, p. 67). As they said, "Of these, the first three are forms of control resting on a legal base and revolve about the right to vote a majority of the voting stock. The last two, minority and management control are extra legal, resting on a factual rather than a legal base" (Berle and Means 1932, p. 67). Bonbright and Means complained, "Often … 'control' is used in the restricted sense of 'legal control', by which is meant the *legal right* to elect at least a majority of the directors, a right resulting usually from the ownership of a majority of the voting stock, or else from the device of the voting trust" (1932, pp. 8–9). This is the Marxian definition (Bryer 2021a, p. 370; 2021b; see also Chapter 9). Adopting it would be "unfortunate" since it would "exclude all companies which possess a 'working control' over other companies by virtue of a minority stock ownership", "place the definition of a holding company on a purely legalistic basis rather than on a factual economic basis" (Bonbright and Means 1932, p. 9).

According to Bonbright and Means control meant, "also those companies which exercise a *material influence* over other companies" (1932, p. 9), accounting theorists' notion of "effective control", effective action control, the ability to supervise in practice, based on Fisher's entity concept (Bryer 2021b). However, "control as something apart from ownership on one hand and from management on the other is a new concept ill-defined in practice … [that] may be held to a greater or less extent by a wide variety of individuals" (Berle and Means 1932, p. 111). They therefore found the "dividing line between control by a minority interest and control by management is not clear, and many companies had to be classified as doubtful" (Berle and Means 1932, p. 85). From their perspective, "Corporate control thus appears in many forms — relatively defined and relatively stable legal positions, loosely defined and somewhat more precarious factual situations", for example, as Paton (1922) had argued, where the "pressure from creditors … may go to the point where a bondholder committee itself may be considered to have control" (Berle and Means 1932, pp. 83–84). They therefore concluded, as Fisher and theorists did, there was no clear distinction between debt and equity. The stockholder "becomes simply a supplier of capital on terms less definite that those customarily given or demanded by bondholders; and the thinking about his position must be qualified by the realization that he is, in a highly modified sense, not dissimilar in kind from the bondholder or lender of money" (Berle and Means 1932, p. 245). Their radical conclusion was that big business meant the "dissolution of the old atom of ownership into its component parts, control and beneficial ownership … [which] destroys the very foundation on which the economic order of the last three centuries has rested" (Berle and Means 1932, p. 8). That is, Adam Smith's "self-interest held in check only by competition and the conditions of supply and demand" (Berle and Means 1932, p. 9). The perplexing problem posed by big business was that managers, who control wealth and "are in a position to secure industrial efficiency and produce profits, are no longer, as owners, entitled to the bulk of those profits", whereas the stockholders who benefit have "surrendered … control" (Berle and Means 1932, p. 9). Big business therefore "is the negation of Adam Smith's world in which many individuals controlled their own physical property and labor" (Berle 1933, p. 37).

Berle and Means did not shrink from the radical conclusion that the separation of ownership and control "posed a significant threat to the legitimacy of private property rights" (Previts and Merino 1998, p. 183). They argued, as Marx (1998, p. 437) had, that when capitalists employed managers profit was no longer justified by entrepreneurial control, the increase in social welfare derived from profit's motivating effect on organising production in the most efficient way to satisfy consumer needs, yet passive shareholders get them (Berle and Means 1932, pp. 9, 300–301). After the passage of the 1933 Securities Act Berle reflected on the central issue, "High Finance: Master or Servant?", asking, "What … is the ethical right of any individual or group of individuals to take this increase [the surplus] as their own" (1933, p. 38). He recognised, "We could elect to give it to managers and workers", or his "own bias … in favour of dividing it up between the community as a whole and the plant staff", but did not advocate this because it "turns on one's social philosophy and has no place in a dispassionate review of the forces at work" (Berle 1933, pp. 38–39).

Accounting and Control

In their "dispassionate review", Berle and Means (1932) saw no possibility of giving individual stockholders control through accounting. Examining the "position of a share of stock under the modern corporate structure as modified by common law doctrines, with primary reference to its participation rights in the assets" (Berle and Means 1932, p. 141) raised the valuation problem. Equity demanded individual stockholders get their "pro-rata" share of a corporation's assets, but this depended on putting a "value" on them, which was a "vague concept": "Only when the term assets is used to refer to a fund of value, — perhaps a sum of values, measured in a chosen unit (money), does pro-rata share come to have meaning. The introduction of value, however, brings with it a multitude of meanings which attach to concept and the fund of value referred to as 'assets' may, therefore refer to quite different things" (Berle and Means 1932, fn. 1, p. 141). "Most commonly, the value fund referred to is 'book value', i.e., the assets as arrived at by the accountant" (Berle and Means 1932, fn. 1, p. 141). However, "it usually appears that the value fund may bear little relation to the book value, being rather the value fund which the whole enterprise represents — still involving a vague concept, but one which frequently leads to results different from book value" (Berle and Means 1932, fn. 1, p. 141). They therefore never entertained the thought that stockholders could control corporations using accounts, which they saw primarily as a means of valuing shares.

Columbia Law School gave an "experimental" course in accounting from 1929 (Berle and Fisher 1932, pp. 573–574).[1] Whether derived from May or accounting colleagues, Berle accepted that share "appraisals ... reflect a measure of the ability of the business to make earnings or profits ... [which] are necessarily based on the ... published accounts varied up or down by more fleeting information" (Berle and Fisher 1932, p. 577). As May, we will see, had undoubtedly taught Berle, for valuation "nothing is a 'fact'; even a balance sheet or income statement is a reflection of the state of mind of the persons issuing it" (Berle and Means 1932, p. 283). There should therefore be "a series of running appraisals or values made up to the best appraisal theory in respect of each piece or type of property", but "Like any other ideal, this is not wholly attainable" (Berle and Fisher 1932, p. 577) partly because following May, we will see, accounts had conflicting uses. Berle and Means thought "an effort suitably to define assets would itself involve a comprehensive study" (1932, fn. 1, p. 141), but perhaps advised by May, they did not undertake it. It is therefore questionable whether they "argued that the separation of ownership from control had rendered traditional accounting profit measurement useless as a means of allocating economic resources" (Previts and Merino 1998, p. 281), because it is doubtful that they understood "traditional accounting". Berle and Means were content to use "the term assets ... in the somewhat ambiguous

[1] Several faculty members were interested, including Frederick S. Fisher Jr. unrelated to Irving Fisher.

sense of a fund of value" (1932, fn. 1, p. 141), and turned instead to the erosion of the individual's legal right of participation, and whether the law could reverse it.

Whereas the "corporate contract was originally regarded as establishing a set of more or less fixed participations", "complete freedom of contract in corporate charters" created "a series of mechanisms which ... have thrown into the hands of the board of directors ... extremely wide powers in varying the original rigid *pro rata* participation in assets and earnings" (Berle and Means 1932, p. 142). Issuing shares for director "appraised" property, the elimination of "pre-emptive rights", introducing "par value" shares, "non-par value" shares, "parasitic" shares, mergers, treasury shares, stock purchase warrants, etc., all gave directors the power to change an individual shareholder's participation in the assets and earnings (Berle and Means 1932, pp. 143–182). Because the law could not give individual shareholders control of pro rata value, like Fisher and accounting theorists they accepted the dispersion of stock ownership in large corporations meant, "No longer are the individuals in control of most of these companies, the dominant owners. Rather, there are no dominant owners, and the control is maintained in large measure apart from ownership" (Berle and Means 1932, pp. 110–111). It was often unclear who actually "controlled", but it was clear legally that "the shareholder in the modern corporation has surrendered a set of definite rights for a set of indefinite expectations", that "control now appears as a separate, separable factor" (Berle and Means 1932, pp. 111, 244). Having in most cases given it up, "The stockholder is therefore left as a matter of law with little more than the loose expectation that a group of men, under a nominal duty to run the enterprise for his benefit and that of others like him, will actually observe this obligation" (Berle and Means 1932, p. 244). Now "the individual interest of the shareholder is subservient to the will of a controlling group of managers .... The legal doctrine that the judgment of the directors must prevail as to the best interests of the enterprise, is in fact tantamount to saying that ... the interests of the individual may be sacrificed to the economic exigencies of the enterprise as a whole" (Berle and Means 1932, p. 244). Stockholders' subservience was comparable to the "communist system" (Berle and Means 1932, p. 245), from which they could see little means of escape, even by legal control of accounting. Far from giving stockholders control, because there were no "uniform rules" or "standards", Berle argued, accounting gave management an additional, powerful means for controlling them, so the law could offer no protection from management's "control of accounting". "Thus far, no case has arisen in which any court has had the temerity to overhaul a corporation's bookkeeping system and upset its accounting practice. Were accounting rules standardized and uniform, this, of course, could not happen; but they are not, and, lacking such standardization, the latitude of the corporate management is complete" (Berle 1927, p. 428).

It was "obvious that the development of the law of corporate finance makes almost mandatory the legal sanction of good accounting practice", but Berle had to accept "the failure of the law to recognise accounting standards is probably due to the lack of agreement among accountants" (Berle and Means 1932, pp. 271–272). He did not offer any hope of "standardized" or "uniform" accounts, probably because, we will see, May convinced him this was impossible, because he accepted, "Control over accounting systems — at least until the science of accountancy reaches a new level — must necessarily remain with the corporate management" (Berle 1927, p. 431). Instead, they "suggested", "Aggrieved investors might … seek redress from a firm's investment bankers, directors, or management under a common-law suit for either fraud or violation of the disclosure requirements of particular states' blue sky laws regulating the sale of securities" (Miranti 1990, p. 142). Because "accountants have failed to work out a series of standard rules", directors had a "powerful weapon" they could use against stockholders, "have a large measure of control over the company's income account" meaning "directors and their accountants may frame their figures, within limits, much as they choose" (Berle and Means 1932, p. 182). They could "route the earnings by merely arranging that in certain years there shall be none, and in other years they shall be large. Among the simplest are the charging or failing to charge depreciation; charging to capital expenses which properly should be charged against income account; including non-recurrent profits as income though their real place is in surplus; and the creation of hidden reserves" (Berle and Means 1932, p. 182). If management had control through subsidiary companies, "The possibility of inter-company transactions …; the routing of profitable business to one subsidiary in preference to another; the concealment of losses or the creation of non-existent deficits, make possible an almost unlimited variation in the resulting income account. How far this power has been used, it is simply impossible to say" because no information was published (Berle and Means 1932, p. 183). They illustrated "the possibility of accounting manipulation for the purpose of showing an abnormal profit", giving seven examples of "the methods which can be used" (Berle and Means 1932, p. 272). These were manipulating inventory and depreciation, issuing bonds with stock or stock warrants, overvaluing assets, charging direct to surplus items that should go to the profit and loss account, eliminating "non-recurring" items, and pushing sales into the current period (Berle and Means 1932, pp. 272–273). Berle and Means accepted, as we will see May did, that accountants had failed to work out a series of standard rules because "may be ... in the nature of things strict rules are out of the question" (1932, p. 182). Thus they thought the best stockholders could expect was "a good faith attempt to approximate the facts", and that "the stock should remain freely marketable at a fair price" (Berle and Means 1932, pp. 114, 182).

Berle and Means claimed "some reason to believe that ... standard[s] of decent accounting ... will ultimately find their place in the legal system" (1932, p. 274). The basis for this optimism was Berle and Fisher's (1932, p. 600) conclusion from a "joint adventure" studying legal cases, "that it does appear that in certain great areas there has been a definite *rapprochement* between the law and accounting". However, as Parrish (1970, p. 201) says, Berle and Fisher (1932) actually revealed "Conflicting state incorporation laws and diverse court decisions [that] compounded the profession's own confusion. Accounting principles, in short, were largely determined by what management desired, state legislators permitted, and courts tolerated". Berle later recommended a "board of accounting appeals", but accepted this was "too visionary" as he then accepted the courts had produced "unsystematic and indefinite ... rules of sound accounting", continued to think that "in many cases there is a real problem whether the record deals with so-called 'facts' at all" (1938, pp. 368–369, 375–376). As, like theorists, he saw accounting as valuation, the key difficulty was "when dealing with value or worth ... it is a matter of opinion ... whenever accounting ceases to be a mere record of an historical transaction solely in cash" (Berle 1938, p. 371). "Conservative" accounting was not the solution because this favoured buyers over sellers (Berle 1938, p. 371). Berle found himself "wishing" for "accounting theory" because "an accountant has both the power and the duty to look behind the strict legal line in drawing his conclusions", beyond contracts, but he anticipated only "slow, steady, self-critical" progress (1938, pp. 371, 377). He accepted lawyers "need the accountant quite as much for our own enlightenment and evolution as for his own peculiar contribution" (Berle 1938, p. 378). Shareholders needed them to pursue a legal remedy, but without a theory accountants' practices were often beyond the law and, we will see, in 1938 there was little prospect of one. Therefore, although he claimed the 1933 Securities Act had "subtended very nearly the whole arc of accounting" within legal rules, and accountants had become "part of the mechanism of government control" (Berle 1938, p. 9), he knew the victory was hollow. It left investors with uncertain remedies from the law of "fiduciary duty", and "ethics" enforced by public opinion.

Social Control of Business

Free market capitalism had gone. In its place, Berle and Means saw the modern corporation as a "major social institution", a "revolution" in "social organization" (1932, pp. 308–309). However, they circumscribed their recognition of the "social" within Fisher's entity theory. To control corporations required "a new concept of business enterprise" based on accepting the view that "the claims to ownership are subdivided in such a fashion, and are so mobile, that the enterprise assumes an independent life, as if it belonged to no one" (Berle and Means 1932, p. 309), Fisher and accounting theorists' economic entity view. As control concentrated in large corporations, "Observable throughout the world … is this insistence that power in economic organization shall be subjected to the … tests of public benefit" (Berle and Means 1932, p. 310). This test appeared as the demand for "communism", "socialism", or "responsible" capitalism, which to them, given their definition of control, were differences only of "degree", differences in the degree of supervision of property (Berle and Means 1932, p. 310).

By taking control, management had, according to Berle and Means, "placed the community in a position to demand that the modern corporation serve not alone the owners or the control, but all society" (1932, p. 312), but as management was in "control", and often operated corporations in their own interests, how was this demand operationalised? Leaving management without social obligations "leads to drastic conclusions", the "danger of a corporate oligarchy, coupled with the probability of an era of corporate plundering", and imposing a legal duty of trusteeship to operate in the interests of stockholders led to "irresponsible" owners and a "diminution of enterprise" (Berle and Means 1932, p. 311). This left a "third possibility", Fisher and accounting theorists' fantasy world that stockholders, having "surrendered control and responsibility over the active property, have surrendered the right that the corporation should be operated in their sole interest" (Berle and Means 1932, p. 312). To stave off oligarchy or socialism Berle and Means saw it as "conceivable, — indeed, it seems almost essential if the corporate system is to survive, — that the 'control' of the great corporations should develop into a purely neutral technocracy" (1932, pp. 312–313). Its role should be "balancing a variety of claims by various groups in the community and assigning to each a portion of the income stream on the basis of public policy rather than private cupidity" (Berle and Means 1932, pp. 312–313). They claimed this was "a wholly new concept of corporate activity", where "neither the claims of ownership nor those of control can stand against the paramount interest of the community" (Berle and Means 1932, p. 312), but it was the same ideological fantasy offered by Fisher's entity theory. This "assumption never received widespread acceptance" (Previts and Merino 1998, p. 281), particularly by the wealthy, but it underwrote Berle and Means idealistic assertion that "It remains only for the claims of the community to be put forward with clarity and force", for a "convincing system of community obligations [to be] worked out ... [that are] generally accepted" 1932, p. 312). The notion that when Americans demanded "corporate leaders ... set forth a program comprising fair wages, security to employees, reasonable service to their public, and stabilization of business, all of which would divert a portion of the profits from the owners of passive property, ... the[ir] interests ... would have to give way" (Berle and Means 1932, p. 312)! Stuck within Fisher's theory, the idea that society could impose its demands, not through popular support and state bureaucratic or legal supervision, but democratic planning and accounting control, never occurred to Berle and Means. Thanks to Fisher's theory, therefore, the 1933 and 1934 Securities Acts did not require British/Marxian stewardship.

The Securities Acts

Securities regulation, Parrish argued, "was only a skirmish on ... [a] larger battlefield", the "seven year struggle over how best to preserve capitalism" (1970, p. 2), Seligman claimed the Acts would only "Ultimately ... transform American capitalism" (1982, p. 13), whereas Merino and Neimark argue they "did not represent a fundamental change in public policy" (1982, p. 49). Passage and implementation of the Securities Acts, what follows argues, was not a skirmish, but a major battle in the war to preserve capitalism. They did not transform American capitalism, were not "fundamental changes in public policy but … part of an ongoing attempt to maintain an ideological, social, and economic *status quo*" (Merino and Neimark 1982, pp. 33, 49). However, rather than explain them as an "attempt" or "design" to maintain the *status quo*, although this was the elite's aim, despite the efforts of the best brains they did not "fundamentally" change public policy because they were framed by Fisher's theory. The wealthy had suffered from the crash so it is implausible that they and their agents "designed" the Acts as an ideological smokescreen. As May said, "heavy losses in corporate securities were sustained by persons in all walks of life" (1937, p. 341), including brokers and dealers in securities as "transactions became scarce" with the loss of "buyers' confidence" (McCraw 1984, p. 168), who had as much incentive as any to restore it. Corporate issues of securities fell from $8 billion in 1929 to $0.325 billion in 1932 and $0.161 billion in 1933, and the volume of sales from 1,125 billion to 425 billion (McCraw 1984, p. 169). The Securities Acts did "influence … the structure of American capitalism for years to come" by leaving business control largely intact, and yet it was a "conservative revolution that nonetheless horrified a great many conservatives" (Parrish 1970, p. 4), because although it threatened government control, the government, its advisers, the profession, NYSE and academics remained trapped within Fisher's theory, which blunted reform. They ditched the view that balance sheets should report economic value, but stayed within Fisher's theory by focusing on "income" and disclosure for economic valuation, as the only way of asserting stockholders' "control". Led by May, we will see, government advisors, etc., saw businesses as the circuit M-M′. The income reported for any particular period was, therefore, May argued, a matter of "opinion", and the methods used "conventions", generally accepted ways of allocating cash flows to periods. Managers make accounting more "useful" to stockholders by choosing conventions that, as Canning (1929) put it, have "predicting value", an argument May successfully used to defend the profession from government control.

May's interpretation did not address, and potentially undermined, the reconstruction of total social capital, American investors' ability to hold management accountable — their inchoate demand for "stewardship". Only at the end of the 1930s, we will see, did the profession accept the SEC's demand for GAAP, epitomised in Paton and Littleton's (1940) monograph. Seligman rightly downplays accounting reform's importance in his "transformation of capitalism", that partly "because of the vagueness of the relevant enabling statutes", and "political considerations", "accounting standard setting and corporate governance consistently have been relegated to the bottom of the SEC's list of priorities" (1982, p. xi). Previts and Merino's suggestion that "negative attitudes about investors' abilities rendered implementation of the legislation less important", that "Regulators had little reason to engage in divisive struggles with accountants and managers about reporting methods if they did not believe that small investors could or would employ financial reports" (1998, p. 274), is less convincing. It assumes the aim was protecting small investors, whereas the wealthy demanded it. The SEC accepted resistance from business and accountants to "uniformity" and opted for disclosure, but only in its early years. From 1937, we will see, it did engage in "divisive struggles", which it won.

The Securities Acts did not produce a fundamental change in public policy or capitalism, but their motivation, if not result, did represent "a major change in attitude toward the (potential) capabilities of investors and the role of corporate disclosure"; their "philosophy of disclosure ... represented a marked departure from pre-regulatory attitudes" (Merino and Neimark 1982, pp. 46–47). Whereas "potential competition" and "disinfecting" bad behaviour had previously justified disclosure, after the Securities Acts the justification was "information" (Merino and Neimark 1982, p. 47). The Acts' aim, as Twentieth Century Fund put it, was "a broad improvement in the quality of investment practice. Armed with the facts, less resort will be had to tips and hearsay. In time, the use of worthwhile information will spread from leading traders and investors through investment services, banks and other financial institutions to all security holders to raise the general level of investors' intelligence" (1935, p. 708). The Acts assumed "investors could be trained to use financial disclosure", that "widespread ownership" was feasible because "it would no longer be necessary to accept a 'two-tiered' market structure" when "all had access to information", which their framers assumed should reduce speculation and insider manipulation (Merino and Neimark 1982, p. 47). Fisher (1930b) shared their view when he argued the speculation stemmed from an ill-informed, "irrational", "lunatic fringe". Thus, rather than impose legal or bureaucratic controls, "In empowering the SEC to regulate ... disclosure, public policy focused its attention on the corporate governance model and what came to be called 'Shareholder Democracy'. ... In this model (1) shareholders as owners ... have ... the absolute right to enjoy the wealth generated by their property, and (2) boards of directors are elected by the shareholders to manage the corporation ... to their benefit, ... [who can] retain, monitor, or replace management" (Merino and Neimark 1982, fn. 37, p. 49). The Acts' framers assumed "if investors could be educated to understand and effectively use financial data, then the stockholder/owner could be presumed to effectively 'control' corporate resources" (Merino and Neimark 1982, p. 47). Berle and Means (1932) and others pointed out this was "not descriptively valid" (Merino and Neimark 1982, fn. 37, p. 49), but it was consistent with Fisher's theory, as Canning (1929) argued, because earnings had "predicting value" so knowledgeable investors could use them with other data to derive a "reliable capital value" to supervise the "proprietor" corporation (Bryer 2021a, pp. 340–342). In this sense, writers who "suggest that passage of securities legislation reflected a change in attitude toward investors" (Previts and Merino 1998, fn. 102, p. 458) are correct. Few thought disclosure would directly benefit all investors, particularly "average" investors (Previts and Merino 1998, fn. 102, p. 458), and most continued to accept the necessity of a "two-tier" market led by the informed, but sought to protect the average investor by education, disclosure and outlawing insider dealing.

Reforming Accounting

Following the October 1929 crash, members of Congress introduced bills to regulate corporate financial statements and stock exchange dealings (Seligman 1982, p. 5), but the market's recovery of half the losses by February 1930 muted Democratic criticism of Republican policies, but they became vociferous from June 1930 as the market began its long slide. In the 1930 congressional elections, the Democrats won control of the House and were within one vote of controlling the Senate (Seligman 1982, p. 8). However, progressive Republicans now also "led the clamour for securities law reform" (Seligman 1982, p. 10).

In September 1930, anticipating legislation, following the NYSE's invitation, the Institute established a Special Committee on Cooperation with the Stock Exchanges of senior partners of five large firms, chaired by May (Grady 1962, p. 59), charged with proposing reforms. The NYSE now cooperated because it "had also become concerned about the variety of accounting methods that were employed by different corporations to reflect similar transactions" (Zeff 1972, p. 121). For the first time it threatened to delist a firm, Allied Chemical and Dye Corporation, if it did not provide "adequate financial information to stockholders" (Zeff 1972, fn. 26, p. 121). Hoxsey, secretary of the NYSE's Committee on Stock List, in May 1930 had complained of "eight different methods for accounting for stock dividends", and "In his celebrated talk before the Institute's annual meeting the following September", which concluded by inviting cooperation, he "announced the discovery of a ninth method" (Zeff 1972, p. 121). In 1931, Hoxsey asked what "degree of responsibility ... accountants would willingly take" for evaluating management's choice of accounting methods, for required disclosures in the profit and loss account, and for "curbing the use of reserves to artificially smooth income" (Previts and Merino 1998, p. 276). As Hoxsey made his motivation clear, "that if we act now ... we may retard unwarranted intrusions", he was probably surprised when "The institute's answer was that accountants could not take responsibility for any of the above" (Previts and Merino 1998, fn. 113, pp. 276, 459). Its reasons were consistent with Fisher's theory. The AIA refused to judge management's methods, refused to necessarily condemn the "deliberate understatement of assets or artificial levelling of income", arguing, "smoothing was not necessarily bad since 'measurement of profits as between years is necessarily in large measure conventional' and soundness of conventions must be based on 'broad considerations'" (Previts and Merino 1998, 278). In its view, "Stabilization of income (income smoothing) was from a broad perspective sound; it modified rather than accentuated the effects of changing economic conditions" (Previts and Merino 1998, p. 278). Disavowing history, "Fearful of those who viewed accounting income as a 'fact' and suggested that accounting could provide a 'true' income number that investors could multiply by 10 or 20 to determine the current value of a firm, practitioners pointed out the arbitrariness of accounting allocations" (Previts and Merino 1998, p. 278). Previts and Merino are sympathetic: "Given the subjective nature of accounting income determination, these disclaimers made a good deal of sense" (1998, p. 278), but this accepts the valuation objective's primacy.

The AIA refused to require disclosure of operating and non-operating income, extraordinary items, or creating and using reserves (Previts and Merino 1998, fn. 122, p. 460). It argued, "the primary responsibility for selection of principles and scope of disclosure must remain that of directors and officers of the corporation", adding that accountants lived in "an age of legal uncertainty" (Previts and Merino 1998, pp. 277, 276), so taking more responsibility would expose them to more legal liabilities.

Accountants were inconsistent when in the 1920s they "legitimately claimed they did not have the power to dictate to clients; but during the thirties they made few coordinated attempts to increase responsibility or power" (Previts and Merino 1998, p. 273). The profession "temporized" even as the NYSE and SEC "offered support to increase the authority of the profession", Previts and Merino argue, because they "were distracted by intraprofessional quarrels" (1998, p. 273). More likely, following May's intervention defending accountants by switching attention from the balance sheet to the income statement, they accepted that management was responsible for accounts, and stressed, like theorists, account's "limitations" (Bryer 2021a).

May's Intervention

In January 1932, May met Hoxsey to explain the Institute's stance, emphasising the "old forms of account" which focused on balance sheets "were designed for proprietors familiar with the business", who had inside information, and were "not at all adapted to the needs of the investor" (Grady 1962, p. 59). A balance sheet was not, May argued, as Ripley (1927) said, an "instantaneous photograph", a collection of homogenous "facts", but "is heterogeneous in character — conventions, history, present value are all bases" (Grady 1962, p. 59). As balance sheets only poorly measured economic value, for the investor, May emphasised, "The income account is a more significant statement; but here again there is a very general misunderstanding because of the disposition to treat the income account as equally significant as an historical statement and as an index of earning capacity, and hence of value" (Grady 1962, p. 60). May knew the "investing public" did not understand accounts were "largely historical", that like history they reported on the past and present, and depended on assumptions of the future, repeatedly calling for "educating" investors about the "limitations" of accounts (1932, p. 343). Only a "limited number of financial and statistical people", he argued, understood that the "fundamental difficulty" facing management and accountants posed by long-term investments was allocating the lifetime profit to particular periods, a task that was "impossible" (Grady 1962, p. 60). In the early-1930s, the Twentieth Century Fund still found a naïve faith in the potential objectivity of earnings by a "great many" stockholders, seen as Fisher's "realized earnings" or net cash flow. "It is probably true today that a great many owners of securities think of the earnings statements of our more responsible corporations ... as being the virtual equivalent of an actual count of the assets automatically priced in some mysterious manner, and of the earnings as determined by reference to the cash register" (Twentieth Century Fund 1935, p. 599). May's notion of "earning capacity" sought to correct this view by linking accounting income with share values by seeing current earnings, in effect, as a steady-state forecast of distributable cash flows, average dividends, assuming the current period's income repeats itself over the firm's lifetime.[2] May argued, in effect, "conventions" approximated steady-state earning capacity, his answer to "textbook writers" who stressed economic valuation in the balance sheet, drawing on Canning's (1929) interpretation of Fisher to focus on earning's role in share valuation. In an unpublished review of Canning (1929), May (1936, p. 405) found it "painstaking, informed, interesting, and stimulating", arguably because his "opinion that the primary value of income statements lay in the light they threw on future earning capacity" (Stabler 1996, p. 408) simplified Canning's "predicting value".

May stressed in a lecture in January 1932, "what has been accomplished in the past is usually the main factual basis for estimating future prospects, and it is certainly no part of the work of the accountant to make estimates of the future", that "annual accounts are historical in their nature. They are not intended to be and cannot properly be regarded as designed to indicate earning capacity" (May 1936, pp. 10, 21). Concluding accounts are not forecasts left the problem of explaining how they are relevant for valuation. Later in 1932, May had his answer. He urged the NYSE to strive to make the "income account more and more

---

[2] We can state May's "earning capacity" idea algebraically. Earnings = the change in the balance sheet equation, $P_t = [A_t - A_{t-1}] - [L_t - L_{t-1}] = E_t - E_{t-1}$, where P_t = earnings attributable to investors before dividends at t, A_t = total assets, L_t = total liabilities, and E_t = net equity. Thus, $P_t = D_t + NA_t - NA_{t-1}$, where D_t = the dividends in t, and NA_t = the book value of net assets in t after dividends. A firm commences with net assets of NA_0 at the end of t_0, and ends its life with NA_T at the end of period T. Sum and average the components of P_t over T years:

$$\frac{1}{T}\sum_{t-1}^{T} P_t = \frac{1}{T}\sum_{t-1}^{T} D_t + \frac{1}{T}\sum_{t-1}^{T} [NA_t - NA_{t-1}].$$

As $\frac{1}{T}\sum_{t=1}^{T}[NA_t - NA_{t-1}] = \frac{NA_T - NA_0}{T}$, and in steady-state earnings, P_t, is constant, and $NA_T = NA_0$, current earnings is the average dividend of the firm over its lifetime in steady-state:

$$P_t = \frac{1}{T}\sum_{t-1}^{T} D_t.$$

valuable as an indication of earning capacity", make it the "best reflection reasonably obtainable of the earning capacity of the business under the conditions existing during the year to which it relates" (May 1936, pp. 118–119). This gave him the role and justification for an "independent" accountant. Because only management had intimate knowledge of a company, the "primary responsibility for the financial statements … rests with the officers and directors" to use their "best judgment", "and the function of the accountant is to advise the shareholders whether, in his opinion, the statements … fairly present the position of the company and the results of its operations" (May 1936, p. 6). In his letter to Hoxsey in January 1932, May argued that earnings were not a forecast, but an expert investor could improve on the "indication" given by modifying it according to their knowledge and beliefs, could "make his own estimates of average earning capacity and value" (Grady 1962, p. 60). Predictably, consistent with Fisher's money capitalist's mentality, May's ideal user of accounts was the investment banker. May explained, "No banker considering an investment would be content with the mere balance sheet and income account. … In the case of the income account … [he] would request such analysis or supplementary information as would give it maximum value as an indication of earnings capacity under the conditions existing during the year, from which he could make his own estimates of average earning capacity and value" (Grady 1962, p. 60).

In his letter to Hoxsey, May proposed a conference on "fundamentals" because, as he predicted, the "protection of the investor is a question which seems bound to receive much attention in the future" (Grady 1962, p. 60). Hoxsey, however, was not convinced that allocating profits was as difficult as May made out because he wrote back to May who replied in February 1932 arguing, "the problem of assigning profits to particular years even in those relatively simple cases is by no means easy" (Grady 1962, pp. 60–61).[3] M.C. Rorty, an associate of Hoxsey, was also not convinced accounting was simply "conventions" and "assumptions", that it was impossible to set rules. In early-1932, in a lecture to the American Management Association, Rorty proposed that the NYSE should "after consulting with managements, accountants and others, lay down accounting rules for listed corporations" (Grady 1962, p. 61), based on the distinction between "capital" and "revenue". By the early summer of 1932, the NYSE was considering forming a committee "on accounting

[3] Grady (1962) omits the letters May received.

standards ... charged with the formulation and periodic revision of the accounting rules necessary to safeguard against recognized errors and misrepresentations in corporate reports and financial statements" (Zeff 1972, p. 122). May, however, was against any "uniformity", even from the NYSE. To rebut Rorty's proposal, consistent with Fisher's abolition of the distinction between capital and income, May wrote to him explaining that because the problem was allocating income over a long lifetime "The fundamental distinction between capital and revenue which lies at the root of all profit accounting is ultimately only a question of degree" (Grady 1962, p. 62). As May later put it, the "distinction ... does not rest on any essential difference ... [but] upon the relation between the length of useful life of the property acquired and the length of the accounting period" (1943, p. 45). When in early-1932 May was in England, he told Rorty, he had discussed regulating accounts, an issue there following the Hatry scandal, and had an idea that finessed criticisms of the profession's resistance to rules specifying accounting methods:

> I made a suggestion (borrowing the idea from bridge), that it might be permissible to use any conventions so long as they are not absolutely unfair, and provided you announce them before the period begins and do not change them without notice in the middle of the period. ... My idea would be that every corporation should adopt a method of accounting described in considerable detail. This method should be certified by its auditors as being in accordance with reasonable standards of business practice, and should be freely disclosed. (Grady 1962, p. 62)

By June, May had Hoxsey's agreement, who thought May's idea was a "great innovation" (Grady 1962, p. 73). By July, May had drafted a letter making this proposal to the NYSE, which the Special Committee on Cooperation with Stock Exchanges sent to the Committee on the Stock List in September 1932. In this letter, undoubtedly "one of the most important documents in the evolution of accounting and auditing practice", he made clear, like the profession generally, he was "philosophically opposed to an 'official' specification of accounting methods" (Zeff 1972, pp. 119, 122). May argued in 1926 in response to Ripley's criticisms that accountants should "assume ... greater responsibilities" to gain greater prestige and income, but particularly to avoid government control, "some form of bureaucratic control" (May 1936, pp. 41–42). He now proposed the mandatory disclosure of accounting policies "certified by its auditors as being in accordance with reasonable standards of business practice", and five "broad principles of accounting that have won fairly general acceptance" to impose broad limits on the choice (Zeff 1972, p. 122). He accepted, "wide variations are possible within the limits of such principles", but argued this was the "trouble with an 'official system' of accounting", "which variation should be adopted is a question on which one cannot rightly be dogmatic" (Zeff 1972, p. 123).

In his September 1932 letter, May castigated "Writers of textbooks on accounting [who] speak of the purpose of the balance sheet as being to reflect the values of the assets and the liabilities on a particular date", which involves "a misconception of the nature of the balance sheet", which was an income statement "residual" (1936, p. 113). He accepted economic value was the investor's aim, but estimating it in the balance sheet was "neither practical nor desirable" because "it is apparent that the real value of the assets of any large business is dependent mainly on the earning capacity of the enterprise" (May 1936, p. 114). The circularity was, "How much of a given expenditure of the current or past year shall be carried forward as an asset cannot possibly be determined by … a valuation. Some method, however, has to be found" (May 1936, p. 113), and by "necessity", had been. "Out of this necessity has grown up a body of conventions, based partly on theoretical and partly on practical considerations, which form the basis of the determination of income and the preparation of balance sheets today" (May 1936, p. 114). To break the circle, the income statement had become primary because its "conventions" helped investors in measuring "earning capacity", which like the banker they could use for valuation.

There was "fairly general agreement on certain broad principles", but the problem was "there remains room for differences", many different methods "supported by respectable argument", "and by usage", so "few, if any … can fairly be claimed to be so inherently superior in merit to possible alternatives" (May 1936, p. 115). Aware of non-accountants' ignorance, in his letter May "sought … to make unequivocally clear the existence of a variety of methods" (1943, p. 41). Straight-line depreciation was most common, but there were more than four different methods, and many more for implementing "the most commonly accepted method of stating inventories … at cost or market whichever is lower" (May 1936, p. 115). In a lecture to the AIA in November 1932, May lamented, "Nothing has astonished me more in conversations with men fairly well versed in financial matters than their failure to appreciate the importance of methods of accounting in relation to corporate earnings and to capital values predicated on earnings. We accountants know how varied are the methods commonly and legitimately employed, how great the effect of a difference of methods on the earnings of a particular short period may be" (1936, p. 84). He gave the "simple case of one of the unemployed who joined the apple-selling rush in the winter of 1931" (May 1936, p. 84) who buys and sells apples for four days. According to May's example, "Looking back over the experience of the four days, it was clear that he had bought four crates of apples at a total cost of $8.25 and had sold contents for a total of $19.00, and thus had made a profit of $10.75. It was apparent, however, that the profit from day to day varied according to the way in which the stock carried over from day to day was treated" (May 1932, p. 84). The movement from M to M′ was clear, but "allocating" this to each of the four days was a judgment. He concluded that within the limits of "accepted principles" corporations should therefore freely choose and publish their methods, use them consistently, and highlight any changes, and independent accountants should certify their reasonableness and use. This was his "procedure by which the variety could be curtailed and the best methods gradually made practically universal …, and gradually bring about the elimination of the less desirable practices by the pressure of public opinion" (May 1943, pp. 41–42). May stressed, "This development seems to me infinitely preferable to the alternative which at once suggests itself of uniform methods imposed by external authority" (1936, p. 91), the state. The letter therefore stressed "principles" and avoided "the word 'rules' [because it] implied the existence of a ruling body", and avoided "convention" because it "would not convey an adequate impression of authority" (May 1943, p. 42).

May's "accepted principles" focussed on the income statement because "in the formulation of methods of accounting the pre-eminent importance of earning capacity should be recognized", that "the value of the income account depends on its being a fair indication of earning capacity" (1936, pp. 91, 93). As the September letter put it, "It is probably fairly well recognised by intelligent investors today that the earning capacity is the fact of crucial importance in the valuation of industrial enterprise, and that therefore the income account is usually far more important than the balance sheet" (May 1936, p. 117). According to May, "The development of accounting conventions has, consciously or unconsciously, been in the main based on acceptance of this proposition. As a rule, the first objective has been to secure a proper charge or credit to the income account for the year, and in general the presumption has been that once this is achieved the residual amount of the expenditure or receipt could properly find its place in the balance sheet" (1936, p. 117). Thus, "the direction of the principal efforts of the Exchange ... should be towards making the income account more and more valuable as an indication of earning capacity" (May 1936, p. 118). His summary of the "principal objects ... the Exchange should keep constantly in mind and do its best to gradually achieve" emphasised the profession's rejection of the balance sheet emphasis (May 1936, p. 119):

> (1) To bring about a better recognition by the investing public of the fact that the balance sheet of a large modern corporation does not and should not be expected to represent an attempt to show present values of the assets and liabilities.
> (2) To emphasise the fact that balance sheets are necessarily to a large extent historical and conventional in character, and to encourage the ... disclos[ure] ... on what basis assets of various kinds are stated ....
> (3) To emphasise the cardinal importance of the income account ... and to take the position that an annual income account is unsatisfactory unless it is so framed as to constitute the best reflection reasonably obtainable of the earning capacity of the business under the conditions existing during the year to which it relates.
> (4) To make universal the acceptance by listed companies of certain broad principles of accounting which have won fairly general acceptance.

Appended to the letter as Exhibit 1 was a list of "principles of accounting", which the AIA membership approved, and two others (Zeff 1984, p. 452). The Institute published them in 1934 in a pamphlet, "Audit of Corporate Accounts", that argued they were principles "so generally accepted that they should be followed by all listed companies" (Carey 1969a, p. 177). These "principles" outlawed some egregious practices, but implicitly were moves towards British conservatism, a trend we will see May later helped to accelerate:

> (1) Unrealized profit should not be credited to income account of the corporation either directly or indirectly.... Profit is deemed to be realized when a sale in the ordinary course of business is effected....

(2) Capital surplus ... should not be used to relieve the income account....
(3) Earned surplus of a subsidiary company created prior to acquisition does not form a part of the consolidated earned surplus of the parent company; nor can any dividend declared out of such a surplus properly be credited to the income account of the parent company.
(4) While it is perhaps in some circumstances permissible to show stock of a corporation held in its own treasure as an asset, if adequately disclosed, the dividends on stock so held should not be treated as a credit to the income account of the company (May 1936, p. 121).

Following this plan, accounting would help stockholders to value shares and discipline management in the only way apparently open to them, by appropriate investment decisions, by buying or selling shares, because May agreed with Berle and Means that dispersed ownership meant supervising or disciplining management for "results" had gone:

> The purpose of furnishing accounts to shareholders must be not only to afford them information in regard to the results being achieved by those to whom they have entrusted the management of the business, but to aid them in taking appropriate action to give effect to the conclusions which they reach regarding such accomplishments. In an earlier day, stockholders who were dissatisfied with the results ... could perhaps move effectively to bring about a change in policy or, failing that, a change in management. With the growth in magnitude of corporations and the present wide diffusion of stock holdings, any such attempt is normally impractical.... The only practical way in which an investor can today give expression to his conclusions ... is by retaining, increasing or disposing of his investment, and accounts are mainly valuable to him in so far as they afford guidance in determining which of these courses he shall pursue. (May 1936, p. 118)

May never advocated British/Marxian results control, we will see, but in effect agreed the objective should be Canning's (1929) "predicting value", making reported income "more and more valuable as an indication of earning capacity". Consistency was important because the longer the period the more valuable the measure and the less the influence of any particular method. Thus, according to May, "the investor would not need to be greatly concerned whether the straight-line or the sinking-fund method of providing for depreciation were being employed by a given corporation provided he knew which method … and that it was being applied in the same way every year" (1936, pp. 116–117). Consistency allowed investors to observe trends in earning capacity, which changes of method could obscure, and "the investor may be grossly deceived unless the change is brought to his notice" (May 1936, p. 117). To prevent deception and highlight other questionable practices, in Exhibit II May's letter required a "clear statement of the principles governing the classification of charges and credits as between (a) balance sheet accounts, (b) income accounts and (c) surplus accounts" (1936, p. 122). There should be "sufficient details of the manner in which these principles are to be applied to enable an investor to judge of the degree of conformity in standard usage and of conservatism of the reporting corporation" (May 1936, p. 122). Exhibit II proposed disclosures to prevent the criticised 1920s practices for consolidations, deferrals, extraordinary items, fixed assets, inventories, liabilities and reserves (May 1936, pp. 122–125).

Political Development

Coinciding with the intensification of May's NYSE discussions, in early-1932 having failed to persuade the NYSE to reform, Hoover reluctantly initiated an investigation into stock exchange practices, "in response to charges that Wall Street had profited from and contributed to" the crash (Merino and Neimark 1982, fn. 29, p. 45). May gave evidence about his firm's investigation into the collapsed Kreuger & Toll Company, but there was little discussion of accounting. Ripley gave evidence stressing the need for more disclosure to restore public confidence and prevent speculation and recommended draft legislation based on Berle and Means (1932) (Miranti 1990, pp. 147–148). The investigation made little progress and the Republican presidential platform did not mention stock exchanges (Seligman 1982, pp. 12–13, 15, 18). Roosevelt, however, made it a key part of his campaign, "committed himself to the long-held populist and progressive goal of superseding lax state corporation laws with more stringent federal standards" (Seligman 1982, p. 42). In radio speech on 30 August 1932, Roosevelt promised major reforms, including of accounting, legislation to "prevent the issue of manufactured and unnecessary securities … and to require … true information as to the investment of principal, … true earnings, true liabilities, and true assets of the corporation itself" (Merino and Neimark 1982, fn. 30, p. 46). Berle and Means documented the reduction in legal protection to individual shareholders by "low par" or "no par" stocks, "watered" stocks, removing "preemptive rights", allowing stock options, etc., which allowed management "the power of confiscation" (Seligman 1982, pp. 42–44), and "blue sky" laws' failure to prevent worthless-offerings. This was high on Roosevelt's list because investigations showed the NYSE had not implemented its model listing requirements "as the number of new stock applications approved increased" rapidly during the boom (Seligman 1982, p. 47).

Roosevelt also promised to regulate holding companies, the stock exchange, and national banks, and separate commercial from investment banking, denouncing "bankers, who he believed had violated the moral trust" (Merino and Neimark 1982, fn. 29, p. 45). In his presidential nomination-acceptance speech, Roosevelt promised a New Deal, but focused on the "dry subject of finance" where he saw "an important place for that prize statement of principle ... for letting in the light of day on the issues of securities" (Seligman 1982, p. 19). During the campaign Roosevelt called for "full publicity", to "let in the light", but although he promised the "truth" this meant "disclosure of data" (Seligman 1982, p. 19) to expose wrongdoers, for "fairness". Roosevelt and his advisors "did not think that investors would benefit greatly by financial reports nor did he think that any legislation could prevent people from making errors in judgment about a firm's prospects" (Previts and Merino 1998, p. 274). They saw the problem of financial reporting as fair valuation, dealing with the "unscrupulous money changers", "that small group of men whose chief outlook ... [to] make huge profits from the lending of money and the marketing of securities" (McElvaine 2009, pp. 139, 127). When Roosevelt attacked the "evils of the old order" he meant legislating for "social values more noble than mere monetary profit" (McElvaine 2009, p. 140), not to create advanced capitalism's necessary superstructure.

The Senate Banking and Currency Committee's investigation of stock exchange practices 1932–1934, usually called the Pecora Hearings after the lead attorney, that led to the Securities Act of 1933 (Seligman 1982, p. 13), focused on and reinforced a popular explanation that "immoral" insider manipulation had caused the crash (Merino and Neimark 1982, p. 45). In early-1933, Pecora interrogated a parade of bankers, most of whom "admitted to a long series of misdeeds" including manipulating share prices through syndicates and pools and using articles in the press, trading in the shares of their own banks, loans to bank officials, tax evasion, etc. (McElvaine 2009, p. 136; Merino and Neimark 1982, p. 41). However, for "more knowledgeable observers" focusing on bankers' moral failings also put auditors in the spotlight because they were integral to the "evils of the old order". In 1932, two events put them in the public eye, the collapse of Kreuger & Toll, and Berle and Means's book (1932), "highly critical of current financial reporting", "which had a great impact in sophisticated circles, and further encouraged demand for legislation regulating the issuance of securities and financial reporting of issuers" (Carey 1979, p. 30). In *The Accounting Review*, Hanson argued it "should be read by all accountants ... [because it] has succeeded in focusing attention on the revolutionary changes which are taking place in the modern corporation and private property. … The theme of the book is that the owners of modern business are not in control of it" (1933, p. 255). Despite May's best efforts, therefore, the "pressure for legislation to protect investors was heightened in 1932" (Carey 1969a, p. 170).

Audits of Corporate Accounts

In April 1932, anticipating legislation the NYSE accepted the commonly used English form of audit report. It required accounts audited by "independent public accountants qualified under the laws of some state or country … certifying as to the correctness of the balance sheet, income statement and surplus statement … [which] must cover all subsidiaries, and the scope must be not less than that indicated in a pamphlet entitled 'Verification of Financial Statements'" (May 1936, pp. 125–126). According to May, the "standard form of audit report or certificate commonly in use … was of English origin. There, the auditor was required to state whether in his opinion the balance sheet … was properly drawn up so as to exhibit a true and correct view" (1943, p. 40). In a lecture in January 1932, May noted, "One view of the questions" about secret reserves "is that directors should always submit accounts that represent as accurately as possible their best judgment of the true profits of the year" (1936, p. 22), which was the British view. "Others take the position that all businesses are subject to many hazards which cannot be accurately measured; that the attribution of profits to years is at best conventional" (May 1936, p. 22), which was his and the AIA's view. Hoxsey queried on 17 September 1932 whether May's letter should include the disclosure of secret reserves (Grady 1962, p. 72). However, May told his audience in January that accountants had no "ethical duty to insist on the disclosure even of the fact that a secret reserve has been created, if he believes that the action was taken in good faith and if the amount involved is not so large that ignoring it completely distorts the earnings picture" (1936, p. 22). This was the British position (Dicksee 1927), but its accountants had to certify the balance sheet exhibited a true and correct view based on the underlying books (Bryer 2021a, pp. 94–98). In January 1933, the NYSE had second thoughts and wrote to the presidents of listed corporations asking about the scope of their audit, and withdrew its requirement for the British opinion of "correctness", a "radical change" (May 1943, p. 40). It asked corporate presidents to ask their auditors, in effect, whether they used May's system (May 1936, p. 128):

> (4) Whether in their opinion the form of the balance sheet and of the income, or profit-and-loss, account is such as fairly to present the financial position and the results of operation.
>
> (5) Whether the accounts are in their opinion fairly determined on the basis of consistent application of the system of accounting regularly employed by the company.
>
> (6) Whether such system in their opinion conforms to accepted accounting practices, and particularly whether it is in any respect inconsistent with any of the principles set forth in the statement attached hereto.

May (1936, p. 137) replied for the AIA in February 1933 that the "essential point is to guard against any substantial overstatement of income, and this can be reasonably assured by the auditor satisfying himself of the correctness of the balance sheets at the beginning and end ... and reviewing the important transactions". "Correctness" did not mean, May later made clear, "the 'true position' of a company" (1943, p. 41). Auditors could not give an opinion of the "correctness" of the income account, and their opinion could not cover whether there was sufficient disclosure because "wide differences of opinion exist" (May 1936, p. 138). May reemphasised, "accounts must be largely expressions of judgment, and that the primary responsibility for forming these judgments must rest on the management of the corporation" (1936, p. 138). The NYSE's January letter also asked about "the principles governing the accounting methods of the corporation and the form of presentation of accounts to shareholders" (May 1936, pp. 127–128). In October 1933, the NYSE reported the replies "have indicated very general acceptance of certain principles", and decided, "they should be followed by all listed companies" (May 1936, p. 129). In December 1933, the AIA wrote to the NYSE agreeing the auditor's report, which should state, "In our opinion, based upon such examination, the accompanying balance sheet and related statements of income and surplus fairly present, in accordance with accepted principles of accounting, consistently maintained ..., its position ... and the results of its operations for the year" (May 1936, p. 143).

Meanwhile, shortly after his election in November 1932, in addition to taking action in his first 100-days to save the banking system, to address the crises in agriculture and industry, unemployment and poverty, Roosevelt set about framing securities legislation. He invited Samuel Untermyer, who became prominent as the attorney to the 1913 Pujo Committee's "money trust" investigations, and asked Berle and economist Charles Taussig to work with him to produce a bill. Untermyer, however, merely modified his 1914 proposal: the bill gave the "Postmaster General sweeping powers to issue regulations and prohibitions concerning transactions on the stock exchanges, new securities issuances, periodic corporate financial statements, and the membership of the stock exchanges" (Parrish 1970, p. 44; see also Seligman 1982, pp. 51–52). Roosevelt, however, "shared Moley's doubt that empowering the Post Office to supervise such matters as a uniform system of accounting would be wise" (Seligman 1982, p. 52). A subsequent draft (known as the "Thompson bill", prepared with assistance by Huston Thompson, former Chairman of the Federal Trade Commission), "embodying many of Berle and Means' recommendations", required management to file audited accounts with the Federal Trade Commission (FTC) for each new security they issued (Miranti 1990, p. 148). Facing strong opposition from investment bankers and corporate management, Moley convinced Roosevelt that the revocation powers given to the FTC, and the broad and heavy liabilities it imposed on management for filing false accounts, were "too far reaching" (Seligman 1982, p. 56; Miranti 1990, pp. 149–150). Critics argued legislators should use the British Companies Acts as the model (Miranti 1990, pp. 149–150). In early 1933, Roosevelt asked Felix Frankfurter, law professor at the Harvard Law School, to supervise the drafting of another securities bill, who enlisted James M. Landis also a law professor from Harvard, and Benjamin V. Cohen and Thomas C. Corcoran, former students and corporate lawyers, to help. Frankfurter, a progressive, sympathetic to labour, oppressed minorities and socialists, was disliked by "eminent legal and financial magnates" for his "alleged radicalism", a view to which a colleague reputedly responded: "Felix a radical? … Hell!! The damn fool is wearing out his heart trying to make capitalism live up to its pretensions" (Parrish 1970, pp. 1–2). The magnates were right, however, the Securities Act he helped formulate did pose a potentially radical threat to capitalism. Nevertheless, as Frankfurter said, he "was a moderating influence" (Parrish 1970, p. 42). Four weeks after assuming power, in April 1933, at the depth of the depression, the US Congress passed "The Truth in Securities Act" to regulate the interstate issue of securities, and another in 1934 to regulate securities trading in national markets, which created the SEC. Both required "full and fair disclosure" of all "material facts", including accounts, imposed liabilities on accountants, and gave the SEC power to specify the auditors and accounting methods.

In 1932, when the AIA's leadership, particularly May, saw that Roosevelt intended to pass securities legislation, it had "lobbied behind the scenes" for independent audit (Previts and Merino 1998, p. 273). It was "behind the scenes" because although in January 1933 "the profession stands today at a critical moment in its history" (May 1936, p. 145), it dare not appear on the public stage. Acutely aware of their image, in January 1933 May wrote to all US and Canadian offices of Price, Waterhouse & Co., on "the importance of insisting on sound methods of accounting and presentation of facts, however difficult the circumstances may be and however important may be the client.... We are perfectly prepared to sacrifice present business and profits to maintain the position of the firm.... Naturally, we do not want to be too technical, nor to attempt to override ruthlessly the judgment of directors and officials; but we must not lay ourselves open to the criticism of being subservient to our clients" (May 1936, p. 145), the public perception. "Perhaps at judge Covington's advice", the AIA's legal counsel in Washington, "the Institute did not appear formally at the hearings on the securities legislation … [because] the profession's record in developing standards of financial reporting was not impressive", so … "[i]f official representatives … had testified…, they might have been subjected to hostile questioning" (Carey 1969a, p. 183; Miranti 1990, p. 147). However, Colonel Arthur H. Carter, known as a "man of action" who would not wilt under fire, not seen as one of the AIA's "inner circle" although a senior Haskins & Sells partner, president of the New York State Society of Certified Public Accountants (NYSSCPA), and a member of May's Stock Exchange Committee (1943, p. 72), telegrammed the Senate Committee on Banking and Finance's chair. Carter approved of Thompson's bill, offered assistance and advice, and asked to testify (Miranti 1990, p. 149). The committee invited Carter to appear (Carey 1969a, p. 185). Carter argued, "the failure to require audits was a major omission in the suggested reforms" (Previts and Merino 1998, p. 273). The draft bill allowed the FTC to require an audit by an independent public accountant only if it initiated an investigation on registration, whereas Carter argued it should be mandatory for all financial statements. He suggest amending the bill: "The accounts … shall have been examined by an independent accountant and his report shall present his certificate wherein he shall express his opinion as to the correctness of the assets, liabilities, reserves, capital and surplus as of the balance sheet date and also the income statement for the period indicated" (Carey 1969a, p. 185).

Everyone knew the only other option was a government auditor. Senator Barkley asked Carter, "Do you not think it is more in the interest of the public that [audits] be done by some government agency rather than by some private association of accountants?" (Carey 1969a, p. 186). Senator Reynolds asked, "After it goes to the Federal Commission they have to check it up to see who is right; they have to go through and audit again. There has to be a government audit, as suggested by Senator Barkley. Would it not be creating more difficulty and more expense and more time for the government if auditing organizations interest themselves in these various and sundry corporations?" (Carey 1969a, p. 187). The FTC would not need to re-perform an independent accountants' audit, Carter responded, arguing, "it is an impractical thing for a government agency to do it effectively … because it requires such a large force" (Carey 1969a, p. 187). However, the expense, which government could recoup from the corporations, was not the deciding issue, which was that "the congressional panel wanted to avoid a direct confrontation with the business community" (Previts and Merino 1998, p. 273) who were adamantly opposed to the control this could give a future government. Carter made clear whose side accountants were on when Senator Reynolds "Suppose[d] that we decide in the final passage of the bill here to employ five or six hundred auditors from your organization, that would be alright, then, would it not?" "I do not think the type of men who are in public practice of accountancy would leave their present practice to go in the government employ" (Carey 1969a, p. 188). May behind the scenes, and Carter on the public stage, drew on theorists' insistence that accounts were subjective valuation statements to highlight the socialist threat.

As Previts and Merino (1998, p. 273, fn. 98, p. 457) put it, "Carter and May did not engage in a 'hard sell'; both men stressed the limitations of independent audits and the limited protection that financial reports would afford to investors". Carter warned, "investors are too prone to regard balance sheets and income accounts as positive and indisputable statements of fact', while accountants knew they were simply a matter of opinion" (Previts and Merino 1998, p. 273, fn. 98, p. 457). If, as May and Carter insisted, neither management nor accountants could verify that "the statements … are correct" (Previts and Merino 1998, p. 277), could give only their opinion, the implication was that future socialist politicians could pressure government auditors to reflect their opinion. Consistent with seeing a balance sheet as a valuation statement, Senator Reynolds asked Carter, "Do you think it proper to insert in there that these independent public accountants should be privileged to state their opinion as to the value of the shares of the company?" (Carey 1969a, pp. 185–186). Carter did not deny accounts were relevant to share valuation, but "We are unable to express an opinion as to the value of securities" (Carey 1969a, p. 186). He deplored "the impression [that] generally prevails that one who reads a balance sheet and an income statement regards the figures in such a statement as a defensible definitely ascertained fact" (Carey 1969a, p. 186). He knew better: "whereas, as a matter of fact in reality it can only be an opinion based upon certain accounting assumptions which must be applied to the opinion of some individual as to value" (Carey 1969a, p. 186). Senator Barkley pursued Carter as to why this opinion should be of a private-sector auditor: "Do you not think it is more in the interest of the public that buy these securities, if there is any checkup or guarantee as to the correctness, that it be done by some government agency rather than by some private association of accountants?" (Carey 1969a, p. 186). Carter replied, "the public accountant was better equipped … than the average government agency" because, unlike a corporation controller who "is in the employ of the company", public accountants were "independent", audited only by "Our conscience" (Carey 1969a, p. 187), implicitly, the pro-private-sector, capitalist "conscience".

Some accountants were more direct. C. Oliver Wellington, the chair of the AIA's Committee on Cooperation with the SEC, "clearly showed the animosity that some practitioners had toward New Deal reforms"; he "denounced New Dealers for promulgating legislation designed to 'set the classes against the masses and vice versa'" (Previts and Merino 1998, p. 279, fn. 122, p. 460). It is a "myth that the testimony before Congress of … Carter … prevented the creation of a government bureaucracy of auditors in the 1933 Securities Act" (Doron 2015, p. 5), but Carter's and the profession's argument, that the "nature" of accounting meant the Act should mandate independent auditing, was decisive. As Carter's testimony was the only formal presentation of the case for independent auditors to the Senate, he formally takes the credit even though May "lobbied behind the scenes for audits" (Previts and Merino 1998, p. 273). Senator Gore asked Carter, "Don't you think we have got to establish some sort of standard of bookkeeping for different lines of industry before we can make any comparisons", to which he replied, "I think it is very hard to establish a standard of bookkeeping. You can rely on principles of accounting" (Carey 1969a, p. 189), which required independent judgement. This argument carried the day. With strong backing from business that "preferred private-sector audits to direct government oversight" (Previts and Merino 1998, p. 270), the 1933 Securities Act required independent audits of corporations issuing securities in more than one state. The Act gave the FTC power to specify auditing procedures and auditors' relationships, and to reject filings it thought deficient (Miranti 1990, pp. 152–153). A mandatory independent private-sector audit was the critical issue. The continuing debate on "uniformity", we will see, was also a debate over government control, which May and others implied, and some said, opened the door to socialism, to control of business. Politicians agreed that this must be avoided. Rayburn drew applause when, concluding his introduction to the bill, he "draped the Securities Act in the flag, claiming it to be a mechanism to restore confidence in American institutions and avoid 'the evils of socialism, bolshevism and communism'" (Seligman 1982, p. 66). The Securities Act avoided government control of the profession, but lack of trust in accountants meant a potential socialist threat remained because, thanks to Frankfurter and his progressive colleagues, it gave the FTC (SEC) the power to determine accounting methods, and to neutralise this "evil" required implementing May's interpretation of accounting.

Roosevelt shifted to the left in 1934, his employment policies having failed. In the 1936 election, he castigated the "economic royalists" who took "other peoples' money" and used it to "impose a new industrial dictatorship", laughing at the forces of "organized money" who "are unanimous in their hate for me — and I welcome their hatred". He declared, "the forces of selfishness and of a lust for power [had] met their match" (Lichtenstein *et al.* 2000, p. 436). He won a landslide, taking 60 percent of the popular vote and increased Democratic majorities in both houses of Congress. Roosevelt's advisers had proposed redistributing income to increase demand by increasing taxation on wealthy individuals and corporations, which provoked the formation of the Liberty League in 1934, a coalition of conservative Democrats led by Jacob Raskob, supported by Wall Street and big business, to resist it, an "elite circle" that invited May to join (Miranti 1990, pp. 163–164). Unity through "associationalism", this coalition convinced May, would "give the profession leverage in dealing with political leaders", that "Increased political power would be useful in trying to countervail against the unwelcome encroachments of an activist federal bureaucracy" (Miranti 1990, pp. 167–168).

To save capitalism, the Securities Acts gave the profession a key position as independent auditors, but given its dismal 1920s record and continued identification with management, it could not be trusted. Accountants continued to earn distrust after the Acts. In 1936, Landis concluded, "the impact of almost daily tilts with accountants, some of them called leaders of their profession, often leaves little doubt that their loyalties to management are stronger than their sense of responsibility to the investor.... Such an experience does not lead readily to acquiescence in the plea ... that the form of statement can be less rigidly controlled and left more largely to professional responsibility alone" (Previts and Merino 1998, p. 279). In 1938, SEC commissioner Robert Healy described accountants "as special pleaders for their most lucrative clients" (Previts and Merino 1998, p. 279). May strenuously argued, "inadequate or misleading reports of established business played but a relatively unimportant part in causing the catastrophic losses that were sustained" (1943, p. 57). He admitted, "the pyramiding of holding companies, unsound treatment of stock dividends", etc., played a part, but argued the "speculative fever which produced the Florida land boom", and "belief in a new economic order encouraged by persons high in the political and economic world, were far more potent influences" (May 1943, p. 58). He stressed, "an improvement in accounting information available, however substantial if measured by comparison with existing standards, can only be of minor value to the investor if this value is measured in relation to the risks necessarily run in speculation or investment in corporate stocks" (May 1943, p. 58). He nevertheless accepted, "the temper of the times demanded control of the dealings of corporate securities, and of corporate reports, and it was felt, with reason, that confidence would not be restored until a drastic measure designed to restore this control had been enacted" (May 1943, p. 58). Unfortunately, in May's view, the "law was … passed under the pressure of public indignation, enhanced by investigations that were lacking in judicial quality" (1943, p. 58). His efforts and aversion to socialism meant "the 1933 Securities Act involved a modest grant of regulatory power" — the FTC had no power to "direct capital", "remarkable considering the sentiments of the day", and required independent auditors — but Section 19 gave it "the power to define accounting concepts" (Seligman 1982, pp. 65, 70), to "prescribe accounting rules" (May 1943, pp. 61–62):

> … the Commission shall have the authority … to prescribe the form or forms in which required information shall be set forth, the items or details to be shown in the balance sheet and earnings statement, and the methods to be followed in the preparation of accounts, in the appraisal or valuation of assets and liabilities, in the determination of depreciation and depletion, in the differentiation of recurring and nonrecurring income, in the differentiation of investment and operating income and in the preparation, where the Commission deems it necessary or desirable, of consolidated balance sheets or income accounts … . (Carey 1969a, pp. 191–192)

Section 19 may have been Cohen's suggestion whose "past experience in the New York business community made him fearful of statutory loopholes", which made him keen to ensure the Act allowed requiring detailed disclosures (Parrish 1970, p. 64). Why did the profession apparently lose this battle over "uniformity", but win the war that protected its "independence"?

The Battle against "Uniformity"

The profession argued against "uniformity" because "rules did not require judgment, and implementation of uniform systems would result in the displacement of CPAs by technicians" (Previts and Merino 1998, p. 275). It repeatedly claimed "uniformity" undermined accountants' independence, from management and government, which remained their "most precious asset"; that their "judgment", their "opinion" of the "fairness" of the accounts gave them a pivotal role, and was their "means of using that asset" (Montgomery 1927, p. 253). When threatened with legislation the profession had lobbied hard for "disclosure", which would allow accountants to exercise "judgment", and against "uniformity". At first sight, therefore, in the face of "the forces unleashed by the Great Depression", May's "very substantial effort to ward off intervention of the federal government in the establishment of accounting principles failed" (Zeff 1984, p. 452). The Acts delegated "administrative authority to prescribe accounting principles and methods. The British Companies Acts had never gone that far" (Carey 1969a, p. 182). The British left this to the profession, with court supervision, but the American profession had badly sullied its reputation. Like Barkley's treatment of Carter, Thompson's testimony before Congress "suggests he had strong reservations about the profession" (Doron 2015, p. 5). May lamented, "the irony of the law was that it gave legal recognition to the function of the *independent* public accountant, and at the same time, gave to a non-expert body powers over the profession which went far to destroy its independence" (May 1943, p. 59). In England, as the Greene Committee said in 1926, in "the matter of accounts ... within reasonable limits companies ... [were] left a free hand" (May 1943, p. 61). May complained, "the grant of powers to prescribe accounting procedure, was as unwise and unnecessary as it was inadequately considered. It struck a wanton and unjustified blow at the development of a profession which, despite lapses, had made remarkable progress in the forty years of its existence" (1943, p. 62). It was "retributive rather than remedial" (May 1943, p. 63).

May complained, "there could be no reason for striking at its professional character" by giving responsibility for accounting principles to "a policy-making body that was not expert", that "The provisions were manifestly written into the law by people who had no adequate understanding of the nature of accounting" (1943, p. 62). May (1943, p. 62) pointed to lawyers like Landis who justified the liabilities the Acts imposed on accountants by arguing that "Accounting, as distinguished from law, has generally been portrayed as an exact science, and its representations have been proffered to the unlearned as representations of fact and not opinion". However, in a late-1933 lecture to the NYSSCPA Landis accepted May's view: "It has been said, and very rightly in my humble opinion, that accounting is after all a matter of opinion rather than anything else" (Carey 1969a, p. 193). His complaint was that this was not how accountants had represented themselves to investors, "accountancy has paraded too largely as being an exact science, and its representations have been proffered to the unlearned as representations of fact, and not opinion" (Carey 1969a, p. 193). He justified the harsh liabilities in the 1933 Act as "fair" "If it [the profession] insists upon such fact representations" (Carey 1969a, p. 193), which according to May they did not. May neglected to acknowledge, however, that this supposedly inadequate "understanding of the nature of accounting" as a "science" grounded in the "facts", stemmed from proprietary theorists like Sprague (Bryer 2021a, Chapter 5). May (1943, p. 63) countered the "exact science" view with a comment of Lord Justice Buckley that "the ascertainment of profit is in every case a matter of estimate and opinion", and with Dickinson, "the leading accounting authority on the … need for and significance of these words". However, he neglected to mention that in Dickinson's view, these "estimates" were of facts and the "opinions" sought were whether the accounts gave a "true and correct" view (Bryer 2021a, Chapter 2). May (1943, p. 53, emphases added) could get Buckley to say only that the rule forbidding paying dividends from capital "*may* in practice raise questions of the utmost difficulty in their solution, and the question what are profits and what is capital *may* be a difficult and sometimes an *almost* impossible problem to solve". Buckley "declined to attempt to treat these questions in the abstract", but clearly thought, "no great difficulty would arise in dealing with any particular case on its own facts and circumstances" (May 1943, p. 53).

To May, however, the origin of the idea that accounts were "factual" was a mystery. "If corporate financial statements had, in fact, been falsely portrayed to the unlearned as purely factual", the solution was simple, to "enlighten the unlearned" (May 1943, p. 63). The problem was that a still powerful body of opinion thought accounts should be "factual". For example, while Carter was a loyal and well-drilled follower of May, under questioning from Senator Gore, he conceded the need for enforced "standards" to enable stockholders to make inter-industry comparisons, which from the stewardship perspective provide the factual basis for target-setting and judging results (Carey 1969a, pp. 189–190):

> SENATOR GORE. Don't you think we have got to establish some sort of standard of bookkeeping for different lines of industry before we can make any comparison?
>
> MR. CARTER. I think it is very hard to establish a standard of bookkeeping. You can rely on principles of accounting.…
>
> SENATOR GORE. I mean the bookkeeping would be standard there so that you could compare one with another, and if they are not standardised give this Commission the power to require them to conform to it?

> MR. CARTER. Take the automobile industry. You could have the reports of the various companies and you could find a great similarity in their bookkeeping.
>
> SENATOR GORE. I know, but unless there is substantial similarity I do not see how comparison could be made. …
>
> MR. CARTER. I think you would have to take each industry by itself and … provide a system in which they would set up their accounts peculiar to that particular industry.
>
> SENATOR GORE. That is what I mean, some sort of standard or set of principles so that each industry and individual instance in each industry could be compared with each other….

The SEC's power to determine accounting rules, Frankfurter was right, made his creation more than a "federal blue sky law. The act's greater import was the opportunity it offered for a modern administrative agency to evolve. Far more significant than Schedule A was the little discussed residual authority granted to the FTC to evolve uniform accounting standards; it was this power, more than any other part of the act, that Frankfurter calculated would 'have far reaching beneficial effects on American corporate practices'" (Seligman 1982, p. 71). However, this claim shows the profession's rhetoric, that the "nature" of accounting meant "uniform standards" could only "evolve", had captured Frankfurter. It had also captured disappointed reformers, such as William O. Douglas, then a young law professor at Yale, who accepted the valuation aim and thinking of individual, middle class investors doubted the relevance of accounting, whether "most investors had 'the time, money, or intelligence to assimilate the mass of information in the registration statement'" (Seligman 1982, p. 71). Douglas wrote-off the Securities Acts (but later changed his mind when he joined the SEC) as "wholly secondary in any thorough-going and comprehensive programme for social control in this field" because it did not "perfect a plan for control of our present forms of organization" (Seligman 1982, p. 71). Berle complained the 1933 Act "leaves unsolved most of the major questions … [f]or that Act and the Blue Sky Acts, generally, do not attempt to solve the problem of who is entitled to the increment of value arising from organization, or the increment of power arising from control" (1933, p. 42). Although he had not challenged it, he criticised the "preoccupation with information enabling buyers and sellers to determine the price at which they are willing to buy or sell", that the act "has essentially little to do with the conduct of a corporation's affairs ..., and prohibiting speculative activity by corporate administrators" (Berle 1967, p. xxxiii). To these critics, the Acts were therefore "a first step, not an ultimate solution", and they continued to argue for "federal incorporation to get at 'the really fundamental problem of the increment of power inherent in the present form of organization'" (Previts and Merino 1998, fn. 100, pp. 457–458).

In a paper presented to the AIA in late 1933, Berle "predicted that a government bureau would be set up to standardize accounting practices in various industries" (Carey 1979, p. 32). According to Carey, the "audience sensed that control of accounting by government was nearer than ever before" (1979, p. 32). They were wrong. In 1933, "Wall Street and business in general were on the defensive", but the "issue, basically ... the political question of who should regulate the economy, or, as Berle wrote, whether high finance would be master or servant" (Seligman 1982, p. 72), had already been decided. May had not won the battle against uniformity because a potential threat to "independence" remained, but he had won the war against government control, for continued management control. Some politicians claimed the British Companies Acts was the Securities Acts' model but they omitted shareholders' legal rights to financial statements and, crucially, the requirement for a "true and fair view" (Bush 2005, p. 9). In Carter's examination, two senators asked if the "English system" required independent auditors (Carey 1969a, pp. 186, 190). Focusing on the harsh liabilities under the 1933 Act, May criticised one "misstatement ... freely made in support of the new laws..., that the law of 1933 was in general character and scope similar to the ... English companies acts — an argument that carried great weight with many persons" (1937, p. 344). The 1933 Act significantly increased auditor liabilities beyond British standards, but the 1934 Act repealed them (Miranti 1990, pp. 151–152; Previts and Merino 1998, p. 272, fn. 96, p. 457). The decision not to give shareholders a legal right to know meant that by British standards the Acts failed to give "any sensible guiding accounting and reporting principles" (Bush 2005, p. 20). Bush says this reflected federal "deference to the states" (2005, p. 9), but these differences are consistent with framing by Fisher's theory, and support May's life-long claim that under his leadership the "profession had 'narrowly avoided' a government takeover (May Papers, 3/4/58, 8/8/52)" (cf. Doron 2011, p. 3).

The profession had theoretically lost its "independence", but after the 1933 Act it continued deploying May's interpretation against "uniformity" to prevent it becoming a reality. The AIA submitted a memorandum to Congress that was considering amendments to the 1933 Act, what became the 1934 Act, which "challenged a provision giving the Commission power to prescribe uniform accounting for industry", but "the power ... was retained" (Carey 1969a, p. 194). The AIA and ASCPA formed a joint committee that in 1934 criticised "the regulator's demands ... for 'uniform accounting principles'", because "uniform accounting was unrealistic and ineffective, its primary virtue being simplicity" (Previts and Merino 1998, p. 275). In January 1935 SEC commissioner George C. Mathews stressed to accountants that the SEC had "carefully avoided requiring uniformity of accounting either as to matters of classification or as to matters of principle" (Carey 1969a, p. 195). Accountants, however, remained wary. C. Aubrey Smith, professor of accounting, University of Texas, warned, "the temper of the present Commission is to permit the accountants to draw up for themselves ... 'accepted accounting principles and practices'. If the practitioners, after sufficient time..., have not come to some substantial agreement as to what are or should be considered accepted accounting principles and practices, we may well expect the Commission's staff accountants to prepare ... what it shall demand in the way of such practices" (1935, p. 327). Facing this threat, the profession led by May endlessly repeated that regulation should be limited "to a few general principles so broadly stated that they will permit wide variation in application to meet different circumstances" (Previts and Merino 1998, p. 275). It now more openly argued that "uniform accounting" would realise the spectre of socialism, the domination and exploitation of the individual investor by the state, the interference of "an external authority", as May now moving in the highest circles, who joined the Liberty League in 1934 (Miranti 1990, pp. 163–164), made clear. He was "convinced that under existing law investors have less to fear in the matter of financial accounts from dishonest managements or complaisant auditors than from efforts to create a system of rigid rules" (May 1937a, p. 358). The threat was that "departures ... would be permissible only upon the approval of an external authority having no interest in nor any responsibility to the investor and is quite unlikely to be permanently free from influences affecting its rulings which would have their foundations elsewhere than in the theory and practice of accounting" (May 1937a, p. 358). Allowing a governmental agency to set accounting rules opened the "danger of methods being prescribed on the basis of policy rather than principle" (May 1943,

p. 65). May repeatedly argued "uniform accounting" was impossible because, to accounting's many other aims, the appearance of dispersed stockholders had added share valuation, which prevented uniformity because economic valuation was impractical and therefore rules could produce misleading results. This balancing act, accepting accounting's relevance to economic valuation through his income statement focus, but thereby denying the practicability of uniformity, was May's major contribution to the debate, to preserving the private-sector profession and prevent government control of accounting.

After the Acts the profession promoted, "what could be called the 'accounting impossibility theorem'. Conflicting user interests made it impossible to be 'fair' to all users when preparing general-purpose financial statements. There simply was no 'right' answer to accounting questions" (Previts and Merino 1998, p. 277). When the SEC solved this theorem by choosing shareholders as the primary group the profession replied it could not formulate general principles for investors in publicly traded shares because this applied to only a minority of businesses (Previts and Merino 1998, p. 277). Within the shareholder group, May added, there was a conflict of interest between current and potential investors, between "permanent" and "speculative" investors. With the "free transferability … of shares … [f]inancial accounts … became called upon to serve a double purpose — … a purely historical report by the management to the proprietors, and, a new purpose of affording an indication to potential buyers as well as to potential sellers of the value of the shares of stock in the corporation" (1937a, p. 340). However, "The points of view and the interests of the permanent investor and the speculative operator in stocks are by no means identical, and much of the difficulty of the problem of deciding on the form of corporate reports is due to this diversity of interests" (May 1937a, p. 340). To the speculator, May accepted, a share's value depended "on what it may be expected to produce in the future"; that "Reports dealing with the past are valuable to the extent that they throw light on this probability" (May 1937a, p. 340). Roosevelt wanted to "reaffirm the primacy of private property rights and to promote economic democracy through widespread stock ownership" (Previts and Merino 1998, p. 274). To offer protection, Section 18 of the 1934 Act exposed executives "who have issued a report which is found to be misleading … to a potential liability to those who have bought or sold stock in the corporation" (May 1937a, p. 367). Therefore, May accepted that management "preparing a report has today to consider … not only its import as a historical record, but also the implications for the future which it may suggest" (1937, p. 340). However, this was "a task of no mean difficulty", in most cases was "impracticable" (May 1937a, p. 348) and therefore "dogmatic" rules were impossible (May 1932, quoted in Zeff 1972, p. 123). The "most theoretically correct concept of the income account is that charges or credits to it accrue from day to day … [i]n many … cases, however, its application is impracticable" (May 1937a, p. 348). In short, "The difficulty of attaining uniformity" was because "the income accounts are designed to serve more than one purpose, and … accounting for income is based on more than one concept" (May 1937a, p. 348). This "impossibility" attitude dominated the Acts' early implementation, but eventually led to strong SEC pushback.

Implementing the Acts

Evidence consistent with management continuing to evade accountability for several years after the Acts is that "dominant corporations … seemed capable of surviving like huge dinosaurs in the swamp of general stagnation" (Dawley 1991, p. 339). Through most of the 1930s, banks and small businesses failed in droves, "Yet virtually none of the great industrial corporations disappeared. In fact, even as profits turned into losses, corporations cannibalized assets to pay dividends" (Dawley 1991, p. 339). Dividends fell from $5.9 billion in 1929 to $2 billion in 1933, but some "now came out of reserves" (Dawley 1991, p. 339).

Solomon Fabricant found a preponderance of write-downs from 1931 to 1934 (1936, Table 5, p. 6), and judged them "conservative", that is, "not justified from an economic perspective" (Previts and Merino 1998, p. 276). In 1932, May thought the "practice … of writing down the property accounts of a corporation and correspondingly reducing the depreciation charges" was justifiable only if "the present value is carefully determined, the excess is substantial, and the management is satisfied that the level of values to which the properties are to be reduced is likely to persist" (1936, p. 95). May insisted, "It is obviously improper … to pave the way for the future inflation of earnings by deliberate understatement of present values", "the new value should be fair" (1936, p. 96). He warned, "Much embarrassment has been occasioned to companies which in the period of inflation wrote up their properties to values which have since proved to be only temporary; and it is easy today to err in the opposite direction" (May 1936, p. 96). He warned of the "danger … that assets would be unduly written down for the purpose of reducing depreciation charges to income" (May 1943, p. 95). He criticised those "corporate officials [who] have stated in recommending such readjustments of book values, that they imply no real loss to the stockholders", because it meant paying dividends out of capital (May 1937a, p. 360). He approved the annual report of Union Carbide and Carbon Corporation for 1931, which wrote off some $40 million from buildings, machinery and equipment against surplus to reduce them to "present replacement value" (May 1936, pp. 96–97). As Union Carbide explained, "Because of the decrease of approximately 21 percent in general construction costs during the past two years, the present book value of many items of property acquired, constructed or appraised during periods of high labor and materials costs exceeds the present replacement cost" (May 1936, p. 97). It wrote off $40 million against surplus, but it gave itself the opportunity to restore a "portion" by treating some of the write-down as "a provision for unidentified obsolescence" (May 1936, p. 97). Consolidated Oil Corporation stated in its annual report for 1931, "It will be noted that the balance sheet valuations of the Consolidated properties have been written down to a very conservative level", but claimed, "the stated values formerly assigned to these assets have been reduced to a figure more nearly conforming to present-day economic conditions" (Hendriksen 1970, p. 58). Consequently, as Studebaker's 1931 annual report admitted, "If a write-down of plant facilities is made, substantial savings would result … in depreciation and other charges, thereby benefiting the profits of future years" (Hendriksen 1970, p. 58). Generally, however, Daniels concluded, "Recent write-downs smack of manipulation. As they are being accounted for, not only will future income be overstated, but to the extent that reductions of capital are a concomitant of the write-down, dividends based on future income will be, in effect, capital distributions. The stockholder has a right to be appraised of the nature of such dividends" (1934, pp. 2–3).

Evidence that few companies heeded May's advice, and few accountants resisted, in 1935 Hoxsey asked the AIA for "an opinion about accounting for fixed assets, asking questions about the degree to which property should be written off; for example, should serviceable plants be written down to nominal amounts? And how should such write-offs be accounted for? The institute's response was not only delayed for a considerable period, but also the AIA decided that auditors could not take responsibility for the items Hoxsey mentioned" (Previts and Merino 1998, fn. 118, p. 460). The flexibility management had to write-down assets to nominal amounts directly to reserves could help mollify angry investors by allowing reporting operating profits to justify restoring dividends. "Conservatism justified procedures such as the write-down of fixed assets to nominal amounts, that relieved future years of significant charges to income, enabling some firms to experience a 'speedy' accounting, if not economic, recovery" (Previts and Merino 1998, p. 276). May commended Union Carbide's 1931 write-off because "the revised value was carefully ascertained …; and the amount written off was charged against a previously existing surplus" (1936, p. 98). As we shall see, it was not until 1937 that the SEC's first Accounting Series Release (ASR) banned fixed asset write-offs against capital surplus (e.g., share premiums).

Dillon (1979, 1984) replicated Fabricant's study for 110 corporations listed on the NYSE and found, with the exception of investments for 1925–1929, the same pattern, that in both periods write-downs far exceeded write-ups (1984, Table VI-8, p. 224). He found that 42 percent of firms in his sample revalued assets upwards or downwards over the period 1925–1929 by an average of 6.1 percent of total assets, with around 27 percent of firms on average revaluing in any one year (Dillon 1984, p. 225; Table VI-9, p. 226). For the sample firms, total write-downs exceeded write-ups by $123 million over the period 1925–1929, and by $544 million for 1929–1934 (Dillon 1984, Table VI-8, p. 224). Fabricant and Dillon's evidence is consistent with the hypothesis that large corporations took a "big bath" in 1931 and 1932 when they reported losses, which was why profits showed apparently healthy growth from 1934 to 1937, as did dividends, which were back to 80 percent of their 1929 peak in 1937, whereas profits had recovered to only 57 percent (Table 5.1).

How much management flattered 1930 reported profit or reduced losses from 1931 to 1933 by smoothing, or how much of the profits growth from 1933 was real, is unclear. Twentieth Century Fund found that since the 1929 Crash, "careful study of annual reports plainly indicates that the doctrines laid down by accountants and auditors themselves during the past year or two are not infrequently ignored" (1935, p. 601). It noted, "The not infrequent excessive write-down of capital assets from surplus for the purpose, implied or expressed, of relieving the income statement of future years of the burden of depreciation charges, bringing inventory down to market or cost and sometimes even lower through charges to surplus" (Twentieth Century Fund 1935, fn. 1, p. 601). It pointed to the "vigorous and sustained effort" of the NYSE since the crash "to eliminate at least the worst evils of American accounting practices" (Twentieth Century Fund 1935, p. 609), much of which showed

Table 5.1: Profits and Dividends 1929–1938

	Corporate profits after tax	Dividends	Undistributed profits
Year	**$m**	**$m**	**$m**
1929	8,259	5,813	2,446
1930	2,480	5,490	−3,101
1931	−1,278	4,088	−5,366
1932	−3,402	2,565	−5,967
1933	−370	2,056	−2,426
1934	972	2,587	−1,615
1935	2,194	2,863	−669
1936	4,331	4,548	−217
1937	4,733	4,685	48
1938	2,271	3,187	−916

Source: Baran and Sweezy (1968, Table 13, p. 238).

continuing lack of accountability. It had "endeavoured to persuade corporate and public accountants" not to change depreciation "rates except where careful study indicates a basis for such change, quite apart from the earnings of any particular period. The fact appears to be, however, that … many corporations continue to vary their depreciation policy with their earnings from year to year" (Twentieth Century Fund 1935, pp. 606–607). It tried to stop them "charging against surplus an undue portion of the plant values for the purpose of avoiding or reducing the weight of charges against income statements in respect of depreciation in future years" (Twentieth Century Fund 1935, p. 607). It had persuaded them to stop charging cash dividends against the capital surplus, and the "practice once rather widely in vogue of treating the earned surplus of a subsidiary at the time of acquisition as part of the earned surplus of the parent company", but was less successful in stopping inventory charge-offs against capital surplus (Twentieth Century Fund 1935, pp. 607–608). The NYSE was also less successful in persuading corporations to desist from taking "profits" on reacquiring a corporation's own stock or resale (Twentieth Century Fund 1935, p. 608). The NYSE "did take a stand against writing off unamortized bond discount and expense against capital surplus" (Twentieth Century Fund 1935, p. 607). However, management could boost profits by for example swapping low interest debt for existing high interest debt and charging the costs of redemption to the earned or capital surplus or absorbing a deficit through "quasi-reorganization" (May 1943, p. 50).

From 1934, management reported increased earnings and found the cash and reserves to pay increasing dividends. Some came from customers as big corporations continued to administer their prices, and unable to raise more capital, they conserved cash by slashing investment "from 16 percent of GNP in 1929 to a mere 2 percent in 1932", from $16.2 billion in 1928 to $800 million in 1932 (Dawley 1991, p. 339; McElvaine 2009, p. 73). Construction expenditure fell by 78 percent over the same period (McElvaine 2009, p. 75). Management closed few plants, preferring to run below capacity, utilisation falling to 42 percent in 1932 before climbing to 83 percent in 1937, still below the average for the 1920s, before falling back to 60 percent in 1938 (Baran and Sweezy 1968, Table 11, p. 232; Table 12, p. 237). Tugwell observed, "It is well known ... that nearly every industry is overequipped with plants, machinery and other material to meet any demand it may legitimately expect", "sometimes twice as much" (1933, pp. 137, 203). Instead, management cut labour costs by shedding jobs, using short time working, and cutting wages (Dawley 1991, p. 350).

Accountants would not enforce management's accountability, and neither at first would the SEC. To appease the "financial community", Roosevelt appointed Joseph P. Kennedy as the SEC's first chairperson when it "faced ... serious opposition from both accountants and businesspeople to the concept of 'uniformity', the SEC opted for the far less controversial concept of full disclosure" (Previts and Merino 1998, p. 274). A still popular view is that by 1936 the SEC had "by the language of its regulations, lent support to the view ... that it is not the business of accountants to reflect the 'value' of properties and plant" (Sanders 1936, p. 72). Watts (2003, p. 217), for example, claims there was a "political backlash against *ex post* overvaluations ... experienced by the early SEC commissioners after the 1929 stock market crash ... who, in response, banned upward revaluations". In fact, Sanders pointed out, "A careful study of the Commission's regulations will show that ... a good deal of latitude will be allowed" (1936, p. 72). No retrospective adjustments were required. "With the assistance of Professor Sanders and the American Institute, the SEC wrote off much of the past and allowed corporations abundant accounting flexibility in the future" (Parrish 1970, p. 205). The "Commission initially accepted the propriety of reporting engineering appraisals in registration statements", in other words, during the first few years the "Commission accepted the use of write-ups and the disclosure of current values" (Walker 1992, pp. 11, 13). For example, in the Northern States Power case, the commission voted 3 to 2 "to accept a registration statement that contained unacceptable write-ups, but the commission decided that disclosure was sufficient" (Previts and Merino 1998, fn. 103, p. 458). This was consistent with the SEC pursuing a general policy that left the content of accounting reports to the profession but required disclosure. The profession, however, resisted even this.

The Committee on Cooperation criticised the SEC for allowing "too few confidentiality exceptions" to protect "competitive advantage", claimed disclosure benefited speculators, and objected to disclosure of sales, gross profit, and the salaries of officers and employees (Previts and Merino 1998, p. 279). It worked, perhaps too hard, to convince SEC lawyers and economists they had "less than a perfect understanding of accounting and auditing", resisting those "tempted to write a rule book establishing uniform accounting.... The Institute committee kept pointing out the hazards of such an approach" (Carey 1979, pp. 35–36). However, realising the profession would not voluntarily act against management, eventually losing patience, in 1937 the SEC changed policy, decided to use its power to set the method for write-downs, and to force accountants to formulate and enforce "generally accepted accounting principles".

The SEC's Change of Policy

During 1935, the SEC's attitude towards accountants remained "conciliatory", it "seemed friendly, tolerant and flexible" (Carey 1969a, pp. 195, 199–200; Miranti 1990, p. 153). The AIA worked with the SEC on filing forms and audit qualification wordings (Miranti 1990, pp. 154–155). However, by the end of 1935 the "era of good feeling" had closed (Miranti 1990, p. 157). By the end of 1936, "The AIA's disclaimers and the practitioners' apparent allegiance to the clients (managers) [had] upset the more proactive commissioners" (Previts and Merino 1998, p. 279), such as Landis who now spoke "of accountants in less endearing terms" (Carey 1969a, p. 201). In December 1936, Carey recalled, "in a speech to the Investment Bankers Associations, [Landis] delivered this wintry blast: 'The choice here of more or less regulation is an open one for the profession. It is a "Hobson's choice" for government'. This threat, without prior warning, was a shock" (Carey 1979, p. 36). Carman Blough, the SEC's first chief accountant began referring major accounting questions with which the SEC took "issue with the accountants who had signed the statements", for discussion with senior technical partners in the large accounting firms, and to the Institute's committee, searching for "best practice" (Carey 1969a, p. 201; Zeff 1972, p. 130). His discovery of "the great diversity of practices used by companies and approved by their auditors in the 1930s led Blough to wonder how … 'general accepted accounting principles' might be ascertained" (Zeff 1972, p. 130). Because "the need to reduce the number and variety of these practices was urgent" (Zeff 1972, p. 130), Blough sought the cooperation of the Institute, the American Accounting Association (AAA) and others. However, on 1 April 1937, after mounting criticism "of the profession's inability or unwillingness to standardize accounting principles" (Zeff 1972, p. 132), the SEC abruptly changed policy, announced it would regulate the content as well as disclosure and the form of accounts (Walker 1992, pp. 15, 17). In ASR 1 the SEC announced "a program for the publication, from time to time, of opinions on accounting principles for the purpose of contributing to the development of uniform standards and practice in major accounting questions" (*Journal of Accountancy* May 1937a, p. 328).

ASR 1 began as a proposed letter "to a corporation indicating that write-downs of plant and equipment should be charged against earned rather than capital surplus" (Walker 1992, p. 16). The SEC issued it because, as Blough said, after reviewing hundreds of financial statements, "apart from the simple rules of double entry bookkeeping, there are very few principles of accounting on which the accountants of this country agree" (Zeff 1972, p. 132). In October 1937, Blough made clear, "if the profession did not reduce areas of difference in accounting practices, the Commission would" (Zeff 1972, p. 132). However, "the AIA was able to parry these attacks successfully and retain private-sector standards" because Blough nevertheless "resisted the demands from the SEC's lawyers for 'uniform accounting'" (Previts and Merino 1998, pp. 279–280; fn. 125, p. 461). The SEC changed policy, but May's interpretation framed it: "By May 1937, May was able to announce that the determination of income 'is now generally recognized as the most important single problem in the field of financial accounting'. The period of mourning for the balance sheet was over" (Gilman 1939, p. 36). Underlying Blough's (1939, pp. 162–163) thinking was May's interpretation: "Securities do not sell and investment judgments are not made on the basis of what has happened in the past except as those events throw light on what may happen in the future". Blough's "recommendations became more and more influential. The SEC dropped the idea of issuing a rule book, for the time being at least" (Carey 1979, p. 37). Academics, accountants and analysts "agreed that the income statement is much more significant and informative to the investor than the balance sheet", was "of cardinal importance, because the 'value' of a business depends, not on the historical costs incurred in the process of building it up, but upon its earning capacity" (Kaplan and Reaugh 1938, p. 206). Professionals accepted "The New Emphasis on Profits", "a fundamental change in … viewpoint", that "Within the last few years … emphasis has shifted somewhat to the profit and loss" (Gilman 1939, p. 25).

May's interpretation had done its work. "By the end of the 1930s, the NYSE, the SEC, and CPAs had come to the view that investors were primarily interested in 'future income' and the income statement must be the focal point of accounting" (Previts and Merino 1998, p. 276), and "Mr. May was respected by most practitioners as the profession's philosopher, planner and strategist" (Carey 1969b, p. 3). To Paton (1981, pp. 91–92), by contrast, probably resenting May's criticisms of textbook writers, he "was a very conceited Englishman", whose "high level of self esteem" was a "major fault". Nevertheless, having "impressed" the SEC "with the difficulty of prescribing uniform standards", which had exercised its power to "prescribe accounting rules … with restraint, and judiciously", May could claim credit that "in spite of all the tensions … corporate accounting and professional auditing remain[ed] in the private-sector" (1943, p. 66; Carey 1969a, p. 202). By providing "a logical and persuasive statement of the nature of corporate accounting, the responsibilities of independent auditors, and the manner in which safeguards might be established against the issuance of misleading financial statements" (Carey 1969b, p. 5; Vangermeersch 1996, p. 597), he played a vital role in saving capitalism. The SEC accomplished more in a month than "years of futile committee work within the professional societies have not been able to produce or begin to produce", but concluding that the "SEC's strategy of using accountants to serve its own ends has been successful" (McCraw 1984, p. 191) oversimplifies because May's interpretation defined the SEC's "own ends". Miranti's (1990, p. 147) view that "The AIA played a minor role in the public debate over the New Deal's securities market legislation", is therefore also an oversimplification.

Why did the SEC change policy in early 1937? Discovering many methods was hardly news. More plausibly, Chapter 6 argues, was the economic and political context. Despite the profession's resistance and the

SEC's initial acquiescence, powerful forces, aggrieved investors and Wall Street's demand for "people's capitalism" to finance growth, pushed for "greater uniformity", requiring the SEC to shift towards British principles in the late-1930s as dwindling share ownership and share issues showed "investor confidence" remained low, putting the SEC under pressure to restore it (Bernstein 1987). Following the crash investors took managements and accountants to court over accounting practices and having previously faced judicial indifference, in the late-1930s won legal support for "greater uniformity" and the opportunity to sue accountants for "gross negligence tantamount to fraud" (Previts and Merino 1998, p. 272). During the 1920s, a lenient legal attitude to management control of accounting and a large increase in accountants who "survived through providing consultancy and tax services to their clients", meant, "the profession's obligation to third parties had been obscured. A series of court decisions in the 1930s forcefully reminded CPAs of this obligation" (Previts and Merino 1998, p. 272). Commissioner Judge Robert Healy warned of the danger in an address to the AIA in late 1937, which "aroused considerable comment in professional circles" (Barr 1940, p. 91). Healy described "a number of situations in which disclosure of improper accounting practices of registrants was acquiesced in by the certifying accountants, but since there was a full disclosure of the procedures followed the statements were accepted" (Barr 1940, p. 91). Now "if an earnings statement and a balance sheet reflected the results of improper accounting, they amounted to misrepresentation or misleading statements in violation of the Securities Act, and … should not have been accepted even though disclosure had been made" (Barr 1940, p. 91).

In 1938, the SEC issued ASR 4, Administrative Policy on Financial Statements, "which would recognize standards used by private-sector accountants", but "some commissioners continued to threaten that the SEC might withdraw this acknowledgement" (Previts and Merino 1998, p. 279). Commissioner Mathews thought, "Despite encouraging developments", management still unduly influenced accountants, which "operate[d] to handicap both independent growth and development of accounting principle and wholly independent reporting. Servitudes, less tangible and influential than earlier servitudes, though no less real, still exist" (1938, p. 230). To free them, Commissioner Barr argued, required "accounting research": "Reduced to its essentials this release [ASR 4] says that the accounting principles followed must have authoritative support.… It is in the controversial field suggested by this release that extensive accounting research is necessary" (1940, pp. 91–92). Responding to pressures, in 1939 under May's guidance the CAP began writing Accounting Research Bulletins based on "stewardship", realisation, matching and HC, and Paton and Littleton (1940), now CAP members, influentially rationalised the shift. The CAP cleaned-up most of the 1920s mess by 1950. The profession's existential crisis was over, but as the rate of profit fell from the mid-1950s, its problems as a private-sector accounting regulator multiplied as management retained discretion and used it.

Concluding Comments

American capitalism survived the Great Crash and Depression, as did much of its production capacity that World War II brought back into use. Whatever lay ahead, accountants "had withstood the threat of loss of professional autonomy" (Previts and Merino 1998, p. 271). Public accountancy had statutory recognition and the demand for accountants soared, the number of CPAs increasing from 192,000 in 1930 to 238,000 in 1940 (McCraw 1984, fn. 70, p. 351). Through the 1930s, nevertheless, "corporate managements retained broad discretion to chose among alternative accounting principles" (Seligman 1982, p. 48), "continued to have great flexibility" (Previts and Merino 1998, p. 271). To deflect criticism from accountants, during the early-1930s, "there would be an effort to divorce accounting from economic theory on 'practical' grounds", and from the later-1930s the work of "valuation theorists" was "ignored" (Previts and Merino 1998, p. 269). In 1936, May accepted, "in the 1920s, accountants fell from grace and took to adjusting capital values on the books … to an extent never before attempted", but in addition to "unsound laws" and a "widespread if unfounded belief in the new order of things", argued, "In extenuation they might [also] plead … unpractical economics" (Previts and Merino 1998, p. 269). May's interpretation explains why, despite this, although "The passage of securities legislation should have changed relationships between accountants and management … [i]t did not" (Previts and Merino 1998, p. 271). To Previts and Merino it was "because the stated objectives of the legislation — to curb managerial power, to promulgate uniform reporting rules, and to provide information that was useful to investors for decision-making — were not implemented" (1998, p. 271). Legislators pursued these aims, but even radical reformers could not escape Fisher's framing. Previts and Merino conclude, "In many respects securities legislation appeared to be symbolic, its primary purpose being to mollify public concern", "a conservative reform, designed to restore public confidence in the economic system" (1998, pp. 271, 273). The legislation possibly mollified middle class investors (Previts and Merino 1998, p. 274), but did not restore "public confidence". It "conferred upon CPAs a legally defined social obligation to assist in creating and sustaining investor confidence in the public capital markets" (Previts and Merino 1998, p. 274), which to the late-1930s they resisted. There was little confidence in economic prospects, which prevented raising capital for growing industries (Bernstein 1987), but also in management's accountability, a problem Littleton highlighted in 1928, which the SEC forced the profession to address only from 1937. Further weakening confidence, militant unions became interested in accounts, demanded a "fair share" of profit and that management "open the books" (Bryer 2016).

The SEC responded in 1937 to the contradictory pressures from capital and labour by requiring the profession to develop GAAP, shifting towards British conservatism to meet investors' inchoate demand for "stewardship", and American "conservatism" to defeat unions, Chapter 6 argues, both necessary for investor "confidence". British "conservatism" would increase management's accountability, but American conservatism and Fisher's theory that justified it would help defeat "organized labor" (Bryer 2016), both necessary, but contradictory elements in re-creating "people's capitalism". Under pressure from academics and the SEC, led by May, in 1939 the profession began writing "research bulletins" based on HC and "stewardship". However, May's acceptance of earning capacity's valuation role and Paton's commitment to valuation meant the shift towards British principles was superficial. By the late-1950s, the CAP's failure to curb management's discretion had undermined its credibility and May's and Paton and Littleton's interpretation, leading to its replacement by the APB, which prompted an intensified search for a theory to meet the demand for GAAP. May saved capitalism, but gave management discretion that it again abused. Because this threatened "people's capitalism" and the profession, with help from a new-generation of theorists it overthrew May's interpretation in the late-1960s by fully embracing Fisher's theory, which revived from the late-1950s, gained professional support, and Chapter 7 argues underlies the FASB's conceptual framework, which Chapter 8 argues facilitated the GFC.

Chapter 6

"People's Capitalism" and the Rise and Fall of GAAP

A falling rate of profit, Marx argued, increases capitalists and management's propensity to "swindling", including manipulating accounts, which this and following chapters argue provides an important context in which to understand the pressure on the profession to limit discretion through accounting regulation, and management's resistance. The rate of profit increased from the early-1940s to historical highs by early-1950s, the beginning of a Golden Age, but it fell in the mid-1950s, and fell steeply from the mid-1960s to low levels during the "profitability crisis" of the 1970s and 1980s, and continued at low levels to the 2008–2009 GFC (Kliman 2012, Figure 5.1, p. 76; Roberts 2016, Figure 1.4, p. 22). The history of accounting regulation reflected these trends, becoming more urgent and more difficult as the rate of profit fell, but it also reflects the perverse influence of Fisher's theory, that justified management discretion, and yet as problems increased theorists saw it as the means for reducing discretion.

In 1929, American accounting notionally had two objectives (Daines 1929), but in practice economic valuation had eclipsed stewardship (Bryer 2021a, pp. 388–404). From the mid-1930s, the chapter argues, the SEC and academics, and the profession from the late-1930s, sought to revive investor confidence in accounting, to promote what became by the 1950s a vision of "people's capitalism", by reviving "stewardship" based on HC, and began searching for GAAP to constrain management discretion. However, Fisher's continuing implicit influence meant accounting, in effect, retained two objectives, "stewardship" and economic valuation, and management retained discretion, which allowed increased manipulations from the mid-1950s as the rate of profit fell, and from the late-1950s explicit interest in Fisher's accounting theory revived. With Fisher's intellectual credentials re-established, from the mid-1960s as the rate of profit fell steeply and management's propensity to engage in "swindling" intensified, his accounting theory became influential as academics and ultimately the FASB sought, in effect, to use it to limit management's discretion, which failed, following chapters argue, during the "profitability crisis", and facilitated the GFC.

The chapter first outlines accounting regulation history in the context of "people's capitalism" and a falling rate of profit, which this and following chapters examine in detail. Second, it analyses the search for GAAP, by the AAA, the AIA and SEC, and its culmination in Paton and Littleton's (1940) influential *Introduction to Corporate Accounting Standards* and G.O. May's *Financial Accounting: A Distillation of Experience* (1943) based on his articles and lectures from 1936, using Marxian accounting as the benchmark. This, it argues, reveals the limits imposed on the revival of "stewardship" by Paton's economic entity concept, the continuing implicit commitment to economic valuation, and the discretion this left management. Management's manipulations, the chapter concludes, explain the failures of the CAP in 1959, and the APB following the profession's 1960s crisis, which led to the Wheat and Trueblood Committees in 1971, the FASB's creation in 1973, and its "conceptual framework" that sought "fundamental truths". The profession eventually overthrew May's compromise and Paton and Littleton's articulation because it left management discretion that it used in its own interests, which threatened "people's capitalism" and the profession's "remarkable economic success story … in the 1960s" (Burton 1971, p. 47), its now lucrative business. The profession's drive for intellectual leadership and ideological hegemony, however, framed by Fisher's theory, Chapter 7 argues, meant the overt power the FASB's framework took away from management it covertly gave back, which Chapter 8 argues allowed banks to account for securitization SPEs off-balance sheet, facilitating the 2008–2009 GFC.

"People's Capitalism", Accounting Regulation and the Rate of Profit

During the 1920s, to stave off the threat of government regulation the NYSE began promoting "universal stock ownership" (Ott 2009, p. 44). It became "the self-styled 'people's market' [that] promulgated an ideology of shareholder democracy … [and] recast the corporation as a democracy of shareholders, the United States as a nation of stock owners, and the stock market as both an analogue and an instrument of political democracy and economic justice" (Ott 2009, p. 44). Fostering widespread share ownership had been an element of the first New Deal. However, continuing mistrust of stock markets and accounting, and low rates of profit during the 1930s, meant "people's capitalism" became an important theme only in post-war ideology, and in NYSE public relations from the mid-1950s (Perlo 1958, p. 333; Ott 2009, p. 70). From the end of World War II, America began an unprecedented economic expansion to the 1970s (Lichtenstein *et al.* 2000, p. 570), based on high rates of profit, which required "people's capitalism" to finance it, which required that capitalists initially restrain their consumption. As Carey put it, "Industry needed massive amounts of capital to expand plants and equipment", and "The best way to raise that capital was … by encouraging investment in common stocks by people of moderate means" (1969b, p. 57), but insiders recognised that widespread ownership "need not be regarded as the most essential part of a people's capitalism" (Perlo 1958, p. 333). From the mid-1950s "Under the banner of 'people's capitalism', the stock exchanges actively promoted such investment" (Carey 1969b, p. 57), but its promotion began in the late-1930s when the SEC pushed accountants to play their part.

By the late-1950s, "It ha[d] become the fashion to classify the economy of the United States as a new form, 'People's Capitalism'", an "expression … developed by the Advertising Council" in 1956, "which prepared a 'People's Capitalism' exhibit, shown internationally under the auspices of the United States Information Agency" (Perlo 1958, p. 333). The Cold War against "Marxist–Leninist dogma" began in 1946 (Lichtenstein 2000, pp. 548–549), and in the mid-1950s corporations used "people's capitalism" as part of the Great Free-Enterprise Campaign against worker militancy (Bryer 2016), and by the late-1950s, "The term is accepted by publicists and widely propagated in corporation reports and advertisements" (Perlo 1958, p. 333). In 1957, General Electric, for example, published a full-page advertisement: "People's Capitalism: The 376,000 owners with savings invested in General Electric are typical of America, where nearly every citizen is a capitalist" (Perlo 1958, p. 334). Standard Oil Company (N.J.) "tells its employees that Karl Marx … 'devised a theory ... [in which] [o]wnership of the mills, as with ownership of the land, was the key to the future. Ownership should, therefore, be vested not in the hands of the few, but with something he identified as

The People. Today, says Standard Oil, this is realized in the United States: Yes, the people own the tools of production.... By his own definition, Karl Marx's prophecy has been realized.... How odd to find that it is here, in the capitalism he reviled, that the promise of the tools has been fulfilled'" (Perlo 1958, p. 334).

"People's Capitalism" was an element of Cold War propaganda, but it reflected America's need to rebuild its capital market, regain the trust of wealthy, well-to-do and middle class investors, to reconstruct total social capital. America had around 4 million stockholders in 1940, dominated by "a heavy concentration of holdings in the hands of a relatively few wealthy people and institutions", which had increased to 7 million by 1952, but leapt to 17 million by 1962, to 20 million by 1965, and 24 million by 1968, "with no sign of faltering" (Carey 1969b, p. 58). This meant, "a large [sic] proportion of the American people had a direct or an indirect stake in the stock market", which increased from c3 percent in 1940 to c12 percent [24 million/200 million] by 1968, which was "unparalleled" (Carey 1969b, p. 58; Lichtenstein *et al.* 2000, p. A16). As "Private investment decisions became a matter of national importance", and as investors used the "traditional formula for valuing common stocks" of applying a multiple to earnings per share, so "the net income figures ... audited by certified public accountants, became a matter of national importance" (Carey 1969b, p. 59). From the late-1930s, to restore investor confidence, to promote what became "people's capitalism", the "accounting principles" used to calculate net income "attracted more attention from the general public and its spokesman, the press, than ever before in the history of the accounting profession" (Carey 1969b, p. 59). Given the 1920s experience, unsurprisingly, the "emphasis in most discussions ... was on 'uniformity'", a term accountants preferred to avoid, eventually accepting the need for "comparability" (Carey 1969b, p. 59).

After the SEC issued ASR 4 in 1937 requiring principles with "substantial authoritative support", the profession came under pressure to clean up the "big mess" inherited from the 1920s (Chapter 5). The CAP's mission "might have been described in 1939 as bringing order out of chaos" (Storey and Storey 1998, p. 15; Carey 1969b, p. 84), and the AIA responded by expanding its membership, and the AAA published Paton and Littleton's *Introduction to Corporate Accounting Standards* in 1940. Under May's direction as vice-chair and "guiding spirit", with Paton and Littleton on board, with high rates of profit lessening management's resistance, and closely cooperating with the SEC, "Most of the questionable practices in evidence in 1938 had completely disappeared by the early 1950s" (Carey 1969b, p. 88; Storey and Storey 1998, p. 30). This generation of accountants and theorists, who witnessed the 1929 crash and the depression, saw investors' wrath and the SEC's threats in the late-1930s, turned in the 1940s and 1950s to emphasise "stewardship" based on HCA. Accounting, however, retained two objectives, "stewardship" and an implicit commitment to economic valuation. Still framed by Fisher's theory, studiously avoiding any "cost theory of value", caught between inchoate demands for "stewardship" and commitments to economic valuation, unsurprisingly, neither May, Paton and Littleton, or the CAP resolved any fundamental problems. New problems proliferated as management, with unquestioned ideological hegemony, responded to the falling rate of profit from the mid-1950s, and opportunities for enrichment offered by a buoyant stock market, by manipulating accounts. The profession came under pressure from the SEC, financial analysts, the financial press, academics, and some leading professionals, to reduce the variety of methods, but management resisted any "uniformity". By the late-1950s, critics were dissatisfied with the CAP, which lost credibility as a source of GAAP to reduce management's discretion. In 1959, the profession replaced the CAP with the APB with more resources for "research" to produce a consistent body of GAAP, which opened the door to a revival of Fisher's accounting theory.

As accounting's role in "people's capitalism" became a national issue during the later-1950s academics, particularly at the University of Chicago, rehabilitated Fisher's reputation, and a new generation of theorists came to see the solution to the profession's problems as embracing his theory and overthrowing May's interpretation and Paton and Littleton's articulation. To deal with increasingly well-publicised criticism, the new generation saw their challenge as operationalising Fisher's theory to eliminate alternative methods in a theoretically rigorous way that management could not resist. These theorists took up Paton's and Canning's work, openly acknowledging their debt to Fisher, dubbed the "normative apriorists" (Mouck 1995, p. 55), a school that peaked in the 1960s and early-1970s that argued for "current value accounting" in various forms (e.g., Edwards and Bell 1961; Staubus 1961; Mattessich 1964; Chambers 1966; Sterling 1970). According to the AAA, "To a significant degree, they may have been influenced by the neoclassical economic theory of the firm" (1977, p. 6). In fact, as Flegm concluded, "the advocates for a change from the historical cost base, both past and present, have concentrated on the data needed to make an investment decision in a given situation based on an economists' view of income", noting "Irving Fisher was the first to attempt to rationalize accounting and economics" (1984, p. 184). They were "never able to agree on the details … or even indeed the general outline of such a theory" (Mouck 1995, p. 63), which led to "decision-usefulness", the "information perspective" that integrated accounting as "information" into Fisher's theory that financial markets equalised preferences for borrowing and lending (Mouck 1995, p. 65). It revived Paton and Canning's view of accounting as economic "statistics", which the profession's leaders and the SEC ultimately accepted. In the early-1960s, however, the SEC rebuffed the APB's attempt to operationalise Fisher's theory as "value in exchange", or "exit prices" (Moonitz 1961; Sprouse and Moonitz 1962), as a dangerously radical departure from practice based on HC. Management resisted the APB's attempts to limit its right to control the accounts. Rising to the challenge, by the mid-1960s, academics and some leading professionals effectively buried "stewardship" by agreeing it meant "decision-usefulness" for "investors", for stockholders and creditors, which they argued was the overriding objective. In 1966, an AAA committee "issued an influential report in which it advocated this 'decision usefulness' approach" (Zeff 2013, p. 89).

During the 1960s and 1970s, whereas the HC rate of profit was trendless, after accounting for "inflation", particularly using "current cost", the rate of profit continued to fall (Kliman 2012, pp. 77, 111, 120; Roberts 2016, p. 22), but management clung to HCA, and continued to resist any erosion of its discretion. Having repeatedly backed-down to management, by the late-1960s the APB had also lost legitimacy, and the AAA's decision-usefulness approach was "carried forward in 1973 by the report of the American Institute of CPAs' Trueblood Committee" (Zeff 2013, p. 89). The AICPA replaced the APB with the FASB in 1973 that used "decision-usefulness" to overthrow May's and Paton and Littleton's "revenue-expense" accounting and write a "conceptual framework". Management's determination to maintain its discretion had eventually pushed the profession into embracing Fisher's theory to mount a war that management could not win, but from which it eventually understood it had nothing to fear. This was a war between so-called "inductivists", who followed May in claiming to derive general principles from practice, which gave management discretion, and "deductivists" who wanted the profession to dictate practice with theory, concluding "that a foundation of fundamental premises ('concepts') necessarily underlies and determines sound practice" (Storey and Storey 1998, p. 1). Looking back over its history, the FASB claimed, "The latter view has been the source of significant advances ... and for more than twenty years has affected financial accounting standards and practice through the FASB's conceptual framework" (Storey and Storey 1998, p. i). It admitted, "accounting practice, however, has continued to be dominated by the former view" (Storey and Storey 1998, p. i), which Chapter 7 argues is because within the framework management retains ideological hegemony and accounting choice.

The view overthrown — the first view — May's "inductive" approach to principles, we will see, was not devoid of theoretical commitments. GAAP, May argued, were a "distillation of experience" (Storey and Storey 1998, p. 3), which management used to choose methods to reflect its estimate of "earning capacity", on which "the value of a business ... mainly ... depended" (Storey and Storey 1998, p. 11). The balance sheet was "to a large extent historical and conventional, largely comprising the residual amounts of expenditures or receipts after first determining the proper charge or credit to the income account for the year" (Storey and Storey 1998, p. 11). Therefore, it "did not ... represent an attempt to show the present values of the assets and liabilities ...; and ... because financial accounting and reporting was necessarily conventional, some variety in accounting methods was inevitable" (Storey and Storey 1998, p. 11). In May's scheme, management chose the methods, but disclosed them, accountants would say whether they were consistent with GAAP, and whether management had applied them consistently. After the experiences of the 1920s and 1930s May was adamant that "accounting rules and principles are founded not on abstract theories or logic, but on utility" (1942, p. 35). The second view was the revival of Fisher's deductive approach that overthrew the "inductive" approach to break management's overt control over accounting that threatened the development of "people's capitalism" and accountants' incomes by weakening the profession's credibility. However, the core concepts of the "asset-liability" approach it produced, Chapter 7 argues, meant management retained control. Chapter 8 explores one of the consequences.

The Search for "Generally Accepted Accounting Principles"

By the mid-1930s, the major challenge facing the profession was clear, as was its reluctance to confront it. Howard C. Greer, president of the

American Association of University Instructors in Accounting (AAUIA) in 1932, recollected, "it had become apparent to almost everyone that the public no longer would accept the philosophy that each company could establish its own accounting principles, and ... auditors were responsible merely for certifying that its practices were consistent" (1956, p. 6). To the SEC and academics the "need for a formal 'code' or principles and practice had become abundantly clear", but given the profession's resistance, the "problem was how to get it written and adopted" (Greer 1956, p. 6). In 1934, Eric K. Kohler, editor of *The Accounting Review* and a practitioner saw a "nervous profession": "Under the spell of rumored drastic regulations of the federal Securities and Exchange Commission, professional accountants are exhibiting a bad case of nerves. Many damage suits against leading firms of practitioners are already in the courts, and reports of more and larger suits are rife" (1934, p. 334). Kohler criticised the profession for "failing to play an active role in developing accounting principles" (Zeff 1972, p. 131). As the "profession is either unwilling or incapable of doing any straightforward thinking on its own behalf", Kohler (1934, p. 334) asked AAUIA members, "Is it impossible for us ... as accountants ... to take any initial responsibility for defining our accountability to the business and financial world and to the investing public?" Should they, he suggested, "begin to engage in the kind of research that had been assumed to come exclusively within the province of the practitioners' organization" (Zeff 1966, p. 37). Kohler, a persistent critic of the profession's failure to curb bad practice, saw in its denial that "standards" were possible the origin of its tarnished image. "The Editor ... has quoted ... statements from leading members of the profession in which the possibility of devising standards of procedure has been vigorously denied" because " 'The accountant's judgment must not be hampered ...'. To the Editor this has always meant and still means no more than that the accountant must be sufficiently pliable to meet the demands of new clients and the new demands of old" (Kohler 1934, p. 334).

In 1935, to the profession's dismay, seizing the opportunity, "anxious to raise their status by promoting research aimed at solving major social problems", lead by Paton, a group of academics formed the AAA, dedicated to the "development of principles for financial reporting to help a demoralized investing public" (Miranti 1990, p. 156; Zeff 1966, pp. 33–34). In December 1935, the AAUIA merged into the AAA with one class of membership, allowing in practitioners (Zeff 1966, pp. 36, 38). In January 1936, Commissioner Mathews discussed with the AAA's executive committee the SEC's "concerns about accounting practice", recited "a list of unanswered question on accounting policy, and asserted the need for an authoritative literature for use by governmental agencies" (Zeff 1966, pp. 30–34, 38–41; 1972, p. 131). In March 1936, the AAA published its "Statement of its Objectives" (1936a, p. 1). These were to "encourage and sponsor research in accounting", to "develop accounting principles and standards, and to seek their endorsement or adoption by business enterprises, public and private accountants, and governmental bodies", and "promote studies of accounting as an agency of control of business enterprise and economic affairs in general" (AAA 1936a, p. 1). The need was clear: "After a quarter-century and more of active discussion and experimentation in this country, many of the simplest and most fundamental problems of accounting remain without an accepted solution. There is still no authoritative statement of essential principles" (AAA 1936a, p. 1). This had given "public accountants ... an almost impossible task. They have been asked to certify to the correctness and adequacy of accounting statements, when no satisfactory criteria of correctness and adequacy have been agreed to", which were necessary to remove the accountant from "this anomalous position" (AAA 1936a, p. 1). To find them the statement accepted, "It is impossible now to escape the social implications of large-scale business enterprise", that its "affairs are matters of public, as well as private, concern" (AAA 1936a, p. 1). Dangling the threat of socialism, "Public accounting must, therefore, assume a full responsibility for the preparation of sound and informative reports on the operations of business, or await the time when the alternative of rigid governmental control of such matters will become an established fact" (AAA 1936a, p. 1).

In June 1936, after several months of intense research and discussion, led by Kohler, Paton, Littleton and Greer, the AAA published "A Tentative Statement of Accounting Principles Affecting Corporate Reports" (Zeff 1972, p. 131; 1966, pp. 40–41). For accounting's objective, "The basic assumption made here is that ... the purpose of the statements is the expression, in financial terms, of the utilization of the economic resources of the enterprise and the resultant changes in and position of creditors and investors" (AAA 1936, p. 188), consistent with stewardship or economic valuation. The Statement did not expand on "the purpose", but denied accounting was "essentially a process of valuation" (AAA 1936, p. 188), which left open the possibility of two objectives, that accounting was also "not essentially" a stewardship process. Accounting, it suggested, should not focus on the balance sheet, but consistent with May's earning capacity theory, was a process of "allocating historical costs and revenues to the current and succeeding fiscal periods" (AAA 1936, p. 188), and should therefore focus on the income statement. Zeff suggests, "It is not at all clear how the committee reached the conclusion that historical costs should govern accounting. Perhaps the implication was that the committee saw accounting as a stewardship function, but they did not use this terminology" (2013, p. 270). Kohler and Littleton, however, "were supporters of the stewardship view, coupled with strict historical cost accounting", and "while Paton favoured the use of current values" (Zeff 2013, fn. 14, p. 315), he also accepted HC as an implicit PV estimate (Bryer 2021a, Chapter 7). As Zeff says, "This difference may not have led to easy discussions within the committee" (2013, fn. 14, p. 315), with Paton defending economic valuation, and Littleton stewardship, which underlay the statement's compromises and, according to Marxian accounting, its weaknesses.

The SEC "was seeking to achieve a greater degree of uniformity" (Zeff 1966, p. 40), which the statement accepted, but left open what it meant. "Every corporate report should be based on accounting principles which are sufficiently uniform and well understood to justify the forming of opinions as to the condition and progress of the business enterprise behind it" (AAA 1936b, p. 187). The statement suggested, "it should … be possible to agree upon a foundation of underlying considerations which will tend to eliminate random variations in accounting procedure" (AAA 1936b, p. 188). That is, changes "resulting not from the peculiarities of individual enterprises, but rather from the varying ideas of financiers and corporate executives as to what will be expedient, plausible, or persuasive to investors" (AAA 1936b, p. 188), from management's discretion. To control it, the statement accepted, required a "single coordinated body of accounting theory", but unable to agree what that was it merely "attempted to set forth some of the bases upon which accounting statements rest; it has not tried to establish the postulates of all accounting theory" (AAA 1936b, p. 187). Rather than theory, the committee offered "a tentative statement of certain basic propositions of accounting which embody standards of adequacy and reasonableness in the presentation of corporate financial statements" (AAA 1936b, p. 188), derived from well-known criticisms of 1920s accounting. "In most instances these principles represent levels of accounting practice departures from which now are viewed with concern by many practitioners and financial analysts" (AAA 1936b, p. 188).

Responding by implicitly adopting a "stewardship" objective, the statement focused on egregious departures, or "difficulties" concerning "Costs and values", "Measurement of income" and "Capital and surplus" (AAA 1936b, p. 187), issues where "business managements as well as public accountants have traditionally permitted themselves much freedom of action" (AAA 1936b, p. 188). The statement admitted it was not a "scholarly inquiry", but a "declaration", a normative statement of "principles that should underlie corporate financial reports" (Zeff 1966, p. 41). It "hoped" to "arouse discussion [so] … a more comprehensive formulation [would] develop" (Zeff 1966, p. 42).

The primary valuation basis should be "cost". For "physical assets" the question was "what part of original cost should be written off to reflect consumed, expired, or lost usefulness, and what part should be carried forward as reasonably applicable to future operations" (AAA 1936b, p. 188). "Cost" was "cash outlay or … the fair market value of property exchanged for shares" (AAA 1936b, p. 188), but the statement did not explain its basis. It insisted, "Recognition invariably should be given to depreciation, depletion, and all other diminutions or expirations of cost, even when the amounts … must be estimated" (AAA 1936b, p. 188), but did not discuss the choice of method. For asset write-downs, it implicitly accepted PV or NRV. "Every business enterprise should eliminate from its accounts those costs which are applicable to assets no longer useful or salable, and should reduce the carrying values of assets in use or ultimately to be marketed to such amounts as may reasonably be expected to be recoverable in the course of future operations" (AAA 1936b, p. 189). The statement accepted, "An extreme change in the value of money might vitiate the usefulness of cost records but there seems to be no sound reason for repeated adjustments of asset values" (AAA 1936b, p. 189). Observers agreed, "Present procedure is unsatisfactory in that it permits periodic revaluation of assets, up or down, in accordance with current price levels and expected business developments … [which] produce in the average financial statement a hodgepodge of unrelated values" (AAA 1936b, p. 189).

For income, the statement advocated the all-inclusive concept: "The income statement for any given period should reflect all revenues properly given accounting recognition and all costs written off during the period, regardless of whether or not they are the results of operations in that period" (AAA 1936b, p. 189), ruling out 1920s reserve accounting. "Income statements for a series of periods should not be distorted or artificially stabilized through the practice of creating large operating reserves in certain periods and charging to such reserves losses in succeeding periods which it is desired not to reflect in the current income statement", particularly for "contingencies" (AAA 1936b, p. 189). For capital and surplus the statement addressed the 1920s practice of blurring the distinction, requiring "Two major divisions of the capital of a corporation should be recognized: paid-in capital and earned surplus" (AAA 1936b, p. 190). It made a series of "propositions" — e.g., reacquired shares were reductions of capital — with "The objective … to make an effective distinction between capital contributed to the corporation by stock-holders and capital accumulated as a result of earnings from operations or from sources other than stock transactions with stock-holders" (AAA 1936b, p. 190). To give "income and profits … any meaning" it was necessary to forbid "accounting procedure [that] permits the creation of various types of operating or surplus reserves to which may be carried expense charges or income credits" (AAA 1936b, p. 191), but the statement had not defined "expense charges" or "income credits". Like May, it argued, the income statement should "be divided into two sections, one showing particulars of operation for the period … and the other showing realized capital gains and losses and extraordinary credits and charges resulting from income realization and cost amortization not connected with the operations of that period" (AAA 1936b, p. 189), but did not define "extraordinary".

It did not use the word "conservatism", but commentators thought the statement "marked the beginning of what many academics believed was a retreat to 'conservatism'", a move "Practitioners generally applauded" (Previts and Merino 1998, p. 280). All its sections pushed towards "conservatism", both British and American. The point of valuation was "what part of the original cost should be written off". The income statement should recognise "all costs written off during the period, regardless of whether or not they are the results of operations in that period"; and the distinction between capital and earned surplus means, "Neither paid-in surplus nor surplus reserves should be availed of for the absorption of losses" (AAA 1936b, pp. 188–189, 191). The first two sections opened the door to American conservatism; the third, by not allowing accounting for asset write-downs to RCs as CMAs, through reserves, also encouraged it. Lorig saw in the statement's prescriptions "an attempt to check a certain recent progressive tendency in accounting and to force accountants back to the old conservatism for conservatism's sake" (1937, p. 401). "They make of conservatism a god so domineering that the objective of accounting providing useful financial information for intelligent guidance is somewhat forgotten" (Lorig 1937, p. 401). He interpreted "Principle No. 1" to say, "the accountant should try to prevent assets from being overvalued, but be indifferent to undervaluation. Thus, hidden values (secret reserves) are knowingly permitted — even brought about by the accountant — the creditor and investor being kept in ignorance" (Lorig 1937, p. 402). Rorem thought, "The committee would seem to be saying: 'be accurate if you possibly can, but in case of doubt, be conservative'" (1937, p. 134), and to DR Scott it gave a "generally conservative interpretation of theory and practice" (1937, pp. 296, 303).

American writers commonly explained and defended "conservative" accounting as necessary against over-optimistic managers and entrepreneurs, as Fisher did, to protect the investing public, but usually did not distinguish between British and American conservatism. An exception was Gilman who saw American accounting "Ruled by the doctrine of conservatism", but discovered, "Oddly enough, the original meaning of conservatism", the British definition, "characterized by a tendency to preserve or keep intact or unchanged", "was quite different from its present connotation" (1939, pp. 130, 233), but did not explore it. He accepted, "The implication of understatement now attaches to conservatism" (1939, p. 233), the American definition. Thus, the accountant "declines to recognize income until such recognition is clearly warranted but, on the other hand, has a tendency to be generous in recognizing costs, expenses and losses and including them in the profit and loss statement of one period even though there may be some doubt as to the fairness of such inclusion" (Gilman 1939, p. 130). Gilman observed, "Conservatism has a tendency which is opposed to the ideal of matching cost with income", but "Few outside of the accounting profession realize the overwhelming importance of the doctrine … and the extent to which that doctrine has understated balance sheet values and distorted profit and loss statements" (1939, pp. 130, 232). Thus, he concluded, since "understatement 'falls below the truth or fact' … conservatism is more of a policy than a principle" (Gilman 1939, p. 233). Gilman saw the most "serious objection to some applications of the doctrine of conservatism" was their "tendency to distort earnings so that during a period or several periods profits will appear unduly small, to be followed by a period or periods when the reverse effect is noticed" (1939, p. 234). This was true for charging "capital expenditure to expense, … overdepreciation … [and] the rule of lower of cost or market", and "another method [that] creates other unduly large reserves, particularly contingency reserves" (Gilman 1939, p. 234). Conservatism was "illogical", Gilman argued, because it gave "only a temporary advantage", but accepted, "insistence by all authorities on the importance of conservatism insures its influence upon accounting and reporting for many years to come. Hence, conservatism is distinctly entitled to a ranking position among accounting doctrines" (1939, pp. 235–236), but not as an "accepted principle". The failure, therefore, of the AAA to "list conservatism among their postulates or to discuss it among their comments appears significant" because "the committee's position seems to be definitely opposed to the policy of … understatement as it is usually understood" (Gilman 1939, p. 203), but its proposals encouraged it.

Scott criticised the AAA's statement for not developing the "control function and the protection of equities function", a theory of financial accounting based on cost accounting, as "an instrument of economic adjustment and social control" (1937, pp. 296–297). HC was insufficient for achieving these aims, for holding management accountable, he argued, and called for the "constructive development of accounting theory" (Scott 1937, p. 303) around this objective. "Thus the control function of accounts takes on a new and quite different form. Instead of being merely a tool of control by business enterprise they become a tool for the control of business enterprise itself" (Scott 1939, p. 399). Consistent with British/Marxian stewardship, Scott argued, "Accounting has emerged as a system of rules or principles and a system of techniques which transcend the authority of the business management. The business manager is not free to charge expenses to asset accounts or the reverse" (Scott 1939, p. 400). The accountant's role was "certification that given financial statements reflect a proper application of accounting methods and principles [which] derives its significance from the protection which it affords the interests of those who are affected by such statements" (Scott 1939, p. 400). The primary "interest" was, in effect, Marx's total social capital: "The public accountant is not a hired man of business management. Just as the lawyer is an officer of the court, so the public accountant is a public officer. He occupies a position of public trust. … In its recognition and regulation of the accounting profession the state gives official sanction to this social control over business enterprise exercised by accounts and accountants" (Scott 1939, p. 400). There was, therefore, a "social" need to develop principles to this end: "With a comprehensive and consistent system of principles, their decisions may be made more intelligently and upon a basis of impersonal principles ... [give] a more effective social control over economic processes" (Scott 1939, p. 401). Scott's stewardship view of accounting's "social" role did find a place in the AAA's and AIA's efforts, but it was precarious and short-lived. Scott did not define what he meant by "social control". ARB 1 accepted accounts must "serve a useful social purpose" (AIA 1939, p. 1), but May criticised its test of "Usefulness ... [as] an indefinite concept" (1943, p. 12).

As he had in 1928, Littleton (1936) continued to argue for HC and realised revenue, and disclosures of economic values. He argued, as May did, for the "primacy" of the income statement, for seeing the balance sheet as a list of residuals from the cost and revenue allocation process. From the value perspective, "profit is a highly intangible, inconclusive event"; "Profit is not a thing in itself ... it is an intellectual concept only and varies from person to person and from time to time" (Littleton 1936, p. 10). Turning the intellectual concept into a monetary measure made no difference, "does not change the illusive nature of profit" (Littleton 1936, p. 12). Accounting should therefore, Littleton argued, focus on "profit" defined as "the excess of the prices received in bargaining exchanges over the prices previously given" (1936, p. 12). "Profit" is the money value of prices received or realized over cost, over "value-in-use", "an expression of the direct utility present", the cost of use-values, not fluctuations in "value-in-exchange", "an expression of the marginal utility", not fluctuations in the market price (Littleton 1935, p. 270). Because before realisation "value-in-exchange is essentially subjective and very fleeting at best", the prime function of accounting is, "as W.A. Paton so well puts it, to record cost-price [sic] as it enters an enterprise and to trace cost-price through many intricate conversions" (Littleton 1935, p. 270). Accounting's foundation was therefore "value-for-use (original cost prices)", not "an estimate of value for exchange (replacement or market prices)" (Littleton 1935, p. 270), that was subjective. Use-values and bargained prices underpinned the objectivity of accrual accounting:

> Those who used accrual accounting recognized the fact that bargained purchase-price, and not cash disbursed, was the element used to represent the thing received; that bargained sale-price, and not cash collected, was the element used to represent the thing given .... [T]hat it was utilization of goods or services, and not the act of acquisition, which marked the appearance of the expense; and that the alienation of goods or the act of rendering a bargained service, rather than the receipt of an object in exchange, marked the appearance of income. (Littleton 1936, p. 12)

In 1940, after much discussion by the AAA's executive (Zeff 1966, pp. 53–54), Paton and Littleton published their "hugely influential monograph, *An Introduction to Corporate Accounting Standards*.... Like its forebear, it was a paean to historical cost accounting" (Zeff 2013, p. 271), and like it, we will see, resolved no fundamental questions because Paton continued to defend his implicit commitment to economic value while Littleton avoided an explicit theory of value. They produced an influential and apparently workable compromise, but these commitments underlay the ultimate failure of the AAA's, AIA's and SEC's attempts to produce GAAP.

The AIA and SEC

Criticised by the SEC for inaction, apparently goaded by the AAA's 1937 competition for the best essay on the Tentative Statement, in 1937 the AIA offered a $500 prize for the best essay on "To What Extent Can the Practice of Accounting Be Reduced to Rules and Standards" (Zeff 1966, pp. 42–43; *Journal of Accountancy* 1937, p. 2). Gilbert R. Byrne CPA won it arguing that the profession could and must "reduce" practice to "principles" (1937). Having agreed to sign-off accounts as "in accordance with accepted principles of accounting", Byrne argued, they must now agree what they were, otherwise "accountants have indeed stultified themselves" (1937, p. 367; Gilman 1939, p. 171). Academics and regulators agreed, but accountants "envisage the impossibility, if not undesirability, of the task" (Byrne 1937, pp. 365–366), citing May as an example. Byrne's definition of a "principle" as a "fundamental truth", May responded, was too exacting (1937b, p. 423). More appropriate was "A general law or rule adopted or professed as a guide to action; a settled ground or basis of conduct or practice", citing the Oxford English Dictionary (May 1937b, p. 423). May (1937b, p. 423) argued, "Mr Byrne seems to assume that in the certificate the word is used in the first of these ... senses, but an examination of the history and development of the certificate will, I think, clearly show that it is used in the second". May's view that an accounting "principle" was a "guide to action" dominated the profession to the late-1960s. He influentially responded to ASR 1 and the AAA in a Harvard lecture series, reprinted in the *Journal of Accountancy* in May 1937, "Improvement in Financial Accounts".

May now accepted accounts should provide some form of "social control", that he elsewhere called "stewardship". The stockholders' need for economic valuation, he had argued many times, prevented *any* "uniformity" in accounting. Now, perhaps because he was "influenced by his new allies" in the coalition of conservative wealthy business leaders and Wall Street elite (Miranti 1990, p. 167), who had lost heavily in the crash, he stressed "accounts may properly differ according to the purposes for which they are prepared" (May 1937a, p. 335).[1] Now he emphasised that differences between accounting methods were not "so much a matter of one accountant being right and another wrong, as of accounts being made up for entirely different purposes" (May 1937a, p. 336). Valuation was one purpose, but May now stressed, "an annual report should be regarded *primarily as a historical report* to stockholders" (1937a, p. 367, emphasis added). In 1932 May had argued, "the balance sheet was largely historical" in "nature" (1936, p. 113), whereas the profit and loss account provided a conventional measure of earning capacity, not that accountants should regard the "annual report" as a "historical report to stockholders", that this should be its objective. Now he argued, "the distinction which I have here suggested", between different accounts for different purposes, that accounts had a "double purpose", "seems to me to have been obscured in the securities act of 1933, and practically ignored in the act of 1934" (May 1937a, pp. 336, 340, 367). Now, he concluded, Section 18 was "open to criticism — because it treats a periodical report too much as if it were a new edition of a prospectus instead of a historical report, and because it assumes a much closer relation between market transactions in a stock and periodical reports than the facts warrant" (May 1937a, p. 367). As "much of the difficulty in the problem of deciding on the form of corporate reports is due to this diversity of interest", the chosen aim(s) would have "an important bearing on the question, what direction improvements in present practice in corporation reports ought to take" (May 1937a, pp. 337, 340). May now argued, "an income account may be designed to show what income has been realised in a given period or what was the earning capacity of the business under the conditions existing during the period — and is, more frequently, something of the nature of a compromise between the two" (1937a, p. 346). He still argued, if "the income account is required to serve a variety of purposes ... uniformity becomes impossible" (May 1937a, p. 349). However, he wanted, with others, to shift the

[1]Bonbright's *The Valuation of Property* (1937), that cited Fisher extensively, stressed the importance of purpose, which influenced May (1937a, pp. 334, 337, 357, 369), and Berle (1938, p. 11).

compromise towards "stewardship", towards HCA, realisation and "conservatism", we will see, and used his concepts of "earning capacity" and "conservatism" to suggest improvements to accounts. He now "recognize[d] the value of a certain degree of uniformity", but did not "believe complete standardization of accounting in the industrial field to be either desirable or attainable at this time, if ever" (May 1937a, p. 359).

The NYSE approved May's general principles, and his opinions on accounting issues were influential, but it did not implement his suggestion that the methods certified by its auditors should be disclosed (Zeff 1972, p. 125; Carey 1969b, p. 6). The Special Committee on the Development of Accounting Principles, formed by the Institute in 1933, with May in the chair, recommended only that the auditor give an opinion of conformity to six general principles and "consistency", not the disclosure of methods in the financial statements, which the SEC accepted.[2] To avoid having to judge management's choice of method, accountants proposed that whatever method it chose was fine if used "consistently", unless they had reason to doubt management's competence or good faith in making the choice (Previts and Merino 1998, pp. 276–277). This meant the "accountant did not have to determine if a technique was preferable, only that it had been accepted in practice and had been consistently applied" (Previts and Merino 1998, p. 275). According to May's earning capacity interpretation, and "widely assumed", consistency "was more important than the particular principle or method" because "from the viewpoint of an individual investor in a single company … it would permit valid comparison of the net income of one period with another" (Carey 1969b, p. 7), and produce meaningful trends of earning capacity. However, this "ignored the growing desire for a basis of comparison of the profits of one corporation with those of another" (Carey 1969b, p. 7), for "comparability" for investors directly or indirectly holding well-diversified portfolios.

SEC Commissioner George Mathews "praised" the Tentative Statement (Miranti 1990, p. 157), which Blough thought had made "a real contribution to the accounting profession" (1937, p. 30). In 1937, after much deliberation, the SEC had decided to leave accounting principles to the profession, but to intervene if necessary to control practice. Disillusioned with academic theories, with the agreement of the NYSE, the Institute's

[2]Corporations had to disclose accounting policies in the SEC's form 8K. US GAAP first required disclosure of methods in financial reports in 1963 (Previts and Merino 1998, p. 276, fn. 111, p. 459).

Special Committee on the Development of Accounting Principles declared, "Principles of accounting cannot be arrived at by pure reasoning, but must find their justification in practical utility" (Carey 1969b, p. 6). In 1938, therefore, SEC commissioner and lawyer "Robert Healy shocked the practicing community when he suggested to accounting academicians that they, as 'disinterested parties', might be better able to establish accounting principles" (Previts and Merino 1998, p. 279). The profession's antipathy to theory meant the AAA's "efforts to develop a conceptual framework created significant tensions among academicians and practitioners" (Previts and Merino 1998, p. 280) for many years. The AIA's committee also agreed that only a "relatively small number of broad principles of accounting should be adopted as a framework within which the validity of specific applications could be tested" (Carey 1969b, p. 6). Nevertheless, the SEC insisted, the agreed standard form of the auditor's report should certify that the financial statements "fairly presented" the position and the results "in accordance with accepted principles of accounting". However, "Since disclosure of the accounting principles or methods followed by individual companies was not required, the phrase 'accepted principles of accounting' became shrouded in ambiguity. What were they? Where could they be found? In these questions lay the seeds of future discontent" (Carey 1969b, p. 7; Zeff 1972, fn. 43, p. 129). If corporations did not publish methods, for investors to have "confidence", specifying "acceptable accounting principles" became critically important. As the Institute's Committee on Cooperation with Stock Exchanges had put it in 1932, to protect investors auditors would have to "display courage and independence when their approval is sought for accounts which are either clearly inadequate or misleading, even if technically accurate" (Carey 1969a, p. 169), which they had not done in the 1920s. The pre-requisite for "courage", even May accepted, was a theory backed by legal powers. In 1926, he accepted a "need for some rational conceptual foundation on which the responsibility of independent auditors could be based" (Carey 1969b, p. 5). He recognised "principle" would more likely overawe management than "conventions", "especially in dealing with those (of whom there are many) who regarded accounting as an esoteric but well established body of learning and chose to bow to its authority rather than display their ignorance of its rules" (May 1943, p. 37).

In 1937, responding to the AAA's challenge, the AIA asked the Haskin & Sells Foundation to commission Hatfield, Sanders, and Moore, to produce a compilation of generally accepted accounting principles (Zeff 1966, p. 45; Miranti 1990, p. 157). It published their *Statement of Accounting Principles* in 1938 as a "countermeasure" to the AAA's Tentative Statement, "which was in large measure a defense of accepted practice", "largely an uncritical acceptance of existing methods" (Zeff 1999, pp. 91, 131; Carey 1969b, p. 14). The report was widely "excoriated for its virtually exclusive reliance on experience and current practice as the basis for its principles, its reluctance to criticize even the most dubious practices, and its implication that accountants had no greater duty than to ratify whatever management wanted … so long as … legal and properly disclosed" (Storey and Storey 1998, pp. 16–17). The AIA's tactic spectacularly backfired because at "the obvious tendency of the authors to surround each proposition with hedging observations" (Paton 1938, p. 206), the SEC lost patience and issued ASR 4 banning financial statements "prepared in accordance with accounting principles for which there was no substantial authoritative support". This sent the "clear and unambiguous" message to the profession that if it did not provide the necessary "authoritative support" the SEC would (Zeff 1972, pp. 134, 139). In 1939, Jerome S. Frank, SEC Chairman, warned accountants, "We want to be sure that the public never has reason to lose faith in the reports of public accountants", and "if they are unwilling or unable, perhaps because of the influence of some of their clients, we won't hesitate to step in" (Zeff 1972, p. 139). In 1939, Landis was not optimistic: "As long as you have the May leadership in the accounting situation, I have very little hope of them accomplishing much" (Parrish 1970, p. 208). Following this display of force, the AAA and the SEC had no problem persuading the AIA in 1939 to enlarge its CAP, formed in 1936, to 21 members. It now included smaller firms, and three leading academics, Roy Kester, Paton, Littleton, and Blough who had left the SEC, and began a research programme (Zeff 1972, p. 134; 1984, p. 456). Chaired by the president of the AIA, but run by May as vice-chair, the CAP began producing ARB's giving non-binding recommendations on particular issues.

ARB 1, *General Introduction*, issued in September 1939, saw accounting as "a machinery created by the people in the belief that, broadly speaking, it will serve a useful social purpose", and be "judged from the standpoint of society as a whole — not from that of any interested parties" (AIA 1939, p. 1), but left open stewardship and/or economic valuation. ARB 1 aimed to "indicate the standpoint from which it has approached the subject", advising readers "present and future pronouncements should be read in the lights of these remarks" (AIA 1939, p. 1), but decided not to attempt a comprehensive statement of accounting principles, and ignored calls that it should (Zeff 1972, p. 137; 1984, p. 459; Storey and Storey 1998, pp. 15–16). It did not discuss stewardship, observing only, "The uses to which the corporate system is put and the controls to which it is subject *change* from time to time, and all parts of the machinery must be adapted to meet such *changes* as they occur" (AIA 1939, p. 1, emphases added). As it said, "In the last forty years the outstanding change ... has been ... converting into liquid and readily transferable form the ownership of large, complex, and more or less permanent business enterprises" (AIA 1939, p. 1). It recognised, "problems have come to be considered more from the standpoint of the current buyer or seller in the market of an interest in the enterprise than from the standpoint of a continuing owner" (AIA 1939, p. 1), but did not endorse it. It accepted the "demand for a larger degree of uniformity in accounting" was "one manifestation" of this development, and the bulletins "soon had a visible influence on corporate accounting", narrowing differences "by indicating preferred treatments" (Carey 1969b, pp. 14, 16). It noted, "'uniformity' has usually connoted a similar treatment of the same item occurring in many cases, in which sense it runs the risk of concealing important differences between the cases", but consistent with stewardship, "Another sense of the word would require that different authorities, working independently, should reach the same conclusions. This at any rate is an ideal which all will agree to strive for, and perhaps is more readily attainable" (AIA 1939, p. 2).

ARB 1 said nothing about valuation, a question the SEC was then considering. In 1938, ASR 8 "constituted a clear signal that the Commission looked critically at write-ups", but although it hardened its attitude against revaluations, it issued no formal rule (Walker 1992, p. 18). However, consistent with pursuing an undeclared policy of "conservative" accounting, by 1940 it had used "stop orders" to ban PV estimates and estimated selling or replacement prices (Walker 1992, pp. 22, 25; Zeff 2007, p. 50). As May later noted, while his 1932 letter to the NYSE included "no prohibition against recording unrealized appreciation", "During the last decade there has been a change of viewpoint which may be regarded as the result of an unusual combination of financial, political and social forces" (1943, p. 92). Banning revaluations was "conservative" in the American sense because it meant write-downs would have to go through earned surplus, whereas according to Marxian accounting most should be CMAs (Bryer 2021a, Chapter 2). However, for those corporations that had written-up assets, ASR 8 conservatively required charging depreciation on the appreciation (Walker 1992, p. 22). In ARB 5, Depreciation on Appreciation, issued in April 1940, "the committee said.... 'Appreciation normally should not be reflected on the books of account of corporations'. It added, however, that ... 'income should be charged with depreciation computed on the new and higher figures'" (Zeff 2007, p. 51).

Walker (1992, p. 25) explained the SEC's effective banishment of all forms of current value accounting from 1938 as "may be" because "the essentially legalistic activities of the Commission imbued the accounting staff with a strong respect for precedent (and correspondingly, made them reluctant to re-examine issues on their merits)". However, the early decisions against appraisals did not set precedents as they concerned faulty valuations, or accounting for valuations, not valuations as such. The basis of the change, Zeff points out, was the 1920s experience, particularly by "The person who effectively cemented the SEC's policy to insist upon historical accounting.... Robert E. Healy" (Zeff 2007, p. 49). Before becoming an SEC commissioner in 1934, Healy was Chief Counsel of the FTC from 1928 to 1934 and a six-year, Congressionally required investigation into the market manipulations by public utility holding companies, "with heavy emphasis on their use of dubious accounting practices during the 1920s" (Zeff 2007, p. 49). This "radicalised the conservative Healy. Shocked to find that 'you can capitalise in some States practically everything except the furnace ashes in the basement', he became committed to historical cost accounting" (Zeff 2007, pp. 49–50). He was not alone. Commissioner Andrew Barr, a student of Littleton, was the "intellectual leader of the historical cost school" and "like-minded commissioners succeeded in instilling in [others] an aversion to upward departures from historical cost if they had not already held that view" (Zeff 2007, p. 50). In 1940, Barr reviewed the history of the change. In January 1935 Commissioner Mathews "did not believe that a balance sheet could properly or practically attempt to reflect current values of fixed assets and that to attempt to do so from year to year would involve the accountant in conjecture which might lead him to run a substantial risk of making misleading statements" (Barr 1940, p. 90). In summer 1937, "Judge Healy endorsed historical cost as the proper basis in accounting for utility properties. In December 1938, Mr. Werntz described some of the difficulties encountered with statements of industrial companies in which fixed assets had been recorded at appraised values" (Barr 1940, p. 90). In Autumn

1939, "Chairman Frank, in discussing the importance to the investor of prospective net earning power, stated that the investor wants to know cost because cost is 'useful to him in making an estimate of what the company's property can and probably will yield — that is, its earning power'" (Barr 1940, p. 90). HC was relevant for valuation, but the SEC's attraction to it also reflected an inchoate demand for accountability, reducing accounts manipulation. Zeff (2007, p. 50) points out, "Healy was livid … not only [at] the write-ups themselves", which had not "incensed him as much as the utilities' follow-on accounting practices" (2007, p. 50). Healy complained of "'write-ups used to create income or to relieve the income accounts of important charges'.... Dividends would sometimes be paid against this unrealised appreciation, and 'Very often unamortised debt discount was charged against a capital surplus so created, thus increasing the reported earnings … in future'" (Zeff 2007, p. 50).

The SEC also arguably encouraged "conservatism" in the late-1930s to reduce reported profits in the face of resurgent conflict between capital and labour (Bryer 2016). Banning revaluation accounting signalled a shift to "conservative" accounting in the British and American senses. Through the 1930s, "Most accountants … advocated conservatism … [and] justified procedures, such as the write down of fixed assets to nominal amounts" (Previts and Merino 1998, p. 276), that is, American "conservatism". Werntz, SEC chief accountant, thought the "accountant's tendency toward conservatism … [u]ndoubtedly … commendable", and objected only "when carried to extremes", and in quasi-reorganisations when "conservatism in today's balance sheets … result[s] … [in] unconservatism in future income statements" (1940, p. 27). Having failed since 1913 to persuade the Internal Revenue Service to allow base stock accounting for tax purposes, supported by the Institute (Zeff 1972, p. 128), in 1938 it allowed some businesses to use LIFO (last-in-first-out), making it generally available in 1939 if used in the accounts (Chatfield 1977, p. 208). Because it deferred taxation when prices rose and resulted in reporting "conservative" income and inventories, LIFO "was widely used for accounting purposes regardless of its theoretical propriety" (Chatfield 1977, p. 209). That is, "propriety" to those like May who, we will see, recognised stewardship and advocated cost in the late-1930s, because everybody knew the LIFO "assumption is clearly in most cases fictional" (1943, p. 175).

Evidence of shifting towards British conservatism is that whereas the realisation "concept of profit was gradually taking form … after the First

World War", it "had become dominant in … accounting … by the late 1930's" (Carey 1969b, p. 232). May thought the cost-realisation "rule of today is the result of a revulsion of feeling, and that it has passed through all the stages from being a postulate to a principle within a decade" (1943, p. 39). Gone was "The old rule, which permitted and in some cases encouraged the recording of unrealized appreciation on the books of corporations" (May 1943, p. 9). This "old rule", May argued, "fell into disrepute because of the abuses that were committed in its name, and because of a change in the general concept of the major objective of accounting from the determination of net worth to the measurement of income and earning capacity" (1943, p. 39), which he had helped to engineer.

Responding to the SEC's rejection of valuation accounting, its demand for GAAP, and for "conservative" accounting, Paton and Littleton, wrote *An Introduction to Corporate Accounting Standards*, which the AAA published in 1940. The product of much deliberation, discussion and committee work in and outside the AAA (Greer 1940, pp. vi–vii), its amplification of the Tentative Statement is widely seen as "an elegant conceptual rationale for the use of historical cost accounting" that "became a standard text … in university accounting curricula and was widely read by practitioners as well" (Zeff 2007, p. 51; 2018, p. 45). The AAA and AIA distributed it to members as a "dividend" (Zeff 1972, p. 140) and, as it articulated many of his views, May thought it was "valuable" (1943, fn.1, p. 156).

An Introduction to Corporate Accounting Standards

Paton and Littleton aimed to deal with the "rather considerable literature which grew up … marked by a wide variety of proposals as to what might be considered 'sound accounting'", bring "order out of … [the] chaos of conflicting ideas and practices" (Greer 1940, p. vi). They sought to dispel "serious misconceptions, not only in the mind of the public, but also in the attitudes of business and financial leaders" (Greer 1940, p. vi). Their book was popular with management and the profession because "it generally rationalized existing practice, providing it with what many saw as a theoretical basis that previously had been lacking" (Storey and Storey 1998, p. 28). In particular, it "gained wide acceptance for the proposition that the matching of costs and revenues was the appropriate basis for income measurement, rather than the process of asset and liability valuation" (Carey 1969b, p. 16). It was, however, a mixture of viewpoints. Paton wrote the majority, Zeff shows, and his name came first, but "a simple count of page totals does not capture the essence of their respective contributions" (2018, p. 64). Littleton's contribution, as Zeff (2018, p. 64) concludes, was as "a philosopher and historian, [who] set the terms for the monograph: the fundamental ideas rooted in the historical cost model, which constituted the framework for the subsequent discussion of the particulars in the financial statements". And Paton's contribution was that he was "trained as an economist and … a 'value' man, was an analyst and critic of specific accounting measurements, classifications, and disclosures in financial reports, and was generous with his policy recommendations for improvement" (Zeff 2018, p. 64). Philosophically, Paton and Littleton rejected "conservatism" (1940, p. 80). However, their "theoretical basis", their mixture of Littleton's HC-approach to "stewardship" and Paton's implicit commitment to economic valuation, what follows argues, undermined their concepts of "costs attach", "long-term matching", "assets", and "cost", which allowed management discretion. This led to criticism and eventual suppression of what many saw, despite their denial, as its implicit "cost theory of value" by the FASB's framework as problems mounted in the 1950s and 1960s that their compromise could not solve, and management refused to relinquish discretion.

Stewardship

Berle and Means (1932) highlighted the separation of ownership from control, emphasised stockholders could not use accounting to control management, that accounting was irrelevant to control, a charge accountants and theorists could not ignore. Paton and Littleton "creatively responded to the challenge posed by Berle and Means (1932)" by arguing that "with the acceptance of entity theory, historic[al] cost measurement was 'natural'" because their "'matching' model for income determination … would enable all external users to assess managerial performance" (Previts and Merino 1998, p. 281). By, in effect, affirming accounting's "stewardship" function Paton and Littleton's "historic[al] cost allocation model … effectively silenced questions about the relevance of accounting profit and reaffirmed the primacy of ownership rights" (Previts and Merino 1998, p. 271). They began with the "Separation of Investment and Management", and claimed that accounting reunited them. They argued, "With a condition of detached and scattered investor-interests the service of accounting has necessarily been expanded; the function of reporting information to absentee owners has been added to that of recording and presenting data for owner-operator use" (Paton and Littleton 1940, p. 1). In the historical context it was clear, "there is a need for developing standards to secure proper protection for the equities of corporate investors" (Paton and Littleton 1940, p. 1). Accounting's "social" function was, in effect, management's accountability for "capital" to investors who directed it to its most profitable use, for the benefit of "society": "accounting is important from the social point of view" because "Capital should flow … [to] the management … capable of using capital effectively" (Paton and Littleton 1940, p. 3).

American accountants rarely used the word "stewardship" until the 1940s, and it usually referred to estate accounting, or accounting for charities, etc., but even in the 1920s some leading accountants and academics used it to refer to management's accountability to shareholders, and several supported the British concept (Bryer 2021a, pp. 388–397). "Stewardship" appeared in the *Journal of Accountancy* nine times in 1930–1939 and 32 times in 1940–1949. In *The Accounting Review*, in 1935 Littleton explained the British view that "Most of the balance sheet items could be objectively verified. This afforded a convenient and tangible basis for the auditor's examination of the stewardship and fidelity of the directors as the stockholders expected him to do" (1935, p. 271), and Paul L. Morrison, professor of accounting, Wisconsin University, agreed, "The management is responsible to the stockholders for a report of its stewardship" (1935, p. 81). In a *Journal of Accountancy* editorial in 1938, Carey argued, "Investors in railroad securities, no less than investors in other securities, have a right to a full accounting of the stewardship of management" (1938, p. 191). In 1939, the SEC decided, "Accountants certificates are required not as a substitute for management's accounting of its stewardship but as a check upon that accounting" (Carey 1939, p. 257). Paton and Littleton (1940) only "got round to stewardship much later in their monograph" (Zeff 2013, p. 271), first used the word towards its end, on page 98, but had made clear their focus on management's accountability to "society" for the "residuum" on "the capital". "Accounting exists primarily as a means of computing a residuum, a balance, the difference between costs (as efforts) and revenues (as accomplishments) for individual companies. This difference reflects managerial effectiveness and is of particular significance to those who furnish the capital and take the ultimate responsibility" (Paton and Littleton 1940, p. 16).

On page 98, in the penultimate chapter on "Surplus", echoing Sprague (1907, see Bryer 2021a, pp. 198–202), Paton and Littleton made clear they had been talking about "stewardship". For "publicly owned corporations wherein a large majority of … investors putting their funds, as it were, in trust with management — it seems best to establish standards of corporate reporting upon the assumption that a fiduciary management is reporting to absentee investors who have no independent means of learning how their representatives are discharging their stewardship" (Paton and Littleton 1940, p. 98). Arthur W. Hanson, professor of accounting at Harvard, praised this objective in his review for the *Journal of Accountancy*, which he thought was then "quite generally accepted in practice" (1940, p. 441). As he said, "It has become commonplace to acknowledge that the income statement is today of more importance and significance than the balance sheet. What is there more revealing for the managing officers to report than an account of stewardship, the story of their success in handling other people's money? (Hanson 1940, p. 441). Hanson had no doubt, "This premise lies at the heart of the present study. … It is quite generally accepted in practice. Its formal statement may help clarify objectives and it may stand until it causes a better general purpose for accounting reports to be evolved" (1940, p. 441). Paton and Littleton retained Paton's entity concept, so Hanson was right they gave only a "formal statement" of stewardship. As Zeff (2013, p. 271) says, "By investors, they meant to encompass shareholders and creditors — that is, all capital suppliers, as used by Paton in his 1922 book, Accounting Theory. They added, 'The corporation's most important responsibility … does not run to one or more owner-operators for each enterprise, but rather to one or more groups or classes of detached investors, present and prospective'". A formal statement supporting stewardship was probably necessary to ensure wide acceptance, because accountants "may be divided into two groups: (1) those who claim that the proprietor owns all of the assets but owes certain amounts to creditors, and (2) those who hold that both liabilities and proprietorship are merely claims against the assets. The former point of view, which is the older of the two, is held by the greatest number" (Gilman 1939, p. 49).

Paton and Littleton (1940) theorised realisation and the matching and attaching of HCs to measure "managerial effectiveness", its stewardship of the acquisition, consumption, production and sale of use-values with bargained prices. "Accounting does not match disbursements and receipts, but efforts and accomplishments, services acquired and service rendered, acquisition price-aggregates and disposition price-aggregates" (Paton and Littleton 1940, p. 16). However, although use-values and bargained prices were objective, because Paton and Littleton had no explicit theory of value, they faced irresolvable problems of cost allocation (and with revenue allocation, not considered here). They admitted, "accounting can never be completely scientific, because its factual materials can never be determined with complete and conclusive objectivity" (Paton and Littleton 1940, p. 19). Management is accountable to "detached investors, present and prospective", but because of "bias in favour of one interest or prejudice against another, inequitable results may follow", so investors needed "standards" to ensure "fair dealing in the midst of flexible rules and techniques" (Paton and Littleton 1940, pp. 2, 5). By "standards", Paton and Littleton meant only "an explanation of what accounting attempts to tell the interested parties", "guideposts to the best in accounting reports", not "standardized accounting", not the "alternative … [of] rigid governmental control and prescription", which imposed "restraint upon the exercise of judgment" (1940, pp. 5–6). Kester highlighted the ideological danger of "standards" because "Inherent in it is the whole philosophy of individualism versus socialism in business. Business in this country is individualistic", so he rejected "the straight-jacket of an artificial philosophy of accounting" (1940, p. 444).

Having apparently abandoned economic value, Paton and Littleton could claim their proposals meant accounts were "objective", if not "complete[ly] and conclusive[ly]". However, the problem they faced was that although recording expenditures, the "inflow of cost", is a matter of observation, without an explicit theory of value "recording the outflow of costs as embodied in revenue is essentially a matter of judgement and interpretation" (Paton and Littleton 1940, p. 69). Littleton (1936, fn.1, p. 13) glossed over this problem, the distinction between capital and revenue expenditure, when like May he reduced it to "principally questions of timing, of whether a given expenditure is an immediate deduction from revenue (an expense) or a postponed deduction from revenue (an asset)". However, he noted the problem that although "Cost accounting forces attention upon the physical cycle of form-changing production activities", "costing is a part of the larger problem of judging the adequacy of the services rendered by comparing the price which the service commands with the cost of rendering the service" (Littleton 1936, fn.1, p. 13). Without an explicit theory of value, "judgement" was required to decide which "Outlay costs

... of use values [were] acquired in the venture of producing an acceptable service" (Littleton 1936, p. 13).

Paton and Littleton faced the same problem: "The basic subject matter of accounting is ... the measured consideration involved in exchange activities, especially those which are related to services acquired (cost, expense) and services rendered (revenue, income)", yet "Earning power — not cost price, not replacement price, not sale or liquidation price — is the significant basis of enterprise value" (1940, pp. 10–12). They were unable to reconcile these contradictory viewpoints, to "reconcile neoclassical economic theory with the separation of ownership and control" (Previts and Merino 1998, p. 317). Consequently, what follows argues, their matching model gave accountants only an aura of "objectivity", "an aura of certitude that masked the arbitrariness of the allocation process" (Previts and Merino 1998, p. 281), allowed subjective and conservative accounting in practice.

"Costs Attach"

Paton (1922) apparently derived the "costs attach" idea from Marx, but made clear he did not accept Marx's explanation, as he understood it, substituting the circuit of implicit PV (Bryer 2021a, pp. 293–296). As this rebuttal was now unavailable, while Paton and Littleton's explanation of "costs attach" is consistent with Marx's theory of value, they made clear they did not accept his circuit of capital, in which costs have the "power of cohesion" because they are the "monetary expression of socially necessary labour time" (Bryer 2017, p. 157). Instead, they substituted Littleton's circuit of use-values to which the accountant attaches "acquisition" or "disposition" prices. "When production activity effects a change in the form of raw materials by the consumption of human labour and machine-power, accounting keeps step by classifying and summarizing appropriate portions of materials cost, labor cost, and machine cost so that together they become product-costs. In other words, it is a basic concept of accounting that costs can be marshalled into new groups that possess real significance. It is as if costs had a power of cohesion when properly brought into contact" (Paton and Littleton 1940, p. 13). Paton and Littleton emphasised, "It is confusing to say that accounting records 'values'. ... It is not necessary to assume a cost theory of value in order to explain the concept that costs cohere. Costs are not marshalled to show value or worth" (1940, pp. 12, 13–14), but that readers could assume this, we will see, Paton later regretted. American Marxist economist Paul Sweezy (1942, p. 63), for example, who assumed a "cost theory of value" when he wrote, "Marx's value theory has ... the great merit, unlike some other value theories, of close correspondence to the actual accounting categories of capitalistic business enterprise".

Paton and Littleton dismissed the "cost theory of value" by deploying Paton's (1922) vulgar argument that it abandons realisation, recognises profit during production. "If cost of production were to represent 'value', it should include an amount for the added utility given to the product by the process of business operation itself. But this is not attempted" (Paton and Littleton 1940, p. 14). "The producer may think that utility has been added and that the product is worth more than the sum of the several costs; but he does not know ... [;] the test comes when a sale is made" (Paton and Littleton 1940, p. 14). Realisation, they argued, disassociated them from the "cost theory of value", but it gave them an asset definition close to Marxian accounting's recoverable cost of controlled use-values (Bryer 2021a, p. 46). "The realization of revenue from sales ... marks the time and measures the amount of (1) recapture of costs previously advanced in productive efforts, and (2) capture of additional assets (income) representing [the] amount of compensation for capital services rendered, responsibility taken, and risk assumed in the process of production" (Paton and Littleton 1940, p. 14). The risk justification of profit contradicted their claim that realisation and matching held management accountable to "society", and Littleton's view that management earned profits by avoiding risks, which left the ideological problem of why it made profits to distribute to shareholders. They sidestepped these contradictions using Paton's entity concept in which "stewardship" meant only management's control of use-values with bargained prices to maximise cash flows to "equities", but this caused problems. Following "the accountant's natural instinct to conceive of business property as belonging to the entity, and income as asset-increment" (Paton and Littleton 1940, p. 9) meant focusing on the circuit of use-values and cost prices. However, rejecting the "cost theory of value" and therefore the productive/non-productive labour distinction, led to irresolvable problems leaving discretion. In Marxian accounting, managers control the valorization process, capital's circulation for profit, for a social proprietor, but Paton and Littleton, like Fisher, saw the entity as primarily a material process of production, a circuit of use-values producing cash flows for a legal entity. "Since the concepts of business entity and continuity predicate an enterprise or institutional point of view, accounting theory likewise is oriented first to the enterprise as a productive unit and only secondly to the investor as a legal claimant to assets" (Paton and Littleton 1940, p. 11).

"Long-Term Matching"

Accounting professionals and textbook writers generally did not accept Paton and Littleton's entity concept "and continued to assume that managers sought to maximize returns to stockholders", and "accounting procedures … continued to be viewed in terms of proprietary, or residual equity theory" (Previts and Merino 1998, pp. 281, 283). However, founding accounting on control of use-values and bargained prices gave them a distinction, superficially consistent with British/Marxian proprietary theory, between "revenue and expense", which included the financial effects of events and transactions within the circuit of use-values, and "capital gains and losses", those occurring outside, that many found useful. This was their "concept of long-term matching" that "leads accounting to include in the calculating process (1) windfall gains, those asset-appearances which are obtained without observable effort and hence are not elements of operating revenue, and (2) non-operating losses, those asset-disappearances which cannot be readily associated with immediate efforts to produce results" (Paton and Littleton 1940, p. 17). According to Marxian accounting, the distinction between windfall gains and non-operating losses follows from Marx's concept of the circuit of capital (2021a, pp. 85–86). Gains or losses within the circuit of capital are "ordinary", whereas gains or losses outside the circuit of capital are non-operating or extraordinary.

Paton and Littleton recognised that distinguishing operating and non-operating gains and losses was not a "technical" issue: "The difficulty lies in developing an acceptable conception of 'operation' in the particular situation. One of the most common mistakes is to assume that the operation in the typical enterprise is synonymous with production in the technical, physical sense" (1940, p. 60), seen as primarily a circuit of use-values. Possibly because use-values was a foundation of their income concept, they offered no alternative conception, concluding only that "[t]o justify segregation as non-operating items, therefore, gains (or losses) should be clearly [sic] extraordinary and connected with the avowed purpose of the business in only an incidental [sic] way" (Paton and Littleton 1940, p. 60; cf. Dicksee 1907). They inevitably left space for management discretion, deciding "clearly" and "incidental", because they necessarily distinguished their "costs attach" in the circuit of use-values from the Marxian "cost theory of value".

"Assets"

According to Marxian accounting, assets are controlled use-values with value, socially necessary costs (Bryer 2021a, p. 49). According to Fisher's entity view, "realized income" is net cash flow and therefore "assets" become, as they did for Hatfield and Paton, any "necessary" expenditure to generate entity cash flows. For example, expenditures on raising capital and creating an enterprise, both unproductive according to Marxian accounting, could be "assets". As Paton and Littleton said, "With the entity concept as a basis, there is no difficulty in accepting the proposition that all costs legitimately incurred by the enterprise are properly included, in the first instance, in the total of assets", and so "organization expenditures, costs of raising capital, and related charges are elements of enterprise assets and capital" (1940, p. 9).

Accountants, according to Marxian accounting, should capitalise production overheads and expense non-productive overheads such as expenses for general management, sales, interest, advertising, research, etc. Paton and Littleton (1940) produced a similar result, but the distinction was fuzzy. "Some costs, like manufacturing overhead, in which an affinity [sic] with a product can be detected, are allocated directly to a product; but other costs, like administrative overhead, in which it is difficult [sic] to detect an affinity with a product, are commonly allocated only to time periods" (Paton and Littleton 1940, p. 14). This implied it might be possible to detect an "affinity" between general management expenses and creating a product, which suppressed the idea of the socially necessary cost of productive labour, and without it, difficult questions arise because "Many units of labor service, considered critically, may not be productive. Are the corresponding items of wages to be segregated as losses? Maintenance charges are heavy because 'green' men are handling the machines. Is the excess over normal a revenue charge or a loss?" (Paton and Littleton 1940, p. 94). "The appropriate answer to such questions is", they argued, management's view, "that all expired costs are chargeable to revenue so long as conditions are not too far out of line with ordinary standards of management" (Paton and Littleton 1940, p. 94). According to Marxian accounting, socially necessary waste is a cost of production, and socially unnecessary waste is a loss, but for Paton and Littleton it depends on management's "ordinary standards", leaving room for discretion. For example, "drilling ... one or more dry holes in the development of a tract of oil land may be unavoidable and may ... be treated as a cost of property" (Paton and Littleton 1940, pp. 94–95), or may not. Because in Marxian accounting assets are use-values with value, management should capitalise only successful efforts, only these costs are productive. Paton and Littleton's concept of depreciation as the allocation of original cost was similarly hazy. According to Marxian accounting, depreciation measures the transfer of value to commodities, which the entity must recover before recognising profit for the circuit to continue (Bryer 2017, Chapter 6). By contrast, "Under accrual accounting, depreciation is not a valuation process nor a means of capturing replacement prices from customers; it is simply a step in the process of associating past cost, which measures the planned effort to produce goods and services, with the revenue actually derived from the goods or services produced" (Paton and Littleton 1940, p. 17). According to Paton and Littleton, therefore, "Depreciation as an expense is analogous to a rental charge", which must be paid whether the asset is used or not (1940, p. 17), simply a long-run cash outflow. To them, therefore, "It does not matter that the simple and convenient straight-line depreciation may not accord with observed physical deterioration nor reflect fluctuating prices for similar equipment" (Paton and Littleton 1940, p. 17), and they recommended its universal use.

Cost

"'Costs' are the fundamental data of accounting", Paton and Littleton insisted, but in the absence of an explicit theory of value, recognising, measuring and classifying them was fraught with irresolvable "complexities" (1940, p. 25). Where market prices are available, they use them, in effect, as the socially necessary cost. In a transaction with a related party accountants must view the prices "with some skepticism" (Paton and Littleton 1940, p. 26) — must seek objective evidence of the "effective market costs". For barter transactions, likewise, the cost of goods or services acquired is "the amount of money implicit in the cash selling value of the goods or services furnished in exchange" (Paton and Littleton 1940,

p. 27). The same applied to the cost of shares issued, gifts and discoveries, and treatment of discounts (Paton and Littleton 1940, pp. 28–30). The market prices of commodities, however, are rarely their only cost — usually, the business must transport, handle, install and test them — and, according to Marxian accounting, management should capitalise only productive expenditures giving control of use-values with value, all productive expenditures, all the socially necessary costs of creating the use-values.

By contrast, Paton and Littleton add expenditures "necessary" to own or otherwise have legal access to use-values, including buying costs. Because to them "All costs incurred to secure services necessary to business organization and operation are essentially homogeneous in their significance to the enterprise … it follows that all service costs incurred, prior to their absorption as charges to revenues, contribute to the total amount of assets of the enterprise" (Paton and Littleton 1940, p. 32). Their test for capitalisation is therefore "when a tangible asset is purchased all cost necessary for acquiring the property and for placing it in a position to serve the particular function for which it is intended should be included in the cost of the property" (Paton and Littleton 1940, p. 31). This captures costs of transportation, installation, tuning, breaking in, engineering services and other production overheads, storage, insurance, and modification, the costs of controlling the use-values. According to Marxian accounting, these are the only costs management should capitalise (Bryer 2021a, Chapter 2). Paton and Littleton's test, however, allowed legal costs, taxes, organization costs, interest charges and the costs of deciding what asset to acquire, negotiating with the seller, specifying legal obligations, raising the necessary money or credit, etc. (1940, pp. 31–32), none of which give control of use-values with value. Whereas transporting an insured machine to a factory, installing, testing it etc., delivers productive use-values, buying costs, hiring lawyers, paying taxes, organizing the business, paying interest, etc., do not create or give control of use-values. None is a socially necessary cost of production. For Paton and Littleton, by contrast, "Any type of cost may be 'deferred' if it … represents a factor from which a future benefit or contribution can reasonably be expected", and similarly, they argued, "The revenues of a particular period should be charged with costs which are reasonably associated with the product represented by such revenues" (1940, pp. 40, 65, 69).

Instead of Marxian accounting's "narrow" definition of matching, setting cost of production against revenue realized from commodities or services transferred to customers, we have a "broad" definition that assumes all costs could "produce" revenue. According to Paton and Littleton, "the cost of any factor utilized in operating activity is chargeable to revenue only as the resulting product is recognized as having produced revenue" (1940, p. 70). Management can, therefore, account for "general development costs, not readily assignable to tangible factors" as "deferred charges" and, in their framework, capitalising "the costs of preliminary advertising campaigns and other expenditures directed toward the building up of future revenues … as a form of goodwill … is not intrinsically unsound" (Paton and Littleton 1940, pp. 74, 92). If we can allocate revenue to the factors supposedly responsible for generating it, "Costs of general administration and of selling represent efforts to produce revenue just as truly as do costs of direct labor and materials, and one class of charges is just as legitimate and significant as the other" (Paton and Littleton 1940, p. 70). They accepted in practice, "the accounting treatments accorded cannot be expected to be strictly comparable unless and until the means of effecting association with particular quantities of revenue are equally well developed" (Paton and Littleton 1940, p. 70), but saw this as possible. Assuming the outlay is for bona fide business purposes, the key question for them is Fisher's and Canning's: "does the charge represent a factor from which a future benefit or contribution can reasonably be anticipated" (Paton and Littleton 1940, p. 75). Paton and Littleton admit, nevertheless, echoing Canning's (1929) concern with joint production, that "there is no means of discovering causal relations between the segments of periodic net income and particular economic factors embodied in the intrinsic services of the enterprise" (Paton and Littleton 1940, p. 122). Paton and Littleton stress matching, but because they "avoid the problem of *which* costs are associated with revenues" (Chatfield 1977, p. 240), their broad definition left management discretion. As became clear, "Acceptance of matching as the basis of income determination did not result in a single theory for its application" (Storey 1964, p. 41).

Paton and Littleton (1940) received wide acclaim and influenced practice: "Generations of accountants learned to use it as scripture" (Storey 1981, p. 90; Storey and Storey 1998, p. 28). Even in the 1970s, American academics "called [it] one of the most important contributions to financial accounting [literature] of the twentieth century" (Beaver 1989, p. 3). It pushed American accounting towards realisation, matching, and HC as the CAP wrote ARBs based on May's interpretation, but this did not prevent management's discretion. The choices its "inductive" approach allowed appeared in May's "distillation of experience", and the increasingly criticised work of the CAP.

A Distillation of Experience

May continued to argue, "financial accounts are always in some measure (and in the case of a complex business, perhaps in a very large measure) based on conventions, estimates and opinions" (1937, p. 334), "the result of common agreement between accountants" (1943, p. 3). May's *Financial Accounting: A Distillation of Experience* (1943) is based on articles and lectures from 1936 that he withheld from publication "until formal ties and official positions which might have deemed to imply more than a personal responsibility for them have been relinquished" (1943, p. vii). He gave "Grateful recognition ... to the guidance, friendship and inspiration of Arthur Lowes Dickinson ... to whom this book is gratefully dedicated" (May 1943, p. viii), some of whose views now came to the fore. To justify shifting towards British principles, from 1936 May argued, "Accounting conventions should be well conceived in relation to at least three things: first, the uses of accounts; second, the social and economic concepts of the time and place, and, third, the modes of thought of the people" (1943, p. 3). Having denied in 1932 that diverse stockholders could hold management to account, May (1943, p. 3) listed 10 "distinguishable uses" of accounts, including "stewardship":

(1) As a report of stewardship;
(2) As a basis for fiscal policy;
(3) To determine the legality of dividends;
(4) As a guide to wise dividend action;
(5) As a basis for the granting of credit;
(6) As information for prospective investors in an enterprise;
(7) As a guide to the value of investments already made;
(8) As an aid to Government supervision;
(9) As a basis for price or rate regulation;
(10) As a basis for taxation.

Before 1936, May had vigorously advocated the income account for uses 6 and 7, a "shift of emphasis from the balance sheet to the income account, that is, perhaps, the most significant change of recent years" (May 1943, p. 24). In 1932, he concluded, like Berle and Means, "The only practical way in which an investor can today give expression to his conclusions in regard to the management of the corporation in which he is interested is by retaining, increasing or disposing of his investment" (AIA 1934, p. 11). It followed, "accounts are mainly valuable to him in so far as they afford guidance in determining which of these courses he shall pursue" (AIA 1934, p. 11). After 1936, however, May lamented that "the use of accounts as a guide to the value of investments already made ... has created the most crucial problems of financial accounting" (1943, p. 21). Therefore, while "May's argument was that ... stewardship was still relevant to shareholders", it understates his shift to say, "the actions available to them suggested also that reporting to the capital market had come to possess equal valence" (Zeff 2013, p. 267). The problems arose from the irreconcilable conflict between "stewardship", historical "reports of progress", and valuation: "the present ferment in accounting thought is very largely due to conflicting objectives of those who would continue to regard financial statements as reports of progress or of stewardship, and those who would treat them as being in the nature of prospectuses" (May 1943, p. 21).

May saw stewardship reports as "reports of progress", as "guides to the profits that may be distributed", but because he saw accounting methods as "conventions", he never suggested stockholders could use "stewardship" accounts for results control. He regretted that "general purpose accounts cannot be expected to serve all purposes equally well — indeed, if they are appropriate for the major purpose it is likely that they will not serve some other purposes even reasonably well" (May 1943, p. 4). There was, for May, obvious conflict between accounts for "stewardship", which cared nothing for prediction, and for economic valuation, which meant having both was impossible. "Whether the experience of a company in the recent past is likely to be repeated in the near future is practically immaterial if financial statements are to be considered as reports of stewardship or as guides to the profits that may be distributed. It is of paramount importance if they are to be used as a guide in determining whether to buy, hold, or sell securities" (May 1943, p. 21). It was necessary to choose "the controlling objectives" taking "cognizance of the social and economic concepts of the time", the currently most important of which was that America had "moved from ... the last days of a pioneer, free-enterprise economy" to large corporations with "the separation of ownership and control" (May 1943, p. 4). Whereas in the pioneering days, "the value approach to accounting had strong appeal" because most capital was in marketable current assets, with large corporations employing large fixed capitals "the valuation approach has become impracticable and resort to cost as the primary line of approach becomes almost inevitable" (May 1943, p. 8). The valuation approach's corollary was "the concept according to which income arises gradually" and that of the cost approach "the concept which treats income as arising at a moment when realization is deemed to have occurred" (May 1943, p. 6). Realisation met both aims when the "distribution … of transactions were exactly uniform" because "an allocation of income according to the proportion of completion of each unit would produce the same result as the attribution of the entire profit to a single stage" (May 1943, p. 30).

The "interesting question" when they did not was "whether accounting is likely to move in the direction of a more complete adherence to the realization concept" (May 1943, p. 7). May had no doubt the social and economic times and modes of thought of the people warranted a shift in emphasis, but this was not a revolution: "Times are changing and accounting conventions will change with them" (1943, p. 9). For example, he thought using the realisation concept for large contracts was fine in "earlier days, when the use of accounts as an indication of earning capacity was not considered, and when conservatism was clearly a virtue" (May 1943, p. 31). Here "conservatism" meant avoiding "taking credit for a profit that may never be earned" (May 1943, p. 30), the British definition. However, he accepted that "in recent years there has developed a much greater readiness to take credit for profits on uncompleted transactions, in order to secure a more useful guide to earning capacity" (May 1943, p. 31). To justify the change towards British principles, May drew on his theory of earning capacity, and on conservatism.

An unpublished Price Waterhouse manuscript written in 1933 made clear May was still arguing that share valuation was the "primary" objective. "In the opinion of May, the value of a business enterprise was dependent, in the main, on its earning capacity. The primary use of the income statement was to determine the capital value of the investment by applying a multiplier to the earnings shown. It was extremely important that this multiplier be applied only to the earnings produced in the ordinary course of business" (Stabler and Dressel 1981, p. 82). After 1936 he still recognised, "The prospective investor is not interested in past earnings as such — they are significant to him only in so far as they are a guide to the future" (May 1943, pp. 21–22). However, he now thought it "intolerable to place upon managements the burden of telling stockholders annually to what extent the recent past should be regarded as a fair indication of the probable future" (May 1943, p. 22). He knew, "In England, the purely historical character of the annual report is not questioned" (May 1943, p. 22), and concluded, "it seems desirable that the annual financial statements of American corporations should also be regarded as historical and in no sense prophetic, notwithstanding that the stock of the company may be listed and freely traded in" (May 1943, pp. 21–22). From the British perspective, echoing Dicksee, "as a report of stewardship … [i]t is natural that the management should account for the assets coming into its charge on the basis of cost to the corporation"; only "on rare occasions, if any, should any reflection of changes in value that have not been realized be considered" (May 1943, p. 24). From May's M-M′ perspective, they were "at best partial adjustments … [that] tend to obscure the true nature of accounting" (1943, p. 50). For example, like Canning, May thought, "It is undoubtedly a grave objection to the reproduction cost theory that there are many properties which no one would reconstruct as and where they exist" (1943, p. 97). May could see a case for "recognizing current values", but only where it was "clear that the existing value is markedly at variance with a book value determined on the basis of cost", and "subject to the approval of the shareholders" (May 1943, p. 102). However, because "an attempt to reflect changes in capital value of prospective income in measuring current income or surplus raises difficult technical problems and important questions as to the significance of the resulting figures", "the accounting for fixed assets should be based on cost" (May 1943, pp. 100, 102).

May highlighted "THE PROBLEM OF MEASURING the capital value of enterprises", that is, calculating their PV — forecasting "reasonable expectations of income", deciding the "degree of probability attaching to the expectations", choosing the "rate of discount deemed appropriate" (1943, p. 103). He concluded, "The more the question is studied, the more convinced accountants must be of the wisdom of avoiding valuation of enterprises or capital assets as far as possible" (May 1943, p. 107). Where valuation was unavoidable, and, presumably, when replacement was contemplated, "fixed properties cannot be regarded as worth more than the cost of replacing them", and in general it "would be neither mandatory nor justifiable to record assets at more than cost of reproduction less a reasonable deduction for depreciation" (May 1943, p. 112). This was the clinching argument for May, that cost was "practical", which was his argument for realisation. Although the "most theoretically correct concept of the income account is that charges or credits to it accrue from day to day", it was "impractical", so "the profit on a sale is taken up when the sale is made, although obviously it is not the product of the moment in time when this occurs" (May 1937a, p. 348). Cost was the only practical basis for most assets, but after purchase (at which point it equalled value), May stressed it was only a "conventional measure of *valuation*", merely a "monetary statement about property" (May 1943, p. 87) that required "historical" judgement. Thus, "depreciation must be based on cost. The life of an enterprise, like that of man, is continuous, and the gains and losses, the successes and failures, of one period are in large measure the result of acts, omissions, and events of the past, and the results achieved cannot be appraised as successes or failures without regard to the future. The historical character of accounting cannot be too strongly emphasised" (May 1943, p. 49). May (1943, p. 26) therefore lamented the use of Fisher's word "income", "a word of many meanings", which had "displaced the older and more suggestive word, 'profit'". Seen historically, "the terms 'profit' and 'profit and loss account' suggests the important truth that gain is usually a difference and must be measured by matching costs and expenses against revenues" (May 1943, p. 26). May therefore concluded, "the desirability of adopting as the concept of income that which is suggested by the word 'profit'" (May 1943, p. 26), based on the realisation and matching conventions.

During the 1920s, May suggested, investors did not understand that "stewardship" should be accounts' primary function. He thought it "undeniable, though not fully recognized outside the profession, that books of large enterprises are kept predominantly on a cost basis and do not, therefore, constitute evidence of the value of either the enterprise as a whole or the separate assets thereof" (May 1943, p. 8). Because a "financial statement, like a word, must be interpreted in relation to all the circumstances attending to its use", "No one has a right to interpret a report of stewardship as though it were an invitation to invest" (May 1943, p. 19). May separated his list of 10 uses into the first five which "might be regarded as the older, and the second five as the more modern, uses of accounting statements", and now stressed, "the distinction between the two is significant" (1943, p. 19). According to May, the older "stewardship" aims justified American "conservatism". "In each case, there is an attempt to appraise the past, and to measure the cumulative achievement to date; there is no attempt to use the past as a measure of the future, nor any great stress on the allocation of past achievements to particular years. For each of these purposes, conservatism (a common term in accounting which may, perhaps, be defined as a disposition to resolve doubts in the measurement of assets or profit on the side of understatement) is a major virtue" (1943, p. 20). In May's "experience … losses from unsound accounting have most commonly resulted from the hopes rather than the achievements of management being allowed to influence accounting dispositions. To me, conservatism is still the first virtue of accounting" (1943, p. 44), and he therefore urged, "The Commission should be concerned to see that accounting is conservative" (1943, p. 68). This was despite having concluded that because of the influence of the "credit grantor", "In the early days, conservatism was the cardinal virtue of accounting; now, the virtue of conservatism is questioned, and the greater emphasis is on consistency" (May 1943, p. 9). Moreover, it was despite recognising that "Conservatism in the statement of results of operations in the past may lead to overstatement of the profits of a later period", which was fine for the "permanent investor", but not for temporary investors who wanted an "accurate apportionment" (May 1943, p. 24).

May wrote about many accounting issues, but some examples will show he resolved them eclectically, judging the relative importance of "stewardship" and "conservatism" variously defined, and his notion of "earning capacity" ("earning power"). He was, as Zeff says, "torn between the 'old' use of accounting, that is, for stewardship, with its emphasis on a historical reckoning for the benefit of the long-term investor (i.e., the existing shareholder), and the 'new' use of accounts, which was to provide a gauge of earning capacity for the trader in the markets" (2013, p. 268). Sometimes he chose earning power over conservatism. He was against any form of writing off or amortisation of intangible assets "when earning power is unimpaired" (May 1943, p. 154). He was against any fixed rule for whether "capital gains and losses should enter into the determination of income", but for excluding them "except where they could be shown or fairly be presumed to result from causes the effects of which are generally regarded as desirable to reflect in concepts of income" (May 1943, p. 154), that is, affected earning power. Usually, however, he used both tests, and conservatism received more weight. Sometimes, they pointed in the same direction. May used conservatism and earning capacity to justify

L-C-M and fixed asset impairments. The "rule may be accepted on a pragmatic basis because of its demonstrated merits" as a conservative measure of profit, because "there are many cases in which value will be preferred to cost if it is the lower of the two, but not if it is higher" (May 1943, p. 87). It was "an outstanding illustration" (May 1943, p. 87). Another justification for L-C-M was the "conservative" rule, which justified British or American conservatism, that "There is not the same insistence on realization as a condition precedent to the recognition in the case of losses as in the case of gains" (May 1943, p. 87). However, "alternatively, it may be defended on the ground that only useful costs should be carried forward, and that the fact of value being less than cost is evidence of a loss or a cessation of utility" (May 1943, p. 87), that is, on the ground that L-C-M gives a better indication of earning capacity.

This he recognised was an argument for LIFO, a choice in effect between the conflicting aims of "stewardship" for capital, or earning capacity for valuation. "The strongest argument for the method is that the value of a business is determined by its income, that the income is best measured if sales and costs are reflected in terms of the same price level .... Critics urge that the balance-sheet figure that results from the use of the method is devoid of significance because it is neither a historical cost figure nor a value figure. They insist that if it is to be adopted there should at least be an appropriate indication of the cost value of similar goods at the date of the balance sheet in the footnotes" (May 1943, pp. 176–177). Implicitly, the critics were proprietary theorists who sought accountability for profit *and capital*. It went against his earning capacity interpretation, but consistent with his shift to stewardship, May could also see serious limitations with LIFO (it required homogenous stocks through time; did not work for long-term contracts; was not conservative if prices fell), concluding, "the method has less usefulness than many of its adherents claim" (1943, p. 176). Earning capacity, however, justified May's view that depreciation was about allocating cost to the decline in a fixed asset's "store of future usefulness" not its fall in value (1943, pp. 118, 145), and his view that a provision for a contingency was a "reservation of profit" (1936, pp. 163–165). It also justified his argument for the traditional "conservative" practice of immediately writing off expenditure on research "even though the research is undertaken with a view to benefits in the future" by "insisting that due weight be given to the probability of the purpose's being actually achieved" (May 1937a, pp. 348–349), which was usually very low.

Committee on Accounting Procedure

In January 1939, with May its *de facto* chair, "a staunch advocate of the common-law approach" (Zeff 1966, p. 48), the CAP's first meeting decided not to produce a comprehensive statement of principles (Storey and Storey 1998, p. 15). There was "increasing pressure on the accounting profession … to eliminate alternative methods … from …: the SEC, the American Accounting Association, the financial analysts, the financial press, and elements within the Institute itself" (Carey 1969b, p. 59). However, "powerful countervailing pressures also developed among some corporate managements and organizations … [like] the National Association of Manufacturers, and the Financial Executives Institute" (Carey 1969b, p. 59). Combined with the CAP's commitment to "matching costs with revenues", "costs are assets", and "avoiding distortions of periodic income", management's propensity to manipulate accounts meant its work became fire-fighting, and its power meant a "plethora of sanctioned alternatives for accounting for similar transactions continued to thrive because … the committee rarely found an accounting principle it did not find acceptable" (Storey and Storey 1998, p. 30).

By 1949, the CAP had published 41 ARBs, but Maurice Stans, fresh from encounters with unions (Bryer 2016), soon to be AIA President, highlighted the "Weakness in Present Accounting Which Inhibits Understanding of Free Enterprise" (Stans 1949, p. 466). The question was "What can accounting do for the economic system", and his answer was tackling "economic illiteracy" and to "examine critically the reasons why corporate statements of today meet with such cynicism and distrust" (Stans 1949, pp. 466–468). The problem of "economic illiteracy" was the "predominant present beliefs of labor and the general public that corporations make exorbitant amounts of profit, that corporations conceal their profits and that capitalists who own them gain unreasonably from the efforts of labor" (Stans 1949, p. 467). Stans knew, however, the problem went deeper. "Economic illiterates" were distrustful of accounts, but so were free-enterprise believers, investors and their agents. The answer to the question "What is wrong with accounting as the public sees it", Stans accepted, was "there is still no broad authoritative code of accounting principles" (1949, p. 469). This was why "the two principal accounting organizations … take opposite positions on many basic issues", why "there is no standardization of terminology", "no fixed standards of minimum disclosure", it was "difficult to compare one company with another", why "many identical transactions are treated in different ways by different companies" (Stans 1949, p. 469). Stans called for "a program of evolutionary advancement of accounting practices" based on the "establishment of an authoritative comprehensive code" (1949, p. 470), to convince investors, but convince or cajole management who resisted any reduction of their "right to manage". As Stans put it, "On the whole, the accounting profession has been far more alert to the need of modernizing financial reporting than have corporate executives" (1949, p. 470). Whereas "Accountants have attempted to legislate against the distortions of reserves for contingencies, of charges for possible future losses, of ambiguous representations of income, and to discourage the use of ambiguous representations of income, and of ambiguous terms such as 'surplus', 'reserves', 'appropriation', and so on", they had not received "the general support of corporate financial officers. Many corporate reports have violated these promulgations" (Stans 1949, p. 470). The problem was management's "rights", "a great many rugged individualists among management who do not concede the right of the independent accounting profession to develop principles or narrow the methods of presentation in financial statements" (Stans 1949, p. 470).

Faced with management insisting on its "rights", methods proliferated as the profession attempted to deal with issues on a case-by-case basis (Storey and Storey 1998, p. 31). Frustration and disagreements mounted during the 1940s and 1950s over deferred taxation, HC versus current value and/or general price-level adjustments, the treatment of unusual items (Zeff 1999, p. 92), and other issues. The CAP and SEC stuck to HC and disclosure, but management stuck to its prerogatives, and new problems emerged that Paton and Littleton's monograph, May's experience, or the collective wisdom expressed in ARBs, could not solve. As Most (1977, p. 73) says, "The shortcomings of the CAP were revealed in the period following World War II, when new financing techniques such as conglomerate acquisitions, equipment leasing, convertible securities and leaseback arrangements created accounting problems which could not be solved from precedents". Increased inflation in the late-1940s and early-1950s added to its problems because it "raised the prospect of the abandonment of historical costs, and changes in technology threw up intangibles of great value, which were inadequately expressed at a memorandum figure of one dollar" (Most 1977, p. 73). Reviewing the CAP's work in 1954, Anson Herrick CPA concluded, "Accountants must recognize that present day accounting is frequently found to be insufficient, particularly when the amount to be stated as net income may depend which of several generally accepted procedures is adopted" (1954, p. 627). In 1955, the AAA engaged in a "Re-examination of that portion of the 1948 'Revision of Concepts and Standards Underlying Corporate Financial Statements' relevant to adequacy of disclosure [that] has been prompted by indications of dissatisfaction with the content of some published corporate reports" (1955, p. 400).

Until the mid-1950s, Carey observed, while "questions were raised by … CPAs … the discussions were kept within the bosom of the family", but "suddenly, the issues were thrust into the public domain" (1969b, p. 74). The renegade was Leonard Spacek, managing partner of Arthur Andersen & Co., who in a speech in March 1956 to the Philadelphia Financial Analysts, which the "press happily reported", asked, if "it has not become heresy to raise the question, 'What are generally accepted accounting principles?'" (Carey 1969b, p. 74). A month later in an address to the Controllers Institute of America in Chicago, "Accounting Has Failed to Prevent Major Misrepresentations", he "referred to 'antiquated accounting principles'", criticising deferred tax and lease accounting (Carey 1969b, p. 75). In October 1956, he told an audience from commerce and industry, "I would like to tell you that our profession is standing steadfast to our principles and responsibilities. This I cannot do", now criticising accelerated depreciation for tax purposes, accounting for stock options, leasebacks, and the effects of inflation on reported profits (Carey 1969b, pp. 75–76). Spacek proposed a "court of accounting principles", which he elaborated to the AAA in 1957 (Carey 1969b, p. 76). Carey observed, "By this time many practicing CPAs were deeply disturbed", "The newspapers were gleefully quoting his colorful phrases, and it was feared that the result might be a loss of confidence in corporate reports" (1969b, p. 76). Spacek remained adamant, "There is only one reason for misleading financial statements. It is the failure or unwillingness of the public accounting profession to square its so-called principles of accounting with its professional responsibilities" (Carey 1969b, p. 77). Spacek "then flung down the gauntlet": "He accused the committee on accounting procedure of yielding to industry pressure on an important principle without public discussion … [and] for failing to issue bulletins in the face of internal dissent. … A wave of indignation greeted this speech" (Carey 1969b, p. 77).

The AIA appointed a committee of inquiry, and the President, Marguis G. Eaton, "thought something affirmative ought to be done about the unfavorable publicity the profession was receiving", and gave a speech which he sent to 50,000 "companies, bankers, economists, educators, business leaders, government officials, labor leaders and others" (Carey 1969b, pp. 77–78). Eaton's speech was a "candid acknowledgment of the limitations of accounting" (Carey 1969b, p. 80). He argued, "this phrase — 'generally accepted accounting principles' — suggests to the ordinary reader the existence of some authoritative code of accounting, which when applied consistently will produce precise and comparable results … we accountants all know that … [they] are far from being a clearly defined, comprehensive set of rules" (Carey 1969b, p. 78). Eaton wondered if "Perhaps comparability in financial reports among companies and industries is unattainable", but asked for "the help of the business and financial community" (Carey 1969b, p. 79). Accountants could "assume sole responsibility", but management "had the primary responsibility for their own statements; government also shared responsibility; and bankers, financial analysts, and others had some responsibility to advise how financial statements might be made more useful for the purposes they were intended to serve" (Carey 1969b, p. 80). Accountants knew the problem was "While pressure for reasonable comparability of earnings came from the SEC, the universities, the analysts, the press, and from the profession itself, a strong, though not so visible, countervailing pressure was persistently exercised by some corporate managements" (Carey 1969b, p. 81). Whenever the CAP "proposed elimination of some alternative procedure … some companies were threatened … and they often resisted … directly, or through the Controllers Institute, the Edison Electric Institute, or other trade organizations" (Carey 1969b, p. 81). Accountants felt powerless because, "After all, the SEC had officially stated that management had primary responsibility for its financial statements. What authority did auditors have to dictate to management the accounting methods it must follow. So long as such methods had authoritative support, why should auditors hesitate to give a clean opinion on the financial statements" (Carey 1969b, p. 81). Accountants knew managements "were developing a greater interest in the market price of their common stocks than ever before", and had strong incentives to use discretion because "Stock options to executives gave them immediate personal interest in the reported earnings of their companies" (Carey 1969b, p. 81). Furthermore, the "continual need for new capital made it obviously desirable to keep the market price of a company's stock as high as possible, and this depended on reported earnings", as did "acquisitions of other companies through exchanges of stock" (Carey 1969b, p. 81). Accountants understood, "it was to be expected that any change in accounting principles that would result in reducing reported earnings of a substantial number of companies would be resisted with vigor" (Carey 1969b, p. 81). In 1959 some utility companies challenged the CAP's legal right to issue any opinions on preferred methods (Carey 1969b, p. 82), which went to the Supreme Court that decided it did, but its legitimacy was shredded. In 1959, the AICPA replaced it with the APB, formally charged with using "research" to "advance the written expression of what constitutes generally accepted accounting principles, for the guidance of members and others" (Carey 1969b, p. 93).

Accounting Principles Board

Fisher had been *persona non grata* since 1929, but Jack Hirschleifer (1958, p. 329), a University of Chicago economist, helped to rehabilitate his intellectual credentials, arguing in an influential paper, "recent works on investment decisions ... suffer from the neglect of Fisher's great contributions". The APB's first research director, Maurice Moonitz, professor of accounting, University of California, "recognized as an outstanding accounting theorist" (Carey 1969b, p. 96), "was strongly influenced by Fisher and Canning" (Most 1977, p. 74). In 1961, Moonitz produced Accounting Research Study (ARS) No.1, *The Basic Postulates of Accounting*. To be a "postulate", he argued, a proposition had to "meet two conditions: it must be 'self-evident', an assertion about the environment in which accounting functions that is universally accepted as valid; and it must be 'fruitful for accounting'" (Storey and Storey 1998, p. 34). The overarching self-evident truth was the economic aim, "the production of wealth (goods and services) ... combining labor, natural resources and capital", Fisher's view that "wealth ... [was] identified with happiness" (Moonitz 1961, pp. 10, 21). Moonitz (1961, pp. 13–14) argued, like Fisher, "'income' ... should not be applied both to natural persons and to business entities ... because the economic theory of income is primarily a theory of the income of natural persons and not of accounting entities", but Paton (1922) and Canning (1929) had shown it could be applied to them.

The first two postulates Moonitz derived from "the environment of accounting" were (1) "Quantitative data are helpful in making *rational economic decisions*", and (2) "Most of the goods and services that are produced are distributed through exchange", which he thought an "extraordinarily fruitful one for accounting" (1961, pp. 21–22). As these "postulates" were, in effect, Adam Smith's economic man in a competitive market, they were "universally accepted", even by management. Starting from the proposition "that the primary basis of accounting lies in records of exchange dealings or their equivalent" (Moonitz 1961, p. 10), like Fisher, Moonitz concluded, "the reasons that accounting is concerned with cash prices and cash flows becomes apparent" (Storey and Storey 1998, p. 35). The "platform from which to start", "a place to stand", Moonitz (1961, p. 45) argued, was therefore market prices, not cost. Current prices were ideal, "the emphasis on exchangeability or 'value in exchange' leads to the observation that difficulties of measurement are reduced if exchange values (market prices) actually exist. This is true because of the 'independent judgment' expressed in the market transaction. The market transaction (exchange) exposes exchange values to the light, as it were, revealing the judgement of the market as to what the values are" (Moonitz 1961, p. 18), its PV estimates. Moonitz concluded, therefore, "The observed stress in present day accounting on 'objectivity' and on 'cost', for example, and the widespread antipathy to 'appraisal' and to value not based on an exchange, are all related to the problem of evidence. Valid as all this is, we must recognise that measurement is not impossible in the absence of exchange, nor is it necessarily less accurate. Exchange does not make values; at best, it merely reveals them" (1961, p. 18). Because, like Fisher, Hatfield, Paton and Canning (Bryer 2021a), PV was his ideal, by "value in exchange" Moonitz "includes cost, selling price, sound value, new, scrap or salvage value, or any other measure … that rests on exchange or derived from it" (1961, p. 19).

Moonitz and Robert T. Sprouse, associate professor of accounting and colleague, produced ARS 3, *A Tentative Set of Broad Accounting Principles for Business Enterprises* in 1962 to implement Moonitz's postulates. They acknowledged the contributions of "Dickinson, Hatfield, May, Paton, Canning, Littleton", but drew heavily on Paton and Canning to conduct "a thorough review of the problems of accounting", principally that "The results of the shift to the earnings statement have been mixed" (Sprouse and Moonitz 1962, p. 5). They felt the "time seems right" to re-examine "the strengths and weaknesses of the balance-sheet and income statement approaches" (Sprouse and Moonitz 1962, p. 5). Consistent with Paton's implicit circuit of PV (see Bryer 2021a, Chapter 7), they advocated shifting towards the balance-sheet approach, starting from the "basis

… that profit is attributable to the whole process of business activity", which meant, "the measurement of the components of profit (revenue, expense, gain, and loss) must accordingly rest on the measurement of assets and liabilities" (Sprouse and Moonitz 1962, pp. 10–11). Like Paton and Canning, they reduced "'realization' [to] a statistical generalization, an assertion about a convenient method of measurement" (Sprouse and Moonitz 1962, p. 15).

ARS 1 and 3 were widely seen as "two polemical papers attempting to move the profession towards basing financial statements on exit values, i.e., valuing assets at market prices" (Most 1977, p. 74). Sprouse and Moonitz advocated current value accounting, putting holding gains through the income statement. The SEC dismissed the studies as "too abstract" and "objectionable" (Zeff 1999, pp. 93–94). The APB "peremptorily rejected the 'radical' recommendations (net realisable value or replacement cost for inventories, replacement cost for plant and equipment, present value for long-term liabilities)" (Zeff 2013, p. 280). However, Moonitz's "postulates", derived from Paton (1922), "the idea that that foundation for accounting principles lies in self-evident propositions about the environment", "became commonplace in the accounting literature", influencing APB 4 (1970) (discussed in what follows), and are an "essential part" of the FASB's conceptual framework (Storey and Storey 1998, p. 36). Sprouse and Moonitz's shift to the balance-sheet approach, their implicit entity view, and definition of assets and liabilities in terms of "future economic benefits", also influenced the FASB's framework (Chapter 7).

Meanwhile, George J. Staubus, who did his PhD at Chicago 1949–1952, and taught at Berkley as Moonitz's colleague, had also started down the road of "self-evident" truths in his influential monograph, *A Theory of Accounting to Investors* (1961). Staubus was one of the first to deal with the problem preventing the development of a coherent theory of accounting, the acceptance of conflicting objectives — stewardship versus economic valuation — by ignoring stewardship. Staubus, with "people's capitalism" growing around him as he studied and taught, faced "Too often the question … in my classroom whether this or that generally accepted accounting practice could produce useful information" (1961, p. vii). To answer his students, he concluded, required "reference to some logically defensible criterion or set of criteria", and that "accountants should explicitly and consciously recognise an objective or objectives of accounting" (Staubus 1961, p. viii). It was clear, "the typical elementary, intermediate, advanced or graduate course in general accounting principles, as well as the widely quoted pronouncements … are largely concerned with accounting to investors", but the question was, "What information do investors' need?" (Staubus 1961, p. viii). The primary objective, like Paton (1922), should be providing "investors", stockholders and creditors, with information "useful in making investment decisions", like Canning (1929), for predicting entity cash flows (1961, p. viii), for "decision-usefulness". He was "the earliest exponent of the decision-usefulness approach to accounting theory and standard setting", first developed in his Chicago doctoral thesis, "An Accounting Concept of Revenue" submitted in 1954 (Zeff 2013, p. 276).

The theorists Staubus (2003, p. 178) "admired most in [his] formative intellectual years were Paton and Canning", and he was well acquainted with Fisher's work. "The present-value view of securities has been recognized by Finance scholars at least since Irving Fisher wrote, in 1906, that 'the value of any capital-good, either of wealth or of property rights, assuming all future income is foreknown, is the discounted value of that income'.... This idea has become … widely accepted.... The business school student learns this proposition early and repeatedly in either the undergraduate or graduate curriculum" (Staubus 1977, p. 95). Staubus did not mention Fisher in his PhD thesis, but Canning (1929) and Alexander (1950) feature strongly. He later acknowledged, "Several economists and economics-oriented accountants greatly illuminated the nature and measurement of income. One approach to income is usually attributed to Irving Fisher (1906) and was developed further by John Canning (1929) and Sidney Alexander (1950) — all economists — and by David Solomons (1962)" (Staubus 1977, p. 334). The alternative to the "income approach to accounting theory" was the "comparative statics" of Sir John Hicks (1946), which Staubus preferred, but its uncited foundation was Fisher's theory.

Leaving aside management accounting, concerned with "efficiency", Staubus (1961, pp. 1–2) focused on financial accounting concerned with "providing information to holders of capital funds in order to help them select the units in the economic organization that can use those funds effectively". Rather than society, from Fisher's financial economics perspective Staubus adopted "the viewpoint of the individual investor" for whom "effective use of capital means use in such a way that the user is able to pay the investor a satisfactory return. .... It is this need of the investor to be able to gauge the economic unit's future capacity to pay that will be our guiding concern" (1961, p. 2). Staubus reviewed the literature and found "surprisingly little attention has been paid to the objective of providing information for investment decisions" (1961, p. 3). Accounting writers, committees of leading accounting organisations, individuals who had "have given lifetimes of serious thought to accounting", he complained made "no special effort to show the relation between accounting and the problems facing investors", had not "bothered" to "specify … just what information can be provided by accountants and also be useful to investors" (Staubus 1961, p. 3). Staubus sees this as a failure of scholarship, overlooking that these writers would not challenge management's right to choose, which was why they remained inductivists. Thus, while the CAP "should be commended for recognizing investors' interest in accounting" in ARB 43, his "point … is that this admirable effort … still omits one step in the reasoning: it does not establish the connection between investors and the income statement, or between investors and the 'clean surplus' doctrine. The bulletin does not tell us what information investors *need* and how they could use it" (Staubus 1961, p. 4, emphasis added), was not overtly *normative* from the investors' perspective. He criticised Paton (1922), who "clearly recognized that 'It is the function of accounting to record values, classify values, and to organize and present value data in such a fashion that the owners and their representatives may utilize wisely the capital at their disposal'. He did not proceed, however, to the next step: determining what 'value data' would be helpful to those users" (Staubus 1961, p. 5); Paton did not specify the "value data" accounts should provide. He criticised May, who "does identify the uses of accounts", and "points out a common characteristic of their use…. 'The sole relevance of accounts of the past is as throwing light on the prospects for the future'", who "could probably have constructed a valuable theoretical system if he had started with these observations … and had made a carefully reasoned analysis of the information needed for those users" (Staubus 1961, p. 6). Staubus ignored May's (1946, p. 8) comment that he supported the "change from a value basis to a cost basis … [which] might be considered a serious defect of accounting … but for two considerations: first, that the value of a business is seldom a material fact; and, secondly, when it is, it can only be measured by looking ahead".

Staubus overlooked or did not understand that Paton, May and most AAA committee members of their generation had put management at the centre of capitalism, and therefore he could see it solely as an intellectual challenge posed by a changing environment, the burgeoning of "people's capitalism". Staubus observed "the seemingly tattered pattern of accounting principles", the need to "repair … the generally accepted pattern of accounting" (1961, pp. vii–viii), but did not blame management. He relegated managers to "administration": "One general class of decisions is related to granting credit to, or investing in the economic unit. The persons making such decisions may be called 'investors'. Another group of decisions relate to the administration of the affairs of the unit. These decisions are made by managers" (Staubus 1961, p. 11). Although he denied it, Staubus adopted Paton's entity view, "the view that 'interest charges … are not operating costs but represent a distribution of income, somewhat akin to dividends'", the "assumption that managers sought to maximize returns to the firm, not to any particular user group" (Staubus 1961, p. 25; Previts and Merino 1998, p. 281). For Staubus this "implies an investors' view of income, not an entity or managerial view" (1961, p. 25). He found "This emphasis upon investors … has, surprisingly enough, often been confused with a managerial point of view", and concluded, "to give greater consideration to the needs of investors than to the needs of managers and governments in discussions of 'general purpose' financial statements is reasonable enough" (Staubus 1961, p. 25).

Staubus seemed unaware that management strongly disagreed, and would push the profession into a threatening situation before it would challenge management's discretion. Only later did Staubus take seriously "manager's control over financial reporting" (1977, p. 7). He then realised the wisdom of distancing his decision-usefulness theory from the entity concept: "The entity point of view is too closely allied with the point of view used to defend diversity in accounting among independent entities [i.e., management's] to be acceptable to those who favor the decision-usefulness objective" (Staubus 1977, p. 460). This did not stop Staubus from implicitly adopting the entity concept, nor the FASB, as we will see. He overlooked that stymieing the development of an accounting theory based on Paton's "value data", was the commitment of May's generation from the late-1930s to conflicting objectives, stewardship and valuation. Staubus had not studied the history of stewardship before he published in 1961, and did not do so subsequently. As he put it, looking back in 2003,

> Accounting did have objectives before 1951, but they were, according to my search, never made explicit. Even the so-called stewardship objective did not appear in the literature until later [sic], and it was never used as a basis for a theory [sic]. If anyone had analyzed it or tried to build a theory on the stewardship objective, both the objective and the GAAP tied to it surely would have been found seriously deficient. For example,

> GAAP measurements were easily "gamed" by managements bent on manipulating earnings — a deficiency that remains substantially intact to this day. Stewardship cannot be evaluated using out-of-date measurements at both the beginning and end of the reporting period. (Staubus 2003, p. 163)

Staubus, in short, would have rejected "stewardship" if he had thought of it. At the time, he criticised Paton and Littleton for not establishing "the connection between" their "excellent discussions of the accountant's duty to the absentee investor and the role of accounting, especially through income computation, in aiding the flow of capital … and the several basic concepts on which the remainder of the monograph is based" (Staubus 1961, p. 5). He criticised their failure to explain how accounting is useful to investors in "aiding the flow of capital", how income is useful for investment decisions, but did not recognise their "stewardship" aim.

Staubus saw "one shining light in the series of AAA committee statements", the Supplementary Statement (of the 1948 revision) No. 8 Standards of Disclosure for Published Financial Reports (1954) (Zeff 2013, p. 271). The 1954 version highlighted investment decisions: "The underlying determinant of adequacy of disclosure in published financial reports is their usefulness in making decisions, particularly with respect to investment problems" (AAA 1955, p. 400). It argued, "the use by investors of published financial statements in making investment decisions and in exercising control over management should be considered of primary importance" (AAA 1957, p. 7), which Staubus "commended" (1958, p. 11; 1961, p. 8). However, he ignored the use of accounts "in exercising control over management", and the fact that, unlike the 1954 version, the 1957 version subsumed stewardship within decision-usefulness. As Zeff (2013, pp. 271–272) says, the 1957 committee adopted Paton's entity concept, "undoubtedly driven by" Sidney Davidson, "one of Paton's leading disciples", which explains, "the joining of investor use and stewardship", whereas the 1954 version separated them: "the traditional emphasis on the requirements of the stockholder group appears to be sound. In considering disclosure standards, therefore, the Committee has been concerned primarily with the use of financial statements (1) in the making of investment decisions and (2) in the exercise of investor control over management" (AAA 1955, p. 401). Ignoring this, Staubus (1958, p. 11) commended the 1957 version for "Recognition of the concept of discounted future cash movements [which] is a major contribution to the current statement and augurs well for future discussions of asset and liability measurement, both within AAA Committees and in other quarters". The 1957 Committee, like "many accounting theorists believe[d] that the discounted present value of the expected cash flows of an asset constitutes the conceptually 'best' measure of an asset's worth for many purposes" (Revsine 1973, p. 82).

Staubus (1961) was preoccupied with what he saw as the 1957 committee's failure to implement decision-usefulness in its development of principles (1977, p. 24). He only later recognised "One question that could be raised about the decision-usefulness objective is whether it includes the control and accountability role of accounting" (Staubus 1977, p. 28). Looking back, he concluded, "The answer seems to be a qualified yes — the qualification being that 'decisions' must be interpreted broadly" (Staubus 1977, pp. 28–29). Only in 2003 did he realise that when the profession eventually dropped stewardship as an independent objective in 1973, it meant crossing a "progressive" Rubicon. "By that point in history (1971–1973), with the APB's troubles in everyone's mind, the time was ripe for a progressive-minded body of practitioners to follow the lead of the academics. Stewardship and historical cost were no longer acceptable to those few thought leaders who had been asked to apply themselves to the issue. The result was that the decision-usefulness theory was presented to a much wider readership" (Staubus 2003, p. 166). Looking back, dropping stewardship was "progressive" for Staubus because "beyond influencing decisions of users", other "effects [of accounting] must be considered distinctly secondary" (1977, p. 29), a view endorsed by the FASB's conceptual framework (Chapter 7). Therefore, rather than not bothering, "none of the contributions to the literature of accounting begins by identifying investors as the major users of accounting information and proceeds with an unbroken chain of reasoning through the problems facing investors" (Staubus 1961, p. 8) because their immersion in stewardship's history, in accounting's "dual role", prevented it. Staubus, unaware of stewardship's history, in the Fisher-friendly environment of Chicago, could grasp the nettle, as the older generation could not. He recalled, "when I was seeking a conceptual base for a serious study of revenue in 1951, the complete absence of an objective of accounting in the literature struck me as a major handicap — one that I must overcome. Feeling the need for a general objective led me to the idea that financial information *should be useful* in making decisions. I am not sure I would have reached that point in my thinking in any environment other than that of The University of Chicago" (Staubus 2003, p. 163, emphasis added).

From a historically unencumbered normative standpoint, he concluded, "The information investors use in making their decisions is inadequate" (Staubus 1961, p. 8), and he took up the challenge to make it better. "*The purpose of accounting is to provide information which will be of assistance in making economic decisions*" (Staubus 1961, p. 10), and in particular, it should help investors make investment decisions. In a Fisher-friendly environment he was on safe ground in arguing, "The ideal information for investors to have when deciding to acquire or to hold an equitable interest in a firm is a schedule of future cash transfers from the firm to the holder of the equity" (Staubus 1961, p. 17). Staubus (1961, p. 26) therefore adopted Paton's accounting equation, "assets equal equities", distinguishing "specific equities": "assets minus specific equities (liabilities, including preferred stock) equal the residual equity". It followed, "To report the amount of the residual equity requires finding and measuring all of the entity's assets and specific equities" (Staubus 1961, p. 26). For valuation, he followed Canning, "The current value of the residual equity is equal to the total of all assets measured on the basis of present value minus the total of all of the specific equities measured at present value" (Staubus 1961, p. 33).

To measure these PVs became, like Moonitz, a question of "The type of evidence available to the accountant regarding the future of net asset items", which "varies" (Staubus 1961, p. 33). "In some cases he may have contractual evidence of a future cash movement. In other cases current market quotations are the best evidence of the item's future serviceability to residual equity holders. In still other situations, current market quotations may not be available and past quotations may have to be used" (Staubus 1961, p. 34). Accountants "should choose that measurement technique the application of which will contribute most to the accurate measurement of the present value of the residual equity" (1961, p. 49). They should "evaluate various kinds of evidence, choose one type that is most appropriate to the circumstances", and could use PV, NRV, RC, adjusted HC, and original HC (Staubus 1961, pp. 34–39). As for Staubus (1961, p. 50, Table 2, p. 51) "The selection of a measurement technique is a selection of the most appropriate type of evidence", so like Fisher, Paton and Canning, any value might have some relevance as a forecast of cash flows. Canning's "clear cut emphasis on future service", highlighted "the role of types of evidence of value and the linkages in the surrogate chain: the economic reasoning that permits net realizable value to be substituted for present value, replacement cost to be substituted for net realizable value, and historical cost to be substituted for replacement cost" (Staubus 1977, p. 122; 2003, p. 167). Ironically, Staubus (1961, p. ix) had the good fortune to have the intellectual freedom to seek to operationalise Fisher's theory in his classroom by ignoring history, or as he put it, by taking "a positive, independent approach to the subject", but history was on his side. The context that would force the profession to adopt his decision-usefulness approach, and make his name, rapidly emerged around him.

The Crisis of the 1960s

At the end of 1962, "the accounting treatment of the tax credit exploded on the scene", the first of three "confrontations between the APB and the combined forces of industry and the administrations of Presidents Kennedy, Johnson and Nixon" (Zeff 1978, p. 58). The APB issued Opinion No. 2 requiring deferring a new investment tax credit, but "found itself undercut two or three weeks later by an SEC release allowing both the deferment and the flow-through methods. A similar situation, but this time involving Congress rather than the SEC, occurred again at the end of 1971 in relation to the same matter, the investment tax credit" (Solomons 1983, p. 117). In 1962, "Corporate managements did not hesitate to make their views known to the Board, to the SEC, and to their own auditors" (Carey 1969b, p. 99). The Board split on how to account for the tax credit (Gore 1992, p. 14). When the SEC sided with management by issuing ASR 96 that allowed deferral or flow through, "the Board threw in the sponge", it was "a field day for the Press", its "prestige and authority … had been badly damaged" (Carey 1969b, p. 104). Thus started the "crisis of the 1960s" (Gore 1992, p. 8) during which "American accountants [were] in no doubt about the political sensitivity of their subject" (Solomons 1983, p. 117). Dominating the APB's history was "endeavouring to understand and cope with the third-party forces which were intervening in the standard-setting process", and its failure "to deal effectively with these forces led to its demise and the establishment in 1973 of the FASB" (Zeff 1978, p. 57; Gore 1992, p. 6).

In response to the investment tax-credit fiasco the AIA's executive committee tentatively approved a proposal that APB Opinions should not be the preferred alternative, but the required method, and auditors must qualify accounts for any departures (Carey 1969b, p. 111). In 1964, a meeting of the Institute's Council to discuss it "was the most animated, most heated, and the most extended which had ever occurred" (Carey 1969b, p. 113). The arguments for the proposal were that if the profession did not set standards the SEC would; that as matter stood the profession was not in control of GAAP. As its spokesperson said, "'Generally accepted accounting principles' sounds like something definite. Actually it means substantial authoritative support. This in turn indicates not only Institute bulletins and SEC releases, but also practices of the business community, textbooks and authoritative precedent. We cannot provide a satisfactory answer to the question, generally accepted by whom — the Institute; the corporations which are being audited; the textbook writers" (Carey 1969b, p. 114). During the "great debate" the major argument against the proposal was that the APB could issue an Opinion that was "highly debatable", "a client refused to follow the APB", and "this decision was concurred in by the auditor" (Carey 1969b, pp. 115, 117). The spokesperson for the opposition "reminded the Council that corporations had the responsibility for their own financial statements and authority over them: the threat of qualifications ... would not compel companies to change reporting methods which they preferred" (Carey 1969b, p. 116). Furthermore, auditors could rebel because it would "violate the dictionary meanings of the words 'generally' and 'accepted'" to require auditors to qualify accounts if they agreed with "the client's method" (Carey 1969b, p. 116). The experience of the investment tax credit showed this was no idle threat. "Talk of 'splits in the profession', 'squabbles', and 'clear defiance' by three of the Big Eight Firms (who had stated that they would not expect their clients to follow Opinion No. 2) clearly undermined any hopes of presenting a united front to the watching world" (Gore 1992, p. 15). After extended debate, by a majority of 124 to 51 the Council voted to appoint a special committee "to review the entire matter *de novo*" (Carey 1969b, p. 117).

A Statement of Basic Accounting Theory

Fellow academics were unwilling to concede Staubus the prize, but his "decision-usefulness" approach fitted well with the emerging new-generation consensus of how to respond to the crisis. In 1966, the AAA issued "A Statement of Basic Accounting Theory" (ASOBAT), "The first sign of institutional acceptance of the decision-usefulness objective" (Zeff 2013, p. 278). The AAA told the ASOBAT committee it "should not feel bound in any way by the format or content of previous statements issued by this or other organizations" (1966, p. v). Staubus' saw his normative, revolutionary zeal for decision-usefulness evident in ASOBAT. He claimed the committee "bought the decision-usefulness approach lock, stock, and barrel" (Staubus 1977, p. 25).[3] In fact, as the Trueblood Committee later put it, ASOBAT "agree[d] with the conclusion drawn by many others that ... [t]he basic objective of financial statements is to provide information useful for economic decision making" (AICPA 1973, p. 61), derived from Canning's view that accounting was the statistics of income measurement and therefore multiple valuations bases could be appropriate. As ASOBAT "equated custodianship with stewardship" (Zeff 2013, p. 278), it effectively abolished May's and Paton and Littleton's notion of stewardship as a report on management's performance, thereby avoiding any conflict with decision-usefulness. It dodged the question of defining stewardship any further by asserting, "The interests of society are paramount in defining this function and have been expressed in the corporation codes of the various states" (AAA 1966, p. 5). It thereby relegated "stewardship" to the vagaries of the state legislatures who "have hardly been vigilant in giving effect to genuine stewardship in US corporate society" (Zeff 2013, p. 279). It "discussed the general principle of the stewardship relationship" seen as legal custodianship, "in which it ventured the view, 'Accountants can prepare meaningful reports of stewardship only to the extent that they are aware of or can postulate accurately the provisions of the agreement between the parties to the stewardship arrangement'" (Zeff 2013, p. 279). "Stewardship" could not therefore be a general objective.

The committee identified a list of external users: "present and potential investors, creditors, employees, stock exchanges, governmental units, customers" and their representatives, "such as security analysts, trade associations, credit rating bureaus, and trade union officers" (AAA 1966, p. 20). It asserted, "Although accounting has often been thought of as

---

[3]George H. Sorter, from the University of Chicago, a committee member, who reviewed Staubus (1961), disputed his claim to originality. Staubus suggested Sorter had read his PhD, and this was the source of the committee's inspiration, which Sorter denied (Zeff 2013, fn. 30, p. 316). As Zeff (2013, p. 278) says, "Sorter was ... already a 'believer' and may well have been the driving force within the committee behind the decision-usefulness approach".

essentially historical in nature, it is important to recognize that emphasis upon those accounting techniques that deal with future plans and expectations has been increasing, and that this trend may be expected to continue" (AAA 1966, p. 5). As Zeff says, "This forward-looking focus certainly set the committee apart from AAA committees that had been issuing statements on accounting principles from 1936 to 1957. For the AAA, this was revolutionary thinking" (2013, p. 279). Because like others it saw the problem as one of "evidence", it produced a list of four "standards for accounting information", measurement standards of "relevance", "verifiability", "freedom from bias", and "quantifiability". HC could be relevant, so it recommended reporting both HC and "current-cost" (RC) information, but included the net gains from current-cost valuations, net of tax, in net income (AAA 1966, pp. 85, 94). Unlike predecessor committees, "Nowhere in the external reporting section of the report was conservatism mentioned" (Zeff 2013, p. 279).

To curb management's power other academics accepted it was necessary to change from May's and Paton and Littleton's inductive approach, reasoning from what "is" to what "ought to be", to the deductive approach, reasoning from what "ought to be" to practice, as Staubus had done. Robert R. Sterling, Associate Professor of Accounting, University of Kansas, highlighted, "The committee's methodology is self-consciously antithetical to the previous inductive or empirical methods. They imply that such methods do not yield a theory: 'many accountants ... equate 'accounting theory' with the sum total of all accounting practices currently in use'" (1967a, p. 96). Because "The function of a theory to them is prescriptive, not descriptive", theory gave the "means of accepting or rejecting accounting methods" (Sterling 1967a, p. 96). By contrast, "the [inductive] theory cannot, in principle, deny anything and, therefore, it is totally useless except as an apology for what is or was. ... Except for some theologies, I know of no discipline other than accounting which induces what ought to be from what is" (Sterling 1967a, pp. 96–97). The committee, he observed, was engaged in a "battle" against "others" with a "propensity to 'conservatism', 'matching and attaching', etc", that is, many accountants, but particularly management who resisted any restrictions: "Eventually the battle will have to be fought at this level of abstraction. One will have to present well-formed arguments about what accounting ought to be" (Sterling 1967a, pp. 97–98). Sterling frankly recognised, "The major problem facing public accounting today is its lack of power ...[;] that the management's power far outweighs the accountant's ...: if accountants are to judge managements, then we must deny management the power to hire and fire accountants and the power to select from diverse principles as they see fit" (1973, p. 66).

To deal with "others", to justify what accounting ought to be, ASOBAT argued it was necessary to start from "user needs", and not from "matching and attaching". Sterling applauded this separation of theory from existing practice, but criticised the AAA because it did not specify what information management ought to provide, and did not completely abandon the cost-allocation matching model. Sterling thought, "It will take a master weaver to weave 'accounting is matching and attaching' together with 'accounting is a measurement-communication system'" (1967a, p. 98), and "expressed doubt as to whether such a weaver could be found" (Previts and Merino 1998, p. 322). Nevertheless, Sterling highlighted the significance of this move, that it signalled the end to the debate over whether accountants had a "cost theory of value", that "it is no longer appropriate to argue about which convention or assumption comes closest to the actual cost or income" (1967a, p. 99). Against May and Paton and Littleton's approach, "It is not appropriate to assume that if we carefully describe (fully disclose) the methods used, then the figures will be meaningful, or that only invested cost or transaction data are the subject matter of accounting, or that by its very name accounting reflects costs" (Sterling 1967a, p. 99). "Under the new view, measurements in accounting are a function of some end. … This is a change in 'world-view' and is the stuff that revolutions are made of" (Sterling 1967a, pp. 99–100). Sterling argued, however, the evidence-approach would not work because different individual users of accounts "may have different decision models" (1967a, p. 105). He ridiculed ASOBAT's claim that HC or RC had predictive relevance (Sterling 1967a, pp. 109–111). Sterling agreed with the decision-usefulness "world-view", but influentially advocated exit price (1967a, fn. 12, p. 111). He criticised the committee because it "suffered from indecisiveness as to what the Statement ought to be" (Sterling 1967a, p. 112, fn. 14), ignoring that the committee probably anticipated, as the SEC quickly made clear, it would not "accept registrants' filings which are predicated on the use of current cost in the financial statements" (Zeff 2013, p. 27). However, overall, Sterling made clear in his "opinion, the new view is the correct one and it has the potential to change accounting from a ritualistic and dogmatic tradition to a vital part of the economic process and an academic discipline with problems that would challenge the greatest intellects" (Sterling 1967a, p. 105) and, by implication, those available to management.

As the AAA were preparing ASOBAT, the APB started to prepare what appeared in 1970, after many watering-down drafts, as "Basic Concepts and Accounting Principles Underlying Financial Statements of Business Enterprises", which was "intended to reach a broad audience and not just professional accountants" (Zeff 2013, p. 280). Pushing the profession, coinciding with "a few widely publicized law-suits against accounting firms, involving well-known companies", Carey complained, "Almost every prestigious financial or business magazine, and almost every columnist who dealt with financial matters found it necessary to publish a critical re-examination of the accounting profession in general, and its 'generally accepted accounting principles' in particular" (1969b, pp. 135–136). Press coverage "mushroomed in the 1960s, especially when the APB moved into controversial territory — accounting for the investment tax credit, leases, pensions, income tax allocation, convertible debt, extraordinary items, and business combinations and goodwill" (Zeff 2003a, p. 196). Critical articles appeared in *Fortune*, *Business Week*, *Forbes*, *Time*, *Newsweek*, *The Wall Street Journal*, *The New York Times*, *Harvard Business Review*, *California Management Review* and newspapers across the country (Zeff 2003a, p. 196). *Forbes* declared, "generally accepted accounting principles mean damn little"; it ran an article with the headline: 'What *Are* Earnings? The Growing Credibility Gap'" (Carey 1969b, p. 136). Law journals published critical articles (Carey 1969b, pp. 137–138). In 1967, the Financial Executives Institute (FEI) with other business groups "organized letter-writing campaigns in opposition to the Opinion", APB 11 *Accounting for Income Taxes*; the insurance industry "mounted an all-out pressure campaign"; "the American Bankers Association opposed a proposed Opinion" (Carey 1969b, pp. 133–134). Carey complained, "Few APB prouncements escaped opposition from some corporations or industry groups" (1969b, p. 134).

Management and the Profession

The APB accelerated its output of Opinions from 1964 to 1969 — producing them for leases, pensions, reporting the results of operations, deferred taxation, bank accounting, convertible debt — and produced nine widely distributed research studies (Carey 1969b, p. 142) — but they dug it deeper into the same hole. To address the threat posed by management's discretion, the AICPA organised the *Seaview Symposium on Financial Reporting* in 1968 in Atlantic City, New Jersey, the "first occasion on which representatives of the two principal suppliers of financial information, management and auditors, confronted spokesmen for the two principal user groups, investors and credit grantors" (Carey 1969b, p. 143). The question was who should select "accounting principles"? Financial executives, "preparers", "emphasized their responsibility in presenting financial statements", "that reporting to the stockholders and the public was an important part of their stewardship function, and must remain so. Accordingly … the ultimate authority to decide reporting principles … should rest with management, subject to the check of public accountants for general acceptability and regulatory agencies for conformity to law" (Burton 1969, p. 35). Management, "the preparers suggested … were in the best position to know what accounting was most meaningful to describe the operations of a company", had "knowledge of a firm's plans, expectations and intentions" (Burton 1969, p. 35). Therefore, "when there are alternative accounting methods", "management should have the freedom to adopt that method which in its judgment best revealed the progress and status of the firm … [and] to adopt a different method when considered necessary to meet changing circumstances or conditions" (Burton 1969, p. 35). To bridge the gap, some suggested, "management should have heavier representation on the board, but the prevailing view seemed to be that it would be preferable to have the Board principally made up of practitioners" (Carey 1969b, p. 143).[4] Practitioners noted "expressions from management people, as well as other user groups, indicating a desire to have a voice at the earliest possible stage in the development of Board Opinions" (Carey 1969b, p. 143). Accountants and analysts persuaded the financial executives that "ground rules were necessary to make reporting useful", and there were "few demands for total flexibility" (Burton 1969, p. 35). Falling back on "disclosure as at least a partial substitute for uniformity", the discussion "led to a consensus that the two points of view were not basically inconsistent" (Burton 1969, p. 35), but there was no attempted reconciliation. In holding the meeting, and holding the line that accountants should decide the principles, Carey (1969b, p. 143) thought the APB had "won its spurs", but the fight for control of principles continued.

In January 1969, the *Wall Street Journal* published an article, "Frustrated CPAs — Accounting Body Fails in Attempts to Change Some

[4]At that time, the Board of 29 had three financial executives (Carey 1969b, p. 99).

Firms' Reporting", claiming "Company resistance has led the accounting profession to back down on several proposals to change the ways many companies tally and report profits" (Carey 1969b, p. 138). Carey accepted as a "fact ... that corporate management was partly to blame for the delays in moving forward" (1969b, p. 139). This was evident in the APB's attempt to ban the pooling-of-interests method in the merger boom then occurring in response to "considerable public interest", stimulated in part by the trenchant and widely read criticisms of Abraham J. Briloff, professor of accounting at Baruch College, New York, and regulate goodwill accounting (Gore 1992, p. 15). It issued an initial draft Opinion in July 1969 proposing banning the pooling method, and another allowing immediately writing-off purchased goodwill against profit or amortising up to 40 years. "When these initial positions became known publicly, a campaign was launched by many in business against the Opinion. This seemingly succeeded, for the next draft approved of pooling under certain defined conditions", and after "a squabble over specific rules" (Gore 1992, p. 15) the APB published Opinion 16 *Business Combinations* allowing pooling, and Opinion 17 *Goodwill* requiring amortisation over a maximum of 40-years. The problems in producing these Opinions precipitated "a movement to undertake a comprehensive review of the procedures for setting accounting standards" (Zeff 1972, p. 16).

Charles T. Horngren (1972, p. 39), an APB member from 1968 to 1973, concluded, "Perhaps the APB should really be renamed the Accounting Principles-Political Action Board. Without public support, which usually means without the widespread support of industry, significant changes are seldom possible"; "both the SEC and the APB" were reduced to "impotence ... when hostility [was] rampant". To Donald J. Kirk (1988, p. 9), former Price Waterhouse partner and FASB member (1973–1977), and chairman (1978–1986), "It had become obvious ... in those 'go-go' years that managers in many instances made accounting choices to serve their own self-interests ... to prop up stock prices, increase borrowing capacity, enhance personal compensation, or maintain or enhance public opinion about managerial skills". Responding to these pressures, having worked on it since 1965, in 1970 the APB issued the AICPA's *Basic Concepts and Accounting Principles Underlying Financial Statements of Business Enterprises, Statement of the Accounting Principles Board No. 4*, at best an equivocal revolutionary tract. It appeared revolutionary when it subsumed "stewardship" within decision-usefulness: "The basic purpose … is to provide quantitative financial information about a business enterprise that is useful to statement users, particularly owners and creditors, in making economic decisions. This purpose includes providing information that can be used in evaluating management's effectiveness in fulfilling its stewardship and other managerial responsibilities" (APB 1970, paragraph 73). Yuji Ijiri, professor of accounting and economics, Carnegie Mellon University, therefore criticised the *Statement* for ignoring the "control function" (1971, p. 46), by which, consistent with Marxian accounting, he meant "accountability", if not for the rate of profit:

> The control function means that the resources of the enterprise are properly controlled by its managers and their accountability to the owners is effectively established. If the function of financial accounting were only informational, financial accounting would be of no use to investors who do not read financial statements. Actually, financial accounting is of great use even for such investors by providing behavioural constraints over managers. … The fact that economic activities are recorded and reported influences economic activities themselves. More responsible or accountable activities are carried out when they are properly recorded. In this sense, accountability has always been one of the bases of sound financial accounting. (Ijiri 1971, pp. 46–47)

By "accountability", like Sprague (1907), Ijiri meant results control: "Accounting measurement may then be characterized as primarily economic performance measurement" (1975, p. 34), but he was almost a lone voice and, like Littleton, was an inductivist with no theory of value. "Ijiri's framework is a rigorous theory for stewardship reporting with the use of historical cost" (Zeff 2013, p. 275). Ijiri accepted, "In the free-enterprise system, one of the central goals of an entity is achieving a certain level of profits. Therefore, it follows that an important objective of financial statements is to report on this achievement" (Cyert and Ijiri 1974, p. 31). However, he was a "functionalist" because he nevertheless also accepted, "The concept of profit is not an easy one to define and quantify", that "It is almost as difficult to quantify as are many goals of society such as freedom, security, or economic prosperity" (Cyert and Ijiri 1974, p. 31)! When Ijiri criticised the "failure to mention the control function", he meant therefore the failure to define it. The *Statement* saw two ways in which investors would use accounts, to "retain, increase, or decrease proportionate ownership; evaluate the use and stewardship of resources by management" (APB 1970, paragraph 44), as though decision-usefulness and stewardship were distinct, but it did not define stewardship. The *Statement* elsewhere said the overarching objective was to provide "information which assists users in estimating earning potential, including information about the past and present which could help users make predictions (paragraphs 77–79)" (Zeff 2013, p. 280). To achieve this it elaborated seven "qualitative objectives": relevance, understandability, verifiability, neutrality, timeliness, comparability, and completeness (paragraphs 87–94). "Conservatism was not mentioned" (Zeff 2013, p. 280). The APB issued APB 4 as a non-mandatory *Statement* and not as an *Opinion*, but it was the first time the profession had acknowledged the decision-useful approach (Zeff 2013, p. 281). However, for many it did not go far enough — its apparent retention of stewardship as a potentially conflicting objective, and its defence of existing GAAP, remained obstacles to a coherent normative revolutionary strategy against management. The APB's timidity, from the revolutionaries' perspective, that it "encased its objectives in a Statement and … devoted most of the contents to an explication of existing GAAP, were an important reason why pressure built on the AICPA in 1970–1971 to establish a blue ribbon committee to prepare a normative statement of the objectives of financial statements" (Zeff 2013, p. 281).

The AAA set up a "Committee on the Establishment of a Commission" in August 1970 into the problems of setting accounting standards. It agreed, "the formulation of accounting principles in an optimal manner … [was] a matter of great importance", there was considerable "dissatisfaction with the present methods of formulating these principles", and "the consideration of possible shortcomings should not be left wholly in the hands of any single interest group" (AAA 1971, p. 610). The terms of reference were "to consider the feasibility and desirability of establishing a Commission to study and recommend an organizational structure for (a) advancing the formulation and modification of generally accepted accounting principles and (b) the issuance of authoritative pronouncements concerning the application of such principles" (AAA 1971, p. 609). In December 1970, after Robert M. Trueblood, chair of Touche Ross & Co., threatened to opt out of the APB and negotiate its own standards with the SEC unless there were major changes (Gore 1992, pp. 19–20), the AICPA called a conference to consider how it could improve accounting standard setting. President Armstrong observed at the conference's opening, "criticism of the profession's current efforts to establish accounting principles — as well as suggestions for new approaches to the task — could not safely be ignored" (*Journal of Accountancy*, February 1971, p. 11). The profession attracted criticism, because as John C. (Sandy) Burton, professor of accounting and finance at Columbia, soon to be the SEC's chief accountant said, "it has given every impression of having attempted to avoid responsibility" (1971, p. 49). It was because the profession had repeatedly emphasised,

> … that auditors attest only to the general acceptability, rather than the desirability of management's choice of accounting principles … that articles critical of the accounting profession are beginning to appear more frequently in the business press. One such article, which appeared recently in *Forbes*, concluded: 'It is becoming increasingly clear that management, not the CPA, is in the driver's seat when it comes to financial statements. CPAs like to say that accounting is an art, not a science. Their critics rejoin that if art it be, the corporate treasurers are the artists. The auditors merely sign the painting — and collect their paychecks'. (Burton 1971, pp. 49–50)

The conference discussed the "option" of the profession ceasing to set standards, handing over to the SEC. This was an outcome "no-one in the private-sector wanted" because it threatened business as well as "the remarkable economic success" of accountants (Burton 1971, p. 47), and the SEC made clear "that it was simply unable to do the job" (Gore 1992, pp. 21–22). Dismissing this "unthinkable" option and the "unacceptable" *status quo*, responding to the "crisis of confidence", the AICPA decided to establish two study groups (Gore 1992, pp. 21, 23; Zeff 2015, p. 147).

One group chaired by Francis M. Wheat produced a report in 1972, *Establishing Financial Accounting Standards*, which "concluded that many of the APB's problems were fatal flaws" (Storey and Storey 1998, p. 45). It had insufficient resources, but the real problems were that the "APB was weakened by nagging doubts about its independence … and the lack of coherence and logic of many of its prouncements, which resulted from having to compromise too many opposing points of view" (Storey and Storey 1998, p. 45). However, management had been particularly responsible, as Horngren (1972, p. 41) made clear: "Whatever the form of a successor body to the APB, I hope that business executives do not have any larger role in setting accounting principles than they now possess", because "there is an inherent conflict between their role as managers and the task of measuring their own performance". Many "business executives have repeatedly claimed that the APB gives insufficient attention to the views of industry", but based on Horngren's "experience, the claims are completely unjustified. On the contrary, the Board is inundated with such views" (1972, p. 41). Industry had representation on the APB, and "the practitioners who dominate the Board ... listen to the views of their clients. ... The opinions of business executives come through sharply and clearly — and they are given conscientious consideration. For example, every recent APB Opinion has changed considerably in response to industry reactions" (Horngren 1972, p. 41). The Wheat Committee proposed dealing with the profession's lack of institutional independence by creating the Financial Accounting Foundation, independent from the AICPA, with trustees who would raise funds and appoint members to a new Financial Accounting Standards Board (FASB). The Committee proposed changing the title to include "standards" rather than "principles" because the latter "has proven to be an extraordinarily elusive term" (AICPA 1972, p. 13).

The Trueblood Committee

The other group, that began work in April 1971 and reported in October 1973, was chaired by Robert Trueblood, former Institute President, "an intellectual leader of the profession" (Zeff 2013, p. 281). The AICPA (1973, p. 67) told the group "the study should not be limited to a refinement of Statement 4" (Zeff 2013, p. 281). Given the APB's failure to stand up to management, the aim was to nail down the decision-usefulness objective and overthrow May's approach based on HC and stewardship. This was the fundamental problem, as Oscar S. Gellein, member of the APB during its last years, put it, "the absence of a structure of fundamental notions that would elevate the level at which debate begins and provide assurance of considerable consistency" (Storey and Storey 1998, p. 46) to assert intellectual leadership over management. The "Trueblood Committee" marshalled the best brains from "accounting, the disciplines of economics, financial analysis, law, management, mathematics and sociology" (AICPA 1973, p. 10). It had three academics, three audit partners, two financial executives and a financial analyst — employed six research staff, headed by George Sorter, assisted by Joshua Ronen, from the University of Chicago, who employed seven consultants, and observers from audit firms and universities (Zeff 2013, p. 282). It undertook "an ambitious programme of research and enquiry" including a public hearing, interviews with "business leaders and important decision makers", and invited papers (Zeff 2013, p. 282). It understood its historic importance, "aware of the far-reaching effects that a study of this type can have on the evolution of financial reporting" (AICPA 1973, p. 9). Its aim was to foster accounting's "adaptation" to a changed "environment", to remove what was "incompatible" or in "conflict" with what "ought to be" (AICPA 1973, p. 13). Accounting, it argued, "is a social system much like language and law … [that] tends to evolve by adapting to its environment; but evolutionary changes may occur which are incompatible or even in conflict with current notions of what the objectives of this system ought to be. An explicit statement of objectives, therefore, is essential to its rational development" (AICPA 1973, p. 13). The study group insisted, "the development of objectives should not be based on the operating needs of the managers of the business", "but on the needs of users of financial information outside enterprises or organizations" (AICPA 1973, pp. 9–10). "Managers … are both preparers and users of financial statements" (AICPA 1973, p. 10), but their discretion would not now be central to their preparation.

The Trueblood Committee's report built on the "decision usefulness" approach of APB 4 and the AAA's "Statement of Basic Accounting Theory" (1966) (AICPA 1973, p. 9). It was dominated by the academics, "the research staff, abetted by the financial analyst member … [who] played a decisive role in driving the key recommendation in the report, namely, that financial statements should provide investors and creditors with information about the cash-generating ability of the enterprise, and eventually the cash flows to them" (Zeff 2016, p. 134). The committee proposed 12 statements about objectives, but "The basic objective of financial statements is to provide information useful for making economic decisions" (AICPA 1973, p. 13); the other 11 implemented that objective. It listed the users, but focused on investors and creditors because, unlike management, they "have limited authority, ability, or resources to obtain information and who rely on financial statements as their principal source of information about an enterprise's economic activities" (AICPA 1973, p. 17). Implicitly adopting Paton's entity concept, like Staubus (1961), the study group asserted, "the information needs of creditors and investors are essentially the same. Both groups are concerned with the enterprise's ability to generate cash flows to them and with their own ability to predict, compare, and evaluate the amount, timing, and related uncertainty of these future cash flows" (AICPA 1973, p. 20). Creditors and shareholders concern themselves as individuals with only the circuit of money capital, M-M′: "the primary and continuing goal of every commercial enterprise is to increase its monetary wealth so that over time it can return the maximum amount of cash to its owners" (AICPA 1973, p. 20). The problem was, "the primary goal can be measured meaningfully only over relatively long periods of time and, with precision, only when the enterprise is ultimately dissolved. But measurements for a time span that runs to dissolution are not useful" (AICPA 1973, p. 20). Thus, "A fundamental purpose of accounting is to provide interim measures of enterprise progress" that "should relate to the enterprise goal of producing the most cash for its owners. These measurements, therefore, should emphasize the actual or prospective disbursement or receipt of cash" (AICPA 1973, p. 22).

In certainty, "economic and accounting earnings as measures of better-offness would be readily determinable and would be identical", simply, as Fisher showed, "the change in the present value of cash flows", "But in the real world" measures of "Earnings are based on conventions and rules.... Present accounting practice seeks to base such measurements on performance — services rendered. Since these measurements are made without benefit of certainty, they are of necessity imprecise because they are based on allocations and similar estimates. ... A significant question, therefore, relates to whether accounting measurements of earnings can in fact be made more useful to those with varying interests in financial statements" (AICPA 1973, p. 22). As all parties were interested in an enterprise's "ability to generate cash in the future", and because "Cash generating ability and earnings are closely related and the longer the period, the closer the relationship", all were interested in its "earning power" (AICPA 1973, p. 23). However, in the short-run, "since the future is uncertain and since users differ in their response to uncertainty, such a measure is necessarily subjective at any time", "Financial statements should provide users with information for predicting, comparing and evaluating earning power" (AICPA 1973, p. 23). The study group therefore concluded, "An objective of financial statements is to provide users with information for predicting, comparing and evaluating earning power" (AICPA 1973, p. 24). Echoing Canning, and following Staubus, accountants should report on "earning power", expected cash-generating ability, by embedding this objective into the measurement of earnings. "Since the goals of an enterprise and its earning process involve the use of cash to generate the maximum amount of cash, earnings cycles should relate cash receipts and disbursements", whether the cycles were "complete, incomplete, or prospective" (AICPA 1973, pp. 27–28). Not accountants' operating cycle, but M-M′: "While users may differ, their economic decisions are similar. Each user measures sacrifices and benefits in terms of the actual or prospective disbursement or receipt of cash" (AICPA 1973, p. 20). A minority, "probably the financial executives", saw earnings cycles as "a simplistic and/or impractical approach to the measurement of accounting earnings" (Zeff 2013, p. 283; AICPA 1973, p. 29). Completed earnings cycles were easy, but assessing the progress of incomplete cycles, "ones where the ultimate cash, for example, from unsold products, has not been received" (Zeff 2013, p. 283), were not. The majority responded that change in the value of assets "may provide the best current indication of the outcome of the cycle" (AICPA 1973, p. 31). The PV ideal "is unattainable by any present direct measurement process", but following Canning and Staubus they argued, "Different approaches to value determination of particular assets and liabilities seem desirable, since no single valuation basis approaches the ideal in every circumstance" (AICPA 1973, pp. 32–33). To move towards the ideal, it suggested, "Various current value measurements could be used as indicators of the prospective benefits of assets and sacrifices for liabilities, and of the current sacrifice or benefit aspects of holding them" (AICPA 1973, p. 35).

The study group accepted, "accountability … is a broad term that encompasses stewardship" (1973, p. 25), and engaged Paul Rosenfield (AICPA) to survey the literature (1974). Rosenfield found "Views … vary widely", but the one "apparently most widely held" was, consistent with British/Marxian accounting, that "stewardship responsibilities reported on in financial statements consist not only of safeguarding assets but also of making progress toward the goals that the stewards are expected to achieve. The view is stated in terms of performance, using assets gainfully, productive use of assets, profitability, success or failure, producing earnings or profits, and so forth" (1974, p. 123). Rosenfield (1974, p. 124) found many writers, including May, arguing stewardship required HCA, but others adopted a PV perspective and argued "holding gains and losses should be part of a report on stewardship". He found "Many apparently believe that reporting on stewardship is the only function of the basic financial statements", but just as many "contend that reporting on stewardship is only one of several major functions" (Rosenfield 1974, pp. 124–125). In popular usage "stewardship" referred to responsibilities over a wide range of organizations and situation: "Synonyms for *steward* … include … *custodian, trustee, guardian, fiduciary and manager*" (Rosenfield 1974, p. 125). Therefore, consistent with Marxian accounting, Cyert and Ijiri (1974) recommended "accountability … to designate the function of financial statements termed *stewardship* … because accountability does not have separate, differing connotations depending on the types of entities and the responsibilities involved" (Rosenfield 1974, p. 125). Rosenfield concluded, "A person who is accountable to another person for his behavior may be required to report his behavior or its results to the other person; in any event he is subject to reward or punishment depending on whether the behavior for which he is accountable fulfils his responsibilities" (1974, p. 125). Applied to businesses it meant accountability for results: "An objective of financial statements is to report on the control and use of resources by those accountable for their control and use to those to whom they are accountable. … Managers of a business enterprise in particular are responsible for achieving the goal of operating the business successfully" (Rosenfield 1974, p. 126). It followed, "the narrow view of some that the subject matter of stewardship reports is confined to the safeguarding of assets does not reflect the requirement.… Persons who are accountable to others are judged by an ideal standard — by behavior or results that would be ideal in the circumstances" (Rosenfield 1974, p. 126). The ideal standard, according to Marxian accounting, is the required rate of profit, which depends on the circumstances, which must be "judged" by the capital market. As Rosenfield pointed out, "Large corporations may have thousands or millions of stockholders, none of whom is able singly to apply sanctions directly to the management. The managers are not unaccountable, however.… Sanctions are available" (1974, p. 128). "Management cannot survive without the confidence of the company's investors. Without that confidence stock prices fall, credit dries up, and one way or another management finds itself restricted or even removed" (Rosenfield 1974, p. 128). Rosenfield also recognised, "Successful discharge of accountability by management … brings them rewards such as acceptance by stockholders of higher management compensation levels, profits from stock options, and increased prestige and opportunities for career enhancement" (1974, pp. 128–129).

Rosenfield's views are consistent with British/Marxian proprietary theory in which the directors are accountable to the capital market for target ROI. Management is punished or rewarded according to results for which investors collectively judge it responsible, for example, by comparing them with sector averages. Consistent with British/Marxian RCA, Rosenfield concluded, “The idea that the function of financial statements as stewardship reports calls for accounting based on historical costs needs re-examination”, arguing, “Standards … that report on the achievement of goals expected of management … should be discovered and adopted” (1974, p. 129). In his view, it was only “Confused terminology and the absence of analysis [that] have deterred accountants from discovering just where it leads” (Rosenfield 1974, p. 132). However, given the study group’s commitment to decision-usefulness, preventing recognition of stewardship as a distinct objective was his other conclusion that “As reports on accountable behavior, financial information should contain information about past events. People are not accountable for the future, as least not until it arrives” (Rosenfield 1974, p. 129).

The study group agreed with Rosenfield, “An objective of financial statements is to supply information useful in judging management’s ability to utilize enterprise resources effectively in achieving the primary enterprise goal” (AICPA 1974, p. 26). It agreed, “Stewardship refers to the efficient administration of resources and the execution of plans for conserving and consuming them. Reporting on management’s stewardship has long been recognized as a principal purpose of financial statements” (AICPA 1973, p. 25). However, contrary to Rosenfield, accounts confined to history could not in its view meet this objective because past events “cannot be assessed without considering their probable outcome”, because “Information about past earnings is significant for evaluating enterprise earning power, except when the past is not a valid portent of the future” (AICPA 1974, p. 23)! Its “accountability” objective was, therefore, to report on future consequences, “about potential as well as actual results” (AICPA 1973, p. 26). It recognised management’s accountability was to “all investors — past, present and potential” (AICPA 1973, p. 25), but as individuals, not collectively: “In the United States, where the economic system emphasizes private enterprise, individuals and enterprises generally attempt to maximize their own wealth. Financial information helps them make sound economic decisions” (AICPA 1973, p. 14). The study group implicitly adopted Fisher’s view that only individuals can have “income”, have the utility of consumption. It gave an example, “in deciding whether to sell a bushel of wheat for cash, the seller can estimate with some precision the expected benefits from sale, that is, the proceeds. Whether the amount of the proceeds is such that the seller is better off, and by how much, is a matter that only he can judge" (AICPA 1973, p. 17). Accounting's function was therefore to give individuals information on an enterprise's cash generating ability, its "earning power", leaving it to them to judge how much "better off" they were. The Trueblood Committee thereby "did much to refocus discussions in the accounting policy arena from stewardship reporting" (Zeff 1999, p. 101), away from the "cost theory of value", following Canning by defining "accountability" to mean for economic value. "Accountability extends beyond the element of stewardship involved in the safekeeping of assets entrusted to custody. ... Management is accountable for the value of assets as well as for their costs. ... Since the principal goal of a commercial enterprise is to maximize cash return to owners, its management is accountable for progress towards this goal" (AICPA 1973, p. 25).

Management fought against the demise of May's system, defending his notion of "stewardship". In 1973, the FEI's Research Foundation offered "its support to the Trueblood Committee", and after "several meetings ... concluded that it could be helpful by doing research on the businessman's view of the purposes of financial statements" (Rice *et al.* 1973, p. v). It interviewed top executives from 65 organisations, mostly large firms, but the Trueblood Committee probably found it unhelpful because 75 percent identified the "*overall* purpose of financial reporting to be accountability for performance, or stewardship" (Rice *et al.* 1973, pp. 11, 14–15), giving "a ringing endorsement of the stewardship objective and, one supposes, of ... historical cost" (Zeff 2013, p. 285). Linking "stewardship" to HC was May's interpretation in which "performance" meant "earning capacity" based on management's selection of accounting methods based on HC. Like May, many thought, "a realistic statement of income is more important in future accounting development than a realistic valuation for balance sheets" (Rice *et al.* 1973, p. 15). The interviewees were resolute in their "insistence that stewardship can be assessed only in the fullness of time [which] implies that *consistent* year-to-year treatment is more important than the specific income measurement technique chosen", "that any one year's statements could give a distorted portrayal of performance" (Rice *et al.* 1973, p. 15). They accepted the focus on profitability meant "financial statements were less than adequate for assessing present financial condition", accepted "that stewardship accounting required an indication of present condition as well as past performance", and saw the solution as "supplemental ... statements or disclosure" (Rice *et al.* 1973, p. 16). However, while the executives' "posture toward ... fuller disclosure ... is flexible", "most seemed to feel that since they are ultimately responsible for the financial statements, to develop disclosure standards ... is their prerogative" (Rice *et al.* 1973, p. 20). Like May, the executives stressed "the limitations of present financial statements", which they accepted were "the historical cost reporting basis and the importance assigned to a single earnings per share figure", but nevertheless, "management was unable to endorse changes in accounting concepts, because they felt that, on balance, none would improve present practice" (Rice *et al.* 1973, p. 19).

The study group's treatment of stewardship also drew criticism from some leading accountants. Hector R. Anton, partner in Haskin & Sells, argued, "First the Objective sets a goal that cannot be met because accounting cannot measure 'management's ability to use resources effectively in achieving the primary enterprise goal'" (Anton 1976, p. 47). This was not just because "the results reported by accounting are clouded by the interaction of management ability and a host of other factors that management cannot control and often cannot even be expected to anticipate" (Anton 1976, p. 47), judging which he, in effect, like Rosenfield, left to the market. As important, "the data are not to be considered in relation to control, but rather in relation to another more basic objective — user decision-making" (Anton 1976, p. 47). Second, therefore, Anton argued, "the objective as stated depends on the assumption that 'the principal goal of a commercial enterprise is to maximize its cash return to owners', a proposition that ... is neither substantiated in the report or generally accepted. Moreover, it probably does not describe the behavior of most enterprises. The assumption of maximization of cash flow to owners is crucial ... because it sets the standard against which stewardship is to be judged" (Anton 1976, p. 47).

Despite criticisms, the FASB had replaced the APB by late 1973, and it used the Trueblood report "as the template for its own concepts statement on the objectives of financial reporting" (Zeff 2013, p. 285). Management had lost overt control of accounting. Robert K Mautz, CPA, Ernst & Ernst partner, Cost Accounting Standards Board member, a HCA supporter, observed the shift of power from management. "Stated in terms of power blocs, the [Trueblood] proposal is that financial analysts rather than financial executives should now have the dominant voice in the substance and form of corporate financial reports.... Because of evidence that managements dislike expansions of disclosure requirements, which they regard as infringements on 'management's right to manage'" (Mautz 1973, p. 8), the study group recommended replacing HC and management choice by specifying the "Valuation (or Measurement) Basis" for each "Informational Requirement", envisaging an expanded role for "Exit Values" and "Discounted Cash Flow" (AICPA 1973, p. 42). Mautz was wrong that financial analysts had become dominant, and management had little to fear from the FASB's conceptual framework.

Concluding Comments

From the late-1930s as the rate of profit recovered, and particularly during the 1940s and 1950s as the Free Enterprise Campaign intensified, management's reputation and ideological power grew as accountants, pushed by the SEC and academics, began the process of regulating accounting. As the rate of profit fell from the mid-1950s, management used its power, exploiting May's, and Paton and Littleton's, compromise between "stewardship" and economic valuation, to resist regulation and engage in "swindling". By the late-1960s, with the rate of profit in steep decline, the profession was in crisis and had no option but to confront management, seek to take control of accounting choice, and for this, paradoxically, it turned to Fisher.

As the rate of profit fell to historical lows and inflation sharply increased from the early-1970s, as the FASB engaged in an "inflation accounting debate" and produced its conceptual framework, academics debated the significance of the "inductivist" and "deductivist" approaches, and now unhelpfully concluded that no generally accepted theory of accounting was possible. Drawing on Thomas Kuhn's (1970) theory of scientific revolutions, the AAA's Committee on Concepts and Standards for External Reporting's interpretation of history was the successive development of three incommensurate competing "theory approaches: (1) 'classical' ('true income' and inductive); (2) 'decision-usefulness'; and (3) 'information economics'" (AAA 1977, p. 5). The irreconcilable conflict between these "paradigms" explained why there was no generally accepted theory, and never would be. Peasnell offered an alternative progressive interpretation, that the "three accounting theory approaches ... represent the dominant interests of key researchers at different stages in the development of accounting thought. ... Each time, the object of *direct* interest — or in the committee's words ... the 'empirical domain' — has shifted. First it was accounting practices; then it moved to users' decision outcomes; and now to economy-wide costs and benefits" (1978, p. 224). However, as the FASB used decision-usefulness to overthrow "inductive" theory, Chapter 7 argues, to assert intellectual and ideological hegemony over management, the change was not a shift in theorists' empirical focus (cf. Peasnell 1978, p. 223). Wells, by contrast, employed Kuhn's theory to offer an optimistic interpretation of history. Academic criticisms of the "doubtful value" of "a priori research", Wells argued, did not appreciate that "the overthrow of outdated ideas and practices … were a necessary step in the revolution currently underway in accounting thought" (1976, p. 471). There was a "revolution" underway, to overthrow of management's discretion, which led to the FASB's framework, but Chapter 7 argues it was a Pyrrhic victory. Chapter 8 explores one major consequence, the FASB framework's role in facilitating the 2008–2009 GFC.

Chapter 7

The Profitability Crisis and the FASB's Conceptual Framework

In May 1973, the AICPA introduced Rule 203 into its professional ethics code forbidding CPAs from signing audit reports attesting that the accounts conform to generally accepted principles if they differed from FASB standards, and later that year the SEC recognised the FASB as the source of required "substantive authoritative support" (Storey and Storey 1998, p. 47). By the end of 1973, the FASB decided to launch its "conceptual framework" project by preparing a statement on the "objectives of financial statements by business enterprises" as its foundation, and start where the Trueblood Committee finished (Storey and Storey 1998, p. 47; Zeff 1999, pp. 101–105). The FASB produced its framework in the context of the "profitability crisis" from the late-1960s to the early-1980s (Roberts 2016, Figure 1.4, p. 22; Figure 4.1, p. 60), which quickly revealed its limitations in curbing management's power.

The US rate of profit fell sharply from the mid-1960s, which produced the "economic crisis and slump of the mid-1970s" (Kliman 2012, p. 48; Figure 6.2, p. 111; Figure 6.5, p. 120). The rate of profit and economic growth, however, failed to recover to Golden Age levels (Kliman 2012, pp. 48–56, Figure 6.2, p. 111, Figure 6.5, p. 120; Roberts 2016, Figure 1.4, p. 22), which appears inconsistent with Marx's theory of crises as self-correcting. Government determination to avoid another Great Depression by expanding debt, Kliman (2012) argues, explains the continuingly low rates of profit that eventually produced the 2008–2009 GFC, because there was insufficient devaluation and destruction of capital during the 1970s and 1980s crises. The chapter supports Kliman's conclusion by examining accounting theory's role in undermining the "current cost accounting" (CCA) introduced by the SEC from the mid-1970s, following the UK government's 1974 appointment of a Committee of Enquiry on "inflation accounting", responding to high inflation which meant reported rates of profit were significantly overstated. The inchoate foundation of CCA is the British/Marxian view that management should be accountable for the RC of tangible assets (Bryer 2021a, pp. 45–57), which accounting theorists endlessly criticised, which empowered management to agitate against, undermine, and ditch CCA in the mid-1980s when inflation fell. Aiding this major defeat, undermining management's accountability for the rate of profit during the 1970s and early-1980s, the FASB's conceptual framework abolished "stewardship", replacing it with "decision-usefulness". It adopted Fisher's theory of balance sheet valuation, replaced HC and "revenue-expense" accounting with "asset-liability" accounting, accommodating Paton's and Canning's "asset" definitions. The framework overtly removed management's control of accounting choice, but its resort to Fisher's framing was, the chapter argues, a Pyrrhic victory because management retained discretion, reinstalled covertly in the framework's "qualitative characteristics" and "elements" of financial statements, and in its analysis of their "measurement attribute".

The chapter first explains the "profitability crisis", which provoked the "inflation accounting debate", the context in which the FASB wrote its conceptual framework, and Marxists debated how to measure the rate of profit, HC or "current cost". The "inflation accounting" and Marxist debates highlight an apparent contradiction between Marx's theory that capitalists should use RCA — governments required published CCA data during the 1970s and early-1980s, which included key elements of RCA — and the fact that management and the capital market continued using HCA. Second, the chapter argues, the explanation is that accounting theory undermined CCA's effectiveness by giving management implementation discretion. This explains why, although according to Marx's theory crises are self-correcting through devaluations stimulated by low RC rates of profit, this did not occur in the 1970s and 1980s recessions, which set the low rate of profit context for the GFC. Third, the chapter examines the development of the FASB's framework statements using Marxian accounting as the benchmark, highlighting its abolition of stewardship and RCA, and institutionalisation of management's discretion in asset-liability accounting. Finally, it examines the difference between the appearance of FASB control of accounting standards and the reality of management's ideological hegemony.

Accounting for the Profitability Crisis

Marxist debate how Marx measured the rate of profit, but according to the accounting interpretation capitalists should use RCA (Bryer 2017, Chapter 4), what Marxists mean by "current cost". Marxists, as Kliman says, measure the rate of profit "in relationship to the actual amounts of money advanced as capital in the past (minus depreciation)" or "to the amount of money that businesses would now need to spend in order to replace their fixed assets — the assets' current cost (replacement cost)" (2012, p. 102; Roberts 2016, p. 274). Accounting theorists and accountants include RC within "current cost accounting", but for them, we will see, it includes NRV and PV, and for some even CPP adjustments. The rate of profit fell, Marxists agree, but they disagree whether to use HCA or RCA. They therefore disagree about whether the rate of profit partially recovered from the early-1980s to the late-1990s, and fell again to the GFC using CCA (Roberts 2016, Figure 1.4, p. 22), or fell to 1990, weakly recovered, and fell again to 2009, using HCA (Kliman 2012, Figure 5.1, pp. 76–77). Marxists should use CCA, but because in Marx's theory crises do not depend on the current trajectory, but on low current rates compared to historical highs, on "low (as distinct from falling) profitability" (Kliman 2012, p. 13), the "secular trend", HCA and CCA both support it (Roberts 2016, p. 274).

Measurement, however, is important in Marx's theory of crises because by "devaluing" capital when the input prices of constant capital fall, RCA delays the fall in the rate of profit. Similarly, revaluing capital if input prices increase accelerates its decrease, as they did in the 1970s and 1980s, which encourages the "devaluation" of capital through reporting lower operating profits or losses and higher capital which leads to its devaluation and destruction through closures, down-sizing, etc., which restores the rate of profit and the conditions for resumed accumulation. Kliman (2012), however, points out that management and investors used HCA, did not react to the divergence between current-cost and HC rates of profit from the early-1980s. As he says, "there has been a remarkably close relationship between U.S. corporations' rate of accumulation and their *actual* rate of profit during the last 40 years" (Kliman 2012, p. 115). Thus, he concludes, "*the divergence between the rate of accumulation and the current-cost 'rate of profit' is actually crucial evidence that the latter is not a rate of profit in any meaningful sense* … [because] corporations' investment behavior was regulated by movements in the actual (historical-cost) rate of profit, not the current-cost rate" (Kliman 2012, pp. 115–116).

While theoretically debatable, consistent with focusing on HC rates of profit rather than CCA that fell much further, is that while sufficient devaluation and destruction of capital eventually took place in the 1930s, in the 1970s and 1980s, as Kliman points out, because no strong recovery occurred, it did not. "During the global economic slumps of the mid-1970s and early 1980s … much less capital value was destroyed than had been destroyed during the Depression and the following World War. … But since so much less capital value was destroyed during the 1970s and early 1980s …, the decline in the rate of profit was not reversed … [so] profitability remained at too low a level to sustain a new boom" (Kliman 2012, p. 3). "Insufficient" devaluation and destruction in the mid-1970s and early-1980s, compared to the 1930s, according to Kliman "is largely a consequence of economic policy" (2012, p. 3), which management favoured, that included large corporate tax cuts. As we saw, "The amount of capital value that was destroyed during the Depression was far greater than advocates of *laissez-faire* policies had expected, and the persistence of severely depressed conditions led to significant radicalization of working people" (Kliman 2012, p. 3). To avoid this, governments intervened with "monetary and fiscal policies … to prevent the full-scale destruction of capital value … by pursuing policies that encourage excessive expansion of debt", which "artificially boosted profitability and economic growth, but … repeatedly led to burst bubbles and debt crises" (Kliman 2012, p. 3).

The interesting question from the Marxian accounting perspective is why the "current-cost" rate of profit was not a "rate of profit in any meaningful sense" to the capital market, the government, and particularly to management, when according to Marx's RCA it should have been. The answer, what follows argues, is management's ideological hegemony over accounting choice. Having sponsored "inflation accounting" to reduce reported profits in the face of wage demands and political threats, management drew on accounting theory to resist CCA, water it down, obfuscate the RC rate of profit with "inflation" adjustments, and stop publishing current-cost data in the mid-1980s. Kliman and others overlook "the extremely tortuous and apparently muddled debate on inflation accounting which has taken place in the last fifteen years or so, particularly in the English-speaking countries" (Tweedie and Whittington 1984, p. 1). "It is clear from this debate that inflation accounting is not a subject which lends itself to solution merely by the rigorous application of logic", but was an "essentially political … process" (Tweedie and Whittington 1984, p. 1), an ideological process framed by Fisher's theory in a political context.

As Kliman says, "almost everyone … uses the term 'rate of profit' to mean profit as a percentage of the actual amount of money invested in the past (net of depreciation)" (2012, p. 11). Mainstream researchers, we will see, agree that "the current-cost 'rate of profit' fails to accurately measure businesses' and investors' expected future rates of return", that HC rates of profit more closely correlate with equity market rates of return (Kliman 2012, p. 115; Table 6.1, p. 117). The focus on HCA is evidence of what "actual capitalist firms and investors care about and mean by profitability" (Kliman 2012, p. 117), but does not explain why they did. The disconnection between the current-cost rate of profit and investment behaviour, following sections argue, is evidence of management's ideological hegemony. Marxian accounting supports Kliman's view that "Replacement-cost versus historical-cost measurement is thus a matter of considerable empirical significance. A choice must be made" (2011, p. 113), but to explain the choice during the profitability crisis we must understand the "inflation accounting" debate as a "political" process dominated by management.

Management and "Inflation Accounting"

In the context of inflation spikes during the late-1940s, early-1950s, and late-1960s (Figure 7.1), what follows argues, some segments of big business wanted "inflation accounting" to reduce the increased profits they published in HCAs that attracted union and political criticism. To accommodate sectors where CPP did not reduce reported profits, following government intervention, the US and the UK, "which led international practice" (Tweedie and Whittington 1997, p. 149), required CCA. In the context of neoliberal governments in the early-1980s who deregulated and adopted policies averting another Great Depression, when in the mid-1980s CCA had achieved its political purposes and inflation fell, management successfully campaigned for its abolition. It succeeded because, in the meantime, the FASB had produced its conceptual framework that abolished stewardship and RCA.

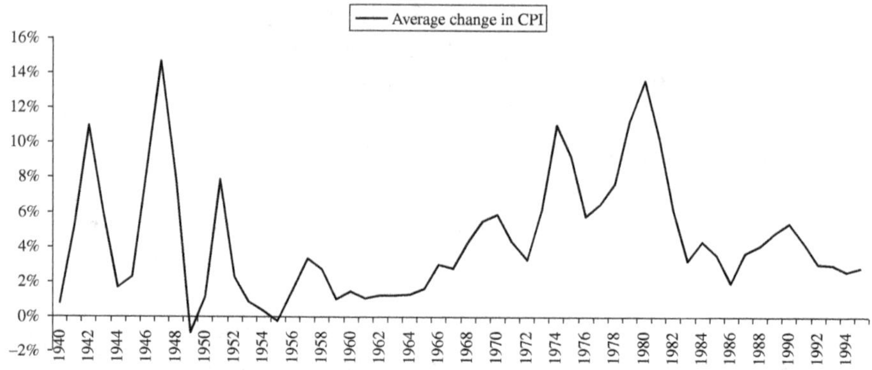

Figure 7.1: US Inflation 1940–1995

Source: https://inflationdata.com/Inflation/Inflation_Rate/HistoricalInflation.aspx#table.

As the RC rate of profit fell from 1946 (Roberts 2016, Figure 1.4, p. 22), post-war inflation "revived the concern of many companies that the historical cost depreciation charge … did not reflect adequately the replacement costs of the assets" (Tweedie and Whittington 1984, p. 38). In 1947, US Steel and DuPont "made supplementary depreciation charges to reflect the decline in the purchasing power of money" (Tweedie and Whittington 1984, p. 38). The CAP did not endorse this accounting, but in 1948 recommended "experimentation with supplementary price-level adjusted statements" (Tweedie and Whittington 1984, p. 38). In December 1948, Carey noted, "The growing public interest in corporate profits, what they mean in relation to prices, wages and the maintenance of productive capacity, was emphasized … by hearings on the subject before a subcommittee of the Joint Congressional Committee on the Economic Report" (1949, p. 4). Economists, business leaders, labour representatives and accountants gave evidence. Noted economist Sumner Slichter, and Paton, argued that reported profits were overstated (Carey 1949, pp. 4–5). Accountants and economists published articles and gave talks arguing high inflation rates made reported profits "illusory", that companies "have in effect been paying dividends out of capital" (Paton 1952, p. 242; Sutton *et al.* 1956, p. 76). In 1953, a Study Group on Business Income, sponsored by the AIA and Rockefeller Foundation, chaired by May, which included prominent accountants, economists and business leaders, encouraged CPP disclosures (Tweedie and Whittington 1984, pp. 38–39). ARB 43 (1953) repeated the 1948 statement, "encouraging the use of supplementary schedules to 'explain the need for retention of earnings in the face of rising price levels'" (Tweedie and Whittington 1984, p. 39), but inflation fell and interest waned.

In 1963, the AICPA published ARS 6 *Reporting the Financial Effects of Price-Level Changes*. Its proposals "were not an advance on the work of Sweeney (1936) or Mason (1956) or material which had appeared in various editions of Paton's textbooks" (Tweedie and Whittington 1984, p. 41), but it "presented actual cases and literature which showed the need for financial statements to reflect the effects of price-level changes" (Waldron *et al.* 1989, p. 20). The 24 cases of published price-level adjusted information included some large US corporations, including Reece Corporation, Indiana Telephone Corporation, Hercules Powder Company, Eastman Kodak Company, and Iowa-Illinois Gas and Electric Company (Waldron *et al.* 1989, p. 20), and it published articles showing the impacts of inflation on US corporations' accounts (AICPA 1963, pp. 169–249). As inflation increased, in 1969 the APB published APB Statement 3 *Financial Statements Restated for General Prince-Level*, based on ARS 6, formalising existing encouragement. However, it was non-binding and because inflation fell, and fully implementing CPP accounting did not necessarily reduce reported income, big business did not universally support it, and only Indiana Telephone Corporation, a long-term enthusiast, implemented it (Tweedie and Whittington 1984, pp. 43, 352), with a notable omission, discussed as follows.

Workers and unions continued to take a keen interest in accounts and were recognised as financial statement users in AAA committee and professional statements (e.g., AAA 1955, p. 401; FASB 1978, paragraph 25). For some the ideological threat from labour was ever-present. In 1973, Paton criticised those who "show American business corporations in the light of a group of gouging, profiteering entities fattening at the expense of employees, consumers, and the 'common people' generally" (1973, p. 14). In 1976, the SEC required supplementary price-level adjusted accounts (discussed in what follows) to counteract "the judgment of some opinion leaders [that] corporate earnings are 'obscene', 'a rip off', etc" (Williams 1978, p. 79). With a sharply falling RC rate of profit (Roberts 2016, Figure 1.4, p. 22), and now steeply rising prices following the 1973 oil crisis, in 1974 the FASB hastily issued an exposure draft, "Financial Reporting in Units of General Purchasing Power". The FASB based its proposals on APB 3, but reflecting academic and business ambivalence towards CPP, it did not "preclude the future introduction of a current value base" (Tweedie and Whittington 1984, p. 43; Zeff 2007, p. 57).

Watts and Zimmerman (1978) studied the motives of 53 companies that commented on the FASB's proposals, which revealed the problem of business acceptability, which for large corporations was that CPP adjustments did not consistently reduce reported profits. Watts and Zimmerman found, "Of the 53 firms, 18 submitted opinions expressing favorable views on general price level adjustments" (1978, p. 122). Given the ideological sensitivity of high profits in a context of attacks on unions, restructuring, and an increasing rate of exploitation, to avoid "political costs" large companies, with most to lose, wanted to report lower earnings. "Political costs" are the potential costs of government regulation, but "Included ... the costs labor unions impose through increased demands generated by large reported profits" (Watts and Zimmerman 1978, p. 115). Adding the "gain" or "loss" on monetary items as part of the profit and loss statement (as in APB 3, see Tweedie and Whittington 1984, p. 43) meant, depending on the composition of assets and the proportion financed by liabilities, that firms could report higher or lower GPLA profits than HCA. ASR 6 recognised a "problem ... of great importance to companies with large amounts of debt outstanding" (AICPA 1963, p. 160). By "recognizing price-level gains on liabilities in the income statement currently, as has been recommended by some sources, ... in some instances such gains will exceed the increase in charges to income from restatement of assets to a common-dollar basis, and net income will be overstated to a greater extent than it would be under historical-dollar accounting" (AICPA 1963, p. 160). One committee member, "Mr. Miller does not favor reporting the net gain or loss on monetary items, 'as a component part of the calculation of net income for the period', as permitted by the study", and Mr Morrison objected to them appearing last as "special credits or charges" which were in effect to "retained earning" (AICPA 1963, p. 250). Most examples and case studies focused on inflation's effects in reducing income, equity, and return on investment, etc. Only some calculated "gains" on net monetary items (AICPA 1963, pp. 240, 245, 247). Reece Corporation's "net income figures do not include gains and losses on monetary items", which "were shown in an analysis of the changes in the stockholders' equity" (AICPA 1963, p. 173); when Indiana Telephone implemented APB 3, it left them out (Tweedie and Whittington 1984, pp. 43, 352).

Watts and Zimmerman predicted, "firms whose earnings are increased by GPLA will oppose GPLA regardless of their size.... However, for firms whose earnings are decreased by GPLA, we predict that they will either support GPLA or will not make a submission depending on … asset size" (1978, p. 124). They found, "The single most important factor explaining managerial … behavior on General Price Level Accounting is firm size (after controlling for the direction of change in earnings). The larger firms, *ceteris paribus*, are more likely to favor GPLA (if earnings decline)" (Watts and Zimmerman 1978, p. 131). The 34 firms Watts and Zimmerman "classified as opposing GPLA … expressed opinions ranging from strong objection to discussions of the merits of current costing to skepticism and feelings that GPLA was premature" (1978, p. 122). Some managements who "opposed" CPP accounting favoured "current costing", but others had concerns at the prospect of "fair value" accounting. In 1973, some of the 62 financial executives from larger companies interviewed by FEI researchers anticipated it would reduce reported profits, and "adopting 'fair value' balance sheets" could mean that "higher asset values would increase management orientation towards operating profits to achieve a respectable return on the presumably higher asset base" (Rice *et al.* 1973, p. 19). Some could see that "fair value" accounting would reduce the rate of profit, implying it would encourage managers to seek to increase "operating profits", which could mean plant closures, wage cuts, price increases, etc. However, in 1973, most admitted they had not "assessed all the implications of adopting 'fair value' balance sheets", and had "different definitions for the term", as accounting theorists did, which the researchers concluded meant for most it was "an interesting theoretical concept but with limited practical application" (Rice *et al.* 1973, pp. 19, 37). They warned, prefiguring the argument widely deployed against CCA in the early-1980s, implicitly adopting Paton's entity theory, "the choice of a basis … would depend on management's plans for the asset.… As a result, the value assigned to the asset would, of necessity, be somewhat subjective" (Rice *et al.* 1973, p. 38). Many saw dangers of increased taxation and demands for dividends from reporting "holding gains", but "several" also argued against "Increasing charges against current income, to reflect higher values of assets being depleted or depreciated" because this "would penalize income for costs not yet incurred, i.e., replacement costs" (Rice *et al.* 1973, p. 39). A "few capital-intensive companies with low profit/sales margins … were concerned that the inevitable inaccuracy in measuring a change of 'fair' value could outweigh normal income from operations" (Rice *et al.* 1973, p. 39), push them into reporting losses. However, by 1974, facing union opposition to closures, and wage demands to keep up with high inflation, conflicted by CPP accounting, big business accepted the need for "current costing".

In 1974, the SEC indicated its preference for RC adjustments, which would typically reduce operating earnings, and in 1976 swept aside self-interested views. The financial controller of the *Caterpillar Tractor Co.* (Peoria) reviewed Rice *et al.* (1973), and "was somewhat … surprise[d] to find that the management people interviewed or surveyed believed that 'fair value accounting to the extent it was even understood is merely theoretical'" (Morgan 1974, p. 215). With high and accelerating inflation (see Figure 7.1), after years of resistance to any upward revaluations, following the appointment in 1972 of Burton as chief accountant, the SEC required supplementary RC disclosures (Zeff 2007, p. 57). Influenced by the UK government's "Sandilands Committee" (1975) (Zeff 1999, p. 117), in March 1976 the SEC published ASR 190 requiring disclosure of "replacement cost information for cost of sales, inventories, depreciation, and productive capacity" (Zeff 2007, p. 57), which typically reduced reported profit. In 1979, the FASB issued Statement No. 33 *Financial Reporting and Changing Prices*, requiring disclosure of "current-cost" and price-level adjusted ("constant dollar") data.

Current Cost Accounting

In late-1973, as UK RC profits sharply diverged from reported HC profits (Figure 7.2), following the profession's recommendation of CPP accounting, the government announced a Committee of Enquiry into "inflation accounting" (Tweedie and Whittington 1984, p. 60), whether this should be CPP or "current cost accounting". The same pattern appeared in the US, where the HC rate of profit remained roughly stable from 1969 to 1979, but the current cost rate fell sharply (Kliman 2012, Figure 5.1, p. 76; Figure 6.2, p. 111; Roberts 2016, Figure 1.4, p. 22). In May 1974, Burton "outlined his preference for a replacement cost approach to the problem of accounting for inflation" (Tweedie and Whittington 1997, p. 156), but not because this would hold management accountable for the RC rate of profit. Burton justified RC's decision-usefulness, asserting it would provide investors "with information relating to 'earning power … defined as the enterprise's cash generating ability'" (Tweedie and Whittington 1997, p. 156).

Burton was a student of Philip W. Bell, professor of accounting at Haverford College, who with Edgar O. Edwards in 1961 published *The Theory and the Measurement of Business Income*, which explained and advocated "replacement cost accounting. Burton was already on record as

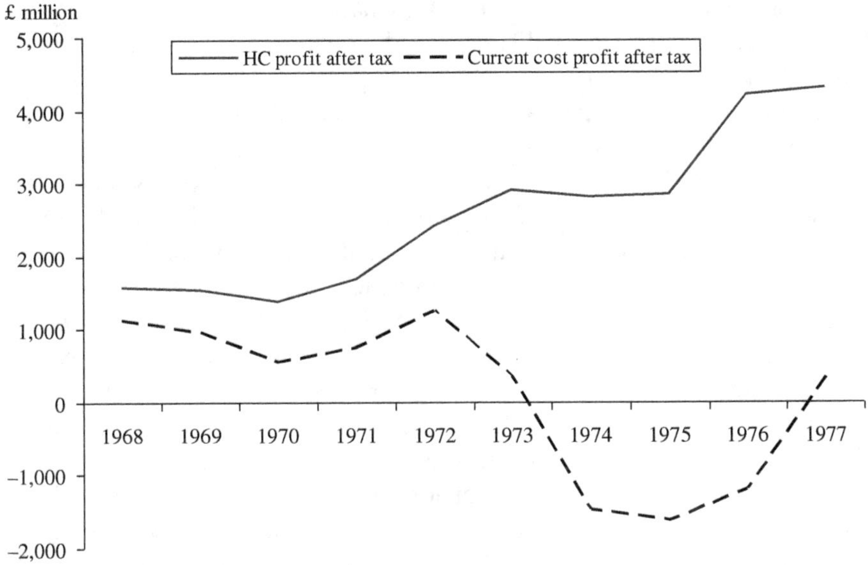

Figure 7.2: UK Historical and Current Cost Profits 1968–1977

Source: Whittington (1983, Table 1.2, p. 19).

favouring a change in the traditional accounting model that would better depict economic reality" and, aged 39, "had not been an accountant during the 1930s and thus would not have been haunted, like his predecessors, by tales of the write-ups during the 1920s" (Zeff 2013, p. 57). Edwards and Bell (1961, pp. vii–viii), however, did not simply explain and advocate "replacement cost accounting", but sought to use RC and other current values to operationalise Fisher's theory, "a reconciliation … which does not at the same time destroy either the subjective approach of the economist or the accountant's emphasis on objective events". Their book "attacks directly problems which, because they fall in that no man's land between economics and accounting, have seldom been explored systematically. And when such efforts have been made, as in the case of Irving Fisher's *The Nature of Capital and Income*, they have not received the attention they deserve" (Edwards and Bell 1961, p. vii). Burton accepted, "users of accounting statements want useful economic information" (1971, p. 50) and "Edwards and Bell's (1961) replacement cost model can be regarded as adopting an informational approach" (Whittington 2010, p. 106). Marxian accounting calculates profit using the RCs of tangible assets, and requires CMAs (Bryer 2017, Chapter 4; 2021a, Chapter 2), but Edwards and Bell (1961) distinguished "operating", "holding", "realized", "unrealized", "nominal" and "real" gains and losses, allowing different "entity" and "proprietary" interpretations of "business income".

The Sandilands Committee influenced the FASB, but it drew on Edwards and Bell (1961), and by giving "prominence to the 'value to the business' (or 'deprival value') approach to current value accounting" (Zeff 1999, p. 117), on American economic theory and valuation practice, also influenced by Fisher. It recommended "current cost accounting" based on the "value to the owner" rules popularised by Bonbright (1937).[1] Bonbright argued, "The value of a property to its owner is identical in amount with the adverse value of the entire loss, direct and indirect, that the owner might expect to suffer if he were deprived of the property" (1937, p. 71). Bonbright's concern was the valuation of property for insurance, the damages courts award for loss of assets, but Professor William Baxter, London School of Economics, who thought his book "should be the bible of theorists in this field", saw its relevance to accounting, which he called "deprival value" (1967, p. 212; 1971, p. 30). "Deprival value" emphasised that according to Bonbright's rule the value of an asset is the *minimum* sum of money required to compensate the owner if deprived of the asset. If the owner was using the asset profitably, the compensation should *not* include the PV of its expected profits because replacing the asset with an equivalent allows the owner to continue seeking those profits. For tangible assets in-use and finished commodities Bonbright's rule coincides with the Marxian stewardship justification for RC, that their use-values are replaceable with equivalents (Bryer 2021a, pp. 49–50), Bonbright's "principle of substitution", which "has led appraisal writers to lay down the rule that the replacement cost of property ordinarily sets the approximate *upper limit* of its value" (1937, pp. 156–157).[2]

A tangible asset's value to a going concern in Marxian accounting is RC because it can substitute equivalent use-values for those currently controlled, and capitalists should write-down to a lower recoverable

---

[1]Bonbright (1937) did not invent the "value to the owner" rules, which are implicit in Fisher (1906) and Paton (1922), and Canning (1929) "devised rules of the value to the owner type for the valuation of fixed assets" (Whittington 1983, p. 131; Bryer 2021a). Bonbright (1937) cites Fisher 19 times.

[2]RC is the "approximate" upper limit because insurance damages would also include "incidental losses" (Bonbright 1937, pp. 157–158).

amount only in exceptional circumstances (Bryer 2021a, pp. 61–62). However, according to Bonbright's rule of compensating the owner with the *minimum* amount necessary on deprival, for *all* assets — tangible, intangible, and monetary — accountants must go beyond RC to "measure ... the value of the benefits conferred by ownership of the asset" (Whittington 1983, p. 131). They must value assets at PV, RC and NRV and select the "value to the owner". If PV and NRV are *higher* than RC, the value to the owner is RC, the minimum necessary compensation for deprival. However, if an asset's PV or NRV are *lower* than its RC, the higher of these values measures deprival value, the *minimum* amount to be "made whole again": "With most types ... the property may be worth to its owner its replacement cost, or its net-selling price, or some amount between these two figures" (Bonbright 1937, p. 92). Because the objective is "to measure the value added to the business by the asset, on the assumption that it is used in the most profitable manner", some see Bonbright's phrase "value to the owner" or "value to the business" as more "apt" (e.g., Whittington 2007, p. 186) than "deprival value". The Sandilands Committee (1974, Table 4, p. 59) summarised Bonbright's analysis by reproducing the table popularised by Solomons (1966, p. 125) and Parker and Harcourt (1969, p. 17), that determined which value, including PV and NRV, was "correct" in each situation (see Table 7.1).

For tangible assets profitably employed, cases 1–4, the value to the owner coincides with Marxian accounting and management should value at RC. In cases 5 and 6 where replacement is not worthwhile, according to Marxian accounting management should also value tangible assets at RC to reveal lower profits or losses until closure or disposal (Bryer 2021a,

Table 7.1: Value to the Owner Rules

Basis of valuation of assets	
In cases where:	**The correct basis of valuation is:**
1 NRV > PV > RC	RC
2 NRV > RC > PV	RC
3 PV > RC > NRV	RC
4 PV > NRV > RC	RC
5 RC > PV > NRV	PV
6 RC > NRV > PV	NRV

Source: Sandilands Committee (1974, Table 4, p. 59).

pp. 57–58). In case 5, for assets whose replacement is not justified, but whose continued operation has a PV greater than NRV, critics of RCA argue, "replacement cost will overstate the value of the asset to the firm. What then can be said about the utility of replacement cost measures when continued operation is warranted but eventual replacement is not" (Revsine 1973, p. 69). The answer, Revsine concluded, consistent with Marxian accounting, is "there is still a reason for showing assets at their replacement costs for balance sheet purposes", because "When these higher replacement costs are matched against realized revenues, the resultant losses will tend to alert the statement reader that, in the long-run, it is uneconomical to replace these assets" (1973, p. 69).

Management, according to Marxian accounting, should account for intangible or monetary assets at HC (Bryer 2021a, pp. 60–66). Bonbright's value to the owner rule, by contrast, applies to *all* assets and liabilities, defining "substitutability" to mean the ability to substitute equivalent economic value. The Sandilands Committee recommended, "the initial standard of Current Cost Accounting should require marketable securities held by a company to be shown in the balance sheet at market value" (1975, p. 177). Furthermore, "The Principles of Current Cost Accounting would require that assets such as patents, goodwill, and expenditures on research and development should be shown at their 'value to the business'", even though it did not recommend this for the initial standard because it envisaged "practical problems" (Sandilands 1975, p. 177). Therefore, although the Sandilands Committee thought RCA for tangible assets met users' major needs, and recommended "a system to be known as Current Cost Accounting" because this portrayed the change as "evolutionary rather than revolutionary" (1975, p. 3), as an evolution from "cost", its theoretical framework required all assets at their value to the owner. Consistent with Marxian accounting it recommended requiring the calculation of operating profit after RC cost of sales and depreciation, and CMAs, but to theorists its foundation in value to the owner meant it was merely a "pragmatic compromise between competing valuation methods" (Whittington 1983, p. 136). Predictably, academic and management criticism of US and UK standards focused on RC.

Criticisms of Replacement Cost

Accounting theorists questioned the economic logic of the value to the owner rule. Whittington articulated the underlying concern that mixing

RC, PV and NRV meant "The aggregation problem is serious, and the connection with opportunity cost is both tenuous and of dubious relevance" (1983, p. 136). From the PV perspective, "The more fundamental problem is, however, that value to the owner has never been demonstrated to arise out of a particular requirement of a potential user, other than that of an insurer. We need to know whether it is intended, in aggregate, as a surrogate for PV or merely a set of piecemeal valuations of individual assets and, if the latter, how it is to be used" (Whittington 1983, p. 136). The same concerns applied to "the properties of the income measures to which it gives rise and why these are to be preferred to income measures based upon replacement cost, net realisable value, or even historical cost" (Whittington 1983, p. 136). Whittington became less "sceptical", accepted value to the owner is "ground[ed] in the economic theory of choice" (2007, p. 186, fn. 21, p. 195), but given its inclusion of RC, still argued the theory was not applied rigorously. According to economic theory, asset values should add up to a company's total PV, but this made RC problematic. Its inclusion meant the "traditional interpretation is counter intuitive in cases 1, 2, and 4. In each of these cases net realizable value is greater than replacement cost, which suggests that it would be profitable for the entity to sell the asset and replace it immediately, yielding a profit (NRV — RC) that is not reflected in deprival value" (Whittington 2007, p. 187). Van Zijl and Whittington (2006) suggested replacing RC with NRV for cases where NRV was greater, to get a "better measure of the economic opportunities of the entity that arise from ownership of the asset" (Whittington 2007, p. 188). In Marxian accounting in cases 1, 2, and 4, RC measures the value of the tangible assets management controls, no pragmatic compromises arise; there is no "problem of aggregation". The aggregate is the recoverable capital management controls, and profit the realised increase in excess of the capital required to maintain current value (Bryer 2021a, pp. 49–51). By contrast, "the capital maintenance concept embodied in SSAP 16 [implementing CCA in the UK] … has no necessary connection with value to the owner" (Whittington 1983, p. 136).

PV and NRV are usually subjective, but "current cost accounting" also attracted criticism for the subjectivity of the required RC calculations (O'Connor and Chandra 1978, p. 6), which provided management with a specific basis for resisting and abolishing CCA, whereas according to Marxian accounting RCs are objective. To measure "value to the owner" for all assets requires management to forecast cash flows from use and discount them to measure recoverable amount as a PV, and estimate selling price and costs for NRV. These values are often subjective, that is, as many commentators have noted (e.g., Whittington 2007, p. 184), are "entity-specific", but Marxian accounting, consistent with valuation practice, does not use management's forecasts. RC is standard practice in valuing property, plant and equipment assets in a business acquisition, "the measurement attribute appraisers utilize in virtually all allocations" (King 2006, p. 88). For stewardship, RC methodology is clear, and its measurements are objective. There are three ways to estimate the RC of a used asset (King 2006, p. 78). The valuer can (a) use the RC of identical assets of the same age and condition, or (b) use the RC of an identical new asset less depreciation, or (c) identify the RC of the least cost "modern equivalent asset". In the absence of an active market in identical used assets, and of significant technical change, (b) is the normal approach for "Value in Use" (VIU). As King says, "The valuation methodology for VIU is straightforward. In theory, we identify all of the assets, determine the cost *new* today, including freight in, installation, testing, and debugging. Then, based on physical inspection of the assets, the professional appraiser determines the age and actual condition of the subject assets and the depreciation from all causes" (2006, p. 78). Active markets exist for many new and used assets, and there are published current RC indices, which "are usually accurate, and the appraisers find this approach provides a concise, yet cost-effective answer" (King 2006, p. 78).

To determine RC management must seek the *minimum* cost of replacing the asset's use-values. RC equals the *minimum* price the least-cost supplier would have charged if replacement had taken place. Therefore, if management could obtain an asset's use-values by a different but cheaper asset not available when it bought the original asset, this lower cost is the relevant RC, the lowest RC of a "substantially identical modern equivalent". The modern equivalent may have a higher RC than replacement with an identical asset, but provide increased outputs, give lower operating costs, and produce outputs with higher quality, etc. According to Marxian accounting, if the modern equivalent provides more use-values than the existing asset, management makes an allowance to derive the "equivalent replacement cost". Assume an asset's HC is £100,000 and RC £150,000. If the modern equivalent costs £220,000, but produces 40,000 units a year compared with the existing asset's 20,000 units, and the useful lives of the assets are identical, the RC of the existing asset is £220,000 × [20,000/40,000] = £110,000.

However, according to the value to the owner framework, if a modern equivalent asset has lower operating costs (or higher quality of output), management must allow for this in calculating the least cost equivalent RC. If, for example, the RC of an identical asset is £50,000, and the cost of the modern equivalent is £70,000 but will save costs over its lifetime with a PV of £30,000, the "equivalent total cost" of the modern equivalent is £40,000. According to Marxian accounting, subject to any allowance for different output levels and depreciation, management is accountable for the RC of the lowest cost modern equivalent asset, that is, for £70,000. By contrast, as the FASB put it in FAS 33, where technology has changed management makes "An estimate of the buying price of a new improved asset less an allowance for the operating disadvantages of the asset owned (higher operating costs or lower output potential) and an allowance for depreciation calculated according to an acceptable accounting method" (1979, paragraph 180). As it said, "This approach yields what may be described as a measurement of the current cost of the *service* potential of the asset owned" (1979, paragraph 180 emphasis added), in Fisher and Canning's sense, of forecast cash flows. Using CCA management reported RC measured as the "value to the owner" of the modern equivalent asset of £40,000 because, from the economics perspective, "*Replacement cost* is the minimum current cost of replacing the economic services provided by the asset to the entity. Its benchmark is the most economic technology currently available" (Whittington 2007, p. 184). From this perspective, while the "advantage" of using RC is that it "represents the current value of the services embodied in the asset, from the perspective of the reporting entity", its current "economic services", or "service potential", this is also its "disadvantage" because this requires subjective "entity-specific" valuation. "Its disadvantage is that, because it is entity-specific, reflecting the economic needs of the entity, its estimation involves a greater degree of judgement, and, in particular, depends upon the expectations and intentions of management, rather than the marketplace. In some cases, for example, the cost of a replacement asset embodying new technology would have to make allowances for consequential changes in the cost of other inputs, such as energy or labour" (Whittington 2007, p. 184). Using value to the owner, therefore, "Discovery of accurate replacement costs is *virtually impossible* in times of changing technologies and newer production alternatives", making it "prohibitively costly" to do continually, and "very difficult" for items with quality variations (Jensen 2007, p. 303). However, according to Marxian accounting, holding management accountable for tangible assets' RC does not depend on intentions, whether or not to replace them. Management makes whatever decisions it thinks are best and the accountant selects the appropriate value to hold it accountable for the results. If management decides to hold a tangible asset in-use accountants values it at RC regardless of whether management intends to replace it with an identical, similar or modern equivalent asset. The accountant selects the RC of the least cost alternative, and seeks independent evidence to support the choice of the least cost modern equivalent if there is one.

According to Marxian accounting, RC measures the current, socially necessary, capital value (Bryer 2017, p. 45; 2021a, p. 49). Management must be accountable for the RC of the least cost modern equivalent because other entities are currently buying this technology at that price expecting to earn the required return, and this is the capital management must therefore recover before recognising profit, despite the fact that its operating costs with the present asset may be higher. Therefore, according to Marxian accounting, the RC of the modern equivalent in the above example is £70,000 to hold management accountable for recovering the value of the capital employed and earning at least the rate of profit that others expect when they buy the same assets at those prices. To accounting theorists, by contrast, RC could be justified as a surrogate for PV. Historically, "One of the strongest arguments … [for] replacement cost measurement is based on the theoretical relationship between the replacement cost … and … discounted present value … [because] at any point in time the replacement cost of an asset is the most objective possible approximation of its discounted present value — the theoretically best measure of an asset's worth" (Revsine 1973, p. 82). During the 1970s and 1980s RC was "usually preferred in the academic literature and by standard setters … because … it represents the current value of the costs avoided by owning the asset rather than having to buy its services in the market" (Whittington 2007, p. 184). In our example, the "current value" of the costs avoided by owning the asset is the £70,000 for a modern equivalent, less the PV of the operating cost saving of £30,000.

Critics of RC argue that markets do not exist for all part-finished or used tangible assets, or market imperfections may mean entry prices are biased. This is not the case for most inventory assets, and using RC for inventory avoids the subjective choice of a cost flow assumption usually required with HCA (Revsine 1973, pp. 78–79). Markets exist or representative quotations are available for most fixed assets. However, if markets for particular fixed assets do not exist or are imperfect, the primary markets for their inputs (labour and materials) always exist, and usually their prices are unbiased, so while the task may be difficult, complex, tedious, and costly, management can always construct an objective measure of an asset's reproduction cost. Whittington, by contrast, argues that the relevance of reproduction cost "to economic decisions is doubtful when the asset is no longer optimal for its purpose and so should not be replaced in its current form" (2007, p. 185). However, to repeat, measuring replacement or reproduction cost does not require that management *intend* to reproduce or replace particular assets. The aim is to hold management accountable for the current value of the assets it decides to use *when* it uses them.

Finally, accounting theorists and management criticised RCA because it made no adjustments for inflationary "gains" and "losses" on monetary assets and liabilities and "holding gains" or "losses" on tangible and other assets. The Sandilands Committee rejected "the use of general price-level indices ... questioning their usefulness" (Tweedie and Whittington 1984, p. 97), but theorists and management argued for "monetary adjustments", and FAS 33 (1979) required CCA and GPLA adjustments (Tweedie and Whittington 1997, pp. 157–158), which apparently mitigated falling CCA rates of profit. By the mid-1980s with inflation abating the US and UK professions ditched CCA arguing, as accounting theorists did, it was not useful, and US management blocked its inclusion in the FASB's conceptual framework.

Ditching CCA

In the UK, "At the time of SSAP 16, companies feared that inflation accounting would systematically lower their profits" (Walton 2007, p. 177), and they sought to mitigate the effect by insisting, with accounting theorists' encouragement, on some form of monetary adjustments. As Gibbs, Percy and Saville of Stockbrokers Phillips and Drew observed, it was "very difficult to justify the introduction of a system of inflation accounting which suggests that large numbers of companies are currently paying dividends out of capital" (1976, p. 62). It was clear, "unless the Sandilands recommendations are modified, or profits rise much more than we are currently expecting, large numbers ... of companies will rapidly have to consider cutting their dividends" (Gibbs *et al.* 1976, pp. 62–63). After an intensive debate (Tweedie and Whittington 1984, pp. 99–148), SSAP 16 (ASC 1980) required a "monetary working capital adjustment" to calculate "operating profit", and a "gearing adjustment" that added back to profit before tax the proportion of "holding gains" supposedly financed by debt, which had a significant effect. Analysts calculated SSAP 16's effects on UK large quoted companies' reported profits from 1968 to 1977, and the effects of making CPP adjustments, calculating "real terms profit" including "real holding gains" (Whittington 1983, Table 1.2, p. 19). Applying RCA, these analysts showed, reduced the reported HCA profits of £24.7 billion over the 10 years, by 97 percent, to £0.94 billion. Including MWCA and gearing adjustments increased total profit to £7.4 billion, and including a "gain on borrowing" and "real holding gains on net assets" increased it to £18.1 billion, a fall from HC profit of 30 percent (Whittington 1983, Table 1.2, p. 19). Despite monetary add-backs, studies of large UK industrial and oil companies in the early-1980s revealed large differences between the rates of return on capital reported using HCA and SSAP 16 (Bank of England 1982; ASC 1986). CCA lowered profits and revealed widespread payment of dividends from capital. The Bank of England found "Around half the [250] companies studied have paid dividends that were not fully covered by current cost profits" (1982, p. 376). It was clear, "A distribution which appears well covered when measured against historical cost profit may appear much well less covered when compared with a measurement of profit which takes account of changing prices" (ASC 1986, p. 9). This was embarrassing in the context of plant closures, high unemployment and wage freezes, but without monetary add-backs it would have looked worse.

As inflation fell in the UK, from 18 percent in 1980 to 4.6 percent in 1984 (Tweedie and Whittington 1997, p. 151), business tolerance of CCA collapsed and it drew on accounting theorists' RC criticisms to justify ditching it. From the Sandilands Committee onwards management had repeatedly "talked about a lack of objectivity in the figures and uncertainty in the valuations" (Walton 2007, p. 177). Auditors joined in, asking "themselves what their legal liabilities were when signing off on subjective figures, and analysts wondered if this was not going to introduce a greater lack of comparability between companies" (Walton 2007, p. 177). To secure management's agreement "SSAP 16 was finally passed, with a condition that it should be reviewed after three years, but preparers continued to lobby against it" (Walton 2007, p. 177). Drawing on accounting theorists' criticisms of RC, "They argued that the figures were too complicated, too costly to prepare, too subjective and neither understood nor used by the analyst community. Some companies refused to prepare the CCA statements" (Walton 2007, p. 177). Compliance fell from 95 percent in 1981 to 34 percent in 1984, the ASC made CCA voluntary in 1985, reducing compliance to 3 percent in 1986, and withdrew it in 1988 (Tweedie and Whittington 1997, Table 8.2, p. 152; Walton 2007, p. 178). This was the "end of the current cost revolution" by management counter-revolution: "The ASC's longest-running, most controversial and most time-consuming project had failed, owing to opposition and non-compliance by preparers of accounts" (Tweedie and Whittington, 1997, p. 156).

America had a parallel history (Tweedie and Whittington 1997, pp. 157–162). In a major FASB-sponsored study, for share valuation Beaver and Landsman (1983) found "historical cost earnings dominated the SFAS 33 earnings variables" (Tweedie and Whittington 1997, p. 159). One reason analysts lost interest in CCA disclosures was because, as Tweedie and Whittington say, "SFAS 33 and SSAP 16 were introduced too late" (1997, p. 151). They appeared just before Reagan became US President in 1981, and Thatcher became UK Prime Minister in 1979, who "intervene[d] with monetary and fiscal policies in order to prevent the full-scale destruction of capital value", which ended the threat of another Great Depression (Kliman 2012, p. 3). This change is consistent with evidence of initially using CCA followed by indifference and hostility. UK evidence suggests management used RC to make closure decisions in the late-1970s and early-1980s in the most vulnerable manufacturing industries (Bryer and Brignall 1986). The ICAEW published four volumes of research on *Current Cost Accounting: The Benefits and the Costs* (Carsberg and Page 1984), that found analysts used it, but for valuation the benefits were small, but so were the costs (Tweedie and Whittington 1997, p. 154). Archer and Steele (1984) found evidence of management's use of CCA in their sample of large companies, but also that "there was strong opposition to CCA amongst preparers" (Tweedie and Whittington 1997, p. 154).

In the US, Berliner (1983) and Norby (1983) found evidence "of limited use of SFAS 33 data by analysts" (Tweedie and Whittington 1997, p. 158). Berliner (1983) found around half had used it, and 10 percent frequently used it, but many had doubts about its "non-comparability", and "about the data's relevance and reliability", and therefore its usefulness because they could obtain better equivalent data from public sources (Tweedie and Whittington 1997, p. 158). Norby (1983) found analysts using CCA data, "if sparingly", in company analyses, but "Once the initial adjustment were reported the subsequent adjustments were predictable" (Tweedie and Whittington 1997, p. 158). In 1984, responding to an FASB exposure draft proposing retaining FAS 33, US analysts, academics and management overwhelmingly opposed it because of "the lack of relevance or reliability of the data", "flexibility of the methods of application", the poor "quality of the information", and preparation costs (Tweedie and Whittington 1997, p. 160). The FASB considered a "comprehensive changing prices model that reflected both current cost and general price-level adjustments", but decided against, first, because the evidence was clear, "there was little interest shown in SFAS 33 information and enterprises generally provided only the minimum" (Tweedie and Whittington 1997, p. 160). Second, there were theoretical problems that meant FAS 33's "opponents may not have accepted any eventual solution", and price-change accounting raised "many complex issues of recognition and measurement ... which remained contentious and unresolved", and third because "Government interest in any requirement to continue the disclosures of SFAS 33 appeared to have diminished" (Tweedie and Whittington 1997, pp. 160–161). Having in the meantime abolished stewardship in SFAC 1 (1978), institutionalised Paton's and Canning's interpretation of Fisher's entity theory in SFAC 3 (1980), and issued SFAC 5 (1984) making CCA discretionary, the FASB withdrew FAS 33 in December 1986, and companies ceased producing price-level adjusted data. The issue was "dead in the water" (Tweedie and Whittington 1997, p. 162).

A management counter-revolution ended the UK "current cost revolution", Tweedie and Whittington accept, highlighting as "particularly important" in explaining CCA's "remarkable decline", "Economic events (notably inflation rates)" and "Self-interest" (1997, p. 150). Management supported CCA to reduce reported profits when inflation was high, but had no interest when inflation was low, even though, as the ASC pointed out, "The limitations of historical cost accounts exist not only in periods of relative rapid price changes but also when prices are changing more slowly" (1986, p. 11). By "self-interest incentives" Tweedie and Whittington mean "the possibility of price controls and penal taxation (the impact of which might be minimised by the use of price change accounting)", which "changes of economic policy, associated with ... Thatcher ... and Reagan" (1997, pp. 150–151) swept away. Their tolerance of mass unemployment and attacks on unions drove down wages, which increased the rate of exploitation (Roberts 2016, p. 61) and reduced inflation. Tweedie and Whittington's "factors" (1997, p. 150), in effect, accept management's power over accounting, but they overlook its resistance to RCA, and accounting theorists' help in burying the Marxian content of

CCA, its inchoate cost theory of value. They also overlook the falling rate of profit as an important "economic event", which management had an incentive to resist.

The US and UK's abandonment of RC were premature according to Marx's theory of crises. In 1982, the US RC rate of profit had fallen to a historical low, but FAS 33's weaknesses combined with expansionary economic policies meant that by 1985 the rate of profit had only weakly recovered, and remained well below Golden Age levels to the 2008–2009 GFC (Roberts 2016, Figure 1.4, p. 22). During and following the 1974–1975 and 1980–1982 recessions, in the US and UK there were high levels of unemployment as plants closed and businesses "restructured". However, the consequences of the "profitability crisis" would have been worse if the capital market and government had allowed the necessary devaluation of capital to restore the RC rate of profit, for which the rigorous application of RCA, with no monetary adjustments and "holding gain" add-backs, would have been necessary. Instead, facing a confusing array of economic concepts and accounting "information", with another Great Depression averted, management and the capital market focused on HCA and, in effect, as theorists argued it could, treated CMAs as distributable "holding gains".

The Conceptual Framework

When the FASB met in 1973 to decide its initial agenda, Donald Kirk (1988, p. 10), influenced by a former colleague at Price Waterhouse, A. Carl Tietjen, "argued that it not be entirely technical". Like others (e.g., Horngren 1981), "Tietjen raised the question of whether pursuing more technical standards was the solution to the perceived ills of financial reporting. His answer was 'no' because he believed 'the root problem in financial reporting is moral and ethical'" (Kirk 1988, p. 10), that is, management's "immoral" and "unethical" accounting. "Others agreed", so the FASB placed "Broad Qualitative Standards for Financial Reporting" on its agenda (Kirk 1988, p. 10). The FASB quickly recognised an objectives statement would not be sufficient to constrain preparers' behaviour. Solomons (1986a, p. 67) found "unconvincing" the Trueblood Committee's claim that "the evolution of accounting to meet some social need can be constrained by an explicit statement of objectives, absent restrictions placed on [the] behavior … of those who prepare financial reports … by some regulatory agency, … [which] seem[ed] quite unlikely to be borne out by events”.[3] Shortly after it received the Trueblood report, the FASB announced it would expand and prioritise this agenda item to “encompass the entire conceptual framework of financial accounting and reporting, including objectives, qualitative characteristics and the information needs of users of accounting information” (Storey and Storey 1998, p. 48). The FASB left ethical infringements to the AICPA, but its “conceptual framework” would, it hoped, provide a framework of normative guidance, of “morals” and “ethics” because “without ethical behavior accounting standards become all-encompassing rules” (Kirk 1988, p. 11).

The FASB intended its framework to “be the ‘relief’ from the so-called ‘fire-fighting’ for which the predecessors of the FASB had been criticized” (Kirk 1988, p. 11), but academic disagreement and management resistance meant it took 10-years to complete, consumed a large proportion of its resources, and disappointed most observers, FASB members, and its employees. It issued a Discussion Memorandum (DM) on objectives in June 1974, its “tentative conclusions” in 1976, and SFAC 1, *Objectives of Financial Reporting*, in November 1978. After many other documents, and gathering and responding to comments, it issued SFAC 2 *Qualitative Characteristics of Accounting Information* in May 1980, SFAC 3 *Elements of Financial Statements of Business Enterprises* in December 1980, and SFAC 5 *Recognition and Measurement in Financial Statements of Business Enterprises* in December 1984.

SFAC 1 Objectives of Financial Reporting

SFAC 1 listed a range of potential users, including managers, auditors, regulators, employees, and the public. It chose “Investors and creditors and their advisors” as “the most obvious prominent external groups who use the information provided by financial reporting and who generally lack the authority to prescribe the information they want” (FASB 1978, paragraph 30). The FASB said its choice recognised that when “ownership is divorced from management, the accountor is in a much stronger position to protect his or her interests than the accountee is” (Solomons 1986a, p. 80). Even Staubus, now FASB Director of Research and Technical

[3] David Solomons, professor of accounting, University of Pennsylvania, worked for the FASB (1978–1980), and was a member of its Advisory Council (1982–1985).

Activities accepted, "Under present GAAP managers appear to enjoy a moderate degree of control over reporting" (1977, p. 8), whereas "the widely held view [was] that accounting policy questions are actually, more often than not, resolved in the interests of … managers" (Solomons 1986a, p. 75). According to APB Opinion 22, *Disclosure of Accounting Policies* (AICPA 1972), still in force, "The *accounting policies* of a reporting entity are the specific accounting principles and the methods of applying principles that are judged by the management of the entity to be the most appropriate in the circumstances" (Solomons 1986a, p. 9). Management could change policies only with justification and auditor support, but "Normally the auditor says that, relying on management's judgment, and in the absence of any criteria established by the FASB for selecting among alternative policies … he or she concurs in the judgment" (Solomons 1986a, p. 18).

Solomons pointed out, "Even within GAAP, numerous choices may still be made by the individual enterprise" (1986a, p. 20), and Staubus added management's scope for "structuring" transactions to take them outside rules, and "cherry picking", selectively selling assets with low HCs to report income (1977, pp. 8–10). Staubus accepted, because "it seems reasonable to assume that management control over reporting of earnings can have … undesirable effects … we feel that, from the standpoint of investors, it is undesirable for managers to be able to choose from among alternative accounting methods" (1977, pp. 11–12). However, rejecting writing more detailed rules, turning standards into an "Internal Revenue Code", the FASB's "framework was undertaken … with the expectation that it would articulate definitions and concepts that would diminish the need for and details in standards" (Kirk 1988, p. 11). The FASB saw "itself [a]s likely to be the major user and thus the most direct beneficiary of the guidance provided by the new series" (1978, p. 6). However, it hoped to reduce the need for rules because "knowledge of the objectives and concepts the Board uses … if used with care may also provide guidance in resolving new or emerging problems of financial accounting and reporting in the absence of applicable authoritative pronouncements" (FASB 1978, p. 6). They would provide guidance for management in such situations for restructured or "new" transactions, and for judgement where standards allowed or required it. This, what follows argues, was an ideological illusion. In reality, management used the framework to design transactions that achieved desired accounting outcomes. Staubus stressed, "auditors are not to blame for the unsatisfactory state of accounting practices", and by implication their clients were also blameless for pursuing their own interests; the problem was that auditors "*have neglected to establish clear and fundamental objectives*" (1977, p. 14). They had been operating without a moral and ethical framework. The first step to pre-empting management discretion, to give it a moral compass without writing detailed rules, was to "acknowledge the preeminence of external users in the determination of accounting standards" (Kirk 1988, p. 13). Following Trueblood, the FASB decided, "Since investors' and creditors' cash flows are related to enterprise cash flows, financial reporting should provide information to help investors, creditors, and others assess the amounts, timing, and uncertainty of prospective net cash inflows to the related enterprise" (1978, p. viii).

A majority of management still rejected this objective. In a speech in 1976 during the objectives DM phase, Marshall S. Armstrong, FASB chair who oversaw the framework project, "reported substantial opposition to adopting the informational perspective. Stewardship was cited most often as the preferred alternative" (Beaver 1989, fn. 6, p. 5). Only 37 percent of respondents supported decision-usefulness, while 63 percent preferred "stewardship", which to Armstrong "indicated that the vested interests of management are threatening the existence of the private-sector's standard-setting body" (*Journal of Accountancy* March 1976, p. 26). By "stewardship", management still meant according to May's approach, which gave it accounting choice. Armstrong observed, management "generally took the position that the basic function of financial statements was to report on management's stewardship of corporate assets and that … [it] can best determine the principles to be employed in reporting on their firms, and that standards … can only impede management in its effort to fulfill this responsibility" (1977, p. 77). He concluded it was "fair to say that some managements have a vested interest in diversity of accounting standards, for diversity means flexibility, and often flexibility opens up options often as diverse as operational choices" (Armstrong 1977, p. 77).

The FASB dealt with management's commitment to "stewardship" by firmly subsuming it under decision-usefulness, claiming it would reduce diversity in accounting by curtailing options. In SFAC 1 "stewardship", which the FASB used interchangeably with "accountability", appeared separately as one of eight statements about objectives, all of them "concerned with decisions" (Solomon 1986a, pp. 68–69). One was "Financial reporting is expected to provide information about an enterprise's financial performance during a period and about how management of an enterprise has discharged its stewardship responsibility to owners" (FASB 1978, p. ix). SFAC 1 elaborated:

> 4. Financial reporting should provide information about how management of an enterprise has discharged its stewardship responsibility to owners (stockholders) for the use of enterprise resources entrusted to it. Management of an enterprise is periodically accountable to the owners not only for the custody and safekeeping of enterprise resources but also for their efficient and profitable use and for protecting them to the extent possible from unfavorable economic impacts of factors in the economy such as inflation or deflation and technological and social changes. To the extent that management offers securities of the enterprise to the public, it voluntarily accepts wider responsibilities for accountability to prospective investors and to the public in general. …

This abolished "stewardship" in Rosenfield's (1974) Marxian sense by equating it with reporting "profitable use" or "earnings" measured as the ability to generate future cash flows. The *Scope and Implications of the* Conceptual *Framework Project* subsumed "stewardship" under decision-usefulness: "financial statements … provide information useful in assessing the prospects for cash flows to the business enterprise on which cash flows to investors and creditors depend and in evaluating enterprise and management performance" (FASB 1976a, p. 11), so "stewardship is subsumed under the informational perspective" (Beaver 1989, fn. 6, p. 5). As Gore (1992, p. 33) says, "running through most of the documents considering objectives was that accountability involved a decision to buy, hold, or sell shares based on the performance of the entity and its management as reported", clear that "the FASB attempted to subsume the accountability or stewardship approach into the adopted decision-usefulness approach".

Staubus' justification was "Everyone familiar with accounting recognizes that it plays a major role in managerial control in general and internal control in particular", and "Without settling on a formal definition of control … suggest[ed] several views on it that include decisions based on accounting information" (1977, pp. 28–29). However, neglecting a control definition meant Staubus confounded action and results control. He equated "reports that compare actual … quantities, such as costs, with standard or budgeted amounts" — where "Actual control" means through "subsequent *decisions*", supervisory decisions, action control — with "an accounting system [that] motivates personnel at all levels to work towards the goals of the firm" — which means affecting "a person's *decisions* about his own behaviour", through results control (Staubus 1977, p. 29). According to Staubus, "These views suggest that, although the control objective is an important part of the decision objective, it need not be stated separately" (1977, p. 29). However, as Solomons (1986a, p. 70), who drafted the Wheat Report, and was an FASB consultant on SFAC 2, put it, because "a balance between the forward-looking and backward-looking uses of accounting is maintained" in SFAC 1, it was not *possible* to state the decision-usefulness and "stewardship" objectives separately. If we measure "performance" according to SFAC 1, as "the amounts, timing, and uncertainty of prospective net cash inflows to the related enterprise", "Performance measurement is necessary, of course, as an input to decision-making" (Solomons 1986a, p. 70).

In its final version, SFAC 1 distinguished "earnings" from "earning power", possibly to remove any suggestion that financial analysts were in control of accounting, and succumbed to pressure to deemphasise cash flows that "troubled some commentators for it seemingly implied a radical shift away from 'traditional' accruals accounting" (Gore 1992, p. 58). To avoid this impression it asserted, "Information about enterprise earnings based on accrual accounting generally provides a better indication of an enterprise's present and continuing ability to generate favorable cash flows than information limited to the financial effects of cash receipts and payments" (FASB 1978, p. 5). However, "earnings", the "ability to generate favorable cash flows" reported in any one year, did not measure management's "stewardship", for which investors would need to estimate "earning power", or a similar measure of "long-term performance":

> 51. Earnings information is commonly the focus for assessing management's stewardship or accountability. Management, owners, and others emphasize enterprise performance or profitability in describing how management has discharged its stewardship accountability. A central question for owners, managers, potential investors, the public, and government is how an enterprise and its owners are faring. Since earnings and its components for a single period are often an insufficient basis for assessing management's stewardship, owners and others may estimate 'earning power' or other average they consider 'representative' of long-term performance. As noted in paragraph 48, however, accrual accounting measures earnings for a period rather than 'earning power' or other financial analysis concepts.

Furthermore, investors could not use earnings to measure management's performance, the FASB concluded, because this had multiple causes:

> 5. Financial reporting, and especially financial statements, usually cannot and does not separate management performance from enterprise performance. … Enterprise successes and failures are the result of the interaction of numerous factors. Management ability and performance are contributing factors, but so are events and circumstances that are often beyond the control of management, such as general economic conditions, supply and demand characteristics of enterprise inputs and outputs, price changes, and fortuitous events and circumstances. … Actions of past managements affect current periods' earnings, and actions of current management affect future periods' earnings. Financial reporting provides information about an enterprise during a period when it was under the direction of a particular management but does not directly provide information about that management's performance. The information is therefore limited for purposes of assessing management performance apart from enterprise performance.

Observers and scholars today agree, "The Board made the important point that financial reporting can provide information about enterprise performance but not directly about a management's performance" (Zeff 2013, p. 286). However, this is only important if the objective is measuring management's "performance" as its contribution to the enterprise's ability to generate future cash flows. According to Marx's theory of capitalism, the board of directors are workers who function as the collective agent of total social capital. As a social functionary, current management is accountable, that is, is subject to punishment or reward for enterprise performance, for its capital and realised profit regardless of past management's contribution, who may remain accountable for future results (e.g., claw back). This would explain why, as SFAC 1 put it, "Management, owners, and others emphasize enterprise performance or profitability in describing how management has discharged its stewardship accountability" (paragraph 51). How much profit an enterprise realises clearly depends partly on management's skill and effort and partly on the circumstances, but providing an objective record of enterprise performance is a necessary condition for assessing management's performance. To judge an agent the principal must adjust the target to reflect the circumstances, just as management routinely do within enterprises by, for example, using flexible budgeting for ROI. For Marx and Rosenfield and, we will see, for others, e.g., Bevis (1965), appraising management's performance was a judgement for the market in the circumstances, not for accounting that measures enterprise performance. Shareholders punish or reward management according to whether they believe they can distinguish management's contribution to the enterprise's results, its ROI, for example, by comparing an enterprise's financial results with industrial sector averages or other benchmarks (e.g., paired comparisons).

William Beaver (1989, pp. 2, 4), professor of accounting at Stanford University, prominently argued that the change from the "stewardship view of management and the concept of economic income" that "dominated financial accounting theory" to the mid-1960s, to "an 'informational' approach" from the late-1960s, culminating in the FASB's decision-usefulness objective, was a "financial reporting revolution". However, while SFAC 1 buried Ijiri and Rosenfield's Marxian stewardship, and its decision-usefulness objective overthrew May's notion of earning capacity, this changed nothing. Ijiri's notion of accountability "mounted quite a different kind of attack on the FASB's list of objectives, by rejecting decision usefulness as the main purpose of accounting" (Solomons 1986a, p. 79), but he undermined its revolutionary potential by questioning the importance of accrual accounting, arguing for cash flow accounting (Ijiri 1978). According to Beaver, by contrast, "the notion that financial statement data ought to provide useful information on the assessment of future cash flows … if taken seriously … has several dramatic implications for financial statement preparation and interpretation" (1989, p. 5). First, it resolved the problem that under uncertainty "the 'ideal' that financial statements are attempting to represent", that is, Fisher's economic income "is not clear conceptually" (Beaver 1989, p. 5). Second, focusing on individual investor's decisions made clear "the selection among financial reporting systems can be viewed essentially as an issue of social choice involving tradeoffs among constituencies" (Beaver 1989, p. 18). However, the "ideal" in uncertainty remained the PV of future economic benefits and, in reality, the mechanism of "social choice", seen as the outcome of individuals competing in a market, remained management dominated. There were no conceptual or social "revolutions". In adopting decision-usefulness, the FASB formally removed management's discretion, but reinstalled it in the "qualitative characteristics" and "elements" of financial statements, and it retained control of the "measurement attribute".

SFAC 2 Qualitative Characteristics of Accounting Information

As Solomons (1986a, p. 86), who wrote SFAC 2 at the FASB's invitation (Zeff 1999, p. 109) said, "Once decision-making is seen as the primary objective" it was "inevitable" that "usefulness ... for making decisions should be the primary quality". Moreover, if these "decisions" require share valuations, with PV as the ideal it was inevitable that the necessary qualities would be subjective. SFAC 2 (FASB 1980a) claimed to narrow the scope for individual choice in accounting by "a hierarchy of accounting qualities", with "understandability" and "decision-usefulness" for "decision makers" at the top, its "primary decision-specific qualities" being "relevance" to forecasting future cash flows, and "reliability", dependability for forecasting. According to SFAC 2 the "Ingredients" of "relevance" are "timeliness", "predictive value", and "feedback value", and the ingredients of "reliability" are "verifiability", "representational faithfulness", and "neutrality", which together it claims produce "comparability and consistency", which are "secondary interactive qualities". Bounding the hierarchy at the top is the "pervasive constraint" that "benefits > costs", and at the bottom "materiality", the "threshold for recognition" (FASB 1980a, Figure 1, p. 20). As all these qualities are subjective, and often conflict — often more relevance means less reliability — SFAC 2 inevitably left it to preparers to operationalise and trade them off (Solomons 1986a, p. 111), leaving the problem that "accounting choices will always have to be made" (Storey and Storey 1998, p. 99).

With PV as the ideal, "relevant" means information could change the estimated PV by changing predictions or giving feedback to make a change. According to SFAC 2, therefore, "relevant" means "capable of making a difference in a decision by helping users to form predictions about the outcomes of past, present, and future events or to confirm or correct prior expectations", and can do this "by improving decision makers' capacities to predict or by providing feedback on earlier expectations" (FASB 1980a, p. 5). With PV as the ideal "reliability" means decision-makers can trust the information to forecast cash flows. To SFAC 2, therefore, reliability "rests on the faithfulness with which it represents what it purports to represent, coupled with an assurance for the user that it has that representational quality. To be useful, information must be reliable as well as relevant" (FASB 1980a, p. 6). To estimate PV, decision-makers need assurance that information is reliable, but inevitably, "Degrees of reliability must be recognized. It is hardly ever a question of black or white, but rather of more reliability or less": more or less verifiability, representational faithfulness, and neutrality (FASB 1980a, p. 6).

The FASB's qualities depend on preparer's perceptions. "Relevance" depends on perceived "predictive" value or "feedback" value to a user's decision model; "reliability" depends on the perceived "representational faithfulness", "accounting's ability to present a picture of 'economic reality' in an enterprise's financial statements" (Solomons 1986a, p. 92), and "verifiability" depends on "consensus" amongst "independent measurers". Although "objectivity was mentioned by several respondents" (paragraph 158) to the DM as a necessary quality, "In the discussion of verifiability, the term 'objectivity' was nowhere to be found, probably", Zeff thought, "to allow for the admissibility of departures from historical cost accounting" (1999, p. 109; Bryer 1999, pp. 579–583). Solomons admitted, "The quotation marks around 'economic reality' … imply that the concept, though useful, is incapable of precise definition" (1986a, p. 92), which left room for "prudence". Fisher argued that "conservatism" means reporting assets at less than PV to "reflect uncertainty", and SFAS 2 in effect institutionalised this by allowing "prudence" (1980a, paragraph 93). It forbade "deliberate understatement" of assets and profits, but this left discretion: "There is a place for a convention such as conservatism — meaning prudence — in financial accounting and reporting, because business and economic activities are surrounded by uncertainty, but it needs to be applied *with care*" (FASB 1980a, paragraph 92, emphasis added).

SFAC 2 avoided using "economic reality" "because its dictionary meaning has become debased in accounting usage and has come to mean whatever the writer or speaker supports" (Kirk 1989, p. 98), but retained the idea. Solomons claimed, "It is in the assertion that the concept of reliability is much more than simply verifiability that the concepts statement makes one of its principal contributions. Representational faithfulness, the other ingredient that makes accounting information reliable, has become a powerful tool that the board now uses in formulating standards" even though he admitted "The goal of representational faithfulness is not invariably achieved" (1986b, p. 120). This was despite its foundation, as Tinker put it, in a "correspondence theory" of truth (1991, p. 297). SFAC 2 defined "representational faithfulness" as "correspondence or agreement between a measure or description and the phenomenon that it purports to represent (sometimes called 'validity')", but the "phenomenon" was the PV of expected cash flows. SFAC 2 stressed the importance of "comparability" and "consistency", from which information "gains greatly in usefulness", but this was comparability between "economic phenomena" and consistency in the method used to represent it: "The quality of information that enables users to identify similarities in and differences between two sets of economic phenomena". As for the trade-off between "costs and benefits", which it recognised was "uniquely" different for each individual, the FASB promised to "do its best" (1980a, paragraph 133).

"Materiality", according to Marxian accounting, is quantitative, whether exclusion changes the reported rate of profit by more than an agreed amount. To SFAC 2, "Materiality is a pervasive concept that relates to the qualitative characteristics", but like "relevance", "defined [it] in terms of what influences or makes a difference to a decision maker". Therefore, "Magnitude by itself, without regard to the nature of the item and the circumstances in which the judgment has to be made, will not generally be a sufficient basis for a materiality judgment". With PV as the ideal this inevitably meant, "The Board's present position is that no general standards of materiality can be formulated to take into account all the considerations that enter into an experienced human judgment" (FASB 1980a, p. 7).

In its *Scope and Implications of the Conceptual Framework Project* the FASB warned, "A conceptual framework does not eliminate judgement in preparing financial statements" (1976a, p. 7), and SFAC 2 amplified this warning. "If alternative accounting methods could be given points for each ingredient of usefulness in a particular situation, it would be an easy matter to add up each method's points and select the one (subject to its cost) that scored highest. ... Unfortunately, neither the Board nor anyone else has such a system ... [so] those who must choose among alternatives are forced to fall back on human judgment to evaluate the relative merits of competing methods" (FASB 1980a, paragraph 6). SFAC 2 nevertheless claimed, "For preparers of financial information, the qualities of useful accounting information should provide guidance in choosing between alternative ways of representing economic events, especially in dealing with situations not yet clearly covered by standards" (paragraph 11). Evidence quickly suggested this was unlikely. Joyce *et al.* (1982) recruited 26 former members of the APB and FASB and tested them with a variety of accounting problems to see if the 11 qualitative characteristics were operational, comprehensive, and parsimonious. They found nine of the 11 "clearly fail the test of operationality", that only "verifiability" and "cost" "have some common meaning to the policy makers. However, the other nine do not and one, representational faithfulness, has no common meaning at all" (Joyce *et al.* 1982, pp. 662, 670). Joyce *et al.* pointed out, "Not only is there considerable disagreement among experienced policy makers on what the qualitative characteristics mean in the context of particular accounting policy issues, there is also considerable disagreement on their relative importance. While the qualitative characteristics appear to comprise a comprehensive set for choosing among accounting alternatives, the set is not a parsimonious one" (1982, p. 670). Therefore, "the Statement fails to meet two out of its three desired criteria … [which] casts doubt on the ability of the qualitative characteristics defined in the Statement to facilitate accounting policy making" (Joyce *et al.* 1982, p. 670). Stanga (1980) found a "moderate" positive correlation between "relevance" and "reliability" in a survey of analysts and bankers, who did not trade them off, which is consistent with one being causal or both concepts measuring a subjective notion of "usefulness". In a report for the ICAEW on the desirability of British adoption of the framework, Richard Macve (1981, p. 12), professor of accounting, Aberystwyth, University of Wales, concluded that the qualitative characteristics "do not offer much practical assistance … to decide questions about accounting methods".

Killing off "Revenue and Expense"

The FASB also sought to reduce management's discretion when it replaced May's and Paton and Littleton's "revenue and expense" accounting with "asset-liability" accounting in SFAC 3 *Elements of Financial Statements of Business Enterprises*. Pushing the FASB down the "asset-liability" road was management's resistance to rules preventing it capitalising research and development expenses, and accruing future losses, important unfinished APB business (Kirk 1988, p. 15). The FASB issued a DM for each topic, and "discovered in the comment letters that many respondents were less interested in what constituted assets and liabilities than in whether capitalizing and amortising research and development costs and accruing self-insurance reserves 'properly matched' costs with revenues and thus did not 'distort periodic net income'" (Storey and Storey 1998, p. 51). "Proper matching", many argued, "required research and development and similar costs to be capitalized and amortized over their useful lives", and "self-insurance and similar costs to be accrued or otherwise 'provided for' each period … [otherwise] periodic income of the affected companies would be distorted" (Storey and Storey 1998, p. 51). To deal with "nondistortion and matching arguments" the FASB first turned to APB 4's definitions of assets and liabilities and found them "useless" (Storey and Storey 1998, pp. 49, 54). To kill off "revenue and expense" accounting it therefore decided an early priority "would have to be providing definitions of assets and liabilities and other elements of financial statements to fill a yawning gap in the authoritative pronouncements" (Storey and Storey 1998, pp. 48–49). To critique "revenue and expense" it turned to the work of Herman W. Bevis, a senior partner of Price Waterhouse, an APB member who articulated and defended "revenue and expense" accounting in *Corporate Financial Reporting in a Competitive Economy* (Bevis 1965). Bevis dedicated his book to G.O. May. The FASB described it as "One of the most complete expositions of the revenue and expense view" (1976b, p. 47). It focused its fire on Bevis' argument that management should allocate revenues and expenses to "minimize distortions of net income which could be attributable to accounting method as opposed to actual transactions and events" (FASB 1965, p. 32). It noted, the "literature of the revenue and expense view and letters of comment show that something akin to the nondistortion guideline is widely used to judge whether … costs and revenues are appropriately matched in specific situations" (FASB 1976b, p. 47). Kirk (1988, p. 9), also a Price Waterhouse partner, thought Bevis' articulations "were widely accepted in the accounting practices of the 1960s".

The FASB criticised Bevis' "nondistortion guideline" because it gave management choice, required "judgment", but it also in effect rejected its implicit cost theory of value. Kirk blamed the guideline for many of the APB's problems. It "explains, at least with hindsight, how, when applied by aggressive managements and approved by willing auditors, assets and liabilities without substance were finding their way into financial statements" (Kirk 1988, p. 9). It "became a rationale for many questionable cost deferrals and accruals in the 1960s … in part … because the tools of the auditors to know income — or nondistorted income — when they saw it — or smelled it — were no match for the corporate chutzpah and creative accounting of those 'go-go' years" (Kirk 1988, p. 9). There were weaknesses in Bevis' articulation of "non-distortion", we will see, but the FASB did not see its British/Marxian stewardship strengths, particularly that Bevis' starting point was society's demand that management be accountable for capital to "those who are, or would be, investors" (1965, p. 9), to the capital market, Marx's total social capital. "Society has … assigned to corporate directors and management the responsibility of employing resources gainfully; after delegating commensurate discretionary authority over the utilization of capital, society expects, and receives, the accounting to which it is entitled" (Bevis 1965, p. 7). To Bevis, therefore, "Corporate financial accounting … is practical … [y]et there runs through most of it a logic distilled from sound business practices and healthy corporation-stockholder-society relationships" (1965, p. 1). The logic was results control: "when a man is obliged to make financial accountings of his activities, the discipline becomes more or less a part of his character and imposes on him much higher ethical standards measured in terms of social responsibility than if there were no reckoning" (1965, p. 8). Rosenfield (1974, pp. 135–136) quoted extensively from Bevis.

Like May and Littleton, Bevis stressed that accountability — "rendering accountings to present stockholders from the stewards of their resources" — was different from and more important than economic decision-making. "[T]he fact that prospective investors may use the information contained in the report to assist them in making projections in connection with investment decisions does not belie the report's essential nature and purpose as an historical accounting of what has taken place" (Bevis 1965, p. 9). Society, Bevis argued, "desires that the corporation create more wealth than the resources of labor and materials it consumes in the process"; "Society, like the stockholder, must hope that the corporation makes a profit" (1965, p. 12). Consistent with Marxian accounting, he articulated the "operating cycle of a corporation", which begins with money capital that management transforms into assets or otherwise spends, that continues with the production of a commodity or service, that it sells for a profit (Bevis 1965, pp. 13–14), or M-C-M′. According to Marxian accounting, accountants report the circulation of capital, the revenues realised and socially necessary expenses incurred over a period, and its composition at a point in time in the various stages of the cycle. Bevis' accrual accounting likewise follows production and realisation, "periodic income determined under the accrual basis … more faithfully reflects this relative steadiness in a corporation's progress, as compared with what would be obtained if annual income were the net result of each year's cash receipts and disbursements alone" (1965, p. 104). Bevis gave "guidelines" for "repetitive operations", operating cycles. The "transaction guideline" that management should recognise transactions and events when they occur, unless the "matching guideline", the "systematic and rational guideline", or the "nondistortion guideline", justified some other period(s). His guidelines came close to Marxian accounting, but because Bevis accepted May's view that an objective was reporting earning power, he necessarily supplemented them with management's "judgement". This gave the FASB the weak spot it was looking for to kill off "revenue and expense" accounting.

Central to Bevis' "matching" was that during production there is a "reasonable expectation that society will value the product at least at the equivalent of the resources of labour and materials directly consumed" (1965, p. 13), a cost theory of value. "The corporation considers that the production process adds value to the raw material processed and … substitutes the asset of inventories for the cash disbursed for labor and materials and for the fixed assets consumed" (Bevis 1965, p. 13). Consistent with Marx's distinction between productive and unproductive labour, for expenditures on promotion, advertising, general administration, all unproductive expenses, Bevis argued, "Society sees no *direct* relationship between these activities and the resources that are being or will be turned over to it by the corporation" (1965, p. 13). Therefore, the "corporation, too, does not consider that expenditures for these functions can be directly related to products or services being produced, or that the value added can be demonstrated" (Bevis 1965, p. 13). Like May, but "in contrast to most accountants of the time, who tended to describe the matching of costs and revenues very broadly", following Paton and Littleton (1940), Bevis took a "restricted" view of matching, warning "Only in part are costs 'matched' against revenues…. [I]t would be more accurate to describe income determination as a process of (1) matching product costs against revenues, and (2) allocating other period costs" (Storey and Storey 1998, p. 56; Bevis 1965, pp. 28–29).

However, because Bevis did not define the cost of production as socially necessary cost, his notion of "period costs" left "gray areas" between direct materials, labour and advertising, and even advertising could be a gray area. He was clear, "the costs of materials directly entering into the finished product, and of labor expended in fabricating and assembling it — which touches it, so to speak — should clearly be included in inventory. At the other end of the scale, the costs of those activities remote from the plant in which the product is produced, such as advertising, should not" (Bevis 1965, p. 112). He was confident, "the applicable guidelines tend to exclude far more 'gray area' costs from inventory than are included. The result is that the amounts added to inventory do not purport to be a fair market value or other such economic value … and, in fact, are usually below any such amounts" (Bevis 1965, p. 113). However, some advertising and promotional expenditures were a possible "gray area" that management could defer. In practice, he knew, "Corporations include in the computation of net income for the year some amounts that benefit future periods. Advertising and other promotional expenditures are examples. How can the three guidelines be reconciled here?" (Bevis 1965, p. 106). They could, he argued, "for repetitive operations of a going concern operating at a fair consistent level, the transaction guideline is also systematic and rational, and produces a nondistorted effect. It is only when the level of transactions changes sharply upward or downward that the effects of the guidelines would differ; then judgement must be applied in selecting an appropriate guideline" (Bevis 1965, p. 106). In other words, to measure earning power management should write off repetitive advertising, but could capitalise unusually high levels if "judgement" sanctioned it.

Under the "transactions principle", consistent with Marxian accounting, Bevis generally stuck to realisation because "From the socioeconomic standpoint, it is only after both development of a useful product *and* its acquisition by a consumer that anyone external to the corporation (society) receives anything of value from the process" (1965, p. 14). Thus, "The matching principle can become potentially dangerous when it attempts to match *today's real costs* with *hopes of tomorrow's revenues*, as in deferring research and development costs to be matched against hoped-for, but speculative, future revenues" (Bevis 1965, p. 101). Here Bevis recognised that between society and the firm "There would be disharmony, for example, if the corporation reported its consumption of resources in research and development as a mere conversion into another asset form … but did not develop a product" (1965, p. 15). However, the transaction date was for Bevis only a guideline, and he allowed cash accounting in the face of collection uncertainty or percentage of completion for "firm orders": the "nondistortion guideline may dictate that … the so-called percentage of completion method be used" (Bevis 1965, p. 108).

Also under the "nondistortion guideline" Bevis, for example, advocated self-insurance provisions, inconsistent with Marxian accounting that insurance is only a cost if the firm buys the security, that is, is pays for a use-value it controls (Bryer 2021a, p. 320). On the other hand, Bevis suggested provisions for dry-docking or blast furnace relines, consistent with Marxian accounting according to which these are costs of production. Where there are additional costs — e.g., scraping off barnacles — Bevis agreed it would not be right to designate a portion of the original asset for this and "depreciate" it, as asset-liability proponents advocate (e.g., Storey and Storey 1998, p. 57). These provisions according to Marxian accounting were not liabilities, any more than depreciation provisions, but are necessary for the "non-distortion" of income, that is, charging the full cost of production (Bryer 2021a, pp. 87–88). Also consistent with Marxian accounting, Bevis rejected the "all-inclusive" or "clean surplus" idea of income and the economic entity concept, and distinguished between "usual" and "unusual" gains and losses, which according to Marxian accounting are extraordinary, unproductive gains and losses, not related to production for profit (Bryer 2021a, pp. 85–86). This principle underlies Bevis' view that unusual items arise because "Plans and programs are changed; supposedly permanent investments are disposed of; plants, products, or product lines are discontinued before their costs are fully recovered. … [T]he gains and losses from liquidating the efforts must be considered unusual. They are 'distortions' in the financial results of the corporation's operations" (1965, p. 37). All Bevis' examples are gains and losses unrelated to the circuit of capital (1965, pp. 132–133), but to fill the conceptual gaps he again introduced judgement: "For many corporations, it is infrequency and size in relation to a single year's operations which render the items unusual in relation to repetitive activities" (1965, p. 38). What mattered was the "nondistortion" of income.

Under the "systematic and rational guideline" Bevis gave the "classic rationale", the British/Marxian theory, for accelerated depreciation "that maintenance and repair costs are higher in later years, offsetting the lower depreciation costs and giving a more even annual total property cost over a property's life" (1965, p. 103; Bryer 2017, pp. 180–195). However, his suggested rationale for straight-line depreciation was that "the passage of time is as good a measure as any of the expiration of the cost", and an alternative rationale for accelerated methods, "that newer equipment has greater utility than older equipment" (Bevis 1965, p. 103), that accounting theorists could agree with. Nevertheless, Bevis generally favoured "use" or "activity" methods, because, consistent with Marxian accounting where value is first produced and then realised, he thought, "It is a fair generalization that the increase or decrease in most corporation's revenues and in the use of their facilities are directly related" (1965, p. 106).

Some of his guidelines produced rules consistent with Marxian accounting, but Bevis' income statement focus meant the "amounts at which many assets and liabilities are stated in the balance sheet are a by-product of the methods designed to produce a fair periodic net income figure" (1965, p. 107). For Bevis (1965, pp. 58–59), like May and Paton and Littleton (1940), because "The objective is not to produce a liquidating value or a current fair market value of assets", "Among all the footnotes explaining and elaborating on the income statement, this makes the balance sheet the biggest footnote of all". In comment letters on the R&D and self-insurance DMs respondents likewise "showed little or no interest" in assets or liabilities (Storey and Storey 1998, p. 60). To attack this view, with the Trueblood Committee's decision-usefulness objective as its "blueprint" (Zeff 1999, p. 101), the FASB concentrated its fire on Paton and Littleton's (1940) and others', like Bevis', "circular" definition of an asset as "economic resources" and "whatever … generally accepted principles recognized and measured as assets" (Storey and Storey 1998, p. 50). This quickly led them to Paton's (1922) "asset-liability" accounting.

Asset-liability Accounting

Paton and Littleton (1940) abandoned "value", but enshrined "matching" and "acquisition prices", HC. At a symposium in 1970 on the "Foundations of Accounting Theory" packed with new-generation scholars, Paton, the "honoured guest", highlighted the problem that haunted his book with Littleton, which he now publicly disowned for veering too close to the "cost theory of value" he had rejected in *Accounting Theory*, to Marx's theory of value, to support "attaching". He admitted, "For a long time I've wished that the Paton and Littleton monograph … had never been written, or had gone out of print twenty-five years or so ago" (Paton 1971, p. xi). He highlighted "The basic difficulty with the idea that cost dollars, as incurred, attach like barnacles to the physical flow of materials and stream of operating activity is that it is at odds with the actual process of valuation in a free competitive market" (Paton 1971, p. xi). From his economics perspective, "The customer does not buy a handful of classified and traced cost dollars; he buys a product, at prevailing market price. And the market price may be above or below any calculated cost figure" (Paton 1971, p. xi). He disowned any Marxian cost theory of value. "Despite any statements in the monograph that seem to hold otherwise, I have never espoused the socialistic, cost-plus interpretation of product pricing, and I apologize humbly, for any apparent veering in this direction by Paton and Littleton" (Paton 1971, p. xi). Paton was "firmly convinced that the most significant measure of any resource is what it is currently worth" (1971,

p. xi), identifying the ideological conflict between "cost is value" and "price is value", and as he always had, choosing "price" as the measure of "economic resources", of "current worth" or PV.

Paton (1971, p. x) was stung into making his "apology" from "Listening to Bob Sprouse take issue with the 'matching' gospel, which the P & L monograph helped to foster, [that] confirmed my dissatisfaction with this publication". Sprouse (1966, p. 45) criticised the APB for not having "established fundamentals … such as the nature of assets and the nature of liabilities", for allowing what he dubbed "what-you-may-call-its", that is, deferred credits and debits, for income smoothing. Sprouse led the attack for the FASB as its vice-chairman from 1973 to 1985 in re-establishing the balance-sheet approach that he and Moonitz had outlined in ARS 3 (1962). In the 1970 symposium Sprouse criticised "the inherent sterility of the matching concept as a basis for resolving accounting issues" (1971, p. 94). He traced its origin to Paton and Littleton (1940), where "The economic concept of income as a change in wealth during a period of time was explicitly rejected, even as an ideal, and the notion of an income associated with each item of goods sold or service rendered was expounded" (Sprouse 1971, p. 92). He complained, "uninhibited by any meaningful concept of assets, liabilities and income, the matching concept may be deemed to supply adequate support for virtually any accounting procedure", reducing accounting to a "beauty contest" (Sprouse 1971, p. 94). From Sprouse's Fisherian perspective, the FASB had little difficulty in ridiculing "revenue and expense", the "pervasive influence of the belief in 'proper matching to avoid distorting periodic income', and the common use of expressions such as 'assets are costs' and 'costs are assets'" (Storey and Storey 1998, p. 49).

Provoking its response was a campaign organised by Professor Robert K. Mautz, an Illinois-educated academic, who had worked on the conceptual framework task force, who represented Ernst & Ernst on the FASB, who argued against asset-liability accounting. Arguing it would lead to "current value accounting", he "produced a lecture on the topic and offered it to the FEI. With their approval, he toured 65–70 FEI chapters presenting his view, roundly criticising the DM and urging rejection of the A&L [asset-liability] view" (Gore 1992, p. 95). Naturally, "the Board and staff were furious", but "Mautz did his work well, and the responses the FASB received on the issue were heavily coloured by his intervention" (Gore 1992, p. 95). The FASB dismissed respondents' "proper matching" argument that managers should decide whether to capitalise and amortise research and development, provide for self-insurance, etc., which "sounded a lot like excuses to justify smoothing reported income, thereby decreasing its volatility" (Storey and Storey 1998, p. 53). As Sprouse (1988, p. 127) said, "Members of the FASB concluded early that references to vague notions such as 'avoiding distortion' and 'better matching' were neither an adequate basis for analyzing and resolving controversial financial accounting issues nor an effective way to communicate". This approach "seemed to make income measurement primarily a matter of individual judgment", and its "basic rationale", May's view, that "the single most important function of financial accounting was the determination of net income and that the function of the balance sheet was not to reflect the values of assets and liabilities", was misplaced (Storey and Storey 1998, pp. 53–54).

The FASB's solution was to reintroduce "value" into accounting and define its measurement ideal, as Fisher, Paton and Canning, and others, had done, as PV. The FASB claimed it provided the "missing boundaries that were needed to bring the accrual accounting system under control" (Storey and Storey 1998, p. 72). The FASB easily found what it wanted, "Definitions ... [that] identified assets with economic resources and wealth, emphasizing the service potential, or benefits, and economic values that an asset confers on the holding or owning entity", including one by Mautz (Storey and Storey 1998, pp. 72–73). In this definition, "service potential" meant, as it did for Fisher and Canning, future economic benefits (cash flows), and like them, HC or current values are PV surrogates. With these foundations, having ditched "revenue and expense" accounting and any idea of social capital, the FASB could theorise accounting using Moonitz's and others' "self-evident propositions about the environment within which accounting functions". "For example, the observation that most of the goods and services produced in the United States are not directly consumed by their producers but are sold for cash or claims to cash" (Storey and Storey 1998, p. 70). To the FASB, this "suggests both why financial accounting is concerned with production and distribution of goods and services and with exchange prices and why investors, creditors, and other users of financial statements are concerned with cash prices and cash flows" (Storey and Storey 1998, pp. 70–71). The objective was helping individual investors make rational economic decisions to sustain a "well-functioning, healthy economy", secure "social good" (Storey and Storey 1998, p. 92), like Canning (1929) in effect legitimating investors' rewards for "controlling" corporations in society's interests.

Underlying these "self-evident" truths is Fisher and Paton's economic entity concept, that the objective is "general purpose financial statements", because "several groups, such as investors, creditors, and other resource providers, have common interests and common information needs" (Storey and Storey 1998, p. 1). According to British/Marxian accounting, by contrast, "general purpose" means accounting to all shareholders, current and potential, as an class for ROI, whereas from Paton's entity perspective it means the business entity accounting to individuals for their interests in expected cash flows. As Sprouse put it, starting from "the notion of an entity", "among the most primitive elements in accounting theory", defined as "an area of economic interest to a particular individual or group", there flowed "the concepts of assets (expected future economic benefits, rights to which have been acquired by the entity ...) and liabilities (the entity's obligations ...)" (1971, p. 100). This was Paton's entity concept, according to which, as Sprouse and Moonitz put it, the objective was "to reflect the claims against and interests in ... entities", so they defined assets as "expected future benefits" and liabilities as "lowest amount for which the obligation could be effectively discharged" (1962, pp. 7, 20, 39), its exit price. The AAA (1965, p. 363) committee (with Sprouse in the chair) emphasised it was an "economic entity", that "*The essence of the entity concept in accounting is an area of economic interest — not legal or administrative form*".

SFAC 3 Elements of Financial Statements of Business Enterprises

The FASB accepted Sprouse's approach in SFAC 3 (December 1980) where it defined "assets", "liabilities", "equity" and "comprehensive income" and its components ("revenues", "expenses", "gains" and "losses"), implicitly using Paton's entity concept. Reed K. Storey, the FASB's assistant director of research and technical activities, "a major contributor to the board's conceptual framework project" (Zeff 1999, fn. 2, p. 90) who "wrote most of SFAC No. 3" (Gore 1992, p. 113), accepted Paton's asset definition, and Canning's, "which is perhaps the most quoted of them all" (Storey 1981, p. 88). According to Canning, who was summarising "the professional accountant's implied definition", "*An asset is any future service in money or any future service convertible into money (except those services arising from contracts the two sides of which are proportionately unperformed) the beneficial interest in which is legally or equitably secured to some person or set of persons*" (1929, p. 22). Storey (1981, p. 88) saw a lineage from Sprague (1907) through Paton (1922) to Canning (1929), but while there was from Paton, Sprague defined "property" as the cost (value) of use-values (Bryer 2021a, pp. 191–195). Like Paton (1922), Canning (1929), and Sprouse and Moonitz (1962), SFAC 3 started from an asset definition: "There is no more fundamental concept in accounting than assets" (Storey and Storey 1998, p. 123). Also like them it defined "assets" as management's effective control of "future economic benefits", but left the option of defining "control" as Paton (1922) did as control of use-values with PV or, like Canning (1929), as legal or equitable access to the expected or "probable" cash flows, not Sprague's legal control of use-values with value (Bryer 2021b, p. 183). According to SFAC 3 "Assets are probable future economic benefits obtained or controlled by a particular entity as a result of past transactions or events" (FASB 1980b, paragraph 7), leaving open what the entity controls, underlying use-values or access to future economic benefits, the "beneficial interest secured". Chapter 8 argues that banks exploited this option to justify off-balance sheet accounting for securitisation SPEs.

In addition to the "capacity… to contribute directly or indirectly to future net cash inflows", an "asset" requires that "a particular entity can obtain the benefit and control others' access to it", and "the transaction or other event giving rise to the entity's right to or control of the benefit has already occurred" (FASB 1980b, paragraph 26). SFAC 3 accepted, "the ability of an entity to obtain benefit from an asset and to control others' access to it generally rests on a foundation of legal rights" (FASB 1980b, paragraph 26). However, like Canning, "legal enforceability of a claim to the benefit is not a prerequisite for a benefit to qualify as an asset if the entity has the ability to obtain and control the benefit in other ways" (FASB 1980b, paragraph 26). Here the FASB followed Ijiri's advice to the Trueblood Committee: "Only those goods and services over which an enterprise has *control* are accounted for in accounting. Thus, the nature of control needs to be delineated. In present financial accounting, control is essentially based on legal property rights. … Furthermore, the concept of control is usually expanded to include expected control and expected release of control" (Ijiri 1971, pp. 45–46). SFAC 3 put management's expected or effective control, its "ability … to obtain benefit", at the heart of accounting, along with its judgements about "probable future economic benefits", which gave rise to a "practical problem" that only management or markets could solve.

As SFAC 3 said, "Uncertainty about business and economic outcomes often clouds whether or not particular items that might be assets have the capacity to provide future economic benefits to the entity" (FASB 1980b, paragraphs 44–48), "sometimes precluding their recognition as assets" (FASB 1980b, paragraph 107). "For example, business enterprises engage in research and development activities, advertise, develop markets, open new branches or divisions, and the like, and spend significant funds to do so. The uncertainty is not about the intent to increase future economic benefits but about whether and, if so, to what extent they succeeded in doing so" (FASB 1980b, paragraph 107). According to the FASB's definition, unlike Marxian accounting, "Since many of the activities described in the preceding paragraph involve incurring costs, the distinction between ... [them] and assets, such as prepaid insurance and prepaid rent ... is often difficult to draw because the two groups tend to shade into each other. Indeed, the distinction is not based on the definition of assets in paragraph 25 but rather on the practical considerations of coping with the effects of uncertainty" (FASB 1980b, paragraph 108). It was happy "If research or development activities or advertising results in an entity's acquiring or increasing future economic benefit, that future economic benefit qualifies as an asset as much as do the future benefits from prepaid insurance or prepaid rent. The practical problem is whether future economic benefit is actually present and, if so, how much — an assessment that is greatly complicated by the feature that the benefits may be realized far in the future, if at all" (FASB 1980b, paragraph 107). To solve this "practical problem" the FASB inevitably turned to management's judgement of the "probable" "value to the entity" of "future economic benefits", or a "market price", but which market and which price also required judgement, leaving "Future economic benefit [a]s the essence of an asset" (1980b, paragraphs 27–31). It accepted, "An asset has the capacity to serve the entity by being exchanged for something else of value to the entity, by being used to produce something of value to the entity, or by being used to settle its liabilities", but this meant, "The most obvious evidence of future economic benefit is a market price" (FASB 1980b, paragraph 8). The questions were exit or entry price, defining them, what to do in the many cases where no market price existed, and the meanings of "ability" and "probable". SFAC 5 did not choose a valuation base, we will see, seeing all values as potentially "relevant". The FASB introduced "probable" "after comments that its omission implied 100 percent certainty was required for an item to be an asset or liability", which was obviously "problematic" (Gore 1992, p. 69). The FASB intended "probable" to mean "less than but near to 100 percent probable", but commentators (largely preparers) insisted it meant "more than 50 percent likelihood" (Gore 1992, p. 68), which the board accepted (FASB 1980b, fn. 9). The same problems arose for liabilities that the FASB defined as "probable future sacrifices of economic benefits" (1980b, p. 6).

SFAC 3 reassured readers there would be no serious practical problems because it expected most assets and liabilities recognised in present practice to "continue to qualify as assets and liabilities under the definitions in this statement" (FASB 1980b, p. xiii). However, it also claimed its definitions "should be especially helpful … in analysing and resolving new financial accounting issues as they arise" (FASB 1980b, p. xiii). Paul Pacter (1983, p. 87) for the FASB argued, "By having defined assets and liabilities, and having defined income in terms of changes in assets and liabilities, Concepts Statement No. 3 provides a frame of reference within which the FASB can question recognition or nonrecognition practices. The asset and liability definitions themselves are likely to have a direct and ongoing impact on accounting practice". However, as Macve pointed out, "it again seems unlikely that they will be of much assistance in resolving individual accounting problems" because "the definitions give the characteristics *necessary* for something to qualify as an element, for example, as an asset — but they are not sufficient to decide whether it is an asset. This also requires consideration of 'recognition criteria' … as well as settling of the 'measurement' and 'presentation' questions.… Moreover, the definitions given are so general that they are unlikely to exclude anything that one might want to include" (1981, p. 62). Solomons thought SFAC 3's definition of an asset was "a distinct improvement on the earlier definitions", but found its mirror image, the definition of a liability, "too broad to provide a clear answer" to problems like pension liabilities (1986b, pp. 120–121). Dopuch and Sunder (1980) and others (e.g., Macve 1981, p. 63) pointed out that the discussion of deferred taxes in the appendix to SFAC 3 conceded that the definition of liabilities was consistent with different methods of accounting (or not accounting) for them. The FASB's EDs on accounting for transfers of debtors with recourse and in-substance defeasance, Denis R. Beresford, a partner with Ernst & Whinney, who became FASB chair in 1987, pointed out, "relied heavily on the concepts statements issued to date but curiously seemed to reach inconsistent conclusions" (1983, p. 59), which Chapter 8 argues helped facilitate the GFC.

SFAC 3 also followed Sprouse and Moonitz (1962) by defining "revenues", "expenses" and "gains" and "losses" in terms of "assets" and "liabilities", and the total as "comprehensive income"; "new terminology" (Zeff 1999, p. 112) describing "the change in equity (net assets) of an entity during a period from transactions and other events and circumstances from nonowner sources" (FASB 1980b, paragraph 56). "Comprehensive income", Fisher's "earnings" concept that included all value changes in the income statement, "caused trepidation, especially among practitioners and financial executives — that the board's adoption of the 'asset and liability view', together with its comprehensive income proposal, would inevitably lead to some form of current value accounting" (Zeff 1999, p. 112). After the publication of SFAC 1, 2 and 3, and in the context of the looming defeat over CCA, "trepidation" turned into resistance in the discussions leading to SFAC 5 in 1984.

SFAC 5 Recognition and Measurement in Financial Statements of Business Enterprises

Miller and Redding (1986, pp. 104–105) noted "as a result of opposition" the FASB did not stick to its "normative" or "prescriptive" approach, even in SFAC 1 where "the Board had to move back and forth between the prescriptive and descriptive approaches", "which very carefully defends traditional accrual accounting".[4] The FASB's aim, they admitted, was to "alleviate fears that the prescriptive approach was going to produce a revolution in accounting practice" (Miller and Redding 1986, p. 105). The FASB also attempted to dispel this fear by changing the objectives to "financial reporting" to allow for disclosure of current value information outside the financial statements. However, fear in the "inevitability" of current value accounting was rekindled by Storey's (1981, p. 93) comment, apparently on the FASB's behalf, that "the handwriting is already on the wall for the present model (which is often mislabelled 'historical cost accounting') because, among other things, it can't cope with everyday complications, such as changing prices and fluctuating foreign exchange rates". To prevent this revolution, to limit any change to "reformation", management organised a "counterreformation" (Miller 1990)

[4]Paul B.W. Miller, professor of accounting at Utah University, was an FASB faculty-member during the recognition and measurement phase (Miller and Redding 1986, p. xi).

that, implicitly, exploited the theoretical fault line in SFAC 3, derived from SFAC 1 and 2, the need for management's subjective judgements. As Sprouse insisted, "the … objectives of financial reporting and the qualitative characteristics of financial information have pervasive impact on the nature of the other three components" (1988, p. 124). The discussions leading to SFAC 5 therefore inevitably ran into the incorrigible problem that SFAC 3 had assigned to management the "practical" judgement of recognition and measurement by defining an asset as its effective control of probable future economic benefits, or to various possible markets, which would also require its judgement. In Fisher's neoclassical, general equilibrium world, market prices equal PVs. However, in the real world of uncertainty and imperfect markets, Fisher's theory cannot logically specify when to recognise an element and how to measure it. The framework inevitably meant, as Macve put it, "standards can lay down procedures but cannot determine how people will estimate the future and therefore what are seen as 'the same economic facts' by different company managements", which made it "inevitable that … managements have some latitude in the calculation of the performance measure by which they are judged" (1981, pp. 10, 76).

The inability to decide recognition and measurement through logical argument by reference to SFAC 1, 2 and 3 allowed "strongly held and ultimately polarizing" opposition from three board members to any current value accounting (Storey and Storey 1998, p. 158), who could remain "convinced that historical costs provide the most important information" (Sprouse 1988, p. 126). John March, for example, who "thought current prices were not relevant, whereas historical costs were" (Gore 1992, p. 108). With inflation decreasing in the early-1980s, restructuring underway or complete, and unions in retreat, management no longer needed "current cost accounting", and business support turned into opposition. In 1984, in response to "A large number of responses to the Invitation to Comment [on *Supplementary Disclosures about the Effects of Changing Prices*] [that] indicate … the costs of preparing the disclosures have outweighed the benefits to date" (Zeff 1999, p. 118), that is, from preparers, the FASB eliminated the requirement for any supplementary disclosures on inflation adjustments. In 1986, after "the most protracted debate the FASB has had on the costs and benefits of a particular Statement" (Kirk 1988, pp. 14, 16), and evidence of only marginal improvements in "decision-usefulness" compared with HC (Walton 2007, p. 174), it removed the requirement for current-cost disclosures. Management's resistance influenced some FASB members, Kirk for example who rejected physical capital maintenance, "could find little reason to endorse on a conceptual level a current value or current cost measurement system for future standards when it appeared that the utility of such a system in Statement 33 was going to be seriously challenged" (1988, p. 16).

Split over whether to allow HC or require current values, to produce an agreed statement the FASB had little option but to restrict itself to describing the "measurement attributes", valuation methods, found in practice; the "thrust of the project had become essentially descriptive" (Miller and Redding 1986, p. 105). SFAC 5 found the usual "Five different attributes of assets (and liabilities) ... used in present practice", HC, current-cost, current market value, net realisable (settlement) value and PV (FASB 1984a, paragraph 67). Therefore, "Rather than attempt to select a single attribute and force changes in practice so that all classes of assets and liabilities use that attribute, this concepts Statement suggests that use of different attributes will continue, and discusses how the Board may select the appropriate attribute in particular cases" (FASB 1984a, paragraph 70). This left selection to management's judgement of the relevance and reliability of current values (FASB 1984a, paragraph 90). As the *Scope and Implications of the Conceptual* Framework *Project* put it, "that trade-off is a key consideration for some who favor replacing historical cost measures with current value measures as well as for others who favor retention of historical cost measures" (FASB 1976b, p. 15). Consequently, SFAC 5 was "severely criticised for saying nothing, merely restating SFAC Nos. 1, 2 and 3 and noting that change will be evolutionary rather than revolutionary" (Gore 1992, pp. 108–109). Solomons regretfully concluded, "Under a rigorous grading system I would give Concepts Statement No. 5 an F and require the board to take the course over again — that is, to scrap the statement and start afresh" (1986b, p. 124). It weakly required that "information based on current prices should be recognized if it is sufficiently relevant and reliable to justify the costs involved and is more relevant than alternative information" (FASB 1984a, paragraph 90). If required to use current prices, "Preparers felt strongly that any unrealized holding gains and losses should not affect earnings", and the FASB agreed, "for Statement 5 to survive", by allowing a split presentation within comprehensive income (Zeff 1999, p. 115). Solomons lamented that accounting for price changes should "properly have been a part of the conceptual framework, though the urgency of the problem in the 1970s no doubt justified its separate treatment. But the problem is less urgent now, and it should have been central to the recognition and measurement project" (1986b).

Many had thought some form of current value accounting was inevitable (Gore 1992, pp. 59, 95; Zeff 1999, p. 112), forcing the FASB in 1976 to state that "Current value accounting is not a foregone conclusion, but thorough consideration of its desirability is one of the most important purposes of the FASB's conceptual framework project" (1976a, p. 19). Current value did not happen, but not because of "thorough consideration". As Gore says, it cannot be "directly attributed to industry pressure", but "Industry did not have to exert pressure: the project developed in such a way that the preparer's wishes were complied with anyway", though a "conservative grouping" helped produce this outcome (Gore 1992, p. 110). In 1982, Robert Sterling, then senior FASB fellow and "in the thick of things during this phase of the project", predicted trouble from management and practitioners because his "case study approach [had] stalled" having "led to some heated exchanges" (Gore 1992, pp. 106–107).[5] He declared himself "a pessimist. ... When the board begins to tackle the ... statements on recognition, measurement and income ... interest in the project is certain to increase. Few managers and practitioners are interested in abstract theory, but nearly all will be most interested in a change in recognizing revenue or valuing assets or adjusting for inflation" (Sterling 1982, p. 104). He was right, "progress towards completion will be accompanied by a crescendo of perceived adversely affected interests, which in turn will be accompanied by a crescendo of resistance and criticism. The resistance may become so great that the board will find it impossible to complete the framework" (Sterling 1982, pp. 104–105). Miller observed that the decision not to disturb the *status quo* "was led by representatives of the preparer constituency, particularly members of the Financial Executives Institute" (1990, p. 28). Storey and Storey criticised "Concepts Statement 5 [a]s a throwback to statements of accounting principles produced by the 'distillation of experience' school of thought" (1998, p. 159), to May's interpretation where management was in charge. In short, after SFAC 5, for measurement management's judgement

[5] Sterling resorted to simplified cases to convince the HC-diehards to accept exit prices, but failed (Gore 1992, p. 106). There was also dissension amongst "current value" supporters, some insisted on exit prices whereas others supported RC (Sprouse 1988, p. 126; Gore 1992, p. 107).

remained, and the same was true for recognition. The FASB used SFAC 2's qualitative characteristics to define the "fundamental recognition criteria" in SFAC 5 (FASB 1984a, paragraph 67), which inevitably therefore also require management's judgements. Decisions whether an element exists, whether if it does management can measure it with "sufficient reliability", and if so whether recognition is "capable of making a difference in user decisions", are inevitably subjective, "somewhat hazy" (Gore 1992, p. 56) judgements the FASB again left to management. SFAC 2 admitted management would retain many choices after the FASB had written more standards, that within its framework "choices arise at every turn" (paragraphs 7–8). This, according to Marxian accounting, was because, as Solomons said, SFAC 5 "bypasses all the difficult areas, such as an analysis of the concept of earnings, the recognition of executory contracts, the treatment of long-term contracts, inventory valuation, depreciation and other matters" (1986b, p. 124). Robert Anthony (1987), professor of accounting at Harvard, criticised it for having "ducked all the big issues in the CF", for not choosing an entity concept and defining capital maintenance and earnings accordingly.

A Financial Reporting "Revolution"?

The FASB and its supporters could claim the conceptual framework was a "revolution" (Beaver 1989) because it removed management's overt control. Many, however, were "sceptical" of the value of SFAC 1, 2 and 3 to practitioners. Beresford, for example, criticised the "minimal return" on the "very large sum spent on this single project", that these statements gave no operational guidance to limit judgement, but provided a template for structuring transactions to achieve desired accounting outcomes (1983, p. 55). Many agreed, "the FASB's bottom's up approach ... has resulted in broad, abstract statements or proposals with little practical applicability. ... To expect preparers and auditors to judge the preferability of accounting alternatives by looking to the objectives of financial reporting or by assessing abstract characteristics such as relevance, understandability, or neutrality, is wishful thinking, particularly since these characteristics are often in the eyes of the beholder" (Beresford 1983, pp. 55, 57–58). Beresford accepted, "the Board has said on many occasions that it — not preparers or auditors — is likely to be the principal user of the framework", but "question[ed] how useful the concepts can be in the Board's own decision-making process" (1983, p. 62). He gave "two recent practice problems", as examples — "transfers of receivables with recourse and 'in-substance defeasance'" (Beresford 1983, p. 58) — problems that had arisen from management's innovations in structuring transactions to put them outside the existing rules.[6] These problems "point out the difficulty the *Board* is having in applying broad concepts to specific accounting questions", so "how can the FASB expect preparers and auditors to consider them useful in dealing with similar issues" (Beresford 1983, p. 58). The FASB's distinction, between its use of the framework and preparers and auditors' use was meaningless because management could structure transactions to create "practice problems" beyond the scope of existing rules. As Sprouse observed in 1988, "The most demanding intellectual challenges for which students need to be prepared arise in accounting practice when new situations or circumstances are encountered that present problems or issues that necessarily must be resolved by utilizing one's individual expertise and experience rather than by merely identifying and applying a prescribed procedure" (1988, p. 121). He accepted, "That is equally true both for accountants who, as members of managements, have the primary responsibility for financial reporting decisions and for public accountants who must express their professional opinions about those decisions" (Sprouse 1988, p. 121). It was, as Sprouse said, the aim of the "Financial Accounting Standards Board and its predecessors to develop such a foundation for analyzing and resolving financial reporting issues" (1988, p. 121).

However, if as Beresford (1983, p. 58) said "no real-life accounting problems … have been solved with the help of any of the concepts statements issued to date", it was futile to think the FASB could use it to solve them. It was therefore futile to think that management would not use the framework's concepts to structure transactions to retain control of accounting. Warren Brown (1980, p. 45), assistant controller of American Telegraph and Telephone Company, warned the FASB, "Nothing can prevent new strategies from surmounting what managers perceive to be the ills of new pronouncements nor from taking advantage of what they perceive to be invitations to new directions". Only the FASB's staunchest supporters claimed the framework (with the exception of SFAC 5) was a conceptual success. Storey, the "real author of much of the CF" (Gore 1992, p. 113),

[6]The FASB's problems with these transactions led to FAS 76 and 77, which Chapter 8 argues underlay SPE accounting that facilitated the 2007 credit-crunch.

conceded, "the FASB's conceptual framework ... is concerned not with a search for ultimate truth", and could not produce "an unequivocally unique solution for each problem", but concluded it had gave "rigorous, internally consistent and useful concepts that are based in the real world" (Storey 1981, p. 96). Paul Pacter, executive assistant to the FASB's chair, claimed that in addition to being useful to the board "the concepts will provide a frame of reference to financial statement preparers and auditors in resolving accounting questions in the absence of established standards. And ultimately the conceptual framework may well reduce the need for some specific standards" (1983, p. 88). Sprouse was right, "the final Statements of objectives, qualitative characteristics, and elements have not been, and are not likely to be, seriously challenged" (1988, p. 124), certainly by management.

Most academics and even FASB's supporters concluded the framework was a conceptual failure (Gore 1992, p. 1). Facing criticism, supporters claimed it was nevertheless a "political" success, a "political reform" (Miller 1990, p. 24; Miller 1985), changed the balance of power. The profession's reactions to the CAP and APB failures show its aim was the "political" overthrow management's control over accounting choice (Chapter 6), and to its supporters SFAC 1 appeared successful. To Miller and Redding, "Perhaps the greatest significance of SFAC 1 lies in its formalization on the conceptual level of the political fact that the Board has to put users' interests first" (1986, p. 114). This was important "because their needs are the source of the SEC's own mandate for setting accounting standards and thus critical to its endorsement of the FASB as the primary standard-setting body" (Miller and Redding 1986, p. 114). The FASB, however, was not successful in even this, the "formalization" of its legally derived mandate from the SEC to put users' needs first. Rather, the framework created the *appearance* of the FASB's ideological hegemony, the appearance of "legitimacy", unquestioned acceptance even by its most radical critics that "the FASB governs", albeit "by negotiation and compromise" (Miller and Redding 1986, p. 26), albeit badly or inappropriately, in users' interests.

Ideological Hegemony: Appearance and Reality

FASB leaders publicly deplored the "political" nature of standard-setting (Armstrong 1977; Kirk 1978, 1986; Wyatt 1986, 1990). The official line was "It is the emphasis on neutrality of information, as well as the independence of the standard setters from undue influence, that ensures the continued success of private-sector standard setting" (Kirk 1988, p. 13). Part of "The aversion to politics in the standard setting process may be attributable to the historic association of politics with government intervention in US standard setting" (Fogarty *et al.* 1994, p. 25), but the profession also wanted to dissuade management from overt displays of political power that could undermine the FASB's legitimacy. Armstrong pleaded with management to "restrict political action to the avenues provided by the procedures of the Board. Employment of other channels must ultimately result in the increased participation of government agencies, and perhaps the legislature; and that, in my view, will spell the demise of this effort" (*Journal of Accountancy* March 1976, p. 26). Kirk insisted, "Sound concepts are essential guides for standard setters beset by lobbying and political pressures to distort what must be, to serve the public interest, an even-handed measurement system", but accepted, "A normative system, however, has definite limits in its ability to point a policy-making body toward incontrovertible solutions to recognition and measurement problems" (1988, p. 17). Kirk saw the need to go beyond a "technical" solution, for preparers to conform to the "moral" and "ethical" standards in the conceptual framework. However, leading academics and some insiders argued that rather than give the FASB conceptual control or moral authority, the framework would give the FASB "political" power.

Based on his APB experience Horngren (1973, p. 61) proposed the "hypothesis ... that the setting of accounting standards is as much a product of political action as of flawless logic or empirical findings. Why? Because the setting of standards is a social decision. Standards place restrictions on behavior; therefore, they must be accepted by the affected parties", which in a "democratic society ... requires skilful marketing in a political arena". Gerboth agreed, "In the face of conflict between competing interests, rationality as well as prudence lies not in seeking final answers but, rather, in compromise — essentially a political process" (1973, p. 479). As the FASB faced "a problem of accounting power", Horngren advised it "to get equipped now" (1973, p. 61). He argued in 1976, "the time for accounting policy makers to issue some formal statement of objectives or conceptual framework is overdue. The more operational, the better" (Horngren 1976, p. 95). In 1981, that the conceptual framework "is likely to help provide power to the [FASB] ... to resolve conflicts among the various constituencies" (Horngren 1981, p. 88). Because the FASB has no coercive power, the conceptual framework's "major role … is to ultimately enhance the likelihood of acceptability of specific statements" (Horngren 1981, pp. 88, 90). However, it was a "desirable but not sufficient" part of the policymaking process given the complexity of economic reality and the limits of deductive reasoning, so the FASB was inevitably involved in the "politics" of social choice (Horngren 1981, p. 95).

In 1983, Solomons, who was British, wrote an article on the "Political Implications of Accounting and Accounting Standard Setting", addressing British academics and professionals, to persuade them to follow the FASB in writing a conceptual framework. Solomons recognised, "The sense that accounting needed a conceptual framework has existed for much longer in the United States than in the UK, and it is today stronger there" (1983, p. 110). To persuade the British to abandon their "recoverable cost model", "matching", etc., the prime benefit from a conceptual framework, he argued, was "political" because it provided "a coherent theoretical base on which to erect accounting standards [which] is an essential weapon in the armoury that can defend accounting from political interference. It may not give complete protection; but it may ward off some attacks and lessen the damage done by others. … The conceptual defence is the provision of a coherent theoretical base from which standards might be derived" (Solomons 1983, pp. 107, 115). American experience, he argued, clearly showed that an accounting standard-setter needed "weapons" for "conceptual defence" against "a sectional interest". "If a standard setting body cannot show that its standards will lead to the production of information having the qualities and characteristics necessary to attain a defined accounting objective, it will have no defence against a sectional interest" (Solomons 1983, p. 115). By "political interference" and "sectional interest", Solomons meant management's power to decide accounting policies, which threatened accounting's "credibility": "there is general agreement that … there can be no return to a state where, from a multiplicity of alternative accounting methods, the managers of each business enterprise can be left entirely free to choose whichever ones suit them" (1983, pp. 107, 114).

The FASB recognised the political problem when it argued in the *Scope and Implications of the Conceptual Framework Project* that it was "a constitution, a coherent system of inter-related objectives and fundamentals that can lead to consistent standards that prescribe the nature, function and limits of financial accounting and financial statements" (1976a, p. 2). It was, the FASB argued, "in the interests of all to enhance the credence of financial statements. A sharpened conceptual framework can do that" because "Some users believe that accounting numbers are prepared on the basis of an amorphous set of principles and rules that permit too much freedom in deciding what financial statements should show" (1976a, pp. 5, 7). It warned, "Skepticism about financial reporting has adverse effects on businesses, on business leaders, and on the public at large. One of those effects is the risk of imposition of government reporting and other regulatory requirements that are not justified" (FASB 1976a, p. 5). Therefore, it was in business leaders' interests "To add credence to financial reporting — to minimize skepticism about financial statements — [which] is a major purpose of a conceptual framework.... Without a conceptual underpinning, periodic earnings and financial statements are essentially matters or judgment and personal opinion" (FASB 1976a, pp. 8–9), that is, management's judgements and opinions. Solomons made explicit the political implication that just as a legislature needed a constitution to protect it from the government, so the standard-setter needed a conceptual framework to protect shareholders ("citizens") from the arbitrary acts of management ("government"). As he put it, "A board or a committee setting standards without a conceptual framework is like a legislature making laws without a constitution to protect citizens from arbitrary acts of government" (Solomons 1983, p. 115). Describing the conceptual framework as a constitution was an apt analogy, Horngren thought, because "When a difference of preference arises, the constitution specifies who will win" (1981, p. 88).

However, the "constitution" quickly proved inadequate to the task of quelling management's resistance to accounting regulation in users' interests, and Solomons by 1986 had changed his mind: "I do not believe that the case for a conceptual framework is strengthened by likening it to a constitution. ... A constitution has the force of law. A conceptual framework has no authority except what flows from its intellectual persuasiveness" (1986b, p. 115), but this had been the case in 1980. Rather than a weapon, it could provide a "Defense against politicization", but this was now conditional on its intellectual robustness: "If the FASB could show that its standards were derived from a coherent and plausible body of concepts, it would greatly enhance the credibility of financial reporting. I know of no better way to reduce accounting's vulnerability to political pressure. How else can the board demonstrate the superiority of a proposed standard over a counterproposal from some sectional interest that is self-serving and not in the public interest?" (Solomons 1986b, p. 116).

Before the recognition and measurement projects completion, Solomons thought it reasonable to "suspend judgment" (1986b, p. 114). By 1986, he judged the completed framework harshly, particularly its failure to deal with recognition and measurement: "If, like me, you think that radical changes are called for, you will think that Concepts Statement No. 5 is a dismal failure" (Solomons 1986b, p. 117). Overall, he judged the framework a lost opportunity: "I had hoped that ... the board would take its eyes off the ground for a while and look to the horizon. But the opportunity to point the way toward the 21st century has been lost. And most of the board's constituents are content to have it that way" (Solomons 1986, p. 123). In fact, the "constitution" came under pressure from the mid-1970s following the official overthrow of stewardship in SFAC 1, from when management changed from its normal "tactical rhetoric" of couching arguments "in terms of ... [t]he traditional model, where management was really seeking to advance its own self-interest" (Zeff 1978, p. 57). Management had used such arguments against the APB (Sprouse 1971) during the 1960s, but in the 1970s "the issue of economic consequences ... surfaced" (Zeff 1978, p. 57).

Economic Consequences

Management began framing its arguments against particular standards in terms of their harmful "economic consequences", that is, "the impact of accounting reports on decision-making behaviour of businesses, governments, unions, investors and creditors" (Zeff 1978, p. 57), reacting to the view that standards could cause a "redistribution of wealth" (Rappaport 1977, p. 89). Academics pointed out that accounts can redistribute the wealth of the "intended recipients" by the impact of reported earnings on share prices (Rappaport 1977, p. 90). They could redistribute wealth by their impact on so-called "free-riders", for example "unions might use financial accounting reports as a basis for labor negotiations", and because "Corporate management, in anticipation of the potential feedback from the behavior of intended recipients and free riders, might choose to alter its own economic behavior" (Rappaport 1977, p. 90).

Faced with many such arguments from preparers, who submitted the majority of comment letters (Miller and Redding 1986, p. 133), the FASB from the mid-1970s effectively accepted "economic consequences" as part of its brief (Zeff 1978, p. 61), even though this contradicted its mandate to set "neutral" standards (Fogarty *et al.* 1994, p. 25). This, Zeff (1978, p. 63) concluded, left the FASB with a "dilemma … which requires a careful balancing of accounting and nonaccounting variables. Although its decisions should rest — and been seen to rest — chiefly on accounting considerations, it must also study — and be seen to study — the possible adverse economic and social consequences". In fact, linking accounting to potential redistributions of wealth created a contradiction, as Rappaport (1977, p. 89) pointed out: "This phenomenon places a particularly heavy burden on the FASB as a private-sector body, because in the final analysis the responsibility of mediating conflicting values in our society rests with Congress rather than with any private-sector organization". Rappaport saw dangers in the FASB's strategy of promoting the framework as the answer to accounting controversies because it would raise expectations, and frustrated constituents would appeal to politicians, which could lead to the demise of private-sector standard-setting. He warned the FASB, "the promotion of the framework as 'the answer' imposes serious and unnecessary risks for the viability of the FASB … [because] corporate executives, investors and other interested parties … [may] view the FASB as being unresponsive to their concerns" (Rappaport 1977, p. 92). These "groups", if they "look increasingly toward the SEC and Congress to redress their grievances … could ultimately lead to the demise of meaningful private-sector involvement in establishing accounting standards" (Rappaport 1977, p. 92). However, the same danger lurked in recognising economic consequences: "The economic impact strategy also involves potential risks. The formal consideration of the potential consequences of measurement and disclosure choices may call into question the 'social legitimacy' of the FASB", and "some might argue that if the consequences of accounting are in fact pervasive, perhaps accounting standards should be legislated by elected officials of our representative government instead of a private-sector organization" (Rappaport 1977, p. 94). Rappaport recommended a "mixed strategy", "a blend of the conceptual framework and economic impact approaches", that on the one hand "recognizes the current limitations of accounting theory to contribute to unambiguous policy choices", and on the other adopts the "responsible position" by giving "explicit consideration" to economic consequences (1977, pp. 94, 98). He thought this mixed strategy was less risky for the survival of the FASB than either pure strategy. It would lower expectations of the framework, yet keeping and developing it provided a common language, "facilitates efficient communication", and recognising economic consequences would "minimize the probability of the Board's issuing an exposure draft of a new Standard that would become so controversial as to threaten the continuing viability of the FASB" (Rappaport 1977, pp. 92, 97).

Rappaport's mixed strategy was, in effect, the FASB's approach, but it insisted on keeping up appearances, on preparers translating economic self-interest into the framework's "neutral" language. Formally it was true, as Solomons put it, that "So far the board has not seriously wavered in its espousal of neutrality and its rejection of the 'economic consequences' school of thought, though pressures on it to abandon neutrality have been strong from time to time" (1986b, p. 120). FASB members "have stated that an appeal based on the economic consequences that a proposed standard might impose on particular interests would not be as favoured as an appeal that was logical, well-reasoned, and of a suitable length" (Fogarty *et al.* 1994, p. 25). However, what this meant was "On one level, the FASB is officially blind to the self-interest of advocates", that is, has formally committed itself to user's needs, but "At the same time, these motivations are tolerated and encouraged *sub rosa* if translated into the neutral language of standard setting and accounting theory" (Fogarty *et al.* 1994, p. 25). Sprouse (1988, p. 124) asserted, "The fundamental nature of the concepts established in those first three Concepts Statements is evident from the frequency with which they are cited, not only in the FASB's own documents, but in the position papers and comment letters that are submitted to the FASB by its constituents". Alternatively, the FASB's constituents quickly "learnt the language", and learnt to exploit its ambiguity because although the framework's concepts became "an agreed language, it has allowed a degree of crosstalk" (Gore 1992, p. 117). The framework became "a tool used by constituents to argue for or against proposed accounting standards" (Ayres 1993, p. 962), and management could use it to structure transactions to avoid standards, as we will see in Chapter 8.

Who Runs the FASB?

Recognising accounting standards "political" nature, when the profession established the FASB it compromised its formal commitment to investors' needs by incorporating management into the standard-setting process, relying on the framework to give it the necessary authority to govern with consent. As the profession saw it, the "only way of escaping" from management control "was by the radical step of partially giving up control", by moving standard-setting "from being the sole preserve of accountants to a concern of the whole business community" (Gore 1992, p. 133), including investors' and management's representatives, within a framework all must accept. To gain management's approval of its Opinions, the APB had consulted financial executives, but the "procedural machinery established for the FASB is even more elaborate" (Zeff 1978, p. 60). In fact, "The history of the APB and the FASB is one of a succession of procedural steps taken to bring the board's deliberations into closer proximity to the opinions and concerns of interested third parties" (Zeff 1978, p. 60), particularly management's.

A major step was when, having cut off management's power through its influence as the "client" of the working partners on the APB (members of the FASB had to cut any affiliations with outside bodies on appointment), management became an institutionalised insider through the appointment of the FEI as a co-sponsor of the FASB. Zeff thought "the incorporation of the FEI in the formal structure of the Financial Accounting Foundation (FAF, the FASB's parent) is one of the most significant advantages which the FASB possesses in relation to its predecessor" (1978, p. 60), because it committed management to the process and its outcomes. However, it also exposed the FASB to management influence because if the "FEI were to lose confidence in the board, it is possible that many of the companies which now contribute to the Financial Accounting Foundation might decline to continue doing so, provoking a crisis that could threaten the board's viability" (Zeff 1978, fn. 25, p. 60). Miller and Redding noted, "approximately 50 percent of the Financial Accounting Foundation's donated funds come from industry", which gave "an appearance of dependency on preparers" (1986, p. 134). Implicitly recognising this latent power, when in 1977 Armstrong was "beginning to sense political action ... designed to retain [accounting] choices", he had little choice but to appeal to the "entire financial community", not only to management, to support the FASB's standards "even when those standards jeopardize traditional management prerogative" (1977, p. 77).

Because it is a "fundamental idea ... that an important purpose for GAAP is to constrain managers against reporting in a biased way", it would be "especially troublesome if financial statement preparers were to become the dominant group because they are the ones who are being regulated" (Miller and Redding 1986, p. 133). Nevertheless, by 1986 Miller and Redding saw "sufficient evidence" that "the first signs of the problem" of preparer dominance "have already emerged" (1986, p. 138). Gore saw it in "structural issues" and the "latent conflict observable in the appointment and composition of the Board, and … attempts to limit board action" (1992, p. 96). With the power to appoint members, trustees could appoint "persons they feel will come up with the 'right' answers" (Gore 1992, p. 96). Gore found evidence industry influenced appointments and a "possible tendency toward preparer domination" in the increase in "industry (preparer) representation" on the board and trustees (1992, pp. 99–100). He concluded, "If one equates … preparers with businessmen who are concerned with accounting changes…, one can see why preparer domination is viewed with concern", for example, by Revsine (1991, pp. 24–25), highlighting sustained efforts by the Business Roundtable that took up "the torch of taming the FASB" (Gore 1992, pp. 100–101; Miller and Redding 1986, pp. 135–136; Van Riper 1994).

The Limits of Accounting Theory

Incorporating management within the accounting process was clearly a risky strategy that depended on a robust conceptual framework to contain management's self-interest. However, as the FASB opened its doors to management participation, and management energetically sought the levers of control, accounting theorists, whose ranks had rapidly increased since the late-1960s, became sceptical that the framework would change anything, that theoretical "closure" was impossible, implying management had nothing to fear from it. In 1977, as the FASB was preparing to publish SFAC 1, the AAA produced a *Statement on Accounting Theory and Theory Acceptance* (SOATATA) that flatly contradicted the "persistent, widely held view among accountants that the accumulation of accounting theory would eventually lead to a compelling basis for specifying the content of external financial reports" (1977, p. 1). The "wide range of thoughtful and talented researchers … attracted" to accounting had "produced new knowledge", which was "exciting and indicative of intellectual growth", but management could take comfort from its conclusion that this was "also frustrating" because it showed "there are no easy theoretical answers to many of the urgent problems faced by the profession" (AAA 1977, Preface). By emphasising the many problems of achieving theory "closure", the committee's goal was that "unrealistic expectations regarding 'authoritative *theory* pronouncements' will be reduced" (AAA 1977, p. 1).

Using ideas from Thomas Kuhn's *The Structure of Scientific Revolutions* (1970), the AAA concluded that the accounting theory literature was a collection of incommensurable "paradigms" or worldviews, from which it derived its "central message" to policy makers "that *until consensus paradigm acceptance occurs, the utility of accounting theories in policy making is partial.* Competing theories merely provide a basis for forming opinions on what must remain inherently subjective judgment" (1977, p. 51). The committee claimed, "accounting theorists do not have a shared paradigm", but noted, "One of the few attitudes that is shared by most contemporary accounting theorists is dissatisfaction with the prevailing matching-attaching paradigm" (AAA 1977, pp. 42–43). "In its place, they have turned to several alternative approaches to answering accounting questions", by which it meant, "the decision-usefulness approach and the economic approach … might each be treated as an alternative paradigm" (AAA 1977, p. 43). However, as they are alternative approaches to operationalising Fisher's theory there are only two competing "paradigms", the cost theory of value and Fisher's theory, but given the impossibility of objectively operationalising Fisher's theory, from Kuhn's perspective it is not a scientific "paradigm" (cf. Peasnell 1978, pp. 218, 220). The conceptual framework therefore, posed no threat to management because, the committee emphasised, "the crucial point is that theory consensus cannot be imposed…. Whatever influence theory has on policy making will be achieved by continuing argumentation, new theory, and debate, not by fiat" (AAA 1977, p. 52). The Committee advised the FASB therefore to abandon the political strategy underlying the framework project, as Rappaport (1977, p. 92) put it, "the anachronistic view that accounting is essentially a field dedicated to the search for 'true' income and 'true' wealth, and, once discovered, the truth will become compellingly apparent to all but the unenlightened". As this strategy would work only in a world of certainty and complete markets, which was unrealistic, but was the Fisherian ideal, resolving this contradiction required accepting "An alternative view … that the very act of choosing one framework rather than another is of itself a value judgment" (Rappaport 1977, p. 92), that "truth" is a value judgement.

Following the publication of SFAC 1 the FASB claimed formal victory over management, but observers, academics, and some insiders, injected a "strong dose of scepticism about how meaningful and consequential the setting of objectives may be" (Zeff 2013, p. 288) into the debate called for by the AAA. Starting as we must in Fisher's theory from the notion of the "social" as collections of individuals, building on the work of Beaver and Demski (1974), and others, Dopuch and Sunder (1980) pointed out that setting objectives for financial statements was "in principle, a fruitless exercise" (Zeff 2013, p. 289). From their perspective, "Financial accounting is a social or multiperson activity. Members of society engage in financial accounting or in other social activities when they are motivated by their individual goals and objectives..... Given a clear definition of the objectives that motivate each individual to engage in an aspect of a social activity, what meaning can we assign to the term 'objective' when it is applied not to individuals or groups, but to the activity itself?" (Dopuch and Sunder 1980, p. 9). Given inevitable conflicts of interests and different preferences for information, they concluded, the only objectives individuals would agree to would be too vague to be useful: "vagueness, while necessary to obtain initial agreement, will reduce the usefulness of a statement of objectives in setting accounting standards" (Dopuch and Sunder 1980, p. 12).

Solomons "doubted whether any statement of objectives would be likely to have much impact on the accounting standard subsequently issued" (1986a, p. 67) because the absence of "more soundly-based" accounting theory had made standard setting political. "Unfortunately, our traditional accounting methods are deficient, and their deficiencies give rise to conflicts between competing economic interests that could be avoided if accounting's theoretical foundations were more soundly based" (Solomons 1986a, p. 246). Kripke concluded SFAC 1 "seems to have had little influence" (1989, p. 11); Burton that it was "ignored" (1989, p. 80); Macve queried whether Statements 1 and 2 would "advance the ability to resolve disputes" (1981, p. 60); and Skinner concluded the statements did not "provide much guidance" (1987, p. 642). Like SOATATA, Macve emphasised, "The chief implication of the uncertainty about what is useful information, and of the need to reconcile the conflicting interests of different parties, is that what is 'good (or better) accounting' is fundamentally a subjective matter", and therefore it "seems idle to hope for an 'agreed conceptual framework' ... that will give explicit guidance" (1981, p. 13). Gore found an analysis of the influence of the framework on three standards "was rather depressing from a pro-CF point of view" (1992, p. 124). Overall, "many observers have argued that it has not met the expectations that were established at its inception" (Miller and Redding 1986, p. 97); "Both observers and those involved felt a great sense of disappointment" (Gore 1992, p. 58). As Fogarty *et al.* say, "The literature that has challenged the sufficiency of the conceptual categories and processes of the FASB is too vast to summarize fairly" (Fogarty *et al.* 1994, p. 26). Many academics concluded that by default, therefore, standard setting "must be political": "the intellectual poverty of conventional FASB doctrine is believed by many to allow accounting to become political" (Fogarty *et al.* 1994, p. 26). However, as Fogarty *et al.* say, "Very little guidance is provided on what the content of political standard setting might be" (1994, p. 26), that is, on the nature of this "politics". Fogarty *et al.*'s conclusion, that "there appears to be great confusion about the role of politics in accounting standard setting despite broad tacit awareness that the process is 'political'" (1994, pp. 29–30), confusion about the political power exercised over the FASB, is consistent with the hypothesis that despite academics' criticisms, the framework has given management ideological hegemony. The many academic criticisms of the framework and inconclusive studies of the FASB's "politics", focused on overt actions and agenda rigging, missed the point that managerial capitalist ideology, its "language of persuasion" (Fogarty *et al.* 1994, p. 30), Fisher's theory, was at its heart. The framework was not, therefore, a total ideological failure for the profession, apparently succeeding as a vehicle for enhancing its "legitimacy" by making the source of management's real power ideologically invisible.

The FASB's "Legitimacy"

As the FASB completed the framework, academic critics who had questioned its legitimacy received severe criticism. Johnson and Solomons (1984, p. 166) reprimanded "Critics of accounting standard-setting in general, and the FASB in particular, [who] … reject the legitimacy of the FASB merely because of alleged deficiencies in the way it operates or in the rules it promulgates or because of its inability to [consistently rank social preferences to] satisfy Arrow's conditions", as Demski (1973, 1974) influentially argued. Theorists' had not rejected the FASB's legitimacy, they concluded, but "the propriety of accounting standard-setting in general" (Johnson and Solomons 1984, p. 180), citing Watts and Zimmerman (1979), who provocatively argued SEC regulation meant normative accounting theories' function was supplying a "market for excuses" (1979, p. 300), and Dopuch and Sunder (1980) who argued it faced an impossible task of social choice. Such theoretical ideals, Johnson and Solomons (1984, p. 166) argued, were "irrelevant" because the "legitimacy of a specific institutional arrangement cannot be meaningfully assessed … without considering the propriety of the function it is intended to perform", which the framework claimed to establish (e.g., Solomons 1983), "and its ability to perform that function, given the … constraints under which it must operate". Other prominent critics, who accepted the need for standards, also failed to undermine the FASB's legitimacy because it produced its framework to answer their well-rehearsed criticisms. A US Senate subcommittee chaired by Senator John E. Moss published a report in October 1976 that was "very critical of the FASB", arguing it "has accomplished virtually nothing toward resolving fundamental accounting problems plaguing the profession" (Zeff 2021, p. 318). It highlighted "the plethora of optional 'generally accepted' accounting principles (GAAPs), the ambiguities inherent in many of those principles, and the manifestations of private accountants' lack of independence with respect to their corporate clients" (quoted by Zeff 2021, p. 318), criticisms the framework claimed to address. The subcommittee recommended, "to the maximum extent practicable, the SEC should prescribe by rule a framework of uniform accounting principles" (quoted by Zeff 2021, p. 318), but the framework was the culmination of academics' and the profession's best efforts since the late-1930s to produce "uniform accounting principles". In December 1976, another U.S. Senate subcommittee, chaired by Senator Lee Metcalf, published a staff report, *The Accounting Establishment*, which was sharply critical of the FASB's domination by the Big Eight accounting firms, the AICPA and the FEI, and proposed government control and democratisation of standard-setting (US Senate 1976, pp. 15, 21). It argued, "Accounting standards involve social and economic issues which can only be resolved effectively through the processes of government responsible solely to the public" (US Senate 1976, p. 21), but "the recommendation was not carried forward into proposed legislation" (Zeff 2021, p. 317). A possible reason was that the Metcalf report's complaint, that "the FASB … is dominated by the very parties it is intended to regulate and is, therefore, incapable of serving the public interest" (Johnson and Solomons 1984, p. 166), was apparently answered by the framework.

The framework did not give the FASB overt political power. However, sympathetic observers and the FASB thought the framework had given its work "public standing", "credibility", or "legitimacy", that is, gave the FASB apparent ideological hegemony over its constituents, over the public and its representatives, but also over critics who recognised its mission and its problems, even if sometimes unsympathetically. Whether they criticised it or not, after the framework most observers believed the FASB had legitimate, derived legal authority to pursue users' needs, even if they disagreed over whether it had control, or what it should do to solve or mitigate its problems. Even non-mainstream academics who argued that standard-setting "could be reorganized in a way that would call attention to its immutable political nature", who accepted, "Such an alteration would recognize the indeterminacy of 'good accounting', the distributive consequences of accounting and the lack of correspondence between desired standard setting and an undisputable economic reality" (Fogarty *et al.* 1994, p. 39). Even these scholars argued, "By making explicit the pressures and constraints that now exist in an implicit and disguised form, accounting standard setting might *enhance* its legitimacy by better conforming to the precepts of democratic decision making", that "Over the longer run … the viability of standard setting might actually be *enhanced*" (Fogarty *et al.* 1994, p. 39, emphases added). Daley and Tranter, for example, who argued, "the Conceptual Framework unrealistically ignores the significant role that economic and political pressures play in the development of accounting standards … [that] are an appropriate means for groups in society who are affected … to be heard" (1990, p. 15), called only for removing the commitment to "neutrality".

Mainstream scholars criticised the framework, but as they typically accepted the FASB's legitimacy, they generally offered their best advice on solving the problems it faced (e.g., Agrawal 1987; Gerboth 1987; Revsine 1991). Revsine (1991, p. 23), for example, argued that because managers, investors, auditors and regulators have economic incentives to allow flexibility in accounting rules, to allow "selective financial misrepresentation", and "accounting cannot be perfect", the FASB should "freeze" standard setting in the private-sector, where market mechanisms limited misrepresentation by anticipating it, and focus on the public sector where they did not. Sceptical professionals accepted the framework had given the FASB's the right to decide accounting standards. Before becoming FASB chair, Beresford was critical of the framework (e.g., 1983). After he became chair, he accepted the FASB must "try for internal consistency within a given pronouncement and overall consistency among all of our pronouncements", that this was "one reason for a conceptual framework", even though "there are no universal objective criteria for judging accounting standards" (Beresford 1990, pp. 82, 84). Accepting the framework's limitations, Beresford (1990, p. 82) emphasised the legitimate right it gave the FASB to decide if "due process" failed to produce an acceptable outcome consistent with its objectives: "Opinions are bound to vary all over the lot. ... Somebody has to find a solution that meets the objectives of financial reporting, and that 'somebody' is the FASB".

Even Marxist critics such as Tony Tinker, professor of accounting, Baruch College, CUNY, not someone "dedicated to the preservation of the FASB", who criticised "accounting's partisanship in social conflicts", its ideological commitment to the notion of "economic reality", and its failure to engage in "praxis" (Tinker 1991, p. 297, fn. 5, p. 299), gave it grudging legitimacy. Tinker was responding to Solomons (1991a, p. 287) who "criticize[d] Radical Accounting, as represented by Tony Tinker's *Paper Prophets*, and others who assert that accounting policies should be chosen for their supposedly desirable economic consequences rather than for their capacity to depict relevant phenomena faithfully". Tinker (1985, p. 111) saw the FASB as the legitimate representative of capitalist accounting, but saw its ideological bias, its adoption of "marginalist economics", as illegitimate from society's viewpoint. As Solomons put it, "Tinker ... attribute[s] what he regards as accounting's antisocial bias to this 'intellectual affiliation' with marginalism. For him, theories are 'weapons of social conflict', and accounting theory is no exception" (Solomons 1991a, p. 288). Solomons rejected this, but history supports Tinker's view that "the desire to measure subjective Fisherian-type income, has presented accountants with a dilemma" (1985, p. 108). As we have seen, "Fisherian and Hicksian income are faithful servants of marginalist value theory in the way they install capital as the 'producer' of value and legitimize profit as the reward for marginal productivity in production" (Tinker 1985, pp. 108–109). This gave the FASB a consistent ideology, but "the affiliations of accounting to these subjective notions of value have drawn accountants into a number of bitter disputes about the way accounting data influence income distribution within and among classes" (Tinker 1985, pp. 108–109).

History also supports Tinker's argument that "Marginalism provides accounting with a slanted picture of reality" (1985, p. 111), and his criticism of Solomons for "attempting to legitimatize the neutrality of the FASB and the *status quo*" (Tinker 1991, p. 297). Tinker rejected the idea of "economic reality", the claim that we can "find and extract pure, uncorrupted, neutral 'facts' from Economic Reality" (1991, p. 298). He criticised Solomons for believing "economic reality exists, independent of our apprehension of it, and that this is the ultimate touchstone of truthfulness and accuracy for accounting symbols" (Tinker 1991, p. 297). He asserted, "many valuation alternatives have been proposed" to market values (Tinker 1991, p. 303), but as Solomons said, here the "emperor simply has no clothes" (1991b, p. 312). Solomons understandably believed that "Tinker espouses a Marxist-Labor Theory of Value, which presumably he thinks would give relative values that would be more to his taste" (1991a, p. 289), but he did not. As Tinker said, "Relative to ... [a] narrow construal of Marxism as a labor theory of value, the four-tier 'value theory of labor' open up a much wider field of vision for social struggle than envisaged by these authors" (1999, p. 659). Although Tinker rejects any idea of economic reality, he says of marginalism, "This slant is ideological insofar as it misconstrues circumstances and events in order to promote certain partisan interests" (1985, p. 111), which appears to accept that "marginalism" does give a "picture of reality", albeit "slanted". Even though he wanted the FASB's revolutionary overthrow, Tinker's rejection of any notion of economic reality implicitly accepted that the FASB, as the representative of capitalist accounting, is legitimately "capitalism's prime adjudicator in social conflict" (Tinker 1985, p. 205). Tinker was right to "underscore the discretionary power of large corporations, including the discretion they exercise over accounting numbers to 'make the world mean' [what they want] to their own political advantage" (1991, p. 302). He was right to "underscore the politicization and capture of the FASB" (1991, fn. 5, p. 299). Moreover, he rightly criticised "the political influence of large corporations who have become enmeshed in the FASB's bureaucratization and institutionalization" (Tinker 1991, p. 303) noting, "Examples of corporate (as well as government) political pressure [on the FASB] are legion" (Tinker 1991, p. 302). However, to restrain corporate discretion, power and pressure, to rescue the FASB for society, but with no alternative theory of value, his solution to standard-setting is "a philosophy of praxis or practical reflexivity that recognizes the arbitrariness of signification, yet *pari passu,* retains a rational basis for warranting social (accounting) practice" (Tinker 1991, p. 297). Marxian accounting, however, agrees with Solomons, "If there is indeed 'nothing to seek', we are really in bad shape, unless we are all willing to become solipsists, and dismiss the external world as fantasy. If signs are 'arbitrary' and are 'independent' of what *is* being signified, then we are all beating the air" (1991b, p. 312).

Accepting the "arbitrariness" of all "signification" means accepting the social legitimacy of the "committee" that inevitably replaces the

FASB, which "adjudicates" the practical meaning of accounting "signs" in its own way. Even Tinker, therefore, believed the FASB, embodying capitalism's problems reflected in accounting distortions, had legitimacy in capitalism as a standard-setting body, which explains why "most of the sins of capitalism … are visited on the heads of accountants" (Solomons 1991a, p. 288). According to Tinker, "capitalism, based on the asymmetrical relationship of wage labor (requiring personal participation in production) and competitive private property accumulation (which does not) is particularly susceptible to biases and distortions in financial reporting" (1991, p. 301), which was a problem of capitalism. Missing from Tinker's radical view, and mainstream critiques of the FASB, is that the "indeterminacy of good accounting", the subjectivity of "economic reality", came not simply from the ideological "desire" to employ Fisher's theory, but also from the need to confront management's power, which perversely installed it at the centre of the framework. According to Marxian accounting this means, despite appearances, the FASB has no capitalist legitimacy, even though it has survived, and may survive for many years. It survives, not as a politically "viable", "capitalist", or "independent" standard-setter dedicated to investors' interests, but because the ideological hegemony of management is invisible.

Management's Invisible Hegemony

Academics, accountants and business leaders implicitly accepted management's ideological hegemony when they supported the FASB's argument that a conceptual framework would help to guard the profession against the ever-present threat of government control of accounting, and implicitly control of business, the threat to management's "right to manage", America's bulwark against socialism (Bryer 2016). Sorter *et al.* argued, "Stating objectives of financial statements would strengthen the accounting profession's position for establishing financial accounting standards in the private-sector" (1974, p. 17). The framework supported the "strong and persistent opposition to government-set accounting" (Fogarty *et al.* 1994, p. 25; Ronen and Schiff, 1978). This was the nearest accounting theorists came to recognising management's continuing ideological hegemony. For most, it was invisible, cloaked by the FASB's legitimacy.

Dopuch and Sunder (1980, p. 17, emphasis added), for example, implicitly envisaged an ideological role for the framework when, seeing no other function, they concluded, "a body like the FASB needs a conceptual framework simply to *boost* its public standing". It could then argue "(1) the objective … is to serve the users … (it is easier to use the public-interest argument for the user group …), and (2) it selects among accounting alternatives on the basis of broadly accepted objectives and not because of pressures applied by various interest groups seeking a favorable ruling from the Board" (Dopuch and Sunder 1980, p. 17). Peasnell similarly concluded, the framework's function was to "raise the moral tone" of the profession, give it "moral" arguments "to which no one could take serious objection" (Peasnell 1982, p. 255), which would in effect give the FASB ideological leadership. As Peasnell argued, "The role of such a tone-raising CF could be a valuable one.... Conflicts of interest are seen to be a serious problem.... One way of dealing with conflicts of interest is to try to encourage a feeling of common destiny and thereby reduce those conflicts (the siege syndrome)" (1982, p. 255). If we mean Fisher's theory, as we have seen, "There is, after all, some evidence to suggest that accountants and businessmen do share beliefs about what is and is not good accounting. Perhaps these shared sentiments could be nurtured and strengthened. In which case, the purpose of a CF should be to encourage what might be called a 'professional attitude'" (Peasnell 1982, p. 255).

Miller and Redding agreed, while "the Conceptual Framework project ... is neither very prescriptive nor descriptive but a combination that may be unsatisfactory for either purpose", it was nonetheless "useful because it defines a number of important terms that the Board can use in its internal and *external* communication" (1986, p. 105, emphasis added). Evidence it was at least partly successful in achieving this public relations function is that Kirk, FASB head from 1978 to 1986, found SFAC 1 and 2 useful as a "mission statement", which as Zeff says, is "interesting" because "A conceptual framework can thus clothe the standard setter with legitimacy" (2013, pp. 288–289). As Kirk (1989, p. 104) put it, "The mission statement of the FASB … has been very effective in explaining to the general satisfaction of the FASB's many publics and overseers, including committees of the Congress of the United States, how the Board attempts to fulfill its public responsibility to improve financial reporting". The framework, as Kirk (1988, p. 13) saw it, had given the FASB legitimacy with its many publics and overseers, had scored a "moral" victory. "The project achieved its goal of identifying, if choice was necessary, the viewpoint that should win out". Management's ideological hegemony was invisible.

Concluding Comments

The CAP's and APB's failures, the weaknesses of the FASB's framework and its institutional construction, show the impossible task the American profession had in challenging management's dominance. In the historical context, it is easy to understand why the profession felt compelled to seek intellectual hegemony over management, why it had no option but to embrace Fisher's theory, and why this handed control back to management. Management's judgements define the space within which the FASB sets standards and auditors judge practice, just as they had according to May's interpretation.

After many years and millions of dollars spent producing 60 documents totalling 4,313 pages, the FASB completed its framework, "a vast undertaking and of great importance to the accounting establishment", "intended to be the intellectual masterpiece ... that would have done much to quieten the critics" (Gore 1992, pp. 48–49). It did not, but the FASB survived and, before "codification" in 2009, had issued 168 standards, and in total the profession had around 25,000 pages of accounting rules (*Business Week*, 3 September 2008), but whether it has reduced accounting policy choice or improved the decision-usefulness of accounting is debatable (e.g., Holthausen and Watts 2001). Even official historians were equivocal about its "considerable success" up to the late-1990s: "The FASB has used the completed parts of the conceptual framework with considerable success. The board's constituents have learned to use the framework .... Both the board and its constituents have ... found that at times the concepts appear to work better than at other times, and undoubtedly they sometimes could have been more soundly applied" (Storey and Storey 1998, p. 161). Solomons claimed, "The definitions of the elements of financial statements formulated in Concepts Statement No. 3 have already been appealed to repeatedly in later board pronouncements" (1986a, p. 116). Arthur Wyatt claimed, "the current FASB members and staff refer to the framework constantly" (Zeff 1999, p. 124). Kirk asserted SFAC 2 and 3 "have proved to be very useful ... to the Board and its staff in analyzing problems and have served as a common language within the Board and in communications between the Board and the various constituent groups that participate in the standard-setting process" (Kirk 1988, pp. 8, 15). The basis of this "common language" was rejection of inchoate Marxian "non-distortion": "To me, the definitions were the missing boundaries that were needed to bring the accrual accounting system back under control. The definitions have, I hope, driven a stake part way through the 'nondistortion' guideline" (Kirk 1988, p. 15). However, even if the FASB found the concepts "useful …as a common language", because this was Fisherian, as Zeff said, "it is difficult to know whether the evolving conceptual framework actually changed minds or was cited in subsequent standards statements to buttress a preconceived view" (1999, p. 124). Agrawal found "Various concepts contained in the framework were used selectively" due, he thought, to its numerous "logical deficiencies" (1987, pp. 174–175).

The FASB could claim its framework had legitimated its work, but nobody has asked whether the price of public relations success has been to weaken management's accountability, is harmful to capitalists' results control, is pathological. Evidence supporting this hypothesis is that during the 1980s, as the Department of Justice and the FTC forced the profession to "deregulate", to change its code of ethics to allow commercial competition, "financial reporting norms came under stress" (Zeff 2003a, p. 202). To boost their bonuses, based on earnings and the value of their stock options, "preparers became more assertive and aggressive, … began to take every advantage of the subjective judgments implicit in accounting choices, thus placing immense pressure on audit engagement partners … to accede to accounting practices arguably beyond the realm of acceptability" (Zeff 2003a, p. 202; 2003b, pp. 273–274, 280). During the 1980s and 1990s, there was "a drive by companies to secure their auditor's approval for creative accounting techniques, especially in the recognition of revenue" (Zeff 2003b, p. 273). Zeff concluded, "auditors in recent years seem to be more susceptible to accommodation and compromise on questionable accounting practices"; that "Few would deny that the U.S. accounting is in a very troubled state" (2003a, p. 189). Zeff attributed this mainly to the "financial incentives given to audit partners" (2003b, p. 280), but an important cause, the final chapter argues, is the framework, which facilitated the 2008–2009 GFC. The history of accounting for "special purpose entities" (SPEs), it concludes, supports Marx's theory of crises and the hypothesis that the framework is pathological because, by providing a template for structuring transactions to achieve accounting results, it undermines management's accountability, which encourages and legitimates "swindling".

Chapter 8

Accounting for the Global Financial Crisis

New Century Financial, the second-largest provider of subprime home mortgages in the US, announced in February 2007 it was restating its accounts for the first three-quarters of 2006 when defaults markedly increased, because it had under-provided for losses. In March 2007, firms with large subprime investments, including Bear Stearns, Lehman Brothers, Merrill Lynch and Citigroup, announced large losses. On 15 September 2007, Lehman Brothers filed for bankruptcy. Through cascading effects, the subprime mortgage collapse led to a significant and prolonged depression, the "Global Financial Crisis" (GFC). The Dow Jones Industrial Index dropped from 14,000 in October 2007 to under 7,000 by March 2009 (Kothari and Lester 2012, p. 336). Observers debate the causes, but the trigger, they agree, was the collapse of the US housing market in 2006 and large subprime loan losses. As the Bank for International Settlements (BIS) put it, "While it is a simplification to suggest that the bursting of the housing bubble in the US was caused by subprime lending, or ... directly led to ... unwind in the credit markets..., it is certainly true that the worldwide financial crisis first manifested itself in the US subprime mortgage market" (2009, p. 6). Observers usually see its origins as "*irredeemably financial*" (Kliman 2012, p. 6), highlighting high debt levels, excessive subprime lending, over-expansion of credit default swaps (CDS), mortgaged-backed securities (MBS), collateralised debt obligations (CDOs), etc., and deregulation. The underlying cause, Marxists argue, was the low rate of profit, which partially recovered from the historical lows in the 1970s and early-1980s, but declined again from the late-1990s to 2009 (Kliman 2012, p. 3; Roberts 2016; Carchedi and Roberts 2018). There are, however, two Marxist explanations.

According to the "conventional Left account", neoliberal economic policies from the 1970s increased the rate of exploitation, which "led to a significant rebound in the rate of profit", but did not increase the rate of accumulation because "financialization" diverted profit into financial investments, leading to low growth, the accumulation of debt, and the GFC (Kliman 2012, p. 5). By implication, the absence of neoliberalism and financialisation would have prevented the 2008 crisis (Kliman 2012, pp. 6–7). By contrast, TSSI proponents explain the GFC as a "crisis of capitalism" (Kliman 2012; Mattick 2011; Roberts 2016), a falling rate of profit and, Kliman argues, government intervention preventing the destruction of sufficient capital in the 1970s and early-1980s crises to increase the rate of profit and sustain a new boom (2012, p. 3). The chapter supports the TSSI's explanation of the GFC, but adds the role of accounting standards for "Special Purpose Entities" (SPEs), justified by the FASB's framework. As some critics feared, it provided a template for banks to design complex financial instruments to achieve accounting results, facilitated "swindling", unscrupulous accounting that allowed removing "securitised" loans, particularly mortgages, risky assets and liabilities, from balance sheets, and increasing earnings by booking a "gain".

SPEs are any legal entity (company, partnership or trust) formed for a "special" or specified activity, such as the construction of a gas pipeline, or in the banks' case purchasing specific bundles of debtors. Historically, they began as joint ventures between a sponsoring company and outside investors, limited by their charters to specified activities that often required any cash flows from the SPE to go only to the investors and not to the sponsoring company for any other purpose. From the early-1980s, as the rate of profit fell to historical lows, the banks used SPEs to "securitise" their loans, to resist it by exploiting the FASB's framework to boost reported profits and reduce gearing. Banks transferred the right to their debtors' cash flows to a legally isolated and contractually determined trust that sold securities to investors based on the collateral of the cash flows from the loans, and used the proceeds to pay the banks. FAS 77's implementation in 1983 allowed banks to treat transfers of debtors with recourse as "sales", book a "gain", and remove risky loans from their balance sheets without adding the debt that financed them. FAS 77 encouraged a sharp increase in banks use of "securitisation" SPEs, which grew "exponentially" from mid-1990s following FAS 125's (FASB 1996) endorsement, which led by the early-2000s to "subprime" lending to risky borrowers who defaulted in large numbers in 2006 triggering the credit-crunch and GFC (BIS 2009, pp. 8–10). While not the underlying cause, and only one source of excessive borrowing, the accounting history of securitisation SPEs supports Marx's theory of crises in which "swindling" is a response to a falling rate of profit, and reveals again the pathological consequences of Fisher's theory in facilitating them.

"Fair value" and "securitisation" accounting, observers argued, contributed to the GFC. Researchers generally exonerate fair value accounting, but securitisation remains "an emerging issue in the accounting and finance literature" (Cerbioni *et al.* 2015, p. 156). Some highlighted the "importance of seemingly mundane accounting rules" governing SPEs, "the extent to which auditors [did not] require firms to consolidate [these] off-balance sheet entities" (Arnold 2009, p. 803). However, only a few papers "deal with the analysis of the accounting rules that may have created a fertile field for the securitisation market in the pre-crisis period" (Cerbioni 2015, p. 156). The chapter goes beyond Cerbioni *et al.*'s (2015, p. 173) conclusion, based on the decision-usefulness perspective, that "securitization accounting and the related disclosure requirements are among the accounting causes of the recent financial crisis". From the Marxian stewardship perspective, it argues, securitisation accounting was *the* direct cause. Under US GAAP, we will see, "it was too easy for originators to eliminate from their balance sheets the assets transferred in a securitization transaction", but it is doubtful that the "information provided to outside investors regarding the real risk associated with these operations was too limited" (Cerbioni *et al.* 2015, p. 173). The chapter explains why US rules were "too easy", and what rules would have prevented this accounting cause of the GFC.

As the rate of profit fell from the mid-1950s US banks invented and corporate managements employed complex "financial instruments" to exploit gaps in standards to "window dress" their accounts. With the profession under pressure from investors and the SEC to respond, theorists applied Paton's and Canning's theories of "assets", "liabilities", "revenues" and "expenses", which rather than limiting management's discretion, institutionalised it. The securitisation accounting that facilitated the GFC, the chapter argues, came from theoretical responses to the increasing use of lease financing for off-balance sheet accounting, which raised fundamental questions for accountants, was "a topic of considerable importance in accounting theory", as SEC chief accountant John Burton (1973, p. 44) put it. This was because leases simultaneously entailed accounting for tangible and financial assets, and financial liabilities, and raised questions of revenue and expense recognition. Professor John Myers (1959, 1962), Northwestern University, made seminal theoretical contributions to lease accounting, which became the basis of accounting standards for securitsation SPEs. Consistent with Paton's (1922) implicit circuit of PV, his definition of an "asset" as a controlled use-value with PV, Myers (1959) proposed an influential "critical events" approach to revenue recognition. Based on Canning's (1929) "asset" definition as control of access to future cash flows, Myers (1962) proposed a "right of use" (ROU) model for lessee accounting. A mixture of these definitions, both possible interpretations of the FASB's asset definition, influenced FAS 13 *Leases* (FASB 1976c). In the 1980s, Myers' critical events interpretation provided the model for early off-balance sheet SPE accounting. When this approach produced inconsistent results, and threatened unwelcome results for bankers, the FASB turned to Canning's definition and applied Myers' ROU "financial components" approach to "securitisations", which in FAS 125 (FASB 1996) allowed the banks to account for transfers of the cash flow rights of mortgages to securitisation SPEs, called "qualifying special purpose entities" (QSPEs), as "sales". Despite the Enron crisis, centred around its extensive use of SPEs for off-balance sheet manipulations, the FASB reproduced FAS 125's QSPE "sales" treatment in FAS 140 *Accounting for Transfers and Servicing of Financial Assets and Extinguishments of Liabilities* (FASB 2000), which fuelled the already "exponential" growth of securitisation SPEs. The chapter's benchmark for judging accounting theory culpable, responsible for facilitating extensive "swindling" leading to the GFC, is Marxian consolidated accounting, based on legal financial results control (Bryer 2021b), which it uses to specify Marxian accounting for securitisation SPEs, which the banks should have consolidated.

Observers agree securitisation SPEs were central to the outbreak of the 2007 credit-crunch. The BIS published a *Report on Special Purpose Entities* (2009) emphasising the historic scale of the crisis, saw its origins as "complex", but highlighted the role of securitisation SPEs in facilitating and exacerbating it. "The current dislocation in the financial markets, which began in mid-2007, is generally considered to be one of the most severe in modern history. The causes are widespread and complex, but include macroeconomic factors, financial market factors, as well as the results of risk disintermediation, often using SPEs. Arguably, the origins of the financial crisis can be traced to the former two factors, but were exacerbated by the usage of SPEs" (BIS 2009, p. 7). The major role of accounting in the crisis, most commentators and researchers argue, was the failure to make the massive growth in securitisation SPEs "transparent" to the capital market, a failure of disclosure. By contrast, the chapter argues, its role was facilitating "swindling", unscrupulous or unprincipled behaviour, opened by influential theorists' interpretations of Fisher's theory, which produced "weak" US accounting rules for securitisation SPEs that allowed and underwrote their rapid growth that created the conditions for the crisis, not poor disclosure.

The problem with US accounting was a familiar refrain in the Comment Letters on the International Accounting Standards Board's (IASB's) proposals to reform consolidated accounting in the wake of the crisis, echoing criticisms of regulators and users "principally in respect of US GAAP (e.g., the use of qualifying special purpose entities) rather than IFRS [International Financial Reporting Standards]" (KPMG, Comment Letter, p. 2). The Hundred Group of UK finance directors was "aware that the Board … [was] under pressure from the G20 and the Financial Stability Forum, which both contended that one of the causes of the financial crisis was weak accounting standards that enabled a proliferation of off-balance sheet special purpose entities" (Comment Letter, p. 1). However, they insisted, "While this is a well documented issue under US GAAP, we do not believe that … IAS 27 'Consolidated and Separate Financial Statements' and SIC-12 'Consolidation — Special Purpose Entities' has been found to be seriously lacking during the course of the financial crisis" (Hundred Group, Comment Letter, p. 1). US GAAP allowed banks and other financial institutions to more easily report "gains" on the "sales" of securitised mortgages, etc., to SPEs than IFRSs, the chapter argues, because IAS 27 and SIC-12 had important elements of Marxian accounting, according to which the banks had retained legal financial results control of these SPEs and should have consolidated them. US GAAP for QSPEs introduced by FAS 125 (FASB 1996) created an incentive for banks to proliferate loans because it allowed banks to transfer loans and the debt raised to finance them off their balance sheets. Did this "mislead" investors, pundits, governments, regulators and the public? Many experts had read and did not question banks' unencumbered balance sheets, the increased profits they reported, and the accounting policies that justified them. It was common knowledge, we will see, that many banks made profits by selling loans to off-balance-sheet trusts, which repackaged them into mortgage-backed securities which they sold to off-balance-sheet vehicles they had created. As the crisis unfolded in 2007, John Gapper of the *Financial Times* observed, "banks came to treat loans as just another kind of tradable security to be packaged, sold and forgotten about" (2007, p. 11), an attitude shared by most observers. *Financial Times* journalists, for example, who took a critical interest only in 2007–2008, when articles mentioning "mortgage-backed-securities" jumped from below 100 each year to 561 and 1002 (ABI/INFORM Global) and the commentary became critical. In June 2008, *Financial Times* journalist Jenifer Hughes, for example, commented on the off-balance sheet accounting criticisms of FAS 140 leading to the FASB decision to abolish QSPEs, "Wizard bankers and accountants have always devised structures to escape certain rules but the credit crunch has highlighted once more the costs of being too clever by half" (2007, p.18). Hughes' conclusion would, we will see, be an appropriate epitaph for the accounting theory that underwrote FAS 140. In 1996, by contrast, the *Financial Times* simply reported, "Europeans join the asset-backed securities club", and accepted, ignoring the accounting attractions, "A combination of factors is driving this trend: the desire by financial institutions to lighten their balance sheets and make better use of their capital; investors' appetite for bonds with high credit ratings and attractive yields" (Middelmann 1996, p. 17). It unquestioningly accepted, "Securitisation is a way for financial institutions or companies to remove assets from their balance sheets, freeing capital and diversifying their funding sources" (Middelmann 1996, p. 17). As the crisis began, in August 2007 Andrew Hill of the *Financial Times* pointed out, "These vehicles are not invisible, for those who know where to look. Rating agencies have examined them and usually give them high marks, based in part on the backing of High Street banks", and admitted that "six weeks ago, whether to bring these entities onto the books would have been a minor issue" (Hill 2007, p. 14). Using SPEs had been urged, its journalists knew, by "Most mainstream economists [who] have long preached the benefits of the securities-based Anglo-American model, in which banks originate loans but sell them on to investors, rather than keeping them on their books" (Guha and Tett 2007, p. 6). The growth of Mortgage Backed Securities (MBS) and Collateralised Debt Obligations (CDO), nevertheless, ceased from around mid-2007, triggered by the collapse of the US housing market (BIS 2009, p. 7). With hindsight, as *Financial Times* journalists Krishna Guha and Gillian Tett (2007, p. 6) now ruefully commented, "After Enron, US rules were changed to bring such programmes back on to bank balance sheets to reduce the chances that they could be used to hide bad debts or other problems. But banks mostly found ways to re-engineer conduits and mainly keep them off balance sheets".

The BIS found the worst excesses in the US. The largest share of issues of Asset Backed Commercial Paper (ABCP) was in the US. "US and European ABCP outstandings peaked at $1,352 billion in 2006 (US outstandings of $1,127 billion and European outstandings of $225 billion). By 2008, outstandings had declined to $731 billion (US outstandings of $664 billion and European outstandings of $67 billion)" (BIS 2009, p. 53). MBS became the single biggest category, also dominated by the US. Fratianni and Marchionne found "US banks … were practically alone in engaging in large amounts of securitization and derivatives" (2009, p. 22). The collapse of the short-term market for commercial paper caused large losses, the world's biggest banks and brokerages reporting more than $1.3 trillion in write-downs and credit losses from early-2007 to early-2008 from off-balance-sheet vehicles (*Financial Times* 30 April 2008). Actual and expected write-downs and losses had significantly increased to around $2.8 trillion by late 2009, the biggest losses appearing in the US (*Financial Times* 1 October 2009). Up to 2009, the US government bailout of banks cost £9.7 trillion compared to Europe's bailout of $1.4 trillion (www: BBC Global Financial Crisis — Global Issues.mht, 2009). US Banks faced further losses as they brought debts back on to their balance sheets (*Financial Times* 21 July 2008, p. 16; Cerbioni *et al.* 2015). In April 2008, the *Financial Stability Forum* published a report to the G7 group of Finance Ministers and Central Bank Governors, making recommendations for "Enhancing Market and Institutional Resilience", which highlighted accounting's potential role in the crisis, and demanded a response. The IASB accelerated its work on the consolidations project with the FASB, but neither accepted any blame. In February 2008, Robert Herz, then FASB chair, admitted US accounting rules for QSPEs were "a fantasy", "didn't work", but claimed this was because banks had "stretched" them (https://www.accountancyage.com/2008/02/08/lenders-stretched-rules-to-get-risk-off-balance-sheet/). Sir David Tweedie, IASB chair, agreed, "The credit crunch isn't an accounting problem, it's a banking problem" (https://www.accountingweb.co.uk/business/financial-reporting/is-accounting-to-blame-for-the-credit-crunch, 23 April 2008).

To show that the crisis was mostly a US accounting problem the chapter first explains and contrasts the Marxian and Fisherian perspectives on consolidated accounts, focusing on their different concepts of "control". According to Marxian accounting, management should consolidate entities over which it has legal financial results control, normally achieved by owning more than 50 percent of voting shares. By contrast, according to Paton (1922) and Canning (1929) "control" means "effective control", action control of use-values with PV (Paton) or access to PV (Canning). Second, it outlines the history of consolidated accounts in America during its transition from an exceptional plutocratic capitalism that appeared in the late-19th century, and its enduring creation, the holding company, which posed the accounting problem, to the British form of advanced capitalism by c. 1930 (see also Bryer 2021a, pp. 138–146). This provides the historical background for the development of the concept of effective control in US GAAP, from ARB 51 *Consolidated Financial Statements* (AICPA 1959) to the early-1980s standards that stimulated securitisation SPEs. The section highlights Paton and Canning's influence on lease accounting standards in the 1960s and 1970s, particularly through Myers (1959, 1962), who proposed the concepts that underlay APB 7 (AICPA 1966) and FAS 13 (FASB 1976), which became the foundation for SPE accounting standards. Third, the chapter outlines the history of SPEs, their nature and purposes, and their extensive use by banks for "off-balance sheet" securitisations from the 1980s, and explains why, according to Marxian accounting, because banks retained legal financial results control, they should have consolidated them. They did not because Paton's and Canning's asset definitions underlay US GAAP for SPEs from the 1980s, and they underlay the FASB's conceptual framework, which it used to justify off-balance sheet accounting for QSPEs in FAS 125 (1996) and FAS 140 (2000, 2003a). Fourth, the chapter explains the weaknesses of the post-Enron reforms, which stemmed from their continued framing by Paton and Canning's interpretations. Finally, it explains the role of SPE accounting in facilitating the "swindling" that led to the "credit-crunch" of 2007, and why subsequent reforms, still framed by Fisher's theory, are unlikely to prevent further swindling.

Consolidated Accounts and Control

SPEs according to Marxian accounting raise the question of "consolidated accounts", the accounts of a "group" of legal "entities", whether a "parent" "controls" other partnerships, companies, or SPEs, whether they are its "subsidiaries"? Defining the boundary of a "group", identifying the entities to include in consolidated accounts, and those excluded, is the key issue, which turns on the meaning of "control", which has been, and remains, controversial because this depends on the objective, stewardship or decision-usefulness. What follows first explains Marxian consolidated accounting's concept of control and contrasts it with Fisher's concept and influential interpretations by Paton (1922) and Canning (1929).

Marxian Accounting and Control

Legal property rights are the basis of the capitalist mode of production's superstructure, according to Marx, which capitalists use in different ways to control their capital. Capitalists use personnel controls, the legal right to hire and fire, action controls, the legal right to supervise people and assets, and results control, the legal right to set targets and punish or reward results. Personnel and action controls are costly, particularly for large capitals, so capitalists typically use legal results control, which takes different forms for different types of capital. Landed capitalists, for example, typically lease their land to a tenant under legal results control, the legal obligation to pay an agreed rent, and money capitalists likewise lend their capital to a borrower under the legal obligation to pay specified interest. The same principle applies to industrial capitalists who typically advance capital to joint stock companies.

Marx's explanation of advanced capitalism is a theory of financial results control, that individual capitals, typically joint stock companies, are accountable to "functioning capitalists", the shareholders as the collective proprietor, representatives of total social capital, for the required rate of profit they realise from the capital they control (Bryer 2017, 2021a). Businesses usually control assets by buying them, but they can control in other ways, for example, by leasing, or controlling the entity that owns them, for joint stock companies by owning more than 50 percent of voting shares, which gives legal results control of 100 percent of their assets. In advanced capitalism, Marx argued, capitalists "all have an equal claim on the common booty, the total surplus value, in proportion to their capital" (1981, pp. 312–313), and therefore demand an "equal return for equal capital" (Bryer 1994, pp. 315, 318, 321), which underlies the rule of "one-share-one-vote", a money-based democracy, which defines the threshold for legal control. Owning shares having more than 50 percent of the votes gives legal financial results control, which defines the boundary of the group requiring consolidation unless a legal contract giving results control to another party overrides majority voting control (e.g., a voting trust transferring legal powers to trustees). The holding company's management is accountable for all the capital it legally controls, but does not own or necessarily actively control. Marxian consolidated accounts make the "controlling interest", Marx's "functioning capitalist" or their agents, accountable to the capital market, for capital owned by the holding company, the "majority interest", and by outsiders, the "minority interest", for its legal control of capital. The parent's management is accountable to minority interests through the subsidiary's accounts that hold its management (i.e., the parent's management) accountable to current and future shareholders for its capital as a separate legal entity.

An agent can be accountable for exercising only legally enforceable powers. To be accountable an agent must have the necessary legal powers to pursue the principal's interests, must have all the owners' rights of "dominion", as Sprague (1907) put it, all the rights to personnel, action and results controls possessed by the capital's owners (Bryer 2017, pp. 34–35; 2021a pp. 23–24). If an agent has the legal power to act, he or she is accountable for the results of exercising or failing to exercise this power. For accountability, it is sufficient that managers (agents) have legal results control, not that they use it, otherwise they could choose whether to control or not to influence reported results. Agents must be independent of third parties, have the legal power to disregard their views or interests, and principals must judge them accordingly. An agent may delegate powers to others, for example, may take advice or instructions from third parties, give others *de facto* or effective control, the ability to control in practice, but the agent with legal power remains accountable for the results. Company directors must exercise all legal powers in shareholders' interests. Directors select personnel, supervise and otherwise control the acquisition and use of assets, and direct activities to produce commodities or services for sale at a profit, or delegate these powers. In short, directors and subordinates control the operations of a business, its acquisition and use of people and resources, and its finances, the circulation of the capital for which they are accountable to shareholders for financial results, for ROI.

The management of a legally controlling entity has the full range of personnel, action, and results controls available for controlling a subsidiary's financial and operating policies, which Table 8.1 divides into their action and results control components. The controlling entity can choose

Table 8.1: Financial and Operating Policies

Policies	Action control	Results control
Financial	**Supervise finance** Acquisition and disposal of investments; budget approvals; credit terms; cash management; raising finance; issue of debt; accounts	**Judge directors** Appoint and dismiss directors; dividend policies; winding up
Operating	**Supervise operations** Strategy; sales; marketing; manufacturing; human resources	**Judge workers** Human resources (including management)

Source: Created by the author.

the subsidiary's personnel, directly manage 100 percent of its operations and finances, and set targets and punish or reward the subsidiary's management for its financial performance. With legal control, the acquirer has the power to decide dividend payouts, raise capital, approve investments, divestments, and determine the pay, conditions and tenure of its directors, etc. Holding the legal powers to decide the distribution of dividends, winding up, appointing, and dismissing directors, gives the controller legal financial results control. The power to decide strategic direction, operating policies, approve expenditures, investment policy, raising finance, marketing, production and personnel policies, etc., are action controls, powers of supervision. Power over "operating policies" gives action control of use-values (land, buildings, equipment, materials, inventories, etc.), including labour, and results control over subordinate labour, the power to set target outputs and punish or reward performance. Power over "financial policies" is the power to set financial targets, design and install control systems, to make dividend, investment, divestment, and financing decisions. Power over financial policy therefore gives the power to supervise capital, action controls, and results control, the power to set financial targets and to require accounts to allow shareholders to judge management's performance.

For stewardship, the legal power to set financial targets and judge performance, of results control, is decisive. In US corporations the shareholders' "principal function is the election of the directors" (Barnes *et al.* 2006, p. 552), so holding more than 50 percent of votes gives them results control. UK majority shareholders have legal results control of financial policies (powers over raising and reducing capital, liquidation, dividends, and directors' appointment, tenure and pay), and only residual action and personnel controls (Mayson *et al.* 2008, pp. 444, 446, 451). Circumstances may give an entity the ability to control another entity in practice, that is, *de facto* or effective control — for example, owning 30 percent of voting capital may in practice give control because the other 70 percent do not vote. However, this does not give legal results control, so according to Marxian accounting, with the "ability" but not the "power" to govern, the *de facto* controller should not consolidate.

Owning a majority of votes is sufficient for financial results control, but not necessary because two entities can make legal agreements giving one control. For example, majority shareholders of a company can contract to pay another company a fee (fixed or performance-related) to manage it in their interests. When consolidated accounts became an issue in the UK in the 1930s, British accountants agreed the key to their preparation was legal control. In English law, controlling a majority of votes gives legal control of the board of directors and this gives control of the company because a long-established English legal principle is that "the board is the company's head and brains" (Gower 1969, p. 197). Directors are the salaried agent or trustee of a legal entity, usually do not own a significant amount of its capital (often have none), and must not use their position in their own interests. In the same way, an entity can be the salaried trustee or agent of the shareholders of another entity and have no ownership or other economic interest in that entity other than receipt of a fee for its management services. The trustee in a trusteeship has the power to deploy the trust's resources within defined limits, whilst the beneficiaries benefit from their deployment. In the same way, the management of one company can contract to manage the capital of another company for a fee for the benefit of its investors and for profits for the benefit of the other entity's investors. Functioning capitalists secure legal financial results control of joint stock companies primarily through controlling votes, but money capitalists secure it through contracts, in the simplest case specifying the legal obligation on borrowers for interest and return of the principal. For SPEs with no share capital, we will see, legal financial results control also came from contracts.

Fisher's Theory of Accounting and Control

Fisher's theory in effect replaced Marx's functioning capitalist with the corporation, with the "economic entity". Rather than a collective of shareholders, Fisher saw corporations as "fictitious persons" whose management control "capital goods", supervise stocks of use-values to produce a stream of "services", cash inflows with market prices or PVs, that provide "incomes" for a variety of stakeholders, with no dominating capitalist proprietor. According to Fisher, "In the old days, when accounting began [sic], the proprietor was a very definite individual with specific liabilities; but today, [there are] a multitude of investment forms and with contracts in which creditors share in profits [sic] and take explicit risks" (1930a, p. 75). To Fisher, therefore, "the whole concept of a proprietor becomes more and more difficult, if indeed it does not vanish into thin air, while the concept of a corporation as a fictitious or artificial person which, for bookkeeping purposes, receives and dispenses all elements of the accounts becomes increasingly useful" (1930a, p. 76). The distinction between stockholders and bondholders, Fisher therefore concluded, "is chiefly one of degree, and may be bridged over by intermediate forms" (1906, p. 85). As from the entity's viewpoint "liabilities" and "equity" were claims against its future income, "obligations" of the entity, in Fisher's theory the qualitative distinction between debt and equity disappeared, and with it the capitalist proprietor. "For a fictitious person … as for instance a corporation or a partnership, the liabilities are always *exactly equal* to the assets; for the balancing item called capital is as truly an obligation from the fictitious person to the real stockholders, as any of the other liabilities" (Fisher 1906, p. 92).

The corporation with numerous and changing "investors", shareholders and creditors, Paton agreed with Fisher, had no "proprietor" (Bryer 2021a, pp. 267–272), that "in view of the present and growing importance of the corporate form of organisation, with all its complexities of ownership, it is becoming more difficult to define proprietorship on any but a conventional basis" (Paton and Stevenson 1918, p. vii). For accounting, Paton concluded, "The stockholder is not the owner; he has merely an equity. The same can be said of the other investors. The managerial view, a conception of the corporation as a legal and economic entity operating a mass of properties in the interests of a whole body of investors of various classes, is the proper starting point" (1922, p. 84). Paton also saw no clear distinction between debt and equity because, like Fisher, by "control" he meant action control, the power to supervise, and in corporations, therefore, there were no necessarily clear-cut "owners". "If all existing corporate stocks and bonds were to be arranged in a series according to degree of risk attaching to each … it would be impossible to draw any hard and fast line of division which followed security types. … And if control or any other aspect of ownership were followed in making the arrangement there would again be no clear-cut line of cleavage" (Paton 1922, p. 73). By "control" he meant the owner-manager's "power to direct", the power of "direct control … of properties", "control of business operations and financial policies" (Paton 1922, pp. 55, 58, 80), not shareholders' legal results control. According to Paton, "one of the elements of ownership is the right to control; ultimate management is a prerogative and responsibility of the owner" (1922, p. 55). In other words, the popular view that "We usually think of the owner of a property, whatever its form, as having the power to direct the method of its use, to hire or lease it as he sees fit, to dispose of it by sale, to destroy it, or withhold it from use if he desires" (Paton 1922, p. 55). However, understanding control as action control, while owners had "ultimate" control because they could appoint themselves as managers, even if they did they would not necessarily have "control", but usually share it with others, particularly significant creditors, and in large corporations this meant dispersed stockholders had little "control", if any. For Paton, therefore, "Undoubtedly there is a sense in which the stockholder is the owner par excellence, for stock ownership carries with it the large elements of direct control and risk; but the bondholder has contingent control and can also properly be thought of as an owner" (1917, p. 11). Defining "ownership" as action control, stockholders are not distinctive because creditors have actual and contingent action controls, and "As has been pointed out many times by various writers on corporate finance, no individual stockholder has any title whatsoever to any corporate asset" (Paton 1922, p. 77). To Paton therefore, "The corporation itself, an entity apart and distinct, legally, from any investor or class of investors, is the owner in about the same sense that the sole-proprietor in an unincorporated business is the owner" (1922, p. 76). Paton's "managerial view" is therefore Fisher's view that a corporation is a legal device for controlling use-values that generate streams of cash inflows to provide "incomes" for various classes of investors, not primarily in the stockholders' interests.

The accounting implication was that "The return to *all* equities constitutes the increase in wealth which, from an accounting standpoint, motivates the business enterprise. The success of an enterprise as an operating unit cannot be directly determined and measured by the return to the stockholders" (Paton 1922, p. 89). Like Fisher, Paton concluded, "from the point of view of economics, the argument that proprietorship and liabilities are simply more or less distinct subdivisions of a larger class, equities or ownership, is easily made" (1922, p. 60), "subdivisions" of "equities", different forms of "property ownership". Because, "property ownership connotes such attributes as control, title, risk-taking, and capital furnishing" accountants must recognise, "Similarly, the status of each interest in the business must be shown periodically to ensure that each owner receives equitable treatment" (Paton 1922, p. 61). Management could not simply maximise stockholders' wealth — located at one end of the control, risk-taking, capital-furnishing continuum — but, as Fisher argued, must provide incomes for all stakeholders: "The return to *all* equities constitutes the increase in wealth which, from the accounting standpoint, motivates business enterprise" (Paton 1922, p. 89). Equity was only quantitatively different from debt measured by its degree of exposure to risks and rewards, not its control of capital, and it was management's job to "control" the entity's use-values to earn "incomes" for investors, and accountants' to report them (Bryer 2021a, pp. 275–294).

Paton's entity concept naturally underlay his asset definition: "What is meant by the term 'properties'? In brief, a property is any consideration, material or otherwise, owned by a specific business enterprise and of value to that enterprise" (1922, p. 30), that is, controlled use-values, "tangible structures and goods, such as land, buildings, machinery, tools, supplies, merchandise, cash, etc., but also of a wide variety of rights", with "value", implicitly PV (Bryer 2021a, pp. 284–288). According to Paton, therefore, management should consolidate an entity if it has the "power to direct" its use-values, has effective control, and uses it to produce PV, current and prospective cash inflows, to increase the incomes and economic value of the group as an economic entity. A managerial concept of control became influential from the 1920s (Bryer 2021b), and Paton's entity concept asset definition, we will see, remains influential.

According to Storey, "Canning's [asset] definition is … more abstract … but agrees in substance with those of Sprague and Paton" (1981, p. 87). However, Canning (1929) pointed out that control of use-values is not necessary for an "asset" according to Fisher's theory. Because for Fisher "The term 'income' is used … interchangeably with 'services'" (Canning 1929, p. 14, fn. 2), Canning's "services", like Fisher's, are expected cash inflows, and Fisher himself had also concluded an "asset" was simply "the right to the chance of obtaining some or all of the future services" (1906, p. 22). Like Fisher, therefore, Canning's asset definition stresses the proprietors' rights to "services", to future cash inflows, and like Hatfield (1909, 1927) (Bryer 2021a, pp. 222–229), focused on their enforceability, ignoring Sprague's (1907) focus on controlled use-values with value.

To Canning, an asset was not necessarily a "material object" or a "legal title": "What is essential is that there must be some anticipated, identifiable, separate (or separable) services (or income) to be had by a proprietor as a matter of legal or equitable right" (1929, p. 14). For Canning, therefore, "An asset is any future service in money or any future service convertible into money" (1929, p. 22). The "nearest foreshadowing" of his definition, he suggested, was Sprague's (1907) that assets "are a storage of services to be received", but Sprague meant controlled use-values with recoverable cost (value) (Bryer 2021a, pp. 192–194). For Canning, by contrast, the use-values "must have a money income consequence" (1929, pp. 21–22), produce a cash inflow, which may be greater or less than cost. Canning's definition of the "operating cycle" therefore ran "from money outflow to money inflow", and for him, "All measures of income for periods less than the … duration of the enterprise are approximate indexes only" (1929, pp. 116, 124). Canning's ideal index of "worth", "His fundamental criterion of valuation is … the present value of future cash flows which are likely to be obtained from the asset, either by sale or by use in the business", and where this "is available, he would prefer to use it" (Whittington 1980, pp. 238–239; Zeff 2000a, p. 7; Bryer 2021a, pp. 323–324). Canning required enforceability of only the "beneficial interest", therefore, and criticised accountants who implicitly defined assets as rights to incomes, but did not recognise "executory contracts … proportionately unperformed" (1929, pp. 18–19, 22). Canning's "asset" required control of access to cash flows, not the use-values.

Effective Control in US GAAP

Reflecting the plutocratic context, dominating early-20th century American consolidations was the objective of "amplifying/extending" the holding company's accounts, and so included entities only with 100 percent or high-levels of ownership and active management, allowing much exclusion (Bryer 2021b). During the 1920s, as America made the transition to advanced capitalism, while the tax authorities, the NYSE and some writers saw the majority-voting test as primary, framed by Fisher's economic entity concept, accounting theorists and writers subsumed the plutocratic perspective and eclipsed the majority of votes test.[1] By 1929, the

[1] In 1919, the NYSE required majority voting-share ownership as the "subsidiary" company definition for financial reporting (Bryer 2021b).

economic entity concept's notion of "effective control" was dominant (Bryer 2021b). However, revulsion against economic valuation after the stock market crash and depression, and the NYSE and SEC's determination to reduce management discretion, caused a retreat to British principles, and by the late-1930s accountants, writers and management reluctantly accepted majority voting, but as the "usual" indicator of effective management control.

In the 1940s and 1950s, under pressure from the NYSE and the SEC to clear up the "big mess", the accounting profession set standards for "stewardship", but this did not mean financial results control (see Chapter 6). ARB 4 (1939) and ARB 43 (1953) implicitly (cf. Nobes 2014, p. 1,006), and ARB 51 (AICPA 1959, paragraph 2) explicitly, recognised "majority voting interest" as the "usual condition for a controlling interest", but not as sufficient, only "a condition pointing toward consolidation", an indicator of effective control (Bryer 2021b). ARB 51 "was primarily descriptive rather than prescriptive — it described what was considered accepted practice at the time, expressing some preferences and presumptions but setting few hard and fast rules" (FASB 1991, p. 3). Accepted practice was "the presumption that consolidated statements are … usually necessary for a fair presentation when one of the companies in the group directly or indirectly has a controlling financial interest in the other companies. … The usual condition for a controlling financial interest is ownership of a majority voting interest, and, therefore, as a general rule … is a condition pointing toward consolidation" (FASB 1991, paragraphs 1–2). ARB 51 allowed exceptions for temporary control, for "non-homogeneity", or if the majority lacked legal control through the entity's bankruptcy or legal reorganisation (FASB 1991, p. 4). It required exclusion for lack of legal control, but left open, remained "unclear about", consolidation with less than a majority of votes (Nobes 2014, p. 1,007), with effective control. This concept, however, underlay the development of lease and SPE accounting. From the late-1930s banks increasingly provided "finance leases" allowing off-balance sheet accounting, reporting "sales" by the lessor, and "rentals" by the lessee, which grew rapidly from the mid-1950s when the rate of profit fell. In response, Myers (1959, 1962) developed theoretical approaches to revenue recognition and lease accounting based on Paton (1922) and Canning (1929), partially implemented in APB 7 (1966) and FAS 13 (1976c), that despite failing to hold management accountable for leases, provided templates for securitised SPE accounting from the early-1980s.

Early Accounting for Leases

From negligible use except in mining and railroads, leases grew in importance from the late-1930s as banks began to promote their tax and accounting benefits. Lessors could gain tax benefits by leasing to an *unprofitable* corporation that gained no tax relief from depreciation, lessees could book profits and secure off-balance sheet finance through sale-and-leaseback, and they could purchase assets off-balance sheet by instalments through leases with a bargain purchase option (Most 1977, p. 335). In 1948, Myers noted, “In recent years a new business procedure has been evolving which requires a reappraisal of today’s body of conventions and principles. It is the acquisition of plant and equipment through use of a long-term lease rather than through the more traditional method of an outright purchase frequently coupled with a long-term mortgage loan” (1948, p. 289). Cannon drew attention to “the growing practice of renting store and warehouse locations on long-term ‘net leases’, as contrasted to outright ownership of the real properties occupied. This technique is not new, but its use is increasing rapidly” (1948, p. 312). Cannon (1948, pp. 313–314) highlighted the effects off-balance sheet accounting for leases had on the financial reports of rapidly expanding major department stores from the late-1930s, acquiring many more stores and warehouses, etc., that reported increased sales and profits on an often smaller base of fixed assets, contributing to large increases in the reported rate of profit on total assets. Cannon knew, “in the aggregate these concerns are occupying more space, and more valuable space, than they were in 1937. But where is it on their balance sheets? And where is the investment that all this realty represents? Where is the debt that in the modern business world the housing of some 4,500 retail establishments would usually entail?” (1948, p. 314). He concluded, “These properties, the equities, and the debts are on someone’s balance-sheets, but not on the chains’. They are on the balance sheets, formal or not, of numerous investor-lessors throughout the nation” (Cannon 1948, p. 314).

In 1949, Myers’, Cannon’s and others’ criticisms pushed the CAP into writing the first lease accounting guidance, ARB 38 *Disclosure of Long-Term Leases in Financial Statements of Lessees* (AIA 1949). ARB 38 analysed leases from management’s perspective, in effect adopted the economic entity perspective, which we will see provided the conceptual foundation for all subsequent lease accounting regulations. Paton was an influential member of the CAP that wrote ARB 38, well known for advocating the entity perspective, emphasising management's decision-making, and hostility to the "proprietary perspective". Because leases did not give legal ownership of assets, from an individual proprietor's perspective none should be capitalised. From the entity's perspective, however, what mattered for capitalisation was not ownership, but effective or *de facto* economic control, effective entity control of an asset's use-values, its "effective purchase". This was Paton's view, seeing leases as evidence of the unimportance of the "proprietorship" concept based on individual ownership, because from the lessor's viewpoint, "by means of a long-term lease the nominal owner may delegate virtually all control to the lessee. The lessor in such a case is still commonly viewed as the owner, but for all practical purposes ownership, in so far as control is an essential, has passed to the lessee. Thus, it is not unreasonable to view the long-term lease as in some respects the equivalent of an outright sale" (Paton 1922, p. 57). Beginning with ARB 38, therefore, "the argument for lease capitalization has relied on the concept of material equity", that the lessee must be "acquiring an implicit equity in the leased asset through the periodic rent payments" (Wolk *et al.* 1992, p. 516), must implicitly purchase the asset. ARB 38 "recommended capitalisation of leases that were, in substance, instalment purchases or *de facto* conditional sales agreements" (Wolk *et al.* 1992, p. 518). It recognised, "Since the lessee … does not have legal title to the property and does not necessarily assume any direct mortgage obligation, it has been argued that any balance-sheet including the property as an asset and any related indebtedness as a liability would be incorrect" (AIA 1949, paragraph 7), the proprietary view. However, "where it is clearly evident that the transaction involved is in substance a purchase, then the 'leased' property should be included among the assets of the lessee with suitable accounting for the corresponding liabilities and for the related charges in the income statement" (AIA 1949, paragraph 7). ARB 38 recommended only a few tests — was there a bargain purchase option, did rentals reduce the purchase price, were they high compared to similar properties in the early periods — to decide whether "A lease arrangement is sometimes, in substance, no more than an installment purchase of the property" (AIA 1949, paragraph 6). From the late-1940s "leasing … emerged as a major means by which many companies finance the use of property and equipment" (Hall 1967, p. 35), but most elided ARB 38, which was almost wholly ineffective (Hennessy 1961; Nelson 1963), contributing to the CAP's loss of credibility by 1959.

The APB chose leases as one of the first topics for its Accounting Research Division, "underlining the importance of the topic" (Nelson

1963, p. 49). Maurice Moonitz, its Research Director, invited Myers to make reform proposals. Qualifying him for the task, in 1948 Myers had proposed that lessees should capitalise all lease assets and liabilities when the lease payments gave the "right to use" the asset, not because they "purchased" it. As Myers said, "The proposal to present on the balance sheet the present value of the liability under a long-term lease is merely a new application of the traditional ... method of presenting long-term bond liabilities. The corresponding asset would be the right to use the premises or equipment for a period of years. It represents an asset as surely as cost would be represented if the asset had been purchased subject to mortgage" (1948, p. 295), but did not develop its theoretical justification. Also qualifying Myers for the task, providing some of the necessary theory to account for leases from an "economics" perspective, in 1959 he had published what became a seminal article, "The Critical Event and Recognition of Net Profit".

Profit Recognition using Paton's Circuit of Present Value

In the context of the crisis over "principles" precipitated by Spacek in the mid-1950s, Myers (1959, p. 528) launched an economics-based critique of Paton and Littleton's "matching of cost and revenue", which "has grown during the past fifteen or twenty years into a cardinal principle of accounting". "Matching" had become arbitrary: "We have learned to postpone or accelerate either cost or revenue ... in order to get all the elements of a single transaction into the same period ... [but] in this effort to sharpen the determination of net income we have given very little attention to the timing of income recognition" (Myers 1959, p. 528). Myers aim was "a principle which is both (1) as clear and uniform in its applicability as that of matching cost and revenue and (2) sound from an economics standpoint" (1959, p. 528). Myers did not cite accounting literature, but what he said is consistent with basing his principle on Paton's implicit circuit of PV. Myers began, in effect, with Fisher's vulgar interpretation of Adam Smith's trinity formula, seeing profit as a rate of interest, to which, as Fisher did, he added "entrepreneurship", decision-making and risk-taking, and asserted this meant accounting profit is "very close to" economists':

> Economic theorists since the days of Adam Smith have spoken of land, labor, and capital as the three factors of production. Compensation to these factors has been known as rent, wages, and interest.... Later

> economists acknowledged a fourth factor of production: entrepreneurship. Its compensation is known as profit. Profit is the reward for bearing risk — the risk of enterprise, the risk of venturing in business, the risk of owning something in hope of selling it later. This profit may be positive or negative depending upon the entrepreneur's decisions as to the directions in which to risk his capital, his labor, and his land. This profit is very close to what the accountant calls profit. (Myers 1959, p. 528)

As Paton had argued, this meant accountants' profit measured the PV increase from taking decisions and risks through the "operating cycle": "Let us assume for accounting purposes that profit is the same as the profit of the economist, a reward for having taken the risks of enterprise. This being the case, profit is earned by the operating cycle, the round trip from one balance sheet position back to that position, whether the starting point be cash or inventory or any other factor" (Myers 1959, p. 528). Because "profit" arises throughout the cycle, "The question arises as to when during that cycle any profit should be recognized", but "to set some limits", Myers "assumed that profit should be recognized at a single moment of time" (1959, pp. 528–529). To "select that moment", "The economist gives a clue in the function of entrepreneurship as the function of directing a business, bearing the pain of the risks, and reaping the rewards of astute decisions. This suggests that profit is earned at the moment of making the most critical decision or of performing the most difficult task in the cycle of a complete transaction" (Myers 1959, p. 529), when the PV increase occurs. Myers admitted, "Just what event this is may not be easy to distinguish in many cases", but it need not be realisation: "Although in most types of business we recognize profit at the moment inventory is converted into accounts receivable, such timing is far from universal" (1959, p. 529). Myers' critical events approach — which, we will see, became known as the widely accepted "risks and rewards" approach to asset and revenue recognition — could justify deferring revenue where "collection was a critical problem", accelerating it to purchase or manufacture for assured sales, and offered a range of bases for magazine publishers to recognise advertising and subscription revenues (1950, pp. 529–531).

Moreover, it could justify banks recognising interest due on a loan as "profit" when they made the loan. "The current practice of recognizing income during the period the loan is outstanding does not seem to agree with the critical function idea. … Perhaps in individual cases the critical function is the decision to loan or not to loan. If that is so, profit probably is earned at that time…" (Myers 1959, p. 532). The same applied to leasing a property, which normally recognised rents as paid, whereas "The critical function theory would seem to demand that all profit for the term of the lease be recognized at this time" (Myers 1959, p. 532). Myers accepted, "This theory may, at first, seem a radical departure from current practice", but pleaded, "If the critical function theory should be correct theoretically, then we must strive to find a way to apply it to the practical situation" (1959, p. 532). Moonitz's invitation allowed its application to leases, for which Myers turned to Canning (1929).

Leases and Canning's Asset Definition

In ARS 4 *Reporting of Leases in Financial Statements*, Myers (1962) had no doubt the motive behind growing lease finance was off-balance sheet accounting. Rather than a legal device to transfer control of an asset, traditionally land and buildings, in return for rent, "Of special interest are those cases where the lease has been used primarily as a financing device. Probably one of the major reasons for the growth in its use is that the lessee has felt it wise to take advantage of the traditional accounting treatment of a lease" (Myers 1962, p. 1). Hennessy agreed, off-balance sheet accounting was "one of the primary objectives" (1961, p. 44). Myers downplayed the importance of tax advantages (1962, pp. 12–13).

Myers made his "Case for Balance-Sheet Disclosure" by lessees of "the present value of future payments" of all leases that gave a "right of use" by comparing hypothetical leases. He observed, "Comment and criticism of financial statements of lessors has been meagre, especially when compared to the discussion of the statements of lessees", which had attracted "widespread public interest" (Myers 1962, p. 63). He argued, "Nevertheless, the same basic issue is present. Is the transaction a transfer of property rights in return for a promise to pay?" (Myers 1962, p. 63). He began with a clear "in-substance purchase", followed by progressive variations, leading to the general case of a "financed purchase" of the "right to use" an asset that was obviously not an "in-substance purchase" of its use-values (see Table 8.2).

A single "rent" in advance equal to the asset's "fair value" was clearly an in-substance purchase. Myers compared cases of leases with varying terms and rent profiles, but in which "the lessee has acquired the right to the asset for its entire useful life for a price equal to the fair value of the asset at the inception of the lease. In these cases, recording the lease

Table 8.2: Myers' In-Substance Purchase and Right of Use Asset

Lease terms	**Let us consider a hypothetical lease in which the lease terms are as follows**	**The terms of the new case are**
Life	Fixed term for the entire estimated useful life of property	Fixed term, at 60 percent of estimated useful life
Property costs (taxes, insurance and maintenance)	Obligation of lessee	Obligation of lessee
Rights at termination	Title to lessee at nominal price	None
Rent	Single payment at beginning of term approximating fair value of property	Instalment payments, present discounted value of which approximates 75 percent of fair value

Source: Myers (1962, pp. 35, 37).

almost in the same manner as the acquisition of property by purchase has been in order" (1962, pp. 35–37). He then considered the general case "where the lessee buys the right to use the asset", for example, "for only 60 percent of its life" (Table 8.2). Myers concluded, "The fact that the right expires before the asset becomes useless to anyone in the economic sense can hardly make a significant difference.... The present value of the payment, therefore, should be recorded, and, over the life of the lease, both the asset and liability should be extinguished" (1962, pp. 37–38). Thus, "Even if the lease were for a minor fraction of the life of an asset, say 5 percent, the basic philosophy is unchanged" (Myers 1962, p. 38). In general, "the present value of contracted lease payments should be placed among the assets and liabilities on a balance sheet *to the extent* that they represent the right to use property. The portion representing periodic services to be performed by the lessor should not be capitalized" (Myers 1962, p. 38).

Myers (1962, p. 40) justified his proposal citing Canning's (1929) asset definition: "An asset is an future service in money or any future service convertible into money (except those services arising from contracts the two sides of which are proportionately unperformed) the beneficial interest in which is legally or equitably secured to some person or set of persons". Myers concluded, "The 'services receivable' in the present case of leases is the right to use the property. The lessor has performed his full obligation; the property has been made available. The lessor's only further duties are to receive and account for the periodic instalments and to permit the lessee quiet enjoyment" (1962, p. 40). This was an "asset", he argued, because it was "an equity in an item" (Kohler, 1957), because "assets represent expected future economic benefits, rights to which have been acquired by the enterprise as the result of some current or past transaction" (Sprouse and Moonitz, 1962) (quoted by Myers 1962, p. 39). From Canning's perspective, seeing no need to control use-values, Myers in effect rejected the whole asset approach (see Monson 2001), which is consistent with Marxian accounting's asset definition, the control of use-values with value. Myers concluded, where "the right to use the asset has not been purchased for its full useful life … [i]t would be incorrect to set up the asset and the liability for the same amounts as before" (1962, p. 37), presumably because the lessor had rights to the residual's future economic benefits. This distinction, which follows from Canning's definition that every legal right to future cash flows is an asset, theorists later called the "financial components" approach, which underlay FAS 125. The asset's full fair value, including residual value, would appear in the lessee's accounts only when this equalled the PV of the lease payments, whereas for short leases nothing would appear (see Table 8.3).

Following Canning, lessees capitalise all non-cancellable payments: "To the extent … that the rental payments represent a means of financing the acquisition of property rights which the lessee has in his possession and under his control, the transaction constitutes the acquisition of an asset with a related obligation to pay for it" (Myers 1962, p. 5). Myers, in short, proposed, "the noncancellability of the lease contract creates legal property rights warranting capitalization" (Wolk *et al.* 1992, pp. 516, 518; Spiller and Gosman 1984, pp. 421–422). However, whereas Canning criticised accountants for ignoring executory contracts, "To the extent … that the rental payments are for services such as maintenance, insurance, property taxes, heat, light, and elevator service, no asset has been acquired, and none should be recorded" (Myers 1962, p. 5).

Moonitz concluded, "Some may assert that Myers goes too far, others that he does not go far enough" (Myers 1962, p. xi). Stewardship supporters could argue Myers had gone too far because he had left subjective judgements required by leases with options, in distinguishing between rentals for "rights of use" and "services", and for "cancellability". Myers accepted, "If there are renewal options, the useful life and value at the end

Table 8.3: Myers' Extreme Lease Examples

Lease terms	The entire amount of rentals is probably a payment for property rights in the case of a lease containing all of the following provisions	On the other hand, only a trifling proportion of the rentals would constitute payment for property rights in a case such as the following
1. Length	The lease covers substantially the entire life of the leased property	The lease covers a very short period of time
2. Option at termination	The lessee may buy the property at the termination of the lease for a nominal price	The lessee has no options at termination specifically open to him under the contract
3. Cancellation provisions	The contract is non-cancellable	The contract may or may not contain a provision for cancellation
4. Rent	The lessee pays fixed amounts (as distinguished from variable) sufficient to return to the lessor his investment in the property under lease plus a fair return	The lease provides that rents shall be set at a level which is competitive with the rents on comparable property and service
5. Taxes, insurance, maintenance	These and other similar costs are to be paid by the lessee	These and other similar costs are paid by the lessor

Source: Myers (1962, pp. 4–5).

of the term of the lease are less clear", but saw this as a problem "no greater than that of predicting useful life and salvage value of any other item of property, plant and equipment" (1962, p. 48). He noted an "objection … that so many subjective judgements are required that the statements will be meaningless or dangerously misleading", but observed, "Estimates are widely used in accounting today" (Myers 1962, p. 7). However, he accepted, from his economics perspective "a decision as to the property rights created in which the lessor has rendered his full service as distinct from those services which the lessor still must perform could be problematic" (Myers 1962, p. 42).

Two members of the advisory committee overseeing his research wrote dissenting comments. Both criticised the subjectivity involved, inchoately that it undermined stewardship. To Ira A. Shur it raised questions about "(a) the theory of commitments in general, and (b) the basic functions of the balance sheet", and "the many practical difficulties of implementing a principle of capitalization may have been passed over too lightly in the study" (Myers 1962, p. 68). Walter R. Staub had "considerable reservation" because a "balance sheet ... does not pretend to reflect all of the economic resources attaching to a business entity". He thought "A principal disadvantage" was the "possibility that the determined capitalized present value may be arbitrary due to the difficulty of determining the portion of rents which should be attributed to bare property rights; certainly the amounts so determined would be largely influenced by subjective considerations" (Myers 1962, p. 69). Staub raised the problem of contingent rentals "dependent to a large degree upon the lessee's revenues or profits" (Myers 1962, p. 69). However, leaving aside problems of subjective judgement, management could and did argue that Myers had gone too far by proposing capitalising many more leases than for "in-substance purchases". Alvin Zises, President of the Bankers Leasing Corporation and Bankers Discount Trust argued, "The job is to implement the rules rather than change them" (1961, p. 37). Zises noted the dissenters' inchoate stewardship criticism: "The accounting profession should recognise ... that such inclusion of commitments within the balance sheet changes the original and basic concept of the balances sheet. Instead of portraying simply what is owned or owed, it will portray material, contingent and continuing charges against revenues", as assets and liabilities (Zises 1961, p. 47). However, unlike the dissenters, possibly seeing no real threat to management's discretion, Zises did not rule out this line of development. He concluded, "time is required to resolve certain problems", for the "concepts of capitalization and the discounted value of money" to be "more widely understood", "perhaps a few decades", to develop "techniques that will be acceptable to analysts and investment officers" (Zises 1961, p. 47).

Lease Accounting Standards

The APB agreed Myers had gone too far. In 1964, it issued APB 5 *Reporting of Leases in Financial Statements of Lessees* (AICPA 1964) to replace ARB 38, but rejected Myers' proposal that "generally favored the capitalization by lessees of the economic effects of long-term financial leases" (Zeff 1972, p. 184). Instead, it "reaffirmed the material equity argument of ARB 38", the "'in-substance a purchase of a property' approach", limiting capitalisation "to lease agreements that are equivalent to instalment purchase or where the lessee is subject to the effective control of the lessor" (Wolk *et al.* 1992, p. 518; Chatfield and Vangermeersch 1996, p. 20; Zeff 1972, p. 184). The APB responded, "The Board agrees that the nature of some lease agreements is such that an asset and a related liability should be shown in the balance sheet, and that it is important to distinguish this type of lease from other leases. The Board believes, however, that the distinction depends on the issue of whether or not the lease is in substance a purchase of the property rather than on the issue of whether or not a property right exists" (AIA 1964, paragraph 5). APB 5 added the test of a renewal option covering the useful economic life of the asset that would justify capitalisation, and partially accepted Myers' proposal for "noncancellability, except upon the occurrence of some remote contingency, as a precondition for capitalization" (Wolk *et al.* 1992, p. 518). APB 5 added some "secondary indicators", such as whether the asset was customised for the lessee, which were "ignored in practice", and "it caused little change in the number of leases that were capitalized, even though it intended to have the opposite effect" (Wolk *et al.* 1992, pp. 518–519).

Moonitz, an APB member, qualified his acceptance of the APB 5: "He does not believe that this Opinion resolves the underlying issue of the nature of assets and of liabilities" (AIA 1964, p. 32). In 1966, the APB issued APB 7 *Accounting for Leases in Financial Statements of Lessors* that did, but was criticised for "obvious inconsistency" with APB 5 (Hall 1967, p. 37), as the APB recognised, "specifically, the question … whether leases accounted for on the financing method by lessors should be capitalized by lessees" (AIA 1966, paragraph 18). APB 7 (AIA 1966, paragraph 7) recommended capitalisation for "noncancellable leases that pass ownership risks and rewards to the lessee", whereas it was "strange but true in most cases, that such leases that pass most of the risks and rewards of ownership to the lessee do not require recognition in the lessee's balance sheet. In effect, the leased property ends up … *on no one's balance sheet*" (Hall 1967, p. 40). The APB's opinions on leasing, observers concluded, "were especially vague and ineffective", which meant, "lessees and lessors had a strong incentive to take advantage of the impotent guidelines" (Spiller and Gosman 1984, p. 410; Hall 1967).

From the late-1960s, as inflation accelerated and the rate of profit fell sharply, lease finance rapidly grew in importance, particularly during the 1970s and 1980s. The SEC criticised lease accounting, and the newly formed FASB responded in 1974 by publishing a DM and, as an early priority, in 1976 it published FAS 13 *Accounting for Leases* as it was developing its conceptual framework, which defined assets as "probable future economic benefits" and liabilities "probable future sacrifices of economic benefits". Given these definitions, some thought it logical to require capitalising *all* leases. A minority on the FASB argued that restricting capitalisation to leases that transfer "substantially all the risks and rewards of ownership" did not fully implement the asset-liability approach. Like Myers (1962), they concluded, "regardless of whether substantially all the benefits and risks of ownership are transferred, a lease, in transferring for its term the right to use property, gives rise to the acquisition of an asset and the incurrence of an obligation by the lessee which should be reflected in his financial statements" (FASB 1976c, paragraph 63). However, under pressure from lessors and lessees, the majority stuck with the "in-substance purchase" argument, rejecting the full implications of the asset-liability view. Only "a lease that transfers *substantially all of the benefits and risks incident on ownership* of property should be accounted for as the acquisition of an asset and the incurrence of an obligation by the lessee and as a sale or financing by the lessor" (FASB 1976c, paragraph 60, emphasis added). FAS 13 defined these as "capital" leases and all other leases as "operating leases" for which lessees accounted only for rentals, leaving the asset and liability off-balance sheet. The FASB devised tests, but "Ambiguities and loopholes in the statement and the ingenuity of lessors eager to please prospective lessees" made capitalisation easy to avoid (Spiller and Gosman 1984, p. 422).

FAS 13 required capitalisation of an asset and liability by the lessee and an asset (receivable) by the lessor if a lease met any of several criteria (paragraph 7). Does it transfer ownership; contain a bargain purchase option; is the term equal to 75 percent or more of the economic life of the leased property; or does the present value of the minimum lease payments at the beginning of the lease term equal or exceed 90 percent of the fair value of the property? Lessees and lessors easily wrote contracts to avoid these "bright lines": "managers have found ways to record most leases as rental arrangements (operating leases) instead of asset purchases (capitalized leases)" (Imhoff *et al.* 1991, p. 51). Lessors, however, could treat leases that transferred "substantially all the risks and rewards of ownership" as sales and book a profit at the lease's inception. The value of leased assets doubled between 1975 and 1980, and in 1982 represented 16.6 percent of company plant and equipment expenditure (Spiller and Gosman 1984, p. 409), consistent with weak US accounting rules allowing management to react to falling rates of profit using leasing to keep assets and liabilities off-balance sheet. "The … freedom given to the parties to the leasing transaction resulted … in billions of dollars of leased items not being shown or depreciated on anyone's books" (Spiller and Gosman 1984, p. 410). Imhoff *et al.* concluded, "The popularity of leasing is due, in part, to management's ability to keep the leased asset and its associated financial obligation off the balance sheet" (1991, p. 51), but probably an important part.

Nevertheless, the "risk and rewards" formulation of Myers' critical events concept and suggested test for capitalisation of which party bears "the incidents of ownership" became influential. Transferring "risks and rewards" influenced IAS 18 *Revenue* (1982) and IAS 39 *Financial Instruments: Recognition and Measurement* (1999), and early US GAAP for SPEs. Myers' ROU asset based on Canning's definition, selectively combined with Paton's, justified standards allowing "in-substance defeasance" (FAS 76) and selling receivables subject to recourse (FAS 77) in 1983, which opened the door to off-balance sheet securitisation SPEs. In FAS 125 (1996) the FASB implemented Myers' "financial components" interpretation of Canning, and combined it with Paton's definition of "control" as the "power to direct", to justify banks accounting for transfers to securitisation SPEs as "sales".

Accounting for Special Purpose Entities

As the rate of profit fell to the early-1980s, there was "nothing short of an explosion in the number of new financial instruments and transactions in the past five years … that has created many accounting issues" (Stewart and Neuhausen 1986, p. 102). Problems arose in "some cases", particularly securitisation SPEs, "a new financial product [that] has been designed to take advantage of the current accounting model" (Stewart and Neuhausen 1986, p. 102), based on the FASB's definition of an "asset". Secured financing has existed for centuries, but "securitisation" developed in the early-1970s in the residential mortgage market (Adhikari and Betancourt 2008, p. 75), the first "consisted of sales of pooled mortgage loans by the Government National Mortgage Association" (BIS 2009, p. 47). In the early-1980s, the Federal Home Loan Mortgage Corporation and the Federal National Mortgage Association "followed with issuances of their own mortgage-backed securities" (BIS 2009, p. 47). SPEs and securitisation, however, first came together during the early-1980s following the implementation of FAS 76 and 77 in 1983 (discussed in what follows) in the financial services industry (Stewart and Neuhausen 1986, p. 107) where they became common in the "asset-backed securities" markets.

During the 1980s, the "variety of securitisation structures expanded beyond mortgage-backed securities (MBS) to include other types of asset-backed securities (ABS), including collateralised mortgage obligations (CMOs) …, credit card receivables, automobile loans and leases, home equity loans, and student loans" (BIS 2009, pp. 47–48). Consistent with American theory as their inspiration and facilitator, "the origins of these forms of securitisations are centred in the US (particularly in the case of MBS and CMOs)", whereas it was only from the mid-1990s that "the securitisation of residential, commercial and consumer assets became increasingly widespread in Europe, Asia, and emerging market economies" (BIS 2009, pp. 47–48). To examine the history of SPE accounting and its influence what follows outlines the "securitisation" process, and as the benchmark against which to judge US GAAP, Marxian accounting for securitisation SPEs.

Securitisation SPEs

Securitisation SPEs are created by a bank or financial institution ("transferor", "originator" or "sponsor") that transfers a pool of financial assets — mortgage loans, automobile loans, etc., — often arranged by brokers, which "is transformed into securities" (Soroosh and Ciesielski 2004, p. 31). Sponsoring or transferor companies create an SPE by forming a legal business entity — a limited partnership, limited liability company, trust, or corporation — and transfer assets to it for a specific purpose, activity or series of transactions. Usually SPEs have little equity, no management or employees, a trustee performs necessary administration, receives and distributes cash according to the contracts, and one party manages any assets according to a servicing agreement (Soroosh and Ciesielski 2004, p. 30). The motive for many was "Financing certain assets or services and keeping the associated debt off the balance sheet of the sponsors", and for the banks, "Transforming certain financial assets, such as trade receivables, loans, or mortgages, into liquid securities. Thus, the originator of the SPV 'securitizes' the assets — turns them from loans into debt instruments" (Soroosh and Ciesielski 2004, p. 30) (Figure 8.1).

SPEs are usually trusts established to convert the pool of financial assets into cash on behalf of the sponsor by issuing debt securities with

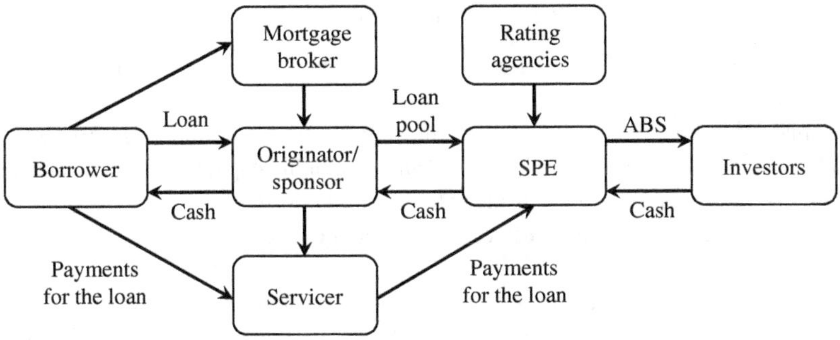

Figure 8.1: The Securitisation Process

Source: Created by the author.

different levels of seniority for cash, which the SPE uses to pay the sponsor for the financial assets. The SPE services the debt from the cash flows generated from the securitised assets (Figure 8.1). The SPE's functions are restricted to receiving pools of mortgages, etc., raising debt capital to purchase the transferred rights to receive the cash flows, receiving cash flows from an appointed debt servicer, and paying the investors their returns, and to enhance their credit-worthiness rating agencies judged the SPEs' "asset-backed securities" (ABS), usually rating them triple A. Table 8.4 lists the common features of SPEs found by the BIS (2009).

Bankers relinquished control of the cash flows to a "brain dead" SPE with limited, contractually determined functions, but to enhance SPEs' credit rating, they often retained interests in its junior securities, and made it "bankruptcy remote", legally isolated from the bank's creditors so if the sponsor becomes bankrupt its creditors cannot seize the SPE's assets (BIS 2009, p. 47).[2] This is a "critical and defining feature of an SPE" (BIS 2009, p. 47) because, we will see, with their design as "limited purpose entities", and structuring transfers as "as a true sale for legal purposes", these elements come together as an "approach" to isolate SPEs legally from the sponsor to support the conclusion that the sponsor does not "control" them. To reinforce this conclusion, first, an SPE has no employees and subcontracts out all services required to maintain and administer the SPE and its assets. All the SPE's activities are set out in "transaction

[2] In the USA, this requires two SPEs, an intermediate and the trust SPE (BIS 2009, p. 17).

Table 8.4: Common Features of SPEs

- Usually created for a single, well-defined and narrow purpose and characterised by share ownership;
- Organised to promote bankruptcy remoteness and a low probability of insolvency ...;
- Auto-pilot arrangements that restrict the decision-making capacity of the governing board and management as well as the activities of the SPE;
- Use of professional directors, trustees, partners and outside administrators rather than employees;
- Thin capitalisation, the proportion of "real" equity is often relatively small and may not support the SPE's overall activities, which are often funded through the issuance of debt securities;
- Absence of an apparent profit-making motive, such that the SPE is engineered to pay out all profits in the form of interest or fees;
- Separateness covenants, such that the SPE will maintain its own books and records, offices, accounts, obligations and assets;
- Debt limitations, such that the SPE should not incur additional debt unless that debt is subordinated to existing obligations ...;
- Sometimes domiciled in offshore jurisdictions;
- May have a specified life or a perpetual life;
- Exists for financial engineering purposes; and
- The creator or sponsor may often transfer assets or liabilities to the SPE in order to derecognise these financial assets or liabilities.

Source: BIS (2009, p. 63).

documents, which provide a measure of the restrictions in place. ... Sponsors appoint corporate service providers for the SPE, and they in turn provide directors, premises, bookkeeping and other corporate administration services required .... This approach ensures that the SPE's directors and operations are independent of the originator in order to satisfy the requirement for bankruptcy remoteness" (BIS 2009, p. 72). Second, the corporate servicer provider "is governed by a corporate services agreement, which can usually be terminated by the SPE (with notice) at any time" (BIS 2009, p. 72). Third, "to fulfil the corporate governance requirement of an independent board of directors, a number of key requirements should be met, e.g., the independence of at least one director" (BIS 2009, p. 72).

Sponsors used SPEs for "for a variety of business purposes", but high among them were increasing earnings, reducing regulatory capital requirements, and balance sheet management (BIS 2009, p. 47). The BIS suggested, "In some cases, sponsoring firms may be motivated to use SPEs to achieve off-balance sheet accounting treatment for assets, leading to improved financial and capital ratios for the firm" (2009, p. 2). However, the evidence, we will see, suggests accounting benefits, rather than economic benefits from isolating risk and lower interest charges, was the major motive. By the early-2000s SPEs were "also referred to as off-balance-sheet arrangements" (Soroosh and Ciesielski 2004, p. 30). After the GFC, many agreed that off-balance sheet accounting for securitisation SPEs was "too easy" under US GAAP and for them the question was appropriate reform. By contrast, according to Marxian accounting the banks should have consolidated their securitisation SPEs, so the questions are why the FASB allowed off-balance sheet accounting, reporting asset transfers to SPEs as "sales", and the consequences.

Marxian SPE Accounting

Assets in Marxian accounting are controlled use-values with value (Bryer 2021a, p. 46). If a banker makes a loan this is an asset because the borrower is legally obliged to pay interest and repay the loan, and its value is the capital amount outstanding. The bank could sell the loan by transferring control of it, that is, the legal ability to collect the contracted cash flows or sell it to another investor. Any borrowing the bank made to finance the loan would appear as a liability. Suppose, however, the banker "securitises" or pools many loans and transfers the rights to collect their cash flows, but not to sell individual debts, to a SPE. The bank transfers the rights to the cash flows to the SPE (Figure 8.1), but in Marxian accounting this is not a sale because, while the bank controls cash it has not realised a profit unless it transfers the right to sell the underlying debts, transfers ownership of the underlying use-values. In law, "A true sale is where there is a legal transfer or equitable assignment of the assets from the originator to the SPE" (BIS 2009, p. 67). Although "The legal assignment will transfer the right to sue the obligor … any obligations can only be transferred if the obligor consents" (BIS 2009, p. 68). Usually, SPEs "are not allowed to sell transferred assets" (Adhikari and Betancourt 2008, p. 81), sell the underlying individual debts because, as the BIS put it, "By using SPEs, originating institutions are … better able to sell assets without selling customer relationships. In many cases, the underlying obligors whose assets have been sold into an SPE will not know that their obligations have been sold, and the originating institution's business relationship with its customer could remain unaffected" (2009, p. 16). The cash inflow is therefore a loan secured against the expected cash flows from the obligations, which remain on the banker's balance sheet. Whether transfers to SPEs are "legal assignments" (or "cash sales"), or "equitable assignments" of the cash flows, both "true sales" for legal purposes (BIS 2009, pp. 67–68), as the transfer is to another legal entity the prior question is whether the bank controls and should consolidate the SPE.

Majority voting control is sufficient in Marxian accounting for legal financial results control and consolidation, but is not necessary. Functioning capitalists secure results control primarily through control of directors, but money capitalists achieve it through contracts, in the simplest case specifying the legal obligation on borrowers for interest and return of the principal. Securitisation SPEs are legally more complicated, but they are contractual arrangements determining the originator or sponsor's returns from financial assets. The SPEs created by the banks delegated operational and financial action controls, and even operational results control, to autopilot mechanisms, but they retained legal financial results control at their creation, and subsequently, for which the bank's managers were accountable for the ROI generated. The banks did not appoint directors or use their employees to operate them, did not actively manage the operations and have direct action control over the SPE. The banks created legal entities that required no active administration, but they had preventative-action controls (Merchant and Van der Stede 2012, p. 85), designed contracts to achieve the target profit in the "autopilot" arrangements, and had powers to respond to results.

The banks could not dictate terms to investors (Perry 1993, p. 79), but they designed the agreed "autopilot" to give them their target profit. As the BIS pointed out, banks could use inside knowledge, "the asymmetric informational advantage of originators … to transfer more risk to other parties than initially perceived…, some advantage in knowing the true risk of a pool of exposures … to structure a deal" to its advantage (2009, pp. 26–27). They could use it, for example, to set the "triggers that measure credit quality and redirect cash flows within an SPE … to benefit it rather than noteholders" (BIS 2009, p. 26). SPEs that hold residential mortgages usually have a "delinquency trigger", a rate of non-payment that redirects the junior notes' cash flows to the senior notes. As the BIS said, if the originator holds the junior notes, "it would be incentivised to ensure that this trigger is set to as high a level as possible…, thus maximising cash flows to the originator" (2009, p. 26). Alternatively, if it held the senior bonds "it would be incentivised to ensure that this trigger is set as low as possible in order to accelerate the likelihood of it being breached, once again maximising cash flows to the originator. Between these two extremes there are multiple interim stages, or alternatively other factors (such as the originator's incentive to receive excess spread from the transaction) that might drive either the level at which the trigger is set or how the trigger is calculated" (BIS 2009, p. 26). Originators could use inside knowledge to seek "excess spread" because, as trusts, "Normally SPEs are set up to not make a profit except for a small notional amount that is given to a charity … to maintain the legal separateness of the SPE" (BIS 2009, p. 91). To maintain this fiction, "various mechanisms are used to extract any profit out of the SPE … either through deferred purchase price back to the seller, through variable interest on the equity tranche or subordinated loan, or through an interest-only tranche which represents excess spread from securitisation", usually distributed to the originator (BIS 2009, p. 91). Alternatively, "the originator of a mortgage securitisation might have some asymmetrical degree of either informational or operational advantage or control over the prepayment behaviour of the underlying mortgage pool that it could use to enhance its own retained positions at the expense of investors" (BIS 2009, p. 26).

In these and other ways the banks retained legal results control over SPEs, had preventative-action controls built into their "autopilots" to give them their required profit, and retained the power to judge and respond to their financial performance. If the SPE did not produce the target results, experienced an "early termination event" or a "default trigger", banks could unwind them (BIS 2009, p. 73), even if they could not vary the "autopilot", and they could change the contracts for new transfers to existing SPEs, or to new SPEs. Alternatively, as the 2007 credit-crunch demonstrated, banks had retained the legal power and the fiduciary duty to act in shareholders' interests, to intervene and support failing SPEs to protect their "reputation", "franchise", and continued access to the capital markets for funding and liquidity, etc. (BIS 2009, pp. 3, 29), or close them, that is, "punish" the SPEs according to their performance. The BIS noted, "A phenomenon of the recent market disruptions was the extent and frequency with which institutions felt compelled to step in and support their sponsored SPEs, even in cases where they had no legal or contractual obligation to do so … [and] experienced substantial funding and liquidity drains" (2009, p. 43). In effect, these debts raised through SPEs were sold "fair value or return". The BIS recommended, "If at inception or at any point during the life of an SPE there is a likelihood or evidence of support by the financial firm, including non-contractual support, then the activities and risks of that SPE should be aggregated with those of the institution for both supervisory assessment and internal risk management purposes" (2009, p. 43). When forced to provide support, many consolidated their SPEs, which "may also have impacted firms' risk profiles" (BIS 2009, p. 43). However, because the banks had legal financial results control built into their autopilots, and powers to intervene, which they used to close many (BIS 2009, p. 7), and support others, according to Marxian accounting they should have consolidated their securitisation SPEs from inception. Avoiding it, "Return on equity and return on assets can be exaggerated if revenue flows are received from SPEs but the assets in those vehicles are not recognised on the balance sheet", and "Leverage ratios may be obscured" (BIS 2009, p. 79).

Early Development of US GAAP

The basis of US rules for SPE accounting from the early-1980s was not legal control, but Paton's and Canning's interpretations of effective economic control, control of the underlying use-values giving exposure to "risks and rewards", or control of access to future economic benefits, which allowed banks to account for their securitisation SPEs off-balance sheet. In 1983, the FASB issued Statements 76 and 77 (FASB 1983a, 1983b) which "began allowing banks to move securitized loans and related debts off their balance sheets and onto the books of these off-balance sheet entities" (Arnold 2009, p. 804). They did because they allowed combining Paton's definition applied to transferring control of assets to a trust (FAS 76), with Canning's definition applied to investors' control of access to future cash flows (FAS 77).

FAS 76 provided "guidance to debtors as to when debt should be considered to be extinguished for financial reporting purposes", which the FASB produced in "response to requests to clarify the circumstances that constitute extinguishment and because the Board learned of growing diversity in practice" (1983a, Summary). For clarification, the FASB turned to the concept of economic "substance". This allowed, it decided, "*in-substance defeasance* — that debt may be accounted for as having been extinguished even though the creditor did not relieve the debtor of the obligation — so long as there are assets placed in trust outside of the debtor's control sufficient to satisfy the obligation" (Hartgraves and Benston 2002, p. 251).[3] In an "in-substance" or "quasi" defeasance, the debtor puts risk-free assets, cash or government bonds, in a trust to meet payments on an outstanding debt (Stewart and Neuhausen 1986, p. 103). FAS 76 allowed the debt to be removed from the balance sheet (with gain or loss) if "(1) the assets are irrevocably placed in trust and (2) the possibility that the debtor will be required to make future payments on its debt is remote (even though the debtor remains primarily obligated)" (Stewart and Neuhausen 1986, p. 103; FASB 1983a, Summary). If the debtor remains obligated, according to Marxian accounting the debtor remains accountable for the debt. FAS 76, however, "followed a risks-and-rewards approach in requiring that (a) it be probable that a debtor would not be required to make future payments with respect to the debt under any guarantees and (b) an in-substance defeasance trust be restricted to owning only monetary assets that are risk free" (FASB 1996, paragraph 105).

The FASB was also "asked to clarify the circumstances under which a transfer of receivables with recourse should be recognized by the transferor as a loan or, alternatively, as a sale", and this time its notion of "economic substance" (1983b, pp. 4, 8) drew on Canning's concept of control to allow sales recognition, which opened the floodgates. According to the British/Marxian realisation principle (Bryer 2021a, pp. 66–67), allowing potential buyers to return products means no sale occurs unless and until the customer accepts the product. Similarly, transferring receivables subject to recourse means the transferor has not realised and therefore not sold them. By contrast, FAS 77 allowed a transferor ("seller") of receivables with recourse to account for the transfer as a *sale* if the seller surrendered "control", the transferor could estimate the recourse obligation, and the transferee ("buyer") could not exceed the recourse provisions (Hartgraves and Benston 2002, p. 251). Drawing on the FASB's framework, FAS 77 defined "control" as "control of the future economic benefits". A "transferor ordinarily should report a sale of receivables with recourse transaction as a sale if (a) the transferor *surrenders its control of the future economic benefits* relating to the receivables, (b) the transferor can reasonably estimate its obligation under the recourse provisions, and (c) the transferee cannot return the receivables to the transferor except pursuant to the recourse provisions. If those conditions do not

[3] "Defeasance" means "undo", "overthrow", "rendering null and void".

exist, the amount of proceeds from the transfer should be reported as a liability" (FASB 1983b, Summary, emphasis added). FAS 77's basis, as the FASB said, was "the determination of whether to derecognize receivables on transfer of control instead of on evaluation of risks and rewards" (1996, paragraph 104), that is, consistent with Canning's definition of an asset as control of access to future cash flows, which recourse and originator participation does not change. Accountants' soon found its influence alarming, that of all the FASB pronouncements on financial instruments, "especially Statement No. 77 … [has] created practice problems and cases of controversial accounting" (Stewart and Neuhausen 1986, p. 106).

FAS 77, Stewart and Neuhausen (1986, pp. 107, 111), Arthur Andersen partners actively involved with the AAA, AICPA and FASB, complained, allowed transactions, for example, where "A company 'sells' with recourse a pool of receivables. The yield to the investor floats or otherwise bears no relationship to the yield (if any) on the receivables pool". Unsurprisingly, "Before Statement No. 77 accountants and others were uncomfortable reporting these transactions as sales because the cash flows and the rights and obligations of the parties are virtually identical to a revolving floating-rate term loan collateralized by receivables" (Stewart and Neuhausen 1986, p. 107), and they remained uncomfortable. More ominously, FAS 77 apparently justified transactions where "A company sells receivables with recourse to a special-purpose company created solely for the purpose of buying the receivables. The special-purpose company isn't owned by the seller-transferor-debtor and, therefore, isn't consolidated" (Stewart and Neuhausen 1986, p. 107). Financial product innovators had grafted the irrevocable trust with restricted functions allowed in FAS 76 (and Bulletin 85-2, discussed in what follows) onto FAS 77's definition of an asset as the control of access to future cash flows.

During the 1980s, banks began using securitisation SPEs to avoid consolidating under ARB 51. Stewart and Neuhausen complained, "Some believe that these special-purpose companies are a consolidation issue rather than a Statement No. 77 issue, but … the problem arose much less frequently between 1959 (when Accounting Research Bulletin No. 51, Consolidated Financial Statements, was issued) and 1984 (when Statement No. 77 became effective)" (1986, p. 107). Because ARB 51's "usual condition for a controlling financial interest is ownership of a majority voting interest", some concluded, "creators of … sophisticated SPEs … [were] able to design entities where sponsors maintain control without owning majority voting power" (Soroosh and Ciesielski 2004,

p. 32). In these entities, some accountants recognised, "The interest of the sponsor, or the sponsor's control, is secured through legal restrictions on the way the SPE uses its assets particularly in regard to what parties the entity may permit access. Consequently, companies ... [were] able to avoid consolidating these entities where in substance they had control, but such control did not meet the definition of ARB 51" (Soroosh and Ciesielski 2004, p. 32). Stewart and Neuhausen observed, "Receivables that weren't commonly or otherwise used as a source of financing before Statement No. 77 are now being converted into freely traded securities. Others are in the planning stages. Examples include automobile loans, automobile lease receivables, commercial bank loans, credit card receivables, short-term trade receivables, other types of lease receivables, commercial mortgages and other consumer receivables" (1986, p. 107). The value of outstanding securitisation securities jumped from $22 billion in 1980 to $269 billion by 1986 (Young 1996, p. 492).

These innovations unscrupulously exploited ambiguities in FASB's concepts, Stewart and Neuhausen (1986, p. 107) implied when they asked, "Given the frequency and magnitude of these potentially off-balance-sheet transactions and considering the risks retained by the entity obtaining financing, it is reasonable to question whether the FASB contemplated this type of activity when it issued Statement No. 77". They singled out, "The notion of control at the heart of Statement No. 77", Canning's definition of access to future cash flows, which in their view, "is far inferior to the approach of accounting for transactions based on which party has the risks and rewards of ownership" (Stewart and Neuhausen 1986, p. 112), Myers' interpretation of Paton's circuit of implicit PV. They complained of "inappropriate accounting arising from a 'pick and choose' approach. Further, they have had unintended consequences, have been applied to unanticipated transactions and have created practice problems. Most important, their *conceptual flaws create questionable accounting* rather than eliminate it" (Stewart and Neuhausen 1986, pp. 110–111, emphasis added). For securitisation SPEs, as Young says generally, "at least some new [financial] instruments were specifically designed to circumvent existing accounting guidance", "to avoid easy classification within existing accounting categories or to take advantage of the ambiguities inherent in any [sic] classification scheme" (1996, p. 494), for SPEs the ambiguity inherent in the FASB's definition of an asset. Facing "potential for perplexity and for varying accounting treatments", Stewart and Neuhausen urged, "The FASB should reconsider Statements Nos. 76 and 77, for they are inadequate to deal with the multitude of new and existing financial products" (1986, pp. 102, 110). Citing "concerns about the increasing variety of new financing instruments and the diversity in practice in accounting for seemingly similar transactions", in May 1986 the FASB started a project to "address financial instruments and off-balance-sheet financing issues" (Young 1996, p. 495; Stewart and Neuhausen 1986, p. 102). The "issues to be addressed in the project" included "when to consider financial assets sold, how to account for instruments and transactions that seek to transfer market and credit risks", and "whether the creation of separate legal entities or trusts would affect these answers" (Young 1996, p. 496). The project took until 1996 to produce the first accounting standard for securitisation SPEs that, we will see, elaborated Canning's definition of control underlying FAS 77, and accepted the graft of Paton's definition, to justify banks accounting for transfers to SPEs as "sales".

The FASB also implicitly turned to Canning's definition, but produced a "glaringly inconsistent" set of rules in Technical Bulletin No. 85-2, *Accounting for Collateralized Mortgage Obligations* (Stewart and Neuhausen 1986, p. 104), by also, in effect, applying the realisation principle. A Collateralized Mortgage Obligation (CMO) is a debt-security collateralised by a pool of mortgage loan receivables. The CMO accumulates the mortgagors' interest and principal and uses them to pay interest and principal to the CMO holders. CMOs were "frequently nonrecourse to the general credit of the borrower; the holders may look only to the cash flow from the mortgage collateral for their interest and principal payments". Technical Bulletin 85-2 allowed the borrower to remove the CMO's assets and debt from the balance sheet with gain or loss "if the cash flows from the assets are irrevocably passed to the creditors and if the borrower can't be required to make any future payment to the creditors. The borrower may not retain even secondary liability to pay the obligations. The technical bulletin doesn't allow off-balance-sheet treatment for passage of partial interests in the assets' future cash flows to creditors unless the interest retained by the borrower is 'trifling'" (Stewart and Neuhausen 1986, p. 104). Allowing the CMO issuer to treat transfers of rights to future cash flows as "sales" is consistent with Canning's definition, but according to Marxian accounting as the issuer does not transfer control of the mortgages themselves there is no realisation, despite the lack of recourse. Bulletin 85-2 was "glaringly inconsistent" with FAS 77, nevertheless, because "Receivables, for example mortgages, transferred in a transaction that purports to be a sale or a participation may be removed from the balance sheet under Statement No. 77 even though there is 100 percent recourse to the seller-transferor for credit losses and the effects of changing interest rates. Further, removal from the balance sheet is allowed even if the seller-transferor retains a substantial undivided interest in the transferred receivables" (Stewart and Neuhausen 1986, p. 104). In 1996, in FAS 125 the FASB abolished Bulletin 85-2 admitting it had created "Confusion and inconsistency in accounting practices" (1996, paragraph 91).

By 1986, Stewart and Neuhausen complained, the FASB's pronouncements had "create[d] a 'pick and choose' accounting environment" (1986, p. 106), which banks exploited. According to the banks, FAS 76 and 77 together allowed off-balance sheet accounting for securitisation SPEs, and particularly for this, but also for other uses, "From the early 1980s until the mid-1990s, SPEs proliferated in business practice", but "without any specific official guidance" from the FASB (Hartgraves and Benston 2002, p. 248). Until 1996, guidance for SPEs came from the Emerging Issues Task Force (EITF), formed by the FASB in 1984 to provide guidance when the Board had not addressed or issued authoritative guidance. By 1986, "about 50 percent of the issues that the FASB emerging-issues task force has considered relate to financial instruments, financial institutions, or off-balance-sheet financing" (Stewart and Neuhausen 1986, p. 102). As the major accounting firms dominated the EITF, and were actively promoting and selling SPEs (Hartgraves and Benston 2002; Arnold 2009, p. 806), the FASB had not delegated its power to an impartial body.

The first specific reference to SPEs appeared in EITF Issue No. 84-30 in 1984 (FASB 1984b), but this failed to reach a consensus, and its call for banks to consolidate SPEs had no impact. It was clear, "banks were creating SPEs, wholly owned by parties not related to the bank, to purchase loan receivables from the bank using funds provided to the SPE by debt and equity investors" (Hartgraves and Benston 2002, p. 251). According to banks' interpretation, "Such SPEs enabled banks to take advantage of the provisions of FASB Statement Nos. 76 and 77, allowing them to remove receivables from their books without recognizing a liability for funds received in exchange for the receivables" (Hartgraves and Benston 2002, p. 251). Reflecting the profession's unease with this accounting, the EITF's Chair "stated that Statement Nos. 76 and 77 were intended to deal with the traditional practice of selling receivables to other financial entities, not to SPEs created by a bank for the sole purpose of buying the bank's receivables" (Hartgraves and Benston 2002, p. 251). "The FASB staff stated … that the assets and liabilities of such SPEs should be consolidated in the financial statements of the transferor of the receivables" (Hartgraves and Benston 2002, p. 251), but it had no effect and SPEs continued to proliferate. The EITF again addressed SPEs in 1989 in Topic D-14 (FASB 1989). To regularise the situation, the EITF this time issued consensus guidance by incorporating effective economic control to "endorse" non-consolidation of "certain SPEs" (Hartgraves and Benston 2002, p. 251). The SEC Observer to the EITF stated, "nonconsolidation and sales recognition by the sponsor or transferor may be appropriate if the majority owner(s) of the SPE: … is an independent third party who made a substantive capital investment in the SPE; … has control of the SPE; and has substantive risks and rewards of ownership in the SPE. … This SEC interpretation laid a broad foundation for future practice favoring nonconsolidation of certain SPEs" (Hartgraves and Benston 2002, p. 251).

Building on D-14, in 1990, the EITF issued guidance on using the rule in *EITF 90-15* and *Topic D-14, Transactions Involving Special Purpose Entities*, stressing the "risks and rewards" control model (FASB 1990). The SEC staff observers expressed "strong concerns" about SPE use, but accepted "nonconsolidation and sales recognition" could be justified (Dharan 2002, p. 19). "Generally, the SEC staff believes that for nonconsolidation … the majority owner (or owners) of the SPE must be an independent third party who has made a substantive capital investment in the SPE, has control of the SPE, and has substantive risks and rewards of ownership of the assets of the SPE (including residuals)" (Dharan 2002, pp. 19–20). This became the "general guidance on nonconsolidation of certain SPEs" (Hartgraves and Benston 2002, p. 252). EITF 90-15 included questions and answers intended to clarify the application of its criteria. The most important was, "What is meant … by the term expected substantive residual risks? What amount qualifies as a substantive residual equity capital investment?" (Munter 2002, p. 87). The answer, which lay at the heart of Enron's SPE accounting, known as the "3 percent rule", founded on effective economic control meaning exposure to the "substantive" risks and rewards of ownership. Nonconsolidation "became possible" in EITF Issue 90-15 "as long as the equity interest of a third-party owner was at least 3 percent of the SPE's total capitalization; at the same time, the majority of equity voting rights cannot reside with the beneficiary" (Soroosh and Ciesielski, 2004, pp. 32–33). "Substantive" generally, but not always, meant the third party equity stake was at least 3 percent of the SPE's total assets (Hartgraves and Benston 2002, pp. 3–4), and if so the sponsor could book "sales" from asset transfers. According to Marxian accounting, by contrast, if the sponsor has legal financial results control it should consolidate the SPE regardless of the percentage of outside equity interests (unless a majority of voting rights). Therefore, asset transfers to an SPE are not sales because, even if the sponsor does not legally own or actively control the individual assets, it controls the SPE.

The Financial Components Approach

Through the 1980s, the FASB adopted Myers' critical events interpretation of Paton's asset definition as controlled use-values with PV; that an asset existed when an entity had all, or substantially all, of the "risks and rewards". This produced inconsistent and unwelcome results, which lead the "Board to seek an alternative to the risks-and-rewards approach and variations to that approach" (FASB 1996, p. 48). The alternative was Myers' ROU interpretation of Canning's asset that focused on controlling access to future economic benefits, already contained in the FASB's asset definition (Chapter 7). In 1993, Raymond E. Perry, Senior FASB Fellow, implicitly drew on Myers' ROU asset to give what became the FASB's justification for accounting for financial asset transfers to securitisation SPEs as sales, and non-consolidation, in FAS 125 and FAS 140. Observing the revolution "During the past decade" in which "asset securitizations have largely replaced traditional financing of loans for purchases of single-family residences and purchases by credit cards", Perry (1993, p. 71) noted, "One of the most vigorously debated accounting questions is whether a securitization is a sale or a financing", citing Stewart and Neuhausen (1986) and Imhoff (1992).

Some argued against the sales and non-consolidation treatment, those Perry (1993) dubbed the "predominant-characteristics paradigm", the inchoate Marxian accounting interpretation. "Some believe that if the originator retains any of the risks or rewards of ownership pertaining to the assets in the SPE, the securitization should be treated as *collateralised borrowing*", but others would allow sale treatment if the interests the originator retains are "limited" without agreeing what that meant (Perry 1993, p. 73). The latter view, consistent with Myers' "significant risks and rewards of ownership", underlay the EITFs. Some argued "an originator guaranteeing senior interests in a securitized pool would recognize all the loans in the securitized pool as assets and all the beneficial interests in the pool as liabilities", whereas "Others would require consolidation only if a majority of the residual interest in the SPE was held by the originator" (Perry 1993, pp. 74, 79). According to this version of the predominant characteristics paradigm, Perry complained, if an originator guaranteed senior interests in a pool it would have to account for all the assets and liabilities, whereas a third party guarantor would account for only the expected losses (1993, p. 74).

Some, however, in effect took the Marxian view that the "predominant characteristic" of a mortgage originator is that its business is to borrow to lend to home buyers, so the SPE is merely a legal vehicle to allow the originator to borrow more cheaply, which supported consolidation by the sponsor. "Some view an SPE in which the originator retains a continuing interest as an extension of the originator rather than an independent entity and would require it to be combined or consolidated with the originator" (Perry 1993, p. 79) because, according to Marxian accounting, the "extension" and "continuing interest" give the originator legal financial results control. Therefore, "Under that approach, all … the SPE's assets and all … its beneficial interests not held by the originator would be recognized in the originator's balance sheet as assets and liabilities" (Perry 1993, p. 79). "Some" went further to "suggest that since the originator of an SPE initiates the provisions of the trust, such initiation constitutes control of the SPE and, therefore, it should be consolidated by the originator" (Perry 1993, p. 79), again according to Marxian accounting because it gave them legal financial results control. Perry countered, "the provisions of the trust agreement are not really dictated by the originator but are a matter of negotiation between the originator and the investors and must be satisfactory to both parties for the securitization to be consummated" (1993, p. 79), but the agreement must give the originator's required returns. Furthermore, while "once the securitization is complete the originator cannot change its provisions" (Perry 1993, p. 79), the originator could use inside knowledge to anticipate future events in the trust agreement, and it could choose to close or support them.

The "alternative", the "financial-components paradigm", justified securitisations as "sales by the originator if legal ownership is transferred to an SPE, with the originator derecognizing the transferred assets and recognizing each interest it retains in (or relationship it has with) the SPE on completion of the securitization" (Perry 1993, p. 74). Perry's financial components approach follows from Canning's asset definition as "*any* future service in money or any future service convertible into money … the beneficial interest in which is legally or equitably secured to some person or set of persons" (1929, 22, emphasis added). Any legal rights to future cash flows are assets, which Myers (1962) accepted for leases, and his "financial components approach" became the focus of lease accounting reform proposals (e.g., McGregor 1996). According to Canning's definition, transferring control of legal rights to cash flows are "sales" if the transferee gets legal control of these rights, if it transfers "the beneficial interest … which is legally or equitably secured to some person or set of persons" (1929, p. 22). This was Perry's justification for treating transfers as "sales", the "crucial" distinction between "selling" and "pledging" assets (1993, p. 74), that whereas a sale allows the buyer to pledge (use as collateral for a loan) or to sell the asset without restriction, secures the buyer's "beneficial interest", a pledge prevents the transferee pledging or selling the asset. It followed, according to Perry, "securitizations are treated as sales by the originator if legal ownership is transferred to an SPE, with the originator derecognizing the transferred assets and recognizing each interest it retains in (or relationship it has with) the SPE upon completion of the securitization" (1993, p. 74).

Because the SPE gets legal ownership of cash flows and its investors can sell or pledge their beneficial interests, asset transfers to securitisation SPEs, Perry concluded, are "sales", at fair value, produce "gain" or "loss", and sponsors who do not retain effective control should not consolidate them. As Perry put it, "In a sale of financial assets the right to receive the cash flows are conveyed to a new owner. In a securitisation, the rights are conveyed to the SPE which then transforms the individual loans into a collective asset in which the beneficiaries (investors in the SPE) have undivided interests. Those beneficiaries are thus able to sell their undivided interests in the assets held in the SPE without restriction" (1993, p. 74). It was a sale because "ownership of the assets has been transferred to an SPE, and the investors in the SPE (the transferee) have the unrestricted right to sell or pledge their undivided interests in the assets held by the SPE, and the transferor has neither the right nor the obligation to reacquire the assets" (Perry 1993, pp. 77–78). Thus, "Completion of a securitization is treated as a completed transaction under the financial-components paradigm. The resulting gain or loss to the originator is the difference between the carrying value of the assets included in the securitization pool and the aggregate fair value of the assets received and liabilities incurred as a result of the securitization" (Perry 1993, p. 78).

Because investors "owned" the cash flow rights held by a legally isolated SPE, Perry concluded, consolidation was not relevant. "Under the financial-components paradigm, the SPE is regarded as a device for holding assets owned by the investor-beneficiaries and for insuring that the proceeds from the securitized assets are protected from claims of creditors of the originator", so no "party holding undivided interests in the SPE … [should] consolidate it. All that is needed is for the holder of beneficial interests in the SPE to recognize such interests" (1993, p. 79). Perry did not distinguish transfer of "legal ownership" of the "beneficial interests" meaning of legal ownership of the cash flows, and the assets' underlying use-values. Usually SPEs cannot sell the underlying assets, so in Marxian accounting usually there was no sale. "Because SPEs are not allowed to sell transferred assets, [under IAS 39, paragraph 20(c), discussed later] the outcome in most securitizations will be the determination that the transferor has retained control" (Adhikari and Betancourt 2008, p. 81), consistent with the British/Marxian realisation principle. To reject consolidation the financial components approach implicitly relies on the absence of management action control and ignores results control. Perry argued, "Unlike the common stockholder, the residual holder is not entitled to any managerial discretion or control over the activities of the entity; control instead rests with the trustee for the benefit of all investors in accordance with the securitization agreement" (1993, p. 79). It was decisive that "The securitization trust is administered by the servicer and the trustee, and their activities are specifically and restrictively defined in the trust agreement and may not be modified by the holders of the residual interests. Moreover, because allocations of all cash inflows are governed by provisions of the underlying agreements, the residual investor (like the senior investor) is entitled to receive only certain cash flows from collection of the securitized loans" (Perry 1993, p. 79). Just like a lessor who "sells" an ROU asset to the lessee, according to Perry (1993) the bank "sells" the rights to cash flows from mortgagees, leaving it controlling its residual interests.

FAS 125 and FAS 140

In 1996, "Recognizing the loopholes in the accounting for securitizations" (Soroosh and Ciesielski 2004), in SFAS 125 the FASB implemented Perry's "financial components" approach, creating the concept of "qualifying special purpose entities" that legitimated the banks' "sales" accounting and non-consolidation. According to the FASB, "the most difficult questions about accounting for transfers of financial assets concern the circumstances in which it is appropriate to remove previously recognized financial assets from the statement of financial position and to recognize gain or loss" (1996, paragraph 99). It considered the available "approaches", the "risks and rewards" and "control" interpretations. It rejected "risks and rewards", the "familiar approach … [that] views each financial asset as a unit that should not be derecognized until the risks and rewards that are embodied in that asset have been surrendered" (FASB 1996, paragraph 99). There were "Variations … [that] attempt to choose which risks and rewards are most critical and whether all or some major portion of those risks and rewards must be surrendered to allow derecognition", but "were unsatisfactory because the result does not faithfully represent the effects of the transfer of assets and because of the potential for inconsistencies" (FASB 1996, paragraphs 99–100). The FASB therefore rejected FAS 76's "risks and rewards" approach, instead taking "a similar approach" to "Statement 77 based [on] the determination of whether to derecognize receivables on transfer of control instead of on evaluation of risks and rewards" (1996, paragraph 104).

To allow derecognition when the sponsor transfers control of use-values to SPEs, but retains some access to risks and rewards, the FASB exercised the option of interpreting its asset definition as Canning's control of access to future economic benefits, rather than Paton's control of use-values with PV, to explain the "Conceptual Basis for the Financial-Components Approach". It reminded readers that "FASB Concepts Statement No. 6, *Elements of Financial Statements,* states … Assets are probable future economic benefits obtained or controlled by a particular entity as a result of past transactions or events" (1996, paragraph 109), stressing the need for "Control by a Particular Entity". Defining "assets" as "control" of "future economic benefits", the FASB emphasised, SFAC 6 (a replacement for SFAC 3 including not-for-profit organisations) meant, "*Every asset is an asset of some entity; moreover, no asset can simultaneously be an asset of more than one entity*" (1996, paragraph 109; 1985, paragraph 183). It was not possible to share particular future economic benefits. However, because an "asset" was not a controlled use-value, "a particular physical thing or other agent [e.g., contractual rights and obligations] that provides future economic benefit may provide separate benefits to two or more entities at the same time" (FASB 1996, paragraph 109; 1985, paragraph 183), for example, to a lessor and lessee.

Adopting Canning's definition, rather than control of use-values, "To have an asset, an entity must control future economic benefit to the extent that it can benefit from the asset and generally can deny or regulate access to that benefit by others, for example, by permitting access only at a price" (FASB 1996, paragraph 109; 1985, paragraph 183). "Thus, *an asset of an entity is the future economic benefit that the entity can control and thus can, within limits set by the nature of the benefit or the entity's right to it, use as it pleases*. The entity having an asset is the one that can exchange it, use it to produce goods or services, exact a price for others' use of it, use it to settle liabilities, hold it, or perhaps distribute it to owners" (FASB 1996, paragraph 109; 1985, paragraph 184). Like Canning, SFAC 6 emphasised, "The definition of assets focuses primarily on the future economic benefit to which an entity has access and only secondarily on the physical things and other agents that provide future economic benefits" (FASB 1996, paragraph 109; 1985, paragraph 185). From his perspective, "*Many physical things and other agents are in effect bundles of future economic benefits that can be unbundled in various ways*" (FASB 1996, paragraph 109; 1985, paragraph 185). It followed, "*two or more entities may have different future economic benefits from the same agent at the same time or the same continuing future economic benefit at different times*" (FASB 1996, paragraph 109; FASB 1985, paragraph 185). For example, "one entity may have the right to the interest from an investment, while another has the right to the principal" (FASB 1996, paragraph 109; FASB 1985, paragraph 185). Or, as SFAS 6 noted, "Leases are common examples of agreements that unbundle the future economic benefits of a single property to give a lessee a right to possess and use the property and give a lessor a right to receive rents and a right to the residual value" (FASB 1985, paragraph 185). In FAS 125, consistent with Myers' interpretation of Canning's "financial components" definition, legally controlling access to future economic benefits, transfers of legal rights in cash flows to SPEs were sales:

> Based on the concepts and definitions [above] …, the Board concluded that the key to applying the financial-components approach can be summarized as follows:
>
> (a) The economic benefits provided by a financial asset (generally, the right to future cash flows) are derived from the contractual provisions that underlie that asset, and the entity that controls those benefits should recognize them as its asset.

(b) A financial asset should be considered sold and therefore should be derecognized if it is transferred and control is surrendered. … (FASB 1996, paragraph 112).

One reason respondents, largely from financial services, "generally supported the financial-components approach" (FASB 1996, paragraph 113) was that it gave management discretion: "assets can be disaggregated into a variety of components whose accounting treatment depends on the transferor's retention of control" (Cerbioni *et al.* 2015, p. 162).

Defining "control" as access to future economic benefits, the FASB recognised, could apply to non-financial assets, but shrank from the radical change this could entail, leaving open Paton's definition for them. "The concepts underlying the financial-components approach could be applied by analogy to accounting for transfers of nonfinancial assets and thus could result in accounting that differs significantly from that required by existing standards and practices" (FASB 1996, paragraph 114). It avoided the problem by highlighting the importance of management's control of use-values in generating future economic benefits from non-financial assets, implicitly drawing on Myers' critical events interpretation of Paton. "However, the Board believes that financial and nonfinancial assets have significantly different characteristics, and it is not clear to what extent the financial-components approach is applicable to nonfinancial assets. Nonfinancial assets have a variety of operational uses, and management skill plays a considerable role in obtaining the greatest value from those assets" (FASB 1996, paragraph 114). By contrast, for financial assets, "management skill" was unimportant because contracts transfer legal control of contractually determined beneficial interests: "financial assets have no operational use. … Once the contract is established, management skill plays a limited role in the entity's ability to realize the value of the instrument" (FASB 1996, paragraph 114).

To remove any taint of management's skill in operating a securitisation SPE, the FASB in effect accepted the 1980s innovators' graft of Paton's definition of control. FAS 125 allowed accounting for financial asset transfers as sales "if the assets were isolated from the transferor, the transferee had unrestricted freedom to pledge the assets, and the transferor did not maintain effective control over the assets through promises to redeem or repurchase the assets" (Hartgraves and Benston 2002,

p. 253). SPEs that met these tests were "qualifying SPEs" (QSPEs) "a type of SPE that, without any further tests, meets a minimum standard for treating the asset transfer as a sale" (Hartgraves and Benston 2002, p. 253). In a QSPE, the "transferee" is "its beneficial interest holders, [who] can freely pledge or exchange the transferred assets or beneficial interests", and it must be "isolated from the transferor and the transferor's creditors" (Adhikari and Betancourt 2008, p. 78). To avoid Paton's definition of control as the active management of use-values, according to FAS 125 "A QSPE is a very limited scope SPE" (Hartgraves and Benston 2002, p. 253). It must be "a … legal entity whose activities are limited to (1) holding title to transferred financial assets, (2) issuing beneficial interests, (3) collecting cash proceeds from assets held, (4) reinvesting proceeds in financial instruments pending distribution to beneficial holders, and (5) distributing proceeds to the holders of its beneficial interests" (Hartgraves and Benston 2002, p. 253). Hartgraves and Benston (2002, p. 253) observed, "In describing the characteristics of a QSPE, the FASB did not mention the 3 percent outside equity requirement or any other requirements regarding outside residual equity investment, only that it have legal standing separate from the transferor. Statement No. 125 also did not specifically address the consolidation issue", which avoided addressing the contradiction that although the FASB in effect adopted Paton's definition of control as the "power to direct" an SPE to avoid consolidation, it rejected Myers' "risks and rewards", critical events interpretation of Paton's definition of an asset as a controlled use-value with PV.

The securitisation "market … expanded exponentially [from] the mid-1990s" (BIS 2009, p. 7), that is, following FAS 125. One important reason was the discretion Canning's interpretation introduced. As the BIS found, "Historically, a motivation for the use of SPEs in securitisation was the accounting treatment following a sale of the assets to the SPE. Originators were *able to recognise the present value of the future cash flows of the assets as profit*. This enabled originators to *manage their profits more effectively*" (2009, pp. 78–79, emphases added). Complaints about "transparency" led in 2000 to FAS 140 a replacement of FAS 125, effective from 31 March 2001, which increased disclosures (Soroosh and Ciesielski 2004). FAS 140 maintained FAS 125's sales tests and merely "expanded the definition … to narrowly limit QSPEs to the types of transactions typically found in a securitization situation", and except for guaranteed MBS, required "outside parties … [to] have at least '10 percent' of the 'fair value of their beneficial interests' (debt or equity)" (Hartgraves and Benston 2002, p. 254). FAS 140 confirmed the non-consolidation of QSPEs (FASB 2000, paragraph 46). Then Enron happened.

Reform of SPE Accounting

The FASB responded to the outcry by reforming SPE accounting, but left QSPEs largely untouched (2003a). Critics argued, "accounting standards dealing with off-balance-sheet entities have produced inconsistent results, because the standards are incomplete and fragmented" (Soroosh and Ciesielski 2004, p. 32). The AAA argued for a "risks and rewards" effective control definition to deal with SPEs because "A primary drawback of the legal approach is that companies can avoid consolidation of SPEs by legal arrangements that obscure the economics of SPE-related transactions" (2003, p. 162). The FASB amended FAS 140 further specifying conditions for QSPEs, but retained their "legal" basis. For non-qualifying SPEs, however, the FASB partially took the AAA's advice in *Interpretation of ARB No. 51, Consolidation of Certain Special-Purpose Entities*. As it said, "Current accounting standards require an enterprise to include subsidiaries in which it has a controlling financial interest … usually … applied to subsidiaries in which an enterprise has a majority voting interest, but in many circumstances, the enterprise's consolidated financial statements do not include SPEs with which it has fundamentally similar relationships" (FASB 2002, p. i). Like Enron, "Some enterprises appear to have used SPEs to avoid reporting assets and liabilities for which they are responsible, to defer the reporting of losses that have already been incurred, or to report gains that are illusory" (FASB 2002, p. 13) using non-equity SPEs. For one of Enron's SPEs, a partnership, the investigating committee found, "The assessment of control under applicable accounting literature was, and continues to be, subjective. In general, there is a rebuttable presumption that a general partner exercises control over a partnership. The presumption can be overcome if the substance of the partnership provides that the general partner is not in control of major operating and financial policies" (Powers *et al.* 2002, p. 48). In 2003 the FASB "responded by issuing a proposed interpretation of existing accounting principles aimed at putting many off-balance-sheet entities back onto the balance sheet of the companies that created them" (Soroosh and Ciesielski 2004, p. 33; Nobes 2014, p. 1,011). FASB Interpretation (FIN) 46 "clarifies the application of Accounting Research Bulletin No. 51", which required "an enterprise to … consolidate … subsidiaries in which it has a controlling financial interest. … Over the years, however, companies have found ways to obtain economic control of other entities without owning 50 percent of the voting stock, thereby avoiding consolidation" (Soroosh and Ciesielski 2004, p. 33). To close this gap, the FASB again drew on Canning's definition of control, but this time to infer Paton's "control" of use-values using the long-standing interpretation of majority voting control as an "indicator" of effective control. It concluded, "The relationship between an SPE and its primary beneficiary results in *control by the primary beneficiary of future benefits from the assets of the SPE* even though the primary beneficiary may not have the direct ability to make decisions about the uses of the assets" (FASB 2002, p. iii, emphasis added).

For these non-qualifying SPEs, the FASB (2003b) implemented the (revised) interpretation FIN 46R covering consolidation of "variable interest entities" (VIEs), designed to prevent non-consolidation of non-equity, non-directed entities, by inferring "control" through exposure to the majority of risks and rewards without control of use-values. As FIN 46R put it, "This interpretation applies to transactions that are currently invisible due to ambiguous ownership, where the voting equity ownership does not give the owners a controlling financial interest", but "specifically excluded … [a] qualifying SPE (QSPE) used in a transfer of financial assets, as dictated in SFAS 140" (Soroosh and Ciesielski 2004, p. 36). FIN 46R required an entity with the majority or the significantly largest amount of "variable financial interest" in a non-QSPE to consolidate it, expanded "the definition of control for consolidation of financial statements to include consolidation based on 'variable interest', as well as consolidation based on voting power" (Soroosh and Ciesielski 2004, p. 34). An SPE could provide a "variable financial interest" by "financial instruments, service contracts, nonvoting ownership interests, or other arrangements" (FASB 2002, p. i). A VIE was an entity that met any one of the following criteria:

(1) The total equity investment at risk is not sufficient to permit the entity to finance its activities without additional subordinated financial support provided by any parties, including equity holders.

(2) The equity investors lack one or more of the following essential characteristics of a controlling financial interest:
   (a) The direct or indirect ability through voting rights or similar rights to make decisions about the entity's activities that have a significant effect on the success of the entity.
   (b) The obligation to absorb the expected losses of the entity.
   (c) The right to receive the expected residual returns of the entity (FASB 2003b, Summary).

Whoever are the "primary beneficiaries of VIEs must consolidate them in their financial statements" (Soroosh and Ciesielski 2004, p. 34). Therefore, although "An entity is a VIE of Group X if X is the primary beneficiary of the VIE because X (instead of the equity holders) receives a majority of residual returns or losses … [which] expanded the scope of US consolidation, it still did not adopt the principle of control. The criterion for inclusion is not control or majority ownership but being subject to the majority of expected losses, expected returns or both" (Nobes 2014, pp. 1,011–1,012). FIN 46(R) would have caught many of Enron's SPEs because "in many cases a guaranty or other form of credit support was required from Enron" (Powers *et al.* 2002, p. 37), and because in "Enron's SPE [hedging] transactions, it was at least debatable whether risk was shifted on the hedged assets owned by Enron" (Schwarz 2002, p. 7). However, it would not catch schemes where management actually controls an SPE but it does not have the majority or largest variable interest — those SPEs that "effectively disperse risks among the parties involved" (FASB 2002, p. ii), that the management of the sponsoring entity would not consolidate under the FASB's test. Investors exposed to the majority of variable financial interests probably usually take care to "control" the operating and financial policies of an SPE, have contracts giving them control, but the FASB simply assumed it. "The Board reasoned that providers of financial support to an SPE would be expected to have risks and opportunities to benefit (risks and rewards) that are of the same character as those of an equity investor. At the same time, they arrange to protect their investment through means other than ownership of voting shares" (FASB 2002, paragraph B15).

For equity-based SPEs, "To help determine 'sufficiency' the interpretation increases the 3 percent threshold to 10 percent", which looks objective, but as with its 3 percent predecessor, "determining the sufficiency of equity investment in a VIE is subject to considerable judgment" (Soroosh and Ciesielski 2004, p. 34). Less than 10 percent could be "sufficient to permit the VIE to finance its activities" if the entity has "demonstrated" it, or shows the industry norm is that it can finance its activities without additional subordinated support, or it exceeds the estimate of the entity's expected losses, based on "reasonable quantitative evidence" (Soroosh and Ciesielski 2004, p. 34). Alternatively, more than 10 percent could be necessary, so "the interpretation leaves room for flexibility in determining what the equity investment in an entity should be in order to avoid consolidation of such an entity by its variable interest holder" (Soroosh and Ciesielski 2004). FIN 46(R) merely required, "The amount of equity investment is sufficient to allow the SPE to finance its activities without relying on support from other variable interest holders. ... Generally, that means that the equity investment should be greater or equal to the expected future losses of the SPE at all times during the SPE's existence" (FASB 2002, paragraph 9(b)). The FASB noted, "*Expected future losses* refers to a probability-weighted estimate of losses without considering possible gains", a subjective forecast.

Accounting for the Credit-Crunch

As the boards deliberated the meaning of "control" (IASB 2004, paragraph 4), the banks continued using QSPEs to sell mortgages to the international bond markets, which led to the credit-crunch in 2007 and 2008–2009 GFC. Banks had used securitisation SPEs to transfer assets and debts off their balance sheets and boost their profits, it quickly became clear, SPEs that many now thought the banks controlled. Some leading US accountants blamed accounting. In 2008 Lynn Turner, SEC chief accountant from 1998 to 2001, saw QSPE accounting as a "scam". He blamed "a critically flawed 1983 decision, [when] the FASB ... started to let the banks take the securitized loans and related debts off their balance sheets. ... It's been clear that in the last two decades, the banks' ability to hide that financing ... in 'special purpose entities' ..., which are nothing more than just a scam to keep things away from investors — has had a very devastating impact" (Turner 2008, np). Robert Herz, then head of the FASB, blamed the assumption that QSPEs were "fairly passive", not seeing that because they "took a lot of management when they went bad" meant the banks had legal financial results control from their inception. According to Herz, "qualified special-purpose entit[ies] ... were fairly passive, and the rules talked about how the powers would be very limited — entirely specified up front — and I think that worked for a fair amount of time" (2008, p. 61), until subprime loans. "I think what we've learned in the last three to five years is in residential mortgages … that these assets are not passive in nature. Certainly, the subprime assets that were put into these vehicles called 'Q's' with a lot of hindsight, because they took a lot of management when they went bad in terms of the servicing or having to restructure the loans, modify them, do all sorts of workouts. … I think the lesson learned here is that they were not actually 'Q-able'" (Herz 2008, p. 61). However, whether for risky assets or not, the FASB banned QSPEs, in effect accepting their accounting underlay the crisis. "What are we doing? We're going to kill Q's … and that will probably result in a lot of the current securitization transactions not qualifying for sale accounting and remaining on the balance sheet" (Herz 2008, p. 61).

Facilitating Swindling

Marxian accounting agrees with Turner that QSPE accounting was a "scam" because it facilitated "swindling", allowed unscrupulous, self-interested managements to manipulate accounts. Academic research supports this interpretation, but while researchers often criticise the consequences, they invariably see the problem as a "difficult conceptual issue", of economic valuation, of decision-usefulness, not accountability. "Guided by its conceptual framework, FASB aims to promulgate standards that are *neutral* in the sense of unbiased and not intended to influence the behavior of a particular group" (Schipper and Yohn 2007, p. 77), but this does not mean particular groups do not use them for swindling. Researchers agree, "understanding banks' incentives for increasing securitization transactions is of fundamental importance in drawing a full picture of the causes of the financial crisis" (Cerbioni *et al.* 2015, p. 156; see also Schipper and Yohn 2007; Dechow *et al.* 2010; Kothari and Lester 2012). However, to explain bankers' behaviour the "fundamental" question, according Marx's theory of crises, is not their "incentives", which were to maximise reported profits and minimise reported assets and liabilities for their economic benefit, but the framework's encouragement of "swindling", which researchers only implicitly recognise in their discussions of "moral hazard". Marxian accounting agrees with Heilpern *et al.* (2009, p. 103), and others, that "banking executives were encouraged to pass on … complex collateralized products to investors to value skim, improve banking returns and their own bonuses", but by accounting rules that legitimated unscrupulous behaviour.

Their motives, banks and economists argue, were "economic" benefits, the "theory [that], because SPEs do not engage in business transactions other than the ones for which they are created, and their activities are backed by their sponsors, they are able to raise funds at lower interest rates than those available to their sponsors" (Soroosh and Ciesielski 2004, p. 30). Therefore, researchers conclude, "It is not clear … whether firms expend resources to structure transactions primarily for accounting, or for economic reasons" (Schipper and Yohn 2007, pp. 68–69, 76). "Some insight can be obtained", Schipper and Yohn accept, "by investigating responses to changes in standards that affect the accounting for financial asset transfers" (2007, p. 77). There is evidence, for example, that US banks responded to FIN 46(R) to avoid consolidation (Schipper and Yohn 2007, p. 77). Accountants, we saw, attributed the increased securitisations in the early-1980s, and mid-1990s, to FAS 77 and FAS 125. To explain an individual's motives for securitisations may be difficult or impossible, but "unscrupulous" or "unprincipled" anti-social behaviour is observable in disjunctures between "principles" and behaviour. The task for securitisations is to explain the behaviour of a relatively small group: "financial asset transfers are economically significant, albeit undertaken by less than 10 percent of U.S. public entities … [and] securitization activities are concentrated among financial services firms" (Schipper and Yohn 2007, p. 68). This group, however, created a very large market: "securities resulting from securitizations were one of the largest segments of the debt market in 2005, totaling $7.4 trillion. By comparison, the Treasury market was valued at $4.1 trillion in 2005" (Dechow *et al.* 2010, p. 2). Within financial services, however, "despite the positive incentives for originators to use securitisation vehicles to transfer some or all of the risks of their loans, many banks did not avail themselves of these opportunities" (BIS 2009, p. 16) for reasons consistent with seeing QSPE accounting as swindling. "One bank", anonymously, but apparently representative of this group, explained its "overarching *principle* was that the institution was *averse* to originating assets that it would not be *comfortable* owning", because it "did not have confidence that it could *reasonably* quantify certain risks that are typically retained in certain securitisation transactions, such as liquidity risk. This bank also noted that the complexity introduced with the *apparent intent of avoiding specific regulatory or accounting requirements* raised a significant *concern*" (BIS 2009, p. 16, emphases added). The evidence supports the bank's social discomfort.

Academic researchers confirm the "opportunistic use of securitization in order to maximize financial statement 'window dressing' and manage earnings (Dechow and Shakespeare 2009; Dechow *et al.* 2010)" (Cerbioni *et al.* 2015, p. 156). "Gains" arose under FAS 140 because it required transfers to SPEs at "fair value". This allowed the transferor to "cherry pick" loans with a lower book value (e.g., issued at a higher rate of interest) or retain an interest which FAS 140 also required the transferor to account for at "fair value", usually at PV, that usually produced "gains" (Dechow *et al.* 2010, pp. 5–9). Consistent with this accounting benefit motive for securitisations, "gains are typical. (Indeed, the Wall Street term for the SFAS No. 140 rules governing securitization accounting is 'gain on sale' accounting)" (Dechow *et al.* 2010, p. 3). Dechow and Shakespeare (2009, p. 100), "investigate whether managers time their securitizations transactions so as to maximize the accounting benefits", and finds they do. Dechow *et al.*, whose "sample consists of firms that retain an interest in the receivables sold … as is very typical for securitizations", "argue that allowing derecognition in such cases provides ample opportunity to manipulate earnings because the retained cash flows must be recorded at fair value even though no active market value is likely to exist" (2010, p. 23). Again consistent with an accounting benefit motive, "Industry specialists state '[t]he thing about gain on sale accounting is that you can create a machine that just manufactures earnings out of thin air'" (Dechow *et al.* 2010, p. 3). This "machine" was highly productive: "the impact of securitizations on earnings is large. In our sample … of 305 firm-year observations, representing 96 firms that report securitization gains …, 13 percent of firms report gains … large enough … to convert an accounting loss to a profit, and the average gain increases reported earnings by more than 38 percent" (Dechow *et al.* 2010, p. 4). Also consistent with an accounting motive, "Selling receivables to obtain cash to relend to new customers is an integral part of the business model for many of these firms" (Dechow *et al.* 2010, p. 5), because to function as a "business" required reporting "gains".

Treating transfers as "sales" when the bank retained significant risk was "swindling", a "scam", because it violated the realisation principle in two ways. First, as Dechow *et al.* put it, while "a conceptual issue is what degree of involvement is permissible to qualify for sale accounting", "firms can easily comply with the sale requirements of SFAS No. 140

even when they retain significant risk, so almost all firms structure securitizations to meet the requirements for sale accounting treatment" (2010, p. 5). They note, "Based on our discussions with structured finance groups at the large accounting firms, it is extremely unusual to structure a securitization as a collateralized borrowing" (Dechow *et al.* 2010, p. 5), consistent with an accounting benefit motive. Their findings, in short, "suggest that firms undertake real transactions, at least in part, for their accounting benefits" (Dechow *et al.* 2010, p. 4), that "managers use the discretion obtained from fair value accounting rules to report larger gains" (2010, p. 23). Second, paying managers "performance" bonuses based on discretionarily determined unrealised "gains", on projected future cash flows, violates the principle that agents must be accountable for objective results. Consistent with swindling, Dechow *et al.* "find that CEO compensation is sensitive to the reported gains and that the gains appear to be treated as a regular earnings component. This suggests that CEOs, on average, are rewarded for the gains they report" (2010, p. 23). Corporate governance arrangements made no difference, in part because those charged with oversight did not fully understand FAS 140 (Dechow *et al.* 2010, p. 4), which violates the principles that directors must act in shareholders' interest, and like auditors, must fully inform themselves.

According to some researchers, the capital market saw through off-balance sheet accounting. Landsman *et al.* (2008) suggest investors treated securitisations as loans rather than sales. Niu and Richardson (2006) show that on average investors saw the off-balance sheet debt from securitisations having the same risk-relevance for explaining the capital asset pricing model beta as on-balance sheet debt; saw securitisation gains as less reliable for valuation than other earnings components; and less reliable the more firms engaged in off-balance sheet securitisations. Dechow *et al.*'s "discussions with debt rating agencies also suggest that in evaluating … risk, rating agencies would consolidate the SPE" (2010, p. 9). This valuation evidence is consistent with investors seeing banks retaining significant risks from asset transfers. However, research has not shown investors seeing "the transferred assets as continuing under the transferor's control", or that while investors became "increasingly skeptical about the value-relevance of the securitization gains as the amount of off-balance sheet debt increases", securitisation gains had no value relevance (Schipper and Yohn 2007, p. 76). As Schipper and Yohn commented, "The research on investor treatment of financial asset transfers, while sparse and sometimes indirect, could suggest that investors tend to view most transfers as secured borrowings, that is, the transferor still has the assets (even though transferred) and has encumbered those assets with a loan. The standard-setting implication of this interpretation, taken to its extreme, is that investors believe the transferor (1) has retained the risk/reward of the assets and presumably controls those assets and (2) has an obligation equal to the loan" (Schipper and Yohn 2007, p. 76), and should be on the balance sheet. This was necessary for accountability, but as Schipper and Yohn pointed out, for valuation it was not that simple: "the transferor has, typically, sold *something*, even if not the entire bundle of risks and rewards that comprise the asset. Specifically, even if the transferor has retained a significant subordinated interest in the transferred assets, it no longer has control of the cash flows of those assets (they are paid first to the investors in the transferred assets)" (2007, p. 76). In addition, "a transferor that retains a subordinated interest in order to absorb most or all of the credit risk … does not have a liability. Rather, it has a potentially low-value asset. Finally, even a transfer of receivables with full recourse does not constitute a present obligation of the transferor to repay the entire loan — the investors must look first to the transferred assets" (Schipper and Yohn 2007, p. 76).

Deep capital market scepticism of QSPE accounting is inconsistent with investors accepting large management bonuses based on it, which were followed by large losses in 2007–2008, but "no executives have been forced to pay back bonuses based on earnings inflated by securitization 'gains'" (Dechow *et al.* 2010, p. 4), because clawback would have been difficult. Executives were following rules based on the decision-usefulness objective, and cancelling the bonuses would require retrospective acceptance of the stewardship objective against which there were no "gains". Evidently, "One of the major issues related to securitization transactions is the lack of information available to investors about the nature and the risk that is undertaken by banks" (Cerbioni *et al.* 2015, p. 160), but they complained loudly about this only after the crisis began, and never demanded accountability information. With hindsight, "The near-absence of information available has made it difficult for banks' and for SPEs' investors to *control and discipline* the process of originating and securitizing risky loans" (Cerbioni *et al.* 2015, p. 160, emphasis added). As Barth and Landsman put it, the "transparency of information associated with measurement and recognition of accounting amounts related to, and disclosure of information about, asset securitizations and derivatives likely *were insufficient* for investors to assess properly the values and riskiness of affected bank assets and liabilities" (2010, p. 401). After the credit-crunch, "Bernanke (2009) criticize[d] the 'lack of transparency' of 'certain innovative products'" (Cerbioni *et al.* 2015, p. 165). According to Cerbioni *et al.* (2015, p. 166), securitisation accounting played three roles "in hiding these risks" (1) by "bypass[ing] risk-based capital adequacy requirements" (discussed in what follows), (2) by "making the financial institution appear wealthy and less risky", and (3) by "inadequate disclosure and representation" of the "banks' exposure to risk", but (1) and (2) are the consequences of non-Marxist accounting. Information for valuation may have been insufficient, but the necessary accountability information did not exist: "required disclosures during our sample period do not provide sufficient information to reconsolidate the receivables and loans, and are therefore not sufficient to undo the accounting" (Dechow *et al.* 2010, p. 19).

Dechow *et al.* (2010, p. 23) recognise their "research raises questions about the appropriateness of the accounting for asset securitizations required by SFAS 140", but from their valuation perspective "Asset derecognition is a difficult conceptual issue (Schipper and Yohn 2007)". The key difficulty for Schipper and Yohn (2007, p. 60) was reconciling the FASB's and IASB's derecognition models, the "divergent concepts and approaches" of FAS 140 which "is based on the surrender of control, while the approach taken in IAS No. 39 is based on the transfer of substantially all risks and rewards". Only a few papers analyse the role of the accounting rules in the securitisation market — Ryan (2008), Barth and Landsman (2010), Kothari and Lester (2012) and Cerbioni *et al.* (2015) — but all assume the valuation objective, and none reconciles "control" with "risks and rewards". Many banks had "practical difficulties" implementing FAS 140, Ryan argues, but "the subprime crisis was caused by firms, investors, and households making bad operating, investing, and financing decisions, managing risks poorly and in some instances committing fraud, not by accounting" (2008, pp. 1,607, 1,609). Barth and Landsman (2010), we saw, criticise disclosures for valuation. Kothari and Lester argue, "Unfortunately, gains generated from securitization of the home loans and from income on the servicing of the loans inflated financial profits, motivating executives of mortgage origination firms to focus on quantity, rather than quality, of borrowers" (2012, p. 336). The gains were "unfortunate" because, according to Kothari and Lester, "income and gains recorded on the securitization transactions inflate earnings and overstated asset balances" (2012, p. 340), that is, were the consequence of not fully applying fair value accounting. They ask, "How is it possible that the sale of an asset originally recorded at one value could generate income and higher asset balances upon merely transferring this asset to another entity? This proposition seems contrary to the economic substance underlying the related transactions, but was the direct result of applying the fair value standards" (2012, p. 340). If the asset had been at "fair value" before the transfer no "gain" was possible, so those reported were partly "incorrect estimates" or not establishing "sufficient loan loss reserves" (Kothari and Lester 2012, p. 343). Thus, "the misapplication of the U.S. accounting standards had some role in the financial crisis" because the "financial statements would not accurately reflect the underlying economics of the securitization transaction" (Kothari and Lester 2012, p. 336), were inadequate for valuation. Cerbioni *et al.* (2015) extend this line of research by arguing that the "interplay" between banking regulations and accounting rules contributed to the crisis.

The underlying cause of crises according to Marx's theory is the falling rate of profit, but "swindling" is directly causal in triggering a financial crisis, stems from an accountability failure. From the valuation perspective, however, accounting is only one source of information and therefore has no directly causal role in crises. Cerbioni *et al.* (2015, p. 156) do not, therefore, claim any direct accounting causality: "we do not aim at demonstrating any causal relation between securitization and the financial crisis, rather we offer several stimuli for reflection about the interplay between accounting rules and bank regulations that might have offered opportunities for opportunistic behavior". By keeping assets and liabilities off-balance sheet, researchers were aware, "banks might securitize assets to manage their regulatory capital" (Schipper and Yohn 2007, p. 69); reduce it to increase the reported rate of profit. Although not necessarily "primarily motivated by the desire to minimize regulatory capital" (Schipper and Yohn 2007, p. 69), as Cerbioni *et al.* say, "If securitization accounting is the tool banks used to transfer risk to outside investors and hide the corresponding risk, regulatory capital regulation provides part of the incentive to do so" (2015, p. 169). They conclude, "the combination of incentives stemming from accounting rules and bank regulation led to a banking business model that introduced high risks to the financial system and that obfuscated the transparency of financial transactions" (Cerbioni *et al.* 2015, p. 155). Not the accounting rules directly, but the business model they and banking regulations fostered, which the banks then applied to more risky loans, without adequate disclosure. Many accept, "The primary contribution of securitization to the financial crisis was to boost the US subprime mortgage market", but whether because "Securitization significantly increased banks' ability and willingness to grant subprime loans since, by securitizing their originated loans, banks could get rid of the associated risk" (Cerbioni *et al.* 2015, p. 158), is debatable.

According to Ryan, "Since early 1995, if not before, bankers and others have used 'subprime' to refer to less than highly creditworthy assets (e.g., subprime mortgages) that yield higher interest rates than do prime assets with similar non-credit risks" (2008, p. 1,609). Previously, "subprime" referred to low risk corporate loans that yielded less than the "prime rate" (Ryan 2008, p. 1,609). The change occurred when "securitization and other markets to sell or transfer the credit risk of credit-risky assets had begun to develop in earnest" (Ryan 2008, p. 1,609), from the mid-1990s, following FAS 125, particularly for mortgages and car loans. These markets developed rapidly, but by 2003, boosting subprime home loans became critical to financial institutions bent on reporting earnings growth because prime mortgage originations and securitisations had peaked (Ryan 2008, p. 1,610). As the prime market hit a plateau, "many large commercial banks changed their strategic focus to retail banking, including subprime mortgage banking", and "Mortgage originators and securitizers that had become accustomed to high volume then turned to subprime mortgages" (Ryan 2008, p. 1,610). Thus, whereas the proportion

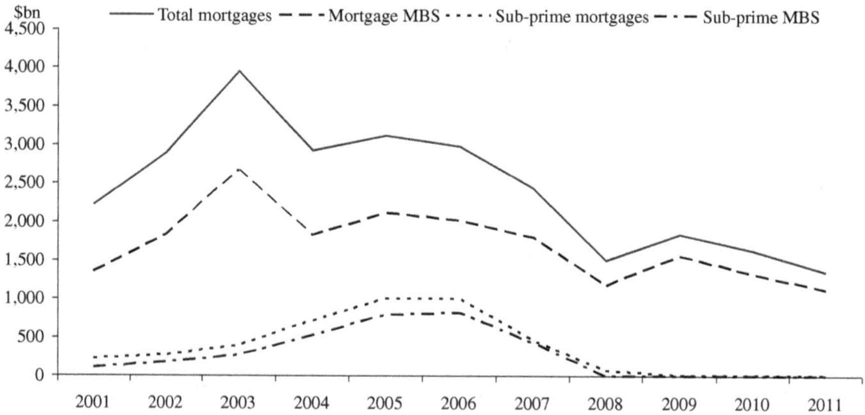

Figure 8.2: Total and Subprime Home Mortgage Originations and Securitisations

Source: Cerbioni *et al.* (2015, Table 1, p. 159).

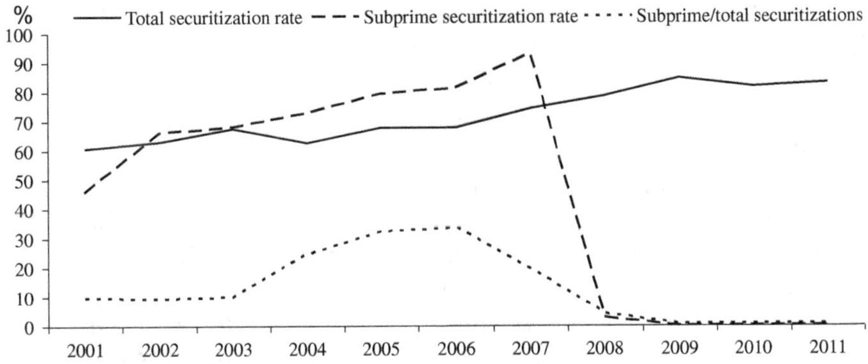

Figure 8.3: Relative Subprime Securitisation Rates

Source: Cerbioni *et al.* (2015, Table 1, p. 159).

of total securitisations remained steady, bankers targeted subprime mortgage securitisations that increased markedly to 2007, their rate of securitisation increasing to high levels (Figures 8.2 and 8.3). Figures 8.2 and 8.3 are consistent with intensifying accounting swindling from 2003 to sustain the mortgage market encouraged by the FASB's reaffirmation of QSPEs, for "gains". There was "Moral hazard and adverse selection in the subprime mortgage market", but directly linked to accounting because allowing off-balance sheet securitisations "created strong incentives for banks to focus on subprime and risky loans" (Cerbioni *et al.* 2015, p. 160). Driving these bankers' behaviour was not regulations or their "business model", but the lure of reporting increased "income" and its benefits. As Cerbioni *et al.* say, "banks could gain substantially more income by selling subprime loans to be securitized into private-label MBS than selling prime loans to be securitized into agency MBS" (2015, p. 160). Swindling occurred in other important credit markets for the same accounting reason, with the same results. This was true particularly for "commercial mortgages and leveraged loans … [where] the extensive use of securitization practices has resulted in a steady decrease in the credit standards required by banks for granting loans, thus creating a credit boom that has been followed by many defaults" (Cerbioni 2015, p. 158). Dechow *et al.* found most securitisations in the financial sector, but "approximately 41 percent of sample firms are from other industries where firms securitize a range of financial assets including store credit cards … and automobile loans and leases" (2010, p. 10).

Other elements of the "money machine" also participated in the swindle. The rating agencies' assumptions were "too optimistic, and the assigned ratings did not reflect the underlying economic risk" (Cerbioni *et al.* 2015, p. 160; Kothari and Lester 2012, p. 336), but if they were sceptical of QSPE accounting, high ratings were unscrupulous. Furthermore, "subscribers had conflicting incentives. They had to undertake accurate due diligence of the financial products subscribed in order to understand the risks ..., but during the ABS boom, they were also able to sell to outside investors the riskiest ABS tranches and avoid bearing any significant part of the risk" (Cerbioni *et al.* 2015, p. 159). This anti-social behaviour, Cerbioni *et al.* implicitly accept, was an accounting effect: "As a consequence, they started cutting costs and enhancing profit by undertaking quick and superficial due diligence, thus imposing huge risks on investors who were actually buying black-box ABSs" (2015, p. 159). However, their critique remains implicit because rather than accountability, trapped within the decision-usefulness framework, they call for "accounting rules that permit [investors] to capture the risk associated with the transactions and operations" (Cerbioni *et al.* 2015, p. 173).

IFRSs versus US GAAP

The BIS observed, "Generally, off-balance sheet treatment is easier to achieve under US GAAP than under IFRS" (2009, p. 2). IFRSs were more effective in limiting off-balance sheet treatment (Adhikari and Betancourt 2008; Cerbioni *et al.* 2015) — that is, according to Marxian accounting, less prone to swindling — which is consistent with IFRSs containing Marxian elements, their legal control focus. Compared to IFRSs, US GAAP made it "easier" to derecognise asset transfers to QSPEs and other SPEs, and avoid consolidation (Adhikari and Betancourt 2008; Cerbioni *et al.* 2015). "Even when banks were not able to create a QSPE, it was sufficient to create a VIE in which the transferor did not hold most of the risks and benefits associated to the entity" (Cerbioni *et al.* 2015, p. 165). According to Cerbioni *et al.*, "from a practical viewpoint, there were no substantial differences in the level of difficulty in derecognizing assets under the two accounting regimes; the real differences were those linked to the consolidation of SPEs, that was easier to avoid under US GAAP" (Cerbioni *et al.* 2015, p. 165). Cerbioni *et al.* (2015) overlook that under IAS 39, paragraph 20(c), "if the entity neither transfers nor retains substantially all the risks and rewards of ownership of the financial asset, the entity shall determine whether it has retained control of the financial asset". IAS 39's Guidance Note explained, "An entity has not retained control of a transferred asset if the transferee has the practical ability to sell the transferred asset". It was "only if the transferee can sell the transferred asset in its entirety to an unrelated third party and is able to exercise that ability unilaterally and without imposing additional restrictions on the transfer" (IASB 2003, paragraphs AG42-AG43). "Because SPEs are not allowed to sell transferred assets", on this test, as Adhikari and Betancourt say, "the outcome in most securitizations will be the determination that the transferor has retained control" (2008, p. 81). Inconsistently, however, another derecognition test under IAS 39 (paragraphs 20 (a)–(b)) was "the principle that a transferor should not retain substantially all the risk and rewards of the cash flows relating to a transferred asset" (BIS 2009, p. 76), which banks could easily arrange.

Under IAS 39 transferors could recognise "profit", but only in the parent's accounts because IAS 39 required management to consider consolidation before derecognition (Cerbioni *et al.* 2015, p. 162), and consolidation of SPEs was more likely under IFRSs than US GAAP because their foundation was legal control. Under US GAAP, traditionally dominated by the parent's accounts, the "parent extension" concept of consolidation (Bryer 2021b), "the sequential logic is reversed because the originator first eliminates from its individual balance sheet the assets that meet the derecognition criteria, and then evaluates whether the SPE must be consolidated" (Cerbioni *et al.* 2015, p. 162), which FAS 140 removed for QSPEs. Legal control, the International Accounting Standards Committee (IASC) discovered when preparing IAS 3 *Consolidated Financial Statements* (IASC 1976) was the core meaning in several continental European countries. It considered whether to require a majority of voting rights, which the chair of the steering committee responsible thought was "unambiguous", or "whether a more general definition should be used based on control of the financial and operating policies of the subsidiary", prevailing practice in "several European countries" (Camfferman and Zeff 2007, pp. 99–100). IAS 3 influenced the EU's Seventh Directive (1983) on consolidated accounts, which in turn influenced the IASC's IAS 27 *Consolidated and Separate Financial Statements* (1989), which it wrote in consultation with the EU (Camfferman and Zeff 2007, p. 268). IAS 27 applied to "the preparation and presentation of consolidated financial statements for a group of entities under the control of a parent" (IASC 1989, paragraph 1). Although it defined "control" as "the power to govern the financial and operating policies of an entity so as to obtain benefits from its activities" (IASC 1989, paragraph 4), leaving open the possibility of articulating Paton's power to direct for economic benefit (taken in IFRS 10, discussed in what follows), IAS 27's tests for control were legal. In the IASB's asset definition, "both control and expected benefits are necessary conditions ..., and ... they are separate issues" (Nobes 2014, p. 1,003). IAS 27 did not allow control through "unified management" or the "actual exercise of a dominant influence", that is, effective control, that EU rules allowed. IAS 27 "presumed" control when the parent owned, directly or indirectly through subsidiaries, more than half of the voting power of another entity. However, a minority of votes gave control, if other legal powers existed: "(a) ... an agreement with other investors; or (b) ... a statute or an agreement; or (c) power to appoint or remove the majority of the ... directors ...; or (d) power to cast the majority of votes at meetings of the directors" (IASB 1989, paragraph 19). IAS 27 (1989, 2004 and 2008) did not recognise effective or *de facto* control. To hold an agent accountable for results, according to Marxian accounting, as IAS 27 put it, the principal needs the "power to govern" the agent, the legal power, and this underlay some of SIC-12's SPE control tests.

SIC-12 Consolidation — Special Purpose Entities

Banks should have consolidated their securitisation SPEs, according to Marxian accounting, because they had legal financial results control of their SPEs, which were not "brain-dead" as they claimed. The banks' SPEs delegated operational and financial action controls, and even operational results control, to autopilot mechanisms, but they did not relinquish legal financial result control. SIC-12 (IASB 1998, paragraph 1) gave the following "indicators" of control, the first two of which are consistent with legal financial results control:

(a) in substance, the activities of the SPE are being conducted on behalf of the enterprise according to specific business needs so that the enterprise obtains benefits from the SPEs operation;
(b) in substance, the entity has the decision-making powers to obtain the majority of the benefits of the activities of the SPE or, by setting up an 'autopilot' mechanism, the enterprise has delegated decision-making powers;

(c) in substance, the entity has the rights to obtain the majority of the benefits of the SPE and therefore may be exposed to risks incident to the activities of the SPE;
(d) in substance, the entity retains the majority of the residual or ownership risks related to the SPE or its assets in order to obtain benefits from its activities.

SIC-12's appendix gave more details, but did not give a definitive test, was "not intended as a 'comprehensive checklist' of conditions that must be met cumulatively in order to require consolidation of an SPE". It required, "An SPE should be consolidated when the substance of the relationship between an enterprise and the SPE indicates that the SPE is controlled by that enterprise" (IASB 1998, paragraph 8). "An individual criterion by itself may not necessarily indicate control, but rather all the indicators and any other relevant facts and circumstances need to be assessed in balance when assessing control of an SPE" (BIS 2009, p. 76), which allowed some discretion, but tests (a) and (b) are consistent with legal financial results control, and if met could not be ignored.

The banks' SPEs met test (a) because they were businesses, a type of "virtual bank" with capital that circulated and made the banks profits. For example, "structured investment vehicles", invented by Citigroup in 1988, made profits by borrowing short term and lending in longer term securities at a higher rate of interest, which they paid to the capital noteholders and to the investment manager, and profits for the bank from fees and pricing the repacked long-term debt. Banks retained significant interests in the results of their SPEs and often gave them credit enhancement. How integral the SPEs were to banks' financial performance is clear from the rapid closure of some during the credit-crunch and from the willingness of others to intervene to bail them out when they got into difficulty, even though they had no legal obligation. The banks' SPEs also met test (b) because they delegated decision-making powers to an "autopilot". The banks retained legal financial results controls over the SPE's operations because they retained the legal power to judge their performance. They retained the power to close the SPE, that is, to punish it, according to its performance. In short, according to these tests the banks, etc., had legal financial results control of SPEs built into their action controls, and should have consolidated them.

Tests (c) and (d), based on "risks and rewards", by contrast, allowed discretion and could easily be met (Adhikari and Betancourt 2008), but they could not be considered in isolation. Overall, after applying SIC-12's control tests, many European banks consolidated their securitisation SPEs even though they may have recognised "sales" and "profit" in the parent's accounts, which increased their distributable reserves. SIC-12 and IAS 39's combined effect "may be that … a securitisation … qualifies as a sale …; but … the 'buyer' is an SPE, so that the asset is immediately re-recognized through consolidation" (Ernst & Young 2009, p. 407). SIC-12's strength, the BIS observed, was that it was "written as an anti-abuse measure to prevent entities from manipulating financial statements through the use of financial engineering … [which] results in consolidation of many vehicles that would have otherwise resulted in off-balance sheet treatment" (BIS 2009, p. 76), largely because of its Marxian content. Predictably, despite its relatively robust performance, following the GFC, revealing the conceptual limits to reform, the IASB abolished SIC-12's Marxian content.

Conceptual Limits to Reform

Under domestic and global fire, in *Preliminary Views* on *The Reporting Entity* (2008) the FASB disowned FAS 140's "control" approach, and with the IASB reformed SPE accounting. As a result, Cerbioni *et al.* argue, "US GAAP … [has] become more similar to IFRS" (2015, p. 171). However, by dropping its focus on legal control and making its latent commitment to Paton's asset definition explicit, IFRS has become more similar to US GAAP, which has become more similar to IFRS by also making Paton's definition explicit. The GFC "cast severe doubt on the appropriateness of securitization accounting", which "led standard-setters to rethink the accounting standards" (Cerbioni *et al.* 2015, p. 171), but the boards remained trapped within Fisher's framework.

In 2008, the FASB decided to abolish QSPEs. Some argued all SPEs should be subject to FIN 46(R)'s "majority of risk and/or reward" approach, in effect, for retaining Canning's "control" definition as access to cash flows, and leaving implicit Paton's definition of control of use-values. Herz (2008, p. 61) argued, "If you do away with the Q, you're left with just the regular SPE that doesn't get his kind of hallway pass, and the rules there are called FASB Interpretation No. 46(R). … And I think they're an OK set of rules". The FASB, however, adopted the British Accounting Standards Board's definition as its "working definition", in effect, Paton's definition. "Control of an entity is the ability to direct the financing and operating policies of an entity, so as to access benefits from that entity (or to reduce the incidence of losses) and increase, maintain or protect the amount of those benefits (or reduce the amount of those losses)" (FASB 2008, paragraph 49).

The FASB tentatively decided, while "there is some overlap between the controlling entity model and the risks and rewards model" (2008, paragraph 103) — because the "controlling entity model" required exposure to benefits (and losses) — the "risk and rewards model" itself "does not provide a conceptually robust basis for determining the composition of a group reporting entity" (2008, paragraph 104). It admitted, "The basic idea is so broad that in order to place what seem like reasonable and necessary limits on which entities should be included in the group, it would be necessary to develop criteria that would involve drawing some bright lines, such as the minimum level of exposure to risks or entitlement to rewards". FAS 166 eliminated QSPEs, but FAS 140's derecognition criteria remain substantially the same (FASB 2009a; Cerbioni *et al.* 2015, p. 172). Having "killed Q's", in FAS 167 the FASB decided to stay with ARB 51's "voting interest model", but revised FIN 46(R), bringing Paton's definition of control, the "power to direct", to the surface. It "replace[d] the quantitative-based risks and rewards calculation … with an approach focused on identifying which enterprise has the power to direct the activities of a variable interest entity that most significantly impact the entity's economic performance and (1) the obligation to absorb losses of the entity or (2) the right to receive benefits from the entity" (FASB 2009b, p. 3). Like Paton's entity concept in which management's judgements are dominant, according to the FASB, "An approach that is expected to be primarily qualitative", that is, based on management's judgements, "will be more effective for identifying which enterprise has a controlling financial interest in a variable interest entity" (2009b, p. 3).

In 2008, the IASB set off down the same conceptual road, but produced its own version. The uncertainties whether an entity "controls" and should consolidate under IAS 27 and SIC-12, it concluded, required an improved definition to remove "inconsistencies", even though many argued SIC-12 had performed well. Unlike IAS 27's legal focus, like the FASB's reforms, the IASB took the opportunity to, in effect, embrace and articulate IAS 27's implicit acceptance of Paton definition, defining "control" as the "link" between the "power to direct" and "exposure to variable returns" to require consolidation for "effective control". Despite many criticisms, the IASB issued *IFRS 10: Consolidated Financial Statements* in 2011, applying its control definition to all aspects of consolidations, including SPEs. Like FAS 167, the IASB's definition has created a complex standard requiring many management judgements, which accountants have warned will be "challenging" to apply (e.g., Ernst & Young 2011).

Concluding Comments

The underlying cause of the GFC was the falling rate of profit, but SPE accounting based on Paton and Canning's interpretations of Fisher's economic entity concept facilitated the 2007 credit-crunch that triggered it. SPE accounting history illustrates the incoherence of the FASB's framework, its failure to deal with securitisation transactions that became "the engine of financial innovation in the pre-crisis years", following its publication in the 1980s, and capital market deregulation, that "gave rise to exotic financial instruments ... [on] commercial and investment bank balance sheets" (Cerbioni *et al.* 2015, p. 155), and the consequences. The incoherence of the FASB's framework is not just that it incorporates both Paton and Canning's definitions. Stuck within Fisher's ideologically distorted, managerial conception of economic society, developed as a critique of Marx, the framework does not reflect the social reality that to prevent accounting swindling from triggering financial crises, management must be accountable to capitalists, current and prospective shareholders, the capital market, for ROI. This, however, would promote the LTFRP, and as there are many other non-accounting sources of swindling possible in modern capitalism, crises would not end even in this unlikely scenario.

Consistent with an inchoate Marxian critique, considering the FASB's record, Turner (2008) doubted the likelihood of effective reform. As he put it, although the FASB and IASB "are working to fix those standards and bring all those off-balance sheet things that have been hidden from view back into full view of investors and the capital markets ... [, u]nfortunately, the FASB has done this about five or six times before" (Turner 2008, np). Apparently sceptical that the FASB's framework would produce the desired result, Turner concluded, "If they aren't successful this time, then, because of the devastation this has wrought on the markets and the economy, I think legislators would be well-served to step in and pass legislation that would require this to be on-balance sheet" (2008, np). Marxian accounting supports Turner's demand that securitisation SPEs should be on balance sheet, and predicts that the FASB and IASB's reforms will not hold management accountable for all the capital it controls through them.

Conclusions

The accounting interpretation of Marx's theory of crises adds to Marxist explanations based on the falling rate of profit (Kliman 2012, Roberts 2016). The historical evidence supports the hypothesis that Fisher's theory framed accounting theorists during the 1920s, which facilitated the 1929 crash and aggravated the Great Depression, and underlies the FASB's framework, which allowed US banks' off-balance sheet accounting for securitization SPEs, which facilitated the 2008–2009 GFC. The history of American accounting theory from c. 1900 to 2007 shows the capture by Fisher's theory of academics, the profession and the capital market, which has prevented accounting reflecting social reality, thus facilitating and aggravating crises. Fisher's theory hinders socially rational accounting because he constructed it as a critique of Marx, an aim that, however inchoately, accounting theorists have supported through their hostility to the "cost theory of value". This hostility, which has no intellectual justification, *Creating the "Big Mess" and Accounting for Crises* have argued, explains why there is no coherent and generally accepted theory of accounting. The history of financial reporting during the 1920s and 1930s reveals the pathological consequences of accounting theory, and the history of SPE accounting from the 1980s illustrates the incoherence of the FASB's framework, which allows divergent interpretations, and its dependence on Paton and Canning shows that accounting theory has not progressed for the last c. 100 years. SPE accounting is one of many examples of how financial accounting has become more dependent on management's judgements, which with a low or falling rate of profit means it is a matter of time before the opportunities for "swindling" available within US GAAP and IFRSs facilitate and aggravate the next financial crisis.

Crises will show workers why, as Marx put it, capitalism must "be gone, and make way for a higher form". Finding that rational accounting has become impossible within capitalist society makes it all the more clear that it should make way for socialism within which it is possible (Bryer 2019, Chapter 8; 2021c). To get there will require critical accountants to provide a historical, social and political critique of all aspects of financial reporting, its concepts, practices and consequences, and develop Marxian accounting founded on a logical and empirically verified theory of value. *Creating the "Big Mess"* and *Accounting for Crises* have used Marx's theory of capitalism, particularly his theory of value as the "essence" of its social relations, to explain Marxian accounting for several accounting issues, ranging from fundamental concepts and principles to their application to specific forms of capital, but much more critical accounting work remains. Completing it will require a concerted, collective effort. Accounting historians and critical accountants have enthusiastically embraced a wide range of social theorists to explain accounting theories and practices (Carnegie *et al.* 2021), and engaged with the world to change it (Bryer 2019, Chapter 9). In the face of 100-years of unanswered criticism of his theory of value, based on Bortkiewicz's claim that his value-price transformation is "inconsistent", scholars have understandably neglected Marx. Building on the TSSI's refutation (Kliman 2007; Bryer 2017, 2022a), accounting historians and critical accountants should give Marx's theory a fair hearing by engaging in "Marxist" accounting history and "Marxian" accounting theory and practice, to test further its coherence and empirical relevance.

Accounting is central to our capitalist world and its functioning. To understand and control it we must explain accounting history as a central element of world history (Bryer 2019), and explain capitalist accounting as a critical element in its functioning, for which researchers need a theory of value (Bryer 2017, 2021a). Today, there are only two contending theories, the neoclassical economists' market price or PV, or Marx's theory of value. Accounting researchers must choose. Armies of neoclassical economists have failed to find a coherent and generally accepted theory of accounting. The army of critical accountants and historians has yet to mobilise around a coherent and relevant research agenda. Marxist accounting history and Marxian accounting theory could provide one.

Bibliography

Accounting Principles Board (1970). *Basic Concepts and Accounting Principles Underlying Financial Statements of Business Enterprises. Statement of the Accounting Principles Board No. 4*. New York: American Institute of Certified Public Accountants.

Accounting Standards Committee (1980). *Statement of Standard Accounting Practice No. 16, Current Cost Accounting*. London.

Accounting Standards Committee (1986). *Accounting for the Effects of Changing Prices: A Handbook*. London.

Accounting Standards Steering Committee (1973). *ED 8: Accounting for Changes in the Purchasing Power of Money*. London.

Adhikari, A. and L. Betancourt (2008). Accounting for securitizations: A comparison of SFAS 140 and IASB 39. *Journal of International Financial Management and Accounting*, 19(1), 73–105.

Agrawal, S. (1987). On the conceptual framework of accounting. *Journal of Accounting Literature*, 6, 165–178.

Alexander, S.S. (1950). Income measurement in a dynamic economy, *Five Monographs on Business Income*. Study Group on Business Income. New York: American Institute of Accountants.

Allen, R.L. (1993). *Irving Fisher: A Biography*. Oxford: Blackwell.

American Accounting Association (1936a). A statement of objectives of the American Accounting Association. *The Accounting Review*, 11(1), 1–4.

American Accounting Association (1936b). A tentative statement of accounting principles affecting corporate reports. *The Accounting Review*, 11(2), 187–191.

American Accounting Association (1955). Standards of Disclosure for Published Financial Reports: Supplementary Statement No. 8, Committee on Concepts and Standards Underlying Corporate Financial Statements. *The Accounting Review*, 30(3), 400–404.

American Accounting Association (1957). *Accounting and Reporting Standards for Corporate Financial Statements and Preceding Statements and Supplements*. Madison, WI: American Accounting Association.

American Accounting Association (1965). Concepts and Standards Research Study Committee — The Business Entity Concept, 'The Entity Concept'. *The Accounting Review*, 40(2), 358–367.

American Accounting Association (1966). *A Statement of Basic Accounting Theory*. Evanston, IL: American Accounting Association.

American Accounting Association (1971). The role of the American Accounting Association in the development of accounting principles. *The Accounting Review*, 46(3), 609–616.

American Accounting Association (1977). *Statement on Accounting Theory and Theory Acceptance. Committee on Concepts and Standards for External Financial Reports*. Sarasota, FL: American Accounting Association.

American Accounting Association Financial Accounting Standards Committee (2003). Comments on the FASB's Proposals on Consolidating Special-Purpose Entities and Related Standard-Setting Issues. *Accounting Horizons*, 17(2), 161–173.

American Institute of Accountants (1934). *Audits of Corporate Accounts*. New York.

American Institute of Accountants (1939). Accounting Research Bulletin No. 1, *General Introduction and Rules Formerly Adopted*. New York: Committee on Accounting Procedure.

American Institute of Accountants (1949). Accounting Research Bulletin No. 38, *Disclosure of Long-Term Leases in Financial Statements of Lessees*. New York: Committee on Accounting Procedure.

American Institute of Accountants (1953). Restatement and Revision of Accounting Research Bulletins, *Accounting Research Bulletin, No. 43*. New York: Committee on Accounting Procedure.

American Institute of Certified Public Accountants (1959). Accounting Research Bulletin No. 51, *Consolidated Financial Statements*. New York: Committee on Accounting Procedure.

American Institute of Certified Public Accountants (1963). Accounting Research Study No. 6, *Reporting the Financial Effects of Price-Level Changes*. New York.

American Institute of Certified Public Accountants (1964). APB Opinion No. 2, *Accounting for the Investment Credit*. New York: Accounting Principles Board.

American Institute of Certified Public Accountants (1964). APB Opinion No. 5, *Reporting of Leases in Financial Statements of Lessees*. New York: Accounting Principles Board.

American Institute of Certified Public Accountants (1966). *APB Opinion No. 7, Accounting for Leases in Financial Statements of Lessors*. New York: Accounting Principles Board.

American Institute of Certified Public Accountants (1967). (APB) Opinion 11, *Accounting for Income Taxes*. New York: Accounting Principles Board.

American Institute of Certified Public Accountants (1970a). (APB) Opinion 16, *Business Combinations*. New York: Accounting Principles Board.

American Institute of Certified Public Accountants (1970b). Accounting Principles Board (APB) Opinion 17, *Goodwill*. New York: Accounting Principles Board.

American Institute of Certified Public Accountants (1972). Establishing Financial Accounting Standards. Report of the Study Group on Establishment of Accounting Principles. New York: American Institute of Certified Public Accountants.

American Institute of Certified Public Accountants (1973). *Report of the Study Group on the Objectives of Financial Statements*. New York: American Institute of Certified Public Accountants.

American Institute of Certified Public Accountants (1974). *Objectives of Financial Statements*, Volume 2, selected papers. New York: American Institute of Certified Public Accountants.

Anthony, R.N. (1987). We don't have the accounting concepts we need. *Harvard Business Review*, January–February, 76–83.

Anton, H.R. (1976). Objectives of financial accounting: Review and analysis. *Journal of Accountancy*, 141(1), 40–51.

Archer, G.S.H. and A. Steele (1984). The implementation of SSAP16, Current Cost Accounting, by UK listed companies. In *Current Cost Accounting: The Benefits and Costs*, B. Carsberg and M. Page (eds.). London: Institute of Chartered Accountants in England and Wales.

Armstrong, M.S. (1977). The politics of establishing accounting standards. *Journal of Accountancy*, 143(2), 76–79.

Arnold, P.J. (2009). Global financial crisis: The challenge to accounting research. *Accounting, Organizations and Society*, 34, 803–809.

Ayres, F.L. (1993). Review of Gore, P. 1992. *The FASB Conceptual Framework Project 1973–1985, An Analysis*. Manchester: Manchester University Press. *Accounting Review*, 68(4), 992–993.

Bank for International Settlements (2009). *Report on Special Purpose Entities*. Basel Committee on Banking Supervision.

Bank of England (1982). Current Cost Accounting, *Bank of England Quarterly Bulletin*, 376–381.

Baran, P.A. and P.M. Sweezy (1968). *Monopoly Capital: An Essay on the American Economic and Social Order*. Harmondsworth: Penguin Books.

Barnes, A.J., T.M. Dworkin and J.D. Richards (2006). *Law for Business*, 9th Edn. New York: McGraw-Hill/Irwin.

Barr, A. (1940). Accounting research in the Securities and Exchange Commission. *The Accounting Review*, 15(1), 89–94.

Barth, M.E. and W.R. Landsman (2010). How did financial reporting contribute to the financial crisis? *European Accounting Review*, 19(3), 399–423.

Baxter, W.T. (1967). Accounting values: Sale price versus replacement cost. *Journal of Accounting Research*, 5(2), 208–214.

Beaver, W.H. (1973). What should be the FASB's objectives? *Journal of Accountancy*, 136(2), 49–56.

Beaver, W.H. (1989). *Financial Reporting: An Accounting Revolution*, 2nd Edn. Englewood Cliffs, NJ: Prentice-Hall International, Inc.

Beaver, W.H. and J.S. Demski (1974). The nature of financial accounting objectives: A summary and synthesis. *Journal of Accounting Research*, 12, 170–187.

Beaver, W.H. and W.R. Landsman (1983). *Incremental Information Content of Statement 33 Disclosures*. FASB.

Benston, G.J. and A.L. Hartgraves (2002). Enron: What happened and what we can learn from it. *Journal of Accounting and Public Policy*, 21(2), 105–127.

Beresford, D.R. (1983). Observations on the FASB's conceptual framework. In *Dr Scott Memorial Lectures in Accountancy, Volume XII*, R. Elam (ed.), pp. 53–69. Curators of the University of Missouri.

Beresford, D.R. (1990). What's right with the FASB: Controversy seems to be part of the process. *Journal of Accountancy*, 169(1), 81–85.

Berle, A.A. (1926). Protection of non-voting stock. *Harvard Business Review*, 4(3), 257–265.

Berle, A.A. (1927). Management power and stockholders' property. *Harvard Business Review*, 5(4), 424–432.

Berle, A.A. (1932). For whom corporate managers are trustees: A note. *Harvard Law Review*, 45, 1365–1372.

Berle, A.A. (1933). High finance: Master or servant. *Yale Review*, 23, 20–43.

Berle, A.A. (1938). Accounting and the law. *The Journal of Accountancy*, 65(5), 368–378.

Berle, A.A. (1968). In *Preface to the Revised Edition*. Berle, A.A. and G.C. Means (eds.). *The Modern Corporation and Private Property*, pp. xix–xxxix. New York: Macmillan.

Berle A.A. and F.S. Fisher Jr. (1932). Elements of the law of business accounting. *Columbia Law Review*, 32(4), 573–622.

Berle, A.A. and G.C. Means (1932). *The Modern Corporation and Private Property*. New York: Macmillan.

Berliner, R.W. (1983). Do analysts use inflation-adjusted information? Results of a survey. *Financial Analysts Journal*, March/April, 65–72.

Bernstein, M.A. (1987). *The Great Depression: Delayed Recovery and Economic Change in America, 1929–1939*. Cambridge: Cambridge University Press.

Bevis, H.W. (1965). *Corporate Financial Reporting in a Competitive Economy*. London: Collier-Macmillan.

Blough, C.G. (1937). The need for accounting principles. *The Accounting Review*. 12(1), 30–37.

Blough, C.G. (1939). Accounting reports and their meaning to the public. *Journal of Accountancy*, 68(3), 162–168.

Bonbright, J.C. (1937). *The Valuation of Property: A Treatise on the Appraisal of Property for Different Legal Purposes*. New York: McGraw-Hill Book Company, Inc.

Bonbright, J.C. and G.C. Means (1932). *The Holding Company: Its Public Significance and Its Regulation*. New York and London: McGraw-Hill Book Company.

Bond, F.D. (1930). *Stock Movements and Speculation*. New York: D. Appleton and Company.

Bortkiewicz, L. von. (1906–1907). Value and price in the Marxian system. *International Economic Papers*, 2, 5–60.

Brody, D. (1980). *Workers in Industrial America: Essays on the Twentieth Century Struggle*. New York and Oxford: Oxford University Press.

Brown, S.J. W.N. Goetzmann and A. Kumar (1998). The Dow Theory: William Peter Hamilton's track record reconsidered. *The Journal of Finance*, 58(4), 1311–1333.

Brown, W.W. (1980). Industry and the conceptual framework. *Journal of Accountancy*, 150(2), 43–47.

Bryer, R.A. (1994). Why Marx's labour theory is superior to the marginalist theory of value: The case from modern financial reporting. *Critical Perspectives on Accounting*, 5(4), 313–340.

Bryer, R.A. (2000). The history of accounting and the transition to capitalism in England – Part one: Theory. *Accounting Organizations and Society*, 25(2), 131–162.

Bryer, R.A. (2006). Accounting and control of the labour process. *Critical Perspectives on Accounting*, 17(5), 551–598.

Bryer, R.A. (2012). Americanism and financial accounting theory. Part 1: Was America born capitalist? *Critical Perspectives on Accounting*, 23(7/8), 511–555.

Bryer, R.A. (2013a). Americanism and financial accounting theory. Part 2: The rise of the 'modern business enterprise', America's transition to capitalism, and the genesis of management accounting. *Critical Perspectives on Accounting*, 24(4/5), 273–318.

Bryer, R.A. (2013b). Americanism and financial accounting theory. Part 3: Adam Smith, the rise and fall of socialism, and Irving Fisher's theory of accounting. *Critical Perspectives on Accounting*, 24(7/8), 572–615.

Bryer, R.A. (2016). Socialism, accounting and the creation of "consensus capitalism" in America, circa. 1935–1955. *Critical Perspectives on Accounting*, 34(1), 1–35.

Bryer, R.A. (2017). *Accounting for Value in Marx's Capital: The Invisible Hand.* Lanham, MD: Lexington Books.

Bryer, R.A. (2019). *Accounting for History in Marx's Capital: The Missing Link.* Lanham, MD: Lexington Books.

Bryer, R.A. (2021a). *Creating the "Big Mess": A Marxist History of American Accounting Theory, c. 1900–1929.* Singapore: World Scientific Publishing.

Bryer, R.A. (2021b). The origins of modern consolidated accounts: Irving Fisher's theory of accounting and America's transition from plutocratic to advanced capitalism, c.1880–1930, Warwick Business School Working Paper.

Bryer, R.A (2021c). Why Lenin failed to implement Marx's concept of socialism: An accounting history of the Russian revolution, c. 1917–1924, *Accounting History Review*, 31(1), 29–71.

Bryer, R.A. (2022a). Dissolving the value-price transformation's Rubik's cube: A response to Steve Toms' review of *Accounting for Value. Accounting History*, 27(1), 147–152.

Bryer, R.A. (2022b). Marx's theory of crises and the railway "mania" of 1845–1846: Revisiting the "swindle hypothesis", Warwick Business School Working Paper.

Bryer, R.A. and T.J. Brignall (1986). Divestment and inflation accounting: An unemployment machine? *Capital and Class*, 10(3), 125–155.

Bush, T. (2005). *Divided by Common Language: Where Economics Meets the Law: US versus Non-US Financial Reporting Models*. London: ICAEW.

Burton, J.C. (1969). The Seaview symposium on financial reporting. *Journal of Accountancy*, 127(1), 33–38.

Burton, J.C. (1971). An educator views the public accounting profession. *Journal of Accountancy*, 132(3), 47–53.

Burton, J.C. (1973). Some general and specific thoughts on the accounting environment. *The Journal of Accountancy*, 136(4), 40–46.

Byrne, G.R. (1937). To what extent can the practice of accounting be reduced to rules and standards? *Journal of Accountancy*, 64(5), 364–379.

Camfferman, K. and S.A. Zeff (2007). *Financial Reporting and Global Capital Markets: A History of the International Accounting Standards Committee, 1973–2000.* Oxford: Oxford University Press.

Canning, J.B. (1929). *The Economics of Accountancy: A Critical Analysis of Accounting Theory*. New York: The Ronald Press Company.

Cannon, A. (1948). Danger signals to accountants in 'net lease' financing. *Journal of Accountancy*, 85(4), 812–819.

Capie, F.H. (2014). British financial crises in the nineteenth and twentieth centuries. In *British Financial Crises Since 1825*, N. Dimsdale and A. Hotson (eds.), pp. 9–23. Oxford University Press.

Carchedi, G. and M. Roberts (2018). The long roots of the present crisis: Keynesians, Austerians, and Marx's law. In *World in Crisis: A Global Analysis of Marx's Law of Profitability*, G. Carchedi and M. Roberts (eds.), pp. 13–35. Chicago: Haymarket Books.

Cardao-Pito, T. and J.S. Ferreira (2018). "Fair Value" accounting as the normative Fisherian phase of accounting. *Accounting History Review*, 28(3), 149–179.

Carey, J.L. (1938). Editorial: A statement of accounting principles. *Journal of Accountancy*, 65(3), 190–191.

Carey, J.L. (1939). Editorial: Interstate Hosiery case. *Journal of Accountancy*, 67(5), 257–258.

Carey, J.L. (1949). Editorial. Congressional committee hears accountants' views on profits. *Journal of Accountancy*, 87(1), 4–5.

Carey, J.L. (1969a). *The Rise of the Accounting Profession: From Technician to Professional, 1896–1936*. New York: American Institute of Certified Public Accountants.

Carey, J.L. (1969b). *The Rise of the Accounting Profession: To Responsibility and Authority, 1937–1969*. New York: American Institute of Certified Public Accountants.

Carey, J.L. (1979). Early encounters between CPAs and the SEC. *The Accounting Historians' Journal*, 6(1), 29–37.

Carnegie G.D., K.M. McBride and C.J. Napier (2020). Accounting history and theorising about organisations. *British Accounting Review*, 52(6), 1–17.

Carsberg, B.E. and M. Page (1984). *Current Cost Accounting: The Benefits and the Costs*. London: ICAEW/Prentice Hall.

Cerbioni, F., M. Fabrizi and A. Parbonetti (2015). Securitizations and the financial crisis: Is accounting the missing link? *Accounting Forum*, 39(3), 155–175.

Chambers, R.J. (1963). Review of Paton. W.A., *Accounting Theory with Special Reference to the Corporate Enterprise* (New York: Ronald Press, 1922, reprinted by Scholars Book Co., Lawrence: Kansas, 1962). *The Accounting Review*, 38(2), 448–449.

Chambers, R.J. (1966). *Accounting, Evaluation, and Economic Behavior*. Englewood Cliffs, NJ: Prentice Hall.

Chambers, R.J. (1975). *Accounting For Inflation, Exposure Draft*. Sydney: University of Sydney.

Chambers, R.J. (1979). Canning's *The Economics of Accountancy* — After 50 years. *The Accounting Review*, 54(4), 764–775.

Chandler A.D. Jr. (1977). *The Visible Hand: The Managerial Revolution in American Business*. Cambridge, MA: Harvard University Press.

Chatfield, M. (1977). *A History of Accounting Thought*. New York: Robert E. Krieger Publishing Company.

Chatfield, M. and R. Vangermeersch (eds.) (1996). *The History of Accounting: An International Encyclopedia*. New York: Garland Publishing Inc.

Clarke, S. (1994). *Marx's Theory of Crisis*. London: Macmillan.

Clarke, S. (2012). Crisis theory. In *The Elgar Companion to Marxist Economics*, A. Saad-Filho, B. Fine and M. Boffo (eds.), pp. 90–95. London: Edward Elgar.

Cobb, C.W. (2015). Editor's introduction: Competing theories of economic crisis. *American Journal of Economics & Sociology*, 74(2), 187–208.

Cullenberg, S. (1994). *The Falling Rate of Profit: Recasting the Marxian Debate*. London: Pluto Press.

Cyert, R.M. and Y. Ijiri (1974). A framework for developing the objectives of financial statements. In *Objectives of Financial Statements*. Vol. 2, selected papers, pp. 30–35. New York: American Institute of Certified Public Accountants.

Daines, H.C. (1929). The changing objectives of accounting. *The Accounting Review*, 4(2), 94–110.

Daley, L.A. and T. Tranter (1990). Limitations on the value of the conceptual framework in evaluating extant accounting standards. *Accounting Horizons*, 4(1), 15–24.

Daniels, M.B. (1934). *Corporation Financial Statements*. Ann Arbor: University of Michigan.

Dawley, A. (1991). *Struggles for Justice: Social Responsibility and the Liberal State*. Cambridge, Mass.: Harvard University Press.

Dechow, P.M. and C. Shakespeare (2009). Do managers time securitization transactions to obtain accounting benefits? *The Accounting Review*, 84(1), 99–132.

Dechow, P.M., L.A. Myers and C. Shakespeare (2010). Fair value accounting and gains from asset securitizations: A convenient earnings management tool with compensation side-benefits. *Journal of Accounting and Economics*, 49(1–2), 2–25.

Deloitte (2008). Business combinations and changes in ownership interests: A guide to the revised IFRS 3 and IAS 27. London.

Deloitte (2011). *iGAAP 2012: IFRS Reporting in the UK*. London: LexisNexis.

De Long, J.B. and A. Shleifer (1991). The stock market bubble of 1929: Evidence from closed-end mutual funds. *The Journal of Economic History*, 51(3), 675–700.

Demski, J.S. (1973). The general impossibility of normative accounting standards. *The Accounting Review*, 48(4), 718–723.

Demski, J.S. (1974). Choice among financial accounting alternatives. *The Accounting Review*, 49(2), 221–232.

Devine, J. (1994). The causes of the 1929–33 Great Collapse: A Marxian interpretation. *Research in Political Economy*, 14, 119–194.

Dharan, B.G. (2002). Financial engineering with special purpose entities. In *Enron Meltdown: Facts, Analysis and Recommendations*, Brazleton, J. (ed.). Commerce Clearing House.

Dicksee, L.R. (1907). *Auditing — A Practical Manual for Auditors*, 7th Edn. London: Gee & Co.

Dicksee, L.R. (1927). *Published Balance Sheets and Window Dressing*. London: Gee & Co.

Dillon, G.J. (1979). Corporate asset revaluations, 1925–1934. *The Accounting Historians' Journal*, 6(1), 1–17.

Dillon, G.J. (1984). *The Role of Accounting in the Stock Market Crash of 1929*. Atlanta: Georgia, Business Publishing Division, College of Business Administration, Georgia State University.

Dimand R.W. and J. Geanakoplos (2005). Celebrating Irving Fisher: The legacy of a great economist. In *Celebrating Irving Fisher: The Legacy of a Great Economist*, R.W. Dimand and J. Geanakoplos (eds.), pp. 3–18. Oxford: Blackwell Publishing.

Dohr, J. (1938). Income divorced from reality. *Journal of Accountancy*, 66(6), 361–371.

Dopuch, N. and S. Sunder (1980). FASB's statements on objectives and elements of financial accounting: A review. *The Accounting Review*, 55(1), 1–21.

Doron, M.E. (2011). The Colonel Carter myth and the Securities Act. Paper presented at World Congress of Accounting Historians, Newcastle University.

Doron, M.E. (2015). The Colonel Carter myth and the Securities Act: Using accounting history to establish institutional legitimacy. *Accounting History*, 20(1), 5–19.

Dreiser, T. (1932). *Tragic America*. London: Constable & Co. Ltd.

Duménil, G. and D. Lévy. (1994). *The US Economy since the Civil War: Sources and Construction of the Series*. Paris: EconomiX PSE.

Duménil, G., M. Glick and J. Rangel (1987). Theories of the Great Depression: Why did profitability matter? *Review of Radical Political Economics*, 19(2), 16–42.

Elbannan, M. and W. McKinley (2006). A theory of the corporate decision to resist FASB standards: An organization theory perspective. *Accounting, Organizations and Society*, 31, 601–622.

Edwards, E.O. and P.W. Bell (1961). *The Theory and Measurement of Business Income*. Berkeley and Los Angeles: University of California Press.

Ely, K. and G. Waymire (1999). Accounting standard-setting organizations and earnings relevance: Longitudinal evidence from NYSE common stocks, 1927–93. *Journal of Accounting Research*, 37(2), 293–317.

Ernst & Young (2009). *International GAAP 2009: Generally Accepted Accounting Practice Under International Financial Reporting Standards*. London: Wiley.

Ernst & Young (2011). *Applying IFRS: Challenges in Adopting & Applying IFRS 10*. London.

Fabricant, S. (1936). Revaluations of fixed assets, 1925–34. *National Bureau of Economic Research Bulletin*, 62 (December), 1–11.

Faulkner, H.U. (1960). *American Economic History*, 8th Edn. New York: Harper & Row Publishers.

Federal Reserve Bank of St Louis (1965). Interest rates, 1914–1965. *Review*, October, 5–12.

Fertig, P.E. (1967). A statement of basic accounting theory. *The New York Certified Public Accountant*, 37(9), 663–671.

Financial Accounting Standards Board (1974). *Exposure Draft, Financial Reporting in Units of General Purchasing Power*. Stamford, Conn.

Financial Accounting Standards Board (1976a). *Scope and Implications of the Conceptual Framework Project*. Stamford, Conn.

Financial Accounting Standards Board (1976b). Discussion Memorandum, *An Analysis of Issues Related to the Conceptual Framework for Financial Accounting and Reporting: Elements of Financial Statements and their Measurement*. Stamford, Conn.

Financial Accounting Standards Board (1976c). *Statement No. 13, Accounting for Leases*. Stamford, Conn.

Financial Accounting Standards Board (1978). *Objectives of Financial Reporting by Business Enterprises*. Statement of Financial Accounting Concepts No.1. Stamford, Conn.

Financial Accounting Standards Board (1979). *Statement No. 33, Financial Reporting and Changing Prices*. Stamford, Conn.

Financial Accounting Standards Board (1980a). *Qualitative Characteristics of Accounting Information*. Statement of Financial Accounting Concepts No. 2. Stamford, Conn.

Financial Accounting Standards Board (1980b). *Elements of Financial Statements of Business Enterprises*. Statement of Financial Accounting Concepts No. 3. Stamford, Conn.

Financial Accounting Standards Board (1983a). *Statement No. 76, Extinguishment of Debt*. Stamford, Conn.

Financial Accounting Standards Board (1983b). *Statement No. 77, Reporting by Transferors for Transfers of Receivables with Recourse*. Stamford, Conn.

Financial Accounting Standards Board (1984a). *Recognition and Measurement in Financial Statements of Business Enterprises*. Statement of Financial Accounting Concepts No. 5. Stamford, Conn.

Financial Accounting Standards Board (1984b). EITF Issue No. 84-30, *Sales of Loans to Special-Purpose Entities*. Stamford, Conn.

Financial Accounting Standards Board (1985). *Elements of Financial Statements, a replacement of FASB Concepts Statement No. 3 (incorporating an amendment of FASB Concepts Statement No. 2)*. Statement of Financial Accounting Concepts No. 6. Stamford, Conn.

Financial Accounting Standards Board (1989). EITF Topic No. D-14, *Transactions Involving Special-Purpose Entities*. Stamford, Conn.

Financial Accounting Standards Board (1990). EITF Issue No. 90-15, *Impact of Nonsubstantive Lessors, Residual Value Guarantees, and Other Provisions in Leasing Transactions*. Stamford, Conn.

Financial Accounting Standards Board (1991). *Discussion Memorandum: An Analysis of Issues Related to Consolidation Policy and Procedures*. Stamford, Conn.

Financial Accounting Standards Board (1996). *Statement No. 125, Accounting for Transfers and Servicing of Financial Assets and Extinguishments of Liabilities*. Stamford, Conn.

Financial Accounting Standards Board (2000). *Statement No. 140, Accounting for Transfers and Servicing of Financial Assets and Extinguishments of Liabilities — A Replacement of FASB Statement No. 125*. Stamford, Conn.

Financial Accounting Standards Board (2002). *Exposure Draft: Proposed Interpretation —Consolidation of Certain Special-Purpose Entities: An Interpretation of ARB No. 51*. Stamford, Conn.

Financial Accounting Standards Board (2003a). *Statement No. 140, Qualifying Special-Purpose Entities and Isolation of Transferred Assets an amendment of Statement 140*. Stamford, Conn.

Financial Accounting Standards Board (2003b). Interpretation 46R, *Consolidation of Variable Interest Entities, and Interpretation of ARB 51*. Stamford, Conn.

Financial Accounting Standards Board (2008). *Preliminary Views on Conceptual Framework for Financial Reporting: The Reporting Entity*. Stamford, Conn.

Financial Accounting Standards Board (2009a). *Statements No. 166, Accounting for Transfers of Financial Assets*. Stamford, Conn.

Financial Accounting Standards Board (2009b). *Statements No. 167, Amendments to FASB Interpretation No. 46(R)*.

Fine, B. (1975). *Marx's Capital*. London: Macmillan.

Fisher, I. (1906). *The Nature of Capital and Income*. New York: Macmillan.

Fisher, I. (1925). *Foreword* to Van Strum, K.S., *Investing in Purchasing Power*, pp. v–vii. New York: Barron's.

Fisher, I. (1930a). The economics of accountancy. *The American Economic Review*, 20(4), 603–618.

Fisher, I. (1930b). *The Stock Market Crash And After*. New York: Macmillan.

Fisher, I.N. (1956). *My Father Irving Fisher*. New York: Comet Press Books.

Flegm, E.H. (1984). *Accounting: How to Meet the Challenges of Relevance and Regulation*. New York: John Wiley & Sons.

Fogarty, T.J., M.E.A. Hussein and J.E. Ketz (1994). Political aspects of financial accounting standard setting in the USA. *Accounting, Auditing and Accountability Journal*, 7(4), 24–46.

Foley, D.K. (1986). *Understanding Capital: Marx's Economic Theory*. Cambridge, Mass.: Harvard University Press.

Fratianni, M. and F. Marchionne (2009). The role of banks in the subprime financial crisis. *Review of Economic Conditions in Italy*, 1, 11–48.

Galambos, L. and J. Pratt (1988). *The Rise of The Corporate Commonwealth*. New York: Basic Books Publishers Inc.

Galbraith, J.K. (1961). *The Great Crash 1929*. Harmondsworth: Penguin Books.

Gapper, J. (2007). Now banks must relearn their craft. *Financial Times*. London (UK), 30th July, p. 11.

Gerboth, D.L. (1973). Research, intuition, and politics in accounting inquiry. *Accounting Review*, 48(3), 475–482.

Gerboth, D.L. (1987). The conceptual framework: Not definitions, but professional values. *Accounting Horizons*, 1(3), 1–8.

Gibbs, M., K. Percy and R. Saville (1976). Sandilands and the effects on dividends. *Accountancy*, August, 62–63.

Gilman, S. (1939). *Accounting Concepts of Profit*. New York: Ronald Press.

Gore, P. (1992). *The FASB Conceptual Framework Project 1973–1985: An Analysis*. Manchester: Manchester University Press.

Gower, L.C.B (1969). *Principles of Modern Company Law*, 3rd Edn. London: Sweet & Maxwell.

Grady, P. (ed.) (1962). *Memoirs and Accounting Thought of George O. May*. New York: Ronald Press Company.

Graham, B. and D. Dodd. (1934). *Security Analysis*. New York: McGraw-Hill.

Greendlinger, L. (1917). *Financial and Business Statements*. New York: Alexander Hamilton Institute.

Greer, H.C. (1940). *Foreword* to Paton, W.A. and A.C. Littleton, *An Introduction to Corporate Accounting Standards*, pp. v–vii. Columbus, Ohio: American Accounting Association.

Greer, H.C. (1956). Benchmarks and beacons. *The Accounting Review*, 31(1), 3–14.

Guha, K. and Tett, G. (2007). Turmoil tests a system that slices up and disperses risk: Questions are being raised about the securities based global financial model. *Financial Times*. London (UK), 15th August, p. 6.

Hall, W.D. (1967). Current problems in accounting for leases. *Journal of Accountancy*, 124(5), 35–42.

Hamilton, W.P. (1922). *The Stock Market Barometer: A Study of Its Forecast Value Based on Charles H. Dow's Theory of the Price Movement*. New York: Barron's.

Hannah, L. (2007). The divorce of ownership from control in 1900: Re-calibrating imagined global historical trends. *Business History*, 49(4), 404–438.

Hanson, A.W. (1933). Review of The Modern Corporation and Private Property. Adolf A. Berle, Jr., and Gardiner C. Means. New York: The Macmillan Company, 1932. *The Accounting Review*, 8(3), 255.

Hanson, A.W. (1940). Comments on 'An Introduction to Corporate Accounting Standards'. *The Journal of Accountancy*, 69(6), 440–442.

Harvey, D. (2006). *The Limits to Capital*. Revised Edition. London: Verso.

Harvey, D. (2013). *A Companion to Marx's Capital: Volume 2*. London: Verso.

Hartgraves, A.L. and G.J. Benston (2002). The evolving accounting standards for special purpose entities and consolidations. *Accounting Horizons*, 16(3), 245–258.

Hatfield, H.R. (1909). *Modern Accounting: Its Principles and Some of Its Problems*. London: D. Appleton and Company.

Hatfield, H.R. (1927). *Accounting: Its Principles and Problems*. New York: D. Appleton-Century Company.

Hawkins, D.F. (1963). The development of modern financial reporting practices among American manufacturing companies. *The Business History Review*, 37(3), 135–168.

Heilpern, E., C. Haslam and T. Andersson (2009). When it comes to the crunch: What are the drivers of the US banking crisis? *Accounting Forum*, 33(2), 99–113.

Hendriksen, E.S. (1970). *Accounting Theory*, Revised Edition. Homewood, Illinois: Richard D. Irwin.

Hennessy, J.L. (1961). Recording of lease obligations and related property rights. *Journal of Accountancy*, 111(3), 40–46.

Herrick, A. (1954). A review of the work of the accounting procedure committee. *Journal of Accountancy*, 98(5), 627–638.

Herz, R. (2008). Dynamic assets don't fit in passive vehicles. *Journal of Accountancy*, 205(6), 61–63.

Hicks, J. (1946). *Value and Capital*, 2nd Edn. Oxford: Clarendon Press.

Hill, A. (2007). Big banks owe it to investors to show their strength. LOMBARD. *Financial Times*. London (UK), 25 August, p. 14.

Hirschleifer J. (1958). On the theory of optimal investment decision. *Journal of Political Economy*, 66, 329–372.

Holthausen, R.W. and R.L. Watts (2001). The relevance of the value-relevance literature for financial accounting standard setting. *Journal of Accounting & Economics*, 31(1–3), 3–75.

Horngren, C.T. (1972). Accounting principles: Private or public sector? *Journal of Accountancy*, 133(5), 37–41.

Horngren, C.T. (1973). The marketing of accounting standards. *Journal of Accountancy*, 136(4), 61–66.

Horngren, C.T. (1976). Will the FASB be here in the 1980s? *Journal of Accountancy*, 142(5), 90–96.

Horngren, C.T. (1981). Uses and limitations of a conceptual framework. *Journal of Accountancy*, 151(4), 86, 88, 90, 92, 94–95.

Hoxsey, J.M.B. (1930). Accounting for investors. *Journal of Accountancy*, 50(5), 251–284.

Hughes, J. (2008). Working out what should be on and off the balance sheet. *Financial Times*. London (UK), 5th June, p. 18.

Hughes, J. and L.P. Cain (1998). *American Economic History*, 5th Edn. New York: Addison-Wesley.

Ijiri, Y. (1971). Critique of the APB fundamentals statement. *The Journal of Accountancy*, 132(5), 43–50.

Ijiri, Y. (1975). *Theory of Accounting Measurement*. Studies in Accounting Research #10. Sarasota, FL: American Accounting Association.

Ijiri, Y. (1978). Cash flow accounting and its structure. *Journal of Accounting, Auditing and Finance*, 1(4), 331–348.

Ijiri, Y. (1983). On the accountability-based conceptual framework of accounting. *Journal of Accounting and Public Policy*, 2(2), 75–81.

Imhoff, E.A. Jr. (1992). Asset securitization: Economic effects and accounting issues. *Accounting Horizons*, 6(1), 5–16.

Imhoff, E.A., R.C. Lipe and D.W. Wright (1991). Operating leases: Impact of constructive capitalization. *Accounting Horizons*, 5(1), 51–63.

International Accounting Standard Committee (1989). *Framework for the Preparation and Presentation of Financial Statements*. London.

International Accounting Standards Board (1998). *SIC — 12: Consolidation — Special Purpose Entities*. London.

International Accounting Standards Board (2003). *Financial Instruments: Recognition and Measurement. International Accounting Standard No. 39*. London.

International Accounting Standards Board (2005). *Exposure Draft of Proposed Amendments to IFRS3: Business Combinations*. London.

International Accounting Standards Committee (1976). *IAS 3 Consolidated Financial Statements*. London.

International Accounting Standards Committee (1989). *IAS 27: Consolidated Financial Statements and Accounting for Investments in Subsidiaries*. London.

Jensen, R.E. (2007). Fair value accounting in the USA. In *The Routledge Companion to Fair Value and Financial Reporting*, P. Walton (ed.), pp. 300–320. London: Routledge.

Johnson S.B. and D. Solomons (1984). Institutional legitimacy and the FASB. *Journal of Accounting and Public Policy*, 3, 165–183.

Jones, S. (2015). Development of financial accounting theory. In *The Routledge Companion to Financial Accounting Theory*, S. Jones (ed.), pp. 1–11. London: Routledge.

Journal of Accountancy (1937). Essay contests. *The Journal of Accountancy*, 64(1), 2.

Journal of Accountancy (1947). What the public thinks about financial statements. *The Journal of Accountancy*, 83(6), 487–489.

Joyce, E.J., R. Libby and S. Sunder (1982). Using the FASB's qualitative characteristics in accounting policy choices. *Journal of Accounting Research*, 20(2), 654–675.

Kahle, J.J. (1993). *American Accountants and their Contributions to Accounting Thought, 1900–1930*. New York: Garland Publishing, Inc.

Kaplan, M.C. and D.M. Reaugh (1939). Accounting, reports to stockholders, and the SEC. *The Accounting Review*, 14(3), 203–236.

Kester, R.B. (1940). Comments on "An Introduction to Corporate Accounting Standards". *The Journal of Accountancy*, 69(6), 442–445.

Kennedy, D. (2001). A clarification of Marx's theory of crisis. *Critique: Journal of Socialist Theory*, 29(1), 49–70.

Keynes, J.M. (1936). *The General Theory of Employment, Interest and Money*. Cambridge.

Kindleberger, C.P. (1978). *Manias, Panics and Crashes: A History of Financial Crises*. New York: Basic Books.

King, A.M. (2006). *Fair Value for Financial Reporting: Meeting the New FASB Requirements*. New York: John Wiley & Sons.

Kirk, D.J. (1978). Business and the FASB: The need for effective interaction. *Management Accounting*, 60(3), 17–20.

Kirk, D.J. (1986). Can you hear me now? *CPA Journal*, 56, 67–70.

Kirk, D.J. (1988). Looking back on fourteen years with the FASB: The education of a standard setter. *Accounting Horizons*, 2(1), 8–17.

Kirk, D.J. (1989). Reflections on a 'Reconceptualization of accounting': A commentary on Parts I-IV of Homer Kripke's paper, 'Reflections on the FASB's conceptual framework for accounting and on auditing'. *Journal of Accounting, Auditing & Finance*, 4(1), 83–105.

Kliman, A. (2007). *Reclaiming Marx's Capital: A Refutation of the Myth of Inconsistency*. Plymouth: Lexington Books.

Kliman, A. (2011). The reproduction schemes as an unbalanced growth model. *Critique of Political Economy*, 1, 33–61.

Kliman, A. (2012). *The Failure of Capitalist Production: Underlying Causes of the Great Recession*. London: Pluto Press.

Kliman, A. (2015). The Great Recession and Marx's crisis theory. *American Journal of Economics and Sociology*, 74, 236–277.

Kliman, A. (2017). Tendency of the rate of profit to fall: Long-term dynamics. In *Routledge Handbook of Marxian Economics*, D.M. Brennan *et al.* (eds.), pp. 225–233. London: Routledge.

Kliman, A., A. Freeman, N. Potts, G. Alexey and B. Cooney (2013). The unmaking of Marx's *Capital*: Heinrich's attempt to eliminate Marx's crisis theory. https://ssrn.com/abstract=2294134 or http://dx.doi.org/10.2139/ssrn.2294134.

Kohler, E.L. (1934). A nervous profession. *The Accounting Review*, 9(4), 334–335.

Kohler, E.L. (1957). *A Dictionary for Accountants*, 2nd Edn. London: Prentice-Hall.

Kothari, S.P. and R. Lester (2012). The role of accounting in the financial crisis: Lessons for the future. *Accounting Horizons*, 26(2), 335–351.

KPMG IFRG Limited, Comment letter on Exposure Draft ED 10, *Consolidated Financial Statements*, 20 March 2009.

Kripke, H. (1989). Reflections on the FASB's conceptual framework for accounting and on auditing. *Journal of Accounting, Auditing & Finance*, 4(3), 3–65.

Kuhn, T. (1962). *The Structure of Scientific Revolutions*. Chicago: University of Chicago Press.

Landsman, W.R., K. Peasnell and C. Shakespeare (2008). Are asset securitizations sales or loans? *The Accounting Review*, 83(5), 1251–1272.

Levy R.A. (1966). Conceptual foundations of technical analysis. *Financial Analysts Journal*, 22(4), 83–89.

Lichtenstein, N., S. Strasser and R. Rosenzweig (2000). *Who Built America? Working People and the Nation's Economy, Politics, Culture, and Society*, Vol. 2. *Since 1877*. New York: Worth Publishers.

Lippmann, W. (1914). *Drift and Mastery*. New York: Mitchell Kennerley.

Littleton, A.C. (1928). What is profit? *Accounting Review*, 3(3), 278–288.

Littleton, A.C. (1935). Value or cost. *The Accounting Review*, 10(3), 269–273.

Littleton, A.C. (1936). Contrasting theories of profit. *The Accounting Review*, 11(1), 10–18.

Lorig, A.N. (1937). Accounting postulates: An analysis of the Tentative Statement of Accounting Principles. *Accounting Review*, 12(4), 401–403.

Macve, R. (1981). A conceptual framework for financial accounting and reporting: The possibilities for an agreed structure. A report prepared for the Institute of Chartered Accountants in England and Wales, at the request of the Accounting Standards Committee (1981). In *A Conceptual Framework for Financial Accounting and Reporting*, R. Macve (ed.) (1997), pp. 27–166. New York: Garland Publishing.

Main, F.W. (1944). Accounting for industry, labor, and the consumer. *Journal of Accountancy,* 78(5), 390–393.

Maltby, J. (2000). The origins of prudence in accounting. *Critical Perspectives on Accounting*, 11, 51–70.

Mautz, R.K. (1973). The Trueblood report: A significant shift in emphasis. *Camagazine*, 103(6), 17–19.

Marx, K. (1969). *Theories of Surplus Value*, Part 2. London: Lawrence & Wishart.

Marx, K. (1973). *Grundrisse*. Harmondsworth: Penguin Books.

Marx, K. (1976). *Capital: A Critique of Political Economy*, Vol. 1. Harmondsworth: Penguin Books.

Marx, K. (1978). *Capital: A Critique of Political Economy*, Vol. 2. Harmondsworth: Penguin Books.

Marx, K. (1981). *Capital: A Critique of Political Economy*, Vol. 3. Harmondsworth: Penguin Books.

Marx, K. (1991). *Economic Manuscript of 1861–1863: A Contribution to a Critique of Political Economy (Continuation)*. Vol. 33, *Karl Marx and Frederick Engels: Collected Works*. London: Lawrence & Wishart.

Marx, K. (1996). *Capital, Vol. 1*. Vol. 35, *Karl Marx and Frederick Engels: Collected Works*. London: Lawrence & Wishart.

Marx, K. (1997). *Capital, Vol. II*. Vol. 36, *Karl Marx and Frederick Engels: Collected Works*. London: Lawrence & Wishart.

Marx, K. (1998). *Capital, Vol. III*. Vol. 37, *Karl Marx and Frederick Engels: Collected Works*. London: Lawrence & Wishart.

Marx, K. and F. Engels. (1985). *Letters, January 1860 — September 1864*. Vol. 41, *Karl Marx and Frederick Engels: Collected Works*. London: Lawrence & Wishart.

Mason, P. (1956). *Price-Level Changes and Financial Statements: Basic Concepts and Methods*. American Accounting Association.

Mathews, G.C. (1938). Accounting in the regulation of security sales. *The Accounting Review*, 13(3), 225–233.

Mattessich, R. (1964). *Accounting and Analytical Methods: Measurement and Projection of Income and Wealth in the Micro- and Macro-Economy*. Homewood, Illinois: Richard D. Irwin, Inc.

Mattick, P. (2008). Review of David Harvey's *The Limits to Capital. Historical Materialism* 16(4), 213–224.

Mattick, P. (2011). *Business as Usual: The Economic Crisis and the Failure of Capitalism*. London: Reaktion Press.

May, G.O. (1926a [1936]). A proper courage in the assumption of responsibility by the accountant, an address to the Society of Certified Public Accountants of the State of New Jersey, October 19. In *Twenty-five Years of Accounting Responsibility 1911–1936*, Vol. 1, G.O. May (ed.), (1936), pp. 44–48. New York: Price, Waterhouse & Co.

May, G.O. (1926). Corporate publicity and the auditor. *The Journal of Accountancy*, 42(5), 321–326.

May, G.O. (1928). Income defined at last. *The Journal of Accountancy*, 45(2), 125–127.

May, G.O. (1932). Influence of the depression on the practice of accountancy. *The Journal of Accountancy*, 54(11), 336–350.

May, G.O. (ed.) (1936). *Twenty-Five Years of Accounting Responsibility 1911–1936*, Vol. 1. New York: Price, Waterhouse & Co.

May, G.O. (1937a). Improvement in financial accounts. *Journal of Accountancy*, 63(5), 333–369.

May, G.O. (1937b). Principles of accounting. *Journal of Accountancy*, 64(6), 423–425.

May, G.O. (1942). Terminology of the balance sheet. *Journal of Accountancy*, 73(1), 35–36.

May, G.O. (1943). *Financial Accounting: A Distillation of Experience*. New York: Macmillan Company.

May, G.O. (1947). Should the LIFO principle be considered in depreciation accounting when prices vary widely. *The Journal of Accountancy*, 84(6), 453–456.

Mayson, S., D. French and C. Ryan (2008). *Company Law*, 25th Edn. Oxford: Oxford University Press.

McCartney, S. and A.J. Arnold. (2003). The Railway Mania of 1845–1847. Market irrationality or collusive swindle based on accounting distortions? *Accounting, Accountability & Auditing Journal*, 16(5), 821–852.

McCraw, T.K. (1984). *Prophets of Regulation*. Cambridge, Mass.: Harvard University Press.

McElvaine, R.S. (2009). *The Great Depression, America, 1929–1941*. New York: Three Rivers Press.

McGregor, W. (1996). Accounting for leases: A new approach: Recognition by lessees of assets and liabilities arising under lease contracts. Stamford, Conn, FASB.

Merchant, K.A. and W.A Van der Stede (2012). *Management Control Systems: Performance Measurement, Evaluation and Incentives*, 3rd Edn. Harlow: Pearson Education,.

Merino, B.G. and M.D. Neimark (1982). Disclosure regulation and public policy: A sociohistorical reappraisal. *Journal of Accounting and Public Policy*, 1, 33–57.

Michie, R.C. (2006). *The Global Securities Market: A History*. Oxford: Oxford University Press.

Middelmann, C. (1996). Europeans join the asset-backed securities club: Recent spate of offerings highlights growing Interest. *Financial Times*. London (UK), 9th July 1996, p. 17.

Miller, P.W.B. (1985). The conceptual framework: Myths and realities. *Journal of Accountancy*, 159(3), 62–71.

Miller, P.W.B. (1990). The conceptual framework as reformation and counter-reformation. *Accounting Horizons*, 4(2), 23–32.

Miller, P.W.B. and R.J. Redding (1986). *The FASB: The People, the Process, and the Politics*. Homewood, Illinois: Irwin.

Mills, P.A. (1994). Henry Rand Hatfield (1886–1945): Life and humor in the dust of ledgers. In *Twentieth Century Accounting Thinkers*, J.R. Edwards (ed.), pp. 293–308. London: Routledge.

Miranti, P.J. (1990). *Accountancy Comes of Age: The Development of the American Profession, 1886–1940*. London: University of North Carolina Press.

Miranti, P.J. (1996). Railroad accounting (U.S.). In *The History of Accounting: An International Encyclopaedia*, M. Chatfield and R. Vangermeersch (eds.), pp. 487–491. New York and London: Garland Publishing.

Monson, D.W. (2001). The conceptual framework and accounting for leases. *Accounting Horizons*, 15(3), 275–287.

Montgomery, R.H. (1927). Accountants' limitations. *The Journal of Accountancy*, 44(4), 245–266.

Moonitz, M. (1961). *The Basic Postulates of Accounting*. New York: American Institute of Certified Public Accountants.

Moonitz, M. (1970). Three contributions to the development of accounting principles prior to 1930. *Journal of Accounting Research*, 8(1), 145–155.

Morgan, R.A. (1974). Review of Rice, C.D., H.C. Ford, R.J. Williams and Silverman, G.W. (1973). *The Businessman's View of The Purposes of Financial Reporting*. New York: Financial Executives Research Foundation. *The Accounting Review*, 49(1), 214–215.

Morrison, P.L. (1935). Reports to stockholders. *The Accounting Review*, 10(1), 77–83.

Most, K.S. (1977). *Accounting Theory*. Columbus, Ohio: Grid Inc.

Mouck, T. (1995). Irving Fisher and the mechanistic character of twentieth century accounting thought. *The Accounting Historians Journal*, 22(2), 43–83.

Munter, P. (2002). Enron post-mortem: Do we need new accounting standards? *The Journal of Corporate Accounting & Finance*, 13(4), 81–89.

Myers, J.H. (1948). Presentation of long term lease liabilities in the balance sheet. *Accounting Review*, 23(3), 289–295.

Myers. J.H. (1959). The critical event and recognition of net profit. *The Accounting Review,* 34(4), 528–532.

Myers, J.H. (1962). Reporting of leases in financial statements, *Accounting Research Study No. 4*. AICPA.

Nelson, A.T. (1963). Capitalizing leases — The effect on financial ratios. *Journal of Accountancy*, 116(1), 49–58.

Niu, F.F. and G.D. Richardson (2006). Earnings quality, off-balance sheet risk, and the financial-components approach to accounting for transfers of financial assets. Working paper, Wilfrid Laurier University and University of Toronto.

Nobes, C.W. (2014). The development of national and transnational regulation on the scope of consolidation. *Accounting, Auditing & Accountability Journal*, 27(6), 995–1025.

Norby, W.C. (1983). Applications of inflation-adjusted data. *Financial Analysts Journal*, March/April, 33–39.

O'Connor, M.C. and G. Chandra (1978). *Replacement Cost Disclosure: A Study of Compliance with the SEC Requirement*. New York: National Association of Accountants.

Okishio, N. (1961). Technical change and the rate of profit. *Kobe Economic Review*, 7, 85–99.

Ott, J.C. (2009). Political ideology and retail brokerage at the New York Stock Exchange, 1913–1933. *The Journal of American History*, 96(1), 44–71.

Pacter, P.A. (1983). The conceptual framework: Make no mystique about it. *Journal of Accountancy*, 156(1), 76–78, 86–88.

Parker, R.H. and G.C. Harcourt (1969). Introduction. In *Readings in the Concept and Measurement of Income*, R.H. Parker and G.C. Harcourt (eds.), pp. 1–30. London: Philip Allen.

Parrish, M.E. (1970). *Securities Regulation and the New Deal*. New Haven and London: Yale University Press.

Paton, W.A. (1917). Theory of the double-entry system. *Journal of Accountancy*, 23(1), 7–26.

Paton, W.A. (1922). *Accounting Theory with Special Reference to the Corporate Enterprise*. New York: Ronald Press.

Paton, W.A. (1928). Limitations of financial and operating ratios. *The Accounting Review*, 3(3), 252–260.

Paton, W.A. (1938). Comments on "A Statement of Accounting Principles". *The Journal of Accountancy*, 65(3), 196–207.

Paton, W.A. (1948). The accountant and private enterprise. *The Journal of Accountancy*, 85(4), 44–58.

Paton, W.A. (1950). Measuring profits under inflation conditions a serious problem for accountants. *The Journal of Accountancy*, 89(1), 16–27.

Paton, W.A. (1952). *Shirtsleeve Economics: A Commonsense Survey*. New York: Appleton-Crofts, Inc.

Paton, W.A. (1964). Foreword to the reissue. In *Stabilized Accounting*, H.W. Sweeney (ed.), pp. xiii–xvi. New York: Holt, Rinehart and Winston Inc.

Paton, W.A. (1971). Introduction. In *Foundations of Accounting Theory: Papers Given at the Symposium University of Florida*, March 1970, W.E. Stone (ed.), pp. ix–xi. Gainesville: University of Florida Press.

Paton, W.A. (1973). Financial misrepresentation and mismeasurement. *Financial Executive*, April, 14–21.

Paton, W.A. (1981). Recalling George Oliver May and me. *The Accounting Historians Journal*, 8(2), 91–95.

Paton, W.A. and A.C. Littleton (1940). *An Introduction to Corporate Accounting Standards*. Columbus, Ohio: American Accounting Association.

Paton, W.A. and R.A. Stevenson (1918). *Principles of Accounting*. New York: The Macmillan Company.

Peasnell, K.V. (1974). Accounting objectives: A critique of the Trueblood report, *ICRA Occasional Paper No. 5. Lancaster: International Centre for Research in Accounting*, University of Lancaster.

Peasnell, K.V. (1978). Statement of accounting theory and theory acceptance: A review article. *Accounting and Business Research*, 8(31), 217–225.

Peasnell, K.V. (1982). The function of a conceptual framework for corporate financial reporting. *Accounting and Business Research*, 12(48), 243–256.

Perlo, V. (1958). "People's Capitalism" and stock-ownership. The *American Economic Review*, 48(3), 333–347.

Perry, R.E. (1993). Accounting for securitizations. *Accounting Horizons*, 7(3), 71–82.

Piketty, T. (2014). *Capital in the Twenty-First Century*. Cambridge, Mass.: Harvard University Press.

Piaget, J. (1971). *Insights and Illusions of Philosophy*. London: The World Publishing Company.

Piott, S.L. (1985). *The Anti-Monopoly Persuasion: Popular Resistance to the Rise of Big Business in the Midwest*. London: Greenwood Press.

Powers, W.C., R.S. Troubh and H.S. Winokur (2002). *Report of Investigation by the Special Investigations Committee of the Board of Directors of Enron Corporation.*

Previts G.J. (1980). *Early 20th Century Development in American Accounting Thought*. New York: Arno Press.

Previts, G.J. and B.D. Merino (1998). *A History of Accountancy in the United States: The Cultural Significance of Accounting*. Columbus: Ohio State University Press.

Rappaport, A. (1977). Economic impact of accounting standards — Implications for the FASB. *Journal of Accountancy*, 143(5), pp. 89–90, 92, 94, 96–98.

Rappoport, P. and E.N. White (1993). Was there a bubble in the 1929 stock market. *The Journal of Economic History*, 53(3), 549–574.

Renshaw, P. (1991). *American Labour and Consensus Capitalism, 1935–1990*. Jackson: University Press of Mississippi.

Revsine, L. (1973). *Replacement Cost Accounting*. New York: Prentice-Hall.

Revsine, L. (1991). The selective financial misrepresentation hypothesis. *Accounting Horizons*, 5(4), 16–27.

Rhea, R. (1932). *The Dow Theory*. New York: Barron's.

Ripley, W.Z. (1927). *Main Street and Wall Street*. Boston: Little Brown.
Rice, C.D., H.C. Ford, R.J. Williams and G.W. Silverman (1973). *The Businessman's View of The Purposes of Financial Reporting*. New York: Financial Executives Research Foundation.
Roberts, M. (2016). *The Long Depression: How It Happened and What Happens Next*. Chicago: Haymarket Books.
Ronen, J. and M. Schiff (1978). The setting of financial accounting standards — Private or public? *Journal of Accountancy*, 145(3), 66–73.
Rorem, C.R. (1937). Accounting theory: A critique of the Tentative Statement of Accounting Principles. *The Accounting Review*, 12(2), 133–138.
Rosenfield, P. (1974). Stewardship. In *Objectives of Financial Statements*. Volume 2, selected papers, 123–140. New York: American Institute of Certified Public Accountants.
Ryan, S.G. (2008). Accounting in and for the subprime crisis. *The Accounting Review*, 83(6), 1605–1638.
Sanders, T.H. (1936). Influence of the Securities and Exchange Commission upon accounting principles. *The Accounting Review*, 11(1), 66–74.
Sanders, T.H., H.R. Hatfield and U. Moore (1938). *A Statement of Accounting Principles*, American Institute of Accountants.
Sandilands, F.E.P. (1974). *Inflation Accounting: Report of the Inflation Accounting Committee*. London: HMSO, Cmnd 6225.
Schipper, K. and T.L. Yohn (2007). Standard-setting issues and academic research related to the accounting for financial asset transfers. *Accounting Horizons*, 21(1), 59–80.
Schlesinger, A.M. Jr. (1957). *The Crisis of the Old Order, 1919–1933*. Boston: Houghton-Mifflin.
Schwarcz, S.L. (2002). Enron, and the use and abuse of special purpose entities in corporate structures. *Duke Law School Public Law and Legal Theory Research Paper Series, Research Paper No. 28*.
Scott D.R. (1937). The tentative statement of principles. *The Accounting Review*, 12(3), 296–303.
Scott D.R. (1939). Responsibilities of accountants in a changing economy. *The Accounting Review*, 14(4), pp. 396–401.
Scott, W.R. (2000). *Financial Accounting Theory*, 2nd Edn. Scarborough, Ontario: Prentice-Hall Canada Inc.
Seligman, J. (1982). *The Transformation of Wall Street: A History of the Securities and Exchange Commission and Modern Corporate Finance*. Boston: Houghton Mifflin Company.
Shaikh, A. (1978). An introduction to the history of crisis theories. In *U.S. Capitalism in Crisis*, pp. 219–241. New York: Union for Radical Political Economics.
Skinner, R.M. (1987). *Accounting Standards in Evolution*. Holt, Rinehart and Winston of Canada.

Smith, C.A. (1935). Accounting practice under the Securities and Exchange Commission. *The Accounting Review*, 10(4), 325–332.

Sobel, R. (1968). *The Great Bull Market: Wall Street in the 1920s*. New York: W.W. Norton & Company.

Solomons, D. (1962). Revision of Alexander, S. Income Measurement in a Dynamic Economy. In *Studies in Accounting Theory*, W.T. Baxter and S. Davidson (eds.), pp.126–200. London: Sweet & Maxwell.

Solomons, D. (1966). Economic and accounting concepts of cost and value. In *Modern Accounting Theory*, M. Backer (ed.), pp. 117–140. Englewood Cliffs, NJ: Prentice-Hall Inc.

Solomons, D. (1983). The political implications of accounting and accounting standard-setting. *Accounting and Business Research*, 13(5), 107–117.

Solomons, D. (1986a). *Making Accounting Policy: The Quest for Credibility in Financial Reporting*. New York and Oxford: Oxford University Press.

Solomons, D. (1986b). The FASB's conceptual framework: An evaluation. The board's dilemma: Radical change or fine-tuning? *Journal of Accountancy*, 161(6), 114–124.

Solomons, D. (1991a). Accounting and social change: A neutralist view. *Accounting, Organizations and Society*, 16(3), 287–295.

Solomons, D. (1991b). A rejoinder. *Accounting, Organizations and Society*, 16(3), 311–312.

Soroosh, J. and J.T. Ciesielski (2004). Accounting for special purpose entities revised: FASB Interpretation 46R. *CPA Journal*, 74(7), 30–37.

Sorter, G.H. and C.T. Horngren (1962). Asset recognition and economic attributes — The relevant costing approach. *The Accounting Review*, 37(3), 391–399.

Sorter, G.H., M.S. Gans, P. Rosenfield, R.M. Shannon and R.G. Streit (1974). Purpose and need for objectives. In *Objectives of Financial Statements*. Vol. 2, selected papers, pp. 13–18. New York: American Institute of Certified Public Accountants.

Spiller, E. and M.L. Gosman (1984). *Financial Accounting: Basic Concepts*, 4th Edn. Homewood: Illinois: Richard D. Irwin.

Sprague, C.E. (1907) [1917]. *The Philosophy of Accounts*. Lawrence, Kansas: Scholars Book Co. (reprint of publication by the author).

Sprouse, R.T. (1966). Accounting for what-you-may-call-its. *The Journal of Accountancy*, 122(4), 45–53.

Sprouse, R.T. (1971). The balance sheet — Embodiment of the most fundamental elements of accounting theory. In *Foundations of Accounting Theory: Papers given at the Symposium University of Florida*, March 1970, W.E. Stone, (ed.), pp. 90–104. Gainesville: University of Florida Press.

Sprouse, R.T. (1988). Commentary on financial reporting — developing a conceptual framework for financial reporting. *Accounting Horizons*, 2(4), 121–127.

Sprouse, R.T. and M. Moonitz (1962). *A Tentative Set of Broad Accounting Principles for Business Enterprises*. Accounting Research Study No. 3. New York: American Institute of Certified Public Accountants.

Stabler, H.F. (1996). May, George Oliver (1878–1961). In *The History of Accounting: An International Encyclopaedia*, M. Chatfield and R. Vangermeersch (eds.), pp. 407–408. New York and London: Garland Publishing.

Stabler, H.F. and N.X. Dressel (1981). May and Paton: Two giants revisited. *The Accounting Historians Journal*, 8(2), 79–90.

Stanga, K.G. (1980). The relationship between relevance and reliability: Some empirical results. *Accounting and Business Research*, 11(41), 29–39.

Stans, M.H. (1949). Weaknesses in present accounting which inhibit understanding of free enterprise. *Journal of Accountancy*, 88(6), 466–471.

Staubus, G.J. (1958). Comments on "Accounting and reporting standards for corporate financial statements — 1957 revision". *The Accounting Review*, 33(1), 11–24.

Staubus, G.J. (1959). The residual equity point of view in accounting. *The Accounting Review*, 34(1), 3–13.

Staubus, G.J. (1961). *A Theory of Accounting to Investors*. Berkeley: University of California Press.

Staubus, G.J. (1972). An analysis of APB Statement No. 4. *The Journal of Accountancy*, 133(2), 36–43.

Staubus, G.J. (1977). *Making Accounting Decisions*. Houston, TX: Scholars Book Company.

Staubus, G.J. (2000). *The Decision-Usefulness Theory of Accounting: A Limited History*. New York: Garland Publishing.

Staubus, G.J. (2003). An accountant's education. *The Accounting Historians Journal*, 30(1), 155–196.

Sterling, R.R. (1967a). A statement of basic accounting theory: A review article. *Journal of Accounting Research*, 5(1), 95–112.

Sterling, R.R. (1967b). Conservatism: The fundamental principle of valuation in traditional accounting. *Abacus*, 3(2), 109–132.

Sterling, R.R. (1970). *Theory of the Measurement of Enterprise Income*. Mt. Vernon, Houston: Scholars Book Co.

Sterling, R.R. (1973). Accounting power. *Journal of Accountancy*, 135(1), 61–67.

Sterling, R.R. (1982). The conceptual framework: An assessment. *Journal of Accountancy*, 154(5), 103–108.

Stewart, J.E. and B.S. Neuhausen (1986). Financial instruments and transactions: The CPA's newest challenge. *The Journal of Accountancy*, 162(2), 101–111.

Storey, R.K. (1964). *Search for Accounting Principles, Today's Problems in Perspective*. AICPA.

Storey, R.K. (1981). Conditions necessary for developing a conceptual framework. *Journal of Accountancy*, 151(6), 84, 86, 88, 90, 92, 94–96.

Storey, R.K. and S. Storey (1998). *The Framework of Financial Accounting Concepts and Standards*. Stanford, Conn.: Financial Accounting Standards Board.

Sutton, F.X., S.E. Harris, C. Kaysen and J. Tobin (1956). *The American Business Creed*. New York: Schocken Books.

Sweeney, H.W. (1936). *Stabilized Accounting*. New York: Harper & Brothers.

Sweezy, P.M. (1942). *The Theory of Capitalist Development: Principles of Marxian Political Economy*. New York: Monthly Review Press.

The Hundred Group of Finance Directors (2009), Comment letter on Exposure Draft ED 10. *Consolidated Financial Statements*, 20 March 2009.

Tinker, A.M. (1984). Theories of the state and the state of accounting: Economic reductionism and political voluntarism in accounting regulation. *Journal of Accounting and Public Policy*, 3, 55–77.

Tinker, A.M. (1985). *Paper Prophets: A Social Critique of Accounting*. London and New York: Holt, Rinehart and Winston.

Tinker, A.M. (1991). The accountant as partisan. *Accounting, Organizations and Society*, 16(3), 297–310.

Tobin J. (2005). Irving Fisher, 1867–1947. In *Celebrating Irving Fisher: The Legacy of a Great Economist*, R.W. Dimand and J. Geanakoplos (eds.), pp. 19–42. Oxford: Blackwell Publishing.

Trigg, A.B. (2017). Marxian reproduction schemes. In *Routledge Handbook of Marxian Economics*, D.M. Brennan *et al.* (eds.), pp. 215–224. London: Routledge.

Tugwell, R.G. (1933). *The Industrial Discipline and the Governmental Arts*. New York: Columbia University Press.

Turner, L. (2008). *Multinational Monitor*, Plunge: How banks aim to obscure their losses: An interview with Lynn Turner, 29(3) (https://www.multinational monitor.org/mm2008/112008/interview-turner.html, np).

Tweedie, D.P. and G. Whittington (1984). *The Debate on Inflation Accounting*. Cambridge: Cambridge University Press.

Tweedie, D.P. and G. Whittington (1997). The end of the current cost revolution. In *The Development of Accounting in an International Context: A Festschrift in Honour of R. H. Parker*, T. E. Cooke, C. W. Nobes (eds.), pp. 149–176. London: Routledge.

Twentieth Century Fund (1934). *Stock Market Control*. New York: Appleton.

Twentieth Century Fund (1935). *The Securities Markets Findings and Recommendations of a Special Staff of the Twentieth Century Fund*. New York: Twentieth Century Fund.

US Congress, Senate. (1955). *Committee on Banking and Currency*, 84th Congress, 1st Session. Hearings on factors affecting the buying and selling of securities. Staff Report.

US Department of Commerce (1975). *Historical Statistics of the United States. Colonial Times to 1970*, 2 Vols. Washington, D.C.: U.S. Government Printing Office.

US Senate (1976). Subcommittee on reports, accounting, and management of the senate committee on governmental operations. *The Accounting Establishment*, Washington, D.C.: Government Printing Office.

Vangermeersch, R. (1996). Uniformity. In *The History of Accounting: An International Encyclopaedia*, M. Chatfield and R. Vangermeersch (eds.), pp. 596–598. New York: Garland Publishing.

Van Antwerp, W.C. (1913). *The Stock Exchange From Within.* New York: Doubleday, Page.

Van Riper, R. (1994). *Setting Standards for Financial Reporting: FASB and the Struggle for Control of a Critical Process*. Westport, CT: Quorum Books.

Van Strum, K.S. (1925). *Investing in Purchasing Power*. New York: Barron's.

Van Strum, K.S. (1927). *Forecasting Stock Market Trends: The General Level of Commodity Prices*. Barron's, March 14, 3, 7, 11.

Van Zijl, T., and G. Whittington (2006). Deprival value and fair value: A reinterpretation and a reconciliation. *Accounting and Business Research*, 16(2), 121–130.

Waldron, M.A., J.E. Shaver and C.E. Jordan (1989). Evolution of inflation accounting in the U.S. *Accounting Historians Notebook*, 12(2), 17–27.

Walker, R.G. (1977). The Hatry affair. *Abacus*, 13(1), 78–82.

Walker, R.G. (1978). *Consolidated Statements: A History and Analysis*. Sidney: Sidney University Press.

Walker, R.G. (1992). The SEC's ban on upward revaluations and the disclosure of current values. *Abacus*, 28(1), 3–33.

Walton, P. (2007). CCA — An unsuccessful attempt to change the measurement basis. In *The Routledge Companion to Fair Value and Financial Reporting*, P. Walton (ed.), pp. 173–180. London: Routledge.

Watts, R.L. and J.L. Zimmerman (1978). Towards a positive theory of the determination of accounting standards. *The Accounting Review*, 53(1), 112–134.

Watts, R. and J. Zimmerman (1979). The demand for the supply of accounting theories: The market for excuses. *The Accounting Review*, 54(2), 273–305.

Wells, M.C. (1976). A revolution in accounting thought? *The Accounting Review*, 51(3), 471–482.

Wells, M.C. (1978). *Accounting for Common Costs*, Centre for international education and research in accounting, Monograph 10. University of Illinois.

Werntz, W.W. (1940). Financial statements for investors. *Journal of Accountancy*, 69(1), 22–29.

White, E. (1990a). The stock market boom and crash of 1929 revisited. *The Journal of Economic Perspectives*, 4(2), 67–83.

White, E. (1990b). When the ticker ran late: The stock market boom and crash of 1929. In *Crashes and Panics: The Lessons From History*, E. White (ed.), pp. 143–187. Homewood: Dow Jones/Irwin.

Whittington, G. (1977). Accounting and economics. In *Current Issues in Accounting*, B. Carsberg and T. Hope (eds.), pp. 192–212. Oxford: Philip Allan Publishers.

Whittington, G. (1980). Pioneers of income measurement and price-level accounting: A review article. *Accounting and Business Research*, 10(38), 232–240.

Whittington G. (1983). *Inflation Accounting: An Introduction to the Debate*. Cambridge: Cambridge University Press.

Whittington, G. (2007). Alternatives to fair value. In *The Routledge Companion to Fair Value and Financial Reporting*, P. Walton (ed.), pp. 181–195. London: Routledge.

Whittington, G. (2010). Measurement in financial reporting. *Abacus*, 46(1), 104–110.

Wiese, R.G. (1928). *Investing for a Business Man*. Barron's, 9 January, 2, 5, 8.

Williams, H.M. (1978). Inflation, corporate financial reporting and economic reality. *The Journal of Accountancy*, 145(3), 79–85.

Williamson, J.E. and F.J. Lipman (1991). Tracing the American concept of stewardship to English antecedents. *The British Accounting Review*, 23(4), 355–368.

Wolk, H.I., J.R. Francis and M.G. Tearney (1992). *Accounting Theory: A Conceptual and Institutional Approach*, 3rd Edn. Cincinnati, Ohio: South Western Publishing Company.

Wyatt, A.R. (1986). Standard setting: Processes and politics. *FASB Viewpoints*, 1–3.

Wyatt, A.R. (1989). Accounting standards and the professional auditor. *Accounting Horizons*, 3(2), 96–102.

Wyatt, A.R. (1990). Accounting standards: Conceptual or political? *Accounting Horizons*, 4(3), 83–88.

Young, J.J. (1996). Institutional thinking: The case of financial instruments. *Accounting, Organizations and Society*, 21(5), 487–512.

Zeff, S.A. (1966). *The American Accounting Association: Its First 50 Years*. American Accounting Association.

Zeff, S.A. (1972). *Forging Accounting Principles in Five Countries: A History and an Analysis of Trends*. Champaign, Illinois: Stipes Publishing Company.

Zeff, S.A. (1978). The rise of "economic consequences". *Journal of Accountancy*, 142(6), 56–63.

Zeff, S.A. (1984). Some junctures in the evolution of the process of establishing accounting principles in the U.S.A.: 1917–1962. *The Accounting Review*, 49(3), 447–468.

Zeff, S.A. (1999). The evolution of the conceptual framework for business enterprises in the United States. *Accounting Historians Journal*, 26(2), 89–131.

Zeff, S.A. (2000a). John B. Canning: A view of his academic career. *Abacus*, 36(1), 4–39.

Zeff, S.A. (2000b). *Henry Rand Hatfield: Humanist, Scholar and Accounting Educator*. Stamford, Conn.: JAI Press.

Zeff, S.A. (2003a). How the U.S. accounting profession got where it is today: Part 1, *Accounting Horizons*, 17(3), 189–205.

Zeff, S.A. (2003b). How the U.S. accounting profession got where it is today: Part 2. *Accounting Horizons*, 17(4), 267–286.

Zeff, S.A. (2007). The SEC rules historical cost accounting. *Accounting and Business Research*, 37 (sup1), 49–62.

Zeff, S.A. (2013). The objectives of financial reporting: A historical survey and analysis. *Accounting and Business Research*, 43(4), 262–327.

Zeff, S.A. (2015). The Wheat Study on Establishment of Accounting Principles (1971–72): A historical study. *Journal of Accounting and Public Policy*, 34, 146–174.

Zeff, S.A. (2016). The Trueblood study group on the objectives of financial statements (1971–73): A historical study. *Journal of Accounting and Public Policy*, 35, 134–161.

Zeff, S.A. (2018). An Introduction to Corporate Accounting Standards: Detecting Paton's and Littleton's influences. *The Accounting Historians Journal*, 45(1), 45–67.

Zeff, S.A. (2021). Evolution of US regulation and the standard-setting process for financial reporting: 1930s to the present. *Foundations and Trends® in Accounting*, 15(3), 263–372.

Zeff, S.A., J. Demski and N. Dopuch (eds.) (1979). *Essays in Honour of William A. Paton: Pioneer Accounting Theorist*. Ann Abor: University of Michigan.

Zises, A. (1961). Disclosure of long-term leases. *Journal of Accountancy*, 111(2), 37–47.

Zieger, R.H. (1994). *American Workers, American Unions*, 2nd Edn. Baltimore and London: John Hopkins Press.

Zijl, T. van and G. Whittington (2006). Deprival value and fair value: A reinterpretation and a reconciliation. *Accounting and Business Research*, 36(2), 121–130.

Index

A

accountability for the rate of profit (*see also* British stewardship; management's accountability; return on investment (ROI)), 27, 56, 262

accounting for value (*see also* accounting interpretation of Marx's theory of value; Marxian accounting; Marx's theory of value), 25

accounting historians, 8, 127, 404

accounting interpretation of Marx's theory of capitalism (*see also* Marxian accounting), 2–3, 24–25, 27, 60, 263

accounting interpretation of Marx's theory of crises (*see also* Marx's theory of crises), 1–3, 16, 21–22, 24–27, 36, 41, 56, 58, 62, 65–67, 70, 83, 403

accounting interpretation of Marx's theory of history (*see also* Marx's theory of history), 9–10, 21, 24, 62

accounting interpretation of Marx's theory of value (*see also* Marx's theory of value), 21

accounting logic of *Capital* (*see also* Capital Volume 1 (Marx); Capital Volume 2 (Marx); Capital Volume 3 (Marx)), 26, 35, 51, 53–54, 63–64

Accounting Principles Board (APB), 6, 13, 183, 186, 189–190, 231, 233, 238, 240–241, 245–247, 249–251, 258, 267, 293–295, 301, 313–314, 317, 320, 331, 351, 358–359

Accounting Principles Board (APB) Opinion 2, *Accounting for the Investment Credit*, 240

Accounting Principles Board (APB) Opinion 5, *Reporting of Leases in Financial Statements of Lessees*, 358–359

Accounting Principles Board (APB) Opinion 7, *Accounting for Leases in Financial Statements of Lessors*, 340, 349, 359

Accounting Principles Board (APB) Opinion 11, *Accounting for Income Taxes*, 245

Accounting Principles Board (APB) Opinion 16, *Business Combinations*, 247

Accounting Principles Board (APB) Opinion 17, *Goodwill*, 247
Accounting Principles Board (APB) Statement 4, *Basic Concepts and Accounting Principles Underlying Financial Statements of Business Enterprises*, 233, 245, 247, 249, 251–252, 295
accounting profession (*see also* accounting profession's legitimacy crises), 13, 188, 197–198, 202, 215, 227–229, 245, 247, 250, 329, 349, 358
accounting profession's legitimacy crises (*see also* accounting profession), 6, 13–14, 18, 186, 240–241, 250, 259
accounting reform in the 1930s (*see also* May, George, O.; Securities Acts 1933 and 1934; Securities Exchange Commission (SEC); uniformity in accounting), 5, 17, 85, 97, 121, 126, 144–145, 162–163, 182–183
accounting regulation (*see also* superstructure), 2, 22, 185–186, 316, 350
Accounting Research Bulletins (ARBs), 13, 182, 199, 204–206, 219, 227–228, 235, 350–351, 358, 370, 384
Accounting Research Bulletin (ARB) 1: *General Introduction and Rules Formerly Adopted*, 199, 204–205
Accounting Research Bulletin (ARB) 5, *Depreciation on Appreciation*, 206
Accounting Research Bulletin (ARB) 38, *Disclosure of Long-Term Leases in Financial Statements of Lessees*, 350–351, 358
Accounting Research Bulletin (ARB) 51, *Consolidated Financial Statements*, 340, 349, 370–371, 401
Accounting Research Study (ARS) 1, *The Basic Postulates of Accounting*, 231–233
Accounting Research Study (ARS) 3, *A Tentative Set of Broad Accounting Principles for Business Enterprises*, 232, 301
Accounting Research Study (ARS) 4, *Reporting of Leases in Financial Statements*, 354–358
Accounting Research Study (ARS) 6, *Reporting the Financial Effects of Price-Level Changes*, 267
Accounting Series Releases (ASRs) (*see also* Securities Exchange Commission (SEC), 175, 179, 181, 188, 200, 204–206, 240, 268, 270
accounting's roles in the credit-crunch and Global Financial Crisis (GFC) (*see also* securitization accounting; swindling; US GAAP for SPEs), 1–3, 6, 13–14, 16, 19, 22, 24, 67, 333–404
accounting's roles in the Great Crash and Great Depression (*see also* criticisms of 1920s accounting; Fisher's new-era theory of investment; investors' confidence in accounting; management discretion; manipulating accounts; smoothing income/profit; swindling), 1, 21–22
Accounting Standards Committee (ASC), 15, 279–282
accounting theorists (*see also* accounting theory), 14, 84, 133, 136, 139, 142, 231, 238, 262–263, 269, 274, 278–280, 282, 299, 321–322, 329, 348, 403
accounting theory (*see also* accounting theorists; American

accounting theory), 2–4, 6, 11, 13, 16–19, 71, 194, 198, 215, 234, 236, 241, 243, 252, 259, 262, 264, 290, 300, 303, 318–319, 321–324, 327, 336, 338, 403
Accounting Theory (Paton), 6, 13–19, 91
action control (*see also* control of use-values; effective control; power to direct), 135–136, 287, 340–341, 343, 345–346, 366–367, 378, 398–399
Adhikari, Ajay, and Luis Betancourt, *Accounting for securitizations: A comparison of SFAS 140 and IASB 39*, 397
advanced capitalism (*see also* America's transition to advanced capitalism; total social capital), 10, 71, 134, 157, 340–341, 348
Agrawal, S., 332
Alexander, Sidney S., 234
Allied Chemical and Dye Corporation, 122, 147
American Accounting Association (AAA), 179, 186, 188–190, 192–193, 198–200, 203–204, 208, 229, 235, 237–238, 241–245, 249, 252, 259, 267, 303, 321–322, 370, 383
American accounting theory (*see also* accounting theory), 2–3, 403
American Association of University Instructors in Accounting (AAUIA), 192
American conservatism (*see also* British conservatism; conservatism), 175, 183, 196–198, 132, 207, 225–226
American Federation of Labor (AFL), 128, 132
American Institute of Accountants (AIA), 121, 147, 152, 154, 158–161, 163, 170–171, 174, 178–181, 186, 188, 199–200, 203–204, 208, 227, 229, 240, 266
American Institute of Certified Public Accountants (AICPA), 18, 190, 231, 242, 245, 247, 249–251, 254, 260, 267, 325, 370
America's transition to advanced capitalism (*see also* transition to capitalism), 8, 10, 134, 340, 348
An Introduction to Corporate Accounting Standards (Paton and Littleton), 18, 186, 188, 200, 208
Anthony, Robert N., 311
Anton, Hector R., 258
Archer, G.S.H., and Anthony Steele, *The implementation of SSAP16, Current Cost Accounting, by UK listed companies*, 281
Armstrong, Marshall S., 250, 286, 313–314
Arthur Andersen & Co., 229
asset-liability accounting (*see also* conceptual framework; decision-usefulness; Paton's asset definition; Paton, William A. Jr.; Statement of Financial Accounting Concepts (SFAC) 3, *Elements of Financial Statements of Business Enterprises*), 19, 126, 191, 262, 294, 299–303, 360
A Statement of Basic Accounting Theory (ASOBAT) (American Accounting Association (AAA)), 241–245, 252
A Tentative Set of Broad Accounting Principles for Business Enterprises (Sprouse and Moonitz), 232
A Tentative Statement of Accounting Principles Affecting Corporate Reports (American Accounting Association (AAA)), 193, 200, 202, 204, 208

A Theory of Accounting to Investors (Staubus), 233
attaching (*see also* matching; Paton, William, A., and A.C. Littleton, *An Introduction to Corporate Accounting Standards*), 211, 223, 243–244, 300, 322, 345, 358
auditing (*see also* auditors; independent audit requirement), 12, 126, 151, 162, 164, 178, 180
Audit of Corporate Accounts (American Institute of Accountants (AIA)), 154
auditors (*see also* auditing; government auditors; independent audit requirement), 5, 151, 158–159, 161–166, 170–171, 174–175, 179–180, 192, 202–203, 230, 240–241, 246, 250, 280, 284–286, 295, 311–313, 326, 331–332, 335, 390
audit report (*see also* auditing; independent audit requirements), 158, 160, 203, 261

B

balance sheet valuation (*see also* asset-liability accounting; decision-usefulness; economic valuation), 18–19, 174, 197, 262, 294
bankers, 10, 19, 67, 85, 97, 99, 113–114, 131, 140, 157–158, 160, 178, 230, 245, 294, 336, 338, 358, 363, 387, 394–395
Bank for International Settlements (BIS) (*see also* Report on Special Purpose Entities (Bank for International Settlements (BIS)); special purpose entities (SPEs)), 333, 335–339, 361–368, 382, 388–389, 396–397, 399–400
Baran, Paul A., and Paul M. Sweezy, *Monopoly Capital: An Essay on the American Economic and Social Order* (*see also* Sweezy, Paul M.), 69–70, 176
Barr, Andrew, 181, 206–207
Barron's Weekly, 93, 101–102, 111, 117–118, 120
Barth, Mary E., and Wayne R. Landsman, *How did financial reporting contribute to the financial crisis*?, 391–392
Baxter, William T., 272
Bear Stearns, 333
Beaver, William H., 290, 323
Beaver, William H., and Joel S. Demski, *The nature of financial accounting objectives: A summary and synthesis*, 323
Beaver, William H., and Wayne R. Landsman, *Incremental Information Content of Statement 33 Disclosures*, 281
Beresford, Denis R., 306, 311–312, 326
Berle, Adolf A. (*see also* Berle Adolf A., and Frederick S. Fisher Jr., *Elements of the law of business accounting*; Berle, Adolf A., and Means, Gardiner, *The Modern Corporation and Private Property*), 17, 130–131, 134–135, 137–141, 169–170, 201
Berle Adolf A., and Frederick .S. Fisher Jr., *Elements of the law of business accounting*, 141
Berle, Adolf A., and Means, Gardiner, *The Modern Corporation and Private Property*, x, 12, 17, 109, 133, 135, 137–138, 141, 143, 146, 155–158, 160, 209, 221
Berliner, Robert W., 15, 281
Bevis, Herman W. (*see also* Corporate Financial Reporting in a

Competitive Economy (Bevis); nondistortion guideline), x, 290, 295–300
Bortkiewicz, Ladislaus, 2, 404
big business, 5–6, 8, 11–12, 71, 97, 110, 119, 121, 126, 128–130, 133–137, 165, 265, 267, 269
big mess (*see also* Creating the "Big Mess" (Bryer)), 4–5, 188, 349
Blough, Carman G., 178–179, 202, 204
Bonbright, James C. (*see also* Bonbright, James C., and Gardiner C. Means, *The Holding Company: Its Public Significance and Its Regulation*; Sandilands Committee; The Valuation of Property: A Treatise on the Appraisal of Property for Different Legal Purposes (Bonbright); value to the owner), 15, 136, 201, 272–274
Bonbright, James C., and Gardiner C. Means, *The Holding Company: Its Public Significance and Its Regulation*, 136
Bonbright, James C., and Gardiner C. Means, *The Holding Company: Its Public Significance and Its Regulation*, 136
Bond, Frederick D., 80, 92, 98–99, 113
Boston Edison, 117–118
brains trust, 17, 79, 129–131
Brandeis, Louis, 131
Briloff, Abraham J., 247
British accounting (*see also* British conservatism; British realisation principle; British stewardship; Marxian accounting), 2–5, 8, 14, 21, 88, 118, 120, 126, 158–159, 167, 170, 181, 183, 210, 220, 222, 315, 344, 349, 400
British capitalism, 2, 11, 21
British Companies Acts, 160, 167, 170
British conservatism (*see also* American conservatism; British accounting; conservatism; Marxian accounting), 18, 154, 183, 197, 207, 226
British financial crises, 4
British railway accounts, 12, 63
British realisation principle (*see also* British accounting; Marxian accounting; realisation), 369, 378
British stewardship (*see also* British accounting; Marxian accounting; stewardship and accounting reform, 1929–1973), 4, 143, 148, 155, 198, 254–256, 262, 295, 303
brokers' loans, 81–82, 106–107, 114
Brown, Donaldson, 28
Brown, Warren, 312
bubble explanation of 1920s stock market boom (*see also* Galbraith, John K.; irrational speculation explanation of 1920s stock market boom; speculation; stock market boom of the 1920s; White, Eugene N.), 5, 7, 17, 74–75, 77–78, 81, 83, 92, 106–107
Burton, John C., 250, 270–271, 323, 336
Bush, Timothy, 170
Byrne, Gilbert R., 200

C

calculative mentality (*see also* Marx's theory of history), 4, 10
Canning, John B. (*see also* Canning's asset definition; control of access to future economic benefits; Economics of Accountancy (Canning); Fisher's theory of accounting; Myers, John H.), 5, 12, 14, 15–16, 18–19, 91, 108–109, 144, 146, 149, 155, 189–190, 219, 223, 231–234, 239, 242, 253–254, 257, 262, 272, 277, 282, 302–304,

335–336, 340–341, 347–349, 354–356, 361, 368–372, 375–377, 379–380, 382, 384, 400, 402–403
Canning's asset definition (*see also* Canning, John B.; Financial Accounting Standard (FAS) 125, *Accounting for Transfers and Servicing of Financial Assets and Extinguishments of Liabilities*; financial components approach; Myers, John H.; Statement of Financial Accounting Concepts (SFAC) 3, *Elements of Financial Statements of Business Enterprises*; US GAAP for SPEs), 15, 19, 262, 303, 336, 340, 347, 354–358, 376, 379
Cannon, Arthur M., 350
capital accumulation (*see also* capitalist accumulation; Marx's theory of crises), 3, 16, 21, 24–25, 33
capital-in-general (*see also* accounting logic of *Capital*; total social capital), 26–28, 50–51
capitalist accumulation (*see also* expanded reproduction; Marx's theory of crises), 3, 16, 24, 27, 29–34, 37, 41, 43, 45, 66
capitalist control (*see also* British stewardship; results control), 2–3, 23–24, 35, 66, 134
capitalist mode of production (*see also* forces of production; Marx's theory of capitalism; Marx's theory of history), 30, 34–35, 53, 57, 62, 64, 341
capital maintenance adjustments (CMAs) (*see also* replacement cost accounting (RCA)), 53, 196, 205, 272, 274, 283
Capital Volume 1 (Marx), 16, 24, 26–27, 29–32, 35, 51, 56, 60, 66
Capital Volume 2 (Marx), 16, 24, 26–27, 29, 34–36, 41, 51, 56, 63, 66
Capital Volume 3 (Marx), 16, 24, 26–27, 29–30, 34–35, 49, 51, 53–56, 60, 63–64, 66
Carey, John L., 134–135, 170, 178, 187, 210, 229, 245–247, 266
Carter, Colonel Arthur H., 161–164, 167–170
Caterpillar Tractor Co., 270
centralisation of capital (*see also* concentration of capital; credit system; joint stock companies; Marx's theory of capitalism; total social capital), 17, 57, 60, 63, 67, 71, 77
Cerbioni, Fabrizio, Michele Fabrizi, and Antonio Parbonetti, *Securitizations and the financial crisis: Is accounting the missing link?*, x, 335, 392–393, 395–396, 400
Chambers, Raymond J., 14, 189
chart reading (*see also* Dow theory; stock market trends trading rule; technical analysis; trend lines), 101–103
circulating capital (*see also* fixed capital), 34, 67
Citigroup, 333, 399
Clarke, Simon, 22, 57–58, 65
Cohen, Benjamin V., 160, 166
Columbia University Law School, 130, 134
Committee on Accounting Procedure (CAP), 5–6, 13, 18, 182–183, 186, 188–189, 204, 219–220, 227–231, 235, 266, 313, 331, 350–351
common stock era, 70, 76–78, 93
concentration of capital (*see also* centralisation of capital; Marx's theory of capitalism), 67, 71, 77 16–17, 57–58, 60–61, 63–64, 67, 71, 77

conceptual framework (*see also* asset-liability accounting; Canning's asset definition; current value accounting; decision-usefulness; Financial Accounting Standard Board (FASB); Financial Accounting Standard Board (FASB) Fisher's theory of accounting; Fisher's theory of accounting; legitimacy of the FASB; non-distortion guideline; Paton's asset definition; revenue and expense accounting; Statement of Financial Accounting Concepts (SFAC) 3, *Elements of Financial Statements of Business Enterprises*; Statement of Financial Accounting Concepts (SFAC) 1, *Objectives of Financial Reporting by Business Enterprises*; Statement of Financial Accounting Concepts (SFAC) 2, *Qualitative Characteristics of Financial Statements*; Statement of Financial Accounting Concepts (SFAC) 5, *Recognition and Measurement in Financial Statements of Business Enterprises*; Statement of Financial Accounting Concepts (SFAC) 5, *Recognition and Measurement in Financial Statements of Business Enterprises*),; stewardship in the FASB's conceptual framework), 6, 14, 18–19, 126, 183, 186, 190–191, 203, 209, 233, 260–332, 334, 340, 360, 369, 387, 402–403

conservatism (*see also* American conservatism; British conservatism), 13, 17–18, 123, 154, 175, 183, 196–198, 202, 207, 222, 225–226, 292

consolidated accounts (*see also* Marxian consolidated accounting), 19, 110, 120, 156, 166, 335–337, 339–342, 344, 347–349, 365–366, 368, 370–371, 373–379, 382–386, 388, 390, 392, 396–401

Consolidated Oil Corporation, 174

constant capital (*see also* fixed capital; Marx's theory of capitalism; variable capital), 25, 28–29, 31–32, 35, 38–40, 44–45, 51, 53, 65, 263

control of access to future cash flows (*see also* Canning's asset definition; control of access to future economic benefits; future economic benefits), 16, 336, 368, 370–371

control of access to future economic benefits (*see also* Canning's asset definition; control of access to future cash flows; future economic benefits), 304, 336, 368, 375, 379–381

control of use-values (*see also* action control; effective control; power to direct), 214–215, 218, 304, 343, 347, 356, 379–381, 384

control of use-values with PV (*see also* Paton's asset definition; present value (PV); present value (PV) measurement ideal;), 16, 304, 340, 375, 379

control of use-values with value, 218, 304, 356

Coolidge, Calvin, 107, 112–113

Corcoran, Thomas C., 160

Corporate Financial Reporting in a Competitive Economy (Bevis), 295

cost theory of value (*see also* Marx's theory of value; Paton, William A. Jr.), 5, 189, 209, 213–214, 216,

244, 257, 283, 295, 297, 300, 322, 403
Creating the "Big Mess" (Bryer), 3–4, 6, 17, 403–404
credit-crunch (*see also* Global Financial Crisis (GFC)), 1–3, 6, 14, 16, 19, 22, 24, 67, 312, 335–336, 339–340, 367, 386–387, 392, 399, 402
credit system (*see also* centralisation of capital; concentration of capital; joint stock companies; Marx's theory of capitalism; money capitalism; total social capital), 32, 51, 60–63, 71
critical accountants, 19, 404
critical events approach (*see also* Myers, John H.), 336, 353, 361, 375, 381–382
criticisms of 1920s accounting, 12, 17, 85, 126, 151, 194
current cost (*see also* current cost accounting (CCA); replacement cost accounting (RCA)), 190, 243–244, 262–265, 269–271, 277, 280, 282, 308–309
current cost accounting (CCA) (*see also* current cost; replacement cost accounting (RCA); Statement of Standard Accounting Practice 16 (SSAP 16)), 14–15, 18–19, 262–263, 265, 269–270, 272, 274–275, 277, 279–283, 307–308
current purchasing power accounting (CPP) (*see also* general price-level accounting (GPLA); general price-level adjustments; inflation accounting), 15, 263, 265–270, 280
current value accounting (*see also* fair value accounting; Statement of Financial Accounting Concepts (SFAC) 5, *Recognition and Measurement in Financial Statements of Business Enterprises*), 13–14, 123, 178, 189, 206, 223, 228, 233, 239, 254, 267, 271–272, 277–278, 301–302, 307–308, 309–310
Cyert, Richard M., and Yugi Ijiri, *A framework for developing the objectives of financial statements*, 255

D

Davidson, Sidney, 237
Dawley, Alan, 9, 73, 132
Debs, Eugene, 131
debt (*see also* broker's loans; financial crises; financial risk; leverage; Marx's theory of crises), 3, 13, 23, 60–61, 66, 70–71, 80–84, 107, 111, 128, 136, 176, 189, 207, 245, 261, 264, 268, 280, 333–334, 337, 343, 345, 347, 350, 362–364, 368–369, 372–373, 383, 388, 390, 399
Dechow, Patricia M., and Catherine Shakespeare, *Do managers time securitization transactions to obtain accounting benefits?*, 389
Dechow, Patricia M., Linda A. Myers and Catherine Shakespeare, *Fair value accounting and gains from asset securitizations: A convenient earnings management tool with compensation side-benefits*, 389, 390, 392, 395
decision-usefulness (*see also* asset-liability accounting; Financial Accounting Standards Board (FASB); Statement of Financial Accounting Concepts (SFAC) 1, *Objectives of Financial Reporting by Business Enterprises*; Staubus, George, G.; stewardship in the

FASB's conceptual framework), 5, 14, 18–19, 190, 234, 236–238, 240–242, 244, 248–249, 251, 256, 259–260, 262, 270, 286–288, 290–291, 300, 308, 322, 331, 335, 341, 387, 396
Demski, Joel S., 324
depreciation accounting, 28, 63, 117–118, 123, 140–141, 152, 156, 166, 173–176, 195, 197, 206, 217, 223–224, 226, 229, 263, 265–266, 270, 274, 276–277, 299, 311, 350
depreciation of values (*see also* Marx's theory of crises), 65
deprival value (*see also* value to the owner), 272–273, 275
devaluation of capital (*see also* Marx's theory of crises), 5, 13, 15, 63, 65, 261–264, 283
Devine, J., 83–84
Dice, Charles, 107
Dickinson, Sir Arthur L., 168, 220, 232
Dicksee, Lawrence, R., 159, 216, 223
Dillon, Gadis J., 96, 108, 175
disproportionality (*see also* Marx's theory of crises), 3, 22–23, 28–29, 57–58
Dopuch, Nicholas, and Shyam Sunder, *FASB's statements on objectives and elements of financial accounting: A review*, 306, 323–324, 329–330
Douglas, William O., 169
Dow, Charles H., 101
Dow Theory (*see also* chart reading; technical analysis; trend lines), 101–103
DuPont, 28, 266
DuPont formula, 28

E

earning capacity (*see also* earning power; May, George O.), 5, 12, 18, 105, 148–150, 152–156, 180, 183, 191, 194, 201–202, 208, 222, 225–226, 257, 290
earning power (*see also* earning capacity), 90, 108, 111, 207, 213, 225, 253, 256–257, 270, 288, 297–298
earnings and share prices (*see also* accounting theory; earning capacity; earnings growth; Fisher's new-era theory of investment; stock market crash 1929), 11–12, 74, 78, 84, 88, 115–117
earnings multiples, 105, 107, 109, 113, 188
earnings growth (*see also* Fisher's new-era theory of investment; stock market crash 1929), 70, 74, 78, 88, 96, 110–111, 113–117, 394
earnings trends (*see also* Fisher's new-era theory of investment), 97–104, 109
Eastman Kodak Company, 267
Eaton, Marguis G., 229–230
economic consequences of accounting (*see also* legitimacy of the FASB), 3, 317–319, 327
economic crises (*see also* financial crises; Global Financial Crises (GFC); Great Depression; Marx's theory of crises), 1, 3, 16, 23, 29, 56, 58–60, 66, 71, 84, 261
economic entity concept (*see also* Fisher's accounting theory; Paton, William A. Jr.), 18, 135–136, 186, 211, 214–216, 236–237, 252, 299, 303, 347–349, 401–402
economic growth (*see also* capital accumulation; expanded reproduction), 1, 13, 18, 21, 23, 36, 47, 74, 261, 264

Economic Manuscripts of 1861–1863: A Contribution to a Critique of Political Economy (Continuation) (Marx), 29, 54
Economics of Accountancy (Canning), 91
economic valuation (*see also* asset-liability accounting; balance sheet valuation; decision-usefulness), 5, 12, 144, 149, 172, 185–186, 189, 193–194, 201, 204, 209, 221, 233, 259, 349, 387
Edwards, Edgar O., and Philip W. Bell, *The Theory and Measurement of Business Income*, 14, 189, 271–272
effective control (*see also* action control; Canning's asset definition; management control of companies; Paton's asset definition; power to direct), 136, 304, 308, 340, 342, 344, 347–349, 359, 377, 381, 383–384, 398, 401
Ely, Kirsten, and Gregory Waymire, *Accounting standard-setting organizations and earnings relevance*, 96
Emerging Issues Task Force (EITF), 373–375
Emerging Issues Task Force (EITF) D-14, *Transactions Involving Special-Purpose Entities*, 374
Emerging Issues Task Force (EITF) 84–30, *Sales of Loans to Special-Purpose Entities*, 373
Emerging Issues Task Force (EITF) 90–15, *Impact of Nonsubstantive Lessors, Residual Value Guarantees, and Other Provisions in Leasing Transactions*, 374
Engels, Frederick, 21, 25, 29, 31, 54
English audit system, 158, 170
English law, 344
Enron, 336, 338, 374, 383, 385
Ernst & Ernst, 258, 301
Ernst & Whinney, 306
Establishing Financial Accounting Standards (American Institute of Certified Public Accountants (AICPA)), 250
executory contracts (*see also* Canning's asset definition), 311, 348, 356
expanded reproduction (*see also* reproduction schemes/schemas; simple reproduction; unbalanced growth), 16, 24, 26, 34–52, 66
extraordinary items, 147, 156, 196, 215, 245, 299

F

Fabricant, Solomon, 173, 175
falling rate of profit (*see also* law of the tendential falling rate of profit (LTFRP)), 5, 13, 16, 22–24, 28–29, 51, 56, 58–59, 61–62, 64, 66, 70, 75–76, 78, 80, 82–83, 93, 185–186, 189, 283, 334–335, 393, 402–403
fair value accounting (*see also* current value accounting; fair value gains), 269–270, 335, 390, 393
fair value gains (*see also* bankers; fair value accounting; securitization accounting), 19, 377, 389–390, 393
Federal Trade Commission (FTC), 160, 162, 164, 166, 169, 206, 332
Federal Reserve, 112, 116
fictitious capital, 62, 66
financial accounting, 1, 6, 14, 23, 60, 63, 67, 122, 179, 191, 198, 219, 221, 234, 248, 250, 284–285, 290, 292, 296, 302, 304, 306, 315, 317, 323, 329, 403

Financial Accounting: A Distillation of Experience (May), 186, 220–226
Financial Accounting Foundation, 251, 320
Financial Accounting Standard (FAS) 13, *Accounting for Leases*, 336, 340, 349, 360
Financial Accounting Standard (FAS) 33, *Financial Reporting and Changing Prices*, 15, 277, 279, 281–283
Financial Accounting Standard (FAS) 76, *Extinguishment of Debt*, 16, 312, 361, 368–370, 373, 379
Financial Accounting Standard (FAS) 77, *Reporting by Transferors for Transfers of Receivables with Recourse*, 16, 334, 361, 368–370, 372, 388
Financial Accounting Standard (FAS) 125, *Accounting for Transfers and Servicing of Financial Assets and Extinguishments of Liabilities*, 16, 335–337, 340, 378–383, 388, 394
Financial Accounting Standard (FAS) 140, *Accounting for Transfers and Servicing of Financial Assets and Extinguishments of Liabilities*, 336, 338, 340, 375, 378–384, 389–390, 392, 397, 400–401
Financial Accounting Standard (FAS) 166, Accounting for Transfers of Financial Assets, 401
Financial Accounting Standard (FAS) 167, Amendments to FASB Interpretation No. 46(R), 401
Financial Accounting Standards Board (FASB) (*see also* conceptual framework; legitimacy of the FASB), 6, 13–15, 18–19, 126, 183, 186, 190–191, 209, 233, 236, 238, 240, 247, 251, 258–263, 265, 267–268, 270, 272, 277, 279, 281–295, 297, 300–322, 324–332, 334, 336, 338–340, 359–361, 365, 368–387, 392, 395, 400–403
financial and operating policies, 342–343, 397–398
financial components approach (*see also* Canning, John B.; Financial Accounting Standard (FAS) 125, *Accounting for Transfers and Servicing of Financial Assets and Extinguishments of Liabilities*; Myers, John H.; Perry, Raymond E.; securitization accounting), 336, 356, 361, 375–381
financial crises (*see also* economic crises; Global Financial Crisis (GFC); Marx's theory of crises), 1, 3–4, 13, 23, 28–29, 59–60, 63, 67, 69, 75, 402
financial executives (*see also* Financial Executives Institute (FEI)), 246, 251, 254, 258, 269, 302, 320
Financial Executives Institute (FEI) (*see also* financial executives), 227, 245, 257, 269, 301, 310, 320, 325
Financial Interpretation (FIN) 46 (R), *Consolidation of Variable Interest Entities, and Interpretation of ARB 51*, 384–386, 388, 400–401
financial reporting revolution (*see also* accounting profession's legitimacy crises; Beaver, William H., stewardship in the FASB's conceptual framework), 242–244, 247, 249, 260, 290, 307, 309, 311–313

financial risk (*see also* debt; Great Collapse; leverage; Marx's theory of crises), 59, 61, 70, 80–82
Financial Times, 338–339
Fisher, Irving (*see also* Fisher's accounting theory; Fisher's new-era theory of investment; The Nature of Capital and Income (Fisher); The Stock Market Crash And After (Fisher)), 3–8, 11–15, 17–19, 67, 74–76, 78, 82, 84–85, 88, 91–96, 98, 100, 106–107, 110–111, 113, 116, 120–123, 126–127, 130–131, 133, 135–136, 38–139, 142–151, 170, 182–183, 185–186, 189–191, 197, 201, 214, 216, 219, 224, 231–232, 234, 238–240, 253, 256, 259, 262, 265, 271–272, 277, 282, 290, 292, 301–303, 307–308, 322, 324, 327, 329–332, 335, 337, 339–341, 344–348, 352, 400, 402–403
Fisher, Frederick S, Jr, 138
Fisher's accounting theory (*see also* accounting theory; Fisher, Irving; Fisher's new-era theory of investment), 3–8, 10, 12, 14–15, 17–19, 67, 75–76, 84, 185–186, 189–190, 234, 240, 262, 265, 271, 308, 322, 324, 329–331, 335, 337, 340, 344–348, 403
Fisher's new-era theory of investment (*see also* Fisher, Irving; Fisher's theory of accounting; New Era), 17, 74, 78, 82, 87–88, 90–93, 96, 99, 103–105, 107–108, 116, 123
fixed capital (*see also* constant capital; circulating capital; depreciation accounting), 8, 29, 34, 44, 47, 65, 67, 78, 83–84, 222
Fogarty, Timothy J., Mohamed .A. Hussein, and J. Edward Ketz, Political aspects of financial accounting standard setting in the USA, 323–324
Foley, Duncan, 49
Forbes, 245
forces of production (*see also* capitalist mode of production; Marx's theory of history), 2, 21, 35, 52, 56, 65
Foster, William T., 79
Frankfurter, Felix, 160–161, 164, 169
Frank, Jerome S., 204, 207
future economic benefits (*see also* asset-liability accounting; Canning's asset definition; conceptual framework; control of access to future cash flows; control of access to future economic benefits; decision-usefulness; Fisher's theory of accounting; Paton's asset definition; right of use asset (ROU)), 233, 290, 302–305, 308, 356, 360, 368–369, 375, 379–381

G

Galbraith, John K. (*see also* irrational speculation explanation; The Great Crash 1929 Galbraith), 7–8, 11, 70, 72–76, 80, 100, 106–107, 112–115, 117–118, 120–121
Gellein, Oscar S., 251
General Electric, 187
general law of capitalist accumulation (*see also* Marx's theory of capitalism; Marx's theory of crises; workers' understanding of crises), 16, 24, 29–34, 66
generally accepted accounting principles (GAAP), 4–5, 17–18, 122, 126, 144, 171, 178–179, 183, 185–186, 189, 191–200, 203, 208, 229–231, 236–237, 241, 245, 249, 285, 320, 325

generally accepted theory of accounting, 259, 403–404
General Motors, 77
general price-level accounting (GPLA) (*see also* current purchasing power accounting (CPP); general price-level adjustments; inflation accounting), 14–15, 268–269, 279
general price-level adjustments (*see also* current purchasing power accounting (CPP); general price-level accounting (GPLA); inflation accounting), 228, 279, 282
Gerboth, Dale L., 314
Gibbs, M., K. Percy and R. Saville, *Sandilands and the effects on dividends*, 279
Gillett Safety Razor Co., 109
Gilman, Stephen, 197–198
Global Financial Crisis (GFC) (*see also*, financial crises), 1–4, 6, 13–16, 19, 22, 24, 66–67, 183, 185–186, 260–263, 283, 306, 332–402
Golden Age (*see also* profitability crisis), 13, 18, 185, 261, 283
goodwill accounting (*see also* Accounting Principles Board (APB)), 219, 245, 247, 274
Gore, Pelham, 287, 310, 321, 323
government auditors (*see also* auditors; independent audit requirement), 162–163
government control of accounting (*see also* government control of business; socialism), 5, 8, 11–12, 17, 122, 126, 135, 142, 144, 151, 164, 170, 172, 325, 329
government control of business (*see also* government control of accounting; socialism), 11, 17
Graham, Benjamin and David Dodd, *Security Analysis*, 88–90, 92–93, 101, 103, 108
Great Collapse (*see also* Great Depression; orthodox Marxist explanations of the Great Depression; stock market crash 1929), 16, 66–67, 69–85
Great Crash (*see also* stock market crash 1929), 2–3, 5, 7–12, 21, 67, 74, 85, 113, 126, 182
Great Depression (*see also* accounting's roles in the Great Crash and Great Depression; Great Collapse; historians' explanations of the 1920s boom, 1929 crash and Great Depression; orthodox Marxist explanations of the Great Depression; underconsumptionist explanations of the Great Depression), 1, 4, 7–8, 11, 13, 15, 17, 21, 69, 84, 125–183, 261, 265, 281, 283, 403
Great Free-Enterprise Campaign, 187
great railway swindle (*see also* swindling, British railway accounts), 63, 66
Green, William, 128
Greer, Howard C., 191–193
Grundrisse (Marx), 23, 25–26, 29, 56–57, 65

H

Hamilton, William P., 101
Hanson, Arthur W., 158, 211
Hartgraves, Al L., and George J. Benston, *The evolving accounting standards for special purpose entities and consolidations*, 382
Harvard University, 160, 200, 211, 245, 311
Harvey, David, 26, 34, 39, 44, 47, 50, 55–57, 65
Haskin & Sells, 203, 258
Hatfield, Henry R., 17–18, 203, 216, 232, 347

Hatry affair, 118–119
Healy, Robert E., 165, 181, 203, 206–207
Hennessy, John L., 354
Hercules Powder Company, 267
Herz, Robert, 339, 386–387, 400
Hicks, Sir John, 234, 327
Hirschleifer, Jack, 231
historians' explanations of the 1920s boom, 1929 crash and Great Depression (*see also* orthodox Marxist explanations of the Great Depression; underconsumptionist explanations of the Great Depression), 7–8, 16, 67, 69–70, 83
historical cost (HC), 13, 18–19, 180, 182–183, 185, 189–190, 194, 198–199, 206–207, 209, 219, 226, 228, 238–241, 243–244, 248, 251, 256–259, 262–266, 270–271, 274–276, 280–281, 300, 302, 308–310
historical cost accounting (HCA) (*see also* May, George O.; Paton, William, A., and A.C. Littleton, *Introduction to Corporate Accounting Standards*; stewardship and accounting reform, 1929–1973), 5, 18–19, 189–190, 194, 200, 202, 206, 208, 254, 258, 262–263, 265, 268, 278, 280, 283, 292, 307
Hoover, Herbert, 111, 113, 120–121, 125, 127–128, 156
Horngren, Charles T., 247, 250–251, 283, 314–316
Hoxsey, J.M.B., 122, 147–148, 150–151, 158, 174

I

ideology (*see also* management's ideological hegemony), 6, 8, 25, 76, 132, 187, 324, 327
IFRS versus US GAAP (*see also* International Financial Reporting Standards (IFRS); US GAAP for SPEs), 337, 396–398, 400–402, 403–404
Ijiri, Yuji, 248, 255, 290, 304
Imhoff, Eugene A., 375
Imhoff, Eugene A., Robert C. Lipe and David W. Wright, *Operating leases: Impact of constructive capitalization*, 361
income statement primacy (*see also* May, George O.; Paton, William, A., and A.C. Littleton, *Introduction to Corporate Accounting Standards*), 152–154, 180, 199, 222
independent audit requirement (*see also* auditing; auditors; government control of accounting), 5, 110, 158, 161, 163–166, 170, 180
Indiana Telephone, 267–268
inevitable crises (*see also* Marx's theory of crises), 2–3, 7–17, 21–23, 28–30, 35, 51–52, 56, 58, 62, 66, 71
inflation accounting (*see also* current purchasing power accounting (CPP); general price-level accounting (GPLA); general price-level adjustments; Sandilands Committee), 13–14, 19, 259, 262, 264–270, 279
information perspective (*see also* decision-usefulness), 14, 190
in-substance defeasance (*see also* Financial Accounting Standard (FAS) 76, Extinguishment of Debt), 16, 306, 312, 361, 368–369
in-substance purchase approach (*see also* lease accounting), 354–355, 358, 360
International Accounting Standard (IAS) 27, *Consolidated and Separate Statements*, 337, 397–398, 401

International Accounting Standard (IAS) 39 *Financial Instruments: Recognition and Measurement*, 361, 397, 400
International Accounting Standards Board (IASB), 337, 339, 392, 398, 400–402
International Financial Reporting Standards (IFRS), 337, 396–398, 400–401, 404
International Accounting Standards Committee (IASC), 397–398
investment tax credit accounting (*see also* Accounting Principles Board (APB)), 240–241, 245
investors' confidence in accounting (*see also* investors' economic confidence), 5, 11, 13, 17, 70, 84–85, 88, 103, 114, 117, 120, 122, 156, 164–165, 181, 183, 185, 188, 203, 229
investors' economic confidence (*see also* investors' confidence in accounting), 8, 11, 13, 17, 70, 74, 85, 88, 114, 116, 126, 183, 185
Iowa-Illinois Gas and Electric Company, 267
irrational speculation explanation of 1920s stock market boom (*see also* Galbraith, John K.; stock market boom of the 1920s), 7–8, 74–75, 78, 121, 145

J

joint stock companies (*see also* credit system; moral hazard; separation of ownership from control; total social capital), 27, 62–63, 341, 344
Journal of Accountancy, 179, 200, 210–211, 250, 286, 314
Joyce, Edward, J., Robert Libby and Shyam Sunder, *Using the FASB's qualitative characteristics in accounting policy choices*, 294

K

Kaehler, Ronald E., 99–100
Keynes, John M., 100
Kindleberger, Charles P., 75
King, Alfred M., 276
Kirk, Donald J., 247, 283–295, 309, 313–314, 330–332
Kliman, Andrew, 13, 22, 36–37, 47, 49, 52–54, 56–59, 61–66, 261–265, 334
Kohler, Eric K., 192–194, 356
Kothari, S.P., and Rebecca Lester, *The role of accounting in the financial crisis: Lessons for the future*, 392–393
Kreuger & Toll Company, 156, 158
Kripke, Homer, 323
Kuhn, Thomas S., 259–260, 322

L

laissez-faire (*see also* ideology; management's ideological hegemony), 8–9, 73, 78, 83, 122, 127, 130–133, 264
Landis, James M, 160, 165, 167, 178, 204
Landsman, Wayne R., Kenneth V. Peasnell and Catherine Shakespeare, *Are asset securitizations sales or loans*?, 390
last-in-first-out (LIFO), 207, 226
law of the tendential falling rate of profit (LTFRP) (*see also* falling rate of profit; Marx's theory of crisis; rate of profit), 2, 6–7, 22–25, 30, 35, 37, 51–62, 66, 402
legal financial results control, 336–337, 340, 342–344, 366, 368, 375–376, 386, 398–399
lease accounting (*see also* Accounting Principles Board (APB) Opinion 7, *Accounting for Leases in Financial Statements of Lessors*; Accounting Principles

Board (APB) Opinion 5, *Reporting of Leases in Financial Statements of Lessees*; Accounting Research Bulletin (ARB) 38, *Disclosure of Long-Term Leases in Financial Statements of* Lessees; Financial Accounting Standard (FAS) 13, *Accounting for Leases*; Myers, John H.; right of use (ROU) asset), 15, 229, 336, 340, 349–350, 358–361, 377
legitimacy of the FASB (*see also* conceptual framework; Financial Accounting Standards Board (FASB); management's ideological hegemony), 318, 324–330
Lehman Brothers, 333
Lenin, Vladimir, 76, 130, 187
lessee accounting (*see also* lease accounting), 336, 349–352, 354–360, 378–380
lessor accounting (*see also* lease accounting), 349–354, 359–360, 378–380
leverage (*see also* debt; financial risk; Marx's theory of crises), 60, 80, 82, 368
Liberty League, 165, 171
Lippmann, Walter, 10
Littleton, A.C. (*see also* A Tentative Statement of Accounting Principles Affecting Corporate Reports (American Accounting Association (AAA)); Paton, William, A., and A.C. Littleton, *Introduction to Corporate Accounting Standards*), 183, 188, 193, 199, 204, 206, 209–210, 212–213, 232, 248
Lorig, Arthur N., 196–197
lower of cost or market (L-C-M) (*see also* British conservatism), 66, 123, 226

M

Macve, Richard H., 294, 306, 308, 323
majority voting control (*see also* Accounting Research Bulletin (ARB) 51, *Consolidated Financial Statements*; Marxian consolidated accounting), 342, 348–349, 366, 370, 383–384
management accounting, 23, 66, 234
management control of accounting, 170, 181, 285, 319
management control of companies, 1, 135–136, 170, 345
management discretion in accounting (*see also* big mess; smoothing income/profit), 4, 6, 13–15, 17–19, 126, 182–183, 185–186, 189–190, 194, 209, 214, 216–217, 219, 230, 236, 245, 252, 260, 262, 282, 286, 290, 292, 294, 328, 335, 349, 358, 381–382, 390, 399
management's accountability (*see also* accountability for the rate of profit), 3, 17, 177, 183, 210, 256, 262, 332
management's ideological hegemony (*see also* ideology; laissez-faire), 18, 189, 191, 263–265, 324, 329–330
managerial capitalism (*see also* managerialism; managerial liberalism; managerial view), 126
managerialism (*see also* managerial capitalism; managerial liberalism; managerial view), 128
managerial liberalism (*see also* managerial capitalism; managerialism; managerial view), 127–129
managerial view (*see also* economic entity concept; managerial capitalism; managerialism;

managerial liberalism; Paton William A.), 236, 345–346
manipulating accounts (*see also* management discretion; smoothing income/profit; swindling), 3, 5, 17, 23, 63, 67, 84–85, 90, 104–105, 109–110, 115–116, 120, 123, 140–141, 174, 185, 189, 207, 227, 237, 336, 387, 389, 400
March, John, 308
Marxian accounting, 4, 6–7, 14, 19, 186, 194, 205, 214–218, 248, 254–255, 262, 264–265, 271–278, 293, 296, 298, 303, 311, 328–329, 336–337, 340–344, 356, 362, 365, 369, 372, 375–376, 378, 387, 396, 398, 402, 404
Marxian accounting for securitisation SPEs, 336, 362, 365–368
Marxian consolidated accounting, 19, 336, 340–344
Marx's accounting theory of crises (*see also* Marx's theory of accounting control; Marx's theory of crises), 21, 27–29
Marx's theory of accounting control (*see also* Marx's accounting theory of crises; Marx's theory of crises), 3, 23, 25–27, 34–35, 37, 41, 51–52, 56, 60, 65–66
Marx's theory of capitalism, 1–3, 5, 16, 21, 52, 56, 289, 404
Marx's theory of crises (*see also* Marx's accounting theory of crises), 1–3, 8, 16, 21–67, 261, 263, 283, 332, 335, 387, 403
Marx's theory of history, 2, 9, 25
Marx's theory of value, 2–3, 22, 25, 41, 66, 213, 300, 328, 404
Mason, Paul, 267
matching (*see also* attaching; Paton, William, A., and A.C. Littleton, *Introduction to Corporate Accounting Standards*), 18, 182, 197, 208–209, 211, 213–216, 218–219, 224, 227, 243–244, 294, 296–298, 300–302, 315, 322, 352
Mathews, George, 171, 181, 192, 202, 206
Mattessich, Richard., 14, 189
Mattick, Paul, 26–27, 50
Mautz, Robert K., 258–259, 301–302
May, George O. (*see also* earning capacity; Financial Accounting: A Distillation of Experience (May); generally accepted accounting principles (GAAP); government control of accounting; income statement primacy; independent audit requirement; May's interpretation of accounting; stewardship and accounting reform, 1929–1973; uniformity in accounting), 5, 10, 12–13, 17–18, 104–105, 121–122, 126–127, 130–131, 133–135, 138, 140–141, 144, 146, 148–156, 158–159, 161–163, 170–175, 179–180, 182–183, 186, 188–192, 196, 199–205, 207–208, 212, 219–228, 232, 235–236, 242–244, 251, 254, 257–259, 286, 290, 294, 296–297, 300, 302, 310, 331
May's interpretation of accounting (*see also* earning capacity; Financial Accounting: A Distillation of Experience (May); generally accepted accounting principles (GAAP); government control of accounting; income statement primacy; independent audit requirement; May, George, O.; stewardship and accounting reform, 1929–1973; uniformity in

accounting), 12, 18, 127, 144, 164, 170–171, 178–180, 182–183, 189, 219, 257, 310, 331
McElvaine, Robert S., 7
Means, Gardiner, 135
Mellon, Andrew W., 112–113
mergers, 109–110, 139
Merino, Barbara G., and Marilyn D. Neimark, *Disclosure regulation and public policy: a sociohistorical reappraisal*, 97–101, 143
Merrill Lynch, 333
middle classes, 8, 10–11, 67, 71, 73, 75–77, 82, 84–85, 87, 104, 107, 109, 111, 169, 183, 188
Miller, Paul W.B., and Rodney J. Redding, *The FASB: The People, the Process, and the Politics*, 307, 313, 320, 330
Miranti, Paul J., 134, 180
Mitchell, Charles E., 113
mode of production (*see also* capitalist mode of production; Marx's theory of history), 2, 30, 34–35, 53–54, 57, 62, 64, 341
Moley, Raymond, 129, 160
money capital, 38, 44, 50–51, 61–62, 91, 253, 296
monetary gains and losses (*see also* current purchasing power accounting (CPP); general price-level accounting (GPLA); general price-level adjustments; inflation accounting; profitability crisis; Sandilands Committee), 15, 268, 279–280, 283
money capitalism (*see also* Fisher's theory of accounting; Marx's theory of crises), 6, 12, 91, 96, 111, 150, 341, 344, 366
Monson, Derek, W., 356
Moonitz, Maurice (*see also* Sprouse, Robert T., and Maurice Moonitz,. *A Tentative Set of Broad Accounting Principles for Business Enterprises*; The Basic Postulates of Accounting (Moonitz), 231–233, 239, 301–302, 352, 354, 356, 359
moral hazard (*see also* joint stock companies; Marx's theory of crises), 61–62, 387, 395
Morrison, Paul, 210, 268
mortgage-backed securities (*see also* bankers; Global Financial Crisis (GFC); securitization accounting; subprime mortgages; US GAAP for SPEs), 337–338, 361–362
Most, Kenneth S., 228
Myers, John H. (*see also* Accounting Research Study (ARS) 4, *Reporting of Leases in Financial Statements*; critical events approach; financial components approach; lease accounting; right of use (ROU) asset), 15, 336, 340, 349–350, 352–361, 371, 375, 377, 380–382

N

neoclassical economics (*see also* Fisher's theory of accounting), 5, 10, 18, 126, 189, 213, 308, 404
net realisable value (NRV) (*see also* value to the owner), 15, 195, 233, 239–240, 263, 273–276
New Deal (*see also* reform of capitalism; Roosevelt, Franklin D.), 9, 11, 129, 131–133, 157, 163, 180, 187
New Era (*see also* Fisher's new-era theory of investment), 70–76, 127–128, 131
New York State Society of Certified Public Accountants (NYSSCPA), 161, 167
New York Stock Exchange (NYSE), 13, 69, 76–77, 80, 82, 98–99, 103,

116, 118–119, 121–122, 135, 144, 146–151, 156–160, 175–176, 180, 186–187, 202, 205, 348–349
Niu, Flora F., and Gordan D. Richardson, *Earnings quality, off-balance sheet risk, and the financial-components approach to accounting for transfers of financial assets*, 390
nondistortion guideline (*see also* Bevis, Herman W.; conceptual framework; Financial Accounting Standards Board (FASB); revenue and expense accounting), 294–296, 298–299, 332
Norby, W.C., 15, 281

O

off-balance sheet accounting (*see also* lease accounting; Marxian accounting for securitisation SPEs; Marxian consolidated accounting; securitization accounting; special purpose entities (SPEs); US GAAP for SPEs), 6, 14, 16, 19, 304, 335–340, 349–350, 354, 360–361, 365, 368, 371–373, 383–384, 390, 393, 395–396, 402–403
Okishio, Nobuo, 2, 53–54
open the books (*see also* unions), 12, 183
Organic Composition of Capital (OCC) (*see also*, falling rate of profit; law of the tendential falling rate of profit (LTFRP); Marx's theory of crisis; rate of profit), 28–29, 30–34, 36, 41–46, 52–54, 56, 70, 79
orthodox Marxists' explanations of the Great Depression (*see also* Devine, J.; historians' explanations of the 1920s boom, 1929 crash and Great Depression; underconsumptionist explanations of the Great Depression; underconsumptionist interpretations of Marx), 16, 22, 24, 82–83
overproduction (*see also* Marx's theory of crises), 3, 22–23, 28–29, 32–34, 57–58, 60–62, 73

P

Paper Prophets: A Social Critique of Accounting (Tinker), 327
Parrish, Michael E., 141, 143
pathological accounting (*see also* Fisher's theory of accounting), 6, 12, 332, 335, 403
Paton's asset definition (*see also* control of use-values with PV; Paton, William Jr; Paton's implicit circuit of PV; Statement of Financial Accounting Concepts (SFAC) 3, *Elements of Financial Statements of Business Enterprises*; US GAAP for SPEs), 15, 19, 262, 303, 336, 340, 347, 375, 379, 398, 400
Paton's implicit circuit of PV (*see also* Paton's asset definition; Paton, William Jr.), 232, 336, 352
Paton, William, A., and A.C. Littleton, *An Introduction to Corporate Accounting Standards*, ix, 18, 144, 182–183, 186, 188–190, 200, 208–219, 228, 237, 242–244, 259, 294, 297, 300–301, 352
Paton, William A. Jr (*see also* Accounting Theory (Paton); asset-liability accounting; A Tentative Statement of Accounting Principles Affecting Corporate Reports (American Accounting Association (AAA); economic entity concept; managerial view; Paton's

asset definition; Paton, William, A., and Littleton, A.C., *Introduction to Corporate Accounting Standards*; power to direct), 6, 14–19, 91, 108, 133, 135–136, 180, 183, 188–190, 192–194, 199–200, 204, 209, 211, 213–214, 216, 231–237, 239, 252, 262, 266–267, 269, 272, 282, 300–304, 335–336, 340–341, 345–347, 349–353, 361, 368, 371–372, 375, 379, 381–382, 384, 398, 400–403
Peasnell, Kenneth V., 259–260, 322, 330
Pecora Hearings, 157–158
people's capitalism, 13, 18, 126, 181, 183, 185–189, 191, 233, 235
Perry, Raymond E., ix, 375–378
phenomenal forms (*see also* Marxian accounting; Marx's theory of value), 4, 10, 24–25
Piaget, Jean, 27
pooling-of-interests accounting (*see also* Accounting Principles Board (APB)), 247
power to direct (*see also* action control; effective control; Paton, William A. Jr.), 133, 135, 346–347, 361, 382, 398, 401
predominant characteristics paradigm (*see also* Perry, Raymond E.; securitization accounting), 375–376
present value (PV) (*see also* control of use-values with PV; Paton's implicit circuit of PV; present value (PV) measurement ideal; value to the owner), 15–16, 91, 117, 148, 154, 173, 191, 194–195, 205, 213, 223, 232–235, 238–240, 253–254, 263, 275, 277–278, 290–293, 301–302, 304, 308–309, 336, 348, 352–356, 358, 360, 371, 375, 379, 382, 389, 404
present value (PV) measurement ideal (*see also* accounting theory; control of use-values with PV; Fisher's theory of accounting; present value (PV); value to the owner), 239, 254, 290–293, 301–302, 322, 348
Previts, Gary J, and Barbara D. Merino, *A History of Accountancy in the United States: The Cultural Significance of Accounting*, x, 143, 147–148, 163, 182
price-earnings ratios (*see also* earnings and share prices; earnings multipliers; Fisher's new-era theory of investment), 95, 108–109
Price Waterhouse, 5, 134, 161, 222, 247, 283, 295
production for the sake of production (*see also* unbalanced growth), 24, 36–37, 41, 46
productive expenditures, 217–218
productive/non-productive labour, 214, 216, 297
profitability crisis (*see also* Current Cost Accounting (CCA); Financial Accounting Standard (FAS) 33, *Financial Reporting and Changing Prices*; law of the tendential falling rate of profit (LTFRP); Marx's theory of crises; replacement cost accounting (RCA); Sandilands Committee; Statement of Standard Accounting Practice 16 (SSAP 16)), 4, 13–14, 18, 185–186, 261, 263, 265, 283

Q

qualifying special purpose entities (QSPEs) (*see also* Financial Accounting Standard (FAS) 125, *Accounting for Transfers and Servicing of Financial Assets and*

Extinguishments of Liabilities; Financial Accounting Standard (FAS) 140, *Accounting for Transfers and Servicing of Financial Assets and Extinguishments of Liabilities*; financial components approach; Perry, Raymond E.; securitization accounting; US GAAP for SPEs), 16, 336–340, 378, 382–384, 386–388, 391, 395–397, 400–401
Quesnay, Francois, 25, 31

R
railroad companies, 78, 110, 210, 350
Rappaport, Alfred, 318–319, 322
Rappoport, Peter, and Eugene N. White, *Was there a bubble in the 1929 stock market*, 106–107
rate of exploitation (*see also* Marx's theory of capitalism rate of profit; rate of surplus value), 17, 29, 39, 53–55, 57–58, 67, 268, 282, 334
rate of profit (*see also* accountability for the rate of profit; falling rate of profit; law of the tendential falling rate of profit (LTFRP); Marx's theory of accounting control; Marx's theory of capitalism), 2–3, 5–6, 11–14, 16–18, 21–29, 32–33, 35, 42–46, 51–67, 70–72, 75–76, 78–80, 82–83, 85, 115, 185, 248, 259, 261–267, 269, 283, 333–335, 341, 349, 361, 393, 402–403
rate of surplus value (*see also* Marx's theory of capitalism; rate of exploitation; rate of profit), 28–29, 31–33, 39, 42–46, 52–54
RCA Corporation, 77–78
realisation (*see also* British realisation principle; Marxian accounting), 18–19, 26–27, 37–38, 182, 196, 199, 202, 207–208, 211, 214, 219, 222, 224, 226, 233, 296, 298, 353, 369, 372, 378, 389
Reagan, Ronald, 281–282
Reece Corporation, 267–268
reformers (*see also* accounting reform in the 1930s; reform of capitalism), 7, 9, 97, 133, 169, 182
reform of capitalism (*see also* accounting reform in the 1930s; Berle, Adolf A.; Berle, Adolf A., and Means, Gardiner, *The Modern Corporation and Private Property*; Marx's theory of crises; New Deal; Roosevelt, Franklin D.), 1, 7, 9, 11, 85, 126, 132–133, 144–146, 156, 182–183
relative surplus value (*see also* Marx's theory of capitalism; rate of profit), 29, 32–33, 35, 51–54, 57–58, 66
relevance of accounting (*see also* Statement of Financial Accounting Concepts (SFAC) 2, *Qualitative Characteristics of Financial Statements*), 169, 172, 209, 235, 239, 243–244, 249, 275, 279, 281–282, 291–294, 309, 311, 390
reliability of accounting (*see also* Statement of Financial Accounting Concepts (SFAC) 2, *Qualitative Characteristics of Financial Statements*), 118, 281–282, 291–292, 294, 309, 311
replacement cost (RC) (*see also* current cost), 15, 66, 174, 233, 239–240, 243–244, 262–264, 266–267, 269, 281, 283, 310
replacement cost accounting (RCA) (*see also* Current Cost Accounting; (CCA) Marxian accounting; Sandilands Committee), 14–15, 19,

53–54, 256, 262–265, 270–271, 274, 279–280, 282–283
Report on Special Purpose Entities (Bank for International Settlements (BIS)), 336
reproduction schemes/schemas (*see also* expanded reproduction), 34, 36–42
results control (*see also* accountability for the rate of profit; British stewardship; Marxian accounting for securitisation SPEs; legal financial results control; Marxian consolidated accounting; Marx's theory of accounting control; Rosenfield, Paul), 16, 24, 41, 52, 155, 221, 248, 287–288, 296, 332, 335–337, 340–344, 346, 349, 366–368, 375–376, 378, 386, 398–399
return on investment (ROI) (*see also* accountability for the rate of profit), 2, 4, 11, 21, 23, 27–29, 35, 50, 52, 57–58, 60, 66–67, 256, 268, 290, 303, 342, 366, 402
revenue and expense accounting (*see also* Bevis, Herman W.; conceptual framework; income statement primacy; May, George O.; Paton, William, A., and A.C. Littleton, *Introduction to Corporate Accounting Standards*), 294, 297, 301–302, 336
Revsine, Lawrence, 274, 321, 326
Rhea, Robert., 101–102
Ricardo, David, 52
right of use (ROU) asset (*see also* Canning's asset definition; Financial Accounting Standard (FAS) 125, *Accounting for Transfers and Servicing of Financial Assets and Extinguishments of Liabilities*; financial components approach; lease accounting; Myers John H.; Perry, Raymond E.), 336, 361, 375, 378
Ripley, William Z., 111, 117–119, 133–135, 148, 151, 156
risks and rewards of ownership approach (*see also* Myers, John H.; US GAAP for SPEs), 353, 359–361, 368, 370–371, 374–375, 379, 382–385, 391–392, 396, 399, 401
Roaring Twenties, 8, 21, 71, 75
Ronen, Joshua, 251
Roosevelt, Franklin D.R., 9–10, 17, 79, 122, 125, 127–132, 156–157, 160–161, 164–165, 172, 177
Rorem, C. Rufus, 197
Rorty, M.C., 150–151
Rosenfield, Paul, 254–256, 258, 287, 290, 296
Ryan, Stephen G., 392, 394

S

Sanders, Thomas H., 177
Sanders, Thomas H., Henry R. Hatfield and Underhill Moore, *A Statement of Accounting Principles*, 203–204
Sandilands Committee (*see also* Current Cost Accounting (CCA); current purchasing power accounting (CPP); inflation accounting; profitability crisis; replacement cost accounting (RCA); value to the owner), 15, 270, 272–274, 279–280
Schipper, Katherine and Teri L. Yohn, *Standard-setting issues and academic research related to the accounting for financial asset transfers*, 388, 390–392
Scott, DR., 197–199

Seaview Symposium on Financial Reporting, 245
Securities Acts of 1933 and 1934, 5, 17, 103, 122, 126, 133, 135, 143–146, 165, 169–170
Securities and Exchange Commission (SEC) (*see also* Securities Acts of 1933 and 1934; uniformity in accounting), 5, 11, 13, 15, 17–18, 96, 122, 126, 145, 148, 161, 163–165, 169, 171–173, 177–181, 183, 185–190, 192, 194, 200, 202–207, 210, 227–228, 230, 233, 240–241, 244, 247, 249–250, 259, 261–262, 267, 270, 313, 318, 324–325, 335–336, 349, 359, 374, 386
securitisation(s) (*see also* securitization accounting; US GAAP for SPEs), 304, 334–338, 340, 361–368, 370–373, 375–377, 381–382, 386, 388–390, 392, 394–395, 398, 400, 402
securitization accounting (*see also* bankers; Financial Accounting Standard (FAS) 125, *Accounting for Transfers and Servicing of Financial Assets and Extinguishments of Liabilities; Financial Accounting Standard (FAS) 140, Accounting for Transfers and Servicing of Financial Assets and Extinguishments of Liabilities*; Perry, Raymond E.; US GAAP for SPEs), 335, 389, 392–393, 400
self-correcting crises (*see also* devaluation of capital; Marx's theory of crises), 11, 24, 64–66
Seligman, Joel, 107, 143–145
Senator Alben W. Barkley, 162–163, 167
Senator John E. Moss, 325
Senator Lee Metcalf, 325
Senator Reynolds, 162–163
Senator Robert Wagner, 132
Senator Thomas P. Gore, 164, 168
separation of ownership from control (*see also* America's transition to advanced capitalism; Berle, Adolf A., and Means, Gardiner, *The Modern Corporation and Private Property*; joint stock companies; Marx's theory of capitalism; moral hazard), 60–63, 71, 133–134, 138, 209, 213, 221
Shaikh, Anwar, 58
Shur, Ira A., 357–358
simple reproduction (*see also* expanded reproduction), 38, 40–43, 49
Slichter, Sumner, 266
Smith, Adam, 37, 52, 64, 67, 126, 137, 232, 352
Smith, C. Aubrey, 171
Smith, Edgar L., 90–92
smoothing income/profit (*see also* management discretion; swindling), 11, 17, 84, 88, 147, 175, 301–302
socialism (*see also* workers' understanding of crises), 2, 6, 8–10, 12, 17, 19, 22–23, 57, 62, 125, 127, 129, 132, 142–143, 164, 166, 171, 193, 212, 329, 404
socially rational accounting, 6, 19, 403
social relations of production (*see also* Marx's theory of capitalism), 2, 4, 10, 24–25, 56, 62
Solomons, David, 234, 273, 283–285, 288, 291–292, 306, 309, 311, 315–317, 319, 323–325, 327–328, 331
Sorter, George, 242, 251, 329
Spacek, Leonard, 229, 352

special purpose entities (SPEs) (*see also* Bank for International Settlements (BIS); Marxian accounting for securitisation SPEs; Report on Special Purpose Entities (Bank for International Settlements (BIS); securitization accounting; Standards Interpretation Committee (SIC) 12, *Consolidation-Special Purpose Entities*; US GAAP for SPEs), 6, 14, 16, 332, 334, 336–337, 361–368, 370, 385–386, 388, 398–400
speculation (*see also* irrational speculation explanation; Marx's theory of crises; stock market boom of the 1920s), 3–4, 7–8, 11, 17, 23, 58, 60–64, 66–67, 70–71, 73–75, 78, 82–84, 88, 90–93, 95, 98–99, 106–108, 111–113, 121, 145, 156, 165
Sprague, Charles E., 168, 211, 248, 304, 342, 347–348
Sprouse, Robert T., 232, 301–303, 308, 310, 312–313, 317, 319
Sprouse, Robert T., and Maurice Moonitz, *A Tentative Set of Broad Accounting Principles for Business Enterprises*, 232–233
S&P 500 Weekly Index, October 1928–October 1934, 114
Standard and Poor's Index of Common Stocks 1920–1934, 70
Standard Oil Company (N.J.), 187–188
Standards Interpretation Committee (SIC) 12, *Consolidation-Special Purpose Entities*, 337, 398, 400–401
Stanga, Keith, G., 294
Stans, Maurice, 227–228
Statement of Financial Accounting Concepts (SFAC) 1, *Objectives of Financial Reporting by Business Enterprises*, ix-x, 282, 284–290, 307–308, 311, 313, 321–323, 330
Statement of Financial Accounting Concepts (SFAC) 2, *Qualitative Characteristics of Financial Statements*, 284, 288, 291–294, 311, 331
Statement of Financial Accounting Concepts (SFAC) 3, *Elements of Financial Statements of Business Enterprises*, 282, 284, 294, 303–308, 379
Statement of Financial Accounting Concepts (SFAC) 5, *Recognition and Measurement in Financial Statements of Business Enterprises*, 282, 284, 305, 307–312
Statement of Financial Accounting Concepts (SFAC) 6, *Elements of Financial Statements of Business Enterprises, a replacement of FASB Concepts Statement No. 3 (incorporating an amendment of FASB Concepts Statement No. 2*), 379–380
Statement of Standard Accounting Practice (SSAP) 16, 15, 275, 279–281
Statement on Accounting Theory and Theory Acceptance (SOATATA) (American Accounting Association (AAA)), 321, 323
Staubus, George G., 14, 189, 233–243, 252–254, 284–285, 287–288
Staub, Walter R., 358
steady-state (*see also* earning capacity; earning power), 5, 105, 149
Sterling, Robert R., 14, 189, 243–244, 310
stewardship and accounting reform, 1929–1973 (*see also* British stewardship; May, George O.;

Paton, William, A., and A.C. Littleton, *Introduction to Corporate Accounting Standards*), 5, 18, 144, 182, 185–186, 189, 193–194, 199, 209–213, 214, 220–221, 223–226, 233, 236–238, 242, 246–249, 251, 254–259
stewardship in the FASB's conceptual framework (*see also* conceptual framework; Financial Accounting Standards Board (FASB); management's accountability; Statement of Financial Accounting Concepts (SFAC) 1, *Objectives of Financial Reporting by Business Enterprises*), 262, 265, 276, 282, 286–290, 295, 317
Stewart, John E., and Benjamin S. Neuhausen, *Financial instruments and transactions: the CPA's newest challenge*, ix, 370–371, 373, 375
stock market boom of the 1920s (*see also* bubble explanation of 1920s stock market boom; earnings and share prices; Fisher's new-era theory of investment; Galbraith, John K.; irrational speculation explanation of 1920s stock market boom), 5, 7–8, 10, 17, 67, 72, 78, 81, 84, 90, 106
stock market crash 1929 (*see also* earnings and share prices; Galbraith, John K.; Great Crash; historians' explanations; investors' confidence in accounting; The Stock Market Crash And After (Fisher)), 1, 5, 7, 10–13, 16–17, 24, 67, 70, 73, 75, 84, 87–123, 175, 177, 189, 349, 403
stock markets in capitalism (*see also* credit system; Marx's theory of capitalism; total social capital), 1–2, 83
stock market trends trading rule (*see also* chart reading; Dow theory; trend lines), 96, 99–100
Studebaker Corporation, 174
Storey, Reed K. (*see also* Storey, Reed K., and Sylvia Storey, *The Framework of Financial Accounting Concepts and Standards)*, 13, 303–304, 307, 312, 347
Storey, Reed K., and Sylvia Storey, *The Framework of Financial Accounting Concepts and Standards* (*see also* Storey, Reed K.), 310–311
subprime mortgages (*see also* bankers; Global Financial Crisis (GFC); mortgage-backed securities; securitization accounting), 333, 335, 387, 392, 394–395
superstructure (*see also* accounting regulation; mode of production), 2–3, 10, 21, 23, 25, 34, 52, 56, 65, 157, 341
surplus value (*see also* Marx's theory of capitalism Marx's theory of value), 2, 23–33, 35–41, 48–55, 57–58, 64–66, 341
Sweeney, Henry W., 15, 267
Sweezy, Paul, 214
swindling (*see also* management discretion; manipulating accounts; Marx's theory of crises; smoothing income/profit), 3–4, 6, 8, 11–12, 16–17, 19, 23, 60, 62–64, 66–67, 71, 76, 82, 84–85, 93, 185–186, 259, 332, 334–337, 340, 387–390, 393, 395–396, 402–403

T

Taussig, Charles, 160
technical analysis (*see also* chart reading; Dow theory; stock market

trends trading rule, trend lines), 101, 103
Temporal Single-System Interpretation (TSSI) (*see also* Kliman, Andrew), 2, 7, 22, 53, 334, 404
Thatcher, Margaret, 281–282
The Accounting Review, 158, 192, 210
The Basic Postulates of Accounting (Moonitz), 231
The Great Crash 1929 (Galbraith), x, 7, 74
The Modern Corporation and Private Property (Berle and Means), 12, 17, 133
The Nature of Capital and Income (Fisher), 271
Theories of Surplus Value (Marx), 64–65
The Stock Market Barometer: A Study of Its Forecast Value Based on Charles H. Dow's Theory of the Price Movement (Hamilton), 101
The Stock Market Crash and After (Fisher), 95, 120
The Structure of Scientific Revolutions (Kuhn), 322
The Valuation of Property: A Treatise on the Appraisal of Property for Different Legal Purposes (Bonbright), 15, 201, 272
Tietjen, A. Carl., 283
Tinker, Anthony M., 292, 327–329
total social capital (*see also* advanced capitalism; America's transition to advanced capitalism; capital-in-general; Marx's theory of capitalism), 2, 16, 21, 24, 26–28, 35, 37, 41, 49–52, 58, 60, 66–67, 71, 133, 144, 188, 198, 289, 295, 341
transition from simple to expanded reproduction (*see also* unbalanced growth), 40–41, 43, 46–47, 49–50
transition to capitalism (*see also* America's transition to advanced capitalism), 8
trend charts (*see also* chart reading; Dow theory; stock market trends trading rule; technical analysis; trend lines), 96–104
trickle down economics, 37
Trueblood Committee, 18, 186, 190, 242, 251–259, 261, 283, 300, 304
Trueblood, Robert M., 249, 251
Tugwell, Rexford, 79, 129–131, 177
Turner, Lynn, 386–387, 402
Tweedie, Sir David., 339
Tweedie, David, and Geoffrey Whittington, *The end of the current cost revolution*, 281–282
Twentieth Century Fund, 87, 100–104, 108, 110–111, 116, 119, 145, 148–149, 176
two-tiered market (*see also* Merino, Barbara G. and Marilyn D. Neimark, *Disclosure regulation and public policy: A sociohistorical reappraisal*), 97, 145

U

unbalanced growth (*see also* production for the sake of production; transition from simple to expanded reproduction), 24, 28, 36–37, 41–52
underconsumption in Marx's theory of crises (*see also* underconsumptionist explanations of the Great Depression; underconsumptionist interpretation of Marx), 3, 17, 22–23, 28–29, 57–58

underconsumptionist explanations of the Great Depression (*see also* historians' explanations of the 1920s boom, 1929 crash and Great Depression; orthodox Marxist explanations of the Great Depression; underconsumption in Marx's theory of crises; underconsumptionist interpretation of Marx), 69–70, 73, 82–83, 126, 129–130
underconsumptionist interpretation of Marx (*see also* historians' explanations of the 1920s boom, 1929 crash and Great Depression; orthodox Marxist explanations of the Great Depression; underconsumption in Marx's theory of crises; underconsumptionist explanations of the Great Depression), 22, 47, 82–83, 126, 130
uniformity in accounting (*see also* government control of accounting; May, George O.; Securities and Exchange Commission (SEC)), 5, 17, 145, 151, 164, 166–173, 177, 181, 188–189, 194, 201–202, 205, 246
Union Carbide and Carbon Corporation, 174–175
unions (*see also* open the books), 9, 12, 34, 78, 128, 131–132, 183, 227, 267–268, 282, 308, 317
University of Chicago, 14, 189, 231, 233–234, 238–239, 242, 251
unproductive expenditures (*see also* productive expenditures; productive/non-productive labour), 216, 297, 299
Untermyer, Samuel, 160
unusual items (*see also* extraordinary items), 13, 228, 299
US GAAP for SPEs (*see also* Financial Accounting Standard (FAS) 125, *Accounting for Transfers and Servicing of Financial Assets and Extinguishments of Liabilities*; Financial Accounting Standard (FAS) 140, *Accounting for Transfers and Servicing of Financial Assets and Extinguishments of Liabilities* securitization accounting; special purpose entities (SPEs)), 19, 186, 304, 335, 337, 340, 348, 361–362, 365, 368–386, 396, 400–401
US Steel, 120, 266

V
value-in-use (VIU), 199, 276
value-price transformation (*see also* accounting logic of *Capital*; Marx's theory of accounting control), 2, 22, 24, 66, 404
value-relevance, 390
value to the owner (*see also* Bonbright, James C.; Sandilands Committee), 15, 272–277
Van Strum, Kenneth S., 91–93
Van Zijl, Tony, and Geoffrey Whittington, *Deprival value and fair value: A reinterpretation and a reconciliation*, 275
variable capital (*see also* constant capital; wages), 28, 30–33, 38–40, 45, 47, 50, 53
variable interest entities (VIEs) (*see also* Paton's asset definition; US GAAP for SPEs), 384–386, 396

W

Wages (*see also* general law of capitalist accumulation; variable capital; workers' understanding of accounting), 16, 24, 28–33, 42–43, 45, 54, 63, 72, 78–79, 83, 130, 132, 143, 177, 216, 266, 282, 352
Walker, Robert G., 119–120, 206
Wall Street, 8, 76, 92, 94, 102–103, 115, 118, 129, 131, 156, 165, 170, 181, 201, 389
Wall Street Journal, 101–102, 104, 245–246
Watts, Ross L., 85, 268–269, 324, 331
Watts, Ross L. and Jerold L. Zimmerman, *The demand for the supply of accounting theories: The Market for Excuses*, 324
Watts, Ross L. and Jerold L. Zimmerman, *Towards a positive theory of the determination of accounting standards*, 268–269
wealthy investors, 8, 11, 67, 71, 73, 76–77, 82, 85, 87, 96, 103–105, 108, 111, 143–145, 188
Werntz, William W., 206–207
Wheat Committee, 186, 251, 288
Wheat, Francis M., 250, 288
White, Eugene N., 74–75, 77–78, 106, 114–116
Whittington, Geoffrey, 274–275, 279
whole asset approach (*see also* lease accounting), 356
Wiese, Robert G., 111–112
workers' understanding of crises (*see also* Marx's theory of crises; socialism), 2, 6–7, 16, 23–24, 26, 30–35, 37, 57
Wright, Charles, 99–100
Wyatt, Arthur R., 313, 331

Y

Yale University, 94, 111, 169
Young, Joni J., 371

Z

Zeff, Stephen A., 194, 206–207, 209, 211, 225, 237, 242–243, 292, 317, 320, 330, 332
Zises, Alvin, 358

www.ingramcontent.com/pod-product-compliance
Lightning Source LLC
LaVergne TN
LVHW011657200926
848484LV00004B/969